Economic and social development

Economic and social development

trends, problems, policies

Adam Szirmai

Prentice Hall
London New York Toronto Sydney Tokyo Singapore
Madrid Mexico City Munich Paris

First published 1997 by
Prentice Hall Europe
Campus 400, Maylands Avenue
Hemel Hempstead
Hertfordshire, HP2 7EZ
A division of
Simon & Schuster International Group

Typeset in 10/12 pt Plantin
by PPS Limited, London Road, Amesbury, Wilts.

Printed and bound in Great Britain by
Redwood Books, Trowbridge, Wiltshire

Library of Congress Cataloging-in-Publication Data

Szirmai, Adam, 1946–
Economic and social development : trends, problems, policies / Adam Szirmai.
p. cm.
Includes bibliographical references and index.
ISBN 0–13–358003–2
1. Economic development. 2. Social change. I. Title.
HD75.S97 1997 96-32837
338.9—dc20 CIP

British Library Cataloguing in Publication Data

A catalogue record for this book is available from
the British Library

ISBN 0-13-358003-2

1 2 3 4 5 01 00 99 98 97

Contents

Figures

Tables

Preface

The aim of this book is to provide a general introduction to the study of development and the problems of developing countries. It is a reflection of interdisciplinary courses on 'issues of development', which the author has been teaching to students of all faculties at the University of Groningen and the Eindhoven University of Technology since 1987. The book is intended for students of universities and other institutions of higher education who come across the problems of developing countries in the course of their own disciplinary studies and who are in need of a general introduction to this field. It is also intended for people pursuing a professional career in developing countries and for readers with a general interest in the problems of development.

The central issue in development, as approached in this book, lies in low levels of per capita income and low standards of living among the mass of the population in the so-called developing countries. The key elements in the book are trends in per capita income, changes in standards of living and welfare, and the factors that affect economic development or economic stagnation in the long term. Though the essence of development has thus been defined in economic terms, the explanatory factors are definitely not limited to economic ones. Historical, institutional, demographic, social, political and ecological factors are all of great importance for the analysis of economic development. They will receive ample attention in the book. It will also be emphasized that the concept of development involves much more than economic aspects only.

The structure of this book takes as its point of departure the three basic factors of production distinguished in economic theories of growth: labour, capital and land. However, in order to do justice to the interdisciplinary nature of development issues, these three factors are interpreted in a very broad fashion. Thus the production factor 'labour' gives rise to a more general discussion of demographic and human factors in development. These include population growth and the interrelationships between population growth and economic development (Chapter 4) and subjects such as health and disease, education and literacy (Chapters 5 and 6). Health and education are important as independent aspects of development in their own right. But the state of health and levels of education also influence the quality of the labour force, the productivity of labour and the economic dynamics in a country.

Modern economic growth is historically associated with capital accumulation in the industrial sector and a structural transformation of agrarian societies into societies in which industry becomes more and more important. With respect to the production factor 'capital', attention will therefore focus on overall processes of industrialization and on industrialization strategies (Chapter 7)

The discussion of the production factor 'land' is broadened to include the whole issue of agricultural and rural development. In Chapter 8 the role of the agricultural sector in economic development will be examined. In Chapter 9 the development of production and productivity in the agricultural sector will be discussed against the background of social change in rural communities as a whole; this chapter will also present a discussion of trends in food consumption.

The discussion of development from the perspective of the three factors of production in Chapters 4 to 9 is preceded and followed by chapters which place development in a historical and international perspective. Chapter 2 focuses on the development of the international economic and political order since the fifteenth century. Chapter 3 deals with theories of growth and stagnation and presents empirical data on economic trends in a sample of twenty-four developing countries, including countries in Asia, Latin America and Africa. The approach in these chapters is historical and comparative. The sample of countries will be used throughout the book to provide an empirical basis for the discussion of theories, patterns and trends in development. The country data are supplemented by aggregate statistics for regions and continents. Chapter 10 focuses on political aspects of development and the role of state formation in development. International aspects of development since World War II are examined in Chapter 11. This chapter presents a discussion of the evolution of international institutions and organizations and of developments in international economic relationships and their implications for developing countries. It also includes a treatment of the debt crisis and the rise of structural adjustment policies. Finally, Chapter 12 focuses on the role of foreign aid in development. Foreign aid is placed in the perspective of international resource flows and is discussed in the context of the many different factors influencing development in the long run.

Despite its considerable length, this book has no pretensions to completeness. It is intended explicitly as an introduction to the ongoing debates on development, rather than as a summary of our knowledge of all different aspects of the subject. In the choice of issues, the emphasis has been on the long-run dynamics of development and the factors that play a role in these dynamics.

I could not have written this book without the support of numerous colleagues and ex-colleagues, who generously let me profit from their knowledge of and insights into the various aspects of development. I have made extensive use of their advice, publications and empirical work. I have both learned from and enjoyed years of fruitful and intensive discussions with them. I would like especially to thank the following persons for their advice and their stimulating comments on previous drafts of the manuscript or portions of it: Bart van Ark, Pierre van der Eng, Peter Druijven,

Jacob de Haan, Niels Hermes, Hans-Paul Klijnsma, Jos Koetsier, Remco Kouwenhoven, Robert Lensink, Angus Maddison, Kees van der Meer, Nanno Mulder, Dirk Pilat and Gé Prince. I am grateful to Harry van Vianen for introducing me to the extensive literature on health care and the demographic aspects of development. Of course, the responsibility for the whole book and its shortcomings rests with the author alone.

In the process of writing this book I have been fortunate to enjoy the support of a series of enthusiastic and talented student assistants. Ida Terluin, Heine van Wieren, Ineke van der Werf, Marcel Timmer, David van Horen and Donné van Engelen helped to collect and organize the statistical materials incorporated in the book. This English edition of the book is a revised version of the Dutch edition which originally appeared in 1994. Ingrid Hadders played an important role in translating the Dutch version into English. Rick van der Kamp provided valuable assistance in updating and revising the statistics. I thank all these people for their help and cooperation. I dedicate this book to my wife Veronika, who had to bear part of its hidden burdens.

Eindhoven
January, 1996

A. Szirmai

Abbreviations

ACP	Asian, Caribbean and Pacific countries
ADB	Asian Development Bank
ASEAN	Association of South East Asian Nations
CGIAR	Consultative Group on International Agricultural Research
CIMMYT	Centro Internacional de Mejoramienta de Maiz y Trigo (International Maize and Wheat Improvement Centre)
CMEA	Council for Mutual Economic Assistance
DAC	Development Assistance Committee (OECD)
DRS	Debt Reporting System (World Bank)
ECLA	United Nations Economic Commission for Latin America
ECOSOC	Economic and Social Council of the UN
EEC	European Economic Community
EC	European Community
ECLA	United Nations Economic Commission for Latin America
EDF	European Development Fund
ESAF	Enhanced Structural Fund Facility (IMF)
ESCAP	United Nations Economic and Social Commission for Asia and the Pacific
EU	European Union
EWLP	Experimental World Literacy Programme
FAO	United Nations Food and Agriculture Organization
GATT	General Agreement on Tariffs and Trade
GDFF	Geographical Distribution of Financial Flows to Developing Countries
GSP	Generalized System of Preferences
HDR	Human Development Report
IADB	Inter-American Development Bank
IBRD	International Bank for Reconstruction and Development (World Bank)

IDA	International Development Association
IFAD	International Fund for Agricultural Development
IFC	International Finance Corporation
ILO	International Labour Organization
IMF	International Monetary Fund
IRRI	International Rice Research Institute
ITO	International Trade Organization
NAFTA	North American Free Trade Association
NATO	North Atlantic Treaty Organization
NGO	Non-governmental organization
NIEO	New International Economic Order
OAU	Organization of African Unity
OAS	Organization of American States
ODA	Official Development Assistance
OECD	Organization for Economic Cooperation and Development
OPEC	Organization of Petroleum Exporting Countries
SAL	Structural adustment loan (World Bank)
SECAL	Sectoral adjustment loan (World Bank)
SAF	Structural adjustment facility (IMF)
UN	United Nations
UNCED	United Nations Conference on Environment and Development
UNCTAD	United Nations Conference on Trade and Development
UNDP	United Nations Development Programme
UNEPTA	United Nations Extended Program of Technical Assistance
UNESCO	United Nations Educational, Scientific and Cultural Organization
UNICEF	United Nations Children's Fund
UNIDO	United Nations Industrial Development Organization
UNITAR	United Nations Institute for Training and Research
UNPF	United Nations Population Fund
USAID	United States Agency for International Development
USSR	Union of Socialist Soviet Republics
WB	World Bank (see IBRD)
WDR	*World Development Report* (World Bank)
WDT	*World Debt Tables* (World Bank)
WFP	World Food Programme
WHO	World Health Organization
WRI	World Resources Institute
WT	*World Tables* (World Bank)
WTO	World Trade Organization

1 Introduction: developing countries and their problems

This introductory chapter focuses on the meaning of the concept of development. The low standard of living of the mass of the population in developing countries is singled out as the key issue in development. The development of per capita income over time and the factors that influence economic development or stagnation are the central topics of this book. However, the interplay between economic and non-economic factors is of great importance for a good understanding of development processes. Economic development cannot be explained by economic factors only, and the concept of development includes more than mere changes in economic indicators.

After a discussion of problems of involvement and detachment in the study of development issues in sections 1.1 and 1.2, in sections 1.3 to 1.6 we will look at the various aspects of the concept of development and at indicators of development. In section 1.7 the differences between developing countries will be discussed. The final section addresses the question: what do developing countries have in common in spite of all the differences between them.

1.1 *Involvement and detachment*

In discussions of development issues two general approaches can be distinguished (see Myint, 1980):

1. *The fight against poverty* This approach focuses on the problems of hunger and misery in developing countries and on the question of what should be done in order to improve the situation in the *short term*.
2. *The analysis of long-term economic and social development* This approach concentrates on comparing developments in different countries, regions and

historical periods in order to gain a better understanding of the factors that have a *long-term* effect on economic growth or stagnation.

One of the characteristics of the first approach is a strong involvement with the problems of developing countries and their inhabitants. Most people who study development issues do so because they feel that present levels of poverty, misery and injustice are unacceptable. Their aim is to arrive at concrete recommendations for action by means of scientific study of the issues. This approach has close links with development policy at international, national, regional or local levels. Some interpret this technocratically, others in a radical-political sense, arguing for political action in order to achieve dramatic changes in the existing order of things.

The drawback of such involvement is a certain degree of trendiness (see van Dam, 1978, 1989). To illustrate this point, I will mention just a few of the many ideas and slogans that have played a role in post-war discussions on development: the idea that large-scale injections of capital are the key to development ('big push'); the notion that the missing link in development is human capital; the green revolution; community development; basic needs; integrated rural development; self-reliance; delinking from the world economy; the New International Economic Order; stimulation of the informal sector; structural adjustment; and sustainable development.

A common characteristic of these recipes for development is their short-term perspective. Time and again, proposals have been put forward in order to reach certain goals, preferably within a decade (see, for example, Brandt, 1980, 1983; Brundtland, 1987). In the meantime, developments that take place irrespective of the fashion of the day are disregarded. These fashions often evoke a brief wave of enthusiasm within the world of politics, policy and science. Soon, however, a period of disenchantment sets in. The issue disappears from the public eye, and new and more appealing solutions are sought after. The greater the involvement, the greater the confusion between desirability and reality, and the greater the disappointment that follows when reality proves less manageable than one had hoped (see Elias, 1970). Sometimes, major mistakes in development policies are a direct consequence of erroneous advice from Western advisers and experts. An example of this is the drive for industrialization at all costs in the 1950s, as a result of which the agricultural sector came to be neglected.

The long-term approach is more detached. One tries to comprehend why, in the long term, such great differences in development have occurred in the different parts of the world (Szirmai, 1993). One tries to identify the factors that may help to explain different patterns of development, such as the accumulation of production factors, the efficiency with which these factors of production are being used, technological changes, external political and economic influences, historical factors and cultural differences. Economic and social policies can be an important factor, but considering policy as one out of many other factors may help to deflate immoderate pretensions of policymakers, politicians and scientific advisers.

Economic growth in its modern form is very much associated with the economic development of the Western countries since the mid-eighteenth century. Therefore, the history of the economic development of prosperous European and North American countries will often serve as a point of reference in our comparisons. This is not simply to advocate the copying of Western solutions by developing countries. Rather we hope to gain an insight into the similarities and differences in development processes.

Economic growth in its modern form is also associated with industrial development and a process that Higgins and Higgins (1979, p. 3) have ironically described as 'getting rid of farmers'. Again this relationship between industrialization and economic growth cannot be applied indiscriminately to developing countries. It does, however, serve as another point of reference. Furthermore, comparisons of the historical development of economically advanced countries and developing countries may teach us a lot about the role of institutions in advancing or impeding economic development. In this context one can think of land tenure relations, property rights, patent institutions, processes of state formation, or financial institutions.

Finally, the historical study of processes of economic growth reveals the importance of processes of saving and investment in the accumulation of factors of production. Such a study leaves us under no illusion with regard to the human costs of economic growth. In the past, economic growth has always been coupled with an enormous increase in the capital–labour ratio. In order to invest in capital goods, a considerable portion of the national income has to be saved. In poor countries, saving means that people, living at subsistence levels, have to postpone present consumption for the sake of investment in future production. This is not easy. In Western countries such savings have been realized through the ruthless workings of the market mechanism of nineteenth-century capitalism, which kept wages low. In the centrally planned economies of the twentieth century, exploitation of people by people through the market has been replaced by direct coercion by the state. Both mechanisms have resulted in the transfer of income to social groups (capitalists, entrepreneurs, government policy makers) that were both able and willing to save and invest. It is not likely that such tough choices can be avoided in the future.

An objection to the long-term approach is that it seldom offers neat solutions to the kind of practical problems policymakers, politicians, entrepreneurs and aid workers are faced with on a day-to-day basis. On the other hand, it is exactly this kind of distance to policy that enables one to analyze problems and developments in a more independent and critical manner. The emphasis on long-term developments can make us more immune to the fashion of the day and it may change our view of reality dramatically.

In this book the emphasis will be more on the detached approach to problems of development. However, there is no absolute contrast between the two approaches. There is a need for both. It is completely legitimate for politics and policy to ask for support and advice from scientific researchers. Besides, strong involvement does not necessarily preclude independent judgement or critical analysis. On the other hand, a long-term approach offers a starting point for the assessment of the effects of the development strategies pursued. It provides us with greater insight into the significance and scope of socio-economic policies amidst the many factors that impinge on processes of development.

Central questions that will be tackled in each chapter are: How do the factors discussed influence the development of per capita income, the standard of living and the conditions of life in poor countries? Which are the factors that contribute to development? Which are the factors that hamper development? What are the explanations for the observed developments and trends? How can the differences between regions and between historical periods be interpreted and explained?

1.2 *Discussion about development issues*

Posing the questions mentioned at the end of section 1.1 is more important than giving unambiguous answers. There is no such thing as scientific certainty, especially not in a field as controversial as that of economic and social development. Although the author's views will undoubtedly leave their imprint on this book, it is primarily intended as an introduction to the *debate on issues of development*. This debate is characterized by numerous clashing perspectives and theories. The results of empirical studies are often contradictory. At times it even seems that empirical research leads to more rather than less uncertainty. I have tried to represent the different views on issues of development in a balanced fashion, providing the reader with suggestions for further reading. Further, I have tried to sketch a picture of developments in post-war thinking on issues of development.

This approach should definitely not result in a noncommittal enumeration of points of view, perspectives and approaches, between which no choices need to be made. It is of great importance to learn to evaluate statements on development critically and to ascertain to what extent they are consistent with or contradicted by the empirical information available to us at present. Therefore, the exposition is illustrated as much as possible with statistics on development in several countries and regions. The purpose of this material is to introduce readers to international statistics and to stimulate them to find out their own way in empirically grounded discussions of the issues of development.

By way of example, I will present a number of statements that are no longer tenable as generalizations in the light of the empirical information presently available to us.

- *Developing countries are trapped in a vicious circle of stagnation; they are condemned to stagnation and poverty.* This stereotypical view of developing countries is generally untrue. As will be indicated in Chapter 3, some developing countries exhibit strong economic growth and dynamics. Besides, one should always remember that each economically advanced country was once a developing country.
- *Given the pace of the population growth, food scarcity in developing countries will always be a problem.* This statement, often associated with horrible pictures of starvation and malnutrition on the African continent, is generally untrue. In the long term, world food production is increasing marginally more rapidly than

world population (see Chapter 9). This is the case in most developing countries. However, this does not mean that hunger and malnutrition can be eliminated in the foreseeable future.

- *Agricultural exports do not contribute to the economic development of a country.* This unfavourable image of agricultural exports originates from the late nineteenth century when tropical developing countries exported agricultural products and industrial countries exported industrial products. Nevertheless, there are many countries where agricultural exports have been the foundation of later economic prosperity.
- *Population growth is a threat to economic development.* There is no need to deny the fact that rapid population growth is a problem in many developing countries. However, as will be discussed in Chapter 4, under certain conditions, a low population density may form an obstacle to economic growth. Sometimes population growth can be a stimulus to economic development and technological change.

1.3 *Growth and development*

In the preceding sections, the term 'development' has already been used frequently. In common parlance the term is used both often and casually: development studies, problems of development, developing countries, less developed countries, development cooperation, underdevelopment, and so on. So what *do* we mean by 'development'?

Implicit in the use of the term 'development' is the notion that some countries and regions of the world are extremely poor, whereas other countries, containing a relatively small percentage of world population, are very prosperous. The discussion of development is always tied up with questions like: Why are poor countries poor and rich countries rich? Why do poor countries lag behind rich countries in the development of their standards of living? How can poor countries become more prosperous? In this sense, 'development' refers to growth of national income per capita.

Development conceived of as economic growth is a quantitative concept and basically means more of the same. Yet economic development is more than economic growth alone. It also refers to qualitative changes in the structure of the economy (Kuznets, 1966). Of special importance are changes in the production structure: an increase of the share of industry in national income and employment and a decrease of the share of agriculture. This implies that economic growth can occur without economic development. An example of this is provided by the oil-exporting countries, which experienced a sharp increase in national income but saw hardly any changes in their economic structure.

In the 1960s the identification of development with economic growth came under increasing criticism. Authors like Dudley Seers, Gunnar Myrdal, Paul Streeten, Hollis Chenery, Mahbub ul Haq and institutions like the International Labour Organization

(ILO) pointed out that developing countries did not experience much change in the living conditions of the masses of the poor in spite of the impressive growth figures in the post-World War II period (Myrdal, 1971; Streeten, 1972; Chenery *et al.*, 1974; ul Haq, 1976; ILO, 1976; Seers, 1979). They came to the conclusion that development involves more than economic growth and structural economic change. Seers formulated three additional requirements for development, namely, that there should be a decrease in poverty and malnutrition, that the income distribution should be equalized, and that the employment situation should improve (Seers, 1979).

Criticism of growth fetishism led to the development of so-called social indicators: life expectancy, literacy, level of education, infant mortality, availability of telephones, hospital beds, licensed doctors, availability of calories, and so forth. Some authors even went so far as to posit an opposition between growth and development. Parallels were drawn between countries such as Sri Lanka where growth was not very rapid but where welfare facilities and the level of education were improving, and countries like Brazil where extremely rapid growth hardly affected poverty levels. Still, most authors reached the conclusion that, especially in the poorest countries, growth is a prerequisite for development, while development involves more than just growth.

Social scientists have stated that development should not be viewed in terms of economics only, and that attention should also be paid to changes in family structures, attitudes and mentalities, cultural changes, demographic developments, the transformation of rural societies and processes of urbanization.

The Swedish Nobel prize winner Gunnar Myrdal has argued that discussions of development have been based on a series of modernization ideals. Opinions differ on the way in which these ideals should be pursued. Nevertheless, according to Myrdal, there is a widespread consensus on the ultimate objectives of development among the members of political elites in developing countries involved in developmental policy (Myrdal, 1968, pp. 57–69). The broad concept of development therefore involves a change of the entire society in the direction of the modernization ideals.

The modernization ideals as described by Myrdal include the following:

- Rationality (in policy, in the application of technological knowledge, in structuring social relations, in thinking about objectives and means).
- Planning for development; searching for a coherent system of policy measures in order to change situations that are considered undesirable.
- An increase in per capita production and production per worker, primarily by industrialization and increasing capital intensity in production.
- An increase in the standard of living.
- An increase in social and economic equality. Development ought to be for the benefit of the people, the masses.
- More efficient institutions and attitudes that are conducive to an increase in productivity and to development in general (for example, institutions that are characterized by mobility, leeway for initiative and entrepreneurship, effective competition, equal opportunities; attitudes like efficiency, diligence, orderliness,

punctuality, economy, honesty, rationality, openness to change, solidarity and future orientedness.
- Consolidation of the national state and national integration.
- National independence.
- Political democratization. The concept of democratization can be interpreted in various ways of which parliamentary democracy is but one. Democratization always implies some notion of involving the masses of the population in political decision-making.
- Social discipline.

At this stage three remarks can be made. First, as Myrdal, Seers and many others noted, development is unavoidably a normative concept. The normative assumptions should therefore be made explicit. Secondly, an increase both in productivity and production per head of population is an essential element of every definition of 'development'; this is even the case with interpretations of the concept that are critical of a narrow economic approach to 'development'. Economic growth always remains one of the necessary conditions for 'long-term development'. Thirdly, the fact that there are modernization ideals, in no way implies that all societies ought to develop in the same manner or that they ought to converge.

1.4 *The desirability of growth and development*

The desirability of economic growth and development is not undisputed. Critics have pointed out the drawbacks of growth, development and modernization. They have pointed to the irreversible disruption of traditional societies and lifestyles, and the spread of a uniform materialistic mass culture, which will lead to cultural shallowness and loss of meaning, and to the increasing exploitation of people as a result of the spread of capitalist market relations. Sometimes it is suggested that people are happier in traditional societies than in modern societies: they would be more in tune with their natural environment, and their needs and wishes would balance their potentialities. There is a strong Malthusian movement which maintains that continued economic growth will disturb the natural balance, and will eventually lead to ecological catastrophes (Meadows *et al.*, 1972; Brundtland, 1987).

Several authors see 'development' as a euphemism for Western penetration and domination of the world, involving great misery and exploitation both in past and present. An eloquent example of this viewpoint is Stanley Diamond's frontal attack (1974) on the concept of civilization, usually associated with development and progress. Diamond argues that processes of civilization have always involved conquest, violence, coercion and oppression with respect to so-called less civilized peoples. For instance, the Indians have been victims of Western penetration into North America, the slaves have been victims of Western penetration into Africa, and the Eskimos have been victims of the spread of Western culture to Alaska. Yet, Diamond does not restrict himself to the results of Western expansion in the world.

Wherever people try to spread their civilization, the fire and the sword are always involved, whether it concerns the expansion of the Greek, the Roman, the Egyptian or the Islamic civilization. Such criticism is valuable though at times one-sided. First, it creates an awareness of the costs involved in development. Secondly – and perhaps most important – it brings to our attention the relation between the 'concept of development' and international power relationships. What one understands under 'development' in a particular historical period is strongly influenced by dominant cultures and powers of that period.

On the other hand, it is no coincidence that criticism of growth and development often emanates from members of the most prosperous classes of the richest countries in the world. When members of traditional tribal societies come in contact with modern consumer goods, their needs turn out to be far from limited. The possession of new goods will be sought for eagerly and widely. If one were to ask poor peasants or residents of urban slums in Africa or Asia whether they would prefer improvement in their productivity and standards of living, an overwhelming majority would respond positively. Only people who have been raised in very affluent societies can afford to have their doubts about the merits of economic growth and material progress.

Criticism of economic growth and development is sometimes dictated by a romantic idealization of an harmonious and balanced society that may never have existed. And even if isolated and socially and ecologically balanced societies did exist in days gone by, they no longer exist today. The problems developing countries are facing today have much to do with the fact that these countries have already been 'opened up' to trade, investment, colonial domination and partial penetration by the money economy for a long time (Myint, 1980). As far as there ever was a choice in whether or not to strive for development, this 'choice' has already been made in the past. Traditional self-sufficient economies have been upset. Modern technologies have contributed to a rapid population growth, which surpasses the capacity of traditional methods of production. Contact with the outer world has led to the emergence of modern preferences and needs. Societies have no choice but to strive for socio-economic development. Given the rapid rate of population growth the alternative would be to sink deeper and deeper into a situation of poverty, misery and starvation, which has for instance been the case in Bangladesh. Although not all modernization ideals are supported by all inhabitants of developing countries, almost everybody longs for the socio-economic side of development (see Lewis, 1950, appendix 1; North and Thomas, 1973, pp. 1–2; Jones, 1988). In turn, socio-economic development is impossible without extensive social modernization and social changes.

The ambivalence concerning development is very obvious in the continuing attempts to develop hybrids of the ideals of sustained growth of welfare and productivity and modernization of social institutions on the one hand, and valued elements of cultural traditions on the other hand. Examples are African socialism as advocated by political leaders such as Nyerere and Senghor, Indian socialism as advocated by Gandhi and Nehru, and the present-day striving for an Islamic development model.

In recent years disturbing reports of global warming, the extinction of rain forests and pollution of air and water have revived the discussion concerning the 'limits to growth' (for example, see Bunyard, 1985; Ettinger *et al.*, 1989; World Bank, 1992). An influential report, written for the United Nations, argues for 'sustainable development', that is, development which does not diminish the life chances of future generations (Brundtland, 1987). However, the effect of such ideas on actual policy has been limited up to now.

1.5 *Development and westernization*

Apart from such elements as economic growth and productivity, it is practically impossible to define the concept of development in an abstract and ahistorical way. The substance and meaning of words like development and modernization are strongly determined by the international political and economic balance of power. Countries that are most prosperous economically and that are politically and culturally dominant, are models for development in the eyes of their own people as well as in the eyes of the peoples trying to break away from their hold. In the last 400 years the 'West' has become the economic and political centre of the world. Western countries have become the models for 'modern' societies. This means that present-day 'development' – which has been described above as a change in society in the direction of specific modernization ideals – and 'westernization' are inevitably entwined. As is illustrated by Myrdal's modernization ideals, notions of development have been derived from the historical development experiences of the present prosperous Western countries.

This conclusion may shock those who criticize a Western ethnocentric view on issues of development. They may consider it another attempt to project the blueprint of Western development on non-Western societies. This is by no means my intention. First, there is no question of Western society being considered 'superior' to other societies. I simply want to note that the explicitly formulated or implicitly present ideals and objectives of development are modelled on the powers that dominate the world economy.

Secondly, the interweavement of development and westernization does not imply that all countries or societies should or can adopt the same course of development. Initial conditions and circumstances are so different for each country, region and historical period, that previous developmental experiences cannot be copied. Besides, at each stage there are alternative paths and options. Furthermore, I do not say that countries or societies will converge. I only observe that the measures for 'developed' or 'less developed' have been highly coloured by the developmental experiences of Western countries.

Thirdly, I nowhere state that the relationship between developmental values and westernization is a lasting one. As the centre of gravity of economic and political power relationships shifts towards Asia, our understanding of the terms 'modern' and 'less modern', 'developed' and 'less developed' will gradually change. At one time British society was the model of a 'developed' and 'modern' society. In the twentieth century this role has been taken over by the United States. At present, we notice that our attention is gradually turning towards Japan as an example of a modern and successful society that might be imitated. Or, to mention yet another example, after the decline of the Soviet empire the world appears to be less attracted to Western ideologies such as Marxism; planning, which was still high on Myrdal's list of modernization ideals, is increasingly dropping out of favour.

In summary, it can be concluded that development is a highly value-laden concept. The meaning of this concept is determined by the societies that are considered dominant or advanced at a particular moment in time.

1.6 *Indicators of development*

The indicator most often used to indicate the degree of 'development' of a country is national income per capita. National income can be calculated in three different ways (for example, see Allen, 1980):

1. As the sum of all incomes – wages, profits, interest, dividend and rent – that have been earned in a country during the period of one year.
2. As the sum of all value added in an economy (national product).
3. As the sum of all expenditures of a country (consumer spending, investment, government expenditures, exports minus expenditures on imports).

In theory, national income, national product and national expenditure are equal. In practice, however, statistical discrepancies often occur. An important conceptual difference is that between gross national product (GNP) and gross domestic product (GDP). The difference between GNP and GDP lies in the balance of foreign income from factors of production and payments to other countries for factors of production. This distinction is very important for developing countries. Since a significant part of investment in developing countries is in foreign hands, there is a net annual outflow of dividends and profits. Therefore, gross national product (or gross national income) will be less than gross domestic product.

There are two kinds of debates on indicators such as per capita GNP or per capita GDP. First, there are all sorts of technical objections to the use of per capita GNP as an adequate indicator of the level of economic development of a country. Secondly, there are substantive objections to the use of per capita GNP as an indicator of development. After all, as mentioned in section 1.3, development involves much more than economic growth alone.

Technical objections to the use of per capita GNP as an indicator of economic development include the following (Bauer, 1976, pp. 55–66; Myint, 1980, pp. 8–10):

- Principally GNP refers to that part of the national income that is traded via the market for money. In developing countries, however, there is widespread subsistence production. If, in the process of economic development, there is a shift from subsistence production to production for the market, it seems as if national income is increasing, whereas in reality there is no increase in production.

- GNP does not allow for differences in climate and conditions of life that require different types of clothing, food, transportation and housing.
- Economic growth and industrialization involve costs that do not occur in other societies: the costs of transporting goods and people, the costs of the disposal of waste, and the costs of fighting environmental pollution. These costs are not accounted for in national income.
- International comparisons of national incomes are usually made with exchange rates. However, these exchange rates do not provide us with a reliable picture of the purchasing-power parity of the currencies of the countries compared. Relative levels of prosperity in developing countries are higher than suggested by official international statistics on national incomes in dollars. One of the reasons for this is that services in developing countries are much cheaper than in prosperous countries (see Kravis *et al.*, 1982).

Substantive objections to the use of GNP as an indicator of development are all based on the fact that development involves a lot more than economic growth only. Even from an economic point of view, GNP does not provide us with a good picture of the changes in the life circumstances of the poor masses. Per capita GNP is an average figure. It does not account for the distribution of income and consumption, which is often very unequal. Furthermore, the level of the national income is not directly related to the standard of living. When a considerable part of a country's national income is invested or used for military spending, consumption of the inhabitants of this country may for many years lag far behind the growth of the national income.

Despite increases in national income, living conditions of the very poorest groups in a society may thus deteriorate. On the other hand, their situation may improve in spite of a stagnation or slow growth of GNP. From this perspective, it is argued that various other economic and social indicators should be used along with GNP. Such economic and social indicators give a more straightforward picture of developments in a country: the number of people below poverty thresholds, data on malnutrition, employment figures, life expectancy at birth, infant mortality, numbers of doctors, nurses and hospital beds for every thousand inhabitants, energy consumption, the degree of illiteracy, years of education, data on income distribution, miles of roads and railways, access to pure water, equal opportunities for both men and women, human rights, and so on. Since 1990 the United Nations Development Programme (UNDP) publishes the *Human Development Report*, which reports on many of these indicators annually. In this report the Human Development Index (HDI) has been introduced. HDI is a non-weighted average of three variables: an index of per capita gross domestic income; life expectancy; and the level of education. In the income index the income categories above the poverty threshold are given progressively lower weights in order to represent the declining marginal utility of higher incomes. The education index is a weighted average of literacy (two-thirds) and the average number of years of schooling (one-third) (see UNDP, 1991, pp. 88–91). When countries are ranked according to the Human Development Index, their position may differ substantially from their position on a per capita income ranking. For example, in 1990, twenty-six countries had a HDI ranking that differed more than 20 points from the ranking according to their per capita income (UNDP, 1991, p. 15).

These indicators are a useful addition to the national income data. Still, in practice, these indicators have not succeeded in superseding per capita GNP. First, the quality of the data is often absolutely inadequate for international comparisons of levels and trends between many countries. In contrast, work on standardization of concepts and measuring techniques with regard to national income has already been continuing for many decades (see UNSO, 1968). Secondly, the weighting of social indicators is rather arbitrary. For instance, if higher incomes get lower weights, one automatically gets a different ranking. Thirdly, in spite of some exceptions many social indicators appear to be closely connected with per capita national income (Beckerman, 1974, 1993). At a given moment, differences may occur between the order based on income and the order based on social indicators. However, if the development of per capita national income stagnates over time, this will sooner or later be reflected in a deterioration of the social indicators.

The development of gross domestic product provides an indication of the development of a country's productive potential. How this capacity will be used cannot be known in advance. For example, it may be used for fulfilment of basic needs, health care, education, military spending, foreign payments, or luxury consumption of the well-to-do. It depends very much on the policies pursued in a country. In any event it is a well-established fact that there can be no long-term improvement of the living conditions of the masses of the population without a growth of productive capacity. As has been shown in section 1.3, an increase in per capita income is one of the important elements in all definitions of the development concept. This view is also endorsed in the *Human Development Report* (UNDP, 1991, p. 1). The chapters in this book on demographics, health care, education and state formation (Chapters 4–6, 10) will explicitly pay attention to the interplay of economic growth and social indicators.

1.7 *The Third World does not exist*

After World War II the term 'Third World' came into vogue as a designation for developing countries (Worsley, 1964). This Third World was contrasted with the First World of the advanced capitalist countries and the Second World of the industrialized socialist countries in Eastern Europe. The use of this term implies that all Third World countries have common characteristics and interests, and that a wide and growing gap separates them from the affluent industrialized countries. The same is implied by terms such as 'North' versus 'South'. With regard to these terms, the similarities and differences in circumstances in developing countries will be discussed. In this section the emphasis will be on the diversity of circumstances; similarities will be discussed in section 1.8.

Table 1.1, derived from the *World Development Report 1995* (World Bank, 1995), shows a greatly diversified world economy with enormous differences in per capita incomes, and great inequality both between rich and poor countries and among poor countries themselves. In Table 1.1, countries have been ranked primarily by income per capita, and have been divided into three categories: low-income countries; middle-income countries; and high-income countries. Moreover, the middle-income countries have been subdivided into lower-middle-income countries and upper-middle-income countries.

Table 1.1 Population and GNP per capita (including growth rates and PPP estimates) in 1993

	Population[a] (millions)	GNP per capita		
		1993 ($)	Average annual growth (%) 1980–93[b]	1993 PPP estimates (international $)
Low-income economies	3,092.7	380	3.7	
China and India	2,076.6	410	6.2	
Others	1,016.1	300	0.1	
1 Mozambique	15.1	90	−1.5	550
2 Tanzania	28.0	90	0.1	580
3 Ethiopia[c]	51.9	100	−1.9	340
4 Sierra Leone	4.5	150	−1.5	750
5 Vietnam	71.3	170		
6 Bhutan[d]	1.5	180	6.3	630
7 Burundi	6.0	180	0.9	740
8 Uganda[e]	18.0	180	2.4	900
9 Nepal	20.8	190	2.0	1,020
10 Cambodia[f]	9.0	200		
11 Malawi	10.5	200	−1.2	690
12 Chad	6.0	210	3.2	720
13 Rwanda	7.6	210	−1.2	740
14 Bangladesh	115.2	220	2.1	1,230
15 Madagascar	13.9	220	−2.6	670
16 Guinea-Bissau	1.0	240	2.8	840
17 Kenya	25.3	270	0.3	1,290
18 Mali	10.1	270	−1.0	520
19 Niger	8.6	270	−4.1	780
20 Lao PDR[g]	4.6	280		1,930
21 Burkina Faso	9.8	300	0.8	770
22 India	898.2	300	3.0	1,220
23 Nigeria	105.3	300	−0.1	1,400
24 Albania	3.4	340	−3.2	
25 Nicaragua	4.1	340	−5.7	1,900
26 Togo	3.9	340	−2.1	1,000
27 Haiti[g]	6.6	370	−2.4	

Table 1.1 (*continued*)

	Population[a] (millions)	GNP per capita		
		1993 ($)	Average annual growth (%) 1980–93[b]	1993 PPP estimates (international $)
28 Zambia	8.9	380	−3.1	
29 Monglia	2.3	390	0.2	2,020
30 Central African Rep.	3.2	400	−1.6	1,010
31 Benin	5.1	430	−0.4	1,620
32 Ghana	16.4	430	0.1	1.970
33 Pakistan	122.8	430	3.1	2,170
34 Tajikistan	5.8	470	−3.6	1,380
35 China	1,178.4	490	8.2	2,330
36 Guinea	6.3	500		
37 Mauritania	2.2	500	−0.8	1,490
38 Yemen, Rep.[f]	13.2	520		
39 Zimbabwe	10.7	520	−0.3	2,000
40 Georgia	5.4	580	−6.6	1,750
41 Honduras	5.3	600	−0.3	1,910
42 Sri Lanka	17.9	600	2.7	2,990
43 Cote d'Ivoire	13.3	630	−4.6	1,400
44 Lesotho	1.9	650	−0.5	1,620
45 Armenia	3.7	660	−4.2	2,040
46 Egypt, Arab Republic	56.4	660	2.8	3,780
Afghanistan[i]	21.5			
Liberia[i]	2.8			
Myanmar[i]	44.6			
Somalia[i]	8.9			
Sudan[i]	26.6			
Zaire[i]	41.2			
Middle-income economies	1,596.3	2,480	0.2	
Lower-middle-income	1,095.8	1,590	−0.5	
47 Azerbaijan	7.4	730	−3.5	2,190
48 Indonesia	187.2	740	4.2	3,150
49 Senegal	7.9	750	0.0	1,650
50 Bolivia	7.1	760	−0.7	2,420
51 Cameroon	12.5	820	−2.2	2,100
52 Kyrgyz Rep.	4.6	850	0.1	2,670
53 Philippines	64.8	850	−0.6	2,670
54 Congo	2.4	950	−0.3	2,440
55 Uzbekistan	21.9	970	−0.2	2,510
56 Morocco	25.9	1,040	1.2	3,090
57 Moldova	4.4	1,060	−2.0	2,870
58 Guatemala	10.0	1,100	−1.2	3,350
59 Papua New Guinea	4.1	1,130	0.6	2,350
60 Bulgaria	8.9	1,140	0.5	4,100
61 Romania	22.8	1,140	−2.4	2,800
62 Syrian Arab Rep.[f]	13.0	1,160	−1.4	

Table 1.1 (*continued*)

	Population[a] (millions)	GNP per capita		
		1993 ($)	Average annual growth (%) 1980–93[b]	1993 PPP estimates (international $)
63 Jordan[m]	4.1	1,190	−5.4	4,100
64 Ecuador	11.0	1,200	0.0	4,240
65 Dominican Rep.	7.5	1,230	0.7	3,630
66 Turkmenistan[c]	3.9	1,230		3,950
67 El Salvador	5.5	1,320	0.2	2,350
68 Lithuania	3.7	1,320	−2.8	3,110
69 Colombia	35.7	1,400	1.5	5,490
70 Jamaica	2.4	1,440	−0.3	3,000
71 Peru	22.9	1,490	−2.7	3,220
72 Paraguay	4.7	1,510	−0.7	3,390
73 Kazakhstan	17.0	1,560	−1.6	3,710
74 Tunisia	8.4	1,720	1.2	4,780
75 Algeria	26.7	1,780	−0.8	5,380
76 Namibia	1.5	1,820	0.7	3,790
77 Slovak Republic	5.3	1,950		6,290
78 Latvia	2.6	2,010	−0.6	5,010
79 Thailand	58.1	2,110	6.4	6,260
80 Costa Rica	3.3	2,150	1.1	5,520
81 Iran, Islamic Rep.[c]	64.2	2,200	−1.4	5,280
82 Ukraine	51.6	2,210	0.2	4,450
83 Poland	38.3	2,260	0.4	5,000
84 Russian Federation	148.7	2,340	−1.0	5,050
85 Panama	2.5	2,600	−0.7	5,840
86 Czech Republic	10.3	2,710		7,550
87 Botswana[j]	1.4	2,790	6.2	5,160
88 Turkey[j]	58.5	2,970	2.4	5,170
Angola[i]	10.3			
Cuba[j]	10.9			
Korea, Dem. Rep.[i]	23.0			
Lebanon[i]	3.9			
Iraq[i]	19.5			
Upper-middle-income	500.5	4,370	0.9	
89 Venezuela	20.9	2,840	−0.7	8,130
90 Belarus	10.2	2,870	2.4	6,240
91 Brazil	156.6	2,930	0.3	5,370
92 South Africa	39.7	2,980	−0.2	
93 Mauritius	1.1	3,030	5.5	12,420
94 Yugoslavia[nhe]	23.9	3,060	2.9	
95 Estonia	1.6	3,080	−2.2	6,320
96 Malaysia	19.0	3,140	3.5	7,930
97 Chile	13.8	3,170	3.6	8,400
98 Hungary	10.2	3,350	1.2	6,050
99 Mexico	90.0	3,610	−0.5	6,810

Table 1.1 (*continued*)

	Population[a] (millions)	GNP per capita		
		1993 ($)	Average annual growth (%) 1980–93[b]	1993 PPP estimates (international $)
100 Trinidad and Tobago	1.3	3,830	−2.8	8,080
101 Uruguay	3.1	3,830	−0.1	6,380
102 Oman	2.0	4,850	3.4	9,020
103 Gabon	1.0	4,960	−1.6	
104 Puerto Rico	3.6	7,000	1.0	10,670
105 Argentina	33.8	7,220	−0.5	6,080
106 Greece	10.4	7,390	0.9	9,000
107 Saudi Arabia[c]	17.4	7,510	−3.3	11,170
108 Korea, Rep.	44.1	7,660	8.2	9,630
109 Portugal[j]	9.8	9,130	3.3	10,710
Libya[i]	5.0			
Low- and middle-income	4,689.0	1,090	0.9	
Sub-Saharan Africa	559.0	520	−0.8	
East Asia & Pacific	1,713.9	820	6.4	
South Asia	1,194.4	310	3.0	
Europe and Central Asia	494.6	2,450	−0.3	
Middle East & N. Africa	262.5	1,950	−2.3	
Latin America & Caribbean	466.3	2,950	−0.1	
Severely indebted countries	385.8	2,640	−1.1	
High-income economies	812.4	23,090	2.2	
110 New Zealand	3.5	12,600	0.7	16,040
111 Ireland	3.5	13,000	3.6	13,490
112 Spain	39.5	13,590	2.7	13,510
113 Israel	5.2	13,920	2.0	14,940
114 Australia	17.6	17,500	1.6	17,910
115 Hong Kong[k]	5.8	18,060	5.4	21,560
116 United Kingdom	57.9	18,060	2.3	17,210
117 Finland	5.1	19,300	1.5	15,530
118 Kuwait	1.8	19,360	−4.3	21,630
119 Italy	57.1	19,840	2.1	17,830
120 Singapore	2.8	19,850	6.1	19,510
121 Canada	28.8	19,970	1.4	20,230
122 Netherlands	15.3	20,950	1.7	17,330
123 United Arab Emirates	1.8	21,430	−4.4	20,940
124 Belgium	10.0	21,650	1.9	19,640
125 France	57.5	22,490	1.6	19,000
126 Austria	7.9	23,510	2.0	19,430
127 Germany	80.7	23,560	2.1	16,850
128 Sweden	8.7	24,740	1.3	17,200

Table 1.1 (*continued*)

	Population[a] (millions)	GNP per capita		
		1993 ($)	Average annual growth (%) 1980–93[b]	1993 PPP estimates (international $)
129 United States	257.8	24,740	1.7	24,740
130 Norway	4.3	25,970	2.2	19,780
131 Denmark	5.2	26,730	2.0	19,560
132 Japan	124.5	31,490	3.4	20,850
133 Switzerland	7.1	35,760	1.1	23,660
World	5,501.5	4,420	1.2	

Notes:
[a] Countries with more than one million inhabitants. Totals and subtotals including countries not in the table and countries with incomplete information, excluding countries added from other WDR issues; see notes.
[b] Category averages weighted by population size.
[c] All GNP data 1992 from *WDR 1994*.
[d] All data 1992 from *WDR 1994*.
[e] Growth rate of GNP per capita 1965–90 from *WDR 1992*.
[f] GNP per capita 1991 from *WDR 1993*.
[g] PPP estimate 1992 from *WDR 1994*.
[h] GNP per capita 1990 from *WDR 1992*.
[i] GNP per capita not available. Countries categorized in income classes based on World Bank estimates.
[j] New estimates; countries still categorized according to former classification.
[k] Data refer to GDP.
[l] Growth rate of GNP refers to the Federal Republic of Germany prior to unification.
[m] Growth rate 1985–1992.
[n] Data refer to former Socialist Federal Republic of Yugoslavia, population 1991 from *WDR 1993*.

Source: If not indicated otherwise, World Bank. *World Development Report 1995*.

Low-income countries

The category of *low-income countries* consists of fifty-two countries with a per capita gross national income of less than 695 dollars in 1993. These countries are also called the *least developed countries* (LDCs). Countries the World Bank has assigned to this category are eligible for aid and loans on more favourable terms than richer developing countries. The total population of the countries in this category is over 3.1 billion people with an average per capita income of 380 dollars in 1993.

Within the low-income category there is a significant difference between Asian countries with huge populations and high population densities and African countries with small populations and low population densities. Among the low-income countries are four Asian countries with very large populations and high population densities: India has 898 million inhabitants and a per capita income of 300 dollars per year; China has 1,178 million inhabitants and a per capita income of 490 dollars; Bangladesh has 115 million inhabitants and a per capita income of 220 dollars; and Pakistan has 123 million inhabitants and a per capita income of 430 dollars. This category further consists of twenty-nine African countries (to the south of the Sahara), most of these with small populations and a relatively low population density. The Asian countries are often characterized by ancient urban civilizations and age-old traditions of centralized political rule and unity. In African countries there have been some historical tendencies towards larger political entities but in comparison with Asian countries it can be stated that political centralization and urban traditions did not develop very far during the precolonial age. In Africa, natural circumstances (climate, rainfall, quality of the soil, tropical diseases) are relatively unfavourable in comparison with other parts of the world (World Bank, 1989b). Mineral wealth is abundant in African countries. However, up till now these potentialities have not been exploited to the full. Among others things, this is due to poorly developed physical infrastructure (roads, transport, communication). An inadequate infrastructure is a barrier to economic development in this region in other respects as well.

Since 1965 there has been considerable economic growth in many large poor Asian countries like Indonesia, China, India and Pakistan (with the notorious exception of Bangladesh). In poor African countries there is stagnation rather than growth. In no less than ten countries there has been a negative growth rate of per capita national income since 1965 (see World Bank, 1989a). In 1987 thirteen countries throughout sub-Saharan Africa had a lower per capita income than they did before their independence (World Bank, 1989b, p. 18). Since 1980 per capita income has decreased in eighteen of the twenty-six African countries, for which data are included in Table 1.1.

Lower-middle-income countries

The developing countries that are less poor are described as the middle-income countries. In this rather heterogeneous category it is customary to distinguish between the 'lower-middle-income countries' with an annual per capita income of 696–2,840 dollars and the 'upper-middle-income countries' with an annual per capita income of 2,840–8,626 dollars.

The division between the lower-middle-income countries (LMICs) and the LDCs is rather arbitrary. This category includes several poor countries that are hardly distinguishable from the LDCs. In the bottom half of the lower-middle-income category, there are again some sub-Saharan African countries with small populations (Cameroon, Congo and Senegal). Further, this category includes several poor countries from Central and South America (Bolivia, Colombia, the Dominican Republic, Ecuador, El Salvador, Guatemala, Paraguay and Peru) and North African and Middle East countries (Algeria, Jordan, Morocco, Syria, and Tunisia). Most of these countries experienced very slow or negative economic growth in the 1980s. An exception to this picture of stagnation in the lower-middle-income categories are the populous Asian countries Thailand and Indonesia. Thailand with 58 million people grew at 6.4 per cent per year; Indonesia with 187.2. million inhabitants, shows a respectable growth rate of 4.2 per cent per year. In 1993 this country graduated from the LDC to the LMIC category. Finally, the lower-middle-income category consists of a striking number of countries that used to be part of the Soviet Union (Azerbaijan, the Kyrgyz Repubic, Lithuania, Moldova, Kazakhstan, the Russian Federation, Turkmenistan and Uzbekistan) and several former communist countries (such as Bulgaria, Poland, Romania, the Czech Republic and the Slovak Republic). Second and Third World, North and South, East and West are all mixed up here. The average annual per capita income in the lower-middle-income category is 1,590 dollars; the total population of these countries is 1,096 million. On average, economic growth in this category has been negative.

Upper-middle-income countries

This category consists of twenty-two countries with a total of 501 million inhabitants and an annual per capita income of 2,840–8,626 dollars. The average annual income is 4,370 dollars. In this category one will find four large and populous Latin American countries: Mexico, Brazil, Argentina and Venezuela, and two smaller ones: Chile and Uruguay. It is striking that these Latin American countries are among the more prosperous of the developing countries, in spite of their history of extreme colonial and neocolonial exploitation. The large Latin American countries are characterized by relatively favourable natural circumstances, great natural wealth and a relatively low population density. Often, comparisons are drawn between these Latin American countries and the North American continent; it is an interesting question why Latin America has experienced a less favourable economic development since the nineteenth century in comparison with countries like the USA and Canada.

In the post-war period, many Latin American countries have experienced rapid economic growth. Compared with Asian countries these countries are characterized by an extremely unequal income distribution, as a result of which the poor masses have benefited very little from average increases in welfare. A country like Brazil is often mentioned as an illustration of the fact that large-scale poverty can coexist together with rapid economic growth.

In the 1980s, growth in Latin America stagnated. Most countries were hit by the debt crisis, which affected their growth performance and their economic prospects negatively. Moreover, countries like Argentina, Brazil and Mexico were characterized by extremely high inflation.

Within the middle-income category one can also find southern European countries like Portugal and Greece, as well as former socialist countries like Hungary and Romania and former Soviet republics such as Lithuania, Belarus, Estonia and Latvia. Five of the important oil-exporting countries belong to this category as well.

High-income countries

The category of *high-income countries* consists of twenty-four countries with a per capita income of over 8,626 dollars annually and a total population of 812 million. From 1989 onwards the World Bank no longer distinguished a separate category of industrialized market economies (the rich Western countries and Japan). In the 1989

World Development Report (World Bank, 1989a) these countries were first categorized together with other affluent countries like Israel, Hong Kong, Singapore, the United Arab Emirates and Kuwait.

Oil-exporting developing countries

A separate category consists of the *oil-exporting developing countries*. Some of these belong to the upper-middle-income category (Libya, Saudi Arabia, Oman, Mexico and Venezuela). As has been mentioned above, countries like the United Arab Emirates and Kuwait[1] are high-income countries. In spite of their high average incomes they can still be considered as developing countries since their economic structure is extremely one-sided. It depends on a single type of exports: oil. The central problem for economies like these is how to realize a *structural transformation* into a more diversified economic structure. The problems involved are not only economic but social as well. Attempts to transform and modernize an economy using oil wealth may evoke great social stress and give rise to social protest groups. To some extent, the rise of Muslim fundamentalism may be viewed in this light.

Newly industrializing countries

Several developing countries – including South Korea, Taiwan, Brazil, Mexico, Hong Kong, Singapore and Israel – have experienced an impressive industrial growth since World War II. They are called the *newly industrializing countries*. These countries have succeeded in building up a modern industrial structure in a short period of time. They are a striking illustration of the thesis that developing countries are not necessarily condemned to primary production and that industrialization is a real option for developing countries. Until recently, all of these countries were classified as middle-income countries. Since 1989 Singapore, Hong Kong and Israel have joined the high-income category; Japan had already succeeded in doing so earlier.

Other countries that have realized a considerable growth in their industrial sector since World War II are Egypt, the Philippines, Colombia, Turkey, Yugoslavia, Portugal, Spain and Greece. These countries are also described as the *semi-industrialized countries* (SICs) (see OECD, 1979). At the moment, Indonesia, Thailand, Malaysia and China are experiencing substantial industrial growth.

Former socialist countries in Europe

Until 1988, socialist countries in Central and Eastern Europe were considered a separate category in the consecutive editions of the *World Development Report*. However, very few comparable statistics on these countries were available. The same applied to centrally planned economies in other parts of the world – and, in fact, often still does. Since 1989 the Eastern European socialist countries are no longer regarded as a separate category. This is partly because of the absence of reliable statistical data and partly because of their transformation into market economies.

Moreover, in 1991 the Soviet Union disintegrated. Many of the former Soviet republics in Asia now appear to have much in common with developing countries in other parts of the world. In 1993, no fewer than thirteen former socialist Eastern European countries and former Soviet republics have been categorized as middle-income countries. Yet the historical process of development of both the former eastern European socialist economies and the former Soviet republics is very different from that of other developing countries in the middle-income category.

Regional distribution of poverty and welfare

Table 1.1 offers an impression of the regional distribution of poverty and welfare. Poverty is primarily concentrated in Asia and sub-Saharan Africa, though Asia, with its large and dense population, shows much more economic dynamism than sparsely populated Africa, which is characterized by stagnation. The implication is that the intuitive association between development problems and Africa conjures up too gloomy a picture of the achievements of developing countries. Although it is understandable that the media often concentrate on hunger in Africa, by far the greatest number of poor people actually live in Asia. In terms of changes in the life situation of the very poor, it is therefore more interesting to look at developments in the populous Asian countries.

The large Latin American countries are much more affluent and come closer to the levels of prosperity of rich Western countries than most other developing countries. To some extent the Latin America development problem can be characterized as a distributive problem: how can the masses share in the increased average welfare, achieved in the course of the twentieth century. This applies less to poor African and Asian countries where there is not much to distribute in the first place. In the 1980s economic growth in Latin America faltered. At the same time many Asian countries experienced continued growth. Differences in economic policy are among the causes of this contrast in development (see Chapter 11). The resumption of growth in Latin America is hampered by the heavy debt burden. The same applies to several of the poorest African countries (see Chapter 11).

International comparisons based on purchasing power parities

The last column of Table 1.1. presents estimates of national income in international dollars, based on so called purchasing-power parities (PPPs). For many years, researchers have been trying to overcome the disadvantages of the use of exchange rates in international comparisons, by calculating measures which explicitly take into account the relative purchasing power of the currencies of the countries being compared (see Kravis *et al.*, 1982; Summers and Heston, 1991). By now PPP-based estimates have become available for many countries, though it should be stressed that the quality and reliability of these estimates still varies substantially. In the *World Development Report* (World Bank, 1995) these PPP-based estimates have been updated to 1993 and are given for as many countries as possible.

The use of purchasing-power parities has several effects. In the first place, the dollar incomes of the poorest countries tend to be three to four times higher than their dollar incomes based on exchange rate conversions. PPP-based comparisons provide a more realistic picture of poverty, because they take into account the relative cheapness of services and basic necessities in developing countries.

A second effect of the use of PPPs is that the ranking between countries can change quite substantially, also amongst developing countries themselves. A difference in ranking of more than 10 points occurs for twenty-five of the 120 countries for which we have estimates in international dollars as well as exchange rate comparisons. For instance, China improves its ranking by 10 points, Indonesia by 13 points, while India's ranking declines by 1 point. The greatest improvement is registered by Egypt (+21 points), the greatest decline by El Salvador (−18 points).

Finally, the inequality of average per capita incomes in the world economy is diminished, as incomes in the poorest countries tend to be higher, while incomes in the richest countries tend to be lower. The same can be seen, within each of the categories of Table 1.1. Of course, the use of PPPs changes nothing about the basic reality of poverty in large parts of the world. However, it does describe poverty (and affluence) more adequately. Without the use of PPPs it is almost impossible to understand how anyone could survive on an income of 300 dollars per year. Therefore, it is likely that PPPs will be used ever more frequently in spite of all the technical problems involved in their estimation.

Summary

This discussion has shown that developing countries differ in many ways, which include the following:

- Great differences in the levels of prosperity amongst developing countries.
- Differences in population size, density and growth.
- Differences in climate, soil quality and natural resources.
- Differences in degrees of industrialization.
- Differences in colonial experience. Some areas have been colonized at an early stage, others at a late stage. Some areas have never been colonized at all. Moreover, there have been great variations in the nature and the intensity of the colonial relationships (see Chapter 2).
- Differences in precolonial history. For a full understanding of present-day developments, one has to take into account the precolonial history and the cultural and religious development of the different societies. In particular I have emphasized the importance of age-old traditions of political centralization and urbanization in countries on the Asian continent.
- Pronounced differences in economic dynamism, with long periods of growth in some regions and long periods of stagnation in others.

In short, the term 'Third World' is an unacceptable simplification which does not do justice to the diversity of circumstances and developmental experiences in various parts of the world.

With respect to the gap between rich and poor countries, two conclusions can be drawn: the first conclusion concerns the degree of inequality between rich and poor countries; the second conclusion refers to the possibilities of bridging the gap between rich and poor countries:

1. *The degree of inequality* Inequality in the world economy is very great. For example, Table 1.1 shows that on average the per capita income of the twenty-four richest countries is sixty-one times the per capita income of the fifty-two poorest countries. Even if one takes into account the fact that the use of exchange rates leads to undervaluation of welfare in developing countries, there is still extreme inequality. In Table 1.1, per capita incomes in international dollars in the twenty-four high-income countries are on average 12 times as high as in the thirty-nine poorest countries for which estimates are available. Distribution of world income over households is even more unequal than distribution of the world income over countries, since incomes within countries are also distributed unequally. Furthermore, income inequality in developing countries is considerably greater than in affluent countries. Berry *et al.* (1983) have estimated the distribution of the world income in 124 countries in 1970. They estimate the share of the bottom half of the world population at 8.4 per cent of world income, whereas the share of the top 10 per cent is no less than 49.4 per cent of world income. Such estimates are subject to many uncertainties. However, they do provide us with a striking illustration of the extremely unequal distribution of the world incomes. Furthermore, inequality between rich and poor countries has grown in the course of time.

2. *Bridging the gap* In spite of the huge differences between welfare in various countries, it is not correct to speak of an insurmountable gap between rich and poor countries. The discussion of Table 1.1 shows that the transition from developing countries to affluent countries is a gradual one. Some developing countries are more affluent than the poorer Western countries or the former socialist countries in Eastern Europe. Countries like Japan, Korea and Taiwan, which used to be considered as developing countries, are now called advanced. Other countries that used to be considered reasonably developed – such as Argentina – are now classified as developing countries. There is a constant process of change in the rank order of countries rather than an impermeable and unchangeable gap between rich and poor countries (see Reynolds, 1986).

1.8 *Problems of developing countries*

In spite of the diversity of circumstances and developmental experiences, developing countries do have several characteristics in common. If we were not able to identify such characteristics, it would not be much use to speak of or write about developing countries. Common characteristics of developing countries include the following:

1. Widespread poverty and malnutrition.
2. A large share of agriculture in output and employment.
3. Pronounced dualism in economic structure.
4. Explosive growth of population.
5. Explosive urbanization.
6. Large-scale underutilization of labour.
7. Political instability.

We will look briefly at each of these characteristics in turn.

Poverty and malnutrition

As shown in Table 1.1, in 1993 over 3 billion persons lived in countries with an annual per capita income of less than 695 dollars. The average annual per capita income of these people amounted to only 380 dollars (or 1,766 international dollars). Even this low average income does not offer a correct impression of the incomes of the very poorest since the income distribution in most developing countries is heavily skewed. In the late 1980s the share in total income or total consumer expenditures of the bottom 20 per cent of the households in the poorest developing countries ranged between 2.4 per cent and 9.7 per cent. The average was 6.2 per cent (World Bank, 1995, p. 220). Poverty is not restricted to the poorest countries. In developing countries with a higher average income, there are also large numbers of extremely poor people as a result of the unequal income distribution. In the lower-middle-income category, the share of the bottom 20 per cent of the households ranges from 2.1 per cent to 8.7 per cent. In the upper-middle-income category, the share of the bottom 20 per cent ranges from 2.1 per cent to 10.9 per cent.[2]

Ahluwalia *et al.* (1979, p. 462 ff.) report that 40 per cent of the total population of the developing countries was living below the absolute poverty threshold in 1975. In the poorest developing countries this was no less than 60 per cent. In 1985 a person would be defined as poor if his or her income was less than 370 dollars a year. In the same year, the number of people in poverty was estimated at 1,116 million (World Bank, 1990, p. 29).

One of the most distressing aspects of poverty in developing countries is absolute malnutrition. Estimates of the numbers of undernourished people differ greatly. But the numbers are certainly high. According to estimates by the FAO, 512 million people in eighty-nine non-communist developing countries were undernourished between 1983 and 1985. This works out at 22 per cent of the total population in these countries (see Alexandratos, 1988). Other sources come to substantially higher estimates (e.g. World Bank, 1986). Most studies indicate that the percentage of malnourished people will decline in the long term. However, in view of the enormous population growth, the absolute number of undernourished people will increase.

Absolute malnutrition is associated with high death rates, bad health, impairment of the mental capacities and low productivity.

Share in production and employment

In developing countries the share of agricultural production in the total production is much higher than in affluent countries. Production techniques in agriculture are less productive than in the industrial sector. The share of the agricultural labour force in the total labour force is therefore even larger than the share of the agricultural production in the total production. This means that in developing countries a larger proportion of the labour force is active in the agricultural sector than in affluent countries. Conversely, the share of the industrial sector in production and employment is smaller.

Dualism

In developing countries there is a wide gap between the modern sector (which includes industry, mining, the production of commercial crops for the world market and modern services) and the traditional sector which uses primitive and low-productivity techniques (e.g. traditional agriculture, in particular food production, and the informal sector in the cities and the country). The modern sector is an enclave closely linked to the international economy, but isolated from the remainder of the domestic economy. The principal problem of *dualism* is the absence of technological diffusion from the modern technologically advanced sector towards the rest of the economy. Apart from a technological dualism, other forms of dualism can also occur such as regional dualism (the traditional and the modern sector have also been divided spatially), cultural dualism, and ethnic dualism (some ethnic groups are active in the modern sector, others in the traditional sector). When all dualisms occur at the same time, problems can be quite extreme, and dualism may lead to conflicts or even to civil wars (Higgins and Higgins, 1979).

Population growth

As a result of a decrease in death rates and a continued high level of birth rates, there is a large excess of births over deaths. The average rate of population growth in developing countries is at a historically unprecedented high of around 2 per cent per year.

Urbanization

Most developing countries experience large-scale migration from rural to urban areas as well as rapid growth of the existing urban population. Urban population growth exceeds the absorption capacity of the urban economy, the urban labour market and the urban infrastructure. Thus widespread slums and uncontrollable megacities come into being; the best-known example of this is Mexico City. In turn the growth of the cities and the relative depopulation of the rural areas reinforce existing dualism. Within urban society, too, there is dualism between the modern formal sector and the small-scale informal sector.

Underutilization of labour

In developing countries open unemployment is relatively low. Given the absence of formal systems of social security few people can afford to be out of work. However, there is large-scale underutilization of labour. Underutilization of labour means either that only part of available labour is utilized, or that labour is being used so unproductively that labourers can hardly make a living despite working very long hours.

Political instability

The nation-state in developing countries is weakly developed. There is a lack of national integration. Feelings of solidarity with a common national culture and society are not fully developed. Loyalties are primarily directed to a specific area, tribe, ethnic group, or family. Many developing countries are racked by ethnic conflicts that are a threat to national unity (Chirot, 1977). The rule of law is poorly developed. The military play a disproportionately large part in politics.

In section 1.7 I emphasized the differences between developing countries. The degree to which common characteristics of developing countries occur in different countries and regions also varies a lot. For example, in some countries the share of agriculture in employment is larger than in other countries. There are substantial differences in the degree of political instability and ethnic tensions. Besides, one should not forget that the differences between developing and economically advanced countries are also but differences of degree. Each affluent country[3] was once a developing country. Still, this list of common characteristics helps us identify the developing countries and their problems which are the focus of this book. Not all characteristics are found in every developing country. But if none of the characteristics applies, it is clear we are not dealing with a developing country.

QUESTIONS FOR REVIEW

1. What are the drawbacks of the use of GNP per capita as an indicator of economic development?
2. Discuss the relationships between 'economic growth' and 'development'.
3. Is development conceivable without economic growth?

4. What are the most important dimensions along which developing countries differ from each other? Is the use of the term 'Third World' justified in the light of these differences?

5. To what extent is there an insurmountable gap between rich and poor countries in the world economy?

6. What are the most important common problems and characteristics of developing countries?

Notes

1. The effects of the 1991 Gulf War have not been included in the data on Kuwait and Iraq.
2. 'Data on income distribution should be interpreted with caution' (World Bank, 1995, p. 220). The reliability of international comparisons of income inequality is not yet very high.
3. I have tried to avoid the use of the term 'developed countries' since this term incorrectly implies that these countries have somehow reached some final point in development.

2 Development of the international economic order, 1500–1993

The differences in income levels that characterize the present-day international economic order are not self-evident. In the past these differences used to be much smaller. Around 1500, by far the greater part of world population made its living in agriculture. Although some countries were richer than others, most people lived close to subsistence levels. The distribution of world income by region was therefore relatively equal (Bairoch, 1980; Cipolla, 1981, p. 220).

How did the present diversity of levels of economic development and welfare in the world economy come about? In order to examine possible answers to this question, this chapter will offer a rough outline of the history of European expansion and the development of the international economic order associated with it.

2.1 *International economic order*

Instead of rendering a formal definition of the slippery concept of international economic order, I will distinguish some of its most significant aspects (Lewis, 1978b; Streeten, 1984; Maddison, 1985, 1989).[1] Among others, the international economic order is characterized by:

1. Flows of goods (final products, capital goods, primary products, semi-finished goods) and services.
2. Financial flows (investments, loans, transfer payments, levies and taxes).
3. Flows of people (voluntary migration, indentured labour, slave trade, migrant labour).
4. The intensity of the economic relationships between the various regions which together form the international economic order. Trade flows, for example, were

small until the second half of the nineteenth century (Lewis, 1978b). The different parts of the world economy were not yet closely related.

5. Relations of dependence between countries and regions. Economic relationships create mutual interdependence. However, in relations of interdependence some areas are more dependent on other areas than vice versa. Dependence on advanced economies is a problem for developing countries.
6. The institutional framework of the economic and political relations between countries and regions. Is an area under direct political domination as a result of colonial rule or is it being influenced indirectly through foreign economic interests? Is the trade regime characterized by free trade or protectionism? What is the role of international organizations and international treaties?
7. The patterns of growth and stagnation in various parts of the world economy which together make up the international economic order.
8. Patterns of income inequality between countries and regions.

2.2 *Economic breakthrough and external expansion from Western Europe*

Since the beginning of the sixteenth century, Western Europe experienced a dual process of internal economic growth and external economic and political expansion. This process of development is unique in two respects. First, in a limited part of the world the age-old vicious circle of struggle for survival at near subsistence levels was broken. Secondly, the European expansion led to the formation of a world economy in which all countries and regions in the world are interrelated in networks of interdependence.

Both statements are in need of clarification and qualification. In the first place, economic history prior to the sixteenth century is by no means exclusively the history of stagnation. It is the rule rather than the exception that, in the long run, production increased sufficiently to maintain a slowly growing population (Boserup, 1981; Maddison, 1982a; Jones, 1988). This is referred to as *extensive growth* (Reynolds, 1986, pp. 7–10). There have also been periods in pre-modern history when total production grew faster than population, leading to growth of per capita income (*intensive growth*). This, for example, was the case in China from the ninth century to the thirteenth century.

Nevertheless, economic growth in the Western world since the sixteenth century is distinguished by the long duration of growth and its rapid pace. For example, per capita income in the rich capitalist countries is now at least thirteen times as high as in 1820 (Maddison, 1982a, p. 17). Already in the first part of the eighteenth century, on the eve of the Industrial Revolution, the average level of prosperity in countries like England and the Netherlands was many times higher than in the rest of the world (Landes, 1969; Maddison, 1983).[2] Growth in Europe has led to an unprecedented and lasting increase in prosperity for great numbers of people, whereas in pre-modern societies malnutrition and starvation were never far away, even in more prosperous periods and regions. Although economic development in Europe was often attended by impoverishment and disruption, in the long run the masses of the poor also profited from the increases in average per capita income. It is in this sense that one may speak of a breakout from the vicious circle of poverty.

Secondly, European expansion since the fifteenth century has been preceded by many processes of expansion. To list but a few examples: the formation of the Hellenistic and the Roman Empires, the spread of the Islamic sphere of influence, the Mongolian conquests which stretched from the Pacific to southern India and Central Europe, and the formation of the Ottoman Empire. The process of European expansion, however, is different from other processes of expansion in several respects. First, the European process of expansion was characterized by the absence of political centralization within Europe. Europe was a multitude of rival nation-states in the making, rather than an integrated empire. Second, the ties between the European countries and the rest of the world were not only political, but also economic (Wallerstein, 1974; Braudel, 1978). Third, the process of interweavement of the world economy and the world society, which was a consequence of the European expansion, is characterized by a certain irreversibility. With the exception of the Chinese Empire, the history of all ancient empires and processes of expansion is characterized by rise and fall, centralization followed by decentralization and disintegration. The European expansion, on the other hand, has resulted in a global economic order of which the constituent parts have become permanently interdependent – for the better or for the worse. They will remain closely interrelated long after the role of the West in the world has come to its term.

If an early-fifteenth-century observer could have taken a look at the twentieth century, he would have been very surprised at the present position of Western countries in the world economy. Around the year 1400 nothing indicated that drastic economic breakthroughs and processes of external expansion would take place especially in Europe. From a military point of view it was by no means obvious that Europe would expand its sphere of influence in the world (Kennedy, 1989). The Moors were not driven out of Spain until 1492. Constantinople fell in 1453. Towards the end of the fifteenth century the Ottoman Turks had occupied Greece, the Ionian Islands, Bosnia, Albania and large parts of the Balkan Peninsula. In 1526 large parts of Hungary were conquered, and Vienna was besieged in 1529. It was not until the eighteenth century that the military balance of power would turn in favour of Christian Europe (Fieldhouse, 1982, p. 10; McNeil, 1989).

If our observer would have ventured to predict the prospects of economic development in 1400, he would probably have put his money on the ancient and highly developed societies in Asia, and, in particular, on China.

In the fourteenth century, China was the most advanced society in the world in terms of technology (Elvin, 1973; Boserup, 1981). China knew firearms, gunpowder, hydraulic clocks, magnetic compasses, navigation techniques, the arts of printing and paper making. Transportation technology was well developed; there were roads and extensive systems of canals and waterways. Money came into circulation at an early stage, along with market relationships. Intensive agriculture was practised, the techniques of which were recorded in handbooks (Perkins, 1968). Complicated irrigation systems were in use. By the twelfth century there was already mass production in manufacturing. Elvin (1973) estimates that in the thirteenth century some 20 per cent of the population was living in towns. There was a highly developed bureaucratic administrative system which would much later serve as a model for the British civil service. China was the first country in the world to have a national system of education with comparative examinations providing for entry into positions in the mandarin bureaucracy. Nevertheless, China was not the first country to experience a major economic breakthrough and nor was it the country from which the rest of the world was penetrated. The penetration of world society started from an insignificant and relatively sparsely populated country in the southwest of Europe: Portugal (Wallerstein, 1974, p. 38 ff.).

It is fascinating to note that at the same time Europeans set out upon their expeditions at the beginning of the fifteenth century, a similar process of expansion started from China. From 1405 to 1433 the famous eunuch admiral Cheng Ho undertook a series of expeditions which took the Chinese to the Indian Ocean, Java, Ceylon, Persia and even to the African east coast. However, after Cheng Ho died in 1433, these expeditions were stopped abruptly. In 1435, shipbuilding was even prohibited by imperial decree. The Chinese fleet was dismantled, and overseas trade was discouraged as much as possible. The empire turned inward (Elvin, 1973; Wallerstein, 1974; Jones, 1988; Kennedy, 1989; McNeil, 1989). Scientific and technological development faltered. The Chinese economy, which had flourished until the middle of the fourteenth century, was caught up in a centuries-long process of stagnation lasting until the communist takeover in 1949. On the other hand, the expansion from Europe continued. Portugal gave the initial impetus to the European penetration of the world and the gradual formation of a coherent world economy, of which the constituent parts would become progressively ever more interrelated in the course of time.

2.3 *Why expansion from Europe instead of from China?*

These historical developments led Immanuel Wallerstein to pose a series of interesting questions which concern the very essence of the issue of development (Wallerstein, 1974, pp. 36–63): Why did the breakthrough of capitalism and the process of economic growth associated with it, take place in Europe? Why did the Chinese economy stagnate from the fourteenth century onwards despite the initial conditions which seemed so promising? Why was there a process of external European expansion, starting in the fifteenth century? Why did the external expansion of China come to a stop after 1433 and why did China develop in an inward-looking fashion?

Following Max Weber (1920), Wallerstein seeks the answer to such questions in the difference between the centralized Chinese Empire and the decentralized feudal system in medieval Europe, which would later generate strong national states and within which capitalist institutions could develop. Maintenance of an empire involves a lot of military and administrative expenses which may eventually hinder economic development. In the world economic system, which developed in Europe after 1500, economic relations were more important than direct political control radiating from a single administrative centre. The European centre of this 'world system' gave rise to powerful national states in fierce competition with each other. These states offered support to enterprising groups and classes that contributed to internal economic development and external expansion.

Wallerstein seeks the incentives for external European expansion in the crisis of feudalism from the fourteenth century onwards. This crisis offered motivations for expansion to several social groups: the nobility, whose traditional sources of revenue were threatened by the crisis; the rising middle classes; the state apparatus that considered external expansion as a source of revenue and prestige; and members of the new urban semi-proletariat who were available for work as soldiers and sailors.

Incentives for expansion, discussed by Wallerstein, include: the demand for gold, silver and precious metals, spices, food, fuels and raw materials, and the search for new sources of income and employment. Gold was needed for luxury imports from Asia such as jewels and spices. The need for food, fuels and raw materials stimulated expansion to the Mediterranean countries, the Atlantic islands, North and West Africa, Eastern Europe, the Russian steppes and Central Asia. Population growth led to an intensification of agriculture which involved the introduction of cash crops, cattle breeding and horticulture (see Chapters 4 and 9). There was an increasing demand for corn imports from less densely populated areas. From the fourteenth century onwards, England and the Netherlands imported corn from the Baltic and Mediterranean areas. Cultivation of sugar cane was the motivation for expansion towards the eastern Mediterranean and the Atlantic islands. Due to increasing deforestation, there was a shortage of wood for fuel and for shipbuilding. The textile industry required materials such as pigment and gum.

These factors were prevalent in various parts of Europe. But a number of factors was specific to Portugal, and, according to Wallerstein, they may explain why expansion originated from Portugal. He mentions, for example, the absence of alternatives for the Portuguese nobility, Portugal's location by the sea, its previous experience with long-distance trade, the availability of capital from the Italian city-states, and the strength and stability of the state machinery. There was a convergence of interests. The sovereign, the nobility, the commercial middle classes and the urban semi-proletariat that had fled the countryside all benefited from external expansion.

To explain the differences between Chinese inward-looking development and European expansionism, Wallerstein points to: the absence of a convergence of interests, such as existed in South Western Europe; the intensification of the food production in China; and the political structure of the centralized Chinese Empire.

The absence of converging interests

In China no consensus existed with respect to the benefits of external expansion. The Confucian mandarins in the state bureaucracy opposed the eunuch admirals whose interests lay in expansion. The central bureaucracy had a great dislike for the expense involved in these foreign expeditions. In due course, the emperor sided with the central bureaucracy. The lack of a colonizing mission also played a part. In the Chinese world view, China was the centre of the world and the Chinese Empire already contained everything of importance in the world. The Chinese were not interested in communication with barbarians, including barbarians from faraway Europe. This world view was to play an important role until the nineteenth century. It is often put forward as an explanation for the half-heartedness of Chinese attempts at modernization in the face of Western challenges in the nineteenth century.

Intensification of food production

In Europe increasing population density led to a pattern of agriculture in which more densely populated areas concentrated on cattle farming, horticulture and cash crops, while importing corn from less densely populated areas. Compared to agriculture, cattle farming is a less efficient way of producing calories and it is only feasible if food stuffs can be imported from elsewhere (Boserup, 1981). Population growth provided an impulse for external expansion for purposes of importing corn from less densely populated peripherous regions. Subsequently, the availability of animal power in Europe, lacking in China, was a stimulus to further economic development.

In south-eastern China an extremely labour-intensive type of agriculture developed (Perkins, 1969) causing a shortage of labour. The high level of agricultural and irrigational technology allowed for intensive agriculture – in particular, cultivation of rice. The increasing demand for labour was an impediment to external expansion.

Political centralization

After the fall of the Roman Empire, a highly decentralized feudal system came into being in Europe (Elias, 1969; Wolf, 1982).[3] Money played a relatively small part in this feudal economy. Economic entities were highly self-sufficient. The feudal system, with its landowners living on the surplus of the agricultural production, was inimical to the rising groups based on trade and industry. In Europe, capitalism had to struggle to survive, which accounts for its strength in later periods. Capitalist activities were centred in the cities, which managed to preserve their autonomy due to the decentralized nature of the feudal system. If political pressure became too much in a particular region, entrepreneurs and merchants could always move to other areas where taxes were lower and economic activities less constrained (McNeil, 1989).

Paradoxically, in the long term highly centralized European states developed out of the feudal system. Some political centres started dominating surrounding regions, and once processes of centralization were well under way, the mysticism, characteristic of feudal relations, was transferred to the central authorities. This mysticism strengthened centralizing tendencies in the emerging absolute monarchies. I should emphasize here that the tendencies towards centralization did not result in the rise of another centralized empire, but rather in a multitude of internally highly centralized national states competing with one another. In this environment the emerging states were also dependent on support offered them by the financial and commercial bourgeoisie, which in turn succeeded in consolidating its position and independence.

Competition among states also contributed to the rapid development of military technology. Each technical or organizational improvement was immediately adopted by other states. In the centralized Chinese, Indian and Ottoman Empires, the rise of firearms and cannons led to the strengthening of central authorities. But the monopolization of technology by these central authorities hampered further technological development. From the middle of the seventeenth century onwards this would result in the increasing military supremacy of the Western powers in comparison with the Asian empires (McNeil, 1989; Kennedy, 1989).

In a recent article Justin Yifu Lin (1995) introduces another interesting explanation, namely, the importance of classical literary training as prerequisite for entry into the mandarin bureaucracy. This created a disincentive for investments in human capital of the kind required for 'modern' scientific research. As a result, China failed to make the transition from traditional experience-based science and technology to modern mathematically and experimentally based science. 'Therefore, despite her early lead in scientific achievement, China failed to have an indigenous scientific revolution' (p. 285).

The Roman Empire fell apart in the fifth century in Western Europe in a process of feudalization. The Chinese Empire never really fell apart (Elvin, 1973). Chinese feudal rulers lived off the land and used serfs as foot soldiers in their military rivalries. Time and again they tried to assert their independence from central authorities. But the central authorities successfully managed to resist decentralizing tendencies. Instead of a feudal structure, China developed a *prebendal structure* (Weber, 1920), in which the central authorities appointed a kind of 'official' to administer far-off regions. These officials did not earn a salary but had to live off revenues collected in their region. Naturally, there were constant tendencies towards feudalization and autonomy, with officials trying to turn their positions into hereditary ones. These tendencies, however, were countered by the central authorities, who developed a system of regularly transferring officials, in order to weaken the ties between them and the regions they had to manage. Thus the emperor and the central authorities succeeded in maintaining a loose form of imperial centralization.

The instinct of an imperial power is to defend its territory. 'This drains attention, energy and profits which could be invested in capital development' (Wallerstein, 1974, p. 60). In the long term, centralization will be at the expense of external expansion. All energy is frittered away in the construction of defensive fortifications like the great Chinese wall. Thus decentralization was one of the preconditions for expansion in Europe, which was lacking in China. European expansion was furthered by the competition between states. '[W]hen the Turks advanced in the east, there was no emperor to recall the Portuguese expeditions' (Wallerstein, 1974, p. 70). Besides, the degree of centralization in the Chinese Empire was quite low in comparison with the centralization of the European nation-states in years to come.

The absence of a feudal mystique in prebendalism made it easier to resist tendencies towards centralization around the person of an absolute ruler.

Initially, the contractual nature of prebendalism was conducive to the development of capitalist groups and activities. However, in part because of this, capitalist tendencies in China did not develop as fully as they did in Europe, where the rising middle classes had to wage a fierce struggle for survival. As opposed to European cities, which developed into independent and autonomous enclaves in feudal society with their own municipal rights, Chinese cities never really became completely independent from the central authorities. Capitalist impulses therefore smothered in a non-feudal bureaucratic environment which was initially far from hostile. Besides, in centralized empires there was an irresistible tendency to tax and regulate economic activities in order to cover the expenses of the central administrative apparatus (Jones, 1988).

Of course, it is not possible to discuss the voluminous literature on these classical questions adequately in this text.[4] Nevertheless, simply posing such questions advances our thinking about the sources of development and stagnation in the very long term.

2.4 *European expansion in the world*

Western expansion in the world proceeded rather unevenly. Some areas were penetrated very early, others much later; some areas already achieved their independence long before colonization even reached other parts of the world.

In his standard work on the history of European colonization, Fieldhouse distinguishes between *settlement colonies* and *colonies of occupation* (Fieldhouse, 1982). Settlement colonies involve immigrants from the mother land settling permanently in a colony; these immigrants attempted to build a society resembling as much as possible the society in their country of origin. Settlement colonies can be subdivided into 'pure' settlement colonies, 'mixed' colonies and plantation colonies. In 'pure' settlement colonies such as the United States, Canada and Australia the original inhabitants – Indians, Aborigines – were completely crowded out by immigrants from Europe, who built another European society in the New World. In 'mixed' colonies (for example, the Spanish colonies in Mexico and Peru) a substantial minority of European colonists settled in the colony, trying to absorb the local population. In plantation colonies a tiny minority of Europeans settled permanently; they imported slave labour from elsewhere in order to establish a plantation economy (e.g., the Portuguese in Brazil).

Colonies of occupation involve an extremely small elite of foreign colonial government officials ruling native inhabitants with a completely different language and culture.

Finally, apart from settlement colonies and colonies of occupation the Europeans also founded many trading posts all over the world.

Before the beginning of the nineteenth century, European expansion in Africa and Asia primarily resulted in the establishment of trading posts by the Portuguese, the Dutch and the British. On the American continent the Spanish, the Portuguese, the British, the French and the Dutch founded settlement colonies. Between 1776 and 1824 almost all the colonies in the Americas gained their independence. The second phase of the European expansion started around 1815 after the Napoleonic Wars and was directed towards Asia and also, at a later stage, towards Africa. During this period the colonies that were carved out were mainly colonies of occupation, where alien peoples were dominated by colonial rulers whose prime loyalties lay in their faraway homelands.

2.4.1 Types of international economic orders

Western expansion has led to economic relations between the Western and the non-Western world. Following Maddison, one can distinguish six international economic orders since 1500 (Maddison, 1982b, 1983, 1985, 1989): conquest imperialism, merchant capitalism, free trade imperialism, conflict and autarky 1913–1950, the post-war golden age, and the economic order since the 1973 oil crisis. Each order is characterized by a specific kind of relationship between the rich Western countries and the developing countries. These orders are set out in chronological sequence, but different orders can overlap. The distinctive features of the six orders will be touched upon only briefly here, but will be discussed in more detail later in this chapter and elsewhere in this book.

Conquest imperialism

The relations between Western countries and the colonies are characterized both by straightforward plundering of the colonized areas' resources and by a transfer of economic surpluses by means of taxation and tribute payments. Such relations existed, for example, between Spain and Mexico from 1500 to 1820.

Merchant capitalism

This type of relationship is characterized by the search for monopolistic profits on the production and export of luxury goods from the penetrated areas by the European powers. Where Western expansion resulted in direct colonial domination, taxation, in addition to monopolistic profits, served to transfer economic surpluses to Western countries. These relationships can be found in the areas penetrated by the Portuguese, the French, the Dutch and the British from 1500 to 1870.

Free trade imperialism

This type of international economic order reached maturity in the period 1870–1913 and is identified with far-reaching liberalization of international trade. In developing countries such liberalization was imposed by force or by the threat of force. During this period the typical colonial pattern of international trade emerged, in which developing countries exported primary products to the rich industrialized countries and industrialized countries exported finished manufactured goods to the developing countries.

Conflict and autarky 1913–1950

Two world wars and an economic depression took place in this period. Free trade was abandoned, and protectionism prevailed. Each country tried to isolate itself from the consequences of the economic crisis at the expense of its trading partners. Partly as a result of this, the volume of world trade fell off, and investment in developing countries decreased dramatically. Economic growth stagnated both in rich countries and in developing countries. In many developing countries, policy attempts to cope with the economic crisis were hampered by colonial relations of dependence.

The post-war golden age

In the period 1950–1973 there was an increase in per capita income in rich countries as well as in developing countries. Indeed, per capita income grew more rapidly than ever before. International trade was highly liberalized, though manufacturing sectors in developing countries remained highly protected. The volume of international trade increased sharply, as did international capital flows. The developing countries received a considerable net inflow of capital consisting of direct investments, loans and development aid.

The international economic order since the 1973 oil crisis

Growth of the world economy as a whole slowed down and differences between patterns of economic performance in various parts of the world increased. After 1982, economic growth in Latin America was hampered by the debt crisis. In some developing countries the debt crisis resulted in a substantial net capital outflow to rich countries. However, in large parts of south and Southeast Asia there was continued economic growth. In sub-Saharan Africa there has been a long period of economic stagnation. There are tendencies towards revival of protectionism, but otherwise than during the interwar period, the principles of free trade have not been abandoned.

In the following sections the historical developments in international economic relations will be discussed in more detail.

2.4.2 The first wave of expansion, 1400–1815

In the fifteenth and sixteenth centuries Portugal and Spain initiated the first wave of expansion directed towards Africa, Asia and Latin America. The Portuguese were the pioneers. They started to found trading posts and bases along the African west coast from 1415 onwards and along the African east coast, in India and the Far East from the late fifteenth century onwards. From these trading posts luxury goods such as gold, ivory, pepper and spices were shipped to Europe. From the second half of the fifteenth century African slaves were transported to sugar plantations on the Atlantic islands and later to plantations in the Caribbean and the American continent. There was no direct colonial rule. Native societies, political systems and the economy were initially left undisturbed. Especially in Asia, Western penetration would have little impact for quite some time. From the beginning of the sixteenth century onwards the Dutch pushed the Portuguese out of the Far East; however, the impact of Dutch presence on local societies was initially also rather weak.

The Spanish colonization of Latin America from the late fifteenth century onwards was of an extremely destructive nature. Initially, straightforward plunder of gold and silver treasures was predominant. Later, large estates were created for the *conquistadores* on which the Indians were forced to work. A large part of the economic surplus was transferred to Spain by means of taxation and tribute payments. The ancient Aztec and Inca civilizations were completely erased. Catholicism was imposed by force. The demographic consequences of the Spanish colonization were disastrous. As a result of wars, heavy labour in mines and on plantations, and especially contagious diseases against which the Indians had no naturally immunity, the original population was decimated (Furtado, 1976).

Present-day Brazil was primarily colonized by the Portuguese after its discovery in 1500 by Cabral.[5] The Portuguese found an extremely sparsely populated area. They founded plantations and initiated exports of wood and other primary products. The demand for labour was met by African slave imports. Portuguese colonialism very much focused on making monopolistic profits through trade. In comparison to Spanish colonialism, which was actually a form of organized plunder, Portuguese colonialism was less destructive since new technologies and products were introduced as well. However, neither the slaves nor the original Indian inhabitants benefited much. After an initial increase in per capita production as a result of the introduction of a plantation economy based on slave labour into a society of hunters and collectors, per capita income remained unchanged for three centuries (Maddison, 1985).

Slaves were also imported to Spanish colonies where the Indian population proved to be unwilling or unsuited to do the heavy work in mines and on plantations. In the nineteenth century the demand for labour in Latin America was also met by the recruitment of indentured labourers from China, India and Java.

The economic history of Latin America is the model for theories of exploitation and underdevelopment; in this model the negative effects of colonialism, neocolonialism and capitalist exploitation account for the backwardness of the poor countries. Not only have economic surpluses been transferred to Europe for several centuries, but also regressive social institutions such as landlordism have been introduced, which were to form an obstacle to economic development long after political independence had been achieved. That exploitation has played an important part in the development of Latin America is beyond dispute. There is, however, a debate on the degree to which present-day economic problems can be explained by adverse colonial experiences and postcolonial foreign influences.

Marxist theorists tend to explain the successful economic development of Western Europe from the perspective of colonial exploitation. It is suggested that gold and silver from Latin America, colonial taxation, monopolistic profits from trade and the revenues of the slave trade figured decisively in the 'original accumulation' which was a prerequisite for the Western European economic breakthrough in later years (Baran, 1957; Williams, 1964). This theory, however, is not very tenable. Domestic savings and a gradual increase in productivity in handicrafts and agriculture have been of more importance to European development than external plunder, taxation and foreign profits (North and Thomas, 1973; Bairoch, 1980; Maddison, 1982a). Colonial exploitation certainly contributed to Western prosperity. But the key question is whether economic surpluses and savings could be transformed into productive investments (Wolf, 1982, p. 120). The countries that first profited from colonial revenues – Spain and Portugal – were not capable of doing so. After the sixteenth century, their role soon came to an end.

In the seventeenth century, economic and political supremacy shifted from southwestern Europe to northwestern Europe. In terms of technological capacity as indicated by per capita income, the Netherlands were the leading economy. For a short period of time the Dutch republic was also the dominant power in world politics. The Dutch penetrated Indonesia where they ousted the Portuguese and established trade monopolies. Dutch expansion was of a mercantilistic nature. They did not strive for direct colonial domination but rather for lucrative trade by means of the Dutch East India Company, founded in 1602. The Dutch also penetrated into the western hemisphere. They founded settlement colonies in North and South America and in the Caribbean.

In addition to the Dutch republic, France and England also started colonizing North America and the Caribbean in the seventeenth century. In the Caribbean the various colonial powers primarily founded plantation economies where sugar was grown with slave labour.

As mentioned above, Dutch colonization in Brazil was not granted a long life. On the North American continent the Dutch were already ousted by the British in 1667. The French and the British continued to compete for control over this area. In the eighteenth century this conflict resulted in a series of wars between the British and the French from which the British emerged as the dominant power on the North American continent. At the end of the Seven Years' War in 1763 the role of France in North America had come to an end. Today only Francophone Quebec reminds one of the French expansion in this part of the world.

In the course of the eighteenth century the leading economic position of the Netherlands was taken over by England. In the second part of the century rapid industrialization took place in England, often referred to by the dramatic term 'Industrial Revolution'.[6] Around 1785 the Netherlands were outdistanced by England in terms of per capita production (Maddison, 1982a, p. 49). The other Western European countries became the followers of British leadership.

In the eighteenth century the British penetration into India gathered momentum. In the seventeenth century the British had already founded trading posts and cities along the Indian coastline. Trade was controlled by the British East India Company, founded in 1600. Until the early eighteenth century India was still a powerful Asian empire, although somewhat past its prime. In 1757 Bengal was conquered after the battle at Plassey and was governed by the East India Company as a satrapy. The French, who penetrated into India at the same time as the British, were eclipsed. However, there still was no question of direct colonial control over the entire Indian subcontinent.

From the late eighteenth century onwards Australia was penetrated, starting with the foundation of a penal colony in Sydney in 1788. The convicts were soon followed by voluntary migrants who would eventually turn Australia into a prosperous settlement colony like the United States and Canada.

As can be seen, therefore, the patterns of penetration in various parts of the world differ considerably during the first phase of European expansion (Fieldhouse, 1982). In Asia the Europeans were faced with ancient established civilizations that were initially neither technologically nor militarily inferior to the Europeans. The Europeans had the advantage at sea, but on land they were initially not stronger than their opponents. The Europeans were concentrated in enclaves along the coast. Their influence on native society was relatively unimportant. On the North American continent the hunting and gathering Indian peoples were totally unable to withstand the European onslaught. The same holds for the large Indian civilizations in Latin America that succumbed to the force of small numbers of Spaniards. European immigrants settled on the American continent. The language and culture of their countries of origin would leave a lasting imprint on the development of colonial and postcolonial society. On the African continent there were initially no permanent settlements, with the exception of Cape Colony and a few other areas. None of the African empires – not even the most developed ones like Benin in West Africa – was a match for the European intruders. However, climate, disease and severe conditions of life were obstacles to European settlement.

2.4.3 The first wave of decolonization

The process of Western expansion would continue in many parts of the world during the nineteenth century, but in various other areas direct European influence was on the decline. The British colonies in America declared their independence in 1776 and formed the United States of America. The Napoleonic Wars sounded the death knell for Iberian colonialism. From 1814 to 1824 all Spanish colonies on the American continent became independent. Brazil declared its independence in 1822 although a member of the Portuguese royal family was crowned as emperor.

The decolonization of the English-speaking colonies in Australia, Canada, New Zealand and South Africa took place more gradually. Traditionally, English colonies used to have substantial autonomy with respect to their mother country. From the middle of the nineteenth century onwards this autonomy was gradually transformed into a *de facto* independence within the framework of the British Commonwealth. The attainment of formal independence can best be dated *circa* 1931 when a statute was passed stating that dominions were no longer subject to decisions of the British Parliament.

2.4.4 The second phase of European expansion, 1815–1913

The nineteenth century was the apex of Western expansion and Western political, economic, military and cultural dominance. Per capita production increased sharply (Maddison, 1982a) among others due to rapid increase in the amount of capital goods per head of population. The differences in the levels of prosperity between the rich countries and the developing countries increased dramatically. Industrialization also consolidated the Western military lead. Moreover, formerly powerful empires in Asia and the Middle East were no longer a match for the West. Western expansion progressed more rapidly than ever before. In 1800 Europe, together with its overseas possessions and former colonies, covered 55 per cent of the surface of the earth. By 1878 this percentage had risen to 67 per cent and by 1914 to 84.4 per cent (Fieldhouse, 1982, p. 178).

The relationships between the colonial powers and the colonized areas were intensified. In India, Indonesia and other Asian countries indirect influence through commercial relations was transformed into formal political domination of colonies of occupation by the mother countries. The consolidation of colonial domination was attended by a series of military conflicts such as the Indian Mutiny in 1857 and the Diponegoro rebellion on Java (1825–1830).

Colonies founded by white migrants in Canada, South Africa, Australia and New Zealand expanded inland at the expense of the native inhabitants. Economic growth in the United States went hand in hand with strong expansionary tendencies. This did not lead to the founding of new colonies, but rather to the annexation of Spanish-speaking areas which became states in the American union. In the mid-nineteenth century tsarist Russia expanded eastward to Central Asia, Siberia and the Far East. France, which had an insignificant colonial empire before the nineteenth century, penetrated into North Africa and Indochina. In 1830 Algiers was conquered, and in the fifty years that followed the whole of Algeria was colonized. The French colonization of Indochina in the second half of the nineteenth century started with the occupation of Saigon on the Mekong Delta in 1859. Between 1829 and 1914 the Ottoman Empire had to recognize the southern and southeastern European Balkan states of Albania, Bulgaria, Greece, Romania and Serbia as independent states. For the better part of the nineteenth century England was the leading world power both economically and politically. In England industrialization had proceeded furthest and British maritime power was undisputed until the 1890s. As a result of British dominance there were few conflicts between colonial powers. This was the era of *Pax Britannica*.

After 1830, free trade became predominant in the English international trade policy. Colonial monopolies on trade were abolished. Colonies could now also trade with countries other than their mother country. England lowered numerous tariffs on imports from colonies. But it also demanded free access for its industrial exports to both colonial and non-colonial markets. Establishing free trade involved quite a lot of force and violence, though. By means of gunboat diplomacy, monarchs and rulers, used to financing their expenditures by royal monopolies on trade, were forced to lower tariffs and to open up their countries to Western exports. Maddison therefore describes this international order as 'free trade imperialism' (Maddison, 1985). Furthermore, England tried to impede industrialization in the colonies wherever her influence reached.

Not all colonial powers adopted the policy of free trade immediately. For example, in 1930 governor van den Bosch introduced the 'culture system' into Java. In this system compulsory production of cash crops – for the benefit of the colonial rulers – was the central element. This 'culture system' may be considered the nineteenth century continuation of the international economic order of merchant capitalism.

Around 1890 the United States, once a British colony, took the economic lead and has held that position ever since. Western Europe, Australia, Canada, New Zealand and Japan became the followers in the race for technological and economic development (Maddison, 1982a). It was not until after World War II that the United States became the dominant power in terms of politics as well. However, it did claim the right to intervene in Latin American affairs as early as the nineteenth century: in 1823 the Monroe doctrine prescribed any intervention by powers other than the United States on the entire American continent.

By the end of the nineteenth century all European powers rushed to obtain new colonies. In doing so, they became more and more entangled in fierce rivalries. The African continent especially, until then hardly penetrated by whites, was colonized rapidly in the famous 'scramble for Africa'. The colonial powers drew straight lines on the map in order to demarcate their possessions. These artificial borders disregarded geographical characteristics and ethnic, cultural and historical dividing lines. Much of the present-day instability of African states has to do with the arbitrariness of these colonial borders (see Chapter 10).

2.4.5 The period 1870–1913

The abolition of the Indonesian 'culture system' in 1870 marked the end of the international economic order based on monopolistic trade relations. Free trade became the predominant characteristic of the next international economic order. Since the mid-nineteenth century, developing countries had opened their borders to international trade – at times under threat of military force. Also, leading countries such as England and the Netherlands had lowered their tariff rates on imports.

From 1870 to 1913 economic relations between rich countries and developing countries intensified; this was a new phenomenon. As Arthur Lewis argues, economic relations between the Western countries and the rest of the world were rather weak before the second half of the nineteenth century (Lewis, 1978a, 1978b). Initially most of the raw materials needed for industrialization were available in Europe. The volume of trade between rich industrialized countries and developing countries was negligible. 'Even in 1883 total imports into the United States and Western Europe from Asia, Africa and Tropical Latin America came to only about a dollar per head of the population of the exporting countries' (Lewis, 1978b, p. 5). The improvement of transportation and communication – railways, iron ships, telegraph – and the opening of the Suez Canal in 1869 changed all this. Both the continuous growth of the population of rich countries and the growth of industrial production caused an increase in the demand for agricultural and mining products. The tropics reacted to this growing demand by greatly increasing the export of primary products (e.g. coffee, tea, palm oil, groundnuts, tropical fruit, jute, sisal, rubber, tobacco, cotton, sugar, mining products). On the one hand, small peasants cultivated surplus land and used part of their surplus labour for the production of cash crops, while on the other, there were Western investments in plantations and mines (Lewis, 1970, 1978b; Myint, 1980). The revenues from exports created a market for industrial products from industrialized countries. Thus there was a sharp increase in the volume of international trade.

The present-day world economy came into being between 1870 and 1913. Western influences were felt everywhere, even in those places where the native lifestyles had remained unaffected until then. The poor countries became involved in the world economy through their exports of agricultural and mining products. They became acquainted with industrial consumer goods that were exported by the industrialized countries. The money economy arose when native inhabitants embarked on the production of commercial crops in addition to the cultivation of food products for their own consumption. Large migration flows established new relationships between the various parts of the world and led to drastic changes in the structure of populations (see section 2.4.6). In several developing countries there was a sharp increase in investment by rich countries. These investments focused on plantations, mines and the creation of an infrastructure of railways, roads and harbours for the benefit of exports and imports. Investment flows also increased among the rich countries themselves. According to Lewis (1970, 1978a, 1978b) and Maddison (1989), the 1870–1913 period was a period of increasing per capita income both in developing and in rich countries. However, as a result of a complex of factors – including colonialism – developing countries did not succeed in using the revenues from exports to achieve lasting economic development and industrialization (Lewis, 1970).

In summary, in the 1870–1913 period an integrated world economy came into being in which the volume of international trade underwent a sharp increase. International trade was of an asymmetric nature. Poor developing countries exported primary agricultural and mining products. Rich and politically powerful countries exported industrial products. After World War II 'industrialisation' became strongly associated with 'economic development', partly because of the historical experiences during the 1870–1913 period. Dependence on primary exports was more and more seen as a symptom of economic weakness. However, this is not always true, as will be shown in Chapter 8: countries like the United States, Canada and New Zealand benefited very much from agricultural exports at some stage in their development.

2.4.6 Migration flows

Following Arthur Lewis, it has been stated above that Western economic influence on the rest of the world was rather limited before the second half of the nineteenth century. Western powers may have had trading posts all over the world, yet in many parts of the world native societies continued to exist unchanged alongside European enclaves. Also the volume of international trade was relatively small. Only in the course of the century did the political penetration intensify and the international trade relations become more important.

In at least two respects however Lewis's argument may lead to an underestimation of the impact of Western penetration in the world before 1870. First, the influence of former Iberian colonialism in Latin America received insufficient emphasis. Secondly, not enough attention has been paid to the slave trade which changed the entire population structure of Latin America and the Caribbean and which has left deep scars on the African continent.

In this section, we will examine migration flows as an important aspect of the international economic order, paying attention to: the slave trade from 1500 to 1870; and migration flows at the end of the nineteenth century.

The slave trade

Tables 2.1 and 2.2 provide rough estimates of the extent of the slave trade and its importance for the development of African and Latin American populations. Table 2.1 shows the numbers of slaves imported into different American regions in different periods. Table 2.2 shows the numbers of slaves exported from three African regions in different periods.

According to Curtin's authoritative estimates (1969), in total 11.3 million African slaves were shipped to America between 1500 and 1870. This number does not include the 175,000 slaves who were exported to the Old World in the sixteenth and seventeenth centuries. The slaves were collected by African states along the coast that prospered among others thanks to the revenues of the slave trade. Trade and transportation of slaves was completely controlled by white people (first the Portuguese and later also the Dutch, the British, the French and even the Spanish). The American demand for slaves rapidly increased. In the fifteenth century 150,000 slaves were imported; in the sixteenth century their number had risen to 1.6 million. The slave trade reached its zenith in the eighteenth century when no fewer than 7.3 million slaves were transported overseas.

In 1807 the British Parliament passed a bill making the slave trade illegal. The holding of slaves in areas controlled by the British was forbidden in 1833. Other nations followed hesitantly, sometimes under British pressure: France in 1848, the Netherlands and the United States waiting until 1863. In spite of this, 2.3 million slaves were transported to America in the nineteenth century, mainly to work on sugar cane and coffee plantations (Hopkins, 1973).[7]

Table 2.1 Slave imports into America, 1500–1870 (thousands)

	North America[a]	Spanish America[b]	Caribbean[c]	Brazil	The Americas	Old World	Total including Old World
Population in 1500		9,350	300	1,000	10,650		
Imports 1500–1600[d]		75		50	125	150	275
Population in 1600		6,900	200	1,000	8,100		
Imports 1601–1700		293	464	560	1,316	25	1,341
Population in 1700	370	7,600	500	1,250	9,720		
Imports 1701–1810	376	579	3,205	1,891	6,052		6,052
Population in 1800	6,040	10,400	2,000	2,500	20,940		
Imports 1811–1870	51	606	96	1,145	1,898		1,898
Population in 1900	23,700	29,600	6,500	18,000	77,800		
Total 1500–1870	427	1,552	3,765	3,647	9,391	175	9,566

Notes:
[a] North America includes Delaware, Georgia, Maryland, North Carolina, South Carolina, Virginia, Kentucky, Mississippi, Alabama, Missouri, Arkansas, Tennessee and Texas. There are no data on Louisiana population. Slave imports into Louisiana have been included in totals for North America.
[b] Spanish America includes Mexico, Central America, Cuba, Peru, Colombia and Venezuela.
[c] The Caribbean includes Jamaica, Barbados, Leeward Island, St Vincent, St Luc, Tobago, Dominica, Trinidad, Grenada, the other Leeward Islands, Santo Domingo, Martinique, Guadeloupe, Guyana, the Netherlands Antilles, and the Danish West Indies.
[d] Curtin defines the first period as 1451–1600. Since Christopher Colombus did not discover America until 1492, it is assumed that the slave trade before 1500 refers to the Old World only.

Sources: Data on population in McEvedy and Jones (1978), and Darby and Fullart (1970). Slave imports from Curtin (1969).

Table 2.2 Slave exports from Africa into America, by region of origin, 1500–1870 (thousands)

	Region of origin					
	West Africa[a]	Western Central Africa[b]	South East Africa[c]	Total	Deceased during voyage (17%)	Arrived in America
Population in 1500	11,000	8,000	7,000	26,000		
Exports 1500–1600		150		150	25	125
Population in 1600	14,000	8,500	8,250	30,750		
Exports 1601–1700[d]	526	1,053		1,579	263	1,316
Population in 1700	18,000	9,000	9,500	36,500		
Exports 1701–1810[e]	4,463	2,787	12	7,262	1,210	6,052
Population in 1800	20,000	10,000	12,000	42,000		
Exports 1811–1870[e]	892	1,085	301	2,278	380	1,898
Population in 1900	27,000	15,000	16,000	58,000		
Total 1500–1870	5,881	5,075	313	11,269	1,878	9,391

Notes:

[a] West Africa includes the coastal areas from Senegal to Benin, and Nigeria.

[b] Western Central Africa includes Cameroon, the Central African Republic, Gabon, Zaire and Angola.

[c] South East Africa includes Uganda, Kenya, Tanzania, Rwanda and Burundi and Mozambique.

[d] The slave exports to the Old World have not been included. Since the better part of the slaves was of Western Central African origin until 1650, it is assumed that between 1500 and 1600 Atlantic slaves were exported from Western Central Africa only. It is assumed that in the seventeenth century two-thirds of the slaves were natives of Western Central Africa, and that one-third was of West African origin.

[e] After 1700 Lovejoy subdivides by region of origin. For the sake of consistency, Curtin's totals have been used. These totals have been subdivided into the various regions with the help of Lovejoy's ratios.

Sources: Population, see Table 2.1; totals of slave exports from Curtin (1969), 268. Subdivision with the help of Lovejoy (1982), 485 and 490.

Nowadays there are, fortunately, no differences of opinion regarding the ethical objectionability of the slave trade. There is, however, a lively debate on the effects of the slave trade on economic development on the African continent. Certainly there has been a considerable demographic blood-letting. The total number of slaves exported throughout the eighteenth century was no less than 17.3 per cent of the population in the year 1800 – and importantly, it was young strong men in particular who were sold as slaves. West Africa was the most important slave exporting region. In the course of the eighteenth century 4.5 million people were shipped from that region. This amounts to no less than 22.5 per cent of the West African population in the year 1800. If one realizes that even within West Africa certain regions and peoples were the special targets of slave expeditions, then the impact there must have been devastating.

Conversely, authors like Fage (1969, 1977) and Hopkins (1973) have pointed out that the annual exports of slaves were less than the natural growth of the population. Even in West Africa there was an absolute increase in the population in the eighteenth century. These authors argue that the European slave trade fits into other patterns of pre-European forms of slavery (see also Wolf, 1982, chapter 7). They state that several African kingdoms prospered thanks to the Atlantic trade, of which the above trade was a part. Therefore, the effects of the slave trade varied from region to region. Nevertheless, it can hardly be denied that, on balance, the slave trade has had a demoralizing impact and has been an obstacle to economic development in Africa.

In Latin America the slave trade has changed the entire structure of the population and thus the entire society. Most slaves have been imported into the Caribbean. In 1700 the total population in the Caribbean was 0.8 million. In the course of the eighteenth century 3.2 million slaves were added to this total. In Brazil, as well, slave imports have been extremely important; in the eighteenth century 1.9 million slaves were added to a total population of 1.25 million in the year 1700. In Spanish America the impact of slave imports in percentage terms has been less important. The population figures of Latin America in 1500 and 1600 illustrate the adverse impact of the Iberian colonization on the development of the population.

Both demographic data and data on the slave trade are surrounded by many uncertainties. The estimates of the entire Indian population in Latin America in 1492 range between 7.5 million and 100 million (Slicher van Bath, 1989). Slicher van Bath estimates the number of Indian inhabitants at 35 to 40 million.[8] Towards the middle of the seventeenth century he estimates that only 10 per cent of the original inhabitants had survived. If this should be true, the negative effects of the Spanish colonization on the native inhabitants are even greater than shown in Table 2.1. For the sake of consistency, the same sources have been used for all periods and regions in both Table 2.1 and Table 2.2. In spite of all uncertainties these figures illustrate the great demographic significance of the slave trade.

Migration flows from Europe and Asia

During the second half of the nineteenth century two enormous migration flows occurred which were characteristic of the international economic order of 1870–1913. One of these migration flows originated in Europe and was destined for regions with a temperate climate. From 1846 to 1932, 58.6 million people left Europe, of whom one-fifth returned home after some time (Palmer and Colton, 1978).[9] Most emigrants – 34 million – left for the United States. Between 1871 and 1915 European emigration amounted to 36 million people, two-thirds of whom emigrated to the United States (Lewis, 1978a, p. 181). Other popular destinations were Argentina, Canada, Brazil, Australia, South Africa and New Zealand.

These 'new worlds' had an abundance of land and were sparsely populated. Everywhere the original inhabitants – Indians, Aborigines, Maoris, Africans – were pushed aside by the immigrants. Tempted, among other things, by the higher wages in these new countries, European migrants left their technologically advanced homelands. Scarcity of labour and the relatively high education of the migrants led to a high capital–labour ratio. Therefore, productivity of labour was high. Many of the countries where European migrants arrived, were originally exporters of primary products. Today these countries are among the world's richest countries.

The other great migration flow is concerned with those migrants that left very densely populated areas in India, China and Java; they emigrated to tropical areas in the Caribbean, Africa and Asia where they were employed in mines, construction works and on plantations. In the Caribbean, the import of indentured labourers from Asia was an alternative to slavery which had been banned by the British in 1833. Quantitatively, however, migration from densely populated areas to sparsely populated areas within Asia was most important.

The estimates of the volume of this second migration flow differ widely. Partly, this is because not all migrants settled permanently in a new country. Considerable numbers of people returned to their homeland, whether voluntarily or not, after varying periods of time. In addition, some studies are concerned with migration between countries, whereas other studies also deal with migration flows within a particular region. The highest estimate is by Lewis (1978b) who – without mentioning any sources – states that the entire migration flow involved about 50 million people. A frequently quoted source is Kingsley Davis (1951), who calculated the gross migration from India between 1846 and 1937 at more than 30 million people – 6 million of them actually settling abroad permanently. Only a minor part of this migration took place before 1871, and not all migration was indentured labour. The most important migration flows went to Burma, Ceylon and Malacca. Migrants from India also ended up in the south and east of Africa where they were to play an important role in trade and commerce. Between 1880 and 1922 the number of Chinese settling in tropical areas outside China increased by 5 million – from 3 million to 8 million. Taking into account remigration, gross migration must have been much greater (Lewis, 1978b, p. 185; see also Baker, 1981). Chinese migrants very often ended up in the Netherlands East Indies, Thailand, Malacca and other parts of Southeast Asia. Finally, there was also a migration flow from Java, which was densely populated, to several other islands of the Indian archipelago.

Breman (1985) stresses the fact that indentured labour was often involuntary. Press gangs, deception and coercion played an important role in the recruitment of indentured labourers. Often migrant labour was the only way to pay the taxes imposed by colonial governments and to pay off debts to landlords. Other authors, however, emphasize the appalling conditions of life in the densely populated countryside of China or India, which provided incentives for voluntary migration. According to Lewis, a salary just above subsistence level was enough to attract an 'unlimited supply of labour' from the densely populated areas (Lewis, 1978b). Migrants made a conscious choice to improve their lot (Emmer, 1986). According to Engerman (1986), the truth is somewhere in the middle: indentured labour had both voluntary as well as involuntary aspects.

The availability of large numbers of uneducated and cheap labourers has had a negative effect on the development of productivity in mines and on plantations. Western entrepreneurs invested little in schooling and educating their inexpensive raw labour. Only little capital was available per worker. According to a well-known theory of Lewis, the availability of an unlimited labour supply forced down the prices of exports from tropical developing countries. This also explains why these countries benefited so little from their primary exports (Lewis, 1954, 1978a, 1978b).

2.4.7 Non-colonized areas

Some countries – China, Tibet, Afghanistan, Turkey, Iran, Thailand, Mongolia and Japan, to name but a few – were never colonized by the West. With the possible exception of Tibet and Mongolia, the non-colonized countries, however, were also confronted with the Western challenge and the need to respond to it. Using gunboat diplomacy, the British forced Thailand to open up to foreign trading in the treaty of Bowring (1855). In 1853 Japan was faced with the American fleet of Admiral Perry who forced the shogun to open up Japan to foreign trade. The Western challenge has, of course, been one of the reasons for the initiation of a large-scale process of modernization in Japan that has led to rapid economic growth. By the end of the nineteenth century Japan had already proved capable of joining the Western game of imperialism (Myers and Peattie, 1984). After the war with China (1894–5) Japan claimed Taiwan as its colony. In 1905 the Russo-Japanese war was won by Japan. In 1910 Korea was officially colonized, and in 1932 the Japanese puppet state of Manchukuo was set up in Manchuria. It was not until the end of World War II that the period of Japanese imperial expansion in Asia was concluded.

During the nineteenth century a terribly weakened China was penetrated from all sides by colonial powers. From 1840 to 1842 the British waged war against China – in the name of free trade – because the Chinese government refused to allow the import of opium from India. England was thus one of the first narco states. After the Opium Wars, 'treaty ports' were created along the coast, where the right of foreigners to trade was guaranteed by treaties. In these treaties Chinese jurisdiction over Western subjects was restricted (extraterritoriality). Towards the end of the nineteenth century several imperial powers, including Russia and also Japan, had carved out spheres of influence in China. It is mainly due to colonial rivalry that China was not completely colonized in this period. It is an interesting question why Japan reacted to the Western challenge with wholesale modernization whereas Chinese attempts at modernization in the face of similar challenges were halfhearted (Boserup, 1981).

2.4.8 Latecomers in the process of economic development

Russia and Japan are well-known latecomers in the process of economic development. During the last quarter of the nineteenth century these two countries began a dramatic modernization of their economies. In a relatively short time they each succeeded in building up a large industrial sector and in ranging themselves among the important industrialized nations. Japan, in particular, has managed to become a new industrial superpower in a short period of time.

With regard to the economic development of Russia, Alexander Gerschenkron (1962) has pointed out the 'advantages of backwardness'. A technological leader has to pay all costs of research and development of new technologies; its followers may copy the newly developed theories at little cost. Under certain circumstances the follower countries can experience a process of rapid catch-up. In post-war years the advantages of backwardness have contributed to rapid productivity growth in Japan and Western Europe.

2.4.9 The period 1913–1950

Maddison (1989) describes the international order between 1913 and 1950 as a period of conflict and autarky. The international economic order underwent dramatic changes as a result of two world wars and a deep economic crisis (1929–32). After the Communist Revolution of 1917 the Soviet Union seceded from the world economy and strove for further industrialization and economic development by means of a centrally planned economy. Attempts to reconstruct the liberal international economic order after World War I did not meet with success.

In many respects, the 1913–50 period was the reverse of the economic order of 1870–1913. Economic growth slackened both in rich countries and in developing countries. Investment flows to developing countries dried up. Latin American countries defaulted on their debts, and the international financial system, based on the gold standard, was disrupted. Free trade was replaced by strong protectionism. Especially after 1929 each country tried to protect its own economy and to saddle other countries with the consequences of the economic crisis. As a result international trade spiralled downwards. The developing countries most involved in international trade from 1870 to 1913 were the most affected. The demand for primary exports of developing countries collapsed; the development of their prices was unfavourable compared with the development of the prices of industrial imports ('deteriorating terms of trade'). In some Latin American countries – Brazil, for example – domestic industries benefited from the fact that industrial imports could no longer be paid for. Moreover, domestic industries were actively stimulated and protected by the government (import substitution).

One of the important ideas rooted in the experiences of developing countries during this period of time is that of 'export pessimism'. Export pessimists argue that primary exports will not lead to lasting economic development since the global demand for these products is not stable and terms of trade with respect to industrial products tend to decline in the long term. Developing countries ought to isolate themselves more from the international economy and they should strive for industrialization with the aid of government intervention. These notions will be discussed in more detail in the chapter on industrialization strategies (Chapter 7).

2.4.10 The period after World War II

From a political point of view the period after World War II marks the end of the process of Western expansion. Rapidly, one colony after the other achieved independence – sometimes through negotiation, sometimes through bloody wars as was the case in Algeria, Vietnam and Indonesia. However, the end of Western supremacy over vast colonial empires did not constitute the end of international relations of dependence. As has already been argued above, Western expansion led to the formation of an integrated world economy with interdependence among its components.

The period 1950–73 is characterized by growth rates of national incomes unprecedented in economic history (Maddison, 1982a, 1989). Both in developing and in rich countries there was strong growth, though not everyone benefited from it to the same degree. One after another, obstacles to international trade were eliminated in rich countries. Liberalization of international trade resulted in a considerable growth of the volume of international trade. International trade benefited from a stable monetary system based on fixed exchange rates, gold and the dollar. Developing countries used their newly achieved autonomy systematically to pursue economic development. A number of developing countries experienced rapid processes of industrialization and some of them even succeeded in producing competitive industrial products for the global market. Almost without exception, industrialization in developing countries involved protection of the young industrial sector; this constituted an exception to the general trend towards liberalization of the international economic order. The volume of investment and capital flows increased sharply. Developing countries benefited from a net capital inflow, in contradiction to the period before World War II.

The 1973 oil crisis heralded an era of uncertainty for both rich and developing countries (Maddison, 1985, 1989). The growth rate of the world economy slackened in comparison with post-war years. Protectionist tendencies re-emerged, though there was no return to pre-war protectionism. After a period of continuous growth in the 1970s, in the 1980s many Latin American countries suffered economic problems under the influence of the debt crisis. In Africa, economic development stagnated seriously. Several countries even experienced an absolute decline in per capita national income. In many countries in south and southeast Asia, however, there was continued economic growth. The dissolution of the Soviet Union in the 1990s was accompanied by an economic collapse. Many of the former Soviet Republics which have become independent show many similarities with developing countries elsewhere in the world. The post-war period will be discussed in more detail in Chapter 11.

2.5 *Two perspectives on developments in the world economy, 1500–1993*

The development of the world economy since the sixteenth century can be viewed from two perspectives: that of the formation and dynamization of the world economy; and that of exploitation and increasing inequality in the world economy.

The perspective of the formation and dynamization of the world economy

Since 1500, we have seen the first instance of a sustained breakthrough from recurring cycles of poverty in economic history. In most historical times, the majority of the people never lived far above subsistence levels. Bad harvests – as a result of wars, drought or too much water – would easily result in famines. The time perspective was short. Most people could not afford to invest in long-term improvement in their living conditions; their first priority was survival in the short term.

In this respect the process of economic growth, which started in Europe, was a breakthrough that demands an explanation. This growth, combined with external expansion, provided a challenge to peoples and societies in other parts of the world. It induced processes of change everywhere. The example of Western economic development and the threat of Western penetration and domination called forth an almost universal pursuit of development in other parts of the world.

The perspective of exploitation and increasing inequality in the emerging world economy

Around 1500 there were no great differences in the level of prosperity between the various countries and regions. In the subsequent centuries there was a constant growth of per capita income in Western countries such as the Netherlands, France and Great Britain. At the same time per capita income stagnated in most developing countries such as, for example, China, India, Indonesia and Mexico. As a result, Western Europe was more prosperous than the rest of the world as early as 1750, that is, before the acceleration of the industrial development in the second part of the eighteenth century. The increasing inequalities went hand in hand with exploitation of poor areas by rich – the rich countries appropriating part of the economic wealth of the poor areas they penetrated.

The income differences increased sharply in the nineteenth and twentieth centuries when growth accelerated in Western countries. Even when per capita income in developing countries increased, growth in rich countries was faster, at least until 1973; as a result, the differences between the rich and the poor countries increased further. According to Maddison, in 1820 GDP per capita in Indonesia was about 40 per cent of that of the most productive country of the time – England. When Japan and Russia began their catch-up around 1870, their national income per capita amounted to about one-third of England's per capita income (Maddison, 1983). In 1993 the average national income per capita in developing countries amounted to less than 1/22 of the national income of the United States. If a comparison of the poorest and the richest countries were to be drawn (as has been done in Chapter 1), the ratio would be 1 : 60.

Considered from this gloomy point of view, the formation of the world economy involved a truly explosive growth of global income inequality. The gap that divides rich and poor countries has widened more and more. In this perspective, the emphasis is on understanding centuries of relative economic stagnation in developing countries and analyzing the role of colonial and neocolonial exploitation in such processes of stagnation.

There are important elements of truth in both perspectives. It is not possible to make an absolute choice between them. Advocates of each perspective should realize that there are different ways of approaching issues of development and stagnation and also that these different perspectives will raise different kinds of interesting questions.

2.6 *Key issues*

The contrast between the world economy of 1993 and that of 1500 as described in this chapter raises several fascinating questions which may help to bring some order to the multitude of schools, theories and approaches concerned with development issues. Three questions will be distinguished here.

First, how is it possible that a certain part of the world has experienced a historically unprecedented process of economic growth and development since 1500?

Two types of explanations can be offered: *internal* and *external*. Internal explanations seek the causes of the Western economic breakthrough in typical factors which distinguish Western countries from non-Western countries: culture, religion, mentality, institutions, population density, climate, natural circumstances, geographical location, political characteristics, policies, and so on. External explanations seek the causes of Western prosperity in Western exploitation of other parts of the world. These explanations see the drain of revenues and wealth resulting from colonial penetration as the decisive factor which put the West and the developing world on different paths of development.

Second, why have other parts of the world lagged behind the rich Western countries in their economic development since 1500? Why didn't the developing countries experience processes of development similar to those in the West?

In answering these questions, one can again distinguish *external* and *internal* explanations. Internal explanations seek the specific factors that have been obstacles to economic development in developing countries: traditional cultures, attitudes, mentalities, institutions that are not conducive to technological progress, savings and investment patterns, unfavourable natural circumstances, ineffective policies. External explanations emphasize the negative effects of Western penetration of the world. The lack of economic growth in developing countries is seen as a result of colonial and neocolonial exploitation. Moderate versions of the perspective tend to emphasize the disadvantages of backwardness. In a global economy dominated by established economic powers, latecomers will find it ever more difficult to initiate successful development.

Third, is it possible for developing countries nowadays to undergo processes of development similar to those experienced by rich countries in the past?

The answers to this last question are of course closely linked to the answers given by different thinkers to the previous questions. Three types of answers are possible:

1. In principle, developing countries can undergo processes of economic and social development similar to those experienced by the rich countries in the past. This answer was primarily given by the theorists of modernization of the 1950s and 1960s. They emphasized the necessity of breaking through traditional structures, attitudes, and institutions that hamper development. Advanced countries may help by providing education, information and financial means for investment in new infrastructures and capital goods.
2. In principle, developing countries cannot pursue the same path as rich countries, since the development of rich countries has been very much associated with (capitalist) exploitation of the rest of the world. It was Marxists and other radical critics of modernization theories who came up with this particular answer. Underdevelopment of the poor countries is the counterpart of development in the West. Only by liberating themselves from the capitalist world economy and by finding their own different path do developing countries have a chance of attaining development.
3. There is no reason to believe that developing countries are in principle incapable of reaching higher levels of prosperity. However, it is rather unlikely that the path to a higher per capita income will be the same as the path rich countries have followed in the past. Initial conditions for development differ in each period and in every phase of development of the international economic and political order. Initial starting conditions have to do with demographic characteristics, development of the world trade, international competition, technological development, the international balance of power, and the nature of the relationships with rich countries. Latecomers in development may face both disadvantages and potential advantages. Apart from the differing initial conditions over time, there are also differences in circumstances between various countries and regions. In addition, policy decisions made in developing countries themselves are of great importance.

QUESTIONS FOR REVIEW

1. List the most important characteristics of the concept of international economic order. Discuss the six types of international economic order which can be distinguished since 1500.
2. Explain the unique features of the Western process of development since the beginning of the sixteenth century, compared to earlier processes of socio-economic development.

3. Why did Chinese economic development stagnate from the fourteenth century onwards, in spite of initial conditions which seemed so promising?
4. Discuss the differences between colonies of settlement and colonies of occupation.
5. What were the characteristics of the international division of labour between rich countries and poor countries which evolved in the period 1870–1913?
6. Discuss the impact of major migration flows on the demographic characteristics of developing countries.
7. Discuss the contrasting perspectives on the role of Western expansion in the formation of the modern world economy.

Notes

1. In discussing the international economic order, it is obvious that attention also has to be paid to international political relationships. Since this book focuses on economic developments and since the term 'international economic and political order' is too cumbersome, I will continue to use the term 'international economic order'.
2. For a dissenting view see Bairoch (1980) who argues that around 1700 developing countries were about as rich as the presently affluent countries at that time.
3. It may be useful to remind readers of the fact that European feudalism was not some sort of primitive initial situation, but that it came into being after the fall of larger politically centralized empires.
4. I have restricted myself for the greater part to paraphrasing Wallerstein (1974) who in turn offers a synthesis of the literature on this subject.
5. For a short period of time in the seventeenth century, the Dutch also played an important role in Brazil. However, their role had been played out by 1655.
6. The term 'Industrial Revolution' tends to misrepresent the gradual nature of the long-term increase in economic productivity.
7. Curtin's statistics have been revised by Lovejoy (1982). According to Lovejoy, Curtin's estimates for the eighteenth century are 5 per cent too high, for the seventeenth century 11.5 per cent too low and for the nineteenth century 18.5 per cent too low . Lovejoy calculates the total number of exported slaves at 9.8 million as compared with Curtin's 9.6 million. Since Lovejoy does not offer a subdivision into importing regions, Curtin's estimates, which are of an earlier date, have been used in the text tables.
8. I am grateful to Gerben Bakker who introduced me to this particular source.
9. This total includes 7 million migrants who left for Asian Russia.

3 Growth and stagnation: theories and experiences

This chapter offers a brief introduction to theories of growth and stagnation (sections 3.1 to 3.4), which are of relevance to the fundamental questions raised at the end of the previous chapter. In addition, empirical information is presented in section 3.5 on long-run economic trends in developing countries.

3.1 *Classical thinking about growth and stagnation*

Since the eighteenth century, classical economists and sociologists have concerned themselves with the mystery of economic growth in the capitalist West. Many of their ideas still play a prominent role in topical discussions on problems of development. Without doing justice to the complexities in the theories of classical authors, I shall touch briefly upon a number of important themes in classical thought, which have retained their relevance for present day discussions.

3.1.1 Adam Smith

In *The Wealth of Nations*, Adam Smith (1723–1790) ranked countries according to their economic performance. The most modern and prosperous country was the Republic of the United Netherlands, followed by England, France, North America, Scotland, and China, with Bengal in the last place. Smith was interested in how differences between countries had come about and how knowledge about the causes of prosperity could help England improve its relative standing *vis-à-vis* the Netherlands. Smith attacked traditional obstacles to free trade and free competition, such as guilds and royal monopolies. The more individuals were left free to pursue their own interests, the more the invisible hand of the market would promote collective welfare. In addition Smith emphasized the importance of specialization, the division of labour in the production process and economies of scale. The division of labour and the associated increase in the scale of production would lead to dramatic increases in productivity.

3.1.2 The classical economists Ricardo, Malthus and Mill

The classical economists David Ricardo (1772–1823), Thomas Malthus (1766–1834) and John Stuart Mill (1806–1873) shared Smith's preference for free markets and *laissez-faire* policies. The government should intervene as little as possible in the economic process. One might say that the classical economists offered an institutional explanation of economic growth. People have an innate tendency to engage in exchange and trade. If social institutions give free play to such tendencies, individual self-interest will stimulate efforts that contribute to economic growth and increasing prosperity for all.

Compared to Smith, the classical economists placed more emphasis on the importance of the stock of capital goods used in the production process and on the importance of international trade. Ricardo formulated his famous *law of comparative advantage*. This law states that all countries entering into international trade will profit from such trade if they concentrate on the production of those products in which they are relatively most efficient. This law is still the keystone of modern arguments for liberalization of international trade.

Compared with the eighteenth century there are also some pessimistic elements present in the work of these authors. Malthus was afraid that food production would not be able to keep up with population growth. In the long run this would result in starvation and widespread famine, which would serve as a check to further population growth. Malthusianism has become the general term for modern pessimistic perspectives, emphasizing the limits to economic growth.

Ricardo feared that economic development would stagnate in the long run. As more and more people work in agriculture, due to population growth, less and less fertile soils are taken into production and the marginal product decreases. When marginal product in agriculture declines, food prices will go up, which in turn exerts an upward pressure on wages in industry. Increasing food prices are translated into higher wage costs. In due time, increasing wages cut into profits and thus into future investment. The engine of economic growth thus grinds to a halt.

Ricardo was in favour of abolishing tariffs on food imports, to keep food prices from rising. Ricardo's theory is a predecessor of modern *two-sector models*, which analyze the relationships between agriculture and industry in economic development.

3.1.3 Friedrich List

Ricardo, Malthus and Mill all lived and wrote at a time when the dominant power in the world economy, England, propagated international free trade. They were convinced of the advantages of free trade. Friedrich List (1789–1846), German by and founder of the 'historical school' in economics, was less enthusiastic about the blessings of free trade. According to him, it was the dominant powers which primarily profited from free trade. Latecomers to economic development such as Germany were hindered in their development by competition from economically advanced countries. List argued for protection of newly founded industries against murderous international competition. This so-called *infant industry argument* would play an important role in the development strategies of developing countries in the twentieth century. List was also convinced that active government intervention was necessary to build up an industrial sector in late-developing economies and to further the structural transformation of agrarian into industrial societies.

3.1.4 Karl Marx

Karl Marx (1818–1883) focused on the dynamic role of capitalism as an explanation of economic developments in the West. Just like List and other representatives of the historical school, Marx postulated a theory of stages of development in which every society sooner or later passes through the same stages. His stages of development were: primitive original communism, slavery, feudalism, capitalism and socialism. Each subsequent stage represented a higher level in the development process. In the West the contradictions within feudalism had for the first time led to the overthrow of a feudal economic system based on ownership of land and its replacement by an economic system based on the ownership of capital goods. Sooner or later societies in other parts of the world would inevitably go through the same transition. Such stage theories underlie the negative attitude of many twentieth-century Marxist regimes to agriculture, which is seen as representing an outmoded stage of development.

In Marxist theories, class contradictions – conflicts of interest between social groups which own the predominant means of production and social groups which do not – play a central role in the explanation of social dynamics. Under capitalism, competition provides the incentive for accumulation of capital and technological progress, on the one hand. But it also leads to an ever-increasing exploitation of the newly created industrial working classes by the capitalist classes. Marx agreed with the classical economists that capitalism had led to a revolutionary increase in productive capacity. Productive potential was liberated from the shackles of feudalism. In due course, however, these liberating tendencies of capitalism were superseded by repressive tendencies. The capitalist system, in the grip of competitive forces and conjunctural fluctuations, was no longer able to make an efficient use of the newly unchained productive capacities. Competition led to increasing exploitation of workers. Exploitation of workers led to decreasing purchasing power for the working class. The economic result was overproduction, declining profit margins and ever-deepening economic crises. The social result was pauperization and increasing revolutionary class consciousness. In the long run, the increased polarization between the capitalist class and the working class would lead to revolution and the collapse of capitalism.

According to Marx, the essence of capitalism is production for profit and reinvestment, rather than production for the satisfaction of human needs. Competition forces entrepreneurs continuously to invest in more and qualitatively better means of production. Thus, just as in classical economic thought, accumulation of capital has a central place in Marxist theory. However, in contradiction to the classical economists, Marx did not see capital accumulation and economic growth as an harmonious process leading to increased collective welfare. Economic development is characterized by continuous exploitation, appropriation of surpluses for the purposes of reinvestment, and social conflict. Competing entrepreneurs can only make a profit by paying their workers no more than a subsistence wage, which barely keeps them alive. One of the Marxist ideas which has considerable relevance for modern thinking about economic development is the relationship between appropriation of economic surplus by certain social groups and the process of reinvestment and accumulation of capital.

3.1.5 Imperialism

Marxist predictions of revolutions which would inevitably break out in the most advanced capitalist countries have failed to come true. Where Communist revolutions materialized, they invariably took place in agrarian societies, with low levels of industrial development, such as the USSR, China, Vietnam, Cambodia and Cuba. A later generation of theorists (Hilferding 1877–1943; Luxemburg 1870–1919; Lenin 1870–1924; Hobson 1858–1940) tried to explain the absence of the predicted revolutions in advanced countries with various theories of imperialism. Such theories state that the Western world succeeded in transferring its internal contradictions to world economy and the developing countries. In the process of imperialist expansion in the second half of the nineteenth century, these countries were colonized and exploited.

Theories of imperialism come in many guises. Some theories explained imperialist expansion by pointing to the lack of investment opportunities in the advanced countries and the search for new investment possibilities in the colonies. Other theories pointed to factors such as the safeguarding of the flow of raw materials as inputs for industrial development, or the search for new markets for industrial products that could not be sold in home markets due to overproduction. Theories of imperialism were drawn up at a time when the Western expansion in the world was at its apex. Without exception, these theories stressed the negative effects of imperialism on the development chances of the poor countries.

Nowadays, the empirical evidence for economic explanations of imperialism is considered to be weak (Fieldhouse, 1973; Chirot, 1977; see also Schumpeter, 1976). Nevertheless, these theories have been a source of inspiration for twentieth-century theorists of underdevelopment.

3.1.6 Max Weber and Joseph Schumpeter

To conclude this short excursion through the history of ideas, I will discuss briefly some ideas of Max Weber and Joseph Schumpeter. These two authors follow Marx in his emphasis on the importance of class relationships and in his analysis of the dynamics of capitalism. But they also offer fundamental criticisms of the Marxian legacy.

While Marx saw the profit motive as the distinctive feature of the capitalist system, Max Weber (1864–1920) emphasized the principle of rationality. According to Weber, the development of capitalism was part of a long-run social trend of rationalization in Western societies. The profit motive is common to all times; it cannot differentiate capitalism from other systems. New in capitalism is the rational organization of production for the purposes of sustained profitability, making use of systematic bookkeeping methods. The emergence of markets is also part of the long-run rationalization trend. Production for the market stimulates businesslike thinking about means and ends and the calculation of financial costs and benefits, irrespective of the individuals involved in the transactions.

Weber explicitly posed the question of why capitalism had broken through in Western Europe, rather than in other parts of the world. Marx saw developments in the economic sphere of society, the 'substructure', as determining developments in culture, religion, politics and law (the 'superstructure'). In contradiction to this, Weber sought the explanation of the rise of capitalism in religious influences. He noted that the first capitalist countries were predominantly Protestant. His famous hypothesis – known as the Weber thesis – states that the Protestant ethic favoured economic development. The combination of diligent work in one's professional 'calling' and religiously motivated sobriety in consumption promoted a high level of savings and the accumulation of capital (see Chapter 7). The Protestant ethic was the factor which distinguished the Western world from other regions where the breakthrough of capitalism did not take place. Thus the Protestant ethic is the determining factor in the rise of capitalism and process of economic growth in the West (Weber, 1969).

A third difference with the Marxist tradition is the greater importance of the political sphere. According to Weber, economic development presupposes the rise of highly centralized state apparatuses, which are able to maintain internal peace and order in a country. Without internal peace and centralization, the market will never be able to function. If trade is unpredictable, if there are all sorts of capricious local rules, taxes and tithes, if the safety of trade is not guaranteed, a rational weighing of costs and benefits is impossible.

While Weber focused on the origins of capitalism, Schumpeter (1883–1950) was primarily interested in twentieth-century capitalism. From Marx he derived the idea of capitalism as an economic system, riven by deep class conflicts. This system was both destructive and extremely dynamic. However, in contradiction to Marx, Schumpeter did not believe capitalism would be destroyed by its own inefficiencies. In the middle of the great depression of the 1930s, Schumpeter predicted a golden age of fifty years of economic growth in the Western World (Schumpeter, 1976).

According to Schumpeter, capitalism is characterized by a 'gale of creative destruction'. Old production techniques are continuously becoming obsolescent and are being replaced by new ones. Schumpeter emphasizes the importance of technological progress. An important role is reserved here for the entrepreneur who realizes 'new combinations': new forms of organization, new production techniques, new products, new markets, new sources of raw materials. Capitalism gives free reign to the entrepreneur and thus creates an ample supply of entrepreneurship. In the long run, Schumpeter thought capitalism would be undermined by its successes rather than its failures. The process of innovation would become routinized. The role of the creative entrepreneur would be taken over by staff departments and research laboratories. Gradually and unnoticeably the system would be transformed into a socialist planning system, through the planning and administrative procedures of the very large firms.

It is not clear whether Schumpeter would consider the present Western mixed economies as capitalist or socialist. But the question whether developing countries have a sufficient supply of entrepreneurship is one of the classical questions, which keep cropping up in post-war theorizing on development.

3.2 *Internal and external approaches*

The classical discussions were primarily concerned with explanations of the economic breakthrough of the presently prosperous countries. The present-day discussion of development focuses on the reasons why the poorer countries could not keep up with the richer ones. At the end of Chapter 2, a distinction was made between internal approaches and external approaches to the problems of development. Both the internal and the external approaches start with the observation that economy and society in developing countries are characterized by *dualism*. The term refers to the existence side by side of a modern and a traditional sector. The modern sector is technologically developed and commercialized, and is located in and around urban centres. The traditional sector is characterized by traditional technologies, low productivity, production for own consumption and is predominantly rural. Dualist structures came into being at the end of the nineteenth century, when developing countries were drawn into international trade. Capitalist enclaves emerged within non-capitalist economic systems.

The main problem of dualism is the economic and social gap between the modern and the traditional sector. The modern sector is oriented to the outside world, rather than to domestic society. There are hardly any linkages between the modern sector and the rest of the economy and society. Thus a developing country as a whole does not profit much from technological and economic development in the modern sector. Also, a traditional hinterland can form an obstacle to the further development of a modern sector which is relatively small in size.

Internal approaches emphasize the factors within a society which promote or hinder development. One of the founding fathers of development economics, J. H. Boeke, thus explained the lack of development of the traditional sector in Indonesia by pointing to the characteristics of oriental man and oriental culture, in which individual economic incentives were not operative. Needs were limited and social needs dominated individual needs (Boeke, 1953). External approaches try to explain the situation in developing countries by reference to negative influences from outside. Dualistic structures are created by external economic and political penetration. These external influences also maintain the dualistic structures. The external and internal perspectives will be discussed in more detail in the following sections.

3.3 *Explanations of economic backwardness*

Internal approaches to the problems of development draw our attention to unfavourable circumstances and factors within a society that form an obstacle for development. In the pessimistic perspective of Boeke there is but little chance of overcoming such obstacles. However, most representatives of internal approaches are more optimistic than Boeke. They think a long-run process of modernization has set in, in which all societies gradually move from traditionality in the direction of modernity. Dualism is due to the fact that modernization has taken place in one part of society, but not yet in society as a whole. The key words are 'not yet'. Less developed countries have a 'lag' compared to more developed countries, just as the less developed traditional sectors lag behind the modern sectors. Once the internal barriers to development have been overcome, the laggards can start overtaking the leaders.

3.3.1 Rostow's theory of the stages of economic growth

One of the best-known representatives of modernization theory is W. W. Rostow. In *The Stages of Economic Growth*, Rostow (1960) has sketched a stage theory of growth in which each society sooner or later passes through the same five stages: traditional society, preconditions to take-off, take-off, drive to maturity and a mass consumption society. In this development process some countries take the lead, others lag behind. Just as in Marxist theory, however, the path of development is the same for all societies.

In traditional societies (stage 1), fatalistic patterns of thought predominate, in which people feel at the mercy of external forces of nature, higher powers or political rulers. The production technology is static.

In the pre-condition stage (stage 2), the stability of the traditional society is undermined, usually as a result of external threats or challenges. In this stage the idea emerges that people can improve their living conditions or those of their children by their own efforts. A beginning is made with the translation of the insights of modern science into production technologies.

In the economic sphere the conditions for industrialization are created in this period. The most important condition is an increase in productivity in one of the non-industrial sectors such as agriculture or mining. This creates a surplus above subsistence that is potentially available for investment in the industrial sector. Especially in agriculture, such an increase in productivity is of the greatest importance. Productivity growth in agriculture frees labour for employment in the industrial sector and fulfils the food requirements of a growing population. Increased earnings in the agrarian sector provide a market for industrial goods, while financial surpluses from agriculture can be invested in industry.

In the precondition stage investments are realized in infrastructure (railways, canals, roads, energy supply, harbours, etc.), which are a prerequisite for industrialization. In the social–political sphere, the pre-condition stage is characterized by the emergence of modernizing elites, which consciously strive for development and industrialisation. Socially, the horizon of expectations expands.

The crucial stage is the take-off stage (stage 3). The analogy is that of an aeroplane which gains sufficient speed on the runway to take off into flight. In the take-off stage the structure of the economy changes very drastically in a short period of ten to twenty years, so that sustained growth can set in after that. In the take-off stage the level of investment needs to be increased substantially. Echoing earlier publications by Lewis (1950, 1954), Rostow writes that investment should increase from less than 5 per cent to more than 10 per cent of net national income. Investment should be directed towards industrial sectors, with the strongest linkages with the rest of the economy. In the past, the role of 'leading sector' has been fulfilled by the textile industry, the military industry, the railway industry and the chemical industry. Other ingredients of the take-off stage are a sufficient supply of entrepreneurship and a sufficient supply of loanable funds that can be channelled into the industrial sector, voluntarily or involuntarily .

In the subsequent 'drive to maturity' stage (stage 4), new production techniques spread from the leading sectors to the rest of the economy. In the last stage, a mass consumption society (stage 5) – which looks surprisingly like Rostow's North American society – the whole population benefits from the increased opportunities for consumption.

Parallel with Rostow's primarily economically oriented theories, the 1950s and 1960s saw the rise of various sociological theories of modernization (Hoselitz, 1960; Moore, 1963; Inkeles, 1969; Inkeles and Smith, 1974). These theories chart the social changes which accompany economic growth, including: urbanization; the transition from extended family structures to nuclear families; increasing division of labour and occupational specialization; rationalization in attitudes; increasing social mobility; the transition from ascription to achievement as the determining principle of social stratification; increasing levels of schooling; and individualization. Like Rostovian theory, modernization theories usually conceive of development as a unilinear path from a traditional to a modern society. Some sociological modernization theories focus on the social disruption accompanying rapid technological and economic change. These theories hark back to the classical Durkheimian tradition in sociology, which analyzes the increasing normlessness (*anomie*) of modern social life (Durkheim, 1973).

An important policy recommendation deriving from Rostovian analysis is the requirement of large-scale investment in industry. Foreign investment, loans and development aid can help compensate for the shortfall in domestic savings compared to investment needs. Development aid, training and education can also help surmount the traditional obstacles to growth and contribute to the realization of the preconditions for take-off.

Rostow's theory of stages of development has been severely criticized in the course of time, just like modernization theory in general. Nevertheless, it is striking how many traces of his theory can be found in the work of later authors.

3.3.2 Kuznets's preconditions for industrialization

According to Kuznets (1965) it is not possible to distinguish Rostow's stages of growth empirically. The changes in investment and growth rates are more gradual than the dramatic term 'take-off' suggests. The concept of traditional society does not do justice to the great diversity of social and economic circumstances in pre-capitalist societies. Finally, Kuznets, along with many authors, has serious objections to the unilinear concept of development, that is, the idea that every society follows one and the same path of development. It makes a big difference, for instance, whether a country is an early or a late industrializer, whether industrialization takes place in a large country with a large domestic market or in a small country with a small domestic market. Also, there is nothing inevitable about stages of development. Countries can move backward as well as forward (Kuznets, 1965).

Nevertheless, there are also some important similarities between Kuznets and Rostow. Like Rostow, Kuznets emphasizes the importance of industrialization in development. *Changes in the structure of production* are among the main characteristics of modern economic development. Furthermore, Kuznets identifies conditions for industrialization which are almost identical to those mentioned by Rostow: productivity increases in other sectors such as mining, agriculture or transport; sufficient supply of labour, capital and entrepreneurship; and sufficient effective demand for industrial products.

3.3.3 Advantages of backwardness

Like Rostow, Alexander Gerschenkron emphasizes the importance of overcoming traditional obstacles to industrialization. For Russia, such obstacles included serfdom and the absence of a disciplined, reliable and stable supply of industrial labour. When industrialization occurs in late developing economies, it happens in leaps or in rapid spurts, concentrated in certain leading sectors of economy (Gerschenkron, 1962).

In two respects Gerschenkron disagrees with Rostow. In the first place, there are important differences between the patterns of industrialization in different countries and different historical periods. In early processes of industrialization, self-financing by firms was the most important source of investable funds. In the economic development of Germany, banks and financial institutions played a far more important role than earlier in England and France. In Russia, only the government was able to mobilize sufficient amounts of financial capital for massive investment in industry and infrastructure. As time went by, technological change required investment on an ever larger scale. This explains why the role of banks, financial institutions and goverment becomes more and more important in late industrialization. Increasing scale also explains the explosive nature of industrialization processes. For industrialization to succeed, very many changes in the economy have to take place simultaneously and in a short period of time. If changes are only partial or limited, the required scale of investment will not be attained and the process of industrialization will stagnate.

Very important is Gerschenkron's idea that economic development of a single country should be studied in a context of international technology transfer. In this respect Gerschenkron transcends the limits of internal perspectives. In Gerschenkron's theory, latecomers in economic development have the opportunity to take over technological know-how from economically advanced countries, without having to bear the burden of the costs of research and development of new technologies. Developing countries can choose from a tremendous arsenal of new production techniques that were not available previously. Thus if the economy and the society is able to absorb new technologies, latecomers in development can experience faster economic growth than early developers because they profit from the *advantages of backwardness*.

3.3.4 Neoclassical theories of growth

Neoclassical economic theories of growth analyze the relationships between the growth of inputs (capital, land, labour, technology) and growth of output, in the form of mathematical models of growth. Compared to the theories discussed so far, the neoclassical economic theory of growth as formulated by Solow (1956, 1957) is not really a theory of growth proper. It has little or nothing to say about the more fundamental mechanisms and institutions underlying accumulation of capital, technical change and growth. Nevertheless, it draws our attention to the contribution to growth of the accumulation of factors of production and of changes in the quality of factors of production. It also emphasizes the importance of an efficient allocation of factors of production in processes of economic development. Free markets and perfect competition are the mechanisms which make for such efficient allocation.

Closely associated with the rise of neoclassical growth theory is the rise of the growth accounting tradition, pioneered by authors such as Denison (1967), Kendrick (1961) and Abramovitz (1956). Growth accounting focuses on the empirical quantification of the contributions of different factors to growth, taking the neoclassical framework as an initial point of departure.[1] Growth accounting makes a distinction between the growth of inputs (increase in the quantity and quality of inputs) and the growth of output per unit of input (see Maddison, 1987). Growth accounting goes on to explain growth of output per unit of input by various factors such as structural shifts from low productivity to high productivity sectors, economies of scale, and technological change. Growth accounting shows that a very considerable part of growth cannot be accounted for by increases in the amount of inputs. An important part of growth can only be explained by technological change.

Neoclassical theory does not focus explicitly on developing countries. Implicitly, however, it predicts that if markets function smoothly and the factors of production can move freely across the world economy, sooner or later rich and poor countries will converge and poor countries will catch up. The focus of both neoclassical theory and growth accounting on the so-called proximate determinants of growth places these approaches squarely within the internal tradition in the analysis of backwardness.

The neoclassical theory of growth assumes maximizing behaviour on the part of economic actors. Firms will continue to use more and more capital and labour in production as long as the marginal costs of these factors of production are less than their marginal returns. Under competitive conditions and perfect information, this will result in equalization of marginal costs and marginal returns. The model assumes constant returns to scale, implying for instance that if the amount of both capital and labour is doubled, output will also double. If one factor of production is held constant while the other increases, the marginal returns to the increasing factor will diminish. The model assumes that the growth of labour depends on population growth and is thus given. The share of savings in national income is assumed constant.

Now as the savings are used to accumulate more and more capital per worker, labour productivity will go up. But as the marginal returns to capital are declining, the rate of increase in labour productivity will decline and productivity growth in the long run will become zero. Then per capita income growth will come to a stop. The only factor which counterbalances this is technological change, the rate of which is determined outside the model and is not explained. Technological change shifts the production function upwards. In the long run, therefore, the growth rate of labour productivity depends on technological change.

As developing countries have less capital per worker than rich countries, the marginal productivity of capital should be higher and labour productivity growth will therefore be more rapid than in rich countries. In the long run, rich and poor countries will tend to converge. This tendency towards convergence in the neoclassical theory is strengthened by the assumption that capital moves freely across the world economy. If returns are higher in developing countries, capital will move there, making for convergence. Technology is also conceived of as a public good that is available to all economies. Therefore, in the long run, rich and poor countries should converge and their growth rate of per capita income should be determined by the rate of technological change.

As we well know, there is little actual convergence to be observed between rich and poor countries in the world economy. This is one of the points of departure for the so-called new or endogenous theory of growth which surfaced since the middle 1980s.

In the older neoclassical growth models, technological change was conceived of as exogenous. New growth theories try to endogenize[2] technological change in two ways (Romer, 1986, 1990; Lucas, 1988; for a recent overview, see Fagerberg, 1994). In the first place, it is assumed that technological change (changes in the stock of knowledge) is automatically associated with investment in capital goods and education

The University of Bolton
The Library
Enquiries 01204 903094

Borrowed Items 12/10/2012 13:42
XXX6755

Item Title	Due Date
460803	
* storm : the world economic	19/10/2012
413376	
* Economic and social devel	02/11/2012

* = Newly borrowed items
Thankyou for using this unit

find us http://www.bolton.ac.uk/library

catalogue http://opac.bolton.ac.uk
PLEASE RETAIN YOUR RECEIPT

through a process of learning by doing. In the second place, one can conceive of investment in a separate sector producing technology and knowledge that becomes available for firms engaged in production of goods and services. The production of various goods and services through the application of increasing amounts of knowledge and technology in production is subject to increasing returns to scale, due to the positive external effects of knowledge in production (spill-over effects). The greater the level of initial investment in knowledge and human capital in a country, the greater the returns to further investment. The only limit to unrestricted growth is that the production of knowledge itself is subject to decreasing returns (in other words, becomes ever more difficult). Thus new growth theory offers an explanation for the divergence in economic performance between rich and poor countries existing in the world economy. Countries with a head start in accumulation of human capital and knowledge will tend to forge ahead. Countries which are backward will tend to stagnate further.

A recent version of these theories stresses the notion of conditional convergence (Baumol *et al.*, 1989). Once certain threshold levels of education or investment have been achieved, backward countries can grow very rapidly as they take over technology from elsewhere (see section 3.3.3). But if they fail to achieve these threshold levels, gaps will tend to widen.

Though the ideas contained in new growth theory are stimulating, the empirical verification of these models has run into great difficulties. It turns out to be almost impossible to discard one model in favour of another on the basis of empirical tests. Even at a theoretical level, Solow, one of the founding fathers of neoclassical growth theory, has pointed out that neoclassical growth theory can also accomodate divergence (Solow, 1991). He argues that the availability of modern technology does not automatically mean that technological diffusion to less developed economies will indeed take place. In the absence of institutional changes, these economies may simply be unable to assimilate new technologies. This brings the argument back to institutional factors.

3.3.5 North and Thomas: efficient institutions

One of the less satisfactory aspects of theories of backwardness discussed so far is the mysterious transition from a traditional to a modern economy. This transition is the central theme of a beautiful study of two economic historians Douglass C. North and Robert P. Thomas (1973). In *The Rise of the Western World* they focus on the emergence of efficient institutions. Efficient institutions are defined as institutions which motivate self-interested individuals to act in ways which contribute to collective welfare. Among the efficient institutions discussed by North and Thomas are well-defined property rights, which guarantee that individuals will profit from the fruits of their own exertions. Only under such conditions will individuals be willing to make risky investments in future productive capacity. Protection of intellectual property (patent rights) is one of the conditions for a continuous stream of innovations. The institution of the joint stock company diminishes the risks of large-scale investments for individuals. Land reforms that create well-defined individual rights to land motivate farmers to invest in increased land productivity.

Efficient institutions do not emerge automatically. The rise of efficient institutions depends on the costs and benefits involved in the creation and maintenance of such institutions for different individuals and groups. When population density increased at the end of the Middle Ages and facilitated the development of interregional trade, a money economy and production for the market become viable alternatives to the traditionally determined exchange mechanisms of feudal economic systems. Previously, these latter mechanisms had been more efficient because the *transaction costs* of market exchanges were too high.

Governments were able to guarantee property rights at lower costs per person than private groups because the costs could be distributed over larger numbers of people. Also, government intervention avoided the problems of *free ridership*. Therefore the development of individual property rights went hand in hand with the increasing importance of state apparatuses in societies. Not all governments, however, promoted more efficient institutions. Sometimes, government policy was determined by social classes, whose interests lay in the preservation of inefficient institutions. The influence of governments on the development of institutions in its turn was influenced by the power relationships between different classes in society. Thus North and Thomas succeed in an ingenious fashion in combining the neoclassical economic analysis of institutional changes in terms of costs and benefits with the historical study of the power relationships between classes and interest groups.

In recent publications, North (1990, 1993) warns us that efficient institutions do not automatically supplant less efficient institutions. When a society has embarked on a certain institutional path, later developments depend on choices made earlier on in the development process. Such *path dependence* is one of the explanations for the increasing divergence of richer and poor societies in the world economy.

3.3.6 Myrdal: institutional reforms

As a last representative of the internal approach to development, I now discuss Gunnar Myrdal. Even more than Kuznets and Gerschenkron, Myrdal (1968) emphasizes that simple unilinear development schemes are misleading. They do not take into account the important differences in institutional structures in different countries, regions and historical periods. They can give rise to fundamentally mistaken policy recommendations. Myrdal attaches considerable importance to differences in initial conditions. The initial conditions in developing countries – climate, demography, technology, position in the international economic order – are so different from those of the presently rich countries that copying earlier development experiences of Western countries is not a viable option.

In spite of his criticisms of Rostow and his recognition of the importance of international power relationships, Myrdal should nevertheless be considered as a representative of the internal approach to development. This is because he considers domestic reforms in developing countries among the most important preconditions for development. One of Myrdal's intellectual contributions is the thesis that extreme social inequality is a powerful obstacle to economic development in poor countries. The unequal distribution of rights to land and large landownership hinders the modernization of agriculture. Poverty and hunger undermine the productivity of workers and peasants. Wealthy non-productive elites consume more than they invest. Both the content and the accessibility of education is geared to the requirements of elites, rather than to the real developmental needs of societies. Finally, inefficient and ineffective state bureaucracies and widespread corruption (for which Myrdal coined the term *soft state*) form a serious obstacle to all developmental efforts. Without drastic internal reforms, therefore, development will stagnate. Redistribution of income and productive assets, and equalization of social and political power, are important aspects of such reforms.

3.4 *Theories of dependence and underdevelopment*

In spite of all their differences of opinion, theorists of backwardness commonly tend to see countries as relatively isolated units. They are primarily searching for the internal characteristics of societies that form obstacles to development and for the internal factors that promote development. Proponents of the external perspective on development believe that developments in different countries and regions are mutually interrelated in the context of the international economic and political order. The possibilities for development in poor countries depend on their relationships with rich countries.

These relationships are sometimes conceived of as advantageous. Thus the theory of comparative advantage states, for instance, that developing countries profit from entering into international trade. The possibility of taking over technology from advanced countries, discussed above, also belongs to the advantages of international relationships.

An influential group of authors argues, however, that exchange relationships between rich and poor countries are detrimental to the developmental chances of the economically and politically weaker parties. The most extreme version of such perspectives is *underdevelopment or dependency theory*.

The choice of the term 'underdevelopment' implies that the low level of development in developing countries is the result of active negative influences from outside. One cannot speak of backwardness, because poor countries do not have the chance to follow the same path of development as the presently prosperous countries. Prosperity in the rich countries is even based on exploitation of the developing countries. Poverty in developing countries is the result of such exploitation. The underdevelopment of the non-Western world is thus the other side of the coin to economic development in the West.

The term *dependence* implies that development in poor countries is subordinated to development in affluent countries. Colman and Nixson (1985) have summarized the characteristics of dependent development as follows:

1. The exports of a dependent economy consist in large part of primary products. The export sector, consisting of mines and plantations, is an enclave within the economy. All its products are exported abroad. Capital goods are imported from abroad. The infrastructure of a dependent economy is completely oriented towards the interests of the export sector. There are few linkages between the export sector and local suppliers and buyers.
2. Industrial products are imported from the affluent countries. Western-oriented elites consume imported products on a large scale. Even if a dependent economy succeeds in building up its own consumer goods industry, it remains dependent on the advanced countries for imports of capital goods and intermediate goods.
3. The economy is dependent on imports of technology.
4. The modern sector of the economy is dominated by foreign multinational firms.
5. Surpluses are repatriated abroad, either through direct transfer of profits or through mechanisms of unequal exchange and transfer pricing.
6. Dependence is not limited to the economic sphere. There are also cultural, psychological and political relations of dependence with the advanced nations.

It is clear that from this perspective the dualistic structure of the economy in developing countries is not only the consequence of Western penetration in the past, but is also maintained by relationships with the rich Western countries in the present. Whether a country is a colony or not does not make much difference. Dependence does not end with political decolonization. In the post-colonial period, economic development is still determined by neocolonial influences from abroad. The only chance to realize goals such as development, growth and industrialization is to withdraw from the network of dependency relations characterizing the capitalist international economic order and to seek alternative paths of development.

Within the underdevelopment theory one can distinguish two partly overlapping theoretical traditions: theories of unequal exchange; and neo-Marxist theories of underdevelopment.

3.4.1 Theories of unequal exchange

Theories of unequal exchange have been formulated both by neo-Marxists such as Samir Amin and Arghiri Emmanuel and by non-Marxist thinkers such as Prebisch and Singer (Prebisch, 1962; Hunt, 1989, chapters 5–7). Theories of unequal exchange reject the orthodox economic proposition that differences in factor endowments in different regions result in mutually advantageous patterns of international trade based on comparative advantage.

According to orthodox views, free trade and specialization in those lines of production in which a country is relatively most efficient, will increase all countries' welfare. In the long run, free movements of factors of production will also result in a gradual equalization of returns to the factors of production in rich and poor countries. Theories of unequal exchange, however, state that participation of developing countries in the international division of labour is detrimental to their chances of economic development. Only the rich countries profit from international trade. These theories emphasize the structural characteristics of the economies of developing countries which hinder the operation of the comparative advantage. Therefore these theories are often called *structuralist theories*.

Various arguments are put forward by theorists of unequal exchange. In the first place, developing countries' comparative advantage is in primary products. The income elasticity of world demand for these products is low. This means that as per capita incomes in the world economy go up, the demand for primary products will lag behind. (For instance, there is a limit to how much more bread rich people can eat.) Prices of primary exports will therefore not keep up with prices of industrial exports for which world demand is much more buoyant. In the second place, high wage levels in the affluent countries stimulate investments in capital and technological development so as to increase labour productivity. The technological gap between rich and poor countries will tend to increase. In the third place, orthodox neoclassical economic theory does not take into account the fact that most investment in developing countries is in foreign hands. Therefore, investment behaviour is determined by foreign rather than by national interests. In the fourth place, Prebisch and Singer state that both well-organized trade unions and monopolistic corporations in the rich countries prevent productivity gains in these countries from being passed on to consumers in poor countries in the form of lower export prices. The absence of such institutions in developing countries means that productivity gains in these countries are passed on to consumers in rich countries. For all these reasons the terms of trade between export and import prices of developing countries show a structural decline over time.

An influential version of this theory was formulated by Nobel Prize winner Arthur Lewis (1954, 1978). He argues that disguised unemployment in the traditional sector of the economy makes for a large flow of cheap labour towards the export sector. This flow of cheap labour has a depressing effect on the export prices of agrarian products from developing countries. In the mining sector, high productivity and low wages make for large profits. As mines are mostly foreign owned, the profits will flow out of the country, which therefore benefits little from mining exports. According to Lewis, international trade offers poor countries an opportunity to stay poor, as incomes earned in export production remain low. Only if productivity in the traditional food-producing sector goes up will the unlimited supply of extremely cheap labour with its depressing effects on export prices come to an end.

3.4.2 Neo-Marxist theories of underdevelopment

In their criticisms of capitalist relations of exploitation, neo-Marxist theories of underdevelopment build on the Marxist tradition. However, classical Marxism was a typical stage theory in which capitalism was considered to be a higher stage than the preceding feudal stage. Therefore, in classical Marxism, Western capitalist penetration in developing countries was considered as a progressive force on the way to the highest stage that would succeed capitalism, namely, socialism. This aspect of classical Marxism is rejected by neo-Marxist thinkers. One of the first theorists of underdevelopment, Paul Baran, argues that capitalism in developing economies functions differently from capitalism in the advanced countries. In the advanced countries, capitalism generates an economic surplus which is appropriated by capitalists and subsequently reinvested (Baran, 1957). This process of reinvestment promotes economic growth and dynamism. In poor countries, the economic surplus is transferred to rich countries by monopolistic firms or is squandered away in luxurious consumption by wasteful elites. The absence of a stream of investments and reinvestments in the domestic economy makes for economic stagnation. Only those investments that benefit the rich countries are realized. Thus, what development there is, is dependent development.

Capitalist penetration in developing countries therefore leads to a distorted form of capitalism: dependent capitalism. Domestic handicraft production is undermined by competition from imported products. Economic surpluses are transferred to rich countries. Simultaneously, a wealthy domestic 'comprador class' is created, which is involved in import and export trade and the interests of which are closely aligned with the interests of the rich capitalist countries. According to Dos Santos (1970), dependence does not only refer to the external economic relations of a country. The class relations within a country are also determined by the external dependency relationships. Therefore a country cannot simply withdraw from relations of dependency. This also requires dramatic changes in internal relationships between groups and classes. Domestic reforms, however, can bring about confrontations with rich countries whose interests are threatened by reform. Latin American history offers many examples of such confrontations.

One of the most developed versions of underdevelopment theory has been put forward by André Gunder Frank (1969, 1971). Frank analyzes a chain of exploitative relationships running from the centre of the world economy to the rural sector in developing economies. He makes a distinction between rich countries at the core or *centre* of the world economy and poor countries at the *periphery*. In between are countries of the semi-periphery. The centre appropriates surplus from the semi-periphery and the peripheral countries. The semi-periphery exploits the periphery. Within dependent peripheral economies, dominant elites emerge, whose interests coincide with those of the centre countries. These elites within the modern sector of the economy exploit the peripheral sectors in their own countries. The last link of exploitation is at the level of the rural sector, where landowners, whose interests coincide with those of members of the urban elites, exploit small peasants and landless rural labourers.

The emphasis on relationships of exploitation within developing countries makes the centre–periphery theory into a theory of regional inequality as well. It offers an alternative explanation of the dualistic structure of developing economies, discussed in paragraph 3.2. From this perspective, the traditional sector is not a lagging sector that has yet to catch up with the modern sector; it comes into being as a result of exploitation by the centre in the modern sector. The so-called traditional sector is artificially maintained as a source of cheap labour, foodstuffs and other products required by the modern sector.

The more an underdeveloped country is integrated into the capitalist world economy, the more it becomes underdeveloped. An autonomous process of industrialization is only possible in periods in which the economic ties with the centre are tloosened or in which the rich countries are in economic crisis.

Among the most valuable aspects of Frank's thought is his criticism of the treatment of 'traditional society' in theories of modernization (Frank, 1969, 1971). Like classical Marxism, modernization theories conceive of traditional feudal societies as a stage preceding modern economic development. Feudal societies contain various cultural and institutional obstacles to development that have to be overcome for development to take place. Dualistic structures are explained by the fact that these traditional obstacles and barriers have not yet been transcended in some parts of the economy and society. Frank gives many interesting counterexamples from Latin American history that show that the traditional society, which is called feudal, is in reality the product of Western and capitalist penetration. The Spaniards and Portuguese introduced forms of large landownership and serfdom that had not existed before. As we saw in Chapter 2, even the population mix is a product of Western penetration. For instance, almost the whole population of Surinam was imported by the Dutch from Africa and Asia to work on capitalist plantations as slaves or bonded labourers. If one rereads Rostow after reading Frank, Rostow's use of the term 'traditional society', which precedes higher stages, makes a very ahistorical impression.

The conclusion of neo-Marxists such as Baran and Frank is that the bourgeoisie cannot play the same dynamic role it played in the earlier development of the presently affluent countries. They argue that a socialist revolution is necessary and that developing countries should extricate themselves from international trade and the international division of labour.

Non-Marxist structuralists draw less radical conclusions with regard to the need for domestic changes. However, they do argue for a development strategy which would make developing countries less dependent on international trade (Urquidi, 1993). To achieve this, they have to build up and protect a domestic industrial sector that can replace imports of industrial goods by domestic production. This strategy, known as the *import substitution strategy*, has been applied with a certain measure of success in Latin American countries between the 1930s and the 1960s. After that, this strategy ran out of steam and is nowadays under heavy criticism (see Chapter 7).

Structuralists believe that free market policies will not work in developing countries due to a variety of structural reasons. These include: the absence of an adequate transport and communications infrastructure; the underdevelopment of the financial system; the lack of market information; and the monopolistic structure of the economy. Both Marxists and structuralists are in favour of government planning and an important role for the state in the development process. This recommendation is a corollary of their critique of the workings of capitalism and the free market. Finally, structuralists are among those calling for the creation of a new international economic order, in which developing countries would have better chances. In the 1980s and 1990s such recommendations, earlier largely unchallenged, have come increasingly under critical fire.

Theories of underdevelopment have been primarily formulated with reference to the development experiences of Latin America. In the history of this subcontinent, colonial and neocolonial exploitation by Spaniards, Portuguese, English, Dutch, Americans and others have played an important role. The artificial creation by Iberian colonists of large landholdings and plantations on the one hand, and a poor rural population of landless labourers, serfs and very small farmers on the other, is prominent in history. The slave trade and the import of bonded labourers changed the total population profile. After the achievement of independence in the early nineteenth century, foreign interests continued to play an important role. Military interventions by the English and the Americans occurred frequently and have continued to do so to this very day. The dualist development of the economy went hand in hand with extreme income inequality. Thus rapid economic growth could coexist with continued widespread poverty.

3.4.3 Underdevelopment theories: a preliminary evaluation

Theories of underdevelopment have undoubtedly increased our insight into the negative aspects of Western penetration in the world. They form a valuable counterweight to the often ahistoric blueprints of modernization theorists. One of the important insights deriving from the underdevelopment tradition is that Western influences can give rise to institutions and constellations of interest groups that form serious obstacles to development in subsequent historical periods. Theories of underdevelopment also help us to understand how rapid capitalist growth in Latin America can sometimes coexist with the continued poverty of large masses of the population.

Nevertheless, underdevelopment theories also have a number of important shortcomings. The most basic shortcoming is the deterministic nature of many of their propositions. From the perspective of underdevelopment theory it is hard to understand how and why former colonies such as the United States, Canada, Australia or New Zealand have achieved such economic success. Neither do the experiences of dynamic capitalist developments in South Korea, Taiwan, Singapore, Thailand, Hong Kong, Malaysia, Indonesia and other newly industrializing countries fit the underdevelopment mould.

Moreover, many of the empirical propositions of underdevelopment theory are unfounded. For instance, as we shall see in section 3.5, it is simply not true that there is always a net outflow of capital from poor to rich countries. Also, empirical data do not support a law of declining terms of trade. Sometimes the terms of trade deteriorate, sometimes they improve. Finally, the proposition that the economic breakthrough in the West was only possible due to colonial exploitation and plunder, is not supported by empirical historical research, which emphasizes the importance of centuries of internal pre-capitalist accumulation and gradual increases in productivity.

Finally, in the present economic situation, underdevelopment theory has little to offer in the way of policy recommendations. Socialist central planning of industrial development is increasingly considered a highly inefficient development strategy. The disadvantages of extreme import substitition and the related neglect of agriculture are increasingly recognized (see Chapters 7 and 11). The advantages of participation in international trade are underlined by the positive development experiences of those developing countries which have shown the strongest export orientation. Thus, though underdevelopment theory has contributed to our understanding of historical development processes, it has little to offer for the formulation of adequate development strategies in the present. The study of historical questions of guilt and responsibility for underdevelopment cannot substitute for the search for appropriate development strategies in the present.

3.5 *Empirical study of development experiences*

In this section I shall present empirical data on processes of economic development in poor countries. These data derive mainly from Angus Maddison's publications, *The World Economy in the Twentieth Century* (1989) and *Monitoring the World Economy* (1995), incidentally supplemented by information from other sources. Here I only present economic indicators. Information about demography, education, health, nutrition and other aspects of economic and social life will be presented in the following chapters.

Much of the literature on development and development studies is based on examples, case studies or metaphors. It is my conviction that the systematic empirical study of long-term trends in economic and social indicators and systematic comparisons of such trends can contribute to a less ideological and more analytical approach to the emotionally highly charged field of development studies and to a strengthening of its empirical foundations.

The data in this section only refer to a sample of twenty-four developing countries. Nevertheless, these twenty-four countries contain more than two thirds of the total population of developing countries within their borders. This means that developments in the selected countries give a picture of changes in the economic circumstances of a large portion of the world population. In each of the tables, arithmetic averages are presented per region for the countries included in the table.

The choice of countries is primarily determined by the quality and availability of empirical data and by the size of the countries. The sample contains ten Asian countries, seven Latin American countries and seven African countries. For African countries the data can usually not be traced back as far as those for other countries.

I do not want to suggest that the summary data in this section give a complete picture of economic developments in poor countries. Neither do I argue that these data can provide any final answers to the theoretical controversies touched upon in the previous pages. The data themselves should be considered as hypotheses rather than as indisputable facts, and are themselves of course open to criticism and discussion. The main purpose of presenting these data is to illustrate that discussion of highly politicized theories and propositions can be fruitfully approached in an empirical fashion.

3.5.1 Growth of income per capita

Table 3.1 presents data on the average growth rate of gross domestic product per capita in the twentieth century. This table shows us that average income per head in developing countries has been increasing every since the beginning of this century. This rather effectively contradicts the myth that growth of per capita income in developing countries is impossible due to vicious circles of poverty. Several developing countries show considerable economic dynamism. The increase in production per head has been realized in spite of very rapid population growth, particularly since 1950.

The periodization of the data in Table 3.1 is the same as in Chapter 2, with the difference that the period 1870–1913 is only represented by data for 1900–1913. Between 1870 and 1913 there was substantial foreign investment in developing countries and the exports of agriculture and mining products increased rapidly. There was growth in both rich and poor countries, though growth was more rapid in the rich countries. Between 1913 and 1950, growth in the world economy stagnated as a result of wars and economic depressions. Developing countries were heavily hit by the economic crises, especially the Asian countries. Between 1950 and 1973, growth of per capita incomes in the world economy was higher than ever before in economic history. Both rich and poor countries profited from the liberalization and growth of world trade and the increase in investment and capital flows. After the oil crisis of 1973, there was a slowdown of growth relative to the golden age of 1950–73 (Maddison, 1989). In comparison with earlier historical periods, however, the growth rate of income per capita was still high. In order to bring out the effects of the debt crisis of 1982, the post-1973 period is split in two. After 1981, growth accelerated in Asia and slowed down in the OECD countries. In African and Latin American countries there was negative growth.

For most of the century the figures in Table 3.1 illustrate that economic developments in rich countries and developing countries tend to run parallel. Otherwise than suggested by theories of underdevelopment, growth in the rich countries is not accompanied by stagnation in developing countries. On the contrary, if the heart of economic growth in the rich countries starts beating at a slower pace, this has negative consequences in other parts of the world economy. If growth in rich countries accelerates, growth in developing countries also increases.

This does not mean that the discussion of underdevelopment theses can be concluded. In the first place, Table 3.1 refers to gross domestic product rather than gross national product. It is conceivable that part of national product of developing countries drains away in the form of factor payments to foreign owners of capital. Not only will national product then be lower than domestic product, but economic growth will also be lower than if the economic surpluses had been reinvested in the domestic economy. In the second place, income per capita is an average figure that disregards the income distribution within a country. Rapid growth can be accom-

Table 3.1 Growth of real gross domestic product per capita, 1900–1993 (Annual average compound growth rates)

	1900–1913	1913–1950	1950–1973	1973–1981	1981–1993
Bangladesh	0.5	−0.3	−0.6	2.8	1.8
China	0.4	−0.3	2.9	2.9	7.3
India	0.5	−0.3	1.6	1.7	2.8
Indonesia	1.6	−0.1	2.5	3.1	3.3
Pakistan	0.5	−0.3	1.8	2.7	2.5
Philippines	2.5	−0.2	1.8	3.2	−1.1
South Korea	0.8	−0.2	5.2	5.4	7.7
Taiwan	0.3	0.4	6.2	6.1	6.4[a]
Thailand	0.3	0.0	3.2	4.5	6.0
Turkey		0.8	3.3	2.2	3.0
Argentina	2.5	0.7	2.1	−0.5	0.4
Brazil	1.4	1.9	3.8	2.8	−0.2
Chile	2.4	1.0	1.2	2.1	2.0
Colombia	1.9	1.4	2.3	2.4	1.6
Mexico	1.8	1.0	3.1	3.7	−0.8
Peru	1.9	2.1	2.5	1.0	−3.0
Venezuela	2.3	5.3	1.6	−1.3	−0.7
Egypt	−0.0	0.0	2.7	6.1	2.3
Ghana	2.6	1.7	0.2	−2.7	0.1
Ivory Coast			3.1	1.3	−4.6
Kenya			1.9	0.8	0.2
Nigeria			3.2	0.1	0.1
Tanzania			1.9	−0.5	−0.4
Zambia				−1.8	−2.7
Average Asian countries	0.8	−0.1	2.8	3.4	4.0
Average Latin American countries	2.0	1.9	2.4	1.5	−0.1
Average African countries			2.2	0.5	−0.7
Average developing countries	1.3	0.8	2.5	2.0	1.2
Average OECD countries[b]	1.7	1.2	3.8	1.9	1.6

Notes:

[a] 1981–1992.

[b] Australia, Austria, Belgium, Canada, Denmark, Finland, France, Germany, Italy, Japan, Netherlands, Norway, Sweden, Switzerland, United Kingdom, United States.

Sources: Maddison, *Monitoring the World Economy 1820–1992*, Paris, 1995, table 4; Asian and African countries updated from 1992 to 1993 with growth rates from World Bank, *World Tables 1995*. Zambia 1973–1993 from *World Tables 1995*. In this table and the following tables in this chapter, the averages are unweighted and refer only to the countries listed in the tables.

panied by immiseration of large parts of the population of a country. In the third place, between 1913–1950, the development experiences of Latin American countries are not inconsistent with underdevelopment theory. In this period imports from Europe stagnated due to wars and economic crises. This gave Latin American countries such as Brazil a chance to build up domestic industries.

Till 1973 income per capita in rich countries grew more rapidly than in poor countries, so that the gap between rich and poor became ever larger. Between 1973 and 1981, average growth in the sample of developing countries was marginally higher than that in OECD countries. In Asian countries and in some large Latin American countries, growth was substantially higher than in the OECD countries in this period, indicating some degree of catch-up. But even with higher growth rates in developing countries, it takes quite some time before the absolute income gap compared with rich countries starts decreasing. At low levels of income, high growth rates result in only modest absolute increases. In the meantime, however, some developing countries such as Taiwan and South Korea, will no longer be classified as developing in the very near future.

After the oil crisis in 1973 Latin American countries followed expansionary fiscal and monetary policies. Growth in most of Latin America was fairly high until 1981. After that, economic development stagnated severely as a result of misguided policies, hyperinflation and the impact of the debt crisis (Maddison, 1989). The average growth rate for the whole period 1973–1991 is a modest 0.5 per cent per annum. Negative growth in Ivory Coast, Tanzania and Zambia reflects the economic stagnation of the African continent since the 1970s. In Asian countries, growth accelerated after 1981 to 4.0 per cent per year, two-and-a-half times as high as in the OECD countries. Thus, from 1973 onwards we see divergent trends in the developing world with catch-up in Asia, stagnation in Africa and a mixed record in Latin America.

3.5.2 Investment

A well-known theory of Lewis and Rostow, discussed briefly in section 3.3.1, states that sustained economic growth will occur when the rate of investment increases from 5 per cent or less to more than 12 per cent of net national income. The data in Table 3.2 refer to gross investment (i.e. before subtraction of depreciation), rather than net investment. However, one may assume that 5 per cent net roughly corresponds to 8 per cent in gross terms (Maddison, 1989). This implies that most of our developing countries were already investing more than the Lewis/Rostow lower bound of 5 per cent in 1950. Since then, most developing economies have succeeded in increasing investment to levels comparable in percentage terms to those of the rich countries. In 1981 and 1993, the average investment rate in developing countries was higher than in OECD countries. In 1993, the highest investment rates were found in the Asian countries (28 per cent of GDP). After the 1982 debt crisis, investment rates in five of the seven Latin American and six of the seven African countries declined sharply. At the same time the investment rates in China, Korea, Thailand and Turkey increased very substantially.

Table 3.2 Gross domestic investment as percentage of GDP (at current market prices)

	1950	1973	1981	1993
Bangladesh	5.5	8.7	15.9	13.8
China	10.4[a]	29.0	20.1	41.2
India	9.9	18.3	25.0	24.1
Indonesia	11.5	20.8	29.6	28.3
Pakistan	5.5	12.9	18.8	20.7
Philippines	15.0	21.8	27.5	24.1
South Korea	5.7	20.8	29.8	34.3
Taiwan	14.5[b]	29.1	29.9	25.3
Thailand	11.8	27.0	29.7	40.0
Turkey	11.3	19.0	22.0	27.1
Argentina	13.3	20.7	22.7	18.4
Brazil	12.3	23.2	23.1	19.2
Chile	8.0	10.5	24.6	28.8
Colombia	16.9	18.3	20.6	21.5
Mexico	14.1	20.0	27.4	21.7
Peru	17.1	20.3	34.5	18.6
Venezuela		31.0	24.4	18.7
Egypt	11.8	13.1	29.5	17.0
Ghana	15.1	9.0	4.5	14.8
Ivory Coast		23.2	25.9	9.3
Kenya		25.8	27.7	16.1
Nigeria	7.2	22.4	23.3	15.1
Tanzania		21.7	24.6	21.8
Zambia		28.9	19.2	15.3
Average Asian countries	10.1	20.7	24.8	27.9
Average Latin American countries	13.6	20.6	25.3	21.0
Average African countries	11.4	20.6	22.1	15.6
Average developing countries	11.4	20.6	24.2	22.3
Average OECD countries	20.9[a]	25.2	22.9	20.4

Notes:
[a] 1952; [b] 1951.
Sources: 1950: Maddison, *The World Economy in the Twentieth Century*, (1989), table 6.6; except Egypt, Ghana, Nigeria and Turkey 1950: World Bank, *World Tables 1980*; 1973–1993: World Bank, *World Tables 1995*, except Tanzania: *World Tables 1993* and Taiwan: DGBAS (1994).

The data in Table 3.2 can be interpreted in more than one way. First, it seems clear from Tables 3.1 and 3.2 that high rates of investment are associated with rapid economic growth in the post-war period. Yet there is no unambiguous causal relationship between investment and growth. Differences in growth performance between individual countries are not directly related to differences in investment efforts. Similar investment rates can result in very different growth outcomes. Some countries use investments much more effectively and productively than others. The 'capacity to absorb investment' is of the greatest importance for the contribution of investment to economic development (Myint, 1980). Wasteful investment in prestige projects, for instance, results in high investment rates but low growth. Two examples of countries with rather high investment rates and negative growth are Tanzania and Zambia after 1973.

Table 3.3 Export performance, 1900–1993 (annual average compound growth rate)

	1900–1913	1913–1950	1950–1973	1973–1993
Bangladesh	4.2	−1.5	2.0	7.0
China	4.7	1.1	2.7	12.7
India	4.2	−1.5	2.5	7.1
Indonesia	4.0	2.3	6.5	3.8
Pakistan	4.2	−1.5	3.6	7.7
Philippines	2.8	3.7	5.9	5.8
South Korea	8.0	−1.3	20.3	12.1
Taiwan	7.4	2.6	16.3	10.8[a]
Thailand	5.0	2.3	4.4	12.1
Turkey				9.3
Argentina	4.2	1.6	3.1	4.6
Brazil	0.4[b]	1.7	4.7	7.6
Chile	3.8	1.4	2.4	10.4
Colombia	7.8	3.9	3.8	6.0
Mexico	4.6	−0.5	4.3	6.6
Peru	6.7	2.7	5.8	−2.5
Venezuela				−0.5[c]
Egypt				6.6
Ghana		3.1	2.8	−1.2
Ivory Coast				3.5
Kenya				2.8
Nigeria			7.4	0.9
Tanzania			6.3	−1.3
Zambia				−1.6
Average Asian countries	4.9	0.7	7.1	8.8
Average Latin American countries	4.6	1.8	4.0	4.6
Average African countries			5.5	1.4
Average developing countries	4.8	1.3	5.8	5.4
Average OECD countries	4.8	1.0	8.6	4.4

Notes:
[a] 1973–1992; [b] 1901–1913; [c] 1974–1993.
Sources: Unless otherwise indicated: Maddison (1989), table 6.1; Ghana 1913–50: data made available by Maddison; Ghana, Nigeria and Tanzania 1950–73: World Bank, *World Tables 1980*; 1973–93: World Bank, *World Tables 1995*, except Taiwan: DGBAS (1993).

3.5.3 Export performance

Tables 3.3 and 3.4 give a picture of export performance in developing countries. In Table 3.3 the characteristics of the main phases are clearly distinguishable. Exports were growing at just below 5 per cent per year till 1913. In the period 1913–1950 growth rates slumped, especially in the Asian countries heavily involved in world trade. In four Asian countries growth was even negative. Between 1950 and 1973,

Table 3.4 Manufactured exports as percentage of total commodity exports

	1953	1993
Bangladesh	1	81
China		81
India	48	75
Indonesia	0	53
Pakistan	1	85
Philippines	8	77
South Korea	0	94
Taiwan	6	93
Thailand	2	73
Turkey	1	72
Argentina	10	32
Brazil	2	60
Chile	2	19
Colombia	1	40
Mexico	8	52
Peru	3	17
Venezuela	0[a]	14
Egypt	4	33
Ghana	10[a]	1[c]
Ivory Coast	1[a]	11[c]
Kenya	12[b]	29[c]
Nigeria	3[a]	1[c]
Tanzania	13[a]	11[d]
Zambia		1[c]
Average Asian countries	7	78
Average Latin American countries	4	33
Average African countries	7	12
Average developing countries	6	46

Notes:
[a] 1960; [b] 1961; [c] 1992 from *WDR 1994*; [d] 1991 from *WDR 1993*.
Sources: 1953: Maddison (1989), table 7.10; Egypt and Turkey from Maddison (1970); Venezuela, Ivory Coast, Ghana, Kenya, Nigeria and Tanzania from World Bank, *World Development Report 1983*. 1993: World Bank, *World Development Report 1995*, except for Tanzania: *WDR 1993*.

exports from OECD countries grew at 8.6 per cent per year. Average export performance in the developing countries was also higher than in the 1900–1913 period. After the 1973 oil crisis, export growth from OECD countries slowed down. The growth of exports from developing countries was somewhat higher than from OECD countries. Asian countries showed exceptionally high growth rates, while exports from African countries stagnated. In Ghana, Tanzania and Zambia the growth rate of exports was even negative.

Table 3.4 shows that the stereotype of developing countries as exporters of primary agricultural or mining products is in need of adjustment. From 1953 to 1993 the share of industrial exports in total exports of goods increased from 6 per cent to 46 per cent. In our Asian countries the increase is even more dramatic, from 7 per cent to 78 per cent.

3.5.4 External finance

At the beginning of this century a typical colony would normally export more than it imported. The surplus on the trade balance would be compensated by an outflow of profits, interest payments, salaries of colonial officials, gold and reserves to banks in the colonial mother country. Compared to the pre-war period, one of the characteristics of the international economic order during most of the post-World War II period is that financial flows were reversed. A net influx of capital compensated for deficits in the trade balances and current account balances. Developing economies were able to import more consumer goods, capital goods and intermediate goods than they could have financed from their export revenues. The capital flows consisted of commercial loans, direct investment and development aid. Net capital inflows served to finance imports. Part of the net inflow was used to service dividend and interest payments on earlier loans and investments.

Together with imports and exports of goods and services and transfer payments, dividends and interest payments belong to the current account of the balance of payments. Deficits or surpluses on the current account are balanced by capital flows on the capital account or changes in the gold reserves or financial reserves of a country.

In principal, it is more advantageous for a developing country to use net capital inflows to finance imports of goods, especially capital goods, than for the payment of dividends and interest. But dividend and interest payments should not be exclusively interpreted as a detrimental drain on resources. If the investments and loans for which factor payments have to be made have made a positive contribution to the productive potential of a country, then factor payments are nothing but payments for the productive services of capital. Less favourable is the case in which loans have been used for purely consumptive purposes, with new inflows of capital required to service the debts, in which circumstance a country can get caught up in an increasing spiral of indebtedness without any improvement in its productive potential.

Table 3.5 offers a rough picture of the importance of external finance in developing countries. External finance is defined here as the net balance of exports

Table 3.5 External finance as percentage of GDP, 1950--1993 (at current market prices)

	1950–1973	1974–1981	1982–1993
Bangladesh	2.5	9.4	9.6
China	0.2[a]	0.4	−0.3
India	1.8	1.4	2.1
Indonesia	3.1[b]	−5.5	−1.7
Pakistan	4.4	10.1	8.7
Philippines	2.1	5.2	2.4
South Korea	8.4	5.5	−1.7
Taiwan	3.1[c]	−0.6	−9.0
Thailand	1.8	4.4	3.4
Turkey		6.2	2.7
Argentina	0.6	−1.2	−3.2
Brazil	1.3	4.7	−4.4
Chile	1.3	2.4	−2.3
Colombia	2.0	−0.7	−1.8
Mexico	1.9	4.3	−2.0
Peru	2.6	3.9	0.3
Venezuela			−4.2
Egypt	4.0	15.2	12.7
Ghana	0.9	0.8	5.7
Ivory Coast			−5.5
Kenya			2.1
Nigeria		−2.9	−2.9
Tanzania		10.3	23.6
Zambia			0.4
Average Asian countries	3.0	3.7	1.6
Average Latin American countries	1.6	2.2	−2.5
Average African countries		5.9	5.2
Average developing countries	2.5	3.7	1.5

Notes:
[a] 1953–1973; [b] 1966–1973; [c] 1951–1973.
Sources: External finance is the net balance on the account for goods and non-factor services of the balance of payments with the sign reversed. Unless otherwise indicated, data are from Maddison (1989), table 6.7. Egypt and Ghana 1950–1973: World Bank, *World Tables 1988/1989*. Egypt, Nigeria, Tanzania, Ghana and Turkey 1974–1981: World Bank, *World Tables 1993*; 1982–1993 (except Taiwan), *World Tables 1993 and 1995*. Taiwan, DGBAS (1994), tables 1 and 15.

and imports of goods and non-factor services, with the sign reversed.[3] This concept shows to what extent inflows of capital allowed developing countries to import more goods and services than they were exporting.[4]

Between 1950 and 1981 there was an unmistakable net inflow of capital, averaging 2.5 to 3.7 per cent of GDP. This inflow is inconsistent with underdevelopment theories, which assume that there is a permanent outflow of capital from poor to rich countries. The debt crisis of 1982 caused the inflow of capital to stagnate, and in particular, the inflow of private capital. After 1982 some countries were faced with a net outflow of capital, creating the paradoxical situation that poor countries were financing rich ones. The net outflow of capital is most marked in Latin American countries between 1982 and 1986. The country average for all developing countries in the table is still positive in this period, but the inflow of capital is lower than earlier in the post-war period. Outflows from Taiwan and South Korea can be interpreted in a more positive sense. They represent repayment of past debts by successful economies.

Table 3.6 presents data on the total value of foreign capital in developing countries derived from Maddison (1989). Between 1870 and 1913 investment in developing countries increased rapidly. The real value of foreign capital in this period increased more than threefold. After 1914 there was a decline in the value of foreign capital. In real terms this value was only 40 per cent higher than in 1870. It was only one-quarter of the value in 1914. After 1950 we see a great increase in the value of foreign capital from 46.6 billion dollars in 1950 to 944 billion dollars in 1985.

Table 3.6 Gross value of foreign capital* in developing countries, 1870–1985 ($bn)

	1870	1900	1914	1938	1950	1973	1985
Total in current prices	5.3	11.4	22.7	24.7	13.6	172.0	1,118.0
Total in 1980 prices	33.2	108.3	179.2	143.4	46.6	319.1	944.0

Note:
* Includes both loans, portfolio investments and direct investment.
Source: Maddison (1989), table 2.4.

How to interpret these figures? A negative interpretation is that the value of foreign capital is a measure of the foreign domination of the economies of developing countries. By this criterion, however, several European advanced economies are also dominated by foreign capital. From our macro perspective, a net inflow of foreign capital gives a positive impulse to the economic development of a country. Periods when the inflow of capital stagnates, such as the period 1914–1950, are usually periods of weak growth performance. Presently, the booming economies in Southeast Asia are also characterized by massive foreign investment. Of course the impact of foreign capital and foreign firms in developing countries needs to be studied in more detail. A positive evaluation of foreign investment does not mean that developing countries should not set stringent conditions for the operation of multinational firms and foreign investors in the domestic economies.

3.5.5 Structural change

Nobel prize winner Simon Kuznets has emphasized that modern economic development implies changes in the structure of the economy. In the process of *structural change*, the importance of the agrarian sector declines, while that of the industrial sector increases. At a later stage the service sector overtakes the industrial sector and becomes the most important sector in terms of its share in employment and production.

Table 3.7 presents information on changes in the structure of employment between 1950 and 1990, and Table 3.8, information on changes in the structure of production between 1950 and 1993.[5] Both tables show how the share of agriculture in developing countries declined between 1950 and the late 1980s. The share of both industry and services increased. As labour productivity in industry is higher than in agriculture, the share of industry in production is always higher than its share in employment. High labour productivity is one of the reasons why the modern industrial sector in developing countries is unable to provide a rapidly growing population with sufficient employment. This is one of the crucial differences between industrialization processes in the nineteenth century and present-day processes of industrialization.

Table 3.7 Distribution of employment by sector, 1950–1900 (in percentages)

	1950			1990[a]		
	Agriculture	Industry	Services	Agriculture	Industry	Services
Bangladesh	77	7	16	65	15	20
China	77[b]	7[b]	16[b]	61	18	21
India	72	10	18	63	14	23
Indonesia	75[c]	8[c]	17[c]	50	16	34
Pakistan	77	7	16	47	20	33
Philippines	71	9	20	45	16	39
South Korea	73[d]	3[d]	24[d]	17	35	48
Taiwan	57	16	27	13	41	46
Thailand	82	3	15	66	12	22
Turkey	77	8	15	49	20	31
Argentina	25	31	44	12[g]	32[g]	56[g]
Brazil	60	18	22	24	23	53
Chile	36	30	34	19	26	55
Colombia	57	18	25	34[h]	24[h]	42[h]
Mexico	61	17	22	23	28	50
Peru	58	20	22	40[h]	18[h]	42[h]
Venezuela				11	28	51
Egypt	64[e]	12[e]	24[e]	42	21	37
Ghana	62[f]	15[f]	23[f]	61[i]	13[i]	26[i]
Ivory Coast				65	8	27
Kenya				81[h]	7[h]	12[h]
Nigeria				45[j]	7[j]	48[j]
Tanzania				86[h]	5[h]	10[h]
Zambia				52[g]	14[g]	34[g]

Table 3.7 (*continued*)

	1950			1990[a]		
	Agriculture	Industry	Services	Agriculture	Industry	Services
Average Asian countries	74	8	18	48	21	32
Average Latin American countries	50	22	28	23	26	50
Average African countries				62	11	28
Average developing countries	64	13	22	45	19	36
Average OECD countries	25	36	39	5	29	66

Notes:
[a] Data for 1990 range from 1988–1993 unless specified otherwise; [b] 1952; [c] 1960; [d] 1951; [e] 1947; [f] 1960; [g] 1980; [h] 1980 from *WDR 1988*; [i] 1984; [j] 1988; [k] excluding Germany.

Sources: 1950: Maddison (1989), table C.11; Egypt 1947 and Ghana 1960; Mitchell (1982); Turkey: Maddison (1986). 1990: World Bank, *WDR 1995*, except Tanzania, Kenya, Colombia and Peru from *WDR 1988* and Taiwan from DGBAS (1994). 'Agriculture' includes agriculture, forestry and fisheries; 'industry' includes mining, manufacturing, construction, gas, water and electricity.

Table 3.7 reveals that in 1990 agriculture was still the largest sector in terms of employment in developing countries. Its average share in total employment was 45 per cent (against 64 per cent in 1950). In countries such as Bangladesh, China, India, Thailand, Ghana, Ivory Coast, Kenya and Tanzania, agrarian employment even accounted for more than 60 per cent of total employment around 1990. The share of agriculture in total employment in Latin American countries (on average 23 per cent) was much lower than in the densely populated Asian countries (on average 48 per cent) and the African countries (on average 62 per cent). In OECD countries the percentage share of agriculture in 1990 was only 5 per cent on average.

For the structure of production, Table 3.8 shows that the share of agriculture in total GDP in developing countries declined from 37 per cent around 1950 to 21 per cent around 1993. Compared to the OECD countries, however, the share of agriculture in developing economies is still seven times as high. The share of industry showed a modest increase. In the early 1990s this share was comparable to that in OECD countries.

It is remarkable how important the service sector has become in developing countries. In part, the high share of services points to a pattern of development which differs from earlier patterns in the advanced countries. Developing countries no longer follow the classical sequence of shifts from agriculture to industry, followed by shifts from industry to services. Rather, the service sector develops parallel to the

Table 3.8 Structure of production, 1950–1993 (value added in agriculture, industry and services, in percentages)

	1950			1993		
	Agriculture	Industry	Services	Agriculture	Industry	Services
Bangladesh	51	21	28	30	18	52
China	39[a]	38[a]	23[a]	19	48	33
India	51	21	28	31	27	41
Indonesia	59[a]	12[a]	29[a]	19	39	42
Pakistan	51	21	28	25	25	50
Philippines	26[b]	28[b]	46[b]	22	33	45
South Korea	46[c]	15[c]	39[c]	7	43	50
Taiwan	32[d]	21[d]	46[d]	4	39	57
Thailand	40[b]	19[b]	41[b]	10	39	51
Turkey	46	15	39	15	30	55
Argentina	14	36	50	6	31	63
Brazil	23	30	47	11[f]	37[f]	52[f]
Chile	15	23	62	6[g]	39[g]	56[g]
Colombia	38	22	40	16[f]	35[f]	50[f]
Mexico	20	30	50	8	28	63
Peru	35	23	41	11	43	46
Venezuela	6[b]	43[be]	51[be]	5	42	53
Egypt	30[b]	24[b]	46[b]	18	22	60
Ghana	41[b]	10[b]	49[b]	48	16	36
Ivory Coast	43[b]	14[b]	42[b]	37	24	39
Kenya	40[c]	20[c]	40[c]	29	18	54
Nigeria	66	6	27	30	43	27
Tanzania	57[b]	11[b]	32[b]	61	8	31
Zambia	9[c]	72[c]	19[c]	34	36	30
Average Asian countries	44	21	35	18	34	48
Average Latin American countries	22	30	49	9	36	55
Average African countries	41	22	36	37	24	40
Average developing countries	37	24	39	21	32	47
Average OECD countries	15	41	44	3	33	64

Notes:
[a] 1965; [b] 1960; [c] 1955; [d] 1951; [e] data only for mining. I calculated the share of industry using proportions from later years; [f] other year than specified; [g] 1983 from *WDR 1986*.
Sources: Developing countries (1950, 1955, 1960, 1965): World Bank, *World Tables 1980*. China 1965: World Bank, *World Development Report 1989*; OECD countries 1950: Maddison (1989); developing countries 1993: World Bank, *World Development Report 1995*; Taiwan 1951 and 1993 from: DGBAS (1994); OECD countries 1993 from: World Bank, *World Development Report 1995*; Canada and USA 1988 from *World Development Report 1990*. 'Agriculture' includes forestry and fisheries; 'industry' includes mining, gas, water and electricity.

industrial sector. In terms of production, the service sector was already the largest sector in 1950. By the 1990s it accounted for no less than 47 per cent of total production.

In part the rapid growth of the service sector can be explained by the expansion of the government sector in developing countries. At present there is a lively debate about the question whether the size and rather low productivity of the government sector in developing countries has become an obstacle to continued economic development.

QUESTIONS FOR REVIEW

1. Compare the internal and external explanations of development and stagnation. Is the use of the term 'less developed' associated with internal or external explanations of the situation of development?
2. What are the main elements of classical liberal explanations of growth and development?
3. How do economic theories of imperialism explain economic stagnation in developing countries?
4. Discuss the concept of dualism. Why is dualism an obstacle to development?
5. Which stages of economic growth are distinguished by Rostow and what are their main characteristics?
6. What are the potential advantages of backwardness?
7. How do North and Thomas define efficient institutions? Give examples of institutions which are considered to be efficient.
8. Discuss the characteristics of dependent development, as emphasized by dependency theorists.
9. Discuss Gunder Frank's criticism of the use of the concept of 'traditional society' in theories of modernization.
10. What are the main phases of development since 1900 and what are the most important characteristics of the different phases?

Notes

1. It is not correct to say that growth accounting is purely neoclassical, because in the empirical analysis neoclassical assumptions are often relaxed.
2. Endogenize, i.e. explain something within a model, instead of taking it as exogenous, or given outside the model.

3. This concept is referred to in *World Tables* (World Bank, various) as resource balar Factor services refer to the services of the production factors labour and capital. They include wages for workers working outside their own country, dividends, profits and interest payments.
4. An alternative concept is external finance as the net balance of the current account of the balance of payments with the sign reversed. This concept includes among others payments for factor services. In Table 3.5 the data for 1950–1966 refer to this concept of external finance. After 1966 they refer to the resource balance concept.
5. If information for the years specified in the tables was lacking, I presented information for the closest years for which information was available.

4 Population and development

The following chapters focus on the various relationships between population and economic development. In this chapter we discuss the relationships between population growth and economic development. Chapters 5 and 6 deal with health and education.

As an introduction to this chapter, we distinguish five types of relationships between demographic and economic developments, as follows:

1. Population growth supplies the labour, which is available as an input into economic production. The availability of labour with various qualifications, levels of education and health, has considerable influence on the productive potential of a society.
2. The growth of population, on the other hand, also gives rise to employment problems. Can economic development provide a rapidly growing labour force with sufficient productive and paid employment, or does open or disguised unemployment increase?
3. The size and growth of the labour force is one of the determinants of the need for savings and investment. If investment lags behind the growth of the labour force, then – with given technology – labour productivity will tend to decline and growth of production will not be able to keep up with the growth of population.
4. The level of consumption in a society depends in part on the relationship between population growth and growth of production. Is the growth of production of goods and services sufficient to provide a growing population with a satisfactory standard of living?
5. A rapidly growing population can stimulate growth of production by providing an expanding market for goods and services.

Apart from population growth, population size and population density are also important variables. Several countries in Latin America and Africa have rapid population growth, but relatively low population density. Low population density discourages large-scale investment in infrastructure. Population size influences the absolute volume of required investment and the size of domestic markets. Countries with large domestic markets can better afford to follow an inward-looking path of economic development than small countries (Myint, 1980).

4.1 *Perspectives on population growth*

In post-war debates on the population problem Malthusian views predominated up to the 1970s. It was thought that rapid growth of population in developing countries threatened their chances of economic development. Researchers and representatives of international organizations warned about the consequences of the 'population explosion' and pleaded for vigorous family planning programmes (Coale and Hoover, 1958).

Representatives of developing countries countered that an overemphasis on population policy deflected attention from the core of development problems, namely, economic underdevelopment. Once economic development accelerated, population growth would automatically slow down, as it had done earlier in the Western countries. In addition, they argued that one-quarter of the world population was using more than 80 per cent of global natural resources. The question was not scarcity of world resources, but their unequal distribution (Todaro, 1981, chapter 6; Keating, 1993).

In recent research, there is no firm empirical support for the conclusion that the effects of population growth on economic development are always negative. In some instances, population growth can even have positive effects on factors such as technological change and growth of output (World Bank, 1984; Birdsall, 1988; Kelley, 1988). High population growth rates notwithstanding, some countries have succeeded in substantially raising their per capita incomes. Other countries with rapid population growth show declines in per capita income.

Both in the political debate and in the empirical scientific discussion the contours of a new consensus have become visible: very rapid growth of population can seriously exacerbate existing economic problems in very poor societies. But these economic problems are usually not caused primarily by population growth. Therefore population policy should not be discussed in isolation. Rather it should be integrated into a wider framework of policies aimed at overall economic and social development (Keating, 1993, chapter 5; UN Population Division, 1994).

4.2 *Growth of world population*

Table 4.1 presents figures on the development of world population in the very long term. This table shows that there has always been some measure of population increase, even in prehistoric times. There was no Malthusian equilibrium in which world population remained stable due to the checks of famine and disease. However, the growth of population before 1750 was very slow. After this date there was a dramatic acceleration of growth, which reached its peak between 1950 and 1975. During this period, world population increased at 2 per cent per annum. At such a growth rate, world population doubles every 35 years.

Table 4.1 Growth of world population

Year	Estimated world population: low and high estimates* (millions)	Estimated world population (millions)	Average annual growth rate (%)	Population: developing countries (millions)	Average annual growth rate: developing countries (%)
10000–8000 BC	5–10	7.5			
AD 0–14	270–330	300	0.04		
1000	275–345	310	0.00		
1250	350–450	400	0.10		
1500	440–540	490	0.08		
1750	735–805	770	0.18		
1850	1,100–1,300	1,200	0.44		
1900	1,650–1,710	1,680	0.68		
1950		2,516	0.81	1,684	
1970		3,697	1.94	2,648	2.29
1975		4,078	1.98	2,983	2.41
1985		4,855	1.76	3,682	2.13
1990		5,266	1.64	4,051	1.93
1995		5,692	1.57	4,448	1.88
2000		6,114	1.44	4,842	1.71
2025		8,121	1.14	6,762	1.34
2035		8,793	0.80	7,425	0.94
2100		10,958	0.34		

Note:
* Durand (1970) presents upper and lower limits of estimates, that have the same degree of plausibility. In the second column we have taken the midpoint of the upper and lower boundaries of Durand's indifference ranges.

Sources: 10000 BC–AD 1750 and 1900 from Durand (1977); 1850: Cipolla (1978); 1950–1985: United Nations (1993a); 1990–2035: World Bank (1994), standard projections.

Figure 4.1 shows that most of population growth takes place in developing countries. In the rich countries, population has almost stabilized. From 1990 to 1995 world population increased by some 426 million persons. In this period, the population of the more developed countries increased by 29 million and the population of developing countries by 397 million, or 79.4 million per year.

After 1975, the rate of population growth began to slow down, but still remained very high from a historical perspective. The projected world population for the year

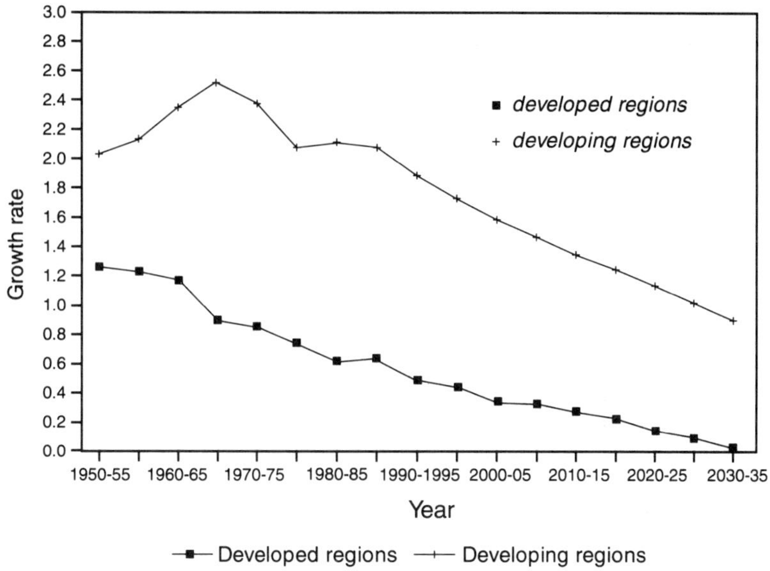

Figure 4.1 Population growth, 1950–2035

2035 is 8.8 billion persons, of which 84 per cent in developing countries. Under the assumption that the decline in growth rates will continue, World Bank projections (World Bank, 1994) suggest that the world population will reach 11 billion persons in the year 2100. Most of the increase will be added between now and the end of the first twenty-five years of the twenty-first century. After that population growth will slow down, both in percentage terms and in absolute terms. But such long term projections are surrounded by uncertainties. Projections for 2100 vary from 9.4 billion to 12.2 billion (World Bank, 1994, figure 8). All these projections assume that fertility rates (see section 4.3) show a continued downward trend. Under the assumption that fertility rates remain constant, a world population of 10.4 billion persons could already be reached by 2020. In Table 4.1, only the 'standard variant' of World Bank projections is reproduced. Projections are heavily influenced by developments in the most populous country in the world, China. When the decline in fertility rates in China was reversed in the late 1980s, projections were revised upwards. In the early 1990s fertility rates dropped again, resulting in lower global projections. The latest projections also incorporate the effects of AIDS on mortality.

4.3 *Demographic transition*

The growth of population is determined by the relation between birth rates and death rates. Acceleration of world population growth is caused by what is optimistically called the *demographic transition*. Figure 4.2 presents a schematic representation of the demographic transition which has earlier taken place in Europe.

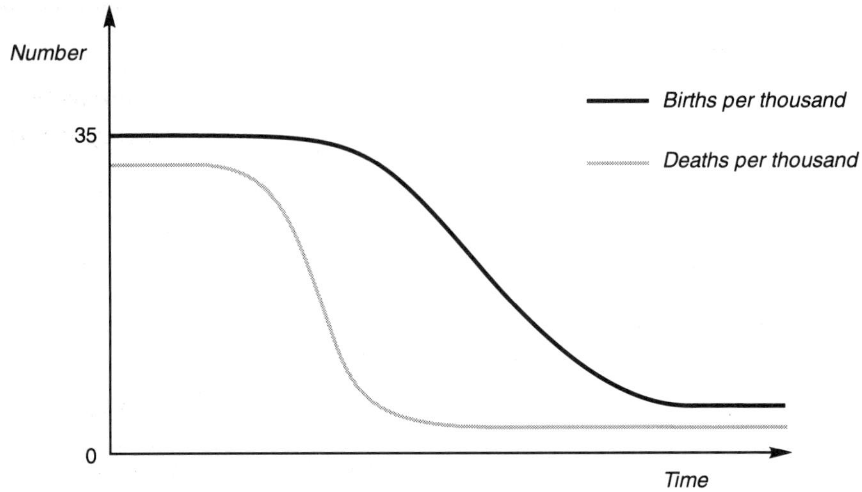

Figure 4.2 Demographic transition

Before the demographic transition, both birth rates and death rates were high. The so-called *crude birth rate* – the annual number of births per 1,000 inhabitants – is around 35 per 1,000, the crude death rate – the annual number of deaths per 1,000 inhabitants – was around 25 to 30 per 1,000. The net excess of births over deaths caused a slow increase of population. In the nineteenth century the death rate gradually declined in the presently prosperous countries, principally as a result of improved nutrition, increases in the overall standard of living and improved hygienic circumstances. As the birth rate did not decline along with the death rate, the excess of births over deaths increased. Population growth in Europe accelerated to the hitherto unknown level of 1 per cent per year. In due course, however, birth rates also started to decline, under the combined influence of urbanization, modernization and increasing standards of living. In the twentieth century a new equilibrium was reached between birth rates and low death rates.

A similar process is presently taking place in developing countries, though even more dramatically. Death rates are declining much faster than they did in Europe in the nineteenth century, primarily due to medical progress. Birth rates of around 45 per 1,000 inhabitants have always been higher than they were in nineteenth-century Europe and, for the time being, they still remain high. The result is an unprecedented rate of population growth. If the earlier pattern of the demographic transition repeats itself, birth rates will start declining in the long run in developing countries and a new equilibrium between birth and death rates will be achieved at a lower level.

In addition to the 'crude birth rate' and the 'crude death rate', two other concepts are important for an understanding of demographic developments, namely, the *total fertility rate* and *life expectation.*

The total fertility rate is the average number of children a woman will bear in the course of the fertile period of her life (World Bank, 1984, p. 66). Together with the age structure of the population, the total fertility rate determines the crude birth rate. A low fertility rate in combination with an age structure with many young women in the fertile period of their life can result in the same crude birth rate as a high fertility rate with relatively few women in their fertile years. Rapid population growth in developing countries is associated with a youthful age structure. This means that population will continue to grow for quite a long time, even if the average number of children per woman has declined to the *replacement level* of two children per woman.

The crude death rate also depends on two factors: the life expectation and the age structure. Life expectation is the average number of years a child is expected to live from birth onwards. This average is strongly influenced by mortality in the first five years of life. A young population with a high life expectation will make for very low death rates. An old population with high life expectations will have higher death rates. Many affluent countries have an increasing number of elderly people in their population, leading to higher death rates in spite of high life expectation.

4.4 *Demographic developments in developing countries*

Tables 4.2 and 4.3 offer a picture of demographic developments in developing countries. Table 4.2 presents growth rates for twenty-four countries, where possible traced back to 1820. These growth rates are compared with those of sixteen OECD countries. Since 1950, population growth in our twenty-four developing countries is more than twice as high as in the OECD countries, since 1973 almost three times as high. Since 1973 the rate of growth in developing countries has started to decelerate, but growth is still extremely rapid.

Present rates of growth of total population in developing countries are more than twice as high as population growth rates in the OECD countries in the nineteenth

Table 4.2 Population growth in selected developing countries, 1820–1993 (%)

	1820–1870	1870–1913	1913–1950	1950–1973	1973–1993
Bangladesh[a]	0.4	0.4	0.8	2.3	2.2
China	−0.1	0.5	0.6	2.1	1.5
India	0.4	0.4	1.0	2.1	2.2
Indonesia	1.0	1.3	1.2	2.0	2.1
Pakistan[a]	0.4	0.4	1.7	2.5	3.1
Philippines	1.7	1.4	2.1	3.1	2.4
South Korea		0.9[b]	1.9	2.2	1.3
Taiwan			2.2	3.0	1.5
Thailand	0.4	1.0	2.2	3.1	2.0
Turkey		0.7[b]	1.3	2.7	2.3
Argentina	2.5	3.4	2.2	1.7	1.4
Brazil	1.6	2.1	2.1	2.9	2.4

Table 4.2 *(continued)*

	1820–1870	1870–1913	1913–1950	1950–1973	1973–1993
Chile	1.6	1.4	1.5	2.2	1.6
Colombia	1.4	1.8	2.3	2.9	2.0
Mexico	0.7	1.1	1.6	3.2	2.4
Peru	1.4	1.2	1.5	2.8	2.4
Venezuela	1.7	1.3	1.5	3.8	3.0
Egypt	1.2	1.7	1.4	2.3	2.3
Ghana		1.0[b]	2.1	3.4	2.8
Ivory Coast			2.1	3.1	3.9
Kenya			2.7	3.0	3.7
Nigeria			2.0	2.0	2.6
Tanzania			2.0	2.5	3.1
Zambia					3.4
Average Asian countries	0.6	0.8	1.5	2.5	2.1
Average Latin American countries	1.5	1.8	1.8	2.8	2.2
Average African countries			2.0	2.7	3.1
Average developing countries	1.1	1.2	1.7	2.6	2.4
Annual growth total population in developing countries	0.1	0.6	1.0	2.3	2.0
Annual growth total population in 16 OECD countries[c]	0.9	1.1	0.9	1.1	0.7

Notes:
[a] Growth rates Bangladesh and Pakistan before 1913 equal to Indian growth rate.
[b] 1900–1913.
[c] Australia, Austria, Belgium, Canada, Finland, France, Italy, Japan, the Netherlands, Norway, United Kingdom, United States, West-Germany, Sweden, Switzerland. For developing countries, both the average growth rate per country and the growth rate of total population have been calculated. For the OECD countries, only the growth rate of total population has been represented.

Sources: Maddison (1995); Asia and Africa, 1992–1993: World Bank, *World Tables 1995*; South Korea, 1900–1913: Maddison (1989); Egypt 1820–1913: Hansen and Marzouk (1965); Ghana 1900–1913: Szereszewski (1965); Turkey 1900–1913: Kirsten *et al.* (1956).

century. We may therefore conclude that the current demographic challenge for developing countries is much greater than that which faced the presently rich countries in the nineteenth century. The acceleration of population growth in the nineteenth century was paralleled by a substantial increase in the demand for industrial labour. Emigration also provided a potential outlet for surplus population.

In developing countries the industrial sector is presently unable to provide the massive influx of new entrants to the labour market with sufficient paid employment.

On the one hand, the influx is so much greater than in the past, while on the other hand, increasing capital intensity in production and productivity augmenting technological change diminishes the demand for labour. Employment will have to be created in other sectors of the economy, such as agriculture, services or the informal sector. For instance, a typical demographic feature of many developing countries is that the absolute size of the rural population is still increasing (see Chapter 9). Emigration on a massive scale is no longer a viable option. A country such as Indonesia still has a large transmigration programme, intended to shift population from the densely populated Java to the outer islands. But the quantitative contribution of such programmes to the population problem is negligible.

Table 4.3 contains a number of important demographic indicators for the post-war period. This table will be used to highlight characteristics of the present demographic situation in developing countries.[1] The demographic transition in developing countries lags about a hundred years behind the transition in presently affluent countries. There are, however, a number of interesting differences between present-day and historical processes of transition.

In the first place, birth rates are substantially higher than they were in the past. Even at their peak, birth rates in the nineteenth century were never above 40 births per 1,000 inhabitants. Between 1950 and 1955 the birth rate in developing countries was no less on average than 45 per 1,000 inhabitants. This figure increased further in the 1960s, before declining to 28 births per 1,000 by 1990–95. This birth rate is comparable to that in many European countries in the nineteenth century. Present-day birth rates are lowest in China and in Latin America. With 41 births per 1,000 inhabitants, the African continent has by far the highest birth rate.

In the second place, the death rate is presently declining much faster than in the past. Historically, death rates declined as a corollary of a general increase in the standard of living, improved nutritional intake, economic growth and modernization of society. Nowadays, death rates are declining in most developing countries, irrespective of their standards of living or economic growth rates. Since 1950, the death rate in developing countries has decreased from 24.4 deaths per 1,000 inhabitants to 9.1 per 1,000. The decline in the death rate proceeded four to five times as fast as in Europe in the nineteenth century (Kuznets, 1980; Kelley, 1988). This decline is not primarily due to an overall improvement in standards of living. Rather, it is explained by medical technical progress – in the treatment of infectious diseases, vaccination, antibiotics, combating animal bearers of diseases (vectors) and by improvements in curative health care, medical services, education, transport and communication.

Population growth in developing countries is now higher than it has ever been in the presently prosperous countries (cf. Table 4.2). Population growth increased throughout the 1950s and 1960s. After the 1960s a decline set in in Asia and Latin America, while growth rates continued to accelerate in Africa. In recent years, the slowdown in the growth of population in Asia has reversed (World Bank, 1994). In the period 1990–95 the growth rates for this region were 0.2 per cent lower than in 1950–55.

Table 4.3 Indicators of demographic changes, 1950–1995, by region

	Africa	Latin America	Asia[a]	Asia, excluding China	Developing countries	More developed countries[b]	World
Population (million)							
1950	222	165	1,294	739	1,684	832	2,516
1990	627	435	2,983	1,849	4,051	1,215	5,266
1995	719	475	3,246	2,047	4,448	1,245	5,692
Annual growth of population (%)							
1950–55	2.25	2.74	1.94	1.98	2.06	1.29	1.81
1990–95	2.78	1.77	1.71	2.06	1.89	0.49	1.57
Birth rate per 1,000							
1950–55	49.2	42.3	44.2	44.6	44.7	22.6	37.5
1990–95	41.0	25.6	25.5	30.3	28.1	13.6	24.8
Mortality rate per 1,000							
1950–55	26.9	15.5	25.1	25.1	24.4	10.1	19.7
1985–90	13.6	6.9	8.5	9.1	9.1	9.7	9.3
Fertility rate							
1950–55	6.7	5.9	6.1	6.1	6.2	2.8	5.0
1990–95	5.7	3.1	3.1	3.7	3.4	1.8	3.1
Percentage of urban population (%)							
1950	14.5	41.6	14.2	16.6	17.0	54.3	29.3
1995	34.7	74.2	32.3	38.2	37.2	74.2	45.2
Percentage of population under 15 years (%)							
1950	42.6	40.4	36.8	39.2	37.9	27.7	34.5
1995	44.2	33.9	32.5	36.2	34.6	20.7	31.5
Percentage of population over 65 years (%)							
1950	3.2	3.5	3.9	3.5	3.8	7.6	5.1
1995	3.1	4.9	5.1	4.4	4.7	13.0	6.6

Notes:
[a] Excluding Japan.
[b] Europe, USSR, North America, Japan, Australia and New Zealand.

Sources: Table derived from Kelley (1988). Instead of Kelley's figures from UN (1986) we have used more recent figures from World Bank (1994) and UN (1993b).

Presently, most rapid growth is found in Africa, with growth rates of around 3 per cent per year (extreme cases being Ivory Coast, Kenya, Tanzania and Zambia). Latin America and south Asia come second. The lowest growth is to be found in east and southeast Asia, and in particular, in populous China. But even for China, the growth rate of 1.5 per cent is higher than that of all European countries in the nineteenth century.

High fertility and rapid population growth have resulted in a very youthful age structure of the population. At present, on average 35 per cent of the population is less than 15 years old. This implies a very high *dependency ratio* – the proportion of the population belonging to age groups that do not make economically productive contributions. The youthful age structure also means that a large proportion of women will be in a reproductive age category in coming years. Thus, even if the fertility rate per woman would go down, birth rates would continue to be high for quite a long time.

Finally, Table 4.3 also contains information on trends in urbanization. Latin America is the most urbanized region, with an urban population of 74 per cent. According to Kelley, urbanization trends in developing countries deviate less from historical patterns than is sometimes suggested. The increase in the share of urban population from 17 per cent to 37 per cent since 1950 is comparable to the speed of urbanization in earlier historical periods. However, in absolute terms the growth of the size of cities proceeds at a much faster pace. The growth of mega cities such as São Paulo and Mexico City confronts policymakers with historically unprecedented challenges. The growth of urban population is not only caused by migration from rural to urban areas, but increasingly by growth of the urban population itself (Kelley, 1988). According to UN projections, the level of urbanization in developing countries is expected to reach 50 per cent in 2015 and 57 per cent in 2025 (UN, 1993b).

4.5 *Economic consequences of population growth*

4.5.1 Pessimistic and optimistic perspectives

Since Thomas Malthus wrote his *Essay on the Principles of Population* in 1798 a debate is raging on the perceived consequences of population growth. Malthusian pessimists believe that population growth threatens human welfare and that there are physical limits to the increase in production, such as availability of land, scarcity of energy and raw materials and the carrying capacity of the global environment (e.g. Meadows *et al.*, 1972; Bruntland, 1987; Ehrlich and Ehrlich, 1990; Keating, 1993; UN, 1994). Optimists argue that scarcity provides a challenge to human creativity. In this view, people will always find new technological solutions to the problems of scarcity. For instance, if the prices of raw materials such as oil go up, it becomes economically feasible to develop alternative sources of energy. Limits to growth are not fixed, but are shifting all the time. Well-known representatives of the optimistic perspective are Simon and Boserup (Boserup, 1965, 1981, 1983; Simon, 1982).

4.5.2 Malthusian analyses

Central to Malthusian thought are two mechanisms, namely, the influence of increasing welfare on population growth on one side and the law of diminishing marginal returns in food production on the other. If the standard of living improves, people will tend to have more children. If increasing numbers of people have to cultivate limited amounts of land, marginal returns will have to decline in the longer term. Food production will be unable to keep up with the growth of population. Famines, malnutrition and epidemics will finally serve as a check on the growth of population.

As we shall show in Chapter 9 (agrarian development), long-run developments clearly contradict Malthusian predictions. In the past there may often have been considerable fluctuations in population size in given regions. Also, in some periods famines and epidemics may have led to depopulation of whole areas. But at a global level, world population never stabilized at any fixed level. In Table 4.1 we saw that the world population has been growing since prehistoric times, albeit at a very slow pace (Boserup, 1981, chapter 4). Since the acceleration of population growth in the nineteenth century, food production has been increasing even more rapidly than population (van der Meer, 1983; World Bank, 1984).

The crucial factor generally neglected in Malthusian thought is technical change. If there were no technical change, it would be correct to assume that marginal returns to labour in agriculture would decline as the man–land ratio goes up. But so far, the threat of declining marginal returns has always stimulated people to develop new production techniques.

4.5.3 *The neo-Malthusian trap*

In the 1950s Leibenstein and Nelson wrote that developing countries were in danger of getting caught in an equilibrium at a low level of economic development (Leibenstein, 1954; Nelson, 1956). This low-level equilibrium, known as the *neo-Malthusian trap*, is represented in Figure 4.3.

The horizontal axis of Figure 4.3 refers to per capita income (Y/C), the vertical axis to growth of population (P) and growth of national income. As per capita income goes up, Malthusian lore states that population growth (P) will increase till the biological maximum of around 3 per cent growth per year is reached. Growth of national income (Y) also depends on per capita income. As people become more prosperous, they are better able to save and invest. Higher investment rates in turn have a positive influence on the rate of growth.

Between points A and B, population is growing faster than income. As a result, income per capita will decline, till a low-level equilibrium is reached at point A. At this point the economy stagnates at a minimum subsistence level. Beyond the intersection point B, national income grows more rapidly than population. Per capita incomes will tend to increase, with a positive influence on the savings rate and further

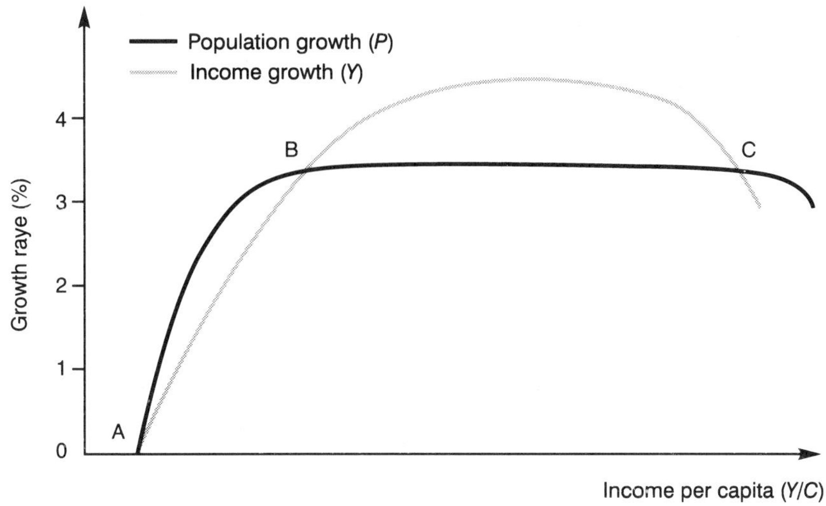

Figure 4.3 The neo-Malthusian trap

economic growth. Thus economic growth becomes self-sustaining. In the very long run, diminishing returns may stabilize per capita incomes at a high-level equilibrium point C. But in the context of developing economies, we are primarily interested in the trajectory between points A and B. Here we see that a small increase in per capita incomes is not sustainable. The economy will be forced back to its low level equilibrium point. Only if the whole economy can jump beyond point B will it be able to realize spontaneous and sustainable economic growth of per capita income.

The policy recommendation deriving from this model is that of the 'big push', the attempt to jump over the neo-Malthusian trap by a gigantic investment programme (see Chapter 7).

Just as in classical Malthusianism, the neo-Malthusian model in Figure 4.3 disregards technical change. As production techniques change, line Y will shift upwards. The intersection point B may even disappear (Myint, 1980, p. 90). Furthermore, we have seen in section 4.4 that the relationship between population growth and income per capita does not obey ahistorical Malthusian laws. Birth rates and fertility rates tend to decline rather than increase as per capita income goes up. With the exception of the African continent, this decline is visible in most developing countries. In the post-war period, death rates have been declining irrespective of income levels. This decline can be seen even in the poorest of developing countries.

4.5.4 Growth of national income, growth of per capita income and the dependency ratio

In an arithmetic sense it is clear that, given the growth rate of national income, a higher figure for population growth implies a lower growth rate of per capita income.

If one compares the growth rates of GDP per capita in Table 3.1 from Chapter 3, with the population growth rates in Table 4.2, it is obvious that production in developing countries grew much more rapidly than production per capita. But one may not conclude automatically that population growth has had a negative effect on the growth of national income per capita. For instance, a growing population may provide incentives to increase production. Nevertheless, we may safely assume that the challenges with which developing countries are confronted become greater as population growth becomes higher.

A rapidly growing population is associated with high percentages of young persons in the age structure of the population. Children do usually not contribute fully to production, but they do participate in consumption. The higher the so-called *dependency ratio* – the proportion of economically non-active to economically active persons – in an economy, the more the active members of the labour force have to produce to attain a given level of welfare.[2] Several theories state that population growth, working through the dependency ratio, has a negative effect on overall economic development.

4.5.5 Dependency ratio and savings

If there are many small children in a household, the consumptive expenditures of the household will tend to be greater and the proportion of household income saved will be smaller. A well-known hypothesis states that a high 'dependency ratio' will result in a low savings rate in an economy.

Surprisingly, however, empirical research provides but little support for this hypothesis (World Bank, 1984; Birdsall, 1988; Kelley, 1988). There are several reasons for this. In the first place, the private household is only one of the sources of savings along with firms, financial institutions and government. The savings decisions of firms and financial institutions are not influenced strongly by the dependency ratio. In the second place, the level of financial savings by households is negligible in poor economies. What savings there are, take a physical form, like using family labour to produce tools and implements, clearing land, or reserving part of output for feed and seed. These kinds of savings will not show up in statistics. Furthermore, many children in poor families often result in lower consumption, rather than lower savings. Finally, large numbers of children can provide incentives to work harder and to produce more in order to be able to feed more mouths. Nevertheless, the World Bank concludes tentatively that a large family size forms a heavy economic burden for a family and may indirectly have negative effects on its long run capacity to save (World Bank, 1984). Also, there is ample evidence that the life chances of children from very large families are less favourable than those of children from smaller families.

4.5.6 Investment

With a lag of some fifteen to twenty years, population growth results in an increased number of entrants to the labour market. This can cause a decline in the amount of capital goods available per person engaged (Coale and Hoover, 1958). If one invests a given percentage of national income while the supply of labour is increasing, the amount of capital per person engaged will decline. In absence of technological change, output per worker will also decline. In such a situation one has to invest a higher percentage of national income in order to forestall a decline in the amount of capital goods (implements, machines, etc.) per worker. In other words, one has to run harder to stay in the same place. A slower rate of population growth would free resources that could be used for an increase in the investments per worker.

Moreover, the increasing share of young people in the population structure might create a competition between resources available for investment in capital goods and those available for investment in schooling and health services (Coale and Hoover, 1958).

Empirical research does not give unequivocal answers to the questions raised here. Theoretically, the effects of population growth on savings and investment depend on numerous assumptions (e.g. assumptions with regard to economies of scale and the degree of substitutability of capital and labour in the production process). According to Birdsall (1988) the effects of population growth on capital accumulation are negligible compared to the effects of the level of national income. Given an investment rate of 18 per cent of national income in 1980, the United States invested $189,000 for every new job. In the same year, Kenya invested 22 per cent of its national income, which amounted to only $4,700 per new job (World Bank, 1984, p. 87).

Empirical uncertainties notwithstanding, we may nevertheless conclude that rapid population growth places additional burdens on already strained economies.

4.5.7 Education and health care

A high-dependency ratio means that a rapidly increasing youthful population has to be supplied with education. Even if nothing is done to improve the present quality of education, more money still needs to be spent on it. Once again, developing countries have to run harder just to stay in the same place.

Since World War II, developing countries have succeeded in substantially increasing educational participation in spite of rapid population growth. At present, however, there is a tendency for educational expenditure per student to decline (see Chapter 6). This threatens the quality of education, which is not very high as it is. If the number of pupils were increasing less rapidly it would be possible to reserve more funds for quality improvement. Also the difficult choices between educational expenditures and investment in physical capital would become less pressing.

Similar dilemmas exist with regard to health care. Rapid population growth means that existing health facilities have to be spread over more and more people, creating new dilemmas with regard to government expenditures.

At family level, finally, the negative effects of population growth are clearly discernible. Children from larger families do less well at school and, due to the pressure on family budgets, have less prospects of enjoying good health (Kelley, 1988).

4.5.8 Employment and income distribution

The influx of large numbers of young people on the labour market makes for both open and disguised unemployment. Open unemployment – not being able to find any gainful employment – is not very common in developing countries, where systems of social security are rudimentary or non-existent. We speak of *disguised unemployment* when labour productivity is so low that people can hardly earn enough to survive, in spite of working very long hours.

The modern sector (comprising the capital intensive industrial sector, government and commercial services) is unable to supply an ever-growing labour force with sufficient employment. Many people are forced to make a living by engaging in low-productive activities in the agrarian sector or in the urban and rural informal sectors of the economy. The large supply of labour thus promotes increasing income inequality. In the first place, the abundant labour supply weakens the position of employees *vis-à-vis* owners of capital. In the second place, income inequality between various categories of labour is also increased. Incomes of unskilled labourers in low-productivity sectors (the informal sector, traditional agriculture) lag behind incomes in the formal sector of the economy.

4.5.9 Population growth and the environment

Human impacts on the environment include the use and depletion of natural resources and the emissions of pollutants into the ecosphere.[3] The environmental effects of human actions can be decomposed into three elements: quantity of resources consumed and pollution per unit of output; output per capita; and population size (UN, 1994, p. 27 ff.).

The first element refers to the technological factor. Technological progress (both in resource use, and in production process technology and products produced) affects the environmental impact per unit of output. Output per capita reflects the affluence effect and population growth the demographic effect. Of course, there is no single indicator for the diversity of environmental effects. But the decomposition technique can be used to analyze various specified environmental effects.

In the prosperous countries the environmental effects of population growth are limited, as population growth in these countries is by now very slow. The most important factor is the growth of production and consumption per capita. The technology factor tends to bring about more efficient use of resources. In developing countries the decomposition studies summarized in UN (1994) suggest that one quarter to one third of increases in pollution are due to population growth. However, the indirect effects of population growth may be even higher and the environmental effects tend to weigh disproportionately on the poorest population groups.

In the analysis of environmental effects of population growth and economic development it is useful to distinguish scarcity of natural resources, localized environmental effects, and global environmental effects.

Contrary to predictions by the Club of Rome in 1972, there is presently no scarcity of raw materials. Where shortages of raw materials occur in the short run, prices are driven up. In the longer run this discourages the use of these raw materials, while making alternative techniques of resource extraction and alternative materials economically more profitable.

It is also not obvious that there is a negative relationship between growth of production per capita in given countries and regions and localized deterioration of the environment. Of course, growth of production implies the emission of various noxious wastes in air and water, which put a severe burden on the environment. On the other hand, however, recent research indicates that pollution of air and surface waters in urban areas of developing countries is far worse than in richer countries (World Bank, 1992, pp. 44–63). Rich countries can afford to reserve an increasing part of their national income for purposes of environmental protection, provision of clean drinking water, disposal of solid wastes, sewage systems and soil decontamination, which are too expensive for developing countries. Concentrations of solid matter and SO_2 in the air above cities in developed countries are generally declining, as is pollution of surface waters.

In developing countries such localized environmental effects are presently very severe and on the increase. In developing countries, 1.2 billion persons have no access to clean water, while 1.7 billion people are not served by adequate sanitary facilities, with tremendous health hazards in consequence. Most urban settlements in developing countries have no sewerage system, and 90 per cent of sewage is discharged without treatment. Air pollution is on the increase (UN, 1994). These localized environmental influences, however disastrous, can be tackled in the long term by technological change and increased investment in pollution abatement, which are positively associated with economic growth.

The environmental limits to economic growth and population growth do not depend, therefore, on the availability of natural resources and raw materials or on the lack of solutions for localized environmental problems. The limits are set mainly by the carrying capacity of the global environment (Brundtland, 1987; Keating; 1993; UN, 1994). There are ever stronger indications that the growth of world population and the associated growth of world production are beginning to form a threat to the environment at a global level, with consequences which may be irreversible. These indications include the following:

1. The rapid disappearance of the tropical rain forests under influence of human exploitation, expansion of agricultural land area, logging and acid rain effects (see Chapter 9). According to some estimates (World Bank, 1994), 1.1 billion square kilometres of forest were lost between 1973–1988. The most important single cause of deforestation was the expansion of agricultural land area under influence of increasing population pressure. Other important causes include cutting of trees for fuelwood in poor countries and logging. In the industrial world, acid rain contributes to a serious deterioration of the quality of forests. Deforestation contributes to increased CO_2 emissions and declining biodiversity.

Land clearing in highland areas leads to land erosion and downstream flooding.

2. The greenhouse effect caused by increased emission of CO_2 and other gases. The greenhouse effect may lead to irreversible mondial climatic changes, such as global warming, the consquences of which for human beings are hard to predict. There is still a lively debate on whether recent climatic changes are natural fluctuations within the same basic pattern or indications of changes in climatic trends. Also, the greenhouse effect itself is still the subject of empirical debate. Critics of Malthusianism such as Beckerman (1993) warn that we should balance unknown future effects of climatic changes against the known huge costs of draconian measures to control CO_2 emissions. On the other hand, the risks of not taking policy measures are so high that governments and international organizations are gradually shifting towards policies aimed at controlling the increase of CO_2 emissions. This is indicated by the resolutions of the international UN conference of world leaders on environment and development convened in Rio de Janeiro in 1992. Progress on paper, however, is greater than in actual practice.
3. The dilution of the ozone layer, which increases the danger of skin cancers.
4. Declining biodiversity. Biodiversity should be seen as a genetic insurance policy against unknown future risks. Declining biodiversity not only means that interesting species are disappearing from the world at an alarming rate, but it may also pose a threat towards continued human existence in the longer term.
5. Land degradation and desertification.

It is estimated that in the past 45 years 1.2 billion hectares, almost 11 per cent of the earth's vegetated surface, have suffered moderate to extreme soil degradation. (Oldeman *et al.*, 1991, quoted in UN, 1994). Land degradation is estimated to cause loss of 12 million tons of grain output per year, equivalent of half the annual increase in production (Brown and Young, 1990, quoted in UN, 1994). The modest impact on overall growth tends to obscure the fact that it is the poorest cultivators who are hardest hit by land degradation.

It is therefore clear that the global environmental effects pose the most serious limits to continued population growth and growth of per capita income. They also provide powerful arguments for effective population policies aimed at reducing growth rates and stabilizing world population. Even so, one should not forget that even global environmental effects also depend on the rate of technological change. For instance, land degradation does not have to be irreversible, if intensification of land use is accompanied by technological change which maintains or improves the productive capacity of land.

To a considerable extent the global environmental effects – especially those mentioned under items 2 and 3 in the above list – are the consequences of industrial growth in the rich countries. However, if one thinks of the billions of people in developing countries striving to attain standards of living comparable to those in the rich countries, the fundamental threat to the global environment in absence of technological change is obvious.

It would be incorrect, however, to blame environmental problems exclusively on growth of population and production. Institutional factors are also important. For instance, desertification and deterioration of agricultural land may also have something to do with poorly defined property rights. In many parts of Africa there are still traditionally defined common rights of land use. Where individual property rights are lacking, individual users of land have little incentive to invest in maintaining or improving land quality. As a result, farmers may continue to apply inappropriate technologies deriving from historical periods with lower population density.

In the case of air pollution, water pollution and deforestation, market imperfections can also play a role. In the market the costs of environmental deteroriation (external effects) are often not charged to producers and consumers. Individual cost-benefit calculations can result in outcomes which are socially unacceptable. Changes in market institutions, leading to internalization of external costs, could contribute to solutions for environmental problems, according to the less pessimistic participants in the environmental debate (Birdsall, 1988).

From this perspective, environmental problems are not only caused by population growth and economic growth but also by inefficient institutional arrangements. Of course, rapid population growth exacerbates existing environmental problems, reducing the time available in which to search for solutions to environmental problems.

4.5.10 Population growth and technological progress

In two books which have received considerable acclaim – *The Conditions of Agricultural Growth* and *Population and Technology* – Ester Boserup (1965, 1981) has drawn attention to the potentially stimulating effects of population growth on economic and technological development. She argues that increasing *population pressure* is a condition for productivity growth in agriculture and for industrialization and technological progress in general. In particular, in the period before 1750, when transport and communication were not so well developed, there was a strong correlation between the level of technological development and population density. But even today, population pressure can exert a positive influence on technological development.

According to Boserup there are two countervailing influences. On the one hand an increase of population leads to increasing pressure on natural resources. If technology does not change, there are diminishing returns. The economic surpluses available for investment and technological change will decline. On the other hand, population pressure is an incentive to develop new productivity enhancing technologies (*innovation*) or take them over from elsewhere (*diffusion*).

Especially in agriculture, population pressure has had a stimulating influence, according to Boserup. As long as population is sparse, people can provide for subsistence by hunting, gathering or by very extensive use of land. As population pressure increases, people are forced to switch to settled agriculture and to the ever more intensive use of land. Intensification implies that one has to work ever harder to increase output per hectare, while maintaining land fertility by weed control, fertilization and water control. The number of harvests per land area also increases gradually from one harvest in 15 to 25 years in forest fallow agriculture, to several harvests per year in areas with high population density. Intensification allows for considerable increase in output per hectare. At the same time, it requires so much extra labour input that there is a strong incentive to develop labour-saving and output-increasing production technologies.

Furthermore, without large population size and fairly high population density, it does not pay to invest in agricultural infrastructure. Similarly, infrastructural investment in water control and irrigation is a condition for further development of agriculture. Infastructural investment in transport and communication facilities is one of the necessary conditions for industrialization (see Chapter 7) and modern economic growth.

Population size and growth are also preconditions for urbanization. Prior to the development of modern transport technologies, only regions which were rich in population could afford to maintain and feed urban centres. These urban centres were the breeding grounds for subsequent technical and scientific progress.

Though the interconnections between population and technology have become less tight since the eighteenth century, Boserup is convinced that population pressure can still exert positive effects on development in present times. For instance, she suggests that the economic problems of many African countries are to some extent related to low population pressure. Low population pressure offers an insufficient basis for the necessary renewal and extension of infrastructure. In such a situation Malthusian mechanisms operate, where a growing population, using traditional agricultural technologies, is confronted with diminishing marginal returns.

Boserup's hypotheses are open to criticism. For instance, there are countries where the hypothesized relationships between population and technological development do not obtain. Nevertheless, her most important contribution is the concept of a race between Malthusian mechanisms of diminishing returns and increasing productivity as a result of technological change. These mechanisms are most clearly visible in the agrarian sector (see Chapter 9).

4.5.11 Conclusion

As we have discussed, there are various schools of thought with regard to the consequences of population growth. The orthodox view emphasizes the dangers of population growth. The 'revisionists' argue that high population growth is not necessarily associated with economic stagnation. They provide empirically founded criticisms of the pessimistic predictions of the Malthusians. Nevertheless, none of the participants in the discussion denies that dramatic population growth provides major challenges to developing countries. Control of population growth is still high on the political agenda, though it is now seen as but one of the many aspects of the development problem.

In the final analysis, the exponential growth of world population is the most convincing argument in favour of control of population growth. As we have seen, many pessimistic predictions concerning the negative consequences of population growth have drawn justifiable criticism. Nevertheless, it is obvious that if we want to provide an ever-increasing world population with an adequate standard of living, the carrying capacity of the natural environment will sooner or later be exceeded.

4.6 *Why do people in developing countries have so many children?*

In section 4.3, we saw that the high rate of population growth in developing countries can be explained by rapid declines in mortality in combination with continued high birth rates. The high birth rates in turn are determined by the youthful age structure of the population and the high number of births per woman (high fertility). For an adequate understanding of the population problems of developing countries, it is important to find out why women in poor countries have so many children.[4]

In this context, Bongaarts has made a useful distinction between the proximate determinants of fertility and the underlying economic, social and cultural determinants of fertility (Bongaarts, 1982; Bongaarts and Potter, 1983). The proximate determinants refer to factors such as age at marriage, breast-feeding, anticonception and abortion, which exert an immediate influence on the biological processes of reproduction. The more ultimate determinants include factors such as the cultural appreciation of children, sexual attitudes, and female–male relationships, as well as the conscious or unconscious economic considerations that play a role in determining family size. The ultimate determinants do not affect fertility directly; they always work through the proximate determinants, which Bongaarts therefore calls '*intermediate fertility variables*'. The Bongaarts model of the effects of intermediate fertility variables is discussed in section 4.6.1. Section 4.6.2 deals with economic explanations of family size; and section 4.6.3 discusses underlying cultural determinants of fertility.

4.6.1 Intermediate determinants of fertility: the Bongaarts model

The point of departure for the Bongaarts model of fertility is the biological maximum number of childbirths a woman could experience in the course of the fertile period of her life. The intermediate fertility variables determine the extent to which realized fertility deviates from this biological maximum.

Bongaarts distinguishes the following seven intermediate fertility variables:

1. The percentage of women in the fertile period of their lives who are married (or who have a stable sexual relationship).
2. The use and the effectiveness of birth control techniques.
3. The practice of induced abortion.
4. The duration of the infertile period after the birth of a child due to lactation and *post-partem infecundability*.

5. Frequency of sexual intercourse (*fecundability*).
6. Occurrence of spontaneous intra-uterine abortion.
7. The prevalence of permanent infertility.

Empirical research has shown that the first four variables are by far the most important in explaining variation in fertility.[5] The effects of these four variables are measured in relation to *total fecundity* (*TF*), which concept measures the combined effects of the last three fertility inhibiting variables (fecundability, spontaneous abortion and infertility). Total fecundity varies from 13 to 17 births per woman, with an average of 15.3. The Bongaarts model can be summarized in the following equation:

$$TFR = \{C_m \cdot C_c \cdot C_a \cdot C_i\} \cdot TF$$

Total fertility (*TFR*, total fertility rate) equals the biological maximum of fertility (*TF*, total fecundity), multiplied by four indexes, varying in value from 0 to 1. If an index has a value of one, fertility will not deviate from total fecundity due to this factor. If any of the indices has a value of 0, total fertility will equal 0. C_m is the marriage index. If all women in fertile age groups are married, then the value of this index is 1. If everyone is single, the value is 0. An important determinant of the marriage index is the age of marriage. In nineteenth-century Europe late marriages were the norm, so that subtantial numbers of women in fertile age groups remained single. In sub-Saharan Africa, people marry very young, which contributes to high realized fertility. C_c is the contraception index which measures the use and effectiveness of birth control techniques. If all fertile women and their sexual partners used modern and effective birth control techniques under all circumstances, the index would take the value 0. The total fertility rate would also be 0. If nobody practised birth control, the value of the index would be 1. C_a is the index for *induced abortion* again running from 1 (abortion is never practised) to 0 (all pregancies are terminated by abortion). C_i is the index for the period of infertility after the birth of a child (*post-partem infecundability*). This infertile period lasts a minimum of two months, but can be substantially longer when women breast-feed their children. Also the cultural practice of sexual abstinence after birth of a child can contribute to a lengthening of post-partem infecundability. The index has a value of 1 in case of complete absence of both breast-feeding and sexual abstinence. It takes a value of 0 in case of complete abstinence by women during their whole fertile life.

This model of Bongaarts has two important advantages. In the first place, it stimulates systematic empirical research concerning the intermediate determinants of fertility in different societies, social classes and historical periods. In the second place, the model structures the investigation of the various underlying economic and cultural variables. These underlying factors can only exert influence on fertility via the intermediate factors. For instance, changes in cultural norms concerning the age at marriage influence the marriage index, which in turn influences fertility. With the help of Bongaarts' analytical model it is possible to analyze, for instance, the extremely high fertility in a country such as Kenya. Here social-cultural changes have led to the disappearance of traditional barriers to high fertility such as lengthy breast-feeding and the practice of sexual abstinence by women after childbirth. The disappearance of traditional obstacles to high fertility is insufficiently compensated by an increase in the use of modern anticonceptive techniques.

4.6.2 Economic explanations of fertility

Economic explanations of fertility assume that people to a certain extent weigh the costs and benefits of having children, whether consciously or unconsciously. Having and raising children costs parents much time, energy and money. If couples have many children, this means that they may have to sacrifice other valued things in life. As most people want to have some children anyway, cost-benefit considerations usually only start playing a role after the birth of a second child.

The following factors can play a role in the decision whether or not to have another child (Becker, 1960; Willis, 1973; Easterlin, 1978; Birdsall, 1988):

1. *The costs of educating children.* The longer children have to go to school and the higher the parents' contribution to the costs of schooling, the higher the costs of children.
2. *The contributions of children to household income.* The earlier children start working – for instance, by helping their parents in agriculture – the greater their economic advantages. In many African societies women need the help of their children in food production.
3. *Financial sacrifices made by parents.* Mothers especially face high opportunity costs when they are unable to take paid jobs outside the home because they have to take care of many children. However, if the opportunities for paid work outside the home are scarce, the sacrifices will be correspondingly lower.
4. *Educational opportunities for women.* The greater the educational opportunities for women, the higher the costs of bearing and having children. Given prevailing male–female relationships, it is difficult for women to participate in education when they have many children. A low level of education in turn diminishes the chance of a woman finding well paid work on the labour market.
5. *The distribution of costs and benefits between men and women.* This depends on the nature of relationships between men and women, on family structures and on patterns of social organization. Often the costs of children are not borne by the biological fathers, but by the mothers or by the extended family system. In such situations biological fathers have little incentive to limit family size.
6. *Provisions for old age.* Children function as a provision for old age in societies where publicly guaranteed systems of old age pensions are lacking. Also, the absence of well-developed financial markets and markets for land in many developing societies makes it difficult to save for one's old age. As traditional communities are opened up in the course of development and the geographic mobility of younger generations increases, the value of children as an investment in old age social security may decrease.

7. *Child mortality*. The higher child mortality is, the more children couples will have in order to ensure a sufficient number of surviving children.

Generalizing broadly, one can reach the following conclusions on the basis of an economic analysis of fertility. The higher household income is, the greater the number of children as well as other desirable things in life one can afford. In this respect higher incomes make for higher fertility. On the other hand, the higher the level of income and education, the higher the opportunity costs of children become compared to the costs of other valued goods and services. Usually, the latter effect dominates the former. Members of wealthy and highly educated social classes tend to opt for a smaller number of better-educated children (Birdsall, 1988).

At lower income levels and in societies with underdeveloped markets, the advantages of children will be relatively greater and the opportunity costs lower. In such contexts, people tend to opt for a large number of children.

Of course, the economic analysis of fertility is open to criticism. One may doubt whether parents have sufficient information about costs and benefits. It is far from certain whether they consciously weigh costs and benefits of children. Nevertheless, the model of economic choice focuses our attention on a number of variables which can be important for population policy. Thus it seems clear that increasing educational opportunities for women makes for lower fertility. Increased educational opportunities for children tend to have the same effects.

4.6.3 Cultural explanations of fertility

The economic model of rational choice can increase our understanding of the considerations affecting family size. However, the model of economic choice is no more than an empty vessel. Decisions and choices are always made within a matrix of cultural preferences of men and women, which directly or indirectly influence the outcomes of their decision-making processes. With no knowledge of culturally determined preferences, we can say little or nothing about the outcomes of processes of economic choice. To give a very simple example, if the cultural value of children is higher in one society than another, then, other things being equal, fertility will be higher in this society.

Cultural factors not only influence choices, they also operate via the intermediate fertility variables. If cultural norms make for early marriage, fertility will be higher than in societies where late marriage is the rule. If there is a religious taboo on the use of contraceptives, fertility will be higher than in societies where such taboos are absent.

In an interesting review article Caldwell and Caldwell (1987, see also 1985) have shown how cultural factors contribute to the extremely high levels of fertility in sub-Saharan Africa. Their central thesis is that traditional belief systems, based on ancestor worship and the continuity of tribe and lineage, continue to be important to the present day in spite of the influences of Christianity and Islam. These cultural systems form a crucial obstacle to the successful introduction and diffusion of modern birth control technologies.

Caldwell and Caldwell discuss the following factors:

1. Ancestor worship. After their death, the spirits of the deceased have to be tended by their descendants. This guarantees the continued existence of both the spirits and the kinship group. Large numbers of children are among the most important conditions for such continuity.
2. High fertility is seen as a reward of higher powers and proof of virtuous behaviour in one's life. The social prestige of women is dependent on having large numbers of children. Infertility is associated with witchcraft, adultery or manifestions of evil. Contraceptive techniques in turn are associated with infertility and are therefore rejected. Fear of infant mortality and concern with the continuity of the lineage further legitimize large numbers of births.
3. Ancestor worship is associated with respect for elders in lineage groups. In traditional African societies there is an upward flow of wealth from younger to older generations. Therefore parents profit from large numbers of children.
4. Decisions concerning reproductive behaviour frequently rest with the males, while the burden of upkeep of the children is on the females. This divorce between benefits and costs makes for high fertility.
5. In several societies, women are not considered to be part of the kinship group of their husbands. Though responsible for the cultivation of the food crops, they have no independent rights to land. Their access to land depends on having children, who can also be used as labour. In this way, women also have an interest in high fertiliy.
6. Furthermore, in traditional societies the costs of raising children are spread over many relatives: aunts, grandmothers, and so on. Adoption is also a frequent phenomenon. Once again this weakens the links between having children and bearing the costs and responsibilities of their education.
7. Lengthy sexual abstinence by women after the birth of a child or grandchild is a traditionally accepted practice. This is sometimes used as a reason for rejecting modern birth control techniques.

According to Caldwell and Caldwell, all these factors together make for high fertility and culturally legitimized opposition to birth control. Cultural barriers explain why birth control programmes in countries such as Kenya and Ghana have met with such little success. They also explain why governments in African countries are so hesitant to start large-scale birth control programmes.

Of course, cultural influences vary from society to society. Nevertheless, we can derive at least three lessons from the studies discussed by Caldwell and Caldwell:

1. Birth control programmes that go against the grain of strong, culturally determined attitudes have little chance of success.
2. Cultural factors influence both the intermediate determinants of fertility and the economic considerations which consciously or unconciously play a role in determining family size.

3. Culturally buttressed attitudes concerning male–female relationships are of great importance in explaining fertility levels and trends. Conversely, one may say that, whatever the cultural context, improvements in the social position of women – in terms of education, economic and social independence, and equality between sexes – contribute to a lowering of birth rates.

4.7 *Policy*

In the long run, one may expect fertility rates in developing countries to decline spontaneously under the influence of economic and social development, as has happened in the presently prosperous countries. The first indications of this trend are now becoming visible (see Table 4.3). Improving standards of living, the penetration of the money economy, urbanization and industrialization all change the cost–benefit ratios of children and make the advantages of large family size less obvious. Culturally legitimized preferences for high fertility are gradually eroded in the process of development. Such patterns of spontaneous fertility decline manifested themselves in the 1960s in countries such as South Korea, Singapore and Hong Kong (World Bank, 1984, p. 106).

In economic development it is not only the growth of per capita income that is important, but also the distribution of incomes and life chances. Success in combating widespread poverty, improvements in the health situation, increasing life expectations, rising educational levels and declining illiteracy are all conducive to a drop in the fertility rate. Thus, between 1965 and 1975 the fertility rate in countries such as Sri Lanka, Thailand and Turkey declined faster than could have been expected on the basis of average economic growth rates.

One may conclude that policies aimed at overall economic development will also contribute to a much needed decline in fertility, especially if the benefits of economic development are evenly distributed over the whole population. However, present birth rates are much too high for policymakers to wait till spontaneous declines set in. Direct measures aimed at limiting the rate of population growth are still urgently required.

Among the determinants of fertility, the cultural determinants are most resistant to policy influences. At best, one can hope that if governments show sufficient conviction in propagating birth control, this may in the long run contribute to a gradual erosion of culturally founded objections to population control. What policy can do most effectively is change the balance of costs and benefits involved in individual choices with regard to family size. Policy can also directly influence the intermediate determinants of fertility.

Table 4.4 summarizes the ways in which policymakers can try to influence reproductive behaviour. In this table a distinction is made between policy and legislation, government expenditures, and tax programmes (World Bank, 1984, p.106).

Of the policy measures set out in the table, the following primarily affect the intermediate determinants of fertility:

Table 4.4 Government policies and birth control

Policies and legislation	Government expenditures	Tax programmes
• Minimum marriage age • Promoting breastfeeding • Improving the status of women • Children's education and work	• Education • Primary health care • Family planning • Incentives for fertility control • Old age security	• Family allowances • Fees for larger families

Source: World Bank, *World Development Report 1984*, p. 106. Copyright © 1984 by the World Bank. Used by permission of Oxford University Press Inc.

1. Policies or legislation aimed at increasing the minimum age of marriage. Late marriages lead to lower fertility rates.
2. Abortion legislation. Legislation can have a direct influence (positive or negative) on Bongaarts' abortion index.
3. Policies aimed at promoting breast-feeding. Breast-feeding lengthens the period of infertility after childbirth.
4. Government expenditure on and government policy concerning birth control. There is a clear relationship between the use of modern birth-control techniques and family size. Expenditure and policy can increase the availability of modern contraceptives and lower the costs for their users. Such policy is especially effective if there is an unfulfilled demand for birth control. This is the case when many couples have more children than they would prefer to have.

Policy can also aim at influencing the choices parents make. The following areas of policy are of interest in this respect:

1. *Improvement in the socio-economic status of women.* There is a strong correlation between improvement in the social status of women and a decline in fertility rates. Status improvement has to do with both educational opportunities and labour market opportunities for women and with more equality in relationships between men and women in general.
2. *Improved educational opportunities for children.* Investment in education increases the costs of having children. When educational opportunities are available, parents will tend to opt for a smaller number of more highly educated children.
3. *Regulating, or even prohibiting, child labour.* This restricts economic activities by children and diminishes their potential economic benefits.
4. *Expenditures for old age pensions and provisions.* The better old age provisions are, the less parents will depend on their children for old age security.
5. *Educational expenditures.* The greater the educational opportunities for women, the greater the sacrifices they have to make in order to have many children. In addition, education increases knowledge of and receptivity to modern birth control techniques among both women and men.

6. *Expenditures for primary health care.* Such expenditures contribute to lower child mortality. The higher child mortality, is the more families will tend to insure themselves against the risk of losing children by having many children.
7. *Rewards and sanctions.* One of the most important ways in which governments can influence choices with regard to family size is through material rewards and sanctions. Positive rewards for families with few children can consist of tax cuts, subsidies, better educational opportunities and better housing. Negative sanctions include the loss of tax advantages and subsidies or even tax levies on children.

Rewards and sanctions change the balance between the costs and benefits of children and can induce people to have smaller families. But there are all kinds of ethical objections to the too blatant use of rewards and sanctions. In the first place, the sanctions tend to place an additional burden on the children from large families, who will be even worse off than before. In the second place, for very poor people incentives and sanctions can end up in a form of coercion, which violates elementary human freedoms. Especially the use of incentives and sanctions to promote irreversible interventions, such as sterilization, raises fundamental moral issues. This is even more the case if there are insufficient guarantees that participation in birth-control programmes is entirely voluntary, as was sometimes the case in countries such as India and China. Thus the World Population Plan of Action adopted by the recent United Nations Conference on Population and Development held in Cairo in September, 1994, reaffirms the basic right of individuals and couples 'to decide freely and responsibly the number and spacing of their children and to have the information, education and means to do so' (UN Population Division, 1994).

Conversely, population pressure in densely populated countries such as China, India, Bangladesh and Indonesia is so excessively high that a system of incentives can well be defended. Some experts argue for the use of 'deferred incentives' in the form of pension schemes for people with small families. With deferred incentives, the burden of the decision rests on the parents rather than on the children.

Of great importance is the conviction with which governments pursue birth-control policies. In the Middle East and in Africa, government efforts to promote birth control have been half-hearted at best. Cultural and religious factors not only impede the execution of existing policies, but also form obstacles to the formulation of new policies.

In Asian countries, population policy has received greater priority than in Africa and Latin America. Especially in China, a marked decline in fertility has been realized since 1979 in the context of the 'one child per family' programme (Goodstadt, 1982). In this programme, extensive use has been made of systems of incentives and sanctions such as described above.

QUESTIONS FOR REVIEW

1. Discuss the concept of the demographic transition.

2. Compare demographic developments in the developing countries with earlier demographic developments in the presently rich countries of Western Europe.
3. Why do people in developing countries frequently have so many children?
4. Is rapid population growth a threat to economic development? Give an overview of the various ways in which population growth could affect the prospects for economic growth.
5. Give examples of how government policies can affect the intermediate determinants of fertility and the choices families make with regard to family size.

Notes

1. These paragraphs are based on World Bank (1984) and Kelley (1988).
2. Here we interpret the dependency ratio as the ratio of young people in the age category 1–14 years to persons in the age category of 15–65 years. Another possible measure is the ratio of all persons under 15 or over 65 to the population aged 15 to 65.
3. The following paragraphs are based on a recent background report (UN, 1994) prepared for the International Conference on Population and Development held in Cairo in September 1994. This report provides a useful summary of recent research on the environmental impacts of population growth.
4. This paragraph is based on lecture notes of Harry van Vianen and Bert van Norren.
5. Bongaarts mentions two criteria for the selection of important factors: 1. variations in a factor should be clearly associated with variation in fertility; 2. factors should vary from society to society. If they do not vary, they will not contribute to explanation of differences in fertility between countries and regions.

5 *Health care*[1]

Health care and education are important aspects of development. They belong to the basic needs every development strategy tries to meet (Deolalikar, 1988). Improving the state of health and the level of education also contributes to the realization of other developmental objectives such as economic growth, increase in labour productivity, responsiveness to innovation, and future orientation. From the perspective of economic development investment in education and health care can be regarded as an investment in human capital (Mushkin, 1962).

In this chapter the main focus will be on the discussion of health-related issues. Trends in child mortality, average life expectancy, and patterns of morbidity and health will be discussed. Attention will be paid to the factors that affect developments in health issues. In the light of these factors attention will be paid to health policies. In Chapter 6 education will be discussed. The following issues will be dealt with: investment in human capital, educational enrolment, literacy, and educational policies. Both chapters will discuss the interactions between the various aspects of development. For example, education can contribute substantially to improvements in health.

5.1 *The state of health in developing countries*

5.1.1 Quantitative indicators of the state of health

Three types of indicators of the state of health can be distinguished (Hardiman and Midgley, 1982), as follows:

1. Demographic indicators such as life expectancy at birth, mortality rates and child mortality rates.

2. Morbidity statistics.
3. Health service dicators: the number of doctors, medical staff or hospital beds, and financial efforts.

Health service indicators present the least reliable picture of the state of health. These indicators refer to the quantity of health services only. They do not provide any information on the functioning and effectiveness of systems of health care. The drawback of demographic indicators such as the mortality rate and average life expectancy is that they do not tell us very much about the state of health of the surviving population. Many diseases in developing countries are chronic. They undermine health and welfare even when they do not result in death. In theory, indicators of morbidity (i.e. diseases) offer the most complete picture of the state of health. In practice, however, not enough information on the prevalence of diseases is available. Even in highly developed countries morbidity registration is unreliable; in developing countries the situation is even worse. Here no full medical records of the population are kept. One has to rely on questionnaires in which people subjectively answer questions concerning their past and present health. The outcomes of these questionnaires undoubtedly reflect important subjective and culturally determined aspects of illness and health, but they are not comparable across countries and regions. This approach cannot provide us with reliable information about the actual prevalence of different types of diseases in different countries or regions. Therefore, demographic indicators are used most often. They are relatively easy to register, and though they do not give a full picture of the state of health, they do reflect some of its very important aspects. Demographic indicators also need to be employed with the greatest care. Data on many developing countries are either extremely incomplete or insufficiently reliable (UN, 1988a, 1988b; Walsh, 1990).

The sections will pay special attention to the following demographic indicators: infant and child mortality; average life expectancy at birth; and patterns of illness as reflected by causes of death.

5.1.2 Infant and child mortality

Mortality is distributed bimodally, with high probabilities of dying in the first years of life (in particular, at birth and immediately afterwards) and a gradually increasing chance of dying after the age of 30. High mortality among infants and children under the age of 5 is considered as one of the important characteristics of the general state of health in developing countries. This, in turn, affects average life expectancy. For these reasons the literature on health issues pays a lot of attention to the topic of infant and child mortality.

Table 5.1 presents data on infant and child mortality. In this table, infant mortality is defined as the chance of dying between the age of 0 and 1 per 1,000 live births. Child mortality is defined here as the chance of dying between the age of 0 and 5 per 1,000 live births.[2]

Table 5.1 Infant and child mortality, 1950–1995 (probability of dying per 1,000)

	1950–1955		1990–1995	
	Probability of dying		Probability of dying	
	between 0–1	between 0–5	between 0–1	between 0–5
Bangladesh	180	312	91	129
China	195	266	31	38
India	190	332	79	106
Indonesia	160	270	66	90
Pakistan	190	332	95	136
Philippines	100	178	40	50
South Korea	115	164	13	16
Taiwan			6	8
Thailand	132	195	26	31
Turkey	233	318	54	69
Argentina	64	84	29	36
Brazil	135	187	57	73
Chile	126	162	17	21
Colombia	123	189	21	25
Mexico	114	193	35	43
Peru	159	268	52	68
Venezuela	106	148	33	39
Egypt	200	350	57	87
Ghana	148	250	81	129
Ivory Coast	216	350	91	129
Kenya	150	254	66	102
Nigeria	207	345	84	183
Tanzania	160	270	92	148
Zambia	150	254	107	178
Average 24 countries	154	247	55	81
Africa	192	322	94	158
Latin America	125	189	44	56
Asia	181	278	60	80
East Asia	181	248	28	34
East Asia excl. Japan			30	37
Southeast Asia	152	244	51	68
South Asia	189	327	84	114
West Asia	202	307	52	68
Developing countries	180	281	67	97
More developed countries	56	73	14	17

Source: 1950–1955: UN (1988b); 1990–95, World Bank, *World Population Projections 1994–95*, 1994b.

In the 1990–95 period the average infant mortality rate per 1,000 live births was 67 in developing countries and 14 in more developed countries. In OECD countries infant mortality was 8 per 1,000 in 1990 (World Bank, 1992). The mortality rate for children under the age of 5 is 97 per 1,000 in developing countries and 17 per 1,000 in more developed countries.

It is not just the extreme contrasts between developing and more developed countries that stand out. There are also great differences among developing countries themselves. For example, the infant mortality rate in countries like Bangladesh, Pakistan, Ivory Coast, Tanzania and Zambia is over 90. In countries such as China, South Korea, Thailand, Argentina, and Chile it is between 13 and 31. Africa has by far the highest infant mortality (94). The lowest infant mortality rate is in East Asia (28) and Latin America (44). The regional distribution of child mortality under the age of 5 shows the same tendency.

Since World War II, infant and child mortality has decreased strongly in developing countries. Even in Africa, which lags behind other developing countries, infant mortality dropped from 192 in 1950–55 to 94 in 1990–95. During the same period child mortality was halved (see also Vallin, 1989). In other parts of the world, especially in Asia, the decrease was even more dramatic.

In *Global Strategy for Health for All by the Year 2000* (WHO, 1981), one stated objective was that infant mortality in the year 2000 should be no higher than 50. For the very poorest countries the 1990 target figure was 120 per 1,000. Table 5.1 shows that the 1990 target for infant mortality has been met. If present trends continue, many regions will also be able to meet the target figure of 50 by the year 2000.[3]

Some observers feel that there has been a worrying deceleration in the decrease in infant mortality during the 1980s (UN, 1984; Caldwell, 1986), although this is denied in other sources (UN, 1988b, p. 19; WHO, 1993). A comparison of the most recent estimates for 1990–95 from *World Population Projections 1994–95* (World Bank, 1994b, included in table 7.1) with estimates for 1985–90 from *World Population Prospects* (UN, 1993a) shows quite marked declines. Infant mortality in developing countries was 79 per 1,000 in 1985–90 and 67 in 1990–95. Child mortality was 119 in 1985–90 and 97 in 1990–95. It may be that part of this decline should be attributed to changes in definitions and data collection methods, but there is no indication at all of slowdown in the decline in infant and child mortality rates. In African countries hardest hit by AIDS (Malawi, Rwanda, Uganda, Zambia) mortality estimates are being revised upwards (UN, 1994), but this mostly affects older age groups.

Despite these positive trends, present levels of infant and child mortality in developing countries are still unacceptably high. In relative terms the gap between developing and rich countries has even widened. In 1950 the probability of an infant in a developing country dying was 3.2 times as high as in rich countries; today the chance is 4.7 times as high. The probability of a child dying before it reaches its fifth birthday in a developing country is no less than 5.7 times as high as in more developed countries. Also the gap between the least developed countries and other developing countries seems to be on the increase (WHO, 1993).

Table 5.2 Life expectancy at birth in selected developing countries, 1920–1992 (in years)

	1920	1930	1940	1950	1970	1992
Bangladesh	20[b]	27[c]	32[d]	34[a]	42	55
China				36[a]	58	69
India		27[e]		34	48	61
Indonesia				34[a]	47	60
Pakistan	20[b]	27[c]	32[d]	34	46	59
Philippines				52	59	65
South Korea		38[a]	41[a]	53	60	71
Taiwan			43	63[g]		
Thailand				51	58	69
Turkey				46[a]	57	67
Argentina				60	68	71
Brazil	37			45	59	66
Chile		37	39	52[h]	62	72
Colombia		33		45[a]	59	69
Mexico			39	47	61	70
Peru				43	53	65
Venezuela				67[j]	63	70
Egypt			39[f]	42[a]	51	62
Ghana				38[i]	50	56
Ivory Coast				40[j]	42	56
Kenya				46[j]	49	59
Nigeria				37[a]	44	52
Tanzania				37[a]	47	51
Zambia				45[j]	45	48
Average 24 countries	26	32	38	45	53	63

Notes:
[a] a Most data for 1950 and before are five-yearly averages. The estimates presented here are simple interpolations.
[b] 1921; [c] 1931; [d] 1941; [e] 1921–1931 average; [f] 1936–1938 average; [g] 1959–1960 average; [h] 1952; [i] 1947/48; [j] 1960 from *WDR 1993*.

Sources: 1920, 1930, 1940: Unless indicated otherwise United Nations (1953); Bangladesh, Pakistan, South Korea: United Nations/ESCAP (1985).
1950: Unless indicated otherwise United Nations (1960); Taiwan, Chile, Ghana, Nigeria: UN (1963); Tanzania, Egypt, Nigeria: United Nations (1986); 1970 World Bank (1983), *World Tables 1983*; 1992, World Bank (1994a,b), *WDR/World Population Projections*.

5.1.3 Life expectancy

Tables 5.2 and 5.3 present data on life expectancy at birth in developing countries. There are clear-cut differences between regions. Particularly in Africa, life expectancy is extremely low. During the 1990–95 period the average life expectancy was 53.9 years. In Table 5.2 this is illustrated by the data for countries like Nigeria, Tanzania and Zambia. In south Asian countries average life expectancy is also comparatively low at 60.3 years. In Table 5.2 this region is represented by India, Pakistan, and Bangladesh. The highest life expectancy can be discerned in east Asia. In 1992 life expectancy in China was 69 years and in South Korea, 71. Within regions there are considerable differences. In some Latin American countries (e.g. Argentina, Chile, Mexico and Venezuela) life expectancy is over 70, while the Latin American average is 68.1.

Today the inhabitants of economically advanced countries live 11.5 years longer on average than the inhabitants of developing countries (74.8 versus 63.3 years). Since 1950 life expectancy at birth in developing countries has increased strongly, to a considerable extent due to the decrease in infant and child mortality. In the twenty-four countries presented in Table 5.2, life expectancy increased from an average 45 years in 1950 to 63 years in 1992. In all developing countries together, life expectancy increased from 41.1 to 63.3 years, that is, a 22-year increase within two generations. In this respect, there is a substantial narrowing of the gap between economically advanced countries and developing countries.

Table 5.3 Life expectancy at birth per region, 1950–1995 (in years)

	1950–1955	1985–1990	1990–1995
Africa	37.8	51.7	53.9
Latin America	51.1	66.5	68.1
Asia	41.2	62.9	65.2
East Asia	42.7	70.3	70.1
Southeast Asia	41.2	61.3	63.3
South Asia	38.9	57.0	60.3
West Asia	45.1	64.6	66.4
Developing countries	41.1	60.7	63.3
More developed countries	65.8	73.3	74.8
OECD countries	68.0	77.0*	77.1

Note: * 1990.

Sources: Developing countries 1950–1955: United Nations (1986); 1985–1990, from United Nations (1993a). OECD 1950–1955: United Nations (1979); OECD 1990: World Bank (1992). All countries 1990–95: World Bank (1994b).

5.1.4 Patterns of disease and health

It is difficult to obtain reliable data on the causes of death in developing countries. There is no complete and systematic registration, and it is often hard to determine the disease a person has died of. Still, some clear patterns can be discerned. In developing countries most people die of infectious intestinal and respiratory diseases. In rich countries neoplasms (cancer), cardiovascular diseases, and degenerative diseases rank high among the causes of death (WHO, 1987).

Table 5.4 presents a broad survey of the most important causes of death in different parts of the world. This table shows that infectious and parasitic diseases caused about 40 per cent of all deaths in 1980. Other sources present even higher estimates. According to Hardiman and Midgley (1982), infectious diseases cause 40 to 50 per cent of all deaths. In a recent study by Walsh (1990) the share of infectious and parasitic diseases in 1986 is estimated to be 35.4 per cent and the share of respiratory diseases 26.8 per cent, adding up to a total 62.2 per cent of all deaths. In 1990 WHO statistics indicate that 44.2 per cent of all deaths in developing countries are due to infectious and parasitic diseases. These diseases especially claim lives of children under the age of 5. Even if these diseases do not result in death, they may permanently impair the development, welfare and general state of health of their victims.

Table 5.4 shows that cardiovascular diseases, other degenerative diseases, and neoplasms cause over two-thirds of all deaths in economically advanced countries. Cardiovascular and degenerative diseases cause over 50 per cent of all deaths (see also UN/ESCAP, 1985), and neoplasms (cancer) about 20 per cent. These diseases are very much age-related, that is, they gain in importance as the population grows older. Cardiovascular diseases and cancer are also typically Western diseases closely related to lifestyle, stress, and eating habits.

These classes of diseases are much less important in developing countries. The diseases characteristic of developing countries manifest themselves primarily amongst children. The diseases characteristic of more developed countries typically occur at more advanced ages; deaths in these countries are concentrated in the higher age groups.

The difference in patterns of morbidity is one of the explanations why life expectancy in developing countries is so much lower than in more developed countries. Moreover, it also explains why the differences in average death rates per 1,000 people are not so large (see Chapter 4); in more developed countries there are more elderly people amongst whom the death rate is evidently much higher than in other age groups.

In the 1980s some new trends emerged in developing countries (WHO, 1993). Cardiovascular diseases and cancer rose as a proportion of all deaths. More than half of all new cancer cases now occur in developing countries, due both to tobacco use and to progress made in tackling other major health problems. But infectious and parasitic diseases still remain the most important ones.

5.1.5 Common diseases in developing countries

In this section diseases have been categorized on the basis of the way they are passed on. Diseases can be transmitted through: contaminated food and drinking

Table 5.4 Causes of death in 1980 by region (× 1,000 and percentages)

Cause	Africa		Latin America		South and Southeast Asia		Eastern Mediterranean region		Western Pacific region*		Developing countries		More developed countries	
	Absolute (000s)	(%)	Absolute (000s)	(%)	Absolute (000s)	(%)	Absolute (000s)	(%)	Absolute (000s)	(%)	Absolute (000s)	(%)	Absolute (000s)	(%)
Infectious and parasitic diseases	3,570	49.7	980	31.2	6,780	43.9	1,760	44.4	2,620	27.3	16,020	39.9	810	7.6
Neoplasms	210	2.9	280	8.9	670	4.3	160	4.0	830	8.6	2,200	5.5	2,050	19.2
Cardiovascular and degenerative diseases	840	11.7	770	24.5	2,410	15.6	560	14.1	2,890	30.0	7,620	19.0	5,710	53.5
Causes related to perinatal period	610	8.5	260	8.3	1,280	8.3	390	9.8	470	4.9	3,080	7.7	170	1.6
Injury and poisoning	270	3.8	200	6.4	660	4.3	160	4.0	650	6.7	1,980	4.9	690	6.5
Remaining and unknown causes	1,680	23.4	650	20.7	3,630	23.5	930	23.5	2,170	22.5	9,240	23.0	1,240	11.6
Total	7,180	100.0	3,140	100.0	15,430	100.0	3,960	100.0	9,630	100.0	40,140	100.0	10,670	100.0

Note: *Including East Asia.

Source: WHO (1987), 72.

water; air; direct physical contact; parasites; and animal bearers of diseases (vectors).

Diseases transmitted through contaminated water or food

Infectious diseases are often transmitted faecally, through direct contact with faeces or through contaminated food or drinking water. Insects and other animal bearers of infections – *vectors* – cause food to rot or water to be contaminated. Poor hygiene, therefore, is among the most serious pathogenic factors. Infectious diseases that are passed on in these ways include the following (Hardiman and Midgley, 1982; WHO, 1987; Maurice and Pearce, 1987):

- *Diarrhoea.* Diarrhoea is a collective name for infections of the digestive system. It is one of the most important causes of death among children in developing countries, claiming 23.3 per cent of child mortality in 1990 (WHO, 1993).
- *Bacterial and viral diseases like cholera, poliomyelitis, hepatitis, and typhus.* Faecally carried diseases like cholera and poliomyelitis are less common as a consequence of vaccination schemes, although they are far from being eradicated.

Airborne diseases

Diseases transmitted by air (e.g. pneumonia, tuberculosis, diphtheria, small pox, meningitis, pertussis (whooping cough), and measles) cause between a fourth and a third of all deaths in developing countries (Hardiman and Midgley, 1982). In 1990, 27.6 per cent of total child mortality was caused by acute infections of the respiratory system alone (WHO,1993). In this respect a vicious circle of undernourishment and infection plays a significant role.

Diseases transmitted through direct physical contact

Other contagious diseases are transmitted through direct physical contact; for example, leprosy (ten to twelve million cases in the 1980s: see Maurice and Pearce, 1987), framboesia and sexually transmissible diseases. Within the latter category, AIDS has become extremely important. It is feared that in years to come the death rate will increase strongly as a result of AIDS, especially on the African continent. In some countries HIV infections are reaching epidemic proportions.

In fifteen African countries in East, Middle, and West Africa the number of HIV-infected persons was 4.5 million in 1990 (UN, 1993a, p. 53 ff.; UN, 1994). This represents 90 per cent of total HIV infections in sub-Saharan Africa and more than half of the world total (UN, 1994). In terms of prevalence of seropositivity, four countries are hardest hit: Malawi, Rwanda, Uganda and Zambia. In terms of projected AIDS-related deaths up to 2005, the hardest-hit countries are Uganda (1.8 million), Zaire (1.4 million), Tanzania (1.3 million) and Zambia (1.1 million). In Uganda and Zambia the trend towards declining death rates has even been reversed.

In other African countries, death rates are declining at a substantially lower rate than they would have done in the absence of AIDS.

HIV infections are most common within the economically most productive age group (25–49). This may have serious economic consequences. In Zambia, for instance, it is estimated that 60 per cent of the important copper industry's labour force will be HIV-infected in 2000. There are also fears that agricultural production will be negatively affected. AIDS infections will impact on patterns of care-giving for both children and the elderly. Moreover, the large number of AIDS patients will be an enormous burden on the health-care system. In spite of AIDS, populations in the fifteen African countries studied will continue to grow rapidly. The projected growth rate between 2000 and 2005 is 2.88 per cent, against 3.13 per cent in the absence of AIDS (UN, 1994).

Parasitic diseases

Parasitic intestinal diseases are also quite common. Approximately one billion people suffer from ascariasis (caused by the roundworm) and ancylostomiasis (caused by hookworms).

Diseases transmitted by animal vectors

Very important are diseases that are transmitted by insects or other animal vectors. Among these diseases are, for example:

- Malaria (transmitted by the malaria mosquito). Malaria has been considerably reduced due to the use of pesticides like DDT. However, in the course of time mosquitoes have become immune to pesticides. The number of malaria cases is estimated to be about 100 million per year (Maurice and Pearce, 1987). The malaria situation is presently deteriorating worldwide.
- *Bilharzia* (schistosomiasis, an infectious disease of the intestines and the urinary tracts caused by worms). Bilharzia can be found in watery areas and is carried by snails. Between 500 and 600 million people are exposed to schistosome infection, with 200 million actually infected (Maurice and Pearce, 1987).
- *Sleeping sickness* (trypanosomiasis). Sleeping sickness occurs in many sub-Saharan African countries and is passed on by tsetse flies. In thirty-six countries, 50 million people are exposed to infection (Maurice and Pearce, 1987), with 16 to 18 million people currently infected (WHO, 1993).
- *Filariasis* (a category of parasitic infectious diseases, transmitted by mosquitoes, flies, and worms). The most important diseases in this category are lymphatic filariasis (its most serious form being elephantiasis), and river blindness (onchocerciasis). An estimated 905 million people are exposed to lymphatic filariasis. with 90 million actually infected. River blindness is common, especially in tropical African countries, where 17 million are actually infected and 78 million are exposed to infection (Maurice and Pearce, 1987).

- *Trachoma* (inflammation of the eye membrane). Hundreds of millions of people suffer from this disease which is passed on by flies and through direct physical contact. Trachoma can result in blindness.

Amongst infectious diseases the so-called undernourishment–infection syndrome merits special attention. Infectious diseases interact with undernourishment, which increases susceptibility to infection. Infectious diseases, and in particular, diarrhoea, cause further undernourishment, thus creating a vicious circle. In the end, diseases that are not dangerous in themselves, may result in death (Mosley, 1985a; van Norren and van Vianen, 1986). In section 5.2.4 this will be discussed in more detail.

5.1.6 Epidemiological transition

The fact that people all over the world live longer today than they did thirty to forty years ago is very much related to the reduction of infectious diseases of the intestines and the respiratory tracts. These are diseases that mainly kill young people. In the affluent countries of today infectious diseases have gradually been reduced from the eighteenth century onwards. At present they are no longer very important. A similar development can be observed today in developing countries.

Such developments are often discussed in the context of the so-called *epidemiological transition*, which is seen as an integral part of an overall process of economic and social development. The transition involves changes from situations characterized by infectious diseases, high fertility rates, high child mortality rates, and low life expectancies to situations characterized by low child mortality rates, few infectious diseases, low fertility rates, high life expectancies and the predominance of cancer and cardiovascular diseases (Frederikson, 1969; Omran, 1971). This epidemiological transition is seen as closely interlinked with the wider process of modernization characterized by increases in prosperity, improvements in nutrition, hygiene and water supply, higher levels of education and improvements in medical technology.

Omran (1971) distinguishes three models of the epidemiological transition:

1. The classical Western model characterized by a gradual decrease of the death rate associated with modernization, improved nutrition and hygiene. By the beginning of the twentieth century infectious diseases were outstripped by other diseases. The decline in the death rate accelerated.
2. The accelerated model of epidemiological transition. The difference with the classical model is mainly that the death rate declines more rapidly and that public hygiene, sanitation and medical factors play a more important role. The pattern of change is similar, however. A typical example of this model is twentieth-century Japan.
3. The decelerated epidemiological transition model. This model refers to today's developing countries and indicates that the transition from older to newer patterns of disease is still unfinished.

Like other modernization theories that assume a unilinear development from a traditional to a modern stage, the simple model of epidemiological transition has proved to be untenable. Changes in patterns of sickness and health never develop along the same path in different societies and during different historical periods (Frenk *et al.*, 1989). For example, in many developing countries cardiovascular diseases, cancer, diabetes and other chronic conditions are on the increase, while infectious diseases continue to remain important (WHO, 1993). Until recently, lifestyle-related diseases such as cardiovascular diseases and cancer were among the most important causes of death in most developed countries.[4] However, in Japan cardiovascular diseases have shown a downward tendency since World War II. They no longer rank first among the causes of death as they do in other rich countries. Also, life expectancy – 77 years – is higher than in other rich countries (UN, 1984, p. 49)

Japan is different in other respects too. In 1900, Japanese life expectancy was similar to the life expectancy in England, whereas per capita income was much lower. According to Johansson and Mosk, this is explained by the exceptional emphasis on public hygiene in Japan in the late nineteenth century. Between 1900 and 1940 life expectancy in Japan hardly changed, whereas in England and in other Western European countries it rose to approximately 60 years. After World War II, Japan embarked on a dramatic process of epidemiological catch-up, which paralleled its economic performance. In health terms it succeeded in overtaking Western Europe and the US (Johansson and Mosk, 1987; Vallin, 1989).

Nevertheless the various patterns of development have some important elements in common. The share of deaths caused by infectious diseases tends to decrease over time, whether gradually or rapidly, while the share of deaths caused by non-infectious diseases tends to increase. What comes in the place of infectious diseases can differ, but the decline in infectious diseases itself is certainly an 'epidemiological transition.'

5.2 Theoretical explanations

To pursue an adequate health-care policy, we need to familiarize ourselves with the determinants of health and morbidity. I will discuss this issue from two different points of view. First, I will concentrate on the various factors that may be of importance to the improvement of the state of health. Second, I will consider several important theoretical ideas. I will then cautiously attempt a synthesis.

Factors affecting the state of health

The following factors may affect the state of health in a particular country:

1. *Improvements in medical technology.* Improvements in curative medicine and the development of effective medicines make it possible to treat diseases that were previously untreatable. Extremely important are, for example, the anti-

biotics that are used to combat various infectious diseases. Preventive medicine based on vaccination is also part of medical technology. Several diseases can be eradicated at relatively modest costs by means of large-scale vaccination schemes. For example, vaccination against smallpox has already been very successful. Most countries have schemes for vaccinating children against diphtheria, whooping cough, tetanus, poliomyelitis, measles, and tuberculosis (WHO, 1987, p. 76). Still, in 1984 four million children died of these diseases, and another four million were crippled for life. Vaccination could have prevented this.

2. *Improvements in water supply, hygiene, and sanitary facilities.* Many diseases are passed on through contaminated water, unhygienic treatment of excrements, and unhealthy living conditions. In developing countries, hundreds of millions of households do not have access to clean drinking water. Facilities for the hygienic treatment of excrements are often woefully inadequate.
3. *Combating animal carriers of diseases (vectors).* An important aspect of health-care policy is controlling vectors that transmit diseases (e.g. flies, mosquitoes, worms, slugs or rats). Chemical substances are often used in combating vectors, although biological methods are applied as well.
4. *Nutrition.* According to some theorists, the importance of medical technology is overrated (McKeown, 1976). Nutrition is the most important factor reducing susceptibility to diseases and reinforcing natural resistance against diseases contracted. In this respect, improvement of the state of health primarily depends on the overall improvement of the economic situation, the standard of living, and the food supply.
5. *Education.* Other authors like Mosley (1983, 1985a) and Caldwell (1984, 1986) emphasize the importance of education, especially the education of mothers. Improving educational levels is positively associated with practices favourable to children's chances of survival – both from a preventive viewpoint (e.g. hygiene, vaccination, food), and in a curative sense (e.g. making better use of the possibilities of the health facilities).
6. *Health-care policy.* Countries that make great efforts with respect to basic health care are relatively more successful in combating diseases, reducing the child mortality rate, and increasing life expectancy. Policy is an important autonomous factor.

The first four factors are of a medical–biological nature. They have direct impacts on processes of disease and treatment. The last two factors are of an indirect nature. oThey influence the availability of direct factors and the ways in which people deal with the direct factors that influence sickness and health. There are many differences of opinion concerning the relative importance of these different factors. Some of the most pronounced theories and models will be discussed in the following sections.

5.2.1 Preston: per capita income and life expectancy

In a pioneering article published in 1975 Samuel Preston studied the relation between per capita income and life expectancy (Preston, 1975). At a given moment in time the level of income and the average life expectancy are closely related. In poor countries life expectancy is much lower than in rich countries. However, in the course of time, life expectancy in all countries increases regardless of the level of income. This is illustrated in Figure 5.1 in which the average life expectancy in a country (on the vertical axis) is compared with per capita income (on the horizontal axis). In this figure there is a positive relation between per capita income and life expectancy, both in 1930 and in 1960. However, the 1960 curve lies above the 1930 curve.

On the basis of his statistical analysis Preston comes to the conclusion that factors other than per capita income account for the 75–90 per cent increase in global life expectancy. Factors like improved nutrition and a higher level of education cannot explain the increase in the average life expectancy either. According to Preston, the rise in life expectancy is explained to a great extent by improvements in health technology. This includes not only vaccination technology, antibiotics, and sulphonamides, but also health policies with respect to vectors, public hygiene, health education and health facilities for mothers and their children.

The conclusion often drawn on the basis of Preston's analysis is that a low level of prosperity does not necessarily hinder improvements in health care and the state of health by application of modern medical technology (e.g. see World Bank, 1984, p. 69). However, Preston also stresses the fact that – after the upward shift of the curve – the relation between per capita income and life expectancy for the poorest developing countries is even closer than before. This may be because when life expectancy increases, the diseases that remain are those most closely related to standard of living – like diarrhoea and other infectious diseases.

5.2.2 McKeown: the importance of nutrition

In a long series of influential publications, Thomas McKeown comes to radically different conclusions (McKeown, 1976, 1978, 1979, 1988). He concentrates on the history of health and health care in England in the eighteenth and nineteenth centuries, and shows that the decreasing number of deaths due to diseases preceded important medical breakthroughs in the treatment of these diseases. McKeown believes that nineteenth-century hospitals contributed more to the spread of diseases than to their effective treatment. Further, he claims that the role of medical technology and medical progress is highly overrated and that one should look for other possible sources of the decline in the death rate and the increase of life expectancy. He stresses the importance of nutrition, and argues that the decreasing death rate in England in the eighteenth and nineteenth centuries was caused to a large extent by increasing immunity against airborne infectious diseases, an immunity that was due to better nutrition.

On the basis of these analyses McKeown and his followers claim that the state of health in developing countries cannot be improved without overall improvement in the standard of living and levels of nutrition. In other words, economic factors are indeed of crucial importance.

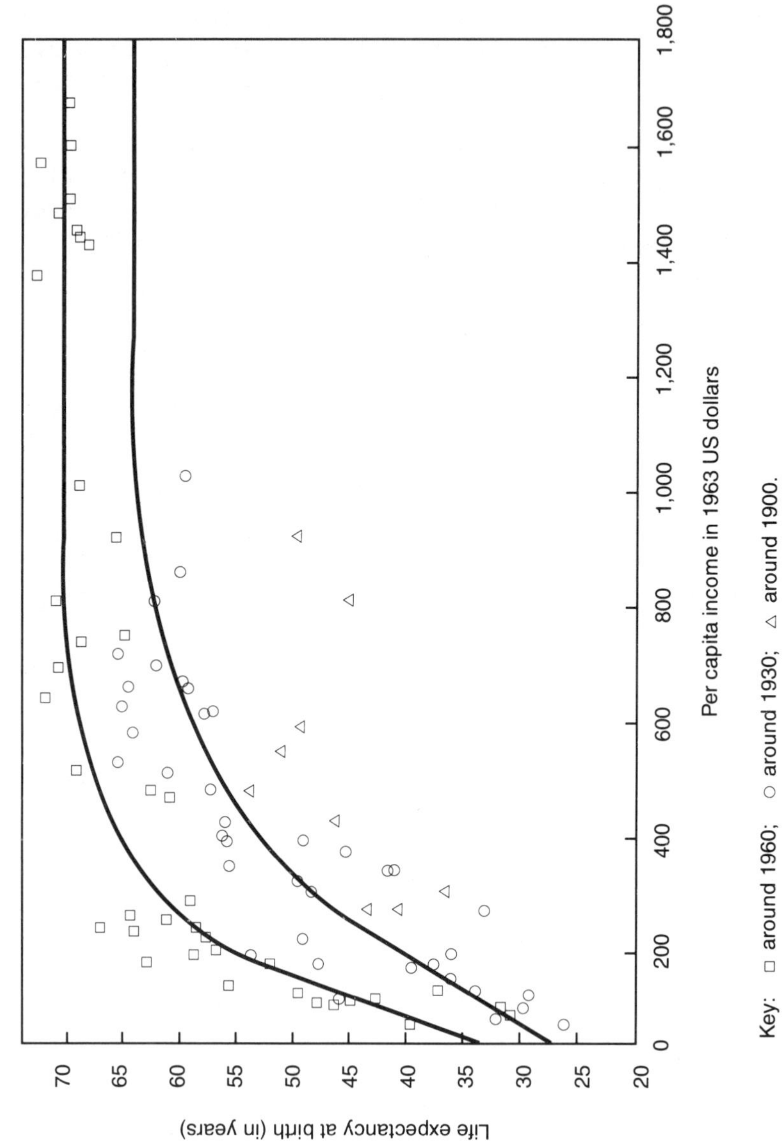

Figure 5.1 The relation between life expectancty at birth and income about 1900, 1930 and 1960 (Source: Preston, 1975)

5.2.3 Preston and McKeown

It is by no means easy to make a choice between the incompatible perspectives of Preston and McKeown and their followers. Still, an attempt will be made.

First, McKeown's statement that only nutrition is of importance can be qualified. Sreter (1988) has convincingly shown that the so-called public health movement in nineteenth-century England contributed greatly to an improved state of health. This movement focused on the amelioration of hygienic conditions, sewers, supplies of clean drinking water, inspection of food quality and housing conditions, and the improvement of preventive medicine. McKeown underestimated the importance of preventive medical technology, in particular vaccination and inoculation. Further, Sreter criticizes McKeown for generalizing on the basis of the health care history of a single country.

However, the difference between Preston and McKeown is not as great as it seems (Vallin, 1989). In Preston's data there is also a clear relation between the level of prosperity and life expectancy at a given moment in time. This relation is especially strong in the case of the poorest developing countries.

One of McKeown's valuable contributions is that he puts the claims of curative medical technology in perspective and stresses the significance of nutrition and undernourishment. The interaction between undernourishment and infectious diseases in particular is very important for a good understanding of the health problems of developing countries. The scepticism about the role of curative medicine may have contributed to the rise of the primary health-care movement (see section 5.3).

On the other hand, the conclusion that medical technology and medical progress are unimportant for developing countries is not justified. We should realize that progress of medical knowledge not only encompasses better techniques of curative treatment for diseases contracted, but also the whole complex of preventive health care, better sanitary conditions, knowledge of the causes of diseases, vaccination, vector control and medication.

5.2.4 The Mosley model and the importance of education

Mosley (1983, see also Mosley, 1984, 1985a, 1985b) has made a significant contribution to the debate on the importance of medical versus socio-economic factors. He concentrates on explanations of child mortality. Like the Bongaarts model presented in Chapter 4, Mosley makes a distinction between underlying social and economic determinants and the intermediate (biological) factors that directly influence the chances of contracting disease and dying. The basic principle is the notion that in a well-protected environment 98 per cent of all children under the age of 5 ought to survive, as in the economically advanced countries. The extent to which this survival rate is not realized should be explained systematically.

A decrease in the chances of survival is the result of primary social and economic determinants. These primary determinants, however, operate through intermediate biological mechanisms, which influence the chances of contracting disease and determine the outcomes of processes of illness. In this model, death is the ultimate result of the multiple episodes of morbidity. It is seldom the result of one isolated instance of illness. The essence of the model is the identification of intermediate variables in order to analyze how primary determinants influence child mortality through the intermediate variables (see also van Norren and van Vianen, 1986).

Mosley's model consists of the following intermediate variables:

1. *Maternal fertility factors*
   (a) Age of childbearing. When mothers are either too young or too old, the children may be at risk.
   (b) Number of children per woman.
   (c) Birth intervals. If intervals between births are short, this may have adverse effects on the state of health. In general, children from large families are more likely to contract diseases than children from small families.
2. *Environmental contamination by infectious agents*
   (a) Contamination of the air.
   (b) Contamination of food, water, or fingers.
   (c) Contamination of the skin (caused by soil or mites).
   (d) Contamination by vectors.
3. *Availability of nutrients for foetus and child*
   (a) Calories.
   (b) Proteins.
   (c) Vitamins.
   (d) Minerals.
4. *Injuries*
   (a) Accidents.
   (b) Injuries inflicted intentionally.
5. *Personal disease control factors:*
   (a) Personal preventive measures.
   (b) Treatment of illnesses once they are contracted.

Figure 5.2 illustrates several significant relationships. First, it shows how behavioural and environmental factors may affect health through the intermediate variables. Thus, the availability and distribution of food within the household affects malnutrition of mothers and their children. Hygienic conditions and circumstances affect susceptibility and resistance to diseases.

In Figure 5.2, prominence is given to the malnutrition–infection syndrome. Malnutrition increases susceptibility and decreases resistance to a variety of (infectious) diseases. Infectious diseases result in metabolic changes and in loss of appetite among children. This causes a decreasing capacity to absorb nutrients, which results in further undernourishment. Child mortality is not the result of any one single factor. Most often there has been a long history of illness leading to retardation of

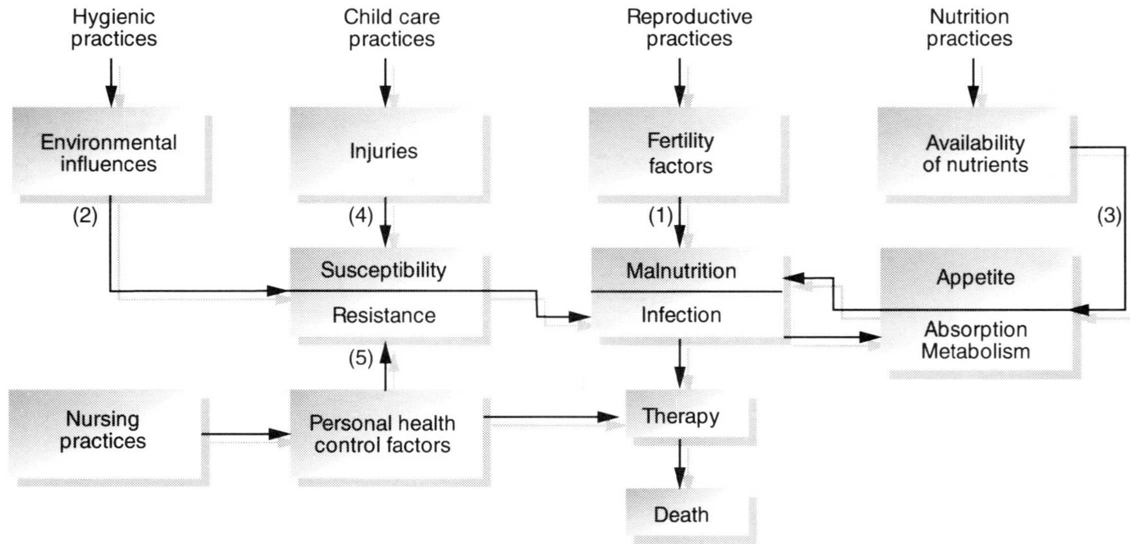

Figure 5.2 Characteristics and behaviour of households which result in sickness and death caused by the five groups of intermediate factors

growth, undernourishment and undermining of a patient's resistance. At the end of the sequence, non-lethal diseases like respiratory infections or diarrhoea may result in death.

Curative health care is just one of the many factors in the model. Often illnesses are not treated until very near the end of the series of illnesses. Many kinds of medication only affect one specific ailment while several diseases contribute to child mortality. Only if a single disease causes high mortality can medical treatments have a substantial, demographic influence (this is the case with combating malaria or vaccinating against tetanus).

Mosley gives two good examples that may serve to put curative medical interventions into perspective. Vaccination against measles prevents people from contracting measles. However, measles is quite a harmless disease, unless one's resistance has already been affected. Treating diarrhoea by means of 'oral rehydration' may prevent children from dying of diarrhoea. Still, this technique does not halt the gradual deterioration and undermining of a patient's health caused by continually recurring bouts of diarrhoea.

Mosley's model refers especially to infant and child mortality. Yet it gives us a more general understanding of the effects of social circumstances on the state of health. De Kadt and Lipton indicate that health risks are greatest in rural areas (de Kadt and Lipton, 1988). Income in rural areas is low, and food supplies are unreliable, especially for those households with insufficient access to land. At the same time, the energy requirements for agricultural labour are immense, in particular during peak periods in the agricultural cycle. If the state of health has been undermined by disease, there is a shortage of energy, just in those periods when it is most needed. Chambers (1982) has shown that a shortfall of food supplies most often occurs when the need for food is greatest, that is, just before harvesting. It is then that food stocks of the previous harvest are depleted, and people need to work hard in preparing for the coming harvest. Furthermore, in tropical regions with a wet climate health conditions are extremely unfavourable in the rainy season, during which much of the agricultural work has to be done. Workers are often exposed to infections, diarrhoea, waterborne parasitic infections, malaria and snakebites (Chambers, 1982). Inhabitants of urban slums are also exposed to serious health risks. In these areas hygienic circumstances in particular are very poor. To some extent this is compensated for by the fact that health services in cities are more accessible than in the countryside.

Although Mosley does not take an explicit stand in the debate on the role of medical technology, he tends to play down the importance of treating specific diseases by means of medical interventions. On the basis of research in Kenya, Mosley concludes that the prime determinant of child mortality is the level of education of the mother. The level of education operates through several intermediate variables: it influences hygienic conditions; it affects the distribution of food within the family; it operates through demographic variables; and it affects the way in which preventive and curative medical services are made use of.

Therefore, a 'primary health care' system should not concentrate merely on medical facilities but rather on the entire complex of nutrition, educational practices, water supply, hygiene, counselling of parents, and so forth. Mosley's argument should not be considered an attack on health care, but rather a plea for considering preventive health care in a broad sense. More attention will be paid to this topic in section 5.3.

5.2.5 Caldwell: the importance of health-care policy

In an interesting article published in 1986 Caldwell raises the question why some developing countries have high scores on health indicators despite low levels of prosperity, while other developing countries with relatively high levels of prosperity have relatively low scores on these health indicators (Caldwell, 1986). Caldwell compared the ranking of countries by their average per capita income in 1982 to their ranking by infant mortality per 1,000 live births, and their ranking by average life expectancy. Caldwell focused on countries whose ranking on health indicators compared favourably with their ranking by per capita income (*superior health achievers*) or unfavourably (*poor health achievers*).

In Table 5.5 Caldwell's method has been applied to more recent data for 1988. Caldwell arranged countries in order of their infant mortality rate and studied those countries whose ranking by infant mortality deviated more than 25 points from their ranking by per capita income. In Table 5.5 the criterion is a rank difference of 15 points. An important difference compared with Caldwell's study is that the ranking by life expectancy deviated more strongly than the ranking by infant mortality. In spite of shifts in ranking since 1982, by and large the more recent data still support Caldwell's conclusions. Among the *superior health achievers* one still finds four of the most important countries with a Buddhist tradition (Thailand, Vietnam, Sri Lanka, and Burma). In the category of *poor health achievers* there is a strikingly large number of Islamic countries. Caldwell associates the positive role of Buddhism with the positive evaluation of education in Buddhism and the Buddhist concept of 'enlightenment'. According to Caldwell, the poor scores of Islamic countries are closely associated with the low social status of women, and with the relatively low appreciation of education in general and female education in particular.

Table 5.5 Comparison of levels of per capita income, infant mortality and life expectancy at birth in 1988

	Per capita GNP ($)	Infant mortality (per 1,000 live births)	Difference in ranking[a]	Life expectancy at birth (in years)	Difference in ranking[b]
Superior health achievements in relation to level of income					
China	330	31	56	70	59
Sri Lanka	420	21	54	71	50
Jamaica	1,070	11	32	73	30
Burundi	240	73	31	49	4
Vietnam[c]	525	44	29	66	29
Zaïre	170	96	27	52	21

Table 5.5 *(continued)*

	Per capita GNP ($)	Infant mortality (per 1,000 live births)	Difference in ranking[a]	Life expectancy at birth (in years)	Difference in ranking[b]
Philippines	630	44	26	64	21
Kenya	370	70	25	59	20
Zambia	290	78	25	53	12
Tanzania	160	104	24	53	30
Thailand	1,000	30	23	65	11
Chile	1,510	20	20	72	21
Indonesia	440	68	19	61	15
Costa Rica	1,690	18	19	75	23
Zimbabwe	650	49	19	63	7
Myanmar (Burma)[c]	525	68	18	60	8
Botswana	1,010	41	16	67	16
Uganda	280	101	16	48	−1
Inferior health achievements in relation to level of income					
Bolivia	570	108	−16	53	−6
Turkey	1,280	75	−18	64	−3
Mauretania	480	125	−19	46	−30
Cameroon	1,010	92	−20	56	−15
Peru	1,300	86	−24	62	−13
Liberia[c]	525	130	−26	50	−18
South Africa	2,290	70	−26	61	−30
Guinea	430	143	−28	43	−30
Yemen	640	128	−30	47	−34
Iran[c]	5,810	64	−30	63	−32
Algeria	2,360	72	−30	64	−16
Congo	910	117	−32	53	−20
Iraq[c]	5,810	68	−35	64	−25
Saudi Arabia	6,200	69	−37	64	−31
Sierra Leone[c]	525	152	−37	42	−38
Libya	5,420	80	−43	61	−38
Gabon	2,970	101	−49	53	−44
Angola[c]	2,225	135	−66	45	−71
OECD	17,449	8		77	

Notes:

[a] Difference between ranking by per capita income and ranking by infant mortality. Ninety-two developing countries have been ranked by the extent of the difference between the two rankings. Only countries with a difference of more than 14 rank positions have been included in the table.

[b] Difference between ranking by per capita income and ranking by life expectancy.

[c] No data on income per capita available in the *World Development Report 1990*. Only the rank number is given. We estimated per capita income as the average of per capita incomes of the countries preceded and following the country in the rank order.

Source: World Bank (1990).

In general, Caldwell sets great store by the educational level of women. Education leads to greater openness with respect to preventive health-care measures and a more effective use of existing health services.

> The key factor seems to be that a woman who goes to school is increasingly seen by both herself and others as being part of a global society with an accepted attitude towards bacterial contamination and corresponding hygienic methods, the use of modern medical facilities and persistence in recommended treatments. . . . [T]hey are more likely to insist that health centres should provide them with adequate treatment. Educated mothers distribute food within the family in closer accord with needs. . . .[T]hey are more likely to behave in accordance with beliefs in bacterial rather than religious pollution. (Caldwell, 1984, p. 108).

Sri Lanka, Costa Rica and the southwest Indian state of Kerala are well-known examples of poor societies with relatively good results in respect to health. Caldwell analyzed the demographic history of these entities and considered the factors that might explain a lower death rate. The factors he identified as important were: autonomy of women; a positive evaluation of education; a relatively open political system; and a tradition of political egalitarianism and radicalism. For Caldwell, the degree of female autonomy is the central factor in mortality declines in poor but open societies. Female autonomy has very positive effects on the quality of child care. The combination of education and political radicalism puts pressure on the political system to develop and maintain good health-care systems. According to Caldwell, investments in the health-care system and progress in medical technology and medical knowledge have contributed greatly to increases in life expectancy, especially in combination with wider social and economic changes.

Centrally planned economies like China, Cuba, and Vietnam also score high on health indicators. In their policies, high priority is given to the realization of effective primary health care systems, accessible to large sections of the population.

The conclusion that can be derived from Caldwell's analysis and from Table 5.5 is that health policy itself is an important explanatory factor. Societies giving high priority to the realization of good health-care systems in the broadest sense were able to achieve excellent results even at low income levels. In this respect, McKeown's idea that only the level of prosperity is of importance proves to be incorrect.

Nevertheless, one should be careful in interpreting the results of an analysis based on the comparison of ranking by per capita income and by health indicators at a given moment in time. A repetition of the exercise in Table 5.5 for different years using data from annual *World Development Reports* shows disturbing shifts from one year to another.[5]

More important, one should also look at the lagged relationships between per capita income and health care. In countries where per capita income shows secular stagnation, sooner or later the economic basis for the maintenance of a good health-care system will inevitably be undermined.

Mosley's thesis that education is more important than medical interventions is also slightly exaggerated. Education – especially education of women – is indeed of great importance. However, the direct effect of education is that the possibilities of the health-care system are utilized more effectively. Therefore, if the health-care facilities themselves are not available, education alone will be of less significance.

Underlying factors like religion and culture are highly important since these factors determine attitudes towards education, the status of women, family planning and a scientific approach to health issues. In an interesting article on the relatively unfavourable state of health in Africa, Vallin has paid a great deal of attention to religious and cultural factors as ultimate determinants of the state of health. Unlike Asian and Latin American societies that were penetrated by great unitary religions like Islam, Christianity, or Buddhism, African societies never experienced the predominance of one single religion or civilization. Rather, there is a patchwork of animistic, Islamic and Christian influences. The extreme cultural, religious, and ethnic diversity in sub-Saharan Africa hampers the effective development of health care services (Vallin, 1989). As adequate knowledge of the cultural backgrounds is lacking, it is difficult to integrate health-care systems into local cultures.

5.3 *Policy*

In building health-care systems after World War II, many developing countries initially copied Western medical institutions. A lot of attention and resources were invested in educating qualified doctors and specialists and in the realization of a system of medical faculties, hospitals, and curative medicine. The attitude towards native, traditional medicine was negative; it was considered non-scientific (Hardiman and Midgley, 1982; Mosley, 1983). Most hospitals were located in national and provincial capitals and were insufficiently accessible to the rural population and to some extent also to the inhabitants of urban slums. In addition, there were 'vertical' campaigns – outside the hospital system – against particular diseases (e.g. malaria, river blindness, tuberculosis, whooping cough) (Netherlands Development Cooperation, 1988). Sometimes these campaigns were fairly successful in the short term, but they were not integrated sufficiently into health care policy as a whole.

There are several objections to such a curative approach to medicine. First, there is too much emphasis on the treatment of diseases (curative medicine) rather than on their prevention. As illustrated by Mosley's model, medical treatment is just one of the many factors influencing disease and mortality.

A second objection is the fact that medical facilities are both expensive and inaccessible to large sections of the population. Medical facilities are heavily concentrated in big cities. Well-trained doctors are seldom willing to work in remote rural areas. Even in urban areas, medical services are predominantly restricted to the more well-to-do sections of society. Paradoxically, there is also an outflow of well-trained doctors to rich countries. Many doctors trained in developing countries are unable or unwilling to find positions in their own country and look for jobs in the affluent countries.

In the course of the 1970s there was increasing criticism of the health strategies pursued up until then. At a large-scale international conference in Alma Ata in 1978, a plea was made for a system of *primary health care*. At this conference it was stated that health is a basic human right and that health care ought to be accessible, affordable, and socially relevant (WHO, 1978).

In the Alma Ata resolutions, primary health care is interpreted in a very broad sense – and rightly so, in the light of the theories discussed in section 5.2. It includes health education and information, adequate food supplies and nutrition, provision of clean water, measures to promote hygiene (sanitation), health care for mothers and their children (including birth control), vaccination against infectious diseases, prevention and control of endemic diseases like malaria, treatment of diseases, adequate supply of medicines, and the promotion of mental health (WHO, 1978, p. 24).

Furthermore, the primary health-care approach emphasizes the reallocation of medical funds to improve the accessibility of medical services. It advocates replacing investments in costly hospitals and medical specialists by investments in cheaper local health-care centres and simply trained paramedic personnel. Health-care policy is seen in relation to other aspects of socio-economic policy; where the benefits of economic development are distributed more equally, the chances of improving health care are greater.

Another important aspect is the participation of the local population in the preparation and execution of health-care policies. Thus health-care workers recruited from the local population will function more effectively. Health-care facilities supported and monitored by the local population will tend to be more effective than similar facilities administered from some inaccessible bureaucratic centre.

For the social relevance and acceptance of primary health care, it is important that health services are adapted to the local culture. Traditional medicine should not to be eradicated or devalued. It should be merged with newer medical insights. People often consult both traditional and modern healers. It pays to train traditional healers in order to narrow the gap between various medical approaches. For example, retraining programmes for traditional midwives have been quite successful.

The Alma Ata conference has been extremely influential. In a series of resolutions of international organizations the recommendations made at the conference have been adopted. National authorities have been urged to implement them. In 1979 the United Nations Assembly endorsed the Alma Ata recommendations. In 1981 the World Health Organisation (WHO) adopted the *Global Strategy for Health for All by the Year 2000* (WHO, 1981). Moreover, the WHO makes use of indicators to monitor the degree to which authorities meet their commitments with respect to health policy (see WHO, 1987, 1993).

In detailed evaluations published in 1987 and 1993, the WHO tried to determine the degree to which the objectives of the *Global Strategy for Health for All by the Year 2000* were actually being realized. As shown in Tables 5.1, 5.2 and 5.3, there have been substantial declines in infant and child mortality and increases in life expectancy – especially in Asia and Latin America. But, the probability of dying before the age of 5 is still 97 out of 1,000 live births. Including perinatal mortality, the WHO indicates that in the least developed countries 200 out of every 1,000 children born alive in 1991 will die before their fifth year.[6] Diarrhoea, acute respiratory infections, undernourishment, and vaccination-preventable diseases are still the most important causes of death for infants and children.

In the 1980s, the economic crisis and cuts in government expenditures resulting from structural adjustment programmes advocated by the World Bank and the IMF affected health care and education budgets negatively (Cornia, 1984). In the second half of the 1980s, the percentage of national income spent on health showed a slight increase, but real educational expenditures per capita declined (WHO, 1993). In sub-Saharan Africa, malnutrition is on the increase and AIDS is placing a heavy burden on already overstressed health-care systems. Health indicators show that sub-Saharan Africa lags further and further behind other regions. Whatever doubts one may have concerning the blessings of economic growth, it is obvious that economic stagnation has deeply unfavourable effects on the state of health. Though death rates are still declining in most African countries and the life expectation is still increasing, this is no longer true in countries most heavily hit by AIDS. There mortality is increasing and life expectancy has started to decline.

The WHO monitoring reports discern slow improvements in the percentage of populations covered by elements of primary health care and in the commitment of governments to primary health-care objectives. The availability of safe drinking and sanitary facilities (e.g. excreta disposal, waste treatment, sewer systems) has improved. But 1,500 million people still lack access to clean water supplies and 2,000 million live without adequate sanitation (WHO, 1993). Vaccination of children against six targeted diseases (diphtheria, tetanus, measles, poliomyelitis, tuberculosis and whooping cough) has clearly improved. There have been noticeable expansions of local community health services. The numbers of health workers, health volunteers, and trained traditional midwives have increased. In some countries there is even an oversupply of medical personnel.

However, there are still significant problems. Though the percentage availability of elements of primary health care has improved, this does not mean that coordinated systems of primary health care have been developed. Also, due to population growth the absolute numbers of people without access to health-care facilities are increasing, rather than decreasing. There is an outflow of highly skilled medical personnel to more developed countries. There is a serious maldistribution of health personnel and health resources. It is still exceedingly difficult to persuade well-qualified doctors to work in rural areas. Semi-skilled medical personnel (community health workers, village counsellors, traditional healers) are paid very poorly. Their motivation is often minimal. Moreover, expectations with respect to briefly trained paramedics were unrealistically high (Netherlands Development Cooperation, 1988).

The ideals of community participation in and democratic control of health services have been insufficiently realized. Local power structures frequently stand in the way of real community participation (Mosley, 1983). The organization of medical systems is still highly centralized and hierarchical. The efficiency of medical systems is low. yThe *broad* concept of primary health care – in which health care is integrated into overall economic and social development policy – is more rhetoric than reality. Insofar as primary health-care services have been established, they remain restricted to medical facilities and services in the *narrow* sense.

Even today insufficient attention is being paid to preventive health care. The emphasis remains – not very surprisingly – on curative medicine (Netherlands Development Cooperation, 1988). Overall, the availability of medical services is inadequate. According to Leisinger, eight out of ten patients in developing countries still consult traditional healers, medicine men, or witch doctors (Leisinger, 1989). Moreover, the desired integration of modern and traditional approaches in medicine has usually turned out to be negligible in practice.

5.3.1 Health and economic development

Much has been written about the relationships between investments in health care and economic development (e.g. see Mushkin, 1962; Baldwin and Weisbrod, 1974; Popkin, 1978; Barlow, 1979; Walsh, 1990; Keyzer, 1993). Despite numerous attempts, though, it has not proved possible to quantify the relation between improvements in the health situation and changes in economic output in a satisfactory way. Most researchers attempt to estimate the losses in output caused by illness and reduction of hours worked due to premature death. But since there is widespread unemployment and underutilization of labour in most developing countires, better health outcomes do not necessarily result in higher employment or output. Moreover, workers may have compensated for low productivity due to illness by working longer hours.

One can distinguish the following relationships between health and economic performance:

1. Illness undermines the productive capacity of individuals. Downright disablement or invalidity make it impossible to work.
2. Illness and malnutrition often lead to loss of body weight and a decrease in human energy. Undernourished and ill people become listless, lethargic and passive. Protracted illness and malnutrition can lead to impairment of mental functions, creativity and learning potential. All this implies direct negative effects on labour productivity. Low labour productivity is important at macroeconomic levels. It is even more important for households that depend on their own labour for their livelihood. Illness leads to lower production in subsistence agriculture (Chambers, 1982; de Kadt and Lipton, 1988), to lower revenues for the self-employed and to lower wage incomes for labourers. It is not hard to imagine the disastrous effects of illness on the life chances of households trying to survive at subsistence level. Illness affects labour productivity in three different ways:

(a) A decrease in the number of hours a person is capable of working per year. Absence from work due to illness is included under this heading.
(b) A decrease in the intensity with which a person can work.
(c) A choice for less productive activities, requiring less energy and effort (Popkin, 1978).

The so-called *efficiency wage theory* is based on such relationships (Leibenstein, 1957; Bardhan, 1993; Keyzer, 1993). This theory states that it may be inefficient to let market relations determine the minimum wage for labour. The market-determined wage level in a labour surplus economy may be too low to guarantee sufficient food and health, so that labour productivity is undermined. Thus it may be economically efficient to set minimum wages above free market rates.

3. The prevalence of diseases such as river blindness may make it impossible or unattractive to open up certain fertile areas for agriculture. Eradication of such diseases can lead to improvements in productive potential in the very short term (Hardiman and Midgley, 1982).
4. High child mortality and low life expectancy could result in a decrease in total labour supply. In the light of widespread underutilization of labour this is not a serious problem for developing counties. However, if mortality is highly concentrated in certain occupational groups, there can be negative effects on production. High infant and child mortality also leads to *replacement fertility.* This involves a decrease in the productive potential of women during pregnancy and the period of breast-feeding.
5. Low life expectancy implies that the number of years a worker can be active is reduced (UN, 1984, p. 4). Low life expectancy is also not conducive to future-oriented attitudes. Further, as mentioned before, illness may lead to a decrease in learning potential. As a result, investments in education and human capital become less attractive. Conversely, investment in education may lead to higher productivity of investment in health care (Mushkin, 1962).

Despite great empirical uncertainties almost all researchers conclude that investment in health care also makes positive contributions to economic development.

QUESTIONS FOR REVIEW

1. Discuss the characteristics of the epidemiological transition. Do the patterns of disease and health change in the same way in all societies, in the course of development?
2. Discuss the relationships between per capita income and life expectation.
3. Do improvements in medical technology provide an adequate explanation of the overall decline in death rates and increases in life expectation in developing countries?

4. What is the malnutrition-infection syndrome? Why is education considered to be an important factor in combating child mortality?

5. What are the most important differences between preventive health care and curative health care in the context of developing countries?

Notes

1. I would like to thank Harry van Vianen for his valuable advice concerning the subject matter of this chapter.
2. Sometimes child mortality is defined in a different fashion, namely, as the chance of dying between the ages of 1 and 5 years for every thousand children who have reached the age of 1.
3. Different statistical sources are unanimous with regard to mortality trends, but not with regard to mortality levels. WHO (1993) infant mortality statistics are higher than those published in *World Population Projections 1994–95* (World Bank, 1994b).
4. During the last couple of years the significance of cardiovascular diseases has decreased significantly (UN, 1984; WHO, 1993).
5. For instance, one of the striking differences between Table 5.5 and Caldwell's 1982 data is that India, one of marked superior achievers in 1982, is no longer among the relatively successful countries in 1988.
6. The WHO (1993) figures are substantially higher than those from *World Population Projections* (World Bank, 1994b). I assume that this is because they include perinatal mortality, which accounts for half of all infant mortality.

6 *Education and development*

Like health, education can be both an end and a means. It is one of the basic human rights and a developmental goal in its own right. At the same time, education can contribute to the realization of other important developmental goals. Functions and tasks generally ascribed to education include the following:

1. Promotion of economic growth and development. Investment in the physical capital stock is not sufficient for economic development; investment in 'human capital' is also required.
2. Modernization of attitudes and mentalities in society.
3. Political socialization, promotion of a sense of civic responsibility, contributing to national integration and national political consciousness in developing countries.
4. Reducing social inequality and increasing social mobility.
5. Contributing to personal growth, development and emancipation.

Immediately after World War II, expectations concerning the role of education in development were high. Expansion and improvement of education were generally considered as essential to development. Governments in developing countries were prepared to invest heavily in education. Families saw education as the main way to improve their children's chances in life. International organizations were eager to provide financial and technical support for the construction of new educational systems. Within a brief time span education became one of the important sources of employment in the modern sector of many developing countries.

However, since the 1970s, optimism about the contribution of education has been shaken. Not all investment in education proved beneficial to development. Resources were often insufficient and the quality of education was disappointing.

This chapter will present a survey of important debates and theories concerning the role of education in development (section 6.1). It will also discuss the educational performance of developing countries in the post-war period (sections 6.2 and 6.3). Important problems and bottlenecks in education are the subject of section 6.4. Throughout the chapter, special attention will be paid to the role of education in the process of economic development.

6.1 *Theories of the contribution of education to economic development*

6.1.1 'Human capital' theory

The notion of education as an investment in economic growth arose in the late 1950s in the United States. Economists such as Abramovitz, Solow and Denison found that the growth of national product in economically advanced countries could not be adequately explained by the growth of the physical capital stock and the growth of the labour force. Considerable part of growth remained unaccounted for (Abramovitz, 1956; Solow, 1957; Denison, 1962). In addition to the growth in physical capital stock, the increase in human capital turned out to be of great importance as well. As people became more and more educated, developed more skills, and improved their reading and writing abilities, it was argued they became more productive and were better able to handle existing and new production techniques. The inclusion of human capital in growth accounting studies substantially reduced the unexplained residual in growth (Maddison, 1987).

Human capital theory developed this line of thought further, particularly at a microlevel (Schultz, 1961, 1971, 1988; Becker, 1964; Blaug, 1972, 1976, 1990). The empirical foundation for this theory was the close relationship observed in many societies between the number of years of education received and a person's income level. The essence of human capital theory was the notion that individuals (supported by their parents) were willing to invest in their own education so that they would be able to earn a higher income in the future. These investments consisted of educational expenses and income forgone due to delayed entry into the labour market. The theoretical link between investment in education and the level of income was labour productivity – just as in the macro approach. Increasing the level of schooling would lead to increased labour productivity. In line with neoclassical economic theory, greater labour productivity would result in higher incomes for the categories of employees concerned.[1]

Not only individuals would benefit from investment in education. Society as a whole would also benefit from an increasing supply of better educated workers and citizens. Such 'external effects' are a justification for public subsidies to education. In almost every country in the world, a considerable part of the cost of education is subsidized by the government.

Recently these ideas have resurfaced in the context of 'endogenous growth theory' (Romer, 1986; Lucas, 1988; Barro, 1991).[2] Endogenous growth theory suggests that investments in technological change, research and development, and human capital are subject to increasing returns, due to spillover effects. The more a country has previously invested in technology, and in human and physical capital, the more it will profit from additional investment. Such theories thus offer an explanation for increasing divergence of economic performance in the world economy.

Another version of these ideas is contained in the notion of 'conditional convergence' (Mankiw *et al.*, 1992; Wolff and Gittleman, 1993). Given characteristics such as a country's initial investment rate and educational attainment, countries with lower initial productivity will tend to converge on countries with higher productivity. However, if the initial conditions are less favourable, economic divergence will tend to prevail.

Though human capital theory was initially developed in the United States and Europe, it was soon applied to developing countries as well. The idea of furthering development by means of education had already achieved considerable popularity, well before the rise of this theory (Foster, 1965a; Krieger, 1988). Many members of the new elites in developing countries had received their education during the colonial period. It was often via education that they had been exposed to ideas about human rights, nationalism and development. At the same time, colonial educational systems had offered them insufficient opportunities to develop their talents. Independence provided an opportunity for rapid improvement in access to education. Education was also regarded as a modernizing force, which would help detach people from traditional cultural influences and social relationships that were seen as obstacles to modernization.

Human capital theory – in both its microeconomic and its macroeconomic guises – provided an additional justification for increased efforts in the field of education. The theory was embraced wholeheartedly by national and international policymakers.

Human capital theory provides a framework for the systematic evaluation of the costs and benefits of different kinds of education. The costs include:

1. School fees, costs of books, teaching materials, school uniforms, and so forth.
2. Income forgone while receiving an education.

The benefits consist of the difference between the lifetime income of an individual with a given amount of education and the lifetime income he would receive if he had not had this education. On the basis of the total costs and benefits one can calculate the average annual return on an educational investment, the so-called *rate of return*.

One of the interesting research findings was the fact that in developing countries the rate of return on investment in education was higher than the rate of return on investment in physical capital (Psacharopoulos, 1985). Another interesting finding was that the rates of return for primary education were consistently higher than those for secondary and higher education (Blaug, 1976; Psacharopoulos, 1985; Schultz,

1988). On these grounds developing countries should give priority to primary education. In practice, however, this has not occurred.

Since governments usually bear the greater part of the costs of education, individual calculations of costs and benefits will differ from social calculations of costs and benefits. Without exception, individual rates of return are higher than social rates of return (Coombs, 1985). This is one of the factors contributing to the explosive growth in the demand for education in developing countries.

Prior to a discussion of criticisms of human capital theory, the question should be raised as to why investment in human capital (education) should lead to higher productivity and economic development. There are a number of possible answers to this question, as follows:

1. Education teaches specific professional skills required for professional practice (training for mechanic, doctor or plumber).
2. Workers who have mastered the three Rs – reading, writing, and arithmetic – are more productive than those who have not. Literate employees are able to read instructions, keep records, make calculations, and so on.
3. Education and literacy lead to changed attitudes which indirectly result in higher productivity (Anderson and Bowman, 1976). For example, increased literacy and education changes people's perceptions of the alternatives open to them. They will start looking for professions or geographic regions where the earnings are higher.
4. Education and literacy contribute to the development of commercial and financial activities. These activities require people who can work as bookkeepers, or clerks, and who can write letters, file papers, or manipulate numbers. Literate people are more likely to utilize paper money, hold bank accounts, and use other financial instruments. Literacy is a prerequisite for the development of financial systems and it influences the supply of savings (Sandberg, 1982).
5. For market mechanisms to function, people have to be able to acquire information and orient themselves amongst alternatives. Education contributes to this. Effectively functioning markets in turn contribute to the efficient allocation of productive resources and thus to increases in productivity.
6. Technological development proceeds at an ever faster pace. It needs well-educated employees to understand and apply the continuous flow of new production techniques. This applies not least to agriculture, where new techniques can lead to dramatic increases in productivity (Schultz, 1988).
7. In general, literacy has positive effects on the dissemination of new ideas and technologies in a society.
8. In modern society the rate of technological development itself depends on continued investment in education, research and development. A sufficient supply of scientific and technical personnel is needed to adapt existing technologies from abroad and develop new ones.
9. Education promotes geographic and occupational mobility (Easterlin, 1981; Sandberg, 1982). Some authors consider the loosening of age-old ties to village

or ancestral occupation as a prerequisite for modernization. Geographic and occupational mobility contribute to a more efficient allocation of the production factor labour. Of course, increased mobility also has drawbacks, such as, for example, unrestricted migration to urban areas.

6.1.2 Criticisms of human capital theory

Though highly influential, human capital theory has also been severely criticized (Blaug, 1976, 1985). The basic points of criticism are the following:

1. The high correlation between education and personal income does not necessarily mean that education makes workers more productive. Nothing is more difficult to measure than marginal productivity (Blaug, 1990).
2. We may have sufficient information on income inequality at a given moment in time, but it is very difficult to draw any conclusions from this concerning the distribution of *lifetime incomes*. Next, it is hard to estimate the income forgone while individuals are being educated. Finally, if we want to calculate the social rate of return of education, we will find the external effects of education difficult to estimate. With so many uncertainties, the whole notion of a cost-benefit analysis of educational investment becomes rather problematic.
3. The benefits of education are not merely economic. Education also increases one's social status and may lead to greater work satisfaction.
4. In most cost-benefit analyses of education, only the number of years of education is taken into account. The quality of education and the type of education (e.g. technical, languages) is disregarded.
5. The demand for education does not only depend on costs and benefits, but also on the ability to pay for education.
6. It is not just the objective relation between costs and benefits that matters, but also the *perception* of this relation. If people believe education will increase their opportunities, they are more likely to make sacrifices for it.
7. Education in itself is not important. Individual talents and characteristics of the parental family are the crucial determinants of one's future income. Education merely translates these characteristics into diplomas.
8. Education is not only investment; it is also consumption. Many people study because they find it enjoyable or intrinsically interesting.

6.1.3 Screening theory

The most extreme version of preceding criticisms of human capital theory is contained in *screening theory* (Berg, 1970; Dore, 1976; Blaug, 1985). This theory argues that education in itself does not contribute to a person's productivity. The knowledge and skills acquired in educational institutions are not applied in one's later career. The specific skills required in a profession are learned on the job rather than at school.

Why, then, are higher-educated employees paid more than less well educated employees? Screening theory states that employers find it hard to predict the future performance of job applicants. They use educational qualifications and diplomas as a screening system for ability, achievement motivation, social background, and the right personality traits. Schooling is an indication of trainability itself. Actual training starts when one starts working.

Thus radical versions of the screening theory argue that education merely 'reproduces' social inequality from generation to generation (Williamson, 1979). The main function of education for the masses is to teach them discipline, respect for authority, punctuality, obediance, ability to cooperate, and concentration (Bowles and Gintis, 1976). Education therefore prepares labourers for inferior level, routine tasks in productive organizations. People from higher social strata are prepared for top level positions in the hierarchical structure. Their education develops personal qualities such as self-reliance, self-esteem, autonomy, flexibility, capacity to assume leadership roles, managerial qualities, and initiative.

The screening theory leads to unfavourable conclusions about the relevance of education for developing countries. Expanding the educational system merely results in diploma inflation and a scramble for the highest diplomas (*credentialism*). On the labour market, people with higher diplomas displace people with lower educational qualifications without any improvement in productivity. For example, university graduates displace graduates of polytechnics, and graduates of polytechnics displace workers with a secondary education, while the latter in turn displace people with a primary education. This process is referred to as *bumping down*.

6.1.4 Criticisms of screening theory

Like human capital theory, screening theory is also open to criticism (Blaug, 1985):

1. If screening theory is right and education does not contribute to productivity, it is hard to explain why self-employed people with a higher education are usually more successful than self-employed people with less education.
2. In screening theory, educational qualifications explain differences in initial earnings. In later stages of a career the relation between education and income should become weaker as employers gain first-hand experience of an employee's productivity. In fact, however, the correlation between education and income persists throughout people's working lives.
3. If selection is the only real function of the educational system, one might as well use less laborious and less expensive methods of selection and recruitment. Psychological tests would serve just as well to identify the right personality traits. However, in practice, applicants are never selected exclusively on the basis of psychological tests.

6.1.5 A preliminary evaluation

The debate between the proponents and critics of human capital theory is still very much open. In particular, the more extreme positions in the debate are based on faith and ideological conviction rather than on empirical evidence.

Since Émile Durkheim, sociologists have emphasized that one of the important functions of education is the transmission of values, standards, attitudes, and knowledge to successive generations. In this sense, education has always had a conserving function and will tend to maintain existing structures of inequality. Yet, we also know that education may often lead to change. A well-known example is the colonial educational system, within which members of future nationalist elites received their education. They later rebelled against colonialism in name of political and humanistic ideals transmitted by Western-style education. Education can also be an importants means of upward social mobility. Groups with few chances of upward mobility within traditional societies were now offered opportunities to improve their positions by way of education.

It is an interesting empirical question which of these influences – the conserving or the change-oriented – predominated in different societies and historical periods. As I will set out below, the dynamic, change-oriented functions of education predominated in developing countries in the post-war period. Here, however, I would like to make a prelimary evaluation of the debate between advocates of the human capital theory and those of screening theory.

Screening theory has drawn our attention to several aspects of education that are also of great importance to developing countries:

1. On the job many employees do not use any of the cognitive knowledge they learned in school. Most skills needed in modern industries can be acquired within a few weeks. In this respect 'on-the-job training' and 'learning by doing' are of great importance.
2. Screening is one of the social functions of education. Given insufficient information, it is plausible to conclude that educational qualifications serve as an important screening device for job applicants.
3. Expanding the educational system does not always contribute to economic development. Especially the rapid expansion of secondary and higher education may lead to 'diploma inflation'. (Of course, it remains perfectly rational for every individual to try to improve his or her life chances by gaining as many educational degrees as possible.)

The conclusion of screening theory, that education adds 'nothing' to already existing personality traits and thus has no autonomous influence on productivity, is no longer tenable. The most important contribution of education is indeed 'learning to learn'. Reading, writing, and arithmetic are basic requirements for being able to learn later on in life.[3] At higher educational levels, learning to think analytically and evaluate information independently are important preconditions for future learning on the job. On the job training is possible in part thanks to the capacity to learn, developed in the formal schooling system.

Evidently, social background and inherited talents also determine one's educational career. However, inherited talent and high status are not sufficient for success in modern societies. It is the schooling system that translates such factors into qualities that are useful for society.

With regard to developing countries, one may even argue that education today is even more important than it used to be in the presently more advanced countries. New production techniques in the industrial and agricultural sector require ever more knowledge and understanding. The pace of technological development is increasing. Only a well-trained labour force can benefit from the opportunities of adopting modern technologies from abroad and adapting these to domestic production processes. Educational investment thus contributes to the building of the technological capabilities of a country (Hobsbawm, 1969; Evenson and Westphal, 1995).

Though much criticism of human capital theory is justified, I therefore conclude that it is worth while for developing countries to invest in further development of their educational systems.

6.1.6 Education as a necessary or sufficient condition for development

Human capital theory takes neoclassical microeconomics as its point of departure and focuses on the costs and benefits of education in a country. An alternative approach is the historical and comparative study of the role of education and schooling in the different processes of economic development.

In a classic study based on international comparisons of indicators of literacy and economic development, Bowman and Anderson (1963) conclude that economic development can only set in once the level of literacy among the adult male population has reached at least 40 per cent. Analogous to Rostow's theory of the stages of economic growth (see Chapter 3) – which argues that modern economic growth will commence only if physical investment exceeds a certain threshold value – Bowman and Anderson argue that literacy is a *necessary condition* for economic growth. Especially in European and North American history, growth of human capital has been more important than has hitherto been recognized. Education, however, is not a *sufficient* condition for growth and development. Without investment in physical capital and the rise of institutions that provide positive incentives to productive efforts there will be no economic development.

Once the 40 per cent threshold has been reached further development of literacy has little impact, according to Bowman and Anderson. It is not until literacy exceeds the 70 per cent level that it will have positive effects on further economic development.

As with human capital, an interesting debate developed concerning the Bowman and Anderson hypothesis (Tortella, 1990). The essential problem is how to determine the direction of causality empirically. It is indisputable that on average the more affluent societies are also more literate and have more training per head of the population. However, this may be explained by the fact that people with higher incomes are willing to pay more for education than people at lower income levels. According to Schultz, the income elasticity of education is 1.4. This means that if the national income rises by 1 per cent, expenditure on education goes up 1.4 per cent.

Some authors try to solve this problem by examining the relations between literacy at an earlier moment in time (A) and national income at a later moment in time (B). For Spain Nuñez (1990) has estimated that the level of literacy affects provincial per capita income with a 35-year lag. Lars Sandberg (1982) even states that for European countries the degree of literacy in 1850 is the best predictor of national income in 1970. In the short run, however, there is no connection between literacy and economic growth.

For Sandberg too, education is only one of the relevant factors in economic development. The volume of investment in physical capital is also of great importance. Sandberg argues that countries will benefit more from physical investment when their initial level of education is higher. Examples supporting this proposition are provided by the currently affluent Scandinavian countries, Sweden and Finland. In the nineteenth century these countries were quite poor but at the same time they had high levels of literacy which were the foundation for their later growth. Japan can also be quoted as an example supporting Sandberg's theory (Hanley, 1990; Pilat, 1994). Around 1869 the Japanese were already highly educated. Since then Japan has continued to invest in education as part of its national development and modernization strategy. The investment in physical capital which started after the Meiji Revolution in 1869 enabled Japan to experience rapid economic growth from the late nineteenth century onwards. Finally, the rapidly industrializing Southeast Asian countries such as South Korea and Taiwan also reached a high level of education at a relatively early stage. This historical work is consistent with the notion of 'conditional convergence' discussed above, in which a high level of education is seen as one of the necessary conditions for catch-up (Mankiw *et al.*, 1992).

Other authors object to the notion of education as a necessary condition for development. Mitch argues that the level of literacy is not as essential to agricultural and industrial development as Bowman and Sanders suppose (Mitch, 1990). Like the critics of the human capital theory, Mitch argues that during the Industrial Revolution it was not important for the working masses to be able to read or write. Literacy only mattered for a limited number of clerks, engineers, bookkeepers, managers, and foremen. Before the twentieth century literacy did not play a major role in agricultural development either. The development of human capacities is important, but this does not always require a formal education. There are 'functional ialternatives' such as working experience, on-the-job training, and 'learning by doing'.

It is also argued that in England and elsewhere the labour force was actually 'deskilled' in the course of the Industrial Revolution. Traditional craftsmanlike skills became obsolete due to the development of mass production (Thompson, 1963; Nicholas, 1990). The educational level of labourers remained unchanged at best. Nicholas, however, does acknowledge the fact that on the eve of the Industrial Revolution England had a high level of education.

In an interesting attempt at synthesis, Sandberg argues that while education has been an important factor in the history of modern European development, there have always been alternatives to education (Sandberg, 1990). Russia, for example, had an extremely low level of education during the nineteenth century. In part it compensated for this by using highly capital intensive methods of production, which reduced the need for skilled labour. In a like fashion, the increased role of government in the mobilization of financial resources compensated for underdeveloped financial markets (Sandberg, 1982).

In this textbook it is not possible to unravel all these controversies in depth and to arrive at authoritative conclusions. However, it is interesting to note that there are two areas of convergence between the various participants in this debate:

1. Since the mid-nineteenth century, education has become increasingly important, as the scientific and technological bases of economic development became more prominent. For instance, investment in education and technology since the late nineteenth century is considered one of the crucial factors in the rise of Germany as an economic power. Insufficient investment in education in England – particularly in technical and vocational training – is seen as contributing to the relative decline of the former economic leader.
2. In developing countries today education is more important than it ever was in Western countries, because it increases the potential to adopt and adapt new technologies. The pace of international technological change is much higher than before. Thus developing countries now have both the opportunity and the necessity to adopt technological innovations very rapidly in order to develop.

6.2 *Indicators of educational development*

Before discussing empirical developments in education in developing countries, the following section will provide a brief discussion of several well-known indicators of educational development (Coombs, 1985).

6.2.1 Indicators of educational enrolment

The *gross enrolment ratio* is the percentage relationship in a given year between the total enrolment at each educational level (primary, secondary, or tertiary) and the total estimated population in the corresponding age bracket. It is a rather inadequate criterion which does not take into account that the numerator includes children outside the relevant age category (e.g. pupils of secondary school age still enrolled in primary education). The gross enrolment ratio, therefore, presents a too rosy picture of educational enrolment. Sometimes it is even higher than 100 per cent. Coombs suggests that this indicator overestimates actual enrolment by 10 to 30 per cent (Coombs, 1985).

The *net enrolment ratio* is a better criterion of enrolment. This ratio indicates what percentage of each school age group is actually somewhere in the school system. The problem with this ratio is that it does not show where in the educational system the pupils actually are.

Indicators of educational enrolment are frequently used. Nevertheless, they have several important defects (Hardiman and Midgley, 1982; Coombs, 1985):

1. Overreporting. Enrolment data are inflated since schools have an interest in high enrolment figures in order to receive more subsidies. The same applies to reports on educational enrolment by national ministries of education to UNESCO.
2. Enrolment data do not show how many students actually finish a particular cycle of education. In fact, not more than 60 per cent of all students actually complete the educational cycle in which they are enrolled. Dropping out of school is quite common. Between 20 and 75 per cent of all students do not get beyond the fourth year of primary school (Coombs, 1985; see also Table 6.3).
3. Enrolment data provide no information on the quality of education. At many schools there is substantial absenteeism. Especially in rural areas school children are expected to work in the fields during agricultural peak periods. Often children are absent for more than one-third of the school year. Besides, the data do not tell us anything about the size of school classes, the poor quality of the teaching materials, and the usually low level of qualification and poor motivation of the teaching staff.

6.2.2 Educational attainments

Data on enrolment tell us something about the efforts made by a society to educate its people. However, they provide little information on the outcomes of the educational process by the time people leave school and enter the labour market. A useful alternative indicator is the average number of years of schooling completed by people in different age categories. This indicator provides information on the quantity of human capital per person. Thus one could look at years of schooling completed for all persons over 15 years of age or all persons over 25 years of age.

Psacharopoulos and Arriagada (1986) have made estimates of years of schooling in the labour force, based on labour force surveys and population censuses. They argue that this is one of the best indicators of the stock of human capital. Psacharopoulos and Arriagada weight the percentages of the labour force that have completed a given educational cycle with the cumulative length in years of that educational cycle. They distinguish six phases or cycles: no education, incomplete primary education, complete primary education, incomplete secondary education, complete secondary education, and higher education (see Table 6.4).

6.2.3 Financial indicators

Financial indicators give us an idea of the efforts of governments and societies to develop educational systems and the resources available for education. Well-known indicators are as follows:

1. Government educational expenditures as a percentage of the national income.
2. Government educational expenditures as a percentage of total government expenditures.
3. Per capita government expenditure on education.

These data refer to government expenditure only. Private expenditure on education is not included.

6.2.4 Physical indicators

Physical indicators refer to numbers of teachers, pupil teacher ratios, numbers of buildings, and so on.

6.2.5 Literacy

Most of the indicators discussed above refer to educational inputs: enrolment, numbers of teachers, amounts of money, and years of education. Far less is known about the results of the educational process. Apparently it is possible to go to school for years without learning to read, write or calculate – even in economically advanced countries.

One of the few indicators of educational outcomes is the degree of literacy. Even here, though, one should be careful. Often literacy is determined by means of survey questions about literacy to which one can answer 'yes' or 'no', without any test of the actual skills themselves. In other estimates of literacy it is assumed that a person is literate when he or she has attended primary school for at least four years. Moreover, literacy itself is defined in very different ways (Ooijens and van Kampen, 1989). According to UNESCO a person is functionally literate, 'if a person is able to engage in all those activities in which literacy is required for effective functioning of his group and community and for enabling him to continue to use reading, writing and calculation for his own and the community's development' (quoted in Ooijens and van Kampen, 1989, p. 2). Most often literacy is expressed as a percentage of the population over 15 years of age.[4]

6.3 *Educational performance in developing countries*

6.3.1 The initial situation after World War II

In most developing countries the state of education after World War II was very poor. Colonial authorities had never invested much in education (Altbach, 1978, 1982; Heinink and Koetsier, 1984). Under colonialism there were two dominant motives for providing education:

1. Religion: missionary work was important in primary education.
2. Educating native elites to fulfil subordinate positions in colonial administration. For members of native elites, a limited number of secondary and higher educational institutions were created, modelled on Western educational institutions. The language of education was the colonial 'mother tongue'. The substance of the curriculum was Western-oriented.

The educational system had a dual structure (Heinink and Koetsier, 1984). Primary education in rural areas emphasized practical and moral training under missionary influence. In addition, there was academically oriented primary, secondary and higher education for children of the foreign colonial elites. This education was also open to very restricted numbers of children of native elites.

In academically oriented education the emphasis was on preparing pupils for employment in the small modern sector of the economy. It was a weak imitation of Western educational systems. In the curriculum the humanities, and, in particular, languages, predominated. Little attention was paid to the natural sciences and to native languages and cultures.

Of course, there were differences between the colonial educational systems. More than the British, the French tried to create small elites of assimilated 'coloured French individuals' by means of education (Altbach, 1982). Of all colonizing powers, the British paid most attention to education; the Belgians and the Portuguese the least. On the eve of independence there were hardly any graduates of higher education in Belgian Congo.

In uncolonized countries such as China and Thailand educational opportunities were also rather limited until World War II. In India and in the Islamic world, pre-colonial, religiously oriented educational systems persisted alongside colonial education, although their importance tended to decline under colonialism. The most favourable situation was to be found in Latin America where decolonialization had been completed early in the nineteenth century and formal education had been developed furthest. Even here, the level of education in the 1950s was still very low.

In the sections below, empirical data will be presented on developments in education since World War II. The educational performance of developing countries should be judged in the light of very poor initial conditions.

6.3.2 Increases in educational enrolment

The data on gross enrolment in Table 6.1 indicate that enrolment in developing countries increased substantially after 1960. With respect to primary education Asian and Latin American countries in particular seem to be on the way to full enrolment. On the African continent as well great progress has been made, though less than on other continents. The data indicate an unambiguous narrowing of the gap between educational levels in developing countries and in more affluent countries (see also Schultz, 1988).

Table 6.1 Gross enrolment ratios[a] by educational level, country, region, 1960–1992[b]

Country/region	Primary education		Secondary education		Higher education	
	1960	1992	1960	1992	1960	1992
Bangladesh	47	77	8	19	1	4
China		123		51		2
India	41	102	23	49	2	6
Indonesia	67	115	6	43	1	10
Pakistan	30	46	6	21	1	3
Philippines	95	110	26	74	13	28
South Korea	94	102	27	93	5	46
Thailand	136	90	8	33	2	19
Turkey	75	113	14	51	3	15
Argentina	98	107	31	71	11	43
Brazil	95	106	11	39	2	12
Chile	109	96	24	70	4	23
Colombia	77	111	12	55	2	15
Mexico	80	113	11	56	3	14
Peru	83	120	18	68	4	39
Venezuela	100	97	21	34	4	30
Egypt	66	101	16	80	5	19
Ghana	59	74	3	38	0	2
Ivory Coast	46	69	2	24	0	3
Kenya	47	95	2	27	0	2
Nigeria	36	76	3	23	0	4
Tanzania	24	68	2	5		0
Zambia	48	95	1	20	0	2
Average	70.6	95.9	12.5	45.4	3.0	14.4
Africa[c]	40.4	72.9	3.5	23.1	0.3	3.2
Asia[c]	85.6	104.7	20.9	48.8	2.6	7.4
Arab countries	48.3	83.6	10.2	50.6	2.0	12.2
Latin America[d]	72.7	106.3	14.6	53.2	3.0	17.7
Developing countries	75.8	97.9	15.7	44.5	2.1	7.7
Developed countries	105.6	101.0	61.1	95.2	13.5	41.7

Notes:

[a] The number of students enrolled per educational level regardless of their age, as a percentage of the number of persons in the relevant age bracket. The age brackets for educational levels differ per country. Percentages over 100 per cent indicate that persons outside the relevant age bracket can also be enrolled.

[b] 1992 or the most recent year after 1988 for which data are available.

[c] Excluding the Arab countries.

[d] Including the Caribbean.

Source: UNESCO (1976, 1994), *Statistical Yearbook*.

The percentage growth of enrolment in secondary and post-secondary education is far higher than in primary education. Between 1960 and 1980 the number of students enrolled in post-secondary education in developing countries increased by a factor 5.2, in secondary education by a factor 3.6, and in primary education by a factor 1.4 (UNESCO, 1983; Coombs, 1985).

Gross enrolment data give a too optimistic picture of primary educational enrolment, as many children over the age of 11 are still in primary school. The net enrolment data in Table 6.2 show that the percentage of pupils enrolled for the 6–11 year age bracket is much lower in all regions. The gross enrolment data would suggest that since 1986 many Latin American and Asian countries have achieved full primary school enrolment. Net enrolment data indicate, however, that even in Latin America 12.5 per cent of all 6- to 11-year-olds do not attend school. The objective of primary education for all is far from being realized, particularly in Africa. One should realize also that even the more modest net enrolment data tend to exaggerate educational performance (see section 6.2.1). Since 1987, net enrolment ratios for Africa have declined at all levels.

Table 6.2 Net enrolment ratios, 1960–1992 (percentage of persons enrolled by age bracket and region)

	6–11 years		12–17 years		18–23 years		6–23 years	
Region	1960	1992	1960	1992	1960	1992	1960	1992
Africa[a]	28.9	51.4	17.1	41.2	1.4	7.3	17.5	36.5
Asia[a]	52.5	81.3	41.0	46.5	8.7	13.6	36.8	47.6
Arab countries	39.1	77.2	18.0	51.8	3.9	19.6	22.8	53.0
Latin America[b]	57.7	87.5	36.3	68.0	5.7	25.4	36.9	62.1
Developing countries	48.1	77.0	35.1	47.3	7.5	14.3	32.9	47.5
Developed countries	91.1	91.9	69.3	86.1	15.1	40.0	61.0	72.5

Notes:
[a] Excluding Arab countries.
[b] Including the Caribbean.

Source: UNESCO (1989, 1994), *Statistical Yearbook*.

For the age categories 12–17 years and 18–23 years, net enrolment figures in Table 6.2 are higher than those in Table 6.1. Evidently this is due to the fact that some of the young people in these age groups are enrolled in lower educational levels.

Although not all educational objectives have been realized, long-run educational achievements of developing countries have been impressive. Despite considerable population growth they have realized very substantial increases in enrolment since 1960. The educational gap between developing and rich countries has been unmistakably narrowed. Indeed, as early as 1960 considerable progress had already been made, in comparison with the unfavourable initial conditions after World War II.

Table 6.3 Highest diploma obtained in eighteen developing countries around 1980 (in percentage of age bracket)

Country	15–19 age bracket					
	No education	Primary education		Secondary education		Higher education
		Incomplete	Complete[a]	Incomplete	Complete	
Bangladesh (1981)	59.8	18.7		16.2	5.4	
China (1982)	9.4		28.2	46.7	15.2	0.5
Philippines (1980)	3.2	17.7	19.6	46.6		12.9
India (1981)	51.6	16.7		31.3		0.4
Indonesia (1980)	11.2	35.5	37.3	14.5	1.6	
Pakistan (1981)	65.6	13.6		20.6		0.3
Thailand (1980)	3.3	60.9	8.9	19.0	7.2	0.7
Turkey (1980)	16.5	56.2		27.2		0.1
South Korea (1980)	0.5	12.7		30.8	52.1	3.9
Argentina (1980)	1.3	21.7	23.8	49.9		3.3
Brazil (1980)	17.0	61.5	9.4	11.6		0.5
Chile (1982)	1.6	47.8		48.3		2.3
Colombia (1973)	11.3	52.7		35.2		0.7
Mexico (1980)	14.2	20.2	20.5	42.6		2.4
Peru (1981)	7.5	19.9	15.6	31.5	16.1	9.4
Egypt (1976)	57.8	37.1		5.1		
Ghana (1970)	28.8	12.4		51.7	7.1	0.0
Tanzania (1978)						

Table 6.3 (*Continued*)

Country	25-plus age bracket					
	No education	Primary education		Secondary education		Higher education
		Incomplete	Complete[a]	Incomplete	Complete	
Bangladesh (1981)	70.4	16.7		7.4	4.2	1.3
China (1982)	44.5		32.7	16.1	5.6	1.0
Philippines (1980)	11.7	31.3	22.8	18.9	15.2	
India (1981)	72.5	11.3		13.7		2.5
Indonesia (1980)	41.1	31.6	16.8	4.7	4.9	0.8
Pakistan (1981)	78.9	8.7		10.5		1.9
Thailand (1980)	20.5	67.3	2.4	4.5	2.3	2.9
Turkey (1980)	52.4	35.3		8.7		3.6
South Korea (1980)	19.7	34.5		18.2	18.7	8.9
Argentina (1980)	7.1	33.4	33.0	20.4		6.1
Brazil (1980)	32.9	50.4	4.9	6.9		5.0
Chile (1982)	9.4	56.6		26.9		7.2
Colombia (1973)	22.4	55.9		18.4		3.3
Mexico (1980)	34.2	31.4	17.2	11.8		5.3
Peru (1981)	24.0	27.3	17.2	10.7	10.7	10.1
Egypt (1976)	86.3	4.7		5.7		3.4
Ghana (1970)	77.7	5.8		12.8	3.3	0.4
Tanzania (1978)	48.6	40.7	8.7	1.6	0.1	0.2

Note:
[a] Some countries do not distinguish between enrolment in secondary education and finishing primary school.

Source: UNESCO (1989), *Statistical Yearbook*.

6.3.3 Education completed

One of the reasons why enrolment data give a too optimistic picture of educational performance is that large numbers of students leave school prematurely without a degree. This is illustrated by Table 6.3. This table shows which proportion of a given age category has completed its primary or secondary education. The percentages are substantially below the enrolment figures. For example, in India 51.6 per cent of all 15- to 19-year-olds had no schooling at all in 1981; 16.7 per cent had an incomplete primary education. This means that only 31.7 per cent had successfully completed a primary education.[5] The situation in countries like Pakistan, Bangladesh, and Egypt was even worse. In these countries respectively 20.8 per cent, 21.5 per cent, and 5.1 per cent had completed primary school. In Brazil only 21.5 per cent of 15- to 19-year-olds had finished primary school; however, the percentage of people with no education at all was much lower here. It is worth while comparing these percentages with the gross enrolment data in Table 6.1, which are sometimes even over 100 per cent.

Countries that score relatively highly in Table 6.3 are South Korea, the Philippines, Peru, and Argentina. Table 6.3 also shows that the degree of schooling of the 15 to 19 age bracket compares favourably with that of the over-25 age bracket.

Table 6.4 Mean years of schooling per Member of the labour force in fourteen developing countries between 1960 and 1980

	Percentage with no education			Mean years of schooling		
	around 1960	around 1970	around 1980	around 1960	around 1970	around 1980
China (1980)			9.3			8.6
India (1961, 1981)	89.9		66.7	0.5		1.9
Indonesia (1980)			26.1			4.9
Pakistan (1975, 1981)		75.8	65.9		1.2	2.5
Thailand (1960, 1974, 1980)	37.4	12.0	10.1	3.3	4.1	4.6
South Korea (1969, 1980)		44.9	14.8		3.9	8.0
Argentina (1960, 1980)	7.0		4.7	6.2		7.4
Brazil (1960, 1980)	48.2		24.7	2.4		5.6
Chile (1969, 1981)		18.6	4.1		5.9	8.1
Colombia (1964, 1973, 1978)	28.9	16.8	16.3	2.8	4.8	5.0
Mexico (1970, 1977)		23.6	26.9		4.2	4.5
Peru (1961, 1981)	31.1		13.5	3.9		7.0
Egypt (1960, 1976)	63.6		53.2	1.7		3.3
Nigeria (1963, 1967)	90.0	86.2		0.5	0.8	
Average	49.5	39.7	25.9	2.7	3.6	5.5

Source: Psacharopoulos and Arriagada (1986).

6.3.4 Years of education per member of the labour force

Table 6.4 shows that the mean number of years of schooling received by members of the labour force has doubled between 1960 and 1980 – from 2.7 years to 5.5 years per person employed. However, there is still a large gap compared to affluent countries, where employees have 12 years of schooling on average.

6.3.5 Educational expenditures

The following two tables refer to government expenditure on education. Table 6.5 brings out clearly how much more is spent per student in secondary and higher education than in primary education. An extreme example is Nigeria where expenditure per student in higher education in 1975 was 244 times as high as in primary education. South Korea and Thailand are the two exceptions to this skewed pattern. In many developing countries real expenditure per student showed a downward trend between 1980 and 1984 due to the economic crisis of the 1980s.

The financial sacrifices that developing countries are willing to make for education are represented in Table 6.6. In 1965, developing countries invested on average 3 per cent of their GNP in education. In 1992, this percentage had increased to 4.1 per cent. In the same year, rich countries invested 5.3 per cent of their GNP in education. Since per capita GNP in developing countries is much lower, this of course means that developing countries can spend less on education per head of the population. In 1987, rich countries spent 704 dollars per head on education, against 29 dollars in developing countries (UNESCO, *Statistical Yearbook 1989*).

6.3.6 Non-formal and informal education

All officially registered indicators refer to formal education. However, there are all kinds of education and schooling which fall outside the scope of formal education. For these, terms such as 'non-formal education' and 'informal education' have come into use.

Non-formal education comprises all forms of organized education that are not included in the regular schooling system: adult education, education for dropouts, literacy projects, agricultural extension or information, occupational training, in-firm training programmes, health education, education for family planning, and so on (Coombs and Ahmed, 1974). Advocates of non-formal education believe that it is more suited to practical everyday needs and requirements. They claim that it offers opportunities to integrate education into wider development strategies.

It is difficult to obtain hard data on non-formal education as it includes such a variety of educational activities financed by various ministries, institutions, and private organizations. Still, studies conducted by UNESCO indicate an upward trend in enrolment in non-formal education. In 1985, about 23 million people were enrolled in non-formal education programmes in developing countries (Hallak, 1990, p. 11).

Table 6.5 Government expenditure on education per student, 1975–1984, for eighteen developing countries (in 1983 $)

Country	1975			1980			1984		
	Primary education	Secondary education	Higher education	Primary education	Secondary education	Higher education	Primary education	Secondary education	Higher education
Bangladesh	4			6	12	106	9	15	78
China		53	837		69	857		97	845
Philippines	31	106	105	37	261	84	27	196	84
India	23	42	99	23					
Pakistan	22	43	369	25	49		23		
Thailand	58	84	526	62	69	425	102	115	147
Turkey				792		11,787	816	1,585	6,453
South Korea	78	57	286	168	148	270	300	226	320
Argentina	114	370	763	220		991	193	210	643
Brazil									
Chile									
Colombia		104		60	88	504	122	151	636
Mexico	93	262	555	102	150	1,113	70	90	931
Peru	89	160	574	86	100	613	64		
Egypt	109		407	107		313			
Ghana	44	138	3,849					11	
Nigeria	77	367	18,782						
Tanzania	56	854	9,924						
Average	61.4	203.1	2,852.0	140.7	105.1	1,551.2	157.9	298.3	1,126.3

Source: Komenan (1987).

Table 6.6 Government expenditure on education as a percentage of gross national product per country and region, 1960–1992

Country/region	1960/61	1965	1970	1975	1980	1985	1990	1992
Bangladesh		1.3		1.1	1.5	1.9	2.0	2.3
China			1.3	1.8	1.9	2.0	1.8	1.7
India	2.3	2.6	2.8	2.8	2.8	3.4	4.0	
Indonesia			2.7	2.7	1.7			2.2
Pakistan	0.9	1.5	1.7	2.2	2.0	2.5	2.7	
Philippines	2.6	2.7	2.6	1.9	1.7	1.4	2.9	
South Korea	3.2	1.8	3.5	2.2	3.7	4.5	3.6	4.4
Thailand	2.5	3.1	3.5	3.6	3.4	3.9	3.6	
Turkey	2.4	3.5	3.0		2.8	2.3	3.1	4.0
Argentina	2.0	3.0	5.0	2.5	2.7	1.5	1.1	3.1
Brazil	2.3	1.1	2.9	3.0	3.6	3.8	4.6[c]	
Chile	2.7	2.7	5.1	4.1	4.6	4.4	2.7	2.9
Colombia	1.8	2.3	1.9	2.2	1.9	2.9	2.8	3.1
Mexico	1.3	1.9	2.5	3.8	4.7	3.9	4.0	5.2
Peru		5.0	3.3	3.4	3.1	2.7	1.5	
Venezuela		3.9	4.7	5.2	4.4	5.1	4.1	5.2
Egypt	4.9	4.6	4.8	5.0	5.7[b]	6.3	3.8	
Ghana	3.4	4.1	4.3	5.9	3.1	2.6	3.1	
Ivory Coast	4.2	5.4	4.9	5.7	7.2			
Kenya		4.6	5.0	6.3	6.8	6.4	7.0	
Nigeria		2.3		2.7[a]		1.2	1.7[c]	
Tanzania			4.5	5.4	4.4	3.5	5.0	
Zambia	1.8	6.0	4.7	6.7	4.5	4.6	2.3	
Africa[d]		2.5	3.4	3.7	5.2	4.9	5.3	5.4
Asia[d]		3.5	3.5	4.2	4.4	4.0	4.1	4.3
Arab countries		4.2	4.7	5.9	4.5	5.8	5.4	5.7
Latin America		3.1	3.3	3.4	3.9	3.9	4.1	4.4
Developing countries		3.0	3.3	3.5	3.7	3.8	3.9	4.1
Developed countries		5.2	5.6	6.0	5.4	5.3	5.3	5.3

Notes:
[a] 1974; [b] 1981; [c] 1989; [d] Excluding the Arab countries

Sources: UNESCO (1972, 1976, 1984, 1992, 1994), *Statistical Yearbook*.

It is well known that schooling and socialization are not limited to schools. Families, churches, associations, work situations, and peer groups can also be very important. *Informal education* refers to the lifelong process of accumulation of knowledge and skills, through experiences in daily life – at play, at work, at home or elsewhere (Coombs and Ahmed, 1974; Coombs, 1985, p. 24). There is no point in considering informal education as part of the educational system. Nevertheless, the rapid rise of new mass media and means of communication, such as newspapers, radio, cinema, television, books, and magazines, may be very important. They can serve as mechanisms of information transfer, influence, education or indoctrination. In particular, radio and television provide considerable opportunities for new modes of education, teaching and dissemination of information.

6.3.7 Summary; comparison with developments in more developed countries

In the post-war period developing countries have given high priority to expanding their educational systems. The increase in schooling and decline in illiteracy proceeded more rapidly than previously in European countries, where primary education expanded very gradually, resulting in universal primary education by the end of the nineteenth century. Developing countries today are on the way to universal primary education. For them, participation in secondary and higher education is higher now than it was in France, England, and Germany in 1950. In Europe, democratization of higher education did not make much headway until after World War II. Before that time, entry to higher education was by and large restricted to the offspring of the upper classes.

One of the characteristics of the educational systems in developing countries is that enrolment in secondary and higher education started increasing long before realization of universal primary education. In this respect, the educational performance of developing countries not only differs from Western development experience, but also from that of the late-developers Japan and the Soviet Union, which both experienced an explosive expansion of education from the late nineteenth century onwards. They, however, gave greater priority to universal primary education. After the Bolshevik revolution large-scale literacy campaigns were organized in the Soviet Union and primary education was expanded very rapidly. Secondary education was only developed after universal primary education had been realized. Higher education was expanded at an even later stage (Lind and Johnston, 1986). In developing countries, however, expansion of secondary and higher education received higher priority.

Despite differences in the patterns of educational development one may conclude that developing countries are engaged in a process of educational catch-up. They have succeeded in training their own educational staff, in decreasing their dependence on foreign teachers and educators, and in developing an educational infrastructure. In the light of the unfavourable initial state of education after World War II, the educational performance of developing countries is quite impressive.

6.4 *Problems*

From the mid-1970s onwards important qualitative shortcomings in the educational systems became more and more visible. In their enthusiasm to create new educational facilities as fast as possible, authorities in developing countries had paid little attention to educational content. The Western-oriented educational systems inherited from the former colonial period were expanded with little or no change; Coombs (1985) calls this a process of 'linear expansion'. In Latin America – where decolonization had been completed early in the nineteenth century – educational systems were also copies of Western models. As a result, educational systems were in many aspects ill-adapted to the conditions and needs of developing countries. The following section will address some of the most important deficiencies in those educational systems.

6.4.1 Growing discrepancies between educational needs and financial resources

Since the late 1970s the pace of growth in educational facilities and educational enrolment has been declining. The scarcity of financial resources increased as a result of the economic problems of the early 1980s and the cutbacks in government spending in the context of structural adjustment programmes. At the same time, the demand for education continued to increase due to population growth and the youthful age structure of the population (Coombs, 1985; Hallak, 1990).

Even without an increase in enrolment, the cost of education tends to rise autonomously. First – if policies are not adjusted – fixed salary structures will lead to increasing salary costs as the teaching staff gets older and as unqualified teachers are replaced by more qualified teachers. Secondly, the costs per student are much higher in secondary and higher education than in primary education. As more students enrol in secondary and higher education, the average expenditure per student increases. In the coming years the gap between the demand for education and the available resources is expected to widen even further.

6.4.2 The quality of education

The quality of education in developing countries has come under increasing criticism (e.g. Naik, 1975). Classes are large, students are often absent from school, drop-out rates are high. In some countries only 10 per cent of all students complete the educational cycle in which they are enrolled. Teachers are underpaid, their training is often insufficient, and their motivation is low. Teaching materials are of poor quality, if available at all. Education is very much focused on preparing for examinations.

The financial problems described in section 6.4.1 may cause the quality of education to deteriorate even further. Educational authorities respond to the budget squeeze by increasing the size of classes, using the same buildings more intensively, and cutting back on expenditures on educational infrastructure, teaching materials, and, where possible, on teacher salaries. These cutbacks primarily affect primary education, which is – unwisely – given low priority.

6.4.3 Lack of relevance

Educational systems in developing countries are often copies of Western educational models. The content of education is Western-oriented; textbooks are Western; examination requirements are derived from Western exams. Little attention is paid to the indigenous history, culture, and society. In many countries the language of instruction is the language of the former colonial power. Education tends to be academically oriented and has little relationship with the life situations of most students.

Radical authors go so far as to characterize Western-oriented education in Africa, Asia, and Latin America as an instrument of oppression and alienation (Freire, 1970; Carnoy, 1974; Illich, 1974). At school, people learn to look down on their own culture. The more successful their educational career, the more students tend to become alienated from their own social backgrounds (Altbach, 1982).

It is indisputable that education has alienating effects and contributes to the formation of rootless elites. Still, it is important to realize that education, as an instrument of modernization, technology transfer and social change, is always a reflection of the educational systems of the dominant nations in world society.[6] An educational system which is in complete harmony with the requirements of a traditional society would not contribute much to 'development'. A modern educational system must to a greater or lesser extent be 'alienating' in a partly traditional society (see the debate on westernization in Chapter 1). The challenge is to develop educational systems that are both relevant to the life situations of people in developing countries and provide meaningful entry into the modern international world of science and technology.

One of the most important shortcomings of education in developing countries is the insufficient attention for agriculture. Many students will spend the rest of their lives in an agricultural environment. Nevertheless, the educational curriculum is oriented almost exclusively to the modern urban sector of society. Primary education is poorly adapted to the educational needs of rural young people. In secondary and higher education, courses with agricultural content are rarely taught. Education reinforces the already low status of physical labour and, in particular, agricultural labour. It contributes to mass migration to urban areas. Almost all authors argue for a more practical orientation of education, with more emphasis on vocational training, work experience and agricultural content.

Most reforms of this nature – however justified – are likely to meet with fierce resistance on the part of students. They rightly consider education as an important means of upward social mobility. This path leads from lower to higher educational levels, which become progressively more academic. In order to gain access to higher educational levels students have to be able to pass academically oriented examinations. Lower vocational education is seen as an obstacle to upward educational mobility, though in fact only a minority of students has a realistic chance of entering higher educational levels (Foster, 1965a, 1965b; Abernethy, 1969). Vocational and practical-oriented education are regarded as second rate by students and their parents (Psacharopoulos, 1989). The major challenge to educationalists in developing countries is how to make education more relevant for the masses of rural children who will never go on to higher education, without diminishing the possibilities of upward educational mobility (Hardiman and Midgley, 1982).

It should be noted that actual experiences with vocational education have often been rather disappointing. The specific occupational skills learned at school are hardly applied in later working life (Foster, 1965b; Psacharopoulos, 1989).

An alternative, presently much in prominence, is so-called non-formal education (see section 6.3.6). Among others, non-formal education comprises adult literacy programmes, agricultural extension, in-firm training programmes, education of school-leavers, health education and education about family planning. Non-formal education offers an opportunity to relate both the form and content of education to the immediate needs and problems of students.

However, it is an illusion to believe that non-formal education could ever replace formal education (Hallak, 1990). Non-formal education supplements and supports formal education rather than provides an alternative to it. The more formal education people have received, the more likely they are to enrol in non-formal programmes and the more likely they are to profit from them. Besides, the costs of non-formal education are by no means lower than those of formal education.

6.4.4 Unequal access to education

Access to educational facilities is distributed very unequally (Williamson, 1979; Hardiman and Midgley, 1982; Coombs, 1985; Ooijens and van Kampen, 1989). In particular, there are great differences between urban and rural areas. In rural areas schools are scarce and of poor quality. Students have to travel great distances to get to school and means of transport are lacking. Both educational participation and the quality of education lag far behind those in urban areas. In the cities there is almost universal primary education. Furthermore, secondary and higher educational institutions are concentrated in urban regions. Rural young people have far less opportunities to follow secondary and higher education than their urban counterparts.

A second significant inequality in educational participation is that between males and females (Coombs, 1985; Schultz, 1988; Fägerlind and Saha, 1989). In particular, in secondary and higher education female participation lags far behind that of males. For example, in 1980 the share of women in higher education in developing countries was only 34 per cent. Women are most disadvantaged in those countries where total enrolment is low. In terms of literacy women are also at a serious disadvantage, especially in Latin America (Ooijens and van Kampen, 1989).

In the chapters on population (Chapter 4) and health (Chapter 5) we have seen that the education of women was a crucial factor in improving the health situation and in the success of family planning efforts. Research by Nuñez has indicated that education of women is also of importance to economic development. In a study of economic development in Spain, she found that regions where male–female differentials in education were smallest were the regions with most rapid growth of income per capita. Also, improvements in female literacy tended to have more positive effects on economic development than improvements in male literacy (Nuñez, 1990).

Over time the educational status of women has shown some improvement. In recent years female participation in all cycles of education has increased (Schultz, 1988; Fägerlind and Saha, 1989).

A third significant form of educational inequality derives from the socio-economic status of the parental family. As in Western societies, children from upper social strata or income groups, or from dominant ethnic groups, are significantly more likely to participate in the highest levels of education. However, in the African context, Foster emphasizes that access to modern education is relatively open. Up until now, education has promoted rather than hampered upward social mobility (Foster, 1980).

6.4.5 Mismatch between education and the labour market

One of the most important points of criticism of education in developing countries is the mismatch between education and the labour market. I have already pointed out that agricultural education is almost non-existent in many countries where agriculture provides the main source of employment and livelihood.

Next, secondary and higher educational enrolment has increased more rapidly than the demand for higher-educated persons on the labour market (Blaug, 1979; Gillis *et al.*, 1992). From the 1960s onwards, many countries trained more doctors than nurses, more engineers than mechanics, and so on. People with higher diplomas displaced people with lower diplomas (see section 6.1.3 on screening theory). As a result, many employees were overqualified for their work.

In the 1950s there were great shortages of well-educated personnel in the civil service, schools, and firms. A task of the educational system was to solve these shortages in a brief period of time. Soon, however, shortages turned into surpluses. Today, swollen government bureaucracies are no longer able to provide jobs for the increasing flows of graduates. Almost all developing countries have extensive academic unemployment. Thus scarce resources are wasted on a large scale on investment in higher education that could be invested more productively in primary education. Academic unemployment and overqualification can lead to serious frustration for both students and graduates. Universities are often hotbeds of political turmoil and instability. One of the most paradoxical results of overschooling is the *brain drain* – the exodus of highly qualified doctors, experts, and scientists from developing countries to rich countries.

Despite widespread unemployment among the educated, there are still severe shortages in specific occupations, especially those requiring technical skills (Psacharopoulos, 1989). Education is still oriented too much to the humanities and social sciences – languages, law, history, sociology, economics – rather than to technical, scientific, and agricultural disciplines. In these areas the services of expatriate experts are often still called upon.

To improve the match between education and the labour market, it is often argued that vocational education and on-the-job training should receive more emphasis in educational policy (see section 6.3.6 on non-formal education). However, students still have a clear preference for academically oriented education. Regardless of the high unemployment rates among graduates of academic institutions, academic education still seems to offer the best career prospects from an individual point of view.

One of the most important recommendations of educationalists is to give higher priority to primary education. Extensive research has shown that both the private and the social returns to investment in primary education are much higher than the returns to investment in secondary and tertiary education (Psacharopoulos, 1993). In primary education, more could be achieved with less resources. Such a policy switch, however, encounters considerable opposition on the part of politically influential groups, who are defending the educational opportunities of their offspring.

Blaug (1979) argues in favour of loosening the ties between educational certificates and paid jobs. Credentialism on the labour market leads to the displacement of people with lower educational qualifications by people with higher qualifications, irrespective of the nature of the jobs involved. It also has very negative effects on the quality of education. All attention is focused on the mechanical preparation for centrally set academic examinations. The content of education is relegated to second place.

6.5 *Literacy*

In a discussion of education the issue of literacy merits special attention, since it is one of the essential outcomes of the educational process. As noted in section 6.1.6, many authors consider a certain threshold level of literacy as a prerequisite for economic development. In preliterate societies, families were the main vehicle of transmission of knowledge and skills to successive generations. As the task of transferring knowledge and skills shifts from families to formal educational institutions in ongoing processes of social differentation, literacy becomes more and more important (Hardiman and Midgley, 1982).

There are several reasons to strive for literacy. Apart from increasing economic productivity, literacy can promote social participation, and it can contribute to cultural education and the realization of humanist goals, and to personal awareness.

In the past, religious groups were particularly active in spreading literacy. An important objective of much religiously oriented education was to teach people to read sacred texts. For example, in Scandinavia Protestantism led to widespread literacy as early as the end of nineteenth century. In developing countries, missionaries played an important role. Ideological movements such as communism also set great store on literacy, as it would enable people to study Marxist writings.

Since its foundation, UNESCO, the United Nations organization for education, science and culture, has placed great emphasis on the battle against illiteracy (Jones,

1988). Between 1946 and 1958 one of the main objectives of UNESCO was *fundamental education*. The essence of fundamental education was that every person had a right to learn the three Rs – reading, writing and arithmetic. But fundamental education was not limited to 'literacy' alone; it also included vocational skills, domestic skills, knowledge of hygiene, knowledge of the principles of science, artistic skill, an understanding of one's social environment, and development of personal skills and moral traits. In the early years it was assumed that there were close links between fundamental education and formal schooling.

Within UNESCO there was a lively debate on the scope of educational objectives. Gradually, the notion of fundamental education was broadened to include development in general. Literacy in the narrow sense was seen as one of the instruments to achieve wider developmental objectives. In practice, however, the main emphasis remained on the formal schooling system, which was being rapidly expanded during this period.

Between 1958 and 1966 the concept of fundamental education was dropped from international rhetoric. Education was no longer to be considered a separate issue. It should be integrated into wider development policies. The new catchphrase was *community development*. In this new context, formal education became less important. The focus shifted to various kinds of adult education. Literacy was also seen as contributing to community development as a whole.

At the second world conference on adult education in Montreal in 1960 the idea emerged for the first time that illiteracy was a manageable problem and that it could be eliminated within a limited number of years (Jones, 1988). At the world conference of education ministers in Tehran in 1965 the objective of eradicating illiteracy was adopted explicitly. Based on this objective, UNESCO launched the 'Experimental World Literacy Program' (EWLP) in 1966.

Both at the 1965 conference and in the EWLP the notion of *functional literacy* was paramount. Functional literacy is not just about reading, writing and calculating, but rather about the contribution of these skills to the economic and social welfare of the individual and the community. In contrast to the broad concept of fundamental education, functional literacy was given a more limited economic interpretation. Literacy should contribute to the productivity and earning capacity of workers. To realize this, literacy education should be related to work practice and vocational training programmes. It should be aimed at specific groups of urban and rural workers. Pupils should learn skills which would be useful for their work and their future careers. It is clear that non-formal education would receive more emphasis in the context of functional literacy.

Between 1966 and 1974 more than one million students participated in the EWLP in some form or other (Coombs, 1985). On balance, the programme turned out to be a total failure. The gap between the high-flown rhetoric of international organizations and the intractable problems in the field proved to be too wide. The main problem was the lack of success in integrating literacy projects into economic and social practice.

Despite its disappointing results, several noteworthy lessons can be derived from the EWLP (Coombs, 1985; Ooijens and van Kampen, 1989), as follows:

1. Literacy programmes are most likely to be successful with people who need literacy in their daily life. Literacy is often most effectively learned in the context of acquiring some other skill to which literacy is incidental (Curle, 1964, quoted in Jones, 1988).
2. Literacy requires that reading materials (newspapers, books, information material) continue to be available after completion of the literacy programmes. Maintaining reading skills requires post-literacy programmes either through formal or non-formal education.
3. Teaching materials should be tailored to the students' environments and interests.
4. Literacy should not be taught in isolation from other subjects. Literacy training should be linked with subjects of strong immediate interest and concern to particular learners. The EWLP did not implement these objectives adequately. It made too much use of standardized teaching programmes and teaching materials in a classroom setting.

Socialist countries, such as the Soviet Union (in the 1920s), Cuba, Nicaragua, and China, have had considerable success with large-scale, politically motivated literacy campaigns. In these programmes the advancement of literacy was closely linked with political mobilization and ideological propaganda. The pedagogical experiments of Paolo Freire in Latin America are also worth mentioning; Freire linked literacy education to political awareness and the emancipation of oppressed groups.

Most of these literacy campaigns are very much rooted in a particular political and social context. They cannot be used as standard recipes irrespective of time and place. They do illustrate the crucial importance of motivation. If people can be motivated to participate in literacy programmes, impressive results can be achieved in very short periods of time.

Ooijens and van Kampen (1989) rightly point out that the best guarantee for literacy is a well functioning and accessible system of primary education. This implies that the main function of non-formal education is to maintain literacy after students have left school. Once again, formal and non-formal education are complementary.

Despite the disappointing results of some literacy programmes, illiteracy shows a clear downward tendency as a joint result of efforts in formal education and in national and international literacy programmes. Since 1946, the percentage of illiterates in the population over 15 years old has declined sharply in all countries. In Latin American countries, in particular, the rate of illiteracy has been reduced drastically. In no less than nine Latin American countries (Argentina, Chile, Uruguay, Trinidad, Grenada, Barbados, Cuba, Costa Rica, and Guyana) the illiteracy rate is below 10 per cent (Ooijens and van Kampen, 1989). The decline in illiteracy in developing countries is much more rapid, than previously in European development (Fägerlind and Saha, 1989, p. 46).

Table 6.7, however, shows that the problems of illiteracy are far from being solved. In many countries levels of illiteracy in 1990 are still unacceptably high. The absolute numbers of illiterates are even increasing as a result of population growth.

In 1985 the average percentage of illiterates among the adult population of developing countries had decreased to 38 per cent (Hallak, 1990). But the absolute number of illiterates increased from 700 million in 1950 to 850 million in 1985.

Table 6.7 Illiterates as a percentage of the population of 15 years and over[a]

Countries	1946–55	1956–65	1966–69	1970–75	1976–80	1981–85	1986–90
Bangladesh		78.4		74.2		70.8	64.7
China						34.5	22.2
India	80.2	72.2		65.9		59.2	56.5
Indonesia		61.0		43.4	32.7		18.4
Pakistan		84.6		79.3	75.6	74.3	70.4
Philippines	40.0	28.1		17.4	16.7		6.4
South Korea	23.2	29.4	31.9	12.4			3.7
Thailand	48.0	32.3		21.4	12.0		9.0
Turkey	68.1	61.9		48.7	34.4	25.8	20.8
Argentina	13.6	8.6		7.4	6.1		4.5
Brazil	50.6	39.0[b]		33.8	25.5	22.2	22.3
Chile	19.8	16.4	11.9	11.0		8.9	6.6
Colombia	37.7	37.7		19.2		14.8	11.9
Mexico	43.2	34.6		25.8	17.0	9.7	12.4
Peru		38.9		27.5		18.1	15.2
Venezuela	47.8	36.7		23.5		15.3	10.0
Egypt	80.1	74.2			61.8		54.2
Ghana		80.6		69.8			46.8
Ivory Coast		95.0			65.0		65.9
Kenya		80.5			52.9		29.1
Nigeria		84.6			66.0		49.3
Tanzania		90.5	71.9		53.7		
Zambia			52.7		46.5		
Average developing countries	46.0	55.5	42.1	36.3	40.4	32.1	28.6

Notes:
[a] Figures refer to the most recent data within each period.
[b] 13 years and over.

Source: UNESCO (1976, 1984, 1989, 1994), *Statistical Yearbooks*.

6.6 *Nation building*

Apart from the economic functions of education, its political functions are also of great importance. After World War II education was expected to contribute to state formation and the creation of a national identity in developing countries. In many of the newly independent states people identified more with tribe, region, lineage, or ethnic group, than with the national state. New political values stood in sharp contrast to traditional ideas about politics. Nationalist leaders fervently hoped that education would contribute to a sense of national awareness and political integration (Hardiman and Midgley, 1982; Krieger, 1988; Fägerlind and Saha, 1989; Psacharopoulos, 1989). Education would further the development of a joint culture and joint political values. Education would familiarize young people with the idea of participation in national political processes. Also, in many countries – particularly those with socialist regimes – education was regarded as a means to achieve political mobilization and increased social consciousness.

In practice, education is often a two-edged sword. Under certain conditions, it can contribute to a sense of national identity. But it can also have very divisive effects. In some states in India, education strengthened feelings of regional identification. Unequal access to education for members of different ethnic, cultural, or religious groups may lead to political frustrations and conflicts. It may undermine the loyalty of underrepresented groups to national institutions. In such settings, different groups can use education to strengthen their own identities and to emphasize their differences. Finally, universities are often hotbeds of political opposition and resistance. In particular, unemployment among the educated is frequently a politically destabilizing factor.

In many former colonies in Africa and Asia the choice for a language of instruction posed a distinct problem. During the colonial period the language of instruction was the language of the colonial power. In view of national integration and national consciousness it would have been preferable to replace this language with a national language. Yet this often proved to be impossible. In many new states several languages were spoken. To adopt one of these languages as the national language would lead to serious opposition from members of the other language groups. Therefore, English, French or Portuguese was often maintained as the language of instruction, especially in secondary and higher education.

Only in a few multilingual countries was a single language accepted as the national tongue, and in these cases, trade languages were chosen which were acceptable to many groups in society: for example, in Indonesia, Bahasa Indonesia; in Tanzania, Kiswahili.

In the long run, education should try to take ethnic, cultural and linguistic diversity into account, which should have more positive results than the forced propagation of a yet weakly developed national culture and identity. An overemphasis on national unity could well have adverse effects. A national political system which is open to regional diversity may well achieve more stability, although this is of course far from certain. If education does not succeed in creating some sense of national belonging, regional diversity in education, language and culture will end up undermining fragile national unity.

6.7 *Policy*

During the first few years after World War II educational policy was mainly concerned with the quantitative expansion of educational facilities. Not much thought was given to the content of the educational curriculum. Education was seen as a driving force in economic development. In this respect, the rapid expansion of education was the counterpart of capital accumulation in the industrialization strategy. In addition, education would contribute to social modernization and political integration.

Plans to expand the educational system were based partly on the political convictions and ideologies of political leaders in post-war developing countries, and also on various educational planning models. In educational planning, three types of analysis have been of importance (Hardiman and Midgley, 1982; Gillis *et al.*, 1992), as follows:

1. Planning based on the social demand for education.
2. Manpower planning.
3. Planning on the basis of cost-benefit analyses.

Planning based on the social demand for education

This type of planning is based on the numbers of students who enrolled in various kinds of education in the past. Past enrolment trends are extrapolated into the future. This kind of planning is the easiest from a political point of view, but it does not always lead to efficient outcomes. The overexpansion of secondary and higher education was to some extent due to planning on the basis of social demand. Members of social elites who want their children to receive a good higher education are more likely to make their voices heard in the political process than powerless rural people who would benefit more from an improvement in primary education.

Manpower planning

Manpower planning tries to determine the social need for employees with different kinds of education. Educational systems are designed to fulfil these needs. For example, estimates are made of the numbers of doctors required. These estimates determine the capacity of medical schools.

In theory, this is a valuable approach. In practice, however, the experiences with manpower planning have been very disappointing, both in developing countries and in more developed countries (Gillis *et al.*, 1992). It seems to be impossible to predict the demand for various categories of employees more than two or three years ahead. Since it takes years for changes in the educational system to be realized, the situation may well have changed by the time new graduates come onto the labour market. Moreover, manpower planning does not pay any attention to the costs of education.

Cost-benefit analysis of education

In keeping with the recommendations of human capital theory, this form of planning calculates *costs* of different types of education for individuals and the community, and the direct and indirect financial *benefits* deriving from that education. This allows one to compare the returns on investment in education to the returns on investment in physical capital stock. One can also determine which kind of educational investment – vocational, general, technical, primary or higher education, and so on – will have the highest returns. Educational planners are of course primarily interested in social rather than private costs and benefits.

Since the 1960s many cost-benefit analyses of education have been performed. Although attractive on theorical grounds, cost-benefit analysis has some serious drawbacks (see section 6.1.2). First, we know the present remuneration of different categories of employees with different levels of schooling, but we do not know how the structure of earnings will develop in the future. Secondly, we cannot be sure that income differentials actually reflect differences in productivity. Thirdly, the indirect benefits of education are very difficult to determine. Finally, cost-benefit analysis usually disregards both the content and the quality of education; analyses have normally been restricted to comparisons between primary, secondary, and higher education. Therefore, in practice cost-benefit analysis does not offer a sound basis for detailed policy-making.[7]

Cost-benefit analyses have shown that the returns to investment in education are higher than returns to investment in physical capital goods. The returns are the highest in countries with the lowest per capita incomes (Psacharapoulos, 1993). One of the most important recommendations derived from cost-benefit analyses is that primary education should be given high priority. The returns to primary education are significantly higher than to secondary and tertiary education (Psacharopoulos, 1993). This recommendation has never been followed by policymakers. In educational planning social demand and political priorities have predominated. With regard to voctional education, recent research indicates that the returns to general secondary education are higher than returns to vocational education (Psacharopoulos, 1993, table 9). This seems to contradict the earlier call for more vocational education. The issue of relevance perhaps depends more on the content of education than on the type of schooling.

Psacharopoulos (1989) pointed out that there is a wide gap between educational planning and educational practice. Often educational plans are formulated in a highly abstract manner, disregarding problems of implementation and resource availability. This actually explains why so many educational reforms never get beyond the drawing-board stage.

Since the early 1970s the debate on educational policy has increasingly centred on the content and quality of education. This debate resulted in a series of proposals and recommendations for reform that will dominate the educational agenda in the coming years. In concluding this chapter I will summarize the most important of those recommendations:

1. Expansion and improvement of primary education in developing countries is argued for almost unanimously. Universal participation in primary education should be a prime objective. The resources to achieve this objective should be transferred from secondary and higher education. Growth of educational

enrolment in secondary and higher education should be limited in order to prevent overschooling and academic unemployment. In higher education students should pay a greater part of the costs of education.
2. Education should be made more relevant to the needs of the labour market.
3. Primary schools in rural areas should pay more attention to subjects that are relevant to the rural population. In secondary and higher education more attention should be paid to agricultural education.
4. In the curriculum more attention should be paid to technical subjects and the natural sciences and less to the humanities and the social sciences.
5. On the labour market educational certificates and diplomas should receive less emphasis. Credentialism results in overschooling.
6. It is no use discussing the content of education without paying attention to the form and content of examinations. Less emphasis in education on the preparation for academically oriented examinations would have positive effects on educational content and relevance.
7. Quality improvement in primary education implies additional (re)training and better payment of the teaching staff.
8. Non-formal education should be further developed as a supplement to and in close relationship with formal primary education. Non-formal education can contribute in particular to further training of people who already have jobs and to increased literacy among adults and school-leavers.

Despite the scarcity of financial means, developing countries should try to provide adequately for the increasing need for education in coming years. Scarce resources should be utilized as efficiently as possible, with due regard for costs. Repetition of past mistakes should be avoided. As shown in this chapter, education is no guarantee for development. The high hopes for education have often not been fulfilled. Nevertheless, education is still one of the important links in the process of development, and developing countries are well advised to continue to invest in it.

QUESTIONS FOR REVIEW

1. What are the most important problems presently facing educational systems in developing countries?

2. What are the non-economic functions of education?

3. Give an overview of human capital theory. Explain the role of productivity in this theory.

4. Discuss the criticisms of human capital theory put forward by proponents of screening theory.

5. Discuss the most common indicators of educational performance and their strengths and weaknesses.

6. What is non-formal education? To what extent is non-formal education an alternative for formal education?

Notes

1. According to neoclassical economic theory, employers will continue to attract labour as long as the marginal returns of additional workers are higher than their gross wages. For the last worker employed, the marginal costs will be equal to the wage rate.
2. The novelty of these ideas has been somewhat exaggerated by the use of the term 'new growth theory'.
3. Too much emphasis on the insignificance of cognitive skills may lead to the neglect of these essentials, in both developing countries and economically advanced countries.
4. Ooijens and Van Kampen argue in favour of also including 11- to 15-year-olds in estimates of literacy (Ooijens and van Kampen, 1989).
5. Some countries only publish data on entry into secondary education. These data probably also include those students that have completed primary school but do not continue their education. Other countries distinguish between finishing primary school and enrolment in secondary education. The percentage of people with a completed primary school education equals 100 minus the percentage with 'no education' and minus the percentage with 'uncompleted primary education'.
6. In Europe, too, modernization of educational systems has always been based on foreign models that are considered successful.
7. In recent research, there has been some improvement in this respect. Returns have been compared for vocational versus general education and for various disciplines in higher education (see Psacharopoulos, 1985, 1993). But content and quality remain hard to measure.

7 Industrialization

As long as people work with their bare hands, their daily production will remain low. This sets a limit to the attainable level of welfare. Economic development is only possible if production per worker (labour productivity) becomes higher. One of the principal ways to increase labour productivity is to provide workers with tools, implements and machines – in other words, through capital accumulation.

In this chapter I will discuss the significance of capital accumulation in the process of economic development. The concept of capital will be introduced in section 7.1. Section 7.2 links capital accumulation with industrialization. In section 7.3 a distinction is introduced between open and closed models of an economy, and the differences between capital accumulation in open and closed models will be discussed. The large-scale industrialization strategies characteristic of the post-war period are associated with closed conceptions of the economy; these strategies are analyzed in section 7.4. In section 7.5 attention will be paid to small-scale activities in the informal sector. Inward-oriented industrialization strategies are compared in section 7.6 with outward-oriented strategies. Finally, outcomes of industrialization policies are discussed briefly in sections 7.7 and 7.8.

7.1 *Capital and capital accumulation*

Physical capital and financial capital

The term 'capital' has two different meanings, one concrete and one financial. The word capital in its concrete sense refers to the physical stock of machines, implements, buildings and devices used in the process of production. Economists usually define capital in this sense as means of production, with a lifetime of at least one year. The financial meaning of the term 'capital' refers to a hoarded amount of financial means and securities. In explaining economic growth, we are primarily interested in the growth of physical stocks of capital per person employed.

Savings and investment

Capital accumulation in both senses is only possible if people are voluntarily willing or are involuntarily forced to refrain from present consumption in order to free resources for investment in future production. This refraining from consumption is called *saving*.

In a subsistence economy, without a developed financial system of banks, financial institutions and money circulation, there is hardly any difference between saving and investing. If an agricultural household saves part of its harvest as seed, rather than eating all of it, this is saving and investment at the same time. A farmer who uses part of his labour to clear new land instead of producing food for consumption is both saving and investing. If a small industrial entrepreneur uses part of his profits to buy new machines and implements rather than consumer goods, his savings equal his investments. The value of his investments is his financial capital. The machines and implements are his physical capital. In early industrialization processes in Europe much of the finance for investment came from within the industrial enterprises themselves.

In a highly developed economy the distance between saving and investing has become much greater. One of the typical problems of developed economies (and of modern economic theory) is the match between the willingness to save and the willingness to invest. Financial intermediaries play an important role here. Savings are often deposited with financial institutions such as banks, pension funds and investment institutions. Through long and complex chains of financial institutions and financial markets, these savings are finally channelled to investors. Today soundly functioning financial institutions and markets are considered to be of significant importance for economic development (World Bank, 1990).

Capital accumulation and industrialization

Capital goods can be used in all sectors of the economy. For instance, the agricultural sector makes use of agricultural machinery and invests in irrigation systems (see Chapter 9). The service sector needs buildings and computers. The transport sector invests in trucks (or ox carts). Nevertheless, when we speak of 'capital accumulation' we tend to think about industry and industrialization. Industry in this sense refers not only to manufacturing, but to the industrial sector in its broadest sense, including mining, construction and the supply of gas, electricity, and water. The dramatic increase in labour productivity in the Western capitalist economies since the mid-eighteenth century is primarily the result of processes of capital accumulation and associated processes of technological change in industry. Naturally, capital accumulation is not the only way to increase labour productivity. Labour productivity may also increase as a result of more efficient working methods, division of labour, specialization in production, economies of scale, schooling or investment in improved health of workers. Still, capital accumulation is one of the important means to increase labour productivity in modern economies.[1] The growth of capital stock is the prime explanation for the fourteenfold growth of per capita income since 1820 (see Maddison, 1991).

7.2 *Arguments in favour of industrialization*

7.2.1 *Economic development and structural transformation*

Since the middle of the eighteenth century modern economic growth has been closely associated with industrialization (Clark, 1940; Kuznets, 1966; Chenery *et al.*, 1986; Syrquin, 1988; Maddison, 1991). In industry it is possible to employ much more capital, so that productivity per person and per hour are much higher than in agriculture. Economies of scale are also of paramount importance. In the large-scale mass production processes characteristic of industry, one can produce more efficiently than in the small-scale production units characteristic of agriculture.

Economic development involves a *structural transformation* in which factors of production are transferred from the sector with the lowest productivity, agriculture, to the industrial sector where productivity is much higher.[2] In the course of this transformation process, the share of agriculture in the total labour force declines, and the share of the industry increases. The importance of the agricultural sector also declines in terms of its share in gross domestic product, while the importance of industry increases. According to authors such as Kuznets, structural transformation involves more than changes in the sector structure alone. It also refers to increases in savings and investment rates, rapid urbanization, accelerating growth of population, and changing social institutions and attitudes (Kuznets, 1971; Syrquin, 1988).

Apart from the productivity differential, a low income elasticity of the demand for agricultural products also plays an important role in the transformation process.[3] As societies become richer, people tend to spend an ever smaller part of their additional income on agricultural products. There is a limit to the amount of food people can consume. Once the basic need for food has been met, people tend to spend more on industrial goods as their incomes go up. Therefore, the share of food consumption in total expenditure will tend to decrease.

The process of structural transformation which took place in the past in the presently rich countries is now taking place in developing countries. Tables 3.7 and 3.8 on pp. 85 and 87 indicate how the shares of the agricultural sector have been declining and the shares of the industrial sector have been increasing. According to Kitching (1982), there is an important element of truth – both theoretical and empirical – in the old orthodoxy that economic development goes hand in hand with industrialization. Benjamin Higgins, one of the early advocates of large-scale industrialization strategies, writes that 'The basic formula for development was "getting rid of farmers"' (Higgins and Higgins, 1979, p. 12).

Whichever indicators one uses, richer countries are on average more industrialized, while the agricultural sector is more important in poorer countries. This is illustrated in Table 7.1 where the share of manufacturing in the total commodity production is set out against a country's per capita gross national income in 1993.

Table 7.1 Industrialization and per capita gross national product in 1993

	Share of manufacturing in total commodity production[a]		GNP/capita ($)	
	%	Ranking	Absolute	Ranking
Japan	56[b]	10	31,490	1
United States	71[c]	3	24,740	2
Germany	69[b]	4	23,560	3
France	69[b]	5	22,490	4
Netherlands	59[b]	6	20,950	5
Canada	52[c]	13	19,970	6
Italy	71[b]	1	19,840	7
United Kingdom	71[b]	2	18,060	8
South Korea	58	7	7,660	9
Argentina	54[b]	12	7,220	10
Mexico	56	11	3,610	11
Turkey	42	15	2,970	12
Brazil	42[b]	16	2,930	13
Venezuela	30	23	2,840	14
Thailand	57	8	2,110	15
Peru	39	18	1,490	16
Colombia	35[b]	20	1,400	17
Philippines	44	14	850	18
Indonesia	38	19	740	19
Egypt	40	17	660	20
Ivory Coast	26[c]	25	630	21
China	57	9	490	22
Ghana	13	28	430	23
Pakistan	34	21	430	24
Zambia	33	22	380	25
India	29	24	300	26
Nigeria	9	29	300	27
Kenya	21	26	270	28
Bangladesh	21	27	220	29
Tanzania	7	30	90	30

Notes:
[a] Value added in manufacturing as a percentage of total value added in commodity production (agriculture, forestry, fishing, mining, manufacturing, construction and utilities).
[b] Other years than specified.
[c] Other years than specified from *WDR 1990*.

Source: World Bank (1995), *World Bank Development Report, 1995*.

The higher per capita income, the larger the share of manufacturing in commodity production. With the exception of China, the poorest countries in the bottom half of the table are the countries with the lowest shares of manufacturing value added. Service production has been excluded in Table 7.1, due to the difficulties in measuring service output.[4] Also the large size of the service sector in both rich and poor countries tends to obscure differences in the relative size of agriculture and industry. If the service sector is included, as in Tables 3.7 and 3.8 in Chapter 3, the differences between more and less developed economies are less prominent.

The differences in the shares of agriculture remain the most pronounced. In Table 3.8 on p. 87 the share of agriculture in value added in the early 1990s was 3 per cent in the OECD countries and 22 per cent in developing countries. The share of industry was 33 per cent in the OECD countries and 31 per cent in developing countries. The sectoral shares in the labour force – Table 3.7, p. 85 – show very clear-cut differences. Around 1990, the average share of agriculture was 5 per cent in the OECD countries and no less than 46 per cent in developing countries. The share of industry in employment was 29 per cent in OECD countries and 18 per cent in developing countries.

Not only are rich countries more industrialized than poor countries, but there are also great differences amongst developing countries themselves. In general, richer and more dynamic developing countries tend to be more industrialized than poorer and stagnating developing countries.

In particular, the poorest developing countries have a very low degree of industrialization. If one could transfer part of the labour force from low-productivity agriculture to a high-productivity sector such as industry, per capita national income would immediately go up. Furthermore, in developing countries labour productivity tends to increase more rapidly in industry than in agriculture due to capital accumulation and technological progress.[5]

Some brief remarks need to be made here about the difficulties in unscrambling capital accumulation and technological change. In itself, the introduction of capital goods in developing countries is an important form of technological change and technological diffusion. But one should distinguish between the increase in the pure volume of capital goods and the shift over time from technologically less sophisticated to technologically more advanced capital goods. This is called *embodied technological change*. Also, in the course of economic development, output per unit of input can increase due to various factors, among which are shifts from one economic sector to another, economies of scale and more efficient allocation of resources within sectors. One of the important factors which can cause increase in output per unit of input is so-called *disembodied technological change*. Disembodied technological change refers to general advances in science and the state of knowledge, that is, increased knowledge about products, markets, raw materials, organization techniques, learning-by-doing effects, and so on.

In economic growth accounting studies the contribution of growth of physical capital to growth of output in post-war advanced economies turns out to be less important than previously thought. Other factors such as growth of employment, growth of human capital and disembodied technological change are very important as well (Maddison, 1987; Thirlwall, 1994, chapter 2). However, for developing countries, physical capital accumulation still seems to be of great importance (Hofman, 1993; Pilat, 1994; Thirlwall, 1994), together with human capital, as discussed in Chapter 6. Also, growth of capital seems to be closely entwined with technological change.

Another economic argument often put forward in favour of industrialization, is that the *linkage* effects are so much stronger than in agriculture and mining. Investment in one branch of industrial activities can have strong positive effects on other branches of the economy (see also sections 7.4.2 and 7.4.4). This increases the economic dynamism of industrialization.

The term *structural transformation* might suggest that all countries experience an identical pattern of change. This is not the case. Several countries show a deviating pattern. Canada, for example, has a relatively low degree of industrialization and a high per capita income. China has a relatively high degree of industrialization at a low level of per capita income, and large Latin American countries like Mexico, Argentina, and Brazil are more industrialized than might be expected on the basis of their average income.

The pattern of industrialization depends among others on factors such as the availability of natural resources, the size of the domestic market, the period at which industrialization commences, and the policies pursued (Chenery *et al.*, 1986; Kirkpatrick, 1987; Syrquin, 1988). Generally, countries with an abundance of natural resources, agricultural or mineral, start industrializing at a relatively late stage. In industrialization, they are likely to develop more capital intensive techniques since wages are higher. Countries that are unable to export primary products will industrialize earlier and are more likely to concentrate on labour-intensive export production.

Furthermore, the timing of industrialization is also of importance. Countries such as Brazil, India, and Egypt have had at least 60 to 70 years' experience with large-scale industry, especially in food processing and textiles. Countries in sub-Saharan Africa had hardly any experience with industrialization before World War II. This is one of the reasons why industrialization in these countries has so far been rather unsuccessful. The countries with rapid industrial growth in the post-war period have all had substantial industrial experience before World War II (Pack, 1988). Syrquin concludes that there is no unique pattern of transition from an agrarian to an industrial economy. Still, he believes that the notion of a global transformation from an agricultural to an industrial society is still undisputed.

7.2.2 The role of the service sector

There is considerable debate about the role of the service sector. In classical theories of structural change the first stage was a shift from agriculture to industry, followed by a shift from industry to services (Clark, 1940). The image of the service sector was quite negative. This sector could only develop once the industrial sector had been able to supply the population with sufficient physical commodities. More recent literature provides a more positive picture of the service sector (Riddle, 1986). The service sector can also make contributions to the process of industrialization. At an early stage the development of communication, transport, trade, and financial services is one of the prerequisites for industrialization. Presently, the development of the financial system is seen as an important factor in economic development. Thus the service sector is seen as playing a more dynamic role. Nevertheless, it remains true that the dramatic expansion of the service industries in advanced economies was preceded by the growth of the industrial sector. In the rich countries the service sector is presently by far the largest sector both in terms of value added and in terms of employment.

In developing countries the historical sequence of industry and services has been reversed. The service sector expanded at an early stage. As shown in Tables 3.7 and 3.8 (see pp. 85 and 87), by the 1990s the shares of the service sector in employment and value added were larger than those of the industrial sector. However, there is reason to doubt the developmental dynamism of the service sector in developing countries. Its size reflects the expansion of employment in the public sector. In many countries the productive contribution of the government apparatus is open to question.

On the other hand, modern industry, with its high capital intensity, provides insufficient employment for the rapidly increasing labour force. The service industries will inevitably have a more important role in employment creation than in past developmental patterns. More of this employment, however, will have to be generated outside the government sector (see section 7.5).

For growth of per capita income, the industrial sector still remains the key factor. There is little correlation between the share of the service sector in national income and the level of national income. It is the industrial sector where the opportunities for increases in productivity through capital accumulation and technological change remain the greatest.

7.2.3 The prestige of industrialization

The high prestige of industrialization is not only based on the empirical relationships between per capita income and the degree of industrialization. It is also grounded in historical experiences. As described in Chapter 2, the late nineteenth century saw the rise of the colonial pattern of international trade; developing countries and colonies exported primary mining and agricultural products, and the rich industrialized Western countries exported manufactured goods. Primary exports came to be associated subjectively with poverty, underdevelopment and dependence. Industry came to be associated with development, power and economic independence.

The unfavourable associations of primary exports were intensified during the 1913–1950 period when the terms of trade for primary exports from developing countries deteriorated dramatically. Countries most dependent on primary exports were hardest hit by the great depression (Maddison, 1989). During this period the notion arose – especially in Latin America – that developing countries should develop their own industries in order to become less dependent on the industrialized world (Furtado, 1976).

After World War II, policymakers in developing countries and Western advisers both considered industrialization to be the royal road to development. Expectations for industrialization were extremely high. In policy, industrialization was given top priority.

7.3 *Accumulation in closed and open models of the economy*

In order to invest in capital accumulation in the modern sector of the economy, savings need to be mobilized. In this context, the term 'modern sector' can mean several things. It can refer to urban as opposed to rural society, to industry as opposed to agriculture, or to the money market economy as opposed to a traditional subsistence economy (see Lewis, 1983b). The latter meaning of 'modern sector' not only includes industry but also commercially oriented agriculture, mining, and the modern service sector. In this chapter our main interest is in investment in manufacturing, mining, construction and in the infrastructure of roads, harbours, railways and telecommunication (see also Chapter 8, section 8.1). The process of capital accumulation in the modern sector of developing countries can be studied in the context of either a closed or an open model of the economy (Lewis, 1954, 1955, 1977; Myint, 1980).

In a closed economy there are no economic ties with the outside world. There is no foreign trade. There are no international flows of profits, loans, or investments, and there is no international migration. In order to invest in the modern sector of a closed economy, all savings need to be earned and mobilized within the boundaries of the domestic economy. The most extreme example of a closed economy is a subsistence agriculture economy. Since the late nineteenth century there are no completely closed economies.

In a closed economy the means for industrialization can only be forthcoming from the agricultural sector. Closed models of industrialization therefore analyze the different mechanisms for transferring resources from agriculture to the industrial sector. These transfer mechanisms are studied within the framework of so-called *two-sector models* of economic development.

In an open economy the export profits may be an important source of savings. There are also financial flows from and to abroad. Capital accumulation may be speeded up by foreign direct investment and bank loans from abroad, but the pace of capital accumulation may also be retarded if resources drain away abroad (Baran, 1957).

For an analysis of the economic history of developing countries since the mid-nineteenth century, an open model is most useful. Most developing countries started their modern economic development in the second half of the nineteenth century by exporting agricultural and mining products. Export revenues and foreign investment served to finance capital accumulation in industry and infrastructure. In Chapter

8, therefore, attention will be paid to the role of primary exports in economic development.

For an understanding of post-war development strategies the closed model is more helpful. Developing countries have tried to reduce their dependence on international trade and primary exports and to replace industrial products imported from Western countries by products manufactured at home (*import substitution*, see section 7.6). In the following sections I will therefore first discuss the industrialization strategy within the framework of a closed model of economic development. The common characteristic of such industrialization strategies is the pursuit of comprehensive industrialization within the borders of the domestic economy.

Later in this chapter I will also pay attention to the criticisms of post-war industrialization strategies. This paves the way for a discussion of more outward-oriented (export-oriented) industrialization strategies. In Chapter 8 the focus shifts to the role of primary exports in economic development and the interactions between agriculture and industry.

7.4 *Industrialization strategies in a closed model*

7.4.1 Economic development with unlimited supplies of labour

In a well-known article 'Economic development with unlimited supplies of labour', Arthur Lewis (1954) has analyzed the process of capital accumulation in a closed two-sector model. Lewis opens with the statement that the classical Marxist tradition has much to teach us about the process of capital accumulation. Following in the footsteps of classical economists, it was Marx who studied the process of capital accumulation in Europe and who focused attention on the role of the entrepreneurial bourgeoisie in this process.

According to Marx, capitalists exploited workers and appropriated the surplus value of their production in the form of profits. These profits were then reinvested in capital accumulation, resulting in an enormous growth of productive capacity. According to Marx, surplus value consisted of the value of production of workers minus a subsistence wage just sufficient for survival. Given the abundance of labour on the labour market, competition ensured that wages were never far above subsistence level.[6]

According to Lewis, there was a similar surplus of labour in densely populated developing countries. The abundant supply of labour would keep wages at a very low level and would contribute to high profits and a rapid rate of capital accumulation.

The sources of unlimited supplies of labour

In densely populated developing countries the majority of the population was initially employed in the agricultural sector where labour productivity was very low. Since too many people worked too little land, Lewis argued that marginal productivity was close to zero.[7] In rural communities traditional forms of solidarity ensured that all members of society would receive sufficient food to survive at the subsistence level. Further, there was also a reserve army of low-paid, low-productivity workers in the informal sector of urban society: household servants, security guards, shoeshine boys, traders, casual workers, handymen, street vendors and so forth.

As soon as the modern capitalist sector of plantations, mines, cities, and manufacturing industries offered wages that slightly exceeded subsistence levels in the traditional sector, there was an enormous flow of labour to the modern sector. Thus Lewis writes that from the mid-nineteenth century to the 1930s some 50 million people migrated from densely populated regions in China, India, and Indonesia to find employment in mines and plantations in the modern sector of the economies of developing countries (Lewis, 1978).

Effects of labour outflow on agricultural production and productivity

The outflow of workers from the agricultural sector does not necessarily result in a decline in production. The marginal productivity of the departing workers after all is assumed to be close to zero. In other words, they do not really contribute to agricultural production. The average productivity of those left behind will increase and the level of production will remain unchanged. Thus there is actually sufficient food to feed workers leaving for the cities and the modern sector, while enough is left for the subsistence needs of the rural population.

Effects of labour inflow into the industrial sector

In the modern industrial sector unlimited supplies of labour cause wages to remain at a low level. Thus great profits can be made. The income distribution changes in favour of capital. If the profits are reinvested in capital goods, a rapid accumulation of capital leads to growth of industrial production. A crucial condition of the Lewis model is that high profits are indeed reinvested by a class of private capitalist entrepreneurs or public managers. Capital accumulation will falter if profits are frittered away on luxury consumption by extravagant elites or wages of non-productive government bureaucrats, used for military expenditures, or spent on beautiful temples, palaces or monuments.

The process of economic development according to Lewis is summarized in Figure 7.1. At a fixed wage (S), slightly above subsistence level in traditional agriculture, an unlimited supply of labour is forthcoming.[8] In the initial situation, capitalist entrepreneurs will expand production until the revenue from the last additional worker (marginal revenue) is equal to the wage level (S). In Figure 7.1 entrepreneurs will increase production until the equilibrium point P is reached. Profits – the shaded part of Figure 7.1 – are reinvested in capital goods so that revenues per worker go up. In the new situation, entrepreneurs will increase production to P′. This process is repeated until the unlimited supplies of labour are exhausted and wage levels start

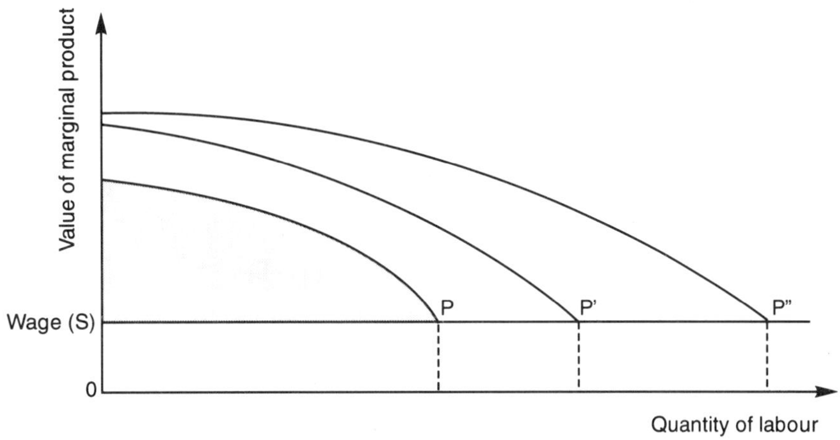

Figure 7.1 The Lewis model

to rise. In the phase of unlimited supplies of labour, capital accumulation in the modern sector can be very rapid.

There is a second mechanism in the Lewis model which can be used to accumulate capital. In a situation where there is an unlimited supply of labour and a shortage of capital, labour can be withdrawn from subsistence agriculture at little or no cost. This labour can be employed to create infrastructure: roads, viaducts, schools, irrigation works, and so on. An example is Maoist China, which succeeded in mobilizing labour from the rural sector in off-season periods for large infrastructural projects (Rawski, 1979). In the context of 'community development', India also tried to mobilize labour during off-season periods for community projects such as building schools, health centres, and digging wells.

According to Lewis, governments can also mobilize investment funds by taxing the agricultural sector or by paying farmers too low prices for food products. Finally, the government may have money printed to finance its investment expenditures. The resulting inflation acts as a tax on agricultural incomes, because the purchasing power of the rural population decreases as prices go up.

The joint element in all these options is the transfer of resources (food, labour, savings) from the agricultural sector to the modern industrial sector in the process of economic development. This is inherent in the logic of the closed model. When the great majority of the labour force is employed in agriculture, the only way to create an industrial sector is to withdraw resources from the agricultural sector and use them to invest in industrialization.

The key assumptions of the model are that resources can be transferred at very low cost and that subsistence levels of consumption in traditional agriculture determine wage levels in industry. If agricultural productivity and agricultural incomes were higher, workers would not be prepared to work at the lowest of wages in mines or factories.

Capital–output ratio

An often quoted thesis from Lewis's 1954 article is the following:

> The central problem in the theory of economic development is to understand the process by which a community which was previously saving 4 or 5 per cent or less of its national income, converts itself into an economy where voluntary saving is running at about 12 to 15 percent of national income or more. (Lewis, 1954, p. 155)

The figures for the required savings rate of 12 to 15 per cent are based on a simple growth model which relates economic growth to annual investment in the capital stock, assuming a fixed ratio between the capital stock and output (the so-called Harrod–Domar model). This model assumes that labour cannot be substituted for capital and that labour is available in abundance. Therefore, the only thing that matters in this model is investment in the capital stock. The fixed ratio between capital and output is called the *capital–output ratio*.[9] Empirical observation indicates that capital–output ratios are usually somewhere between 3 to 1 and 4 to 1. A capital-output ratio of 4 to 1 means that a net investment of $100 (after depreciation) is required to realize $25 increase in annual output.

The example in Table 7.2 shows that with a capital–output ratio of 3 to 1 and an annual population growth of 2 per cent – not unusual for developing countries – a savings and investment rate of 6 per cent of net national income is just enough to keep per capita income unchanged. If investment drops to 5 per cent or less, per capita income will decline. If a country aims at an annual growth of per capita income of 2 per cent,[10] at least 12 per cent of national income needs to be saved and invested. If the capital–output ratio is more than 3 to 1, the percentage of savings has to be over 12 per cent.

Table 7.2 Capital–output ratio

	Country A	Country B
National income	1,000	1,000
Savings/investment	60	120
Savings ratio	0.06	0.12
Capital-output ratio	3	3
Increase output	20	40
Increase national income	2%	4%
Population growth	2%	2%
Growth per capita income	0%	2%

Economic development and income inequality

Where can the required savings be found? In the closed model of the accumulation process, income inequality increases at the expense of workers in agriculture and industry in favour of capitalists in the modern sector. People who are trying to survive at subsistence level cannot afford to save. The increasing income inequality implies a redistribution of income from poor people, who consume most of their incomes, to rich classes, who are better able to save. However, increasing inequality in itself does not automatically result in an increase in savings. Ability to save does not necessarily imply a willingness to save. According to Lewis, a prerequisite for an increase in savings is the rise of a capitalist class of entrepreneurs with an urge to save and to invest the savings productively (Lewis, 1954, p. 159).[11]

The Lewis model offers a possible explanation for the frequently observed phenomenon of increasing income inequality in the course of economic development. Inequality only starts to decline once labour becomes scarce and wages start increasing in later stages of development.

A similar sequence is sketched by Kuznets (1955) who claims that industrialization and urbanization initially lead to increases in income inequality, followed by a decline in inequality at later stages of development. Usually incomes in cities are higher than in the countryside, while the income inequality within urban communities tends to be greater than in rural communities. This implies that a transfer of population to the urban-industrial sector in the early stages of industrialization automatically results in greater aggregate income inequality. At a later stage of economic development the income distribution becomes more equal as a result of demographic factors, democratization and the rise of trade unions and political lobby groups in the modern sector of the economy. The Kuznets hypothesis, often called the *inverted U-curve hypothesis*, has found support in international comparative research. Without exception, the income distribution is more equal in rich countries than in poor countries (Bacha, 1979; World Bank, 1985). Whether we may also conclude from such comparative studies, that inequality will decrease within individual countries as per capita income increases, is still a matter of considerable debate (Rubinson, 1976; Bacha, 1979; Gillis *et al.*, 1992, pp. 84–100).

The thesis that economic development and industrialization are inevitably associated with increasing inequality has been strongly criticized (Ahluwalia, 1976). The crucial assumption is that the rich have a high propensity to save and to invest their savings productively within the domestic economy. If profits are deposited in Swiss banks or if they are frittered away in luxury consumption by extravagant elites, inequality will contribute nothing to economic development. In these cases redistribution may be necessary for increased savings and more productive investments. It has often been noted that the Asian countries that experienced successful industrialization (e.g. South Korea and Taiwan) were characterized by a rather equal initial distribution of income.

Shortage of capital, surplus of labour

The pioneering article by Lewis set the tone for the post-war debate on the role of capital in development. Labour in developing countries was said to be abundant and almost costless (see also Fei and Ranis, 1964). Capital was the scarce factor and therefore the most prominent bottleneck in the process of development. In an economy without much of a modern sector, the agricultural sector is the only possible source of savings. Therefore, in a closed model the ultimate objective is to squeeze resources out of the agricultural sector and use them to create a modern industrial sector. Some exploitation of the agricultural sector is inherent in the closed model of development.

The two-gap model

In an open economy, foreign finance and direct investment are alternative sources of savings. In post-war development planning, rough estimates were made of the total amount of savings required for targeted growth rates. The savings requirements were based on aggregate capital–output ratios, as described above. The difference between aggregate savings requirements and the savings which could be mobilized in the domestic economy was the so-called *savings gap*. The savings gap is a first indication of the required foreign capital inflow. This inflow can be supplied either by direct foreign investment, loans from private banks or by official financial flows, including development aid.

Developing economies not only require foreign finance to supplement domestic savings, but also have a shortage of foreign exchange. Foreign exchange is needed to finance the imports of capital goods for investment in industry, and imports of semi-finished goods and raw materials which are used as inputs in industry. Foreign exchange can be earned by exports. Typically, however, exports in post-war developing economies are less than imports. The difference between the value of exports and the value of imports is the *trade gap* or foreign exchange gap. This is a second indication of the amount of foreign finance required for growth.

In so-called *two-gap models* (Chenery and Adelman, 1966; Chenery and MacEwan, 1966; Chenery and Strout, 1966; Bruton, 1969), the need for foreign finance is determined by the largest of the two gaps. Two-gap models also provide an important rationale for development aid (see Chapter 12). Given target growth rates, the amount of development aid needed to supplement private capital flows can be calculated.

In the long run, two-gap analysis assumes that the need for foreign finance will become less. If the investment programmes are successful, income per capita will go up and domestic savings will increase. Further, as the economy develops, it will be able to substitute some domestically produced capital goods for imported capital goods and it will start expanding its exports. Thus the foreign exchange gap will also decrease.

Actually two-gap models make reference to a third gap, a *technology gap*. To be able to make productive use of imported capital goods, a developing economy also needs a complementary supply of technical assistance. Further, the capital–output ratio depends on the productivity of capital. As the technological capability of a country increases – through investment in human capital, the founding of research and development institutes, and learning by doing – capital productivity can increase and the capital–output ratio can go down. Other things being equal, the amount of investment required for a given growth rate will then tend to diminish. A supply of technical assistance can contribute to increased technological capabilities.

7.4.2 Large-scale industrialization[12]

In post-war industrialization strategies, three related elements have been prominent: large scale; government planning; and import substitution.

1. *Large scale* It was thought that there should be a minimum size for the required investment effort. If a country was to industrialize successfully, a wide range of activities should be undertaken simultaneously. Industrialization is a large-scale activity almost by definition. Piecemeal industrialization is destined to fail. If an economy is to change drastically, large-scale industrialization is the only solution.

3. *Government planning* After World War II there was widespread distrust of the capitalist market economy. Leaders of developing countries associated capitalism with the imperialism and colonialism from which their countries had suffered so painfully. They found inspiration in the experiences of the Soviet Union, which had succeeded in achieving accelerated industrialization in the twentieth century through central planning. Non-communist countries like India also drew up five-year plans and assigned a crucial role to the government in industrialization policies. The basic idea was that the anarchistic market – where every entrepreneur pursues his individual interests and goals – would be unable to coordinate all activities effectively within the framework of large-scale industrialization. Positive external effects would play no role in the decisions of private investors. Thus many investment opportunities would remain unexploited in a market economy. Through central planning and regulation the government should be able to coordinate and stimulate the economic process. Moreover, it was believed that an active enterpreneurial class had not yet developed – in part, due to the suffocating effects of colonialism. The government was forced to compensate for the lack of private entrepreneurial initiatives. Finally, it was thought that the scale of required investment effort had become so large that only the government was able to mobilize sufficient means for investment.

3. *Import substitution* The third element of post-war industrialization strategies was import substitution. There was a strong reaction against the nineteenth-century pattern of international trade, in which developing countries exported primary (unprocessed) agricultural and mining products and had to import all manufactured products from Western countries. By setting up domestic industries, a country would become less dependent on industrial imports. To prevent the newly developed industries from collapsing under cut-throat international competition, they had to be protected in the initial stages of production (the *infant industry argument*). The instruments of protection were tariffs, import quotas, import licences and subsidies. It is clear that import substitution also leads to more government regulation of the economy.

Arguments in favour of large-scale industrialization

Advocates of industrialization were convinced that there was a critical minimum size for the investment effort, required for successful industrialization. Several arguments were put forward in favour of large-scale industrialization.

Rostow (1971) and his followers were of the opinion that sustained economic development could only be realized if investment was increased dramatically within a short period of time (see section 3.3.1). In the 'take-off' phase, an enormous investment boost would set in motion the flywheel of economic development. According to Rostow, historical experiences of Western countries supported the Lewis hypothesis that investment should increase from less than 5 per cent to more than 12 per cent of net national income.

The neo-Malthusian trap discussed in Chapter 4, also leads to the conclusion that large-scale efforts are required for development (Leibenstein, 1954; Nelson, 1956). This model (see Figure 4.3) is based on a race between population growth and per capita income growth. When per capita income increases moderately, population growth will exceed growth of per capita income. Per capita income will then decline until a low level equilibrium is reached. Only if one succeeds in suddenly increasing the level of investment so much that per capita income growth exceeds the growth of the population, will sustained growth be the outcome.

Important arguments in favour of large-scale industrialization policies are the so-called *complementarity arguments* (Higgins, 1968; Myint, 1980, chapter 7). The central idea here is that different economic activities will stimulate each other if they are undertaken simultaneously. Government planning may ensure that the various activities are indeed undertaken simultaneously so that their mutual positive effects are strongest. The emphasis on complementarities in large-scale industrialization is the main characteristic of *balanced growth* theory (Nurkse, 1953).

Balanced growth

In his discussion of *balanced growth* Myint distinguishes between three types of complementarities: complementarities in demand; complementarities between infrastructure and industry; and complementarities in industrial production.

1. *Complementarities in demand* In the oldest version of the balanced growth strategy, Rosenstein-Rodan (1943) argued for the simultaneous setting up of a large number of factories for consumer goods. A single factory in an otherwise traditional economy will never be able to survive, for no one will be able to buy its products. If many factories start production at the same time, the wages paid to the workers will create sufficient purchasing power. Thus there will be a demand for the output of all factories together, while a single factory would go bankrupt.

2. *Complementarities with infrastructure* For industrial production it is essential that there is an uninterrupted supply of raw materials, semi-finished goods, energy and water, and an uninterrupted outflow of the goods produced. Without an adequate

infrastructure of transport, communications, and energy supply no industry can function properly. Therefore, investment in industry has its complement in investment in infrastructure. Infrastructural investment is inevitably large scale. Half a dam cannot produce any hydroelectric energy; an incomplete railway line will not help solve transport problems. Industrialization, therefore, requires simultaneous investment in a wide range of consumer goods industries and large-scale investment in infrastructure.

3. *Complementarities in production* Consumers are not the only buyers of industrial output. Industries also buy one another's products. A car manufacturer, for instance, needs machines, steel, tyres, spare parts, screws and semi-finished products. Industrial enterprises are dependent on each other via technical input–output relations, the so-called *vertical linkages*. When capital goods industries, intermediate industries and consumer goods industries are set up at the same time, all these industries will benefit from one another's demand and the availability of one another's inputs.

The 'big push' development strategy

The most comprehensive development strategy within the framework of the balanced growth approach is the *big push* strategy (Rosenstein-Rodan, 1961; Higgins, 1968). The 'big push' strategy is a comprehensive industrialization plan in which investments in the capital goods sector, the intermediate sector, and various consumer goods industries take place simultaneously. All positive 'external effects' can be realized in the form of technical complementarities in the production process, income effects on the market for consumer goods, and complementarities between infrastructure and industrial production.

Private entrepreneurs cannot be expected to coordinate all their activities. They are only interested in their own profits, costs and benefits and not in the possible positive 'external effects' of their activities on other activities. For example, investment in infrastructure is of great importance to economic development as a whole, but not very profitable in itself. The government therefore needs to play an important role, partly by investing itself and partly by coordinating activities of private entrepreneurs by planning and regulation.

It is also clear that all these new industrial activities cannot be immediately internationally competitive. Initially, they need to be protected on the domestic market by means of protectionist policies and instruments.

7.4.3 Criticism of industrialization strategies

The industrialization strategies described above have the following characteristics in common:

1. Their large-scale nature.
2. Emphasis on capital as the scarce factor in development and labour as the abundant factor.
3. Priority of industry over agriculture.
4. Distrust of the market, faith in government planning.
5. Protection of the domestic market.

All these characteristics are rooted in a coherent industrialization ideology. In the mean time, however, the initial enthusiasm for unbridled industrialization has been tempered (Pack, 1988). In some countries industrialization never got off the ground. In other countries isolated industrial enclaves developed, claiming disproportionate shares of available resources without contributing much to employment or national welfare.

Below, the various assumptions underlying post-war industrialization strategies are subjected to critical scrutiny in order to arrive at well-balanced conclusions with regard to industrialization.

Criticism of the assumption that labour can be withdrawn from the agricultural sector at no cost

One of the central assumptions in the Lewis model is that there is disguised unemployment in the traditional subsistence agriculture. Therefore, labour can be withdrawn from this sector without any loss of production. This leads to the optimistic notion of 'costless development', where developing countries can freely utilize their surplus labour.

It is certainly true that there is underemployment in traditional agricultural systems during part of the year, but this is highly seasonable. During peak periods in the agricultural cycle – brief periods of harvesting and sowing – there are often acute shortages of labour rather than the opposite. When too much labour is permanently withdrawn from the agricultural sector, agricultural output will be affected. This is what occurred in several African countries where young males left the rural areas in search of employment in the modern sector, while women and the elderly were left behind to work the fields.

A low marginal product of an agricultural worker does not mean that he or she does not do any productive work.[13] Agricultural tasks are divided among all workers (I abstract here from the division of labour between men and women in agriculture; see Chapter 9). Though the average number of hours worked per person may not be that high, when somebody leaves, output will decrease, unless the people staying behind start working harder. They will only do this if they can sell their surplus production at reasonable prices on the market and can use the additional income to acquire new industrial products. When there are no economic incentives, peasants will only produce for subsistence and will not produce a surplus to feed the urban population.

The industrialization ideology assumes that agricultural surpluses should be transferred to the urban economy as much as possible. One can do this by taxing agriculture in kind or in money, by keeping food prices artificially low, or by monetary financing of government expenditures, which erodes rural purchasing power through inflation. But if the rural population is exploited too heavily, it will have no motivation at all to produce a food surplus for the urban population. It will only produce for its own subsistence needs.

Frequently, coercive measures are used as an alternative to positive financial incentives. In many countries government policy has included the compulsory delivery of food by farmers to the urban population. If necessary, compliance is achieved by the use or the threat of terror. That this is a possible option is well illustrated by the history of the Soviet Union. However, both the human and the economic costs are unacceptably high, and such a policy may result in permanent disruption of the agricultural sector.

Ester Boserup (1965) pointed out that under certain circumstances an increase in agricultural production per hectare will result in an increase in the demand for labour (see also Chapter 9). If farmers have to spend more time on irrigation, weed control, or fertilization, or if they increase the number of harvests per year, the demand for labour will increase. Withdrawing labour from the rural sector may therefore cause the growth of agricultural production to stagnate.

Finally, employing labour in the urban-industrial sector involves all sorts of additional costs for housing, transport, equipment and urban standards of consumption. Wage levels in industry may well be substantially above those in subsistence agriculture.

All in all, one may conclude that there is no such thing as a costless withdrawal of labour from the agricultural sector. Lewis's classical notion of an unutilized labour reserve should be amended in a neoclassical direction. The neoclassical perspective in economics states that production factors are fully utilized. One can never transfer resources from one activity to another without incurring alternative costs in terms of some loss of output. One has carefully to weigh the costs and benefits of a transfer of resources from one sector to another.

Criticism of the assumption of a constant low wage level in industry

Contrary to the assumption in Lewis's original model, wages in urban areas are not determined by the standard of living in rural areas. In wage determination, political considerations and bargaining with powerful urban trade unions play an important role. As a result, urban wages are relatively high. A small elite has emerged, consisting of relatively well-paid employees in industry and government. This elite profits from cheap and subsidized food supplies. Political survival dictates that governments in developing countries do not challenge these privileges.

The combination of too high wages and subsidies on investment in capital has led to a pattern of investment that uses relatively too much capital and too little labour. Due to the capital-intensive nature of production, the modern sector has proved unable to absorb the inflow of labour from the rural sector.[14] Substantial urban unemployment has arisen, and many migrants try to survive in the informal sector of the urban economy (see section 7.5). The expectation embedded in the Lewis model, that low wages and a high rate of reinvestment would eventually absorb surplus labour, has not been realized in most developing countries.[15]

Criticism of the use of fixed capital–output ratios

Post-war industrialization strategies emphasized the shortage of savings and investments. Raising the rate of capital accumulation would automatically result in increases in production. Applying fixed capital–output ratios, the levels of investment and saving required to achieve target growth rates could be calculated.

However, the real state of affairs is more complicated. Not all investments are equally effective or efficient. When a steel plant operates at one-third of its capacity, the capital–output ratio will be much higher than when it operates at full capacity. When an airport is built without adequate roads leading to it, its contribution to the economy may be marginal. The returns to investment in large-scale prestige projects are often very low. Investments in activities with few linkages with the rest of the economy will not have very positive effects on growth. Much depends on the sectors selected for investment.

During the post-war period, savings and investment rates have increased in all countries. The effects on growth have, however, been mixed. The *capacity to absorb investment* differs widely from country to country (Myint, 1980, p. 107). Countries differ in the efficiency of their governments, the degree of corruption, political stability, monetary stability, and the skills of the labour force. The level of schooling of the labour force and the length of experience with industrialization are of particular importance (Pack, 1988). Some countries in Southeast Asia have shown a great capacity to absorb investments. In other countries, especially on the African continent, investment efforts have had much less positive effects.

Criticism of large-scale industrialization

Several authors have criticized the emphasis on scale in thinking about industrialization. Industrialization is rarely a question of all or nothing. It is more important to think carefully about the most appropriate investments. Myint (1980) has deftly summarized the criticisms of various versions of balanced-growth strategies.

1. *Complementarity in demand* When total demand increases due to the simultaneous setting up of several factories and the payments of wages to their employees, this does not necessarily mean that the sales of a single factory will increase as well. If a new factory does not produce more efficiently than traditional craft industries, it will never be able to sell its products. Also, part of the increased purchasing power may well leak away to other sectors or abroad via the purchase of imported consumer goods. On the other hand, if a factor efficiently produces goods which are in high

demand, it will be able to make a profit, irrespective of how many other factories are being set up. There is always some demand, even at low levels of industrialization (see Thirlwall, 1994, p. 181). Thus the efficiency of investment is as least as important as the size of the investment effort.

2. *Infrastructure* It is true that infrastructural investment is inherently large scale. But again, it is never a question of all or nothing. There is always some infrastructure present. One has to choose between improving a dirt track and constructing a four-lane highway. One should be aware that it takes years before large-scale infrastructural projects – such as the Aswan Dam in Egypt – are completed and start paying off. It is far from easy to coordinate such investments with investments in consumer goods industries. At each stage of development one is faced with choices concerning the most optimal patterns of investment.

3. *'Big push'* The advocates of the 'big push' strategy avoid the choices between more and less efficient investments by arguing that everything should be done simultaneously: investing in consumer goods industries, capital goods industries and infrastructure. As a result, this strategy denies the scarcity of resources and the need to choose between alternative options on the basis of their costs and benefits. It disregards the fact that the size of the investment effort may drive up factor prices. The greater the scale, the greater the risk of expensive mistakes and inefficient investments. Moreover, the emphasis on government planning in 'big push' strategies places unrealistic demands on the administrative capacities of weakly developed administrative systems. If there is a shortage of entrepreneurship in the private sector, why should one expect an abundance of such talents in the public sector? Thus the idea of a big push proved to be too easy. An investment boost does not automatically lead to economic growth. Economic growth also requires, among others, fundamental changes in institutional structures, attitudes, mentalities and educational levels and less hostile relations between the public sector and the business community. The balanced-growth approach is too optimistic about the possibilities of rapidly constructing a totally new industrial structure on the foundations of a traditional economy. At the same time the approach is too pessimistic about the possibilities of gradually replacing traditional crafts production by more productive modern industrial activities (Hirschman, 1988, p. 53).

7.4.4 Unbalanced growth

The 'big push' approach is a typical example of a development strategy that tries to identify prime movers or crucial bottlenecks in the process of development. When the scarce or missing factor – whether capital, education or technology – is made available, development should follow almost automatically. According to Hirschman (1988), this approach is flawed. It is impossible to draw up a list of the necessary conditions for growth and development. First, there are alternatives to each prerequisite or factor. Second, the presence of a set of prerequisites does not necessarily result in growth.

In the process of economic development Hirschman argues that attitudes and value systems favourable to entrepreneurship and economic initiative are of crucial importance. But such attitudes should not be seen as prerequisites for development. Wherever economic opportunities arise, entrepreneurship will sooner or later emerge. There will always be individuals coming forward – members of ethnic minorities or of indigenous populations – who will start exploiting new opportunities. If economic opportunities are lacking in a traditional society, however, entrepreneurship and initiative will remain dormant. Thus Hirschman rephrases the notion of the vicious circles of underdevelopment. Economic initiative is necessary for economic development, but initiative will not be forthcoming in a traditional subsistence economy. When large amounts of capital are poured into a traditional economy where entrepreneurship is lacking, it is not surprising that the outcomes will be disappointing.

The main challenge in devising a development strategy is not the search for missing factors (savings, capital, education, entrepreneurship) or obstacles (risk aversion, land tenure systems) but rather the identification of pressures and inducement mechanisms that call forth hidden resources and abilities. In principle, there is no serious shortage of savings. In the early stages of economic development sufficient savings can easily be mobilized. More important is the development of the capabilities to invest savings productively.

The essence of the theory of *unbalanced growth* is that investments are made in strategic key sectors of the economy. These investments should cause dynamic tensions, shortages and imbalances that call forth entrepreneurship and investment in other sectors. As the modern sector of the economy becomes larger and more dynamic, there will be ever greater opportunities for new investment. This will elicit new entrepreneurship. Thus growth sets positive virtuous circles in motion.

Like the advocates of balanced growth, Hirschman assumes the existence of various complementarities between economic activities. First, there are purely technical complementarities. When a factory produces reinforced concrete, it needs steel. More indirect complementarities occur in the construction of office buildings. Empty office buildings create a demand for office furniture. Further, there are complementarities associated with economies of scale in production. When the production of good A increases, the costs will usually decrease. Product B, which uses product A as an input, will benefit from these lower costs. Another sequence is when the production of good A increases the demand for inputs of good C increases. This may allow economies of scale to be realized in the production of C. Thus C can also be produced at lower cost.

Hirschman's main thesis is that it is neither possible nor desirable to plan all these activities ahead. If we look at an economy at two different points in time, T_1 and T_2, it seems in retrospect that all activities were related in a process of balanced growth. However, in reality, the path from T_1 to T_2 is a dynamic one. Shortages and imbalances at one point in time continuously elicit new activities and investments at a later point in time, which create new shortages and imbalances. A shortage of steel for the production of reinforced concrete or cars will create profitable investment opportunities in the steel sector. As the number of factories increases, the need for an adequate infrastructure will grow stronger, and so on. Development policy should create such dynamic imbalances. It is the movement from imbalance to imbalance which calls forth a stream of entrepreneurship and new investment.

Backward and forward linkages

Hirschman distinguishes two different kinds of linkages between economic activities: *forward linkages* and *backward linkages.*

Backward linkages occur when an economic activity requires inputs that can be supplied by other enterprises. Often, inputs are initially imported. Later, local enterprises may emerge which can produce the imported inputs more efficiently in the domestic economy.

Forward linkages occur when the availability of a product, which is an input into another production process, calls forth investment in this other line of production. For example, the establishment of a basic iron and steel industry may stimulate the rise of fabricated metals industries. The availability of agricultural products may stimulate the rise of food processing industries.

Hirschman also makes a distinction between the strength and the importance of a linkage. Sometimes a linkage is very strong, but not very important because the new activity has a low value added. For example, there is a strong linkage between the production of car parts and the assembly of these parts. But, the value added of assembly is quite modest and therefore contributes little to national income.

The relation between infrastructure and industrial production is another example of a forward linkage. Infrastructure may facilitate the rise of industries, but the strength of this linkage is not very great. The availability of infrastructure is permissive. It allows for other economic activities, but does not compel them. There are many examples of infrastructural investment which did not result in greatly increased industrial activity. Conversely, investments in industry do have a compelling effect on infrastructure, through backward linkages. It is absolutely essential for a factory to have uninterrupted supplies of energy and means of transport. It will exert all possible pressure on the government to realize improved infrastructure in energy and transport. Such pressures can presently be observed in the booming economies of Thailand and Indonesia.

The notion of linkages offers opportunities to investigate the dynamic effects of investments, through the use of input–output tables. Such studies help us identify the key sectors in the economy with the strongest and most important linkages. These are the sectors which should receive priority in an unbalanced growth strategy.

Weak linkages

An objection that is often heard to development strategies based on primary exports is that the linkages involved are so weak. Export-oriented investments in mines, oil wells and plantations have only very limited linkages with the rest of the economy. They can result in enclave economies, with a small modern sector oriented towards the international economy and a traditional sector isolated from the modern sector.

In a country with no industry, industrialization can only start in consumer goods industries delivering to final demand. In the early stages of industrialization, therefore, one will find two kinds of industries: industries transforming domestic or imported primary products into consumer goods, or industries transforming imported semi-manufactured goods into final consumer goods (Hirschman, 1988, chapter 6).

The first industrializing European countries had no choice but to take the first road. The first industries in these countries were in textiles, iron, steel, and pottery. In developing countries that followed this pattern, textiles, food processing and construction materials were of significance.

However, present-day developing countries also have the option of assembling or providing the final touches to almost finished intermediate products imported from abroad. This option is increasingly being preferred. Foreign investors make use of surplus labour and low wages to transfer assembly activities to developing countries. Hirschman calls this option 'enclave-import industries' since it adds little value to the production and is completely dependent on imports. As with enclave-export industries, the linkages with the domestic economy are initially weak. However, in the course of industrialization one may gradually work one's way back from these so-called final industries to intermediate industries, basic industries and even capital goods industries. When sufficient consumer goods are being produced domestically, there is a growing market for producers of intermediate goods and capital goods.

Unbalanced and balanced growth

The theory of unbalanced growth attributes a different and less central role to government in the process of capital accumulation. The market becomes more important. There is less emphasis on the shortage of capital and more emphasis on entrepreneurship and private initiative. The government's role is to maintain and stimulate dynamic imbalances and to identify key sectors for investment. Investment in infrastructure receives a lower priority. It should follow rather than precede other activities. Imports are seen in a more positive light than in balanced growth strategies. They stimulate demand and create the opportunities for later import substitution.

Despite the differences between balanced and unbalanced growth strategies there are also some interesting similarities. In both strategies, complementarities and linkages between industrial activities are seen as important. Unbalanced growth also assumes that the success of industrialization depends on large-scale efforts, a wide range of industrial activities and acceleration of the investment process. The most important similarity lies in the high priority given to industrialization. Both balanced and unbalanced growth tend to ignore the importance of the agricultural sector and the interactions between agriculture and industry.

7.5 *The urban informal sector*

Unlike nineteenth-century Europe, the industrial sector in today's developing countries is unable to provide the stream of labour from agriculture with sufficient paid employment. There are various reasons for this. First, the pace of population growth in developing countries is significantly higher than it used to be in the Western world. Second, technological developments have led to capital intensive production techniques, requiring less and less labour. Third, industrial wages are relatively high due to trade unions and political pressure groups. The costs of capital are relatively low due to cheap credit, subsidies and overvalued exchange rates. This results in the adoption of too capital-intensive production techniques in spite of the abundance of labour.

In most developing countries, industrialization so far has contributed only marginally to solving the problems of unemployment. Alongside formal employment in industry, commercial services and government, an *urban informal sector* has emerged where large numbers of people try to make a living in low-productivity activities.

Migration to the cities

The expansion of employment in the public sector has not been sufficient to compensate for the slow growth of employment in the modern industrial sector. Still people continue to migrate to the cities, in spite of insufficient employment opportunities. Why is this so?

In his well-known model of labour migration, Todaro (1969) argues that the attractiveness of a job in the modern sector is so great that people will migrate to the city, even though the chances of finding a job in the modern sector are slight. They are willing to remain unemployed for years in the hope of finally finding a position in the modern sector. In the meantime, they can depend on traditional forms of solidarity (based on family, ethnic or regional ties), which continue to exist in the city.

In one of his later publications Arthur Lewis recognizes the growing levels of urban unemployment. The prime explanation for this is the large gap between formal urban income levels and rural income levels (Lewis, 1983b). Further, increasing levels of education create unrealistically high expectations. Education is associated with chances of an urban career. Finally, government expenditures on health, education, welfare and development are disproportionately concentrated in urban areas.

The feeling that rural life holds little future for young people also plays a role in migration. When young people come in contact with modern lifestyles through mass communication media, the traditional constraints and hierarchies of rural societies become hard to bear. Also, in many countries the economic prospects in rural areas are so poor, that people prefer the risks of urban existence to the certainties of rural poverty.

The significance of the informal sector for economic development

In a society with no formal systems of social security, people cannot afford to be *openly* unemployed. A large *informal sector* has come into being in which people try to make some kind of a living. The informal sector acts as an employment buffer in the urban economy, providing some minimum of employment for the enormous supply of labour coming both from the countryside and from within the cities themselves.

The informal sector covers a wide range of activities, such as soft drinks vendors, tiny food stalls, small traders, street hawkers, household servants, prostitutes, messenger boys, rickshaw drivers, shoeshine boys, casual workers, car attendants, postcard sellers, and so forth. However, this sector also includes small enterprises: for example, clothing producers, repair shops, small garages, photocopy shops, potteries, breweries, and cabinet makers, to name but a few.

It is hard to give an unambiguous definition of the rich variety of activities in the informal sector. Frequently mentioned characteristics include: labour intensive technology, low levels of productivity, preponderence of family labour, irregular working hours, restricted use of capital, lack of legal protection and regulation, little formal schooling, absence of bookkeeping procedures, few barriers to entry, personal relations with clients, a small and usually poor clientele, lack of access to credit, and lack of government support (van Dijk, 1980; Breman, 1980).

The term *informal sector* was first introduced by Hart (1973) and it soon penetrated into official terminology. Initially, the informal sector was defined in a purely negative sense as everything that did not belong to the 'modern sector'. This undifferentiating view of the informal sector as a 'buffer' for surplus labour has been criticized by Breman (1980). He points to the heterogeneity of the 'informal sector' and to the links between activities in the rural sector, the modern sector, and the informal sector. Activities in the informal sector are dependent on and subordinated to those in the modern sector. The distinction between formal and informal is not clear-cut. Formal activities can easily become informalized when competition becomes fierce. The inflow into the informal sector does not only come from the countryside but also from the growing urban population. Entry is not as free as is often assumed. Different ethnic or social groups succeed in monopolizing certain activities.

The attention paid to the informal sector in government policy is inversely related to its size and importance. While large companies have access to subsidized credit and are supported by the government, small firms cannot borrow any money from formal financial institutions. They are dependent on informal sources of credit, where exorbitant rates of interest are charged due to the high risks of default. The informal sector is also deprived in terms of schooling opportunities, access to information and technology, and government support. At times, entrepreneurs in the informal sector are actively hindered by the government.

Since the 1990s it has frequently been suggested that the informal sector could fulfil a dynamic function in the wider economy and that policy ought to give it more priority. Government should help provide cheaper credit, management know-how, upgrading of skills, market information and supply of raw materials. Discriminatory regulations should be repealed (ILO, 1972). There is something to be said for these suggestions, but they also involve a lot of wishful thinking. Much of the informal sector consists of very marginal activities of people struggling for bare survival; from morning to night they try to scrape together a living. There is little economic dynamism involved. Lewis's assumption of a marginal productivity close to zero seems to apply here. Breman is afraid that the absorption capacity of the informal sector is limited and that further impoverishment will set in as more and more people enter the sector (Breman, 1980).

On the other hand, some other informal activities like small production or maintenance firms could benefit from cheaper credit, technical and managerial support, and education. They might be able to provide increasing numbers of workers with gainful and productive employment. More attention to the developmental potential of the informal sector could therefore be worth while.

7.6 *Import substitution versus export orientation*

The first step from a closed model of an economy to a more open conception is to realize that the resources for industrial investment do not necessarily have to be transferred directly from agriculture. An alternative is the reinvestment of revenues from agricultural exports. This will be discussed in more detail in Chapter 8. Foreign finance can also provide means for investment, as in two-gap models.

A second step towards an open model is to relinquish the objective of producing the whole range of industrial goods within the domestic economy. Instead a country should concentrate on those lines of production in which it has a comparative advantage and in which it is internationally competitive. These products can be exported. Other products can be imported. This strategy is called *export-oriented industrialization.*

The large-scale industrialization policies described in section 7.4.2 assume that a country invests in infrastructure, capital goods industries, intermediate industries, and as many consumer goods industries as possible. The underlying ideal is to reduce a country's dependence on industrial imports. India is an example of a large country that has pursued such an industrialization policy (see Bardhan, 1984).

In order to realize this ideal, domestic industries are given all possible protection. Imports are limited by the imposition of high import tariffs, quotas and import licensing systems. The effect of these measures is that prices go up and domestic industries have a chance to survive. Protection also makes it interesting for foreign companies to invest in a country, because they may thus penetrate or even capture a protected domestic market. Protection through tariffs affects the prices of industrial outputs (*nominal protection*). But protection can also aim at making inputs cheaper, either through direct subsidies or by maintaining overvalued exchange rates which make imported inputs cheaper for domestic firms. The *effective rate of protection* which takes into account both input and output prices may thus be much higher than the nominal rates of protection. Import substituting industries are also supported by subsidies on investment, cheap credit and various tax benefits. Overvalued exchange rates also make imported capital goods cheaper. This complex of policy measures is called *import-substituting industrialization* (ISI). It discriminates in favour of import substituting industries, discourages imports and discriminates against exporters of industrial and primary goods.

The chief justification for import substitution is the *infant industry* argument. Newly established enterprises are unable to compete with their experienced international rivals. In order to industrialize successfully, domestic enterprises first have to gain experience on a protected domestic market. Through learning by doing, these enterprises will gradually become more efficient and productive, until they become internationally competitive and can dispense with protection.

There is an important element of validity in the *infant industry* argument. In developing countries, import substitution is an essential initial phase in the process of industrialization. Without exception, developing countries that have been successful in developing a substantial industrial sector started out with import substitution. In the late nineteenth century the revenues from primary agricultural and mining exports created a small market for industrial consumer goods. These goods were imported from abroad. Once these markets had been established, they could be captured by developing a domestic import-substituting industry and protecting it from foreign competition. Especially the Latin American experiences in the 1930s have been quite significant in this respect. When international trade collapsed as a result of the international economic crisis, countries like Brazil and Argentina managed to develop an impressive domestic industry.

There are also a number of important objections to import substitution (see, for example, Kirkpatrick, 1987; Pack, 1988). First, protection of domestic industries should ideally be restricted to the early stages of production. Once an industry has learned to produce efficiently and has started reaping economies of scale, protection should be discontinued. Countries that follow the path of protection too long will be saddled with inefficient, wasteful and non-competitive industries. When inputs and outputs of such industries are valued at international prices, their net contribution to national income may even be negative.

A second objection to import substitution is that the objective of reducing dependence on foreign imports is seldom realized. Usually, one type of dependence is simply exchanged for another. The dependence on imported consumer goods decreases. The dependence on imports of capital goods, semi-manufactured goods and raw materials tends to increase. When developing countries try to build up their capital goods industries, they become more dependent on imports of technology.

A third objection is that the size of the domestic market is restricted. In dualistic economies, incomes outside the modern sector are too low to create sufficient demand. In smaller countries in particular, import substitution will soon reach its limits, but even in large countries such as Brazil the limited size of the market can cause serious problems.

A fourth objection is that import substitution may give rise to domestic monopolies, which may lead to even higher prices and more restricted supply. These domestic monopolies have a vested interest in maintaining protection indefinitely and will exert maximum political pressure to resist change.

A final objection is that large-scale industrialization policies and import substitution policies allow economies to postpone the necessary choices between more efficient and less efficient industrial actitivities. An economy should concentrate on those products which it can produce relatively efficiently. These products can also be exported to international markets. The export revenues can be used to import products the domestic industry is unable to produce efficiently.[16]

Thus a country should not try to produce 'everything under one roof' but rather concentrate on producing what it is best at. This type of policy is also called the *export-oriented industrialization policy*.

An export-oriented policy makes it more attractive for firms to focus on the international market. In order to achieve this, overvalued exchange rates have to be devalued to make exports cheaper for foreign customers. Protection of the domestic market should be reduced so that entrepreneurs have more incentive to look abroad. Reduced protection may raise the efficiency of domestic firms when they are forced to compete with foreign competitors. Finally, exporting industries can also be subsidized.

In practice, export orientation does not mean that the economy is completely liberalized or that all forms of protection and regulation are abolished. An important aim is a greater degree of balance between the profitability of domestic activities and of export activities. If industries producing for the domestic market are subsidized, export-oriented industries should be subsidized to a similar extent. Further, protection will be given less unconditionally. The efficiency and market conformity of protected industries is monitored. Protection of inefficient and loss-making activities will eventually be discontinued (Verbruggen, 1985; Amsden, 1989).

Industrialization policy in developing countries starts with import substitution. A new industry must gain experience on a protected domestic market before venturing into the world market. But too prolonged protection results in an inefficient allocation of factors of production and technical inefficiency (Little *et al.*, 1970; Pack, 1988). The most successful industrializers among the developing countries switched from import substituting industrialization to export-oriented industrialization in the 1960s (Verbruggen, 1985). Making good use of abundant supplies of cheap labour, they concentrated on labour intensive production. Export-oriented activities were supported by a variety of policy measures, including subsidies, tax reduction schemes and export-processing zones. In those branches where they were competitive due to low labour costs, they successfully managed to penetrate international markets.

The main advantage of an export-oriented industrialization strategy is that one is no longer constrained by the limited size of the domestic market. Export-oriented countries also tend to make better use of their abundant labour resources. The linkages between industry and the rest of the economy tend to be stronger than in import substitution. The tendency towards dualism tends to be weaker.

Of course, export-oriented policies can also be criticized. They have sometimes attracted so-called footloose industries, which temporarily profit from absurdly low wages, tax holidays and unrestricted profit repatriation. These industries move on when conditions are better elsewhere without making a lasting contribution to economic development. Also some authors doubt whether the world market is large enough to allow other economies to follow the example of the Asian *newly industrializing countries* (NICs) in expanding their industrial exports (Cline, 1982).

On the whole, however, the record of export orientation has been positive. Countries with a strong export orientation have experienced substantially higher growth rates of industrial production than countries that have stuck with import substitution (Kreuger, 1978, 1984; Pack, 1988; Krueger *et al.*, 1989). Countries which switched to export orientation at an early stage – such as South Korea, Taiwan, Singapore, Hong Kong, and, to a lesser extent, Thailand and Malaysia – have experienced rapid economic growth. Countries which pursued import-substitution policies for too long – such as Brazil, Mexico, Argentina and India – experienced relative stagnation (Maddison, 1989).

The choice between import substitution and export orientation depends to some extent on the size of a country. In very large countries such as India and China the case for balanced growth and import substitution is more convincing, provided one maintains a sufficient degree of competition on the vast domestic market. For the small economies of Singapore, Hong Kong, and Taiwan, a strong export orientation seems inevitable. But even in China and India the choice for a more outward-looking economic development in the 1990s has led to acceleration of economic growth.

7.7 Urban industrial bias

Since the 1960s there has been growing criticism of development strategies which at all costs favoured industry over agriculture and cities over the countryside. The *urban industrial bias* in policy had numerous adverse effects on both urban and rural areas, and also on the economy as a whole.

As discussed in sections 7.4.3 and 7.5, protection and discrimination in favour of industry in the post-war period resulted in excessively large-scale and inefficient industrialization. A great deal of resources were wasted on non-profitable prestige projects. As protected industries could obtain their capital goods too cheaply, production was too capital intensive and created little employment. Scant attention was paid to the vast numbers of workers in the informal sector and to relatively small-scale industries. A small elite of industrial workers came into being. Industrial workers secured their positions through trade unions and political parties, and consequently were paid better wages than the rural population and workers in the informal sector. Inefficient factories suffered from idle capacity. At international prices their contribution to national income could even be negative (i.e. the value of their inputs at international prices was higher than the value of their outputs). The industrial sector remained dependent on imported capital goods.

Agriculture and the rural sector were highly neglected. All attention was directed to the formal urban sector. Food prices were kept artificially low by means of price controls, compulsory deliveries and marketing boards. Overvalued exchange rates hampered agricultural exports. Moreover, revenues from agricultural exports were heavily taxed in order to finance goverment expenditures. Credit facilities for the rural population were underdeveloped. Farmers could only obtain loans by borrowing from informal moneylenders at exorbitant interest rates. Government subsidies for agricultural investment were scarce. The bulk of public facilities – schools, health centres, and so forth – was located in the cities.

All these factors together had adverse effects on the agricultural sector and resulted in stagnating agricultural production and productivity. Due to the neglect of agriculture, many African countries that had been self-supporting in food were forced to start importing foodstuffs. The same was true in Asia for India and Bangladesh and in Latin America for the former food-exporting countries, Argentina and Chile. The lopsided focus on industrialization reinforced the economic *dualism* between the modern industrial sector and the stagnating rural sector. From the 1970s onwards, arguments were advanced for a more healthy balance between the agricultural and industrial sectors (Bos, 1984). These arguments will be discussed in more detail in Chapter 8.

7.8 *Outcomes of industrialization strategies*

In the post-war period many developing countries increased their savings and investment rates. In many cases, the recommendations of Lewis and Rostow to invest at least 12 to 15 per cent of net national income were met (see Table 3.2, p. 79), and a substantial part of all investment went to industry. But the results of industrialization policies varied substantially from country to country and region to region.

On balance, a rapid process of industrialization has taken place in developing countries. Table 7.3 presents data on the growth of industrial production and the share of industry in gross domestic product. Between 1960 and 1980 there was rapid growth in both industry (including mining, manufacturing, construction and utilities) and in manufacturing proper. Between 1960 and 1970 growth was most rapid in the upper middle income countries. Between 1970 and 1980 the growth rates in low income and middle income countries tended to be rather similar. China registered exceptionally high growth throughout the whole period covered in the table.[17] In the manufacturing sector the increase in production was not restricted to consumer goods only. The share of intermediate goods and capital goods also increased over time. For example, the share of capital goods increased from 20.8 per cent in 1963 to 31.2 per cent in 1979 (Kirkpatrick, 1987).

After 1980 the pace of industrial growth in middle income countries slowed down dramatically. It was influenced by the weak performance of Latin American industrial economies after the debt crisis of 1982. Between 1980 and 1993 the annual growth rate in middle-income countries was only 2 per cent for industry and 3.5 per cent for manufacturing. On the other hand, growth in low-income countries accelerated after 1980. Especially China, and to a lesser degree India, showed rapid growth. Excluding India and China, growth for industry in low-income countries

Table 7.3 Growth of production in industry and manufacturing, 1960–1993

	Growth rate of production						Share in national income			
	Industry[a]			Manufacturing			Industry[a]		Manufacturing	
	1960–70[b]	1970–80	1980–93	1960–70[b]	1970–80	1980–93	1965	1993	1965	1993
Low income countries	6.6	6.3	7.6	5.5	7.3	8.6	26.0	35.0	19.0	25.0
Excluding India and China	6.6	5.3	2.2	6.3[c]	5.7[c]	6.8	20.0	25.0	8.0	13.0
India	5.4	4.5	6.5	4.7	4.7	6.3	22.0	27.0	16.0	17.0
China	11.2	8.9	11.5	–	10.8	11.1	35.0	48.0	28.0	38.0
Middle income countries	7.4	6.7[d]	2.0	7.3	–	3.5[e]	34.0	37.0	20.0	–
Lower-middle income countries	6.2	5.0[d]	1.8	6.5	6.1[d]	2.5[e]	32.0	31.0[f]	20.0	23.0[f]
Upper-middle income countries	9.1	6.1	2.3	8.4	6.6	2.5	36.0	40.0[f]	19.0	25.0[f]

Notes:

[a] Industry includes mining, manufacturing, construction and public utilities.

[b] For the period 1960–1970, the median of growth rates is presented; for later periods, the average. After 1970, the classification of countries is slightly different.

[c] 1970–80 and 1980–92 from *WDR 1994*; [d] 1965–80; [e] 1980–90; [f] 1990.

Sources: 1960–1970 from *World Development Report 1984*; 1970–1993 from *WDR 1995*. Footnoted figures from WDR various issues.

was much lower at 2.2 per cent per year. But growth of manufacturing remained very impressive at 6.8 per cent per year.

With the exception of the lower-middle-income countries, the share of industry in total GDP between 1965 and 1993 increased in all groups. The share of manufacturing also increased substantially.

At a conference of the United Nations Organization for Industrialization (UNIDO) in Lima in 1975, an objective was adopted to the effect that the share of developing countries in total world production of manufactured goods should be at least 25 per cent by the year 2000 (Bos, 1984). If one includes China, this objective of the Lima declaration has been realized by 1992. Table 7.4 presents recent data on the shares of developing countries in world production of manufactured goods. The share of developing countries, excluding China, increased from 10.9 per cent in 1970 to 16.7 per cent in 1992. The share of West Asia tripled between 1960 and 1988. The share of South and Southeast Asia has almost quadrupled since 1960 from 2.0 per cent to 7.8 per cent. On the African continent the share in total production stagnated at around 1 per cent.

Table 7.4 Share of developing countries in world manufacturing value added (%)

Year	Africa	West Asia	South and East Asia	China	Latin America	Developing countries total[a]
Excluding China						
1960	0.8	0.4	2.0		5.0	
1970	0.8	0.7	2.7		6.2	10.9
1980	0.9	0.9	4.1		7.1	13.7
1990	1.0	1.3[b]	6.8		5.7	15.3
1992	1.1		7.8		6.1	16.7
Including China						
1981	0.9	1.0	4.2	3.9	6.5	17.1
1988	0.9	1.1	5.7	7.2	5.6	21.2
1992	1.0		7.0	10.5	5.5	25.5

Notes:
[a] Total including Malta and former Yugoslavia.
[b] 1988 from UNIDO (1990).

Source: 1960: Gosh (1984, p. 351); 1970 and after: UNIDO (1995), except West Asia from UNIDO (1990).

UNIDO data on China are only presented for the years since 1981 and are still far from reliable. The share of developing countries, including China, in the world production of manufactured goods increased from 17.5 per cent in 1981 to 25.5 per cent in 1992.

The nineteenth-century pattern of international trade, in which developing countries only exported unprocessed agricultural and mining products, no longer exists. An increasing part of developing countries' exports consists of manufactures.

The share of manufactured goods in total commodity exports has increased in all developing countries (see Table 3.4, p. 81). In some countries, especially in Asia, manufactured goods are by far the most important exports. Most of these manufactures are sold on the markets of the rich Western countries.

Although aggregate figures thus point to a successful process of industrialization, industrial production has been concentrated in a relatively small number of countries, which include Brazil, Mexico, Argentina, China, India, South Korea, Taiwan, Singapore, Hong Kong, and Turkey. The largest share of industrial exports comes from only a few countries, including Hong Kong, Singapore, Korea, Taiwan, Brazil, India, Mexico, and, in recent years, Malaysia and Thailand.

In the course of the 1980s Latin American industrial economies experienced great difficulties, due to the debt crisis and continued import substitution. In India the industrial sector suffered from considerable inefficiency and low capacity utilization. In Africa, industrialization never really took off despite substantial efforts.

In the previous sections the drawbacks of forced industrialization have been highlighted: an uneven development of economy and society, waste of scarce resources, and neglect of the agricultural sector and small-scale informal activities. However, I do not mean to say that industrialization is no longer important as a policy goal. The old arguments in favour of industrialization, discussed at the beginning of this chapter, still retain their force. But what is needed are more balanced policies which do not neglect other sectors of the economy and which pay more attention to the capacity of a society to absorb industrial investment.

Since World War II, developing countries have made substantial progress in industrialization. Not all new industries were particularly efficient or productive. Nevertheless, in the long run, success in industrialization can only be achieved through learning by doing.

QUESTIONS FOR REVIEW

1. Does economic development necessarily imply industrialization? Provide theoretical and empirical justifications for your answer.
2. Discuss the main characteristics of Arthur Lewis's model of economic development with unlimited supplies of labour. What are the most important criticisms levelled against the Lewis model?
3. Provide an overview of the theoretical arguments for large-scale industrialization in developing countries.
4. Analyze the relationships between large-scale import substitution and government planning in post-war industrialization strategies.
5. Summarize the most important criticisms of post-war industrialization strategies.
6. What is the difference between unbalanced and balanced industrialization strategies?

7. Why is there less emphasis on the scale of the investment effort in export-oriented industrialization, than in import substituting industrialization strategies?
8. To what extent have industrialization strategies in developing countries been successful in the post-war period?

Notes

1. I abstract here from the complex issue of the distinction between growth of the capital stock and technological change.
2. The definition of the relevant economic sectors depends on the context of discussion. It is extremely important to know which definition an author is using when discussing 'structural transformation'. When one focuses on the decreasing importance of the agricultural sector and the increasing importance of the industrial sector, one refers to the industrial sector in its broadest possible sense. This includes mining, manufacturing, construction, and utilities (gas, water and electricity). The service sector includes all remaining activities: government, telecommunication, trade, transport, personal services, and business and financial services. However, when one refers to the differences between the primary, the secondary and the tertiary sector, mining is included in the primary sector together with agriculture, animal husbandry, fishing, and forestry. Within the industrial sector special attention is often paid to the most dynamic subsector, manufacturing.
3. The income elasticity of the demand for agricultural products is the percentage increase in the consumption of agricultural products divided by the percentage increase in real income per capita. If income elasticity is less than one, the share of agricultural products in total expenditure will decrease as per capita income rises; if income elasticity is less than one, it will go up.
4. Unfortunately, it was not possible to exclude utilities from the commodity producing sector as a whole.
5. In the richest countries of the world, growth of labour productivity in agriculture in the post-war period has been higher than in industry – particularly due to biotechnological innovation (see Maddison, 1991, 150–1). However, this is an exception to the general pattern. Even here, the level of labour productivity in industry is much higher than in agriculture.
6. By now we know that wages did rise under capitalism. In the long run, the working classes shared in the increase in prosperity.
7. Marginal productivity is the extra contribution to production made by the last worker (or hour) added to the production process. If marginal productivity is zero, the last person employed makes no further contribution to production.
8. Lewis emphasizes the voluntary nature of migration. Other authors argue that coercion also played an important role (see Chapter 3).
9. One can distinguish between the average capital–output ratio and the incremental capital–output ratio. Here I assume that incremental capital–output ratio and average capital–output ratio are equal.
10. If per capita income increases by 2 per cent per year, per capita national income will double every 35 years.
11. Lewis also emphasizes the fact that the government may perform this function of saving and investing.
12. In his well-known textbook, *The Economics of Development*, Myint (1980) has admirably summarized the debate on large-scale industrialization strategies and balanced growth. The following sections are primarily based on Myint's discussion of these issues.

13. In a later article Lewis actually acknowledges this (Lewis, 1983b). Still, he maintains that workers remaining in agriculture can maintain previous levels of production.
14. It would not be correct to say that there would be no urban unemployment if more labour intensive techniques were employed. Technological change has made industrial production generally more capital intensive. However, an inappropriate choice of techniques certainly worsens employment prospects.
15. South Korea is one of the few countries where labour surpluses have been successfully absorbed.
16. The theory of comparative advantage states that all countries which participate in international trade will benefit if they concentrate on exporting those products they can produce relatively efficiently.
17. Official Chinese growth rates tend to be overestimated, but growth is undoubtedly very rapid (Szirmai and Ren, 1995)

8 Industrialization and agricultural development

Chapter 7 presented criticisms of development strategies that focused exclusively on the industrial sector and neglected other sectors of the economy. These strategies tended to reinforce the already existing economic dualism between the modern urban industrial sector and the stagnating rural sector. This chapter centres on the relations between agricultural and industrial development. The starting point of the analysis remains the fact that in the process of economic development the share of the agricultural sector in production and employment declines and the share of the industrial sector increases. However, in comparison with development strategies that give precedence to industry at all cost, a more positive picture is presented of agriculture and its role in economic development.

The argument consists of two main elements. First, successful industrialization processes are usually preceded by increases in agricultural productivity. Second, in later stages of development a stagnating agricultural sector will be an obstacle to further development of the entire economy. Therefore, a more balanced approach to agriculture and industry is called for in development strategies.

8.1 *Industry and agriculture*

8.1.1 Definitions of economic sectors

Discussions of dualism and intersectoral relationships often suffer from a lack of clarity in sectoral demarcations. At least four kinds of sectoral contrasts can be distinguished, as follows:

1. *The primary versus the secondary sector* The primary sector includes the production of foodstuffs, non-food crops, fishing, hunting, forestry, and mining

(Lundahl, 1985). The secondary sector uses primary products which are directly extracted from nature and converts them into manufactured products. The secondary sector consists of manufacturing and construction. Often utilities, providing gas, water, and electricity, are also included in the secondary sector.

2. *Agriculture versus industry* Besides agriculture proper, the agricultural sector usually also includes hunting, fisheries and forestry. Industry includes mining, manufacturing, construction and utilities. Thus industry equals the secondary sector plus mining.

3. *The traditional sector versus the modern sector* The traditional sector includes subsistence agriculture, traditional crafts production, and the rural and urban informal sector. The modern sector includes manufacturing, construction and mining, but also commercial agriculture (including plantations), the modern service sector and government. The modern sector is characterized by a monetary economy, production for the market and higher levels of productivity and technological sophistication.

4. *The rural versus the urban sector* The distinction between the countryside (rural areas) and the urban sector is a spatial one. Cities and towns are locations characterized by higher population densities than rural areas. Industrial activities are more important in the urban sector, and agricultural activities more important in the rural sector. In rural areas one finds both subsistence agriculture and commercial agriculture. The rural sector, however, is not exclusively agricultural (see Chapter 9), and in rural areas one also finds rural industries, traditional crafts production, wage labour, sometimes mining, services, and a rural informal sector.

These four distinctions differ considerably. But in the literature they are often used in a loose and careless manner. For some theories the distinction between the traditional sector and the modern commercial sector is the most important. Strictly speaking this holds for Lewis's (1954) theory of 'unlimited supplies of labour'. But often the Lewis model is used to analyze the relationships between agriculture and industry. Other theories focus on the relationships between primary and secondary production. When one is talking about the *urban-industrial bias* (Lipton, 1977), the important distinction is between urban and rural communities. The term *rural development* is also based on the rural–urban distinction. It indicates that the rural community comprises more than agricultural activities only (see Chapter 9).

In sections 8.1 to 8.3 of this chapter, the main emphasis is on the distinction between agriculture and industry and the relationships between them in the course of economic development. Agriculture consists of subsistence production and market production of foodstuffs and other agricultural products by both smallholders and large commercial farms and plantations. Forestry and fishing will not be dealt with explicitly, although they also belong to the agricultural sector. In sections 8.4 to 8.8, where we discuss the role of primary exports in economic development, the focus shifts to the distinction between the primary and the secondary sector. Of course, agricultural exports are important in primary exports and much of the argument in this chapter will focus on agricultural exports, but primary exports also include mining exports.

8.1.2 Open and closed models of the economy: early and late stages of development

To structure the discussion in the following sections, I will make a rough distinction between earlier and later stages of industrialization; and between open and closed models of economic development (Lewis, 1954; Nicholls, 1964; Myint, 1975, 1980; Timmer, 1988).

Earlier and later stages of industrialization

Before industrialization starts the great majority of the population finds its livelihood in agriculture. The agricultural sector is the only domestic sector that can provide labour and savings which can be used to start industrialization. The construction of a modern industrial sector inevitably starts with a transfer of productive resources from agriculture to the industrial sector.

At later stages of development the agricultural and the industrial sectors exist alongside each other. Strategic choices have to be made with respect to the priority given to either agriculture or industry in economic policy.

Open and closed models of development

Just as in Chapter 7, I distinguish between open and closed models of economic development. In closed models there are no relations with other countries in the world economy. Within the framework of a closed model, several *two-sector models* have been developed that focus on the interactions and resource flows between agricultural and industrial sectors in different stages of economic development.

In open models, attention is paid to the relations with the international economy. Some of the interactions between agriculture and industry take place via the outside world. In this context, I will discuss the contributions of agricultural exports to economic development. Agricultural exports earn revenues and foreign exchange that are potentially available for reinvestment in the industrial sector.[1] In open models there is also the possibility of foreign direct investment and foreign capital flows providing an impetus for industrialization.

An open model also assumes a transfer of resources from agriculture to industry during the initial stages of industrialization. Here export profits are reinvested in industry. Once industry has started developing, strategic decisions have to be faced in open models just as in closed models. Does policy continue to give priority to industry over agriculture or not?

8.2 *The development of agriculture as a prerequisite for industrialization*

8.2.1 The necessity of an agricultural surplus in early stages of development

In pre-industrial societies the majority of the population is active in the agricultural sector. In a closed economy the means required for developing a domestic industry can only be found in the agricultural sector. Prior to industrialization, productivity in the agricultural sector must increase sufficiently to produce a surplus over the subsistence needs of the agrarian population. Only when such a surplus has become available can processes of transfer to the industrial sector be initiated. Several authors (development economists, economic historians, and agronomists) therefore argue that an increase in labour productivity in agriculture is a necessary condition for industrialization (Rostow, 1960; Kuznets, 1965; Boserup, 1981; Timmer, 1988; Ranis, 1989).

In an open economy the agricultural sector contributes to economic development through the revenues from agricultural exports that are available for investment in the industrial sector. Again, the agricultural sector must produce a surplus over its subsistence needs.

This implies a more positive view of the agricultural sector, even in the early stages of industrialization. Agriculture is a dynamic sector in its own right, with an important contribution to make to economic development. Prior to industrialization there has to be an agrarian revolution.[2]

8.2.2 The agricultural sector: stagnant or dynamic sector

In the industrialization strategies discussed in Chapter 7, the agricultural sector is mainly considered in negative terms as a reservoir of labour, food and savings (financial capital) which can be transferred to the industrial sector. The agricultural sector itself is regarded as traditional, stagnant, and characterized by low productivity and low potential. The dynamic sector is the industrial sector which, for this very reason, should be developed as soon as possible.

Arthur Lewis's (1954) well-known model of 'economic development with unlimited supplies of labour' is an example of this view. This model assumes an extremely low marginal productivity in agriculture. Therefore labour can very simply be withdrawn from agriculture and be employed more productively in industry. In the same article, though, Lewis does acknowledge the fact that agriculture needs to grow along with the industrial sector in order to prevent economic development from grinding to a halt. If agricultural production stagnates, food prices will increase, and the internal terms of trade (the ratio of agricultural to industrial prices) will turn against the industrial sector.[3] Nevertheless, it cannot be denied that the Lewis model assumes a low agricultural productivity in the initial stages of industrialization. His assumption is that labour productivity will automatically increase in agriculture when surplus labour is removed.

Is there any synthesis possible between these conflicting views, that is, transfer of surpluses from a productive agricultural system or squeezing resources out of a low-productive agricultural sector? In a criticism of negative perspectives on agriculture, Reynolds (1975b, p. 14) makes a helpful distinction between transfer of resources from a static agricultural system and transfer of resources from a dynamic agricultural system.

In an economy where agricultural productivity prior to industrialization is stagnant there can still be surpluses of labour time, food, and savings. These surpluses may be withdrawn from the agricultural sector as part of the industrialization strategy. Forced transfer of surpluses, however, leads to the impoverishment of the rural population and possibly even to famine. Transfer in a more dynamic context implies that agricultural production and productivity can continue to increase as a result of agricultural investment, technological progress, positive incentives and intensification of production. Part of the increment in agricultural output and agricultural real incomes is available for transfer to industry. But sufficient portions of additional earnings are ploughed back into agriculture, to maintain its dynamic momentum.

In the history of European industrialization, increases in agricultural productivity preceded industrialization. In developing countries, average agricultural output per worker in the 1960s was much lower than in Western countries between 1810 and 1860 (Bairoch, 1975). Their experience provides an instance of transfer of resources out of a relatively static agricultural sector.[4] Both the stagnation of agricultural development in sub-Saharan Africa and the disappointing outcomes of industrialization should be interpreted in this perspective (World Bank, 1989).

8.2.3 The role of agriculture in early stages of development

In early stages of development one can distinguish the following important contributions of the agricultural sector to the process of economic development (Johnston and Mellor, 1961; Nicholls, 1964; Reynolds, 1975a; Lewis, 1978b; Boserup, 1981; Timmer, 1988):

1. *Agriculture as a source of domestic savings* Until a modern sector has developed, there is no alternative source of domestic savings other than revenues from the sale of agricultural surpluses. The agricultural sector provides the necessary savings for investment in industry and infrastructure.

2. *Agriculture as a source of industrial labour* In early stages of development labour has to be withdrawn from the agricultural sector to create an urban industrial labour force. Labour can also be withdrawn from agriculture for work on infrastructural projects.

3. *Agriculture as a supplier of food for domestic consumption* In early stages of development poor countries are characterized by a rapidly increasing demand for food. On the one hand, the demand for food is determined by the rapidly growing

population, and on the other, by rising per capita incomes (Johnston and Mellor, 1961). Poor people tend to spend a large part of their additional income on food.[5] Since the industrial sector withdraws labour from the agricultural sector, the growing demand for food must be met by the workers remaining in the agricultural sector. This will not cause great problems if the agricultural sector is already quite productive before the onset of industrialization, but if productivity is low and shows no improvement, urban food shortages will push food prices up. High food prices will exert an upward pressure on the costs of labour in the industrial sector.

4. *Agricultural exports as a source of foreign currency* The above-mentioned three functions of agriculture are typical of a closed model of economic development. The debate on the role of agricultural exports is based on an open model of the economy (Myint, 1975). In early stages of economic development agricultural exports are the most likely source of foreign exchange earnings. Foreign exchange is needed to finance imports of the capital goods and intermediate goods required for industrialization.

In theory, an open economy could concentrate on export production. It could meet the demand for food by exporting manufactures, mining products and cash crops, using part of the proceeds to import food (Myint, 1975). Even so, an increase in productivity in domestic food production would lead to considerable savings in scarce foreign exchange, which would otherwise have had to be used for food imports (Nicholls, 1964, p. 12). Agricultural exports will be discussed in more detail in section 8.4.

5. *The agricultural sector as a market for industrial products* Newly established industries are seldom successful in penetrating international markets. They first have to gain experience on their domestic markets. When a large proportion of the population is active within the agricultural sector, an increase in agricultural incomes will create a market for products of the new industries. However, the function of the agricultural sector as a market conflicts with its function as provider of savings. The more people consume, the less they will be able to save. According to Nicholls, the savings function is more important than the market function in the early stages of industrialization. The first industrial products are sold on urban rather than rural markets.

8.2.4 Historical examples[6]

England and Western Europe

From the eighteenth century onwards, a productive agricultural sector provided a sound basis for industrialization in Western Europe. In the eighteenth century English agriculture was the most productive in Europe.[7] Farmers switched to more intensive forms of land use, annual harvests and crop rotation, instead of letting part of the land area lie fallow for one or more years. New high-quality food crops like turnips and potatoes were introduced. Farmers switched to intensive cattle breeding. Part of the farm land was used for the systematic production of fodder crops. Animal manure was used to maintain the fertility of the land. Agriculture became commercialized. Until the 1930s this highly efficient agricultural system was capable of feeding the expanding urban population. There was also a flow of labour from agriculture to the urban centres.

America and Australia

The initial conditions in agriculture in sparsely populated countries such as the United States, Canada, Argentina, and Australia were extremely favourable. At an early stage these countries were able to realize high labour productivity in agriculture, compensating for the scarcity of labour by employing much capital (Baldwin, 1956). The agricultural sector produced considerable surpluses of food and other agricultural products which could be exported. At a later stage the export revenues were available to finance industrialization. Immigration and foreign investment were incentives for economic development.

Such countries provide interesting examples of successful primary export-led economic development. But such development does not follow automatically, as can be seen from the disappointing experience of countries such as Argentina and Brazil. In these countries the long-term development of the agricultural sector was hampered by inefficient institutions such as large landownership. Investments in infrastructure and industry were delayed.

Russia

Russia is an example of a country that started its industrialization under relatively favourable initial conditions. Russian agriculture was – and still is – potentially one of the most productive in the world. This potential, however, has never been fully realized. Until 1861 a system of serfdom was maintained under which labour was tied to the land in an unproductive fashion. After the abolition of serfdom in 1861 large capitalist landowners benefited most from the land reforms. They made high profits, but output increased less than it would have if smaller farmers had been allowed to work the lands more intensively. Rural poverty increased rather than decreased.

Large landowners invested part of their profits in infrastructure, railways, and the industrial sector. The imposition of taxes forced smaller farmers to produce cash crops so that Russia could export wheat.

The Russian pattern of rapid industrialization and heavy exploitation of the peasantry was continued in the communist Soviet Union. Despite resistance by the rural population, agriculture was collectivized. Coercion was used to force the agricultural sector to provide the growing urban population with cheap food.

From the perspective of industrialization, the process of transferring resources from agriculture to industry was fairly successful – though it involved immense human sacrifices. Within a short time the Soviet Union succeeded in building an extensive industrial sector. But the overexploitation of the agrarian sector resulted in an agricultural sector performing far below potential, to this very day.

8.2.5 Conclusion

The lesson to be derived from this section is that it pays for developing countries to try to increase output and productivity in the agricultural sector, even at early stages of development. A dynamic agriculture, producing surpluses, helps combat rural poverty; it also creates favourable conditions for the development of industry.

8.3 *Closed model: a balance between agricultural and industrial development*

8.3.1 Introduction

In the initial stages of industrialization a transfer of resources from agriculture to industry can be justified. That the establishment of a new industrial sector should receive priority can also be defended. But once the process of industrialization is under way, policy is inevitably confronted with difficult choices between investments in agriculture or industry. Should all resources continue to be channelled towards the industrial sector, or should the agricultural sector receive more priority? Post-war advocates of large-scale industrialization and the 'big push', like Leibenstein, Higgins, and Hirschman, argue that industrialization must be given top priority. This implies that the transfer of resources from agriculture to industry should be continued. Most developing countries have taken this advice and have given preference to industry over agriculture in the development strategies of the 1950s and 1960s.

8.3.2 Transfer mechanisms

In the process of resource transfer from agriculture to industry, government policy played an important role. Imposition of taxes was one of the ways to induce subsistence farmers to start producing for the market. They were forced to earn cash money in order to meet their tax obligations. Moreover, taxes skimmed off a considerable part of productivity increases and thus functioned as a kind of forced saving. Prices were kept artificially low by government intervention for the benefit of the industrial sector. Often governments made use of 'marketing boards', which bought up the entire agricultural production at prices fixed below market rates. In several countries, compulsory deliveries of rice and food grains were used to secure the supplies of food to the urban population. Deficit finance or increase of the money supply provided governments with funds to invest in the modern sector, while the resulting inflation functioned as a tax on agricultural incomes.

Government expenditure patterns were also biased in favour of industry. Industrial activities were subsidized, protected by tariffs, provided with cheap credit and underpriced inputs. Investment funds for agriculture were relatively scarce and credit facilities expensive and limited.

Resource transfers sometimes also took place in the private sector, whenever large landowners reinvested their profits in the industrial sector or in infrastructure while paying their agriculture labourers low wages.

8.3.3 Balance between agriculture and industry

Since the 1960s a more balanced approach to both agriculture and industry was put forward as an alternative to post-war industrial *balanced growth strategies* (Mellor, 1976). This approach was called the balanced growth path (Myint, 1980, chapter 8). The basic idea of the balanced growth path is that the pace of economic development of a country depends on a balance between the rate of output growth in different sectors. When the growth of one sector lags behind the requirements of other sectors, these other sectors will be affected negatively as well. Thus economic development in a closed economy depends on the rate of growth of the slowest growing sector. If agriculture stagnates as a result of the too heavy burdens imposed upon it, this will also have adverse effects on industrial development. When industrialization fails to take off, this will limit the developmental opportunities of the agricultural sector. Just as within industry, there are also numerous linkages and complementarities between agricultural and industrial activities. In a closed model of the economy, successful economic development therefore implies that the growth of production in agriculture and industry should be kept in balance (Myint, 1980, pp. 109–10).[8] In the course of the 1960s, countries such as India, Indonesia, and China changed course and started to pay more attention to agriculture. In other developing countries, neglect of the agricultural sector continued despite some changes in official rhetoric.

In the following section, the various interactions between agriculture and industry will be discussed more systematically.

Contributions of the agricultural sector

1. *Food* The industrial sector cannot continue to grow, unless the production of food stays in step. If food production falls short, food prices will go up. This causes inflation. Inflation will start off a wage–price spiral which has negative effects on profits and investment rates in the industrial sector. When food has to be imported to meet urban food requirements, this squanders scarce foreign exchange, which could have been used for investment. This happened in India in the 1960s. In this country the attainment of economic objectives was impeded by recurring food shortages that necessitated food imports (Cassen, 1978; Bardhan, 1984).

In absence of positive incentives and technological change, farmers remaining in the countryside will not be willing to work harder to produce additional food for the urban population. They will only do so if they can sell their agricultural surpluses at reasonable prices and have the opportunity of buying industrial goods, with the money thus earned.

This is one of the essential points of difference between so-called *classical two-sector models* (Lewis, 1954; Fei and Ranis, 1964) and *neoclassical two-sector models* (Jorgenson, 1961, 1967, 1969). The classical approach has been discussed in the previous chapter. It states that labour can be withdrawn from the agricultural sector 'free of charge' since this labour is being 'wasted' and has little or no opportunity costs. The neoclassical point of view argues that factors are fully employed. One can never withdraw factors of production from a sector of the economy without some loss in output. This means that a transfer of resources from agriculture to industry involves costs. Among others these costs include the rewards that have to motivate those remaining in agriculture to increase their output.

Higher prices for agricultural products can contribute to technological progress and productivity increases in the agricultural sector. In the long term, increasing food supplies will stabilize agricultural prices. The opposite is true when agricultural prices are kept low artificially. This causes food shortages and upward pressures on food prices. For political reasons (e.g. fear of political turmoil) governments start subsidizing food for the urban population. In many countries these subsidies are an increasing burden on government budgets.

Of course, the neo-classical assumption that increasing prices would automatically result in increased supplies of food can also be criticized. Markets in developing countries do not function perfectly. There are all sorts of supply constraints such as lack of infrastructure, storage facilities or insufficient information (Helleiner, 1992; see also the discussion of structural adjustment programmes in Chapter 11). Nevertheless, the neoclassical critique of the concept of costless development has served as a welcome counterbalance to the post-war neglect of agriculture.

2. *Primary inputs for the industrial sector* Just as within the industrial sector, there are technical complementarities between agriculture and industry. Agricultural products such as food, wood, fibres or rubber serve as inputs for the food-processing industry, the furniture industry, the textile industry or the rubber industry. The first two industries to emerge in developing countries are often textiles and food processing.

3. *Markets for industrial consumer goods and producer goods* In countries where most of the labour force is in the agricultural sector, the size of the urban market is limited. If industrialization depends exclusively on the urban market, the momentum of industrialization will soon falter. An increase in agricultural incomes may create an internal market of sufficient size, both for industrial consumer goods and for agricultural machinery, implements, industrially produced fertilizers and chemical inputs. This enlarged market provides an important stimulus to continued growth in the industrial sector. Conversely, stagnating agricultural incomes will have adverse effects on the growth of industrial production. Sometimes, proponents of the *balanced*

growth path approach also argue that in balanced growth, industry will be more oriented to the provision of the basic needs of the rural population, rather than the luxury needs of urban elites.

4. *Agriculture as a source of savings* Otherwise than in the very early stages of development, the industrial sector no longer depends exclusively on the agricultural sector for savings. Reinvestment of retained profits and urban savings are alternative domestic sources. But a dynamic agricultural sector can also be a source of savings in later stages of development, provided that a sufficient part of the savings is available for reinvestment in agriculture itself.

5. *Employment* In later stages of development, the agricultural sector no longer has to supply labour to the industrial sector. In the urban sectors there is widespread unemployment and underemployment. A new role for the agricultural sector is to provide additional employment opportunities. China, for example, has tried to discourage migration to the cities and to create more rural employment – both within agriculture and in other sectors of the rural economy (Rawski, 1979).

The contributions of agriculture discussed here are somewhat similar to those in earlier stages of economic development. But there are important differences in emphasis. In early stages of development supplies of food, labour, and savings are of prime importance. The first markets for industrial products are found in urban enclaves. Even the inputs for new industries are often imported (Hirschman, 1988). In the later stages of development the agricultural sector becomes more important as a market and as a supplier of inputs to industry. The agricultural sector also generates new employment. Finally, the linkages no longer run only from agriculture to industry. Agricultural development becomes ever more dependent on industrial inputs. Domestic industry is a potential supplier of such inputs.

Contributions of industry to the agricultural sector

1. *Consumer goods* Just as agriculture provides food for the industrial labour force and the urban population, the industrial sector provides the agricultural population with consumer goods. The possibility of acquiring industrially produced consumer goods is one of the important positive incentives for the rural population to increase its production. There are complementarities in demand not only within industry, but also between agriculture and industry (Myint, 1980).

2. *Agricultural producer goods* The agricultural sector has an urgent need for industrial inputs, including farm implements, farming machinery, inorganic fertilizers, water pumps, pesticides, herbicides, electrical energy, irrigation systems, and industrially developed seeds. In the absence of inputs from the industrial sector, productivity growth in the agricultural sector will eventually stagnate and food prices will start increasing. This is an example of technical complementarities between the two sectors.

8.3.4 Conclusion: negative and positive incentives

In the preceding section it was assumed that higher prices would motivate farmers to increase production. As already indicated, this thesis is not without its critics. Under certain conditions, higher prices will lead to increased rural consumption, rather than investment in productive capacity.

When governments do not provide new infrastructure, new inputs, agricultural research and development, agricultural credit, and agricultural extension, agricultural production is unlikely to respond strongly to price increases (Islam, 1989a). Recent research in sub-Saharan Africa shows that the terms of trade between agricultural and industrial products can improve, while agricultural production stagnates. Higher relative prices are in fact caused by shortfalls in agricultural production. These shortfalls in turn are the result of insufficient investment in agricultural infrastructure (Bautista, 1989).

Price increases may also aggravate rural income inequality. Those who benefit from higher prices are the large, market-oriented farmers. Peasants producing for their own consumption will not profit much. Farm labourers and other rural inhabitants who have to purchase their food on the market will be negatively affected by price increases.

In China, and in other centrally planned economies, the government for a long time took on the task of providing capital goods, machinery, energy, irrigation, and inputs. The farmers were compelled to provide the urban population with food.

Proponents of a market-oriented approach to agriculture acknowledge the significance of infrastructural investment. However, they argue with some justification that farmers will only make optimal use of the available infrastructure, technology and institutions if price incentives are positive. Thus newly developed technologies will spread only if price relations make it attractive for farmers to apply them (Islam, 1989a).

Many countries have therefore elected to employ a mix of negative and positive incentives (Myint, 1980). Negative incentives include taxes and compulsory delivery of part of the output. These are combined with positive incentives such as investment in infrastructure, investment in agricultural research, education and agricultural extension, provision of new inputs, and the right to sell all production exceeding compulsory quotas at free market prices.

Japan in the late nineteenth century (Ohkawa and Rosovsky, 1964) and Taiwan and South Korea during the post-war period provide interesting examples of a policy of 'walking on two legs'. In such a policy, both industrial and agricultural development receive sufficient attention. Tax measures and other negative sanctions ensure that the benefits of agricultural development policy are not exclusively appropriated by the agricultural labour force.

In Japan, and in Korea and Taiwan, redistribution of land stimulated small and medium-size farmers to increase their investment. A great deal of research was carried out on new seeds and new production techniques. Much attention was paid to education and to passing on new production techniques to the farmers. At the same time, tax measures skimmed off part of the agricultural surplus. Taiwan maintained the compulsory delivery of a portion of the harvest to the urban population. Part of the taxed surplus was invested in the industrial sector; another part, however, was channelled back into the agricultural sector in the form of expenditures for research, development, and irrigation.

After the liberalization of Chinese agriculture in 1978, the terms of trade of agricultural products to industrial products improved considerably. Agricultural output and productivity soared. However, some observers fear that the increased revenues of farmers may be consumed and that agricultural investments may be neglected in the long term (Griffin, 1987). In the early 1990s, the urban–rural divide seems to be growing again under the impact of very rapid industrialization.

In summary, agricultural development is hampered when the internal terms of trade become too unfavourable to the agricultural sector. In the long run, this also affects industrial development adversely. However, if the terms of trade swing too much in favour of agriculture, urban standards of living and wage levels will come under pressure. The strategy of balanced intersectoral growth therefore requires a search for a delicate dynamic equilibrium between the growth paths of the different sectors. Characteristic of such an approach is making optimal use of the complementarities between sectors and trying to realize parallel increases in output and productivity in both sectors. Intersectoral linkages are most effective when industrial activities are decentralized, rather than concentrated in a few large urban centres (Ranis, 1989).

In addition to balanced terms of trade between agriculture and industry, policy should aim at a reasonable balance in the allocation of resources (credit, funds for research and development, subsidies on capital and inputs) to agriculture and industry, and a balance in the imposition of taxes and other burdens.

As will be shown in Chapter 9, relatively cheap investments in the agricultural sector may have high payoffs. For instance, there are possibilities for land-saving investments which make use of the abundant supplies of labour. Therefore, a more balanced approach to agriculture and industry would also be desirable from the point of view of employment creation. Further, in countries where agriculture still accounts for a large part of national income and employment, growth of agricultural output and productivity will have significant positive effects on income per capita. In sub-Saharan Africa, GDP is still very much determined by the agricultural sector. For instance, in Tanzania the share of agriculture in GDP was 61 per cent in 1993 (see Table 3.8). A revitalization of agriculture in sub-Saharan Africa may be one of the prerequisites for an improvement of the region's standard of living (Lensink, 1995).

In the course of economic development the industrial sector gains in relative importance, whereas the agricultural sector becomes relatively less important. Yet on the road to economic development, it is important to maintain and improve agricultural productivity and dynamism. A dynamic agricultural sector will also create new rural employment possibilities outside agriculture and is conducive to sustainable patterns of industrialization (Ranis, 1989, p. 43).

8.4 *Open model: agricultural exports*

8.4.1 Introduction

The discussion of the balance between agriculture and industry assumes a closed model in which everything is produced within the confines of the domestic economy. However, in an open model, developing countries have the option of exporting agricultural products. The revenues from these exports may be reinvested in other sectors. For a proper understanding of the economic history of developing countries, an open model is of great importance (Islam, 1989a). The modern economic development of these countries commenced with the export of cash crops and other primary exports.

In the early stages of development, the export of cash crops is an alternative to direct processes of resource transfer from agriculture to industry in the closed model. In the first place, agricultural exports result in increases in per capita income. In the second place, the increased earnings of people involved in the export sector create a market for imported industrial consumer goods. In due time this market can be captured by import-substituting domestic industries. In the third place, agricultural exports generate savings which can be used for investment in industry and infrastructure. Finally, agricultural exports are a means of obtaining foreign exchange, which can be used to finance imports of the capital goods and intermediate inputs required for industrialization. Like resource transfers in closed models, agricultural exports presume the availability of a surplus over subsistence needs in the agricultural sector that can potentially be utilized for developmental purposes.

At later stages of development, the more open an economy, the more domestic imbalances it can afford. In an open economy, countries will concentrate on those lines of production in which they have a comparative advantage. The goods in which a country is relatively unproductive can be imported (Myint, 1975). For example, a country can export non-food cash crops or certain industrial products and import its food. Other countries will export food and labour-intensive manufactured products and import raw materials and capital goods, and so on. The smaller a country and the larger the share of foreign trade in national income, the more suitable an open model will be. For large, densely populated countries like India and China, a closed model will be of more use.

Still, the contrast between an open economy which concentrates on comparative advantage and a closed economy in which balanced growth is the prime goal should not be exaggerated. Gustav Ranis pointed out that import-substituting industrialization actually tended to increase the gaps between modern capital-intensive urban enclaves and the agricultural countryside. Conversely, Southeast Asian countries that opted for labour-intensive export production of manufactures succeeded in developing more positive mutual linkages between agriculture and industry. Thus the internal balance between agriculture and industry – initially associated with a closed model – is positively correlated with an open, outward-oriented industrial development (Ranis, 1989).

In the following sections I will discuss the role of agricultural exports in economic development in more detail. The high prestige of industrialization in the post-war period resulted in an underestimation of the positive role that primary agricultural exports have played in developing countries in the past and could still play in the future.

8.4.2 Vent for surplus

In developing countries agricultural exports have played a crucial part in initiating changes in the economy (Lewis, 1969, 1970, 1978b; Maddison, 1989). By modern standards, the volume of international trade between poor and rich countries before the middle of the nineteenth century was negligible (see Chapter 2). Prior to the rise of the railways, the interior of developing countries was isolated from the outside world. With the improvement of transport and communication and the growing demand for primary products in industrialized countries, there was an explosive growth in exports of cash crops from developing countries (cotton, oilseeds, cocoa, coffee, tea, bananas, rubber, ananas, fibres, copra, and so on) between 1870 and 1913.

Following Adam Smith, authors like Caves and Myint (Myint, 1959; Caves, 1965) use the term *vent for surplus* to characterize agricultural exports during this period. In a subsistence economy, peasants produce food for their own needs. In general, they have a good deal of spare time. Not all agricultural land is being cultivated intensively. If new opportunities arise, peasants can easily use surplus time and land to cultivate new crops, without reducing their subsistence production of food crops. Hence the term *vent for surplus:* unused factors of production are now employed for the first time. As in the previous section, a distinction can be made between the classical and the neoclassical approach to agricultural exports. The classical approach centres on the availability of unutilized production factors which may be employed in the process of development. In the neoclassical approach production factors are fully employed. To produce new goods, one has to sacrifice part of existing output. Resources are switched from one line of production to another. The vent for surplus theory typically belongs to the classical tradition. Production of cash crops can be expanded with no loss in food production.

Through agricultural exports a money economy is introduced into traditional subsistence agriculture. In the beginning peasants produce food crops for their own needs and produce additional cash crops in their spare time. They have one leg in the subsistence economy and another in the money economy. The sale of their export crops provides them with money with which to buy imported manufactured goods. Later, some peasants specialize in production of export crops and others in food crops, which are sold to those specializing in non-food crops. Thus the money economy penetrates deeper into the traditional peasant economy (Myint, 1980, chapter 2). Compulsion also played a role in the expansion of peasant exports. Under colonial rule, peasants were sometimes forced to grow cash crops, as under the cultivation system in the Dutch East Indies; or they had to grow cash crops in order to meet their financial tax obligations. Another source of agricultural exports were large-scale plantations owned by colonial expatriates. Coolie labour was recruited from densely populated areas and set to work on these plantations.

Arthur Lewis has analyzed the factors that explain why some countries benefited so much more from the new export opportunities than others (Lewis, 1970). The most important of these factors were the following:

1. Internal law and order.
2. Availability of land.
3. Systems of land tenure.
4. Availability of water.
5. Government policy.

Internal pacification and the maintenance of law and order are among the most important prerequisites for economic growth (see Chapter 10). Second in importance are the availability of sufficient water and land. Peasants will only start producing for export if there is still unused farmland or if they can easily increase the number of crops harvested per acre. Land tenure systems are also important. Latin America had abundant land, but systems of large landownership restricted access to that land. Large landowners could also produce for export products on their plantations, but did not always do so. Another factor affecting export growth was government policy. Governments determined who had access to land, and were also responsible for the construction of infrastructure.

The most rapid expansion of exports was to be found in countries with abundant land and large-scale immigration, such as Malaysia, Brazil and Ceylon, or in countries with sufficient land and surplus labour, such as Thailand (Manarungsan, 1989), Burma, Colombia, and Ghana. Slowest export growth could be observed in densely populated regions such as India and Java where land was scarce, or in countries where the government left monopolies in landownership unchallenged (Venezuela and the Philippines).

Lewis explicitly excludes differences in entrepreneurial talents and attitudes as an explanation of export performance. Wherever peasants in developing countries had opportunities to improve their economic situation permanently by producing for export, they were eager to take them.

8.4.3 Why disappointing industrialization?

On balance, the 1870–1913 period was a dynamic period for developing countries, with rapid increases in investment and per capita income (Lewis, 1978a; Maddison, 1989). The conditions for investment in industry and infrastructure were quite favourable. Why did industrialization make so little headway in this period, in spite of favourable initial conditions? Only a few countries such as Brazil, Ceylon, India, and Colombia experienced some measure of industrialization. How can this be explained?

According to Lewis, the most important answer lies in the overwhelming profitability of agricultural exports. The incentive to embark on a difficult process of industrialization was not very great when agricultural exports were such an easy alternative. Also, foreign trading houses had vested interests in imports and exports and resisted attempts at industrialization. They were supported by agricultural oligarchies, whose power and influence were threatened by industrialization. Finally, Lewis believes it takes at least one generation to grow a class of domestic industrial entrepreneurs in a country without an industrial tradition. Industrial entrepreneurship is less easily available than agricultural entrepreneurship.

More than Lewis, other authors emphasize the opposition of colonial authorities to industrialization and the destructive impact of international competition on traditional handicraft industries in such countries as India. Instead of impeding industrialization, governments should have protected domestic industries and should have invested more in infrastructure and education. In most colonies, governments did too little in these areas. In independent Latin American countries, industrialization was hampered by the political influence of groups with interests in agriculture and foreign trade.

All in all, the contributions from agricultural exports to industrialization were disappointing. Nevertheless, Lewis argues that important improvements were realized in this period in the fields of education, infrastructure, and industrialization. Though more could have been done, he concludes that the foundations of modern economic development in developing countries were laid during this period.

8.4.4 Primary exports as the engine of growth?

The vent for surplus theory extends our understanding of the process of economic development in a particular period in history. This theory is part of a wider category of theories that emphasize the positive contributions of primary mining and agricultural exports. Gillis *et al.* (1992, pp. 421–3) distinguish three potential benefits of primary exports, as follows:

1. Exports result in improved utilization of existing production factors. If there are surpluses of land or labour, as in the vent for surplus model, export demand provides a stimulus to employ the unused production factors. If production factors are already fully utilized, exports may result in a more efficient allocation of production factors as countries concentrate on their comparative advantage.[9]
2. Export opportunities expand the stock of production factors. When export opportunities increase, this may lead to inflows of foreign capital, increases in domestic savings, and immigration of skilled and unskilled labour.
3. Linkages. Primary exports can have positive linkages with other sectors of the economy (Hirschman, 1977).

On the third point, one can distinguish the following linkages:

1. *Forward and backward linkages in the production process.* Primary exports can provide a positive stimulus to the establishment of industries that process primary agricultural and mining products (forward linkages). Examples are food processing, furniture and plywood industries, or oil refining. Backward linkages occur, for example, when agricultural exports call forth investment in railways, or when fishery exports stimulate shipbuilding.
2. *Consumption linkages.* Incomes earned in export production may be spent in the domestic economy, which can provide a stimulus for other activities. This was the historical sequence in most developing countries. Exports revenues created a market for industrial products. These were initally imported from abroad. Later, imports were replaced by domestic industrial production in a process of import substitution (Hirschman, 1977, 1988).
3. *Fiscal linkages.* Taxes on mining and agricultural exports are an important source of government revenue. These means can be employed to finance development in other areas such as infrastructure, industry, or education.
4. *Contributions to the balance of payments.* Primary exports are an important source of foreign exchange which can be used to import the capital goods and intermediate goods needed for industrialization.

8.5 *Export pessimism*

In the 1930s the developing countries that were most involved in the international economy through primary exports were hit hardest by the effects of the great depression. International trade collapsed and the terms of trade (the ratio of export prices to import prices) of primary exports deteriorated considerably. These historical experiences reinforced negative attitudes towards agriculture and stimulated the pursuit of import-substituting industrialization. After World War II several theories were formulated which stated that developing countries did not benefit from primary exports and international trade, contrary to the experience of countries like the United States, Australia, and Canada in the nineteenth century (Prebisch, 1950; Singer, 1950; Myrdal, 1957; Bhagwati, 1958; Nurkse, 1962; Lewis, 1969; Emmanuel, 1972; Amin, 1974). Trade was no longer seen as an 'engine of growth'. Export pessimists give several reasons why dependence on primary exports is bad for developing countries (Meier, 1989).

Stagnating world demand

Growth of world demand for primary agricultural exports is sluggish. Demand for these exports will not keep up with the growth of per capita income in rich importing countries. As incomes rise, the share of food consumption in expenditure tends to decrease.

With regard to non-food agricultural exports, technological advances result in the substitution of synthetic products for natural products like rubber or vegetable fibres. Furthermore, technological progress reduces the amount of raw materials used per unit of output.

Instability of prices and export earnings

When developing countries export a limited range of primary products, they are vulnerable to the effects of fluctuations in prices on the world market. Prices of primary products are highly unstable. The resulting instability of export revenues is a threat to the overall development of a country.

Deteriorating terms of trade

In the long term, prices of primary exports are believed to fall relative to prices of imported industrial products. The prospects for a developing country that is too dependent on primary exports are unfavourable. There are several versions of the theory of deteriorating terms of trade (Thoburn, 1977; Gillis *et al.*, 1992; Meier, 1968; Sarkar, 1986):

1. *Terms of trade of the prices of final goods* The first version of the theory of deteriorating terms of trade refers to changes in the ratio of the prices of exported and imported goods (*net barter terms of trade*). The prime explanation of the deteriorating terms of trade lies in the above-mentioned fact that the demand for agricultural products does not keep up with increases in per capita income in advanced countries, while the demand for manufactured goods tends to increase at higher levels of income.

2. *Income terms of trade* Usually, when the price of a product goes down, more of this product will be bought. When decreasing prices are compensated for by an increase in the quantities demanded, total export revenues will increase. The so-called *income terms of trade* are defined as the change in revenues from exports divided by the change in the prices of imports. Improving income terms of trade signify that total revenues from exports rise more than the prices of imports. Therefore a country can afford more imports, on the basis of its exports.

However, when a country has a large share of the world market for a given product, an increase in its production may cause world prices to decrease to such an extent that total export revenues decrease. Economists say this country is faced by an 'inelastic demand'. Consequently, this country can import less and less, while exporting more and more. Bhagwati (1958) calls this a process of 'immiserizing growth'.

3. *Factoral terms of trade* A third version of the theory of terms of trade refers to the ratio of the rewards for factors of production in developing countries and the

rewards in economically advanced countries. This debate focuses in particular on the earnings of the production factor labour in rich and poor countries. When the incomes of workers in the export sector of developing countries lag behind those of workers in the export sector in rich industrial countries, we say there is a downward trend in the factoral terms of trade.

Another way of looking at the factoral terms of trade is to ask who benefits from increased productivity in export production, the producers of exports or the consumers of imports? Under perfect competition and given demand, technological changes which increase productivity will result in falling prices. Consumers will benefit from lower prices. However, in advanced industrial economies, powerful trade unions succeed in translating increased industrial productivity into higher wages, rather than lower prices. Monopolistic manufacturers pass on these increased wages in higher prices charged to consumers in poor developing countries. In developing countries, the immense surplus of labour keeps wages low. Fierce international competition depresses export prices. Thus, according to authors like Prebisch (1950) and Singer (1950), the benefits of increased productivity in export production are passed on to the consumers in the rich countries in the form of lower prices. The institutional differences between rich and poor countries (trade unions, powerful monopolistic corporations, the oligopolistic structure of international trade) offer further explanations for the deteriorating trend in the terms of trade. Rich countries benefit more from international trade than poor countries. International exchanges are unequal.

A special version of the theory of unequal exchange was formulated, once again, by Arthur Lewis (1969, 1978a). As long as productivity in the traditional subsistence agriculture sector is low, labour will be available at very low cost for export production. This keeps wages down. Lewis's theory of the 'factoral terms of trade' predicts that the incomes of workers in the export sector of developing countries will lag behind labour incomes in the economically advanced countries. Competition on export markets translates low wages into low export prices. Therefore, prices of exports will also lag behind prices of imports. It is not until labour productivity in food production increases that the labour incomes in the export sector start to rise.

Although this theory has its weaknesses (e.g. the role of demand in international trade is not mentioned at all), it leads to an interesting conclusion: improvement of export prices requires an increase in productivity in traditional food production. This is the theory of the balanced growth path in another guise. Productivity in traditional agriculture has to be increased in order to reverse the declining trend in the factoral terms of trade.

Lewis also observes that developing countries concentrate on a rather limited range of primary export products. They export either products that only grow in tropical conditions or products where low wages compensate for the difference in productivity compared to economically more advanced countries.[10] The resulting overspecialization in a few export products explains in part why developing countries are so vulnerable to export price instability.

Profit repatriation

A slightly different situation exists with respect to mining exports. In mining, productivity is high and minerals and energy sources are in high demand on world markets. Furthermore, the number of producers in mining is much smaller than in agriculture. Producers are sometimes able to form cartels to keep prices high. Thus the factoral terms of trade for mining should be more positive than for agriculture.

However, the orthodox theory of international trade pays too little attention to the fact that mining and oil extraction were until very recently predominantly foreign owned. Foreign investors were the main beneficiaries of productivity increases and export earnings. A substantial part of these profits was repatriated abroad. Plantations producing export crops for foreign markets were also mainly controlled by foreign interests. Profits again tended to be repatriated.

The costs of labour in mines and plantations remained low due to the abundant supplies of labour. Thus domestic labour and the domestic economy profited very little from these primary exports.

Ineffective linkages

The linkage effects of export agriculture and mining are limited (Horesh and Joekes, 1985; Hirschman, 1988; Gillis *et al.*, 1992). The consumption linkages are weak, because incomes of workers in export production are modest. Fiscal linkages are disappointing, primarily because governments do not employ the revenues from export taxes very productively. Often they use them to finance current deficits on the government budget, rather than for additional government investment. Export tax revenues allow politicians to postpone painful choices and decisions.

Stagnating food production

Critics of agricultural exports often claim that the production of cash crops expands at the expense of the production of food crops. Land once used for food production is now used to grow cash crops. Traditional food producers are believed to lose their land to capitalist export farmers. As a result of export production, the local population will become more impoverished.

Boserup (1985) points to the fact that in Africa men concentrate on prestigious cash crops, whereas women are usually responsible for food production. As a result of expansion of export production, women have to use more distant plots of land of inferior quality to cultivate food, and have also to travel long distances. Since women are forced to combine food production with housework, food production will suffer in the long run. However, according to Boserup, intensification of agricultural production and investment in agriculture offer possibilities to expand both food production and the production of cash crops simultaneously. Of course, this requires greater attention to agriculture in government policy.

Overvalued exchange rates

The export of primary products, in particular mining and oil products, may lead to appreciation of the exchange rate. Higher exchange rates make exports more expensive and imports cheaper. Thus the prospects of non-oil and non-mining exports are diminished.

Protectionism by the rich countries

Export opportunities for developing countries are limited due to protectionist measures in rich, economically advanced countries (McBean, 1989). Especially with respect to agriculture, domestic producers in the European Union and the United States are very much protected. Both consumers in rich countries and producers in developing countries would benefit if agricultural protectionism were reduced.

In summary, export pessimists claim that participation in international trade contributes little to the economic development of poor countries. Per capita incomes do not increase. No savings are generated. The market for domestic industry is not enlarged. Under such conditions, 'trade gives poor countries an opportunity to stay poor'.

8.6 *Export pessimism and policy*

Export pessimist theories gave a powerful theoretical underpinning to the import-substituting industrialization policies discussed in Chapter 7. They also contributed to the general climate in which industry received preferential treatment and agriculture was neglected. Agricultural exports were taxed heavily, without the government providing additional means for investment, research, and development. Therefore, it is not surprising that the share of developing countries in world trade of primary products decreased during the past decades (McBean, 1989).

In international relations, export pessimism triggered the call for a new international economic order (NIEO). International commodity agreements and policy measures should stabilize and, where possible, increase prices of raw materials and primary exports, and also improve access to developed country markets, so that developing countries can derive more benefit from international trade (see Chapter 11).

8.6.1 Rehabilitation of primary exports

Since the 1970s, the disappointing results of import-substituting industrialization led to renewed attention to the developmental potential of primary exports (Thoburn, 1977). Though not all arguments of export pessimists have been refuted, conclusions regarding primary exports have generally tended to be less negative.

The question of the trends in the terms of trade is an empirical one. It should be investigated systematically for different periods, regions and countries. In an exhaustive survey of the available empirical data, Spraos (1980) comes to the conclusion that authors such as Singer and Prebisch overestimated the deterioration in the terms of trade. From 1870 to 1937 net barter terms of trade of primary exports from developing countries deteriorated. However, this deterioration was not as substantial as Prebisch and Singer suggested. For the whole 1870–1980 period no clear trends can be discerned. Thoburn (1977) also comes to the conclusion that there was a certain deterioration in the terms of trade until the eve of World War II. However, the terms of trade in 1950 were similar to those at the end of the nineteenth century. After World War II, developments in the terms of trade differed strongly from country to country. Until the 1960s the income terms of trade showed a marked improvement.

An estimation of the terms of trade involves a number of thorny problems (Spraos, 1980; Sarkar, 1986). First, if the quality of industrial products increases more rapidly than the quality of primary products, the deterioration of the net barter terms of trade of primary products might be overestimated. Second, shipping freights have declined substantially. As imports of primary exports to industrial countries are valued with cost, freight and insurance included (c.i.f.) and exports of industrial products free on board (f.o.b.), the deterioration of the terms of trade might be overestimated.[11] Third, it depends very much on which products are included or excluded in the calculation of the terms of trade. Terms of trade will be very different when exports of oil products or industrial products are not included. The composition of exports differs for each country and during each period of time. Among the most striking characteristics of the post-war period is the growth of the share of industrial products in total developing country exports (see Table 3.4, p. 81).

Authors like Thoburn, Spraos, and Myint reach the conclusion that in the long run there has been no systematic deterioration in the terms of trade of developing countries. In recent years, though, there has been a spate of articles which come to the defence of the original Prebisch–Singer thesis (Sapsford, 1985, 1988; Sarkar, 1986; textbooks such as Thirlwall, 1994 and Gillis *et al.*, 1992). Using similar data sets to Spraos, Sapsford argues that terms of trade were declining both in the pre-war period and in the post-war period. During the war years there was a sudden upward shift in the terms of trade of primary products, after which the downward trend resumed. If one combines the pre-war and post-war series in a single series, it seems as if there is no long-run trend. But if one looks at the two periods separately, the downward trend becomes visible.

Sarkar (1986) defends the Singer–Prebisch hypothesis against various critical objections (freight costs, quality changes, and so forth) and concludes that declining terms of trade for developing countries are a reality. Sarkar pays special attention to the counter-argument that the terms of trade between developing and developed countries cannot be equated with those between primary exporters and industrial exporters. This argument states that industrialized countries also export primary products and developing countries also export manufactured products. Sarkar convincingly shows that in the trade between developing and industrialized countries, primary exports predominate in the exports of developing countries and manufactures predominate in the exports of the developed regions. He concludes that at the aggregate level the terms of trade between primary and manufactured goods are still representative for the terms of trade between developing and developed countries. However, as the share of manufactures in developing-country exports continues to increase, this argument of Sarkar will gradually lose its force.

Grilli and Maw (1988) take an intermediate position. Their newly constructed indices of price movements from 1900 to 1986 confirm the long-run decline of prices of primary commodities relative to those of manufactures. But they qualify Sarkar's conclusion that the terms of trade of primary versus manufactured exports are representative for the terms of trade of developing versus more developed countries. They estimate the average annual decline of the net barter terms of trade of developing countries at less than one-third of the decline in the primary commodity terms of trade. They also emphasize the differences between various primary commodities. Finally, they indicate that the income terms of trade of developing countries in the post-war period have been positive rather than negative.

A serious weakness of the modern proponents of the Singer–Prebisch thesis is their tendency to exclude oil 'as a special case' (Sarkar, 1986, p. 365). There is nothing special about oil exports, other than that their prices rose tremendously in 1973 and 1979 and declined thereafter. Another problem is their exclusive focus on net barter terms of trade. To evaluate the pros and cons of developing countries participating in international trade, the income terms of trade are at least as interesting.

Tables 8.1 and 8.2 present some rough calculations on the development of the *net barter terms of trade* and the *income terms of trade* in post-war years. Figures from the IMF *International Financial Statistics* have been reproduced on the price movements of all export products (including agricultural products, mining products, oil products, and manufactures) in relation to the price movements of all imported products. It should be stressed that these tables are of little relevance to the debate on the terms of trade of primary versus manufactured exports, or to the debate on the terms of trade of developing countries versus developed countries. All exports and all imports are included, irrespective of their sectoral origin or geographic destination. The data do have some bearing on the question of whether participation in international trade is beneficial to developing countries.

The main conclusion to be derived from these tables is that few patterns can be discerned. The barter terms of trade for most individual countries in Table 8.1 show a downward tendency during the post-war period. However, this does not apply to India and South Korea. Until 1980, the aggregate data for all developing countries together actually show an upward tendency. After 1980, there is an unmistakable deterioration in the terms of trade for developing countries.

The long-term income terms of trade show a sharply increasing trend. Even after 1980 the income terms of trade kept improving for most countries and regions. An exception is Africa, where income terms of trade fell by 19 per cent between 1980 and 1993.

Table 8.1 Barter terms of trade by region and for selected countries, 1950–1993 (1980 = 100)[a]

Country/Region	1950	1955	1960	1965	1970	1975	1980	1985	1990	1991	1993
Brazil				133	136	116	100	88	86	89	
Burkina Faso					104	91	100	98			
Colombia			88	65	75	76	100	86	70	68	
India		135	130	129	136	100	100	113	105	115	139
Ivory Coast					95[b]	77	100	94			
Kenya		187	149	142	151	97	100	75	58	67	72
Pakistan					114	80	100	91	84	81	83
Philippines	254	208	213	185	173	128	100	81	89	95	
South Korea				114	134	92	100	106	125	126	132
Tanzania		144	128	114	106	90	100	113			
Thailand		131	127	129	132	116	100	78	79	78	79
Turkey					160	137	100	96[c]	127	130	140
Developing countries			46	47	77	100	95	95	83	91	
Africa	74	67	76	73	73	92	100	98	86	86	83
Asia				89	93	86	100	92	89	89	90
Non-oil exporting developing countries			112	116	101	100	91	107	107	108	
Industrialized countries	108	108	118	120	123	111	100	103	115	115	119

Notes:
[a] Calculated as the ratio of indices of export unit values to indices of import unit values.
[b] 1971; [c] 1984.

Source: 1950 and 1955, Colombia 1960–65, Tanzania 1955–85 and Turkey 1970–85: *International Financial Statistics Yearbook*, IMF (1986); 1960: IMF (1990) except India: IMF (1991). 1960–1991: IMF (1993), except Kenya and non-oil developing countries 1991: IMF (1995). 1992–93: IMF (1995); Brazil, Tanzania and Turkey, 1985–90: World Bank, *World Tables 1995*.

Table 8.2 Income terms of trade by region and for selected countries, 1950–1993 (1980 = 100)[a]

Country/Region	1950	1955	1960	1965	1970	1975	1980	1985	1990	1991	1993
Brazil				33	53	75	100	140	145	158	
Burkina Faso				57[b]	68	69	100	94			
Colombia			41	38	49	56	100	87	175	196	
India		42	51	60	78	72	100	118	198	220	195
Ivory Coast					55[c]	63	100	129			
Kenya		37	51	102	130	97	100	75	52	51	33
Pakistan					55	59	100	113	181	216	184
Philippines	33	37	56	56	69	65	100	79	147	167	
South Korea				3	16	45	100	192	365	404	432
Tanzania		86	94	151	177	117	100	54			
Thailand		21	25	39	45	59	100	115	281	331	432
Turkey					102	111	100	318	492	532	654
Developing countries			26	37	67	100	94	153	161	196	
Africa		30	29	34	49	69	100	91	90	87	81
Asia				26	37	53	100	139	257	300	385
Non-oil exporting developing countries			38	52	67	100	124[d]	207	222	272	
Industrialized countries		18	27	40	65	84	100	119	173	179	198

Notes:
[a] Index number of export value, divided by index number of import unit value.
[b] 1966; [c] 1971; [d] 1984.

Sources: See Table 8.1.

It would seem that the empirical debate on long-run trends in the terms of trade is still undecided. Much depends on the products included in the analysis, the specific countries selected and the kinds of terms of trade examined. As industrial exports become more important in developing countries the relevance of the debate on primary exports diminishes. For countries still overwhelmingly dependent on primary exports, however, it may still be of importance.

My main objection to the declining terms of trade hypothesis is not so much empirical, but rather that it has been used as an ideological justification for the continuation of industrialization policies which have proved to be ineffective and sometimes disastrous. The general conclusion that developing countries should not participate in international trade because it is detrimental to their developmental prospects is certainly not justified.

The focus on the terms of trade has distracted our attention from the fact that the share of developing countries in world trade in primary exports has decreased during the past decades. Between 1961–1963 and 1982–1984 the share of developing countries in global primary exports fell from 63 to 48 per cent (McBean, 1989). This is in part due to agricultural protectionism in the rich countries. However, it is also caused by the fact that developing countries themselves neglected their agricultural sectors. If governments in developing countries would tax export production less heavily and would invest more in agricultural infrastructure and improvement of production techniques, developing countries could expand the volume of their exports. For example, the share of farmers in Tanzanian export revenues fell from 70 per cent to 41 per cent as a result of export taxes and payments to 'marketing boards' (McBean, 1989). The same argument holds for exports of mining products.

Myint (1980) argues that one should not focus so much on total world demand for agricultural and mining products. From a developing country's perspective it is more interesting to analyze the demand for that country's specific export products. A similar conclusion can be derived from the Grilli and Maw (1988) study. An efficiently producing country may increase its share in the world market for products in which it has a comparative advantage at the expense of its developed country rivals (Lord, 1989; McBean, 1989). Also, the total world demand for various more exotic agricultural products (such as kiwis or mangoes) seems to increase rather than decrease with income.

For countries which in the past could benefit from vent for surplus exports, more investment in agriculture is of great importance. Vent for surplus is a once and for all effect. With no changes in technology, unused production factors are brought in to use. Once all production factors are fully employed, export growth will stagnate unless there is investment in technological change. Just like the closed model of development, the open model of development requires choices between investment alternatives in later stages of development. Primary exports may be taxed in favour of industrial investment at the risk of stagnation of primary export growth. However, part of export revenues may also be reinvested in the agricultural sector. As long as a developing country succeeds in diversifying its export package and does not remain dependent on one or two exports, it may still derive considerable benefit from continued agricultural and primary exports, even today.

More investment in the agricultural sector may also help countries avoid the choice between food production and production for export. Food crops and export crops are often grown in rotation on one and the same piece of land. According to Boserup, more intensive production techniques may expand both food production and the production of cash crops. But this does require investment in agricultural infrastructure (irrigation, water control) and changes in production techniques (Islam, 1989a). In addition, the option of importing part of food requirements using export revenues from cash crops is of course also still available.

Just as in the closed model, the priority given to domestic industrialization over agricultural and mining exports did not always have positive results. Especially in sub-Saharan Africa, industrialization was not very successful while the primary export sector languished due to charges, taxes, and price regulations (Lensink, 1995). The World Bank (1989) report, *Sub-Saharan Africa: From crisis to sustainable growth*, states that the decrease in export revenues in sub-Saharan Africa was caused more by a fall in the volume of exports than by unfavourable developments in the terms of trade. The report therefore argues in favour of renewed efforts to expand export production of both agricultural and mining products.

QUESTIONS FOR REVIEW

1. What are the contributions of agriculture to industrial development in earlier stages of economic development? Why is an agricultural surplus often considered to be a precondition for industrialization?

2. Discuss the policy differences between the strategy of a balanced growth path between industry and agriculture and the post-war large scale industrialization strategies. Why is a balance between the agricultural sector and the industrial sector considered to be advantageous for economic development in later stages of development?

3. What are the main characteristics of the vent for surplus model of primary exports? To what extent did primary exports contribute to the economic dynamism of developing countries between 1870 and 1913?

4. Give three definitions of the terms of trade.

5. Provide a summary of the theoretical and empirical debate on the contribution of primary exports to economic development. Discuss the potential benefits of primary exports to economic development. Discuss the arguments of the export pessimists, who deny that primary exports can serve as an engine of growth.

6. Why has the World Bank in recent years argued in favour of expansion of primary exports from sub-Saharan Africa?

Notes

1. The same applies to mining exports. Theories that centre on primary agricultural and mining exports are called *theories of primary export-led growth.*
2. Ester Boserup objects to the term 'agricultural revolution' and emphasizes a more gradual nature of long-run processes of productivity increase and intensification of production in the agricultural sector (Boserup, 1981).
3. When food prices increase, wages in the industrial sector must increase in order to compensate for higher prices; thus the share of profits in value added will tend to decline.
4. The difference may be explained as follows. In a completely closed economy, transfer from the agricultural sector is only possible when the agricultural sector produces a surplus exceeding subsistence needs in agriculture. This is more or less what happened in eighteenth-century England. In developing countries the foundations for industrialization were laid in the late nineteenth century, in the context of an open model, with large amounts of foreign investment which subsequently attracted labour from the agricultural sector.
5. In economic terminology the income elasticity of the demand for food is rather high. The income elasticity of the demand for a product is the percentage increase in the demanded quantity of a good, divided by the percentage increase in income.
6. This section is primarily based on Nicholls (1964), 16–26.
7. Ester Boserup (1981: 114–17) claims that there was no agricultural revolution in the eighteenth century. Rather, there was a gradual increase in output per hectare due to an increase in population density and a greater use of labour per unit of land. Still, Boserup agrees that British agriculture was the most productive agriculture in Europe.
8. Though Arthur Lewis (1954) is the spiritual father of the notion that production factors can be withdrawn from agriculture at little cost, he elswhere emphasizes the need for balance between agriculture and industry (e.g. Lewis, 1969). I have no satisfactory explanation for this seeming inconsistency in Lewis's thought. In the context of agricultural exports, Lewis also stresses the importance of productivity increases in food production (see section 8.6).
9. The orthodox theory of international trade states that it pays for countries to concentrate on exporting those products they can produce relatively cheaply. Even if a country produces all products less efficiently than another country, it is still worth while for both countries to export those products in which they are more efficient in relative terms (see Chapter 10).
10. Tobacco and cotton are examples of such products. If there had been no slavery in the United States, with its artificially low remuneration of labour, the South of the United States would not have been able to compete in these products.
11. The debate on the pre-war terms of trade is primarily based on British data.

9 Agricultural development and rural development

In Chapter 8 the relations between the agricultural and the industrial sector were discussed. In the first half of this chapter the agricultural sector itself is the focus of attention. Other sectors are only mentioned in as far as they contribute to agricultural development. In sections 9.1 and 9.2 we analyze long-term trends in agricultural production and identify some of the factors influencing these trends. Theories of agricultural development are also discussed here. Special attention will be paid to the debate on the 'green revolution'. Section 9.3 will centre on food consumption.

In the second half of this chapter the focus shifts from agriculture to rural development. The concept of rural development is introduced in section 9.4. Rural society is primarily characterized by the significance of agricultural activities within rural society. Nevertheless, rural development is broader than agricultural development. First, various non-agricultural economic activities take place in rural areas. Second, rural development refers to the transformation of rural society as a whole, rather than only to the economic aspects of rural life. In sections 9.5 and 9.6, land reform, agricultural collectivization and agricultural cooperatives will be discussed, and in section 9.7 we will examine integrated rural development.

9.1 *Trends in agricultural production*

To set the stage for a discussion of agricultural development, Table 9.1 presents data on world growth of agricultural production from 1934 to 1994. The data derive from the FAO *Production Yearbooks*. The table distinguishes between food production and total agricultural production, and between production and production per capita. It illustrates some interesting trends, as follows:

Table 9.1 Indices of agricultural production, 1934–1994 (1979/1981 = 100)

	World total[a]		Developed countries total[b]		North America		Western Europe[c]		Eastern Europe/ Soviet Union[c]		(Former) Soviet Union[d]		Developing countries total[e]		Developing countries total excluding CPE[f]	
	T	PC	T	PC	T	PC	T	PC	T	PC	T	PC	T	PC	T	PC
Total agricultural production																
1934/39	40	82	–	–	40	74	47	63	41	55	–	–	–	–	37	94
1948/52	46	80	–	–	54	84	48	60	41	58	–	–	–	–	42	84
1959/61	62	91	–	–	63	82	66	75	67	81	69	84	–	–	58	96
1969/71	80	95	–	–	76	85	83	87	87	95	91	98	–	–	77	99
1979/81	100	100	100	100	100	100	100	100	100	100	100	100	100	100	100	100
1985	114	105	108	104	108	103	106	105	110	107	111	106	121	109	114	103
1986/88	117	104	107	102	103	93	106	105	116	111	117	110	126	109	117	100
1989/90	123	105	110	103	105	97	–	–	–	–	120	110	137	112	–	–
1992	129	105	107	99	115	103	–	–	–	–	106	97	146	114	–	–
1994	129	102	–	–	–	–	–	–	–	–	–	–	–	–	–	
Food production																
1934/39	39	79	–	–	36	63	47	63	40	56	–	–	–	–	35	92
1948/52	45	77	–	–	50	76	47	60	42	59	–	–	–	–	41	83
1959/61	62	89	–	–	60	76	66	76	67	81	70	85	–	–	57	93
1969/71	80	95	–	–	75	82	84	88	87	95	91	100	–	–	76	97
1979/81	100	100	100	100	100	100	100	100	100	100	100	100	100	100	100	100
1985	115	105	108	105	108	103	107	106	110	107	111	106	120	108	117	103
1986/88	117	104	108	102	99	93	107	105	117	112	119	112	127	109	120	101
1989/90	124	105	110	103	106	97	–	–	–	–	122	113	137	112	–	–
1992	129	105	108	99	116	103	–	–	–	–	108	98	147	115	–	–
1994	130	103	–	–	–	–	–	–	–	–	–	–	–	–	–	–

Table 9.1 *(continued)*

	Africa[g]		Latin America		Near East		Far East excluding centrally planned economies[f]		India		Indonesia		Asian centrally planned economies[f]		China	
	T	PC	T	PC	T	PC	T	PC	T	PC	T	PC	T	PC	T	PC
Total agricultural production																
1934/39	38	110	33	102	33	84	39	94	–	–	–	–	–	–	–	–
1948/52	49	105	40	90	37	81	41	97	–	–	–	–	–	–	–	–
1959/61	67	114	56	96	54	94	57	91	64	105	51	82	56	77	55	75
1969/71	86	115	74	96	75	98	75	94	79	101	67	85	74	87	74	86
1979/81	100	100	100	100	100	100	100	100	100	100	100	100	100	100	100	100
1985	114	98	113	102	117	100	121	107	123	111	126	114	132	123	132	124
1986/88	121	99	115	99	124	100	123	105	127	110	140	121	139	127	141	129
1989/90	129	97	122	100	122	92	–	–	146	119	155	128	–	–	154	135
1992	134	93	128	100	136	96	–	–	159	124	171	137	–	–	171	145
1994	–	–	–	–	–	–	–	–	166	125	174	135	–	–	185	153
Food production																
1934/39	40	114	31	93	32	81	38	90	–	–	–	–	–	–	–	–
1948/52	50	108	39	86	36	79	40	78	–	–	–	–	–	–	–	–
1959/61	67	115	53	89	54	93	57	91	64	101	49	78	57	79	56	77
1969/71	86	115	73	94	73	95	75	95	80	100	66	82	75	88	74	86
1979/81	100	100	100	100	100	100	100	100	100	100	100	100	100	100	100	100
1985	114	99	114	102	118	101	121	107	124	111	128	115	128	121	129	122
1986/88	121	99	117	101	126	102	124	105	129	113	141	122	137	125	139	127
1989/90	129	98	125	102	123	93	–	–	147	120	130	129	–	–	152	134
1992	134	93	132	103	139	98	–	–	161	125	176	141	–	–	170	143
1994	–	–	–	–	–	–	–	–	168	126	179	139	–	–	187	154

Notes:
T = Total production; PC = Per capita production.
[a] World total until 1961, excluding China.
[b] North America, Europe, Australia, New Zealand, the former Soviet Union, Israel, Japan and South Africa.
[c] The distinction between Western and Eastern Europe was discontinued starting with vol. 44 of the *Production Yearbook* in 1990.
[d] Data for 1992 refer to 1991. The data for the former Soviet Union were discontinued after 1991.
[e] Excluding the Asian republics of the former USSR. The series for total developing countries was discontinued after 1992.
[f] Starting with vol. 44 of the *Production Yearbook*, the distinction between centrally planned economies and market economies was discontinued.
[g] Africa excluding Egypt, Sudan, Libya and South Africa.

Sources: FAO, *Production Yearbook*, various issues.

- Since 1979–81 the rate of growth of agricultural production, whether in absolute terms or per capita, was more rapid in developing countries than in economically more developed countries. The same applies to food production.
- Despite very rapid growth of world population, per capita production of food in developing countries showed a gradual increase. This is contrary to gloomy Malthusian predictions, which state that the production of food will lag behind the growth of population.
- Noteworthy is the increase of per capita food production in densely populated countries such as China, India and Indonesia. Countries such as Indonesia and India, which were dependent on food imports in the 1960s, have now become self-sufficient in food. As will be explained in section 9.2.2, population growth may provide incentives for technological change and intensification of agricultural production so that total production increases faster than population.
- The only region where the increase in food production did not keep up with population growth was Africa. Here the race between population growth and growth of production was won by population growth.
- The trends in the production of food crops are not all that different from the trends in total agricultural production. Food production per head is growing at a slightly faster pace than total production per head. At this very high level of aggregation there seems to be no competition between food production and production of non-food agricultural crops.

It is often claimed that expansion of the production of export crops will be at the expense of food production. Dixon (1990), for example, states that the most fertile and best irrigated lands are often used for growing cash crops and export crops. Moreover, these crops are said to use disproportionate shares of modern inputs, investment, and subsidies. In particular, when export crops are not food crops[1] and when two kinds of crops compete for scarce land and labour, expansion of cash crops may lead to a decreasing food production.

The data in Table 9.1 do not confirm this picture. Rather they imply that in a dynamic agricultural system both food production and non-food production can increase.[2] At the same time, in a less dynamic agricultural system both food production and export production will stagnate. However, this does not preclude competition between food production and the production of export crops at local levels.

From a technical point of view there is no reason to assume that food production cannot continue to grow faster than the population, despite the rapid growth of world population. However, as will be shown in section 9.3, an increase in the average per capita food production does not necessarily mean that each person will receive more food or that the absolute numbers of undernourished people will decline.

A warning is in order with regard to the reliability of the data in Table 9.1. In her book, *Development Economics on Trial*, the anthropologist Polly Hill (1986) severely criticized standardized methods of data collection such as those applied by the FAO, on the basis of her field experience in West Africa and south India. She elaborates on the shortcomings of the basic data.

In West Africa and south India, farmers questioned by surveyors seldom know how much land they actually cultivate and how much food and other agricultural products they produce. Farmers often work several scattered plots of land, some of which lie fallow for long periods of time. The amounts produced are hard to assess since many crops are interplanted. Some root crops like cassava are not harvested at once, but are rather dug up when food is actually needed. It is also hard to obtain reliable information on the amount and value of products used for household consumption, that is, products not traded on the market.

Usually only the male head of the household is questioned in agricultural surveys. In West Africa in particular, food production is the preserve of female members of the household, and the male head knows little about this subject. Furthermore, farmers are not used to aggregating income flows over longer periods of time, like a month or a year. Finally, the surveyors are usually underpaid, poorly trained, and marginally supervised. Hill comes to the conclusion that the margin of error involved in such data is so wide that qualitative statements should be preferred over misleading quantitative data.

This criticism should be taken seriously, but I completely disagree with Polly Hill's conclusion. Qualitative verbal statements about trends are quantitative statements in disguise. They are usually based on case studies and examples. They are even more difficult to check or verify than statistical time series, the sources and methods of which can be documented with considerable precision. Statistical series should not be regarded as conclusive statements about reality, but rather as working hypotheses which are used until replaced by better estimates. They represent the most advanced state of our knowledge. Therefore, we should indicate as precisely as possible how these series have been constructed and we should distrust statistics where such information is lacking. Furthermore, the striving for aggregation and identification of global trends offers an important counterbalance to the possible biases involved in formulating general statements on the basis of intimate experiences at the microlevel in local settings. Therefore, the statistical working hypotheses contained in Table 9.1 and other tables in this chapter will serve as starting points for the discussion of agricultural development.

9.2 *Growth of agricultural production*

Expansion of agricultural production can be realized in three different ways (van der Meer, 1983),[3] as follows:

1. Expansion of cultivated area.
2. Intensification of land use by shortening the period of fallowing or by harvesting more than one crop per year on the same piece of land (multicropping). Intensification will cause average returns per hectare to increase.

3. Increasing the returns per harvest per hectare:
   (a) When labour is scarce, returns per harvest may be increased by using mechanised equipment. Generally, investment in mechanisation is labour saving.
   (b) When land is scarce, returns per harvest may be increased by making land-substituting investments, like investment in irrigation, organic and chemical fertilizers, and the development of high-productivity seeds. In general, land-substituting investments are landsaving and labour intensive.

In the following sections these means of increasing production will be discussed in further detail.

9.2.1 Expansion of cultivated agricultural land

Table 9.2 presents information on the expansion of the cultivated area since 1978. This table shows that during the fifteen years between 1978 and 1993 the cultivated area increased by 1.9 per cent. The largest expansion can be observed in Australia and Oceania (9.1 per cent), followed by Africa (7.8 per cent) and South America (6.0 per cent). Compared to data for the period 1974–89 from an earlier issue of the *Production Yearbook* (FAO, 1990), the rate of expansion of the cultivated area seems to be slowing down.[4]

The opportunities for further expansion of the cultivated area are still far from exhausted. Currently, 54.6 per cent of all potential agricultural land in the world, outside the humid tropics, is in use. Including potential agricultural land area in humid tropical areas, the figure is 46.0 per cent. Especially in Africa, South America, and Australia/Oceania, only a limited part of all potential agricultural land is presently being cultivated.

Expansion of cultivated area, however, competes with woodlands, pastures and other land used for urban development, construction and roads. Particularly in humid tropical areas, potential farm land consists to an important extent of land covered by tropical rain forests. Table 9.2 provides a first rough indication of the decline of woodland area on a world scale (see also section 9.2.2).

The potential amount of land for agricultural use is determined by such factors as climate, soil conditions and the availability of water (Revelle, 1975). Land has to be frost-free for at least one complete crop cycle. Soil conditions must meet certain standards, like permeability to water and retention of water and nutrients. The land should not be too acidic or too alkaline, neither too steep nor too rocky. On the basis of climatic and soil conditions, potential farm land globally amounts to approximately 3.2 billion hectares. However, water is not equally available in the different parts of the world. Only 30 per cent of the land that is potentially suitable for irrigated agriculture can be actually irrigated. Thus potential farm land is reduced to 2.9 billion hectares. Furthermore, the quality of much agricultural land not yet taken into use is so poor that huge investments are necessary before it can be cultivated. Activities other than agriculture also compete for potential agricultural land.

Table 9.2 Cultivated area, potential agricultural land, pastures, woodlands (million ha)[a]

	Cultivated area[b]		Meadows pastures		Forests and woodland		Potential agricultural land		Cultivated area as % of potential area	
							Excluding humid areas[c] I	Including humid areas[c] II	I	II
	1978	1993	1978	1993	1978	1993	1993	1993	1993	1993
Africa	174.3	187.9	846.4	852.6	787.4	760.8	620.0	730.0	30.3	25.7
Asia	455.6	468.7	680.8	800.1	559.1	535.5	540.0	620.0	86.8	75.6
Australia and Oceania	47.2	51.5	448.5	427.9	161.7	200.0	150.0	150.0	34.3	34.3
Europe	141.8	136.0	86.6	79.8	155.2	158.4	170.0	170.0	80.0	80.0
North and Central America	272.5	271.4	355.2	362.1	711.7	855.4	450.0	460.0	60.3	59.0
South America	97.0	102.8	469.0	495.3	897.3	846.4	370.0	670.0	27.8	15.3
USSR	232.0	228.2	321.1	344.1	1,050.0	823.3	350.0	350.0	65.2	65.2
Total	1,420.4	1,447.5	3,207.5	3,361.7	4,322.3	4,179.8	2,650.0	3,150.0	54.6	46.0

Notes:

[a] Total land area, excluding surface waters, comprises: (1) cultivated area; (2) permanent meadows and pastures; (3) forests and woodland, including cleared woodland that has been reforested; and (4) other land, including roads, cities, and wastelands.

[b] Cultivated area comprises 'arable land' (land planted with temporary crops, agricultural land lying fallow, land temporarily used for mowing and pasture, and land used for horticultural crops, including cultivation under glass), and land under permanent crops (coffee, cocoa, rubber, fruit trees, nuts).

[c] Potential land for agricultural use, either including or excluding humid tropical land area. 'Humid tropical areas' refer in particular to tropical rain forests. Besides woodland, potential land for agricultural use also includes meadows and pastures.

Sources: Cultivated area from FAO, *Production Yearbook*, Vol. 48, 1994. Potential agricultural land from Revelle (1975), table 4.

According to Boserup (1990, quoted in Barrow, 1995), 75 per cent of the cereals that have fed growing populations in developing countries between the 1930s and the 1960s came from expansion of cultivated area. Despite the increasing costs of further land reclamation, even in recent years a considerable part of the growth of production in developing countries can be attributed to the expansion of cultivated land area. During the late 1980s, on average 8 per cent of the total increase in production of cereal products is explained by the expansion of agricultural land. In sub-Saharan Africa this percentage amounts to no less than 47 per cent, in Latin America to 30 per cent (see World Bank, 1992a, p. 135). The rest of the increase in production can be attributed to a combination of a more intensive use of land and an increase in the returns per harvest.

Desertification and land degradation

The extent to which potential agricultural land is utilized is affected negatively by desertification and soil degradation (Barrow, 1995, chapter 6). Desertification is a rather ill-defined catch-phrase referring to dryland and semi-arid land degradation. As the end result is 'desert like' it is called desertification, but Barrow warns that one should not think of deserts spreading outwards. Desertification is the result of combined effects of climatic conditions and human actions, which reduce the carrying capacity of soils. Desertification is on the increase, but the estimates vary considerably. UNEP (1993, quoted in Barrow, 1995) estimates that some 7–9 per cent of world land surface may have become desertified. However, some observers suggest that desertification may have been overestimated by a factor 3.

Soil degradation refers to the decline of soil fertility and erosion, the loss of soil organic matter. It is a component of desertification, but is not limited to drylands and does not always result in desert-like conditions. One recent assessment (Harrison, 1992, quoted in Barrow, 1995) suggests that between 1945 and 1990 12.2 million square kilometres of agricultural land suffered serious loss of productivity. Though estimates, as usual, vary considerably, the figures quoted serve to indicate the seriousness of the problem.

Human causes of desertification include increasing population density in combination with unchanged agricultural technologies, overgrazing and fuelwood collection. Causes of soil degradation include pollution, use of inappropriate agricultural machinery, overuse of fertilizer, and deforestation (Barrow, 1995).

As will be emphasized below, land degradation is not necessarily irreversible. A switch to appropriate agricultural techniques and soil conservation policies can reclaim degraded soils, though sometimes at considerable cost.

Competition between agricultural land and woodland

In many developing countries the expansion of the cultivated area is an important way of increasing agricultural production (Dixon, 1990). Even in India, which is extremely densely populated, 20 per cent of production growth of cereal products in the 1970s was attributable to the expansion of agricultural land. In some parts of

South America and Africa at least 80 per cent of production growth was due to the expansion of agricultural land.

Of Africa's 160 million hectares of tropical rain forest an annual 1.3 million hectares are converted to agricultural land. The situation in the Amazon region is even more extreme: here 180,000 square kilometres of tropical rain forests are cut down every year (Leite and Furley, 1985, quoted in Dixon, 1990).

Of the three main causes of deforestation – logging, collection of fuelwood and expansion of agricultural land – expansion of agricultural land is by far the most important. Given the vital function of the remaining tropical rain forests in preserving biodiversity and a global ecological equilibrium, it is obvious that there are limits to this continued expansion at the expense of forested area.

Estimates of the pace of deforestation depend, apart from the empirical problems involved, on the definitions used (see Jepma, 1993). The FAO and the WRI define deforestation as the complete disappearance of closed or open forests and the use of the land for other purposes (see Table 9.2).[5] Biologists, ecologists, and environmentalists employ a broader definition of deforestation, which also includes serious degradation of the quality of forests and woodlands due to forestry, environmental damage and agriculture. The estimates of rates of deforestation in tropical rain forests

Table 9.3 Deforestation in humid tropical areas in the 1980s

	Woodlands (000s ha)		Average annual deforestation in the 1980s			
	WRI	Myers	WRI		Myers	
			(000s ha)	%	(000s ha)	%
Latin America*				1.4		1.7
Bolivia	66,760	7,000	117	0.2	150	2.1
Brazil	514,480	220,000	9,050	1.8	5,000	2.3
Colombia	51,700	27,850	890	1.7	650	2.3
Africa*				0.5		1.0
Cameroon	23,300	16,400	190	0.8	200	1.2
Congo	21,340	9,000	22	0.1	70	0.8
Nigeria	14,750	2,800	400	2.7	400	14.3
Zaire	177,590	100,000	370	0.2	400	0.4
Asia				1.0		2.2
Indonesia	116,895	86,000	920	0.8	1,200	1.4
Malaysia	20,996	15,700	255	1.2	270	5.4
Philippines	9,510	5,000	143	1.5	270	5.4
Thailand	15,675	7,400	397	2.5	600	8.4

Note:
* Regional totals are based on those countries for which data were available. Therefore, only percentage changes have been represented. By way of illustration, both absolute numbers and percentages have been reproduced for a few interesting countries in each region.

Sources: World Resources Institute (1990), table 19.1, pp. 292–3; Myers (1991), table 1, p. 6, quoted in Jepma (1993), p. 22. WRI data refer to the early 1980s; Myers's data refer to the latter part of the 1980s.

vary from an annual 0.4 per cent (FAO, 1988) to an annual 1.8 per cent (Myers, 1989). There are also great differences in the estimates of the remaining land areas covered by tropical rain forests – as can be seen in Table 9.3.

Table 9.3 presents alternative estimates of the rate of deforestation derived from Jepma (1993, table 1.1). The two estimates in Table 9.3 are extremes. Even the relatively cautious estimates of the World Resources Institute indicate rapid deforestation. Among the most extreme cases is Thailand, where the most conservative estimates predict that within forty years the last tropical rain forests in this country will have disappeared if current trends are continued. In general, the more recent the estimates, the higher the rates of deforestation.

9.2.2 Intensification of land use

Prior to the nineteenth century, the growth of agricultural production was to a large extent determined by two factors: the expansion of the land area used for agriculture, and intensification of land use (see Boserup, 1965, 1981, 1990). When population increased and further expansion of cultivated area was not possible, increasing population density resulted in more intensive techniques of land use.

In a series of pioneering publications Ester Boserup criticized the Malthusian notion that the natural environment sets unrelenting limits to the growth of food production. Increasing population density induces changes in agricultural technology, which primarily imply a more intensive use of 'natural' resources.

Boserup distinguishes six vegetable food supply systems, which can be ranked according to length of fallowing (Boserup, 1981, p. 19). These are presented in Table 9.4.

Table 9.4 Systems of supply for vegetable food

System	Description	Frequency of cropping (in %)[a]
Gathering	Wild plants, roots, fruits and nuts are gathered	0
Forest-fallow	One or two crops followed by 15–25 years' fallow	0–10
Bush-fallow[b]	Two or more crops followed by 8–10 years' fallow	10–40
Short-fallow	One or two crops followed by one or two years' fallow	40–80
Annual cropping	One crop each year with only a few months' fallow	0–100
Multicropping	Two or more crops in the same fields each year without any fallow	200–400

Notes:
[a] Frequency of cropping is average cultivated area as percentage of cultivated plus fallow area.
[b] Bush-fallow is often deceptively referred to as 'shifting cultivation'. In fact, it is a form of sedentary agriculture, where agriculturists with fixed dwellings alternately work different plots of land (Hill, 1986).

Source: Boserup (1981), table 3.2, p. 19. Reproduced with permission of the University of Chicago Press.

Letting land lie fallow serves the following functions:

1. Prevention of soil fertility exhaustion. During the period of fallow the soil recovers its fertility. Trees and bushes grow back.
2. Prevention of hillside erosion, by forest fallowing.
3. Controlling weed growth; bushes and trees limit the growth of weeds and grasses.
4. Limiting the spread of plant diseases and pests.

As population density increases, the period the land can be left fallow becomes shorter. The functions of fallowing increasingly have to be replaced by human operations. The production process becomes more and more labour intensive. Soil fertility is maintained by the application of animal manure and vegetable matter. Parasites or affected plants are removed by hand. Weeds are removed or ploughed under. Seeds are transplanted by hand (e.g. in rice cultivation). Ever more water is required. Water has to be transported to the fields. Also, surplus water has to be drained away. For water control and prevention of erosion, land has to be terraced and levelled, and canals and irrigation works dug and maintained. All this makes for increasing inputs of labour per hectare.

Since the nineteenth century many of these functions can also be fulfilled by industrial inputs: herbicides, pesticides, chemical fertilizers, agricultural machinery, pumps, and so forth. Before the nineteenth century, intensification of land use was the most viable alternative to fallowing in Western countries. In many developing countries this is still the case. The transition from extensive to more intensive forms of cultivation involves an increasing demand for labour in agricultural production. This demand is fulfilled by increasing the number of workers per hectare or by working more hours per person per year. Rawski (1979), for example, calculated that in the Chinese agricultural sector the number of days worked per person increased from 119 per year to 250 per year between 1949 and 1978. In the process of intensification, returns per hectare increase sharply as fallowing is reduced and cropping intensity increases. However, since the hours worked per person tend to increase, returns per hour worked may well decline (Boserup, 1965).

Boserup also points to the correlation between livestock breeding and population density. Meat and dairy production are rather inefficient ways of producing calories. Many of the calories consumed by cattle and poultry are lost in the transformation into meat and dairy products. As the population continues to grow and space becomes scarce, the number of cattle per head of the population tends to decrease.

A low population density allows wild game and cattle to thrive in their natural habitat. When land is cultivated more intensively, this becomes more difficult. But land lying fallow can be used systematically as pasture for cattle. The manure from cattle contributes to the fertility of the soil, and cattle can be used as draft animals to work the soil more intensively. When there are annual harvests, farmers have to switch to intensive livestock breeding – part of the land being used for the production of fodder crops. Fodder may also be produced industrially or it can be imported from regions with lower population densities. As land is cultivated more intensively, the share of animal food in the diet tends to decline.

Boserup (1981, p. 23) combines intensification of animal husbandry and intensification of agriculture in a typology consisting of seven systems of food supply, ranked according to increasing population density:

1. Hunting-gathering systems.
2. (Nomadic) pastoralism.
3. Forest-fallow.
4. Bush-fallow.
5. Short-fallow with domestic animals.
6. Annual harvesting with intensive animal husbandry.
7. Multicropping with little animal food.

This classification applies to societies at lower technological levels. At high technological levels a society has the option of producing fodder industrially or transporting it over long distances. After the onset of industrialization from the eighteenth century onwards, the correlations between population density and agricultural systems become weaker.

The transition from the first two systems of foods supply to sedentary systems of cultivation first took place some 10,000 years ago. It is one of the fundamental technological transitions in the history of mankind (see Goudsblom, 1992).

In the agricultural history of pre-industrial Europe, England was the technological leader. Between the ninth and the fourteenth centuries, the three-course rotation system was introduced. For two consecutive years different cereal crops would be grown on one piece of land; in the third year the land would lie fallow. Fallow land was used in common to let domestic cattle graze, the droppings of the cattle serving as manure for the land. The cattle also provided animal traction for tillage. In the eighteenth century there was a transition to annual harvesting. This is sometimes referred to as the 'agricultural revolution', but this term disregards the gradualistic nature of the process of intensification.

The system of annual harvesting was characterized by crop rotation, the introduction of new root crops such as the potato, reserving part of the land for production of cattle fodder and a systematic use of manure.

In the course of the nineteenth century a second agricultural revolution took place which resulted in farmers applying industrially produced chemical inputs and agricultural machinery. For the first time, the inputs came from outside the agricultural sector. Further, there was greater specialization in agricultural production and foodstuffs were often imported from abroad. This second 'agricultural revolution' falls outside the scope of the process of intensification analyzed by Boserup.

In the course of the intensification process the demand for labour increased in the agricultural sector. The transition to annual harvests also involved a reinforcement of individual rights to land (of ownership or use), and increased investment in agriculture (Hayami and Ruttan, 1985, p. 46). Previously, fallow land had been in common use for cattle grazing. Intensification, however, demanded a more precise delimitation of ownership rights (cf. North and Thomas, 1973). The so-called enclosure movement, which took place in England from the second half of the seventeenth century onwards, involved large-scale and fierce social conflicts between villagers who were losing their rights to graze cattle on the commons and (large) landowners who were trying to gain exclusive rights of ownership. Frequently, the acquired ownership titles were used for sheep raising. Currently, similar processes are taking place in Africa where joint rights to land are being transformed into individual ownership titles.

It should be stressed that the transition to more intensive cultivation practices is not uniform. Depending on differences in natural conditions and local circumstances, different systems of cultivation can coexist in one and the same area (Boserup, 1965, chapter 5).

Various lessons can be derived from Boserup's analysis that may deepen our understanding of agricultural issues in developing countries:

1. Intensification of agriculture requires hard work on the part of farmers. As long as sufficient land is available for more extensive kinds of agriculture, these will be preferred. People will only switch to more intensive methods of agricultural production when extensive methods become unsustainable due to increased population density. The sufficient availability of land may, for example, provide an explanation for disappointing results of irrigation projects in northeast Thailand. Farmers preferred to migrate to other areas, rather than participate in intensive irrigated agriculture (van der Meer, 1981; Dixon, 1990).
2. Much of our 'natural' environment is not natural. It is the result of centuries of interaction between people and their environments. The characteristics of the natural environment change under the influence of human interventions and actions. These may result in deforestation or reforestation, erosion or land reclamation, the creation of polders below sea level, desertification or irrigation. This approach puts the whole notion of fixed Malthusian limits to production in a different perspective.
3. Intensification of agriculture requires greater inputs of labour, in the form of more persons employed, more hours worked, or both. Intensification also requires increasing investment in infrastructure and water control.
4. The previous point implies a criticism of the notion of 'disguised unemployment' in agriculture. During peak periods in the agricultural cycle, such as sowing or harvesting, there is often an acute shortage of labour, rather than a surplus. This is particularly true for densely populated areas where multicropping and other forms of intensive agriculture are practised. (The assumption of low productivity per hour worked still seems to be justified.)
5. Production per hectare may increase sharply as a result of intensification. Intensification can contribute substantially to growth of agricultural output.
6. Nowadays, inputs from outside the agricultural sector, such as new seeds, chemical fertilizers, pesticides or herbicides are available. These inputs, together with investments in water control and agricultural infrastructure may contribute to further intensification of agriculture.

7. Subsidized food imports from economically advanced regions such as the European Union or the United States have negative effects on the development of agricultural production and productivity in developing countries. They form a disincentive for agricultural development in developing countries, and allow those countries to postpone the difficult and backbreaking process of agricultural intensification (Boserup, 1983).
8. Low population density may be a disadvantage for agricultural development since a minimum degree of density is required to support infrastructural investment. Without infrastructural investment (e.g. in water control or land preparation), it is hard to intensify agriculture. When there is rapid population growth in a situation of low initial population density, farmers may continue to use extensive methods of agriculture in spite of diminishing supplies of land. Fallow is too short to allow the land to regenerate. The continuation of extensive agricultural practices may thus result in land degradation. A vicious circle arises in which the increase in agricultural production lags behind population growth. Circumstances like this seem to apply in several countries in sub-Saharan Africa.

Cropping intensity

Table 9.5 presents data on cropping intensity by region. A cropping intensity of 1.0 means that there is one harvest per year on a given plot of land. Table 9.5 illustrates the huge differences in cropping intensity between irrigated and non-irrigated land and the differences between regions. Cropping intensity in the Far East is much higher than in Africa and Latin America. The table shows that there is still considerable potential for further intensification.

Table 9.5 Cropping intensity in developing countries[a]

	Nonirrigated			Irrigated		
	1974–76	1982–84	2000	1974–76	1982–84	2000
Total 93 countries[b]	0.70	0.71	0.74	1.07	1.18	1.23
Africa	0.51	0.54	0.59	1.03	0.84	0.89
Far East. excl. China	1.02	1.00	1.11	1.18	1.29	1.29
Latin America	0.59	0.59	0.63	0.92	1.02	1.06
Near East	0.56	0.62	0.68	0.82	0.98	1.09

Notes:
[a] Ratio of the annually harvested area to the total area in use.
[b] 1974–76: 90 countries.

Sources: 1974–76: FAO (1981), annex table 9; 1982–84 and 2000: Alexandratos (1988), 130.

Irrigation contributes both to increased returns per crop and to increased frequency of cropping. Without regulated water supply, new varieties with higher returns per harvest cannot flourish. Irrigation also makes it possible to have more than one harvest per year, for example in rice production. Table 9.6 provides information on irrigation intensity, derived from FAO statistics. The table shows that there is a steady growth of irrigation intensity in all regions. The table also illustrates the large differences between low irrigation intensity in Africa and Latin America, and high irrigation intensity in Asia. In the Far East irrigation intensity has reached 35.2 per cent. With respect to developing countries it is estimated that a total of 22.9 per cent of all agricultural land was irrigated in 1991.

Table 9.6 Irrigated area in developing countries

	Irrigated area (000s ha)				% irrigated area*			
	1976	1981	1986	1991	1976	1981	1986	1991
Africa	3,885	4,534	5,105	5,429	2.0	2.8	3.5	3.6
Latin America	12,462	13,852	14,940	15,889	9.6	9.9	10.3	10.4
Near East	18,011	17,857	19,062	20,484	21.4	21.4	22.7	24.2
Far East	107,467	117,521	124,473	135,839	28.6	30.9	32.6	35.2
Total	141,825	153,764	163,580	177,641	18.1	19.4	21.6	22.9

Note:
*Irrigated area as a percentage of actually cultivated area.

Source: FAO (1993a).

There are great differences in the quality of irrigation systems that are not reflected in FAO statistics. Irrigation systems vary from simple traditional techniques to large-scale modern systems (van der Eng, 1993, chapter 3). The percentage of irrigated land also depends on the definitions used. Dixon (1990) presents a much lower figure than FAO. He gives an estimate of 112 million hectares of irrigated land in developing countries, 14 per cent of the entire area cultivated. In spite of these substantial differences, it is obvious that the capacity to expand irrigation has not yet been exhausted.

Unequal availability of water does set a limit to continued expansion of irrigation. Dixon rightly remarks that locations most suited to irrigation, like river deltas, are already irrigated. Technically another 400–600 million hectares could still be irrigated (Alexandratos, 1988; Dixon, 1990), but it is not always economically profitable to do so. Many farmers in developing countries will remain dependent on rain-fed agriculture.

9.2.3 Hayami and Ruttan's models of agricultural development

In their authoritative study, *Agricultural Development: An international perspective,* Hayami and Ruttan (1971, 1985) distinguish five models of agricultural development: the resource exploitation model; the conservation model; the urban industrial impact model; the diffusion model; and the high-payoff input model. These models show some resemblance to the ways of expanding agricultural output discussed in the previous section. But, they place more emphasis on the analysis of the mechanisms operating in agricultural growth and development. They also clarify the distinction between the increase in returns per harvested crop and more traditional ways of expanding production.

The resource exploitation model

The resource exploitation model corresponds to the process of expanding the cultivated agricultural area as described in section 9.2.1. During most of agricultural history, expansion of cultivated area was the prime method to expand total production. In *frontier societies* like the United States, the frontier of the cultivated area expanded towards the west at the expense of Indian hunters and gatherers, and nomadic pastoralists. Hayami and Ruttan also include the vent for surplus model – discussed in Chapter 8 – under the heading 'resource exploitation'. According to the vent for surplus model, farmers have reacted to the increasing demand for primary products since the middle of the nineteenth century by taking hitherto uncultivated land into use. As explained above, this route to growth of production has not yet been completely exhausted, but in different parts of the world the limits to further expansion of cultivated area are becoming visible.

A drawback of the resource exploitation model is that it makes too absolute a distinction between cultivated and non-cultivated area. In section 9.2.2 it was emphasized that there was a gradual increase in cropping intensity. From a Boserupian perspective even land harvested only once every twenty years is in use. When fallowing is disregarded, the amounts of uncultivated land will be overestimated.

The conservation model

In the transition to annual crops in eighteenth-century England, animal manure and organic wastes played an important role in maintaining soil fertility. The inputs into the agricultural system were all supplied from within the agricultural sector.

On the basis of this agricultural system in England, German agronomists in particular developed the concept of soil exhaustion. In the conservation model, the development of agricultural production involves a struggle to maintain the fertility of the soils. Whatever is taken out of the soil has to be put back later on. If one continues to add other production factors to limited amounts of land, farmers will sooner or later run into diminishing returns.

This is a rather static representation in which nature sets a limit to agricultural production. However, the theories of Boserup illustrate that soil fertility can also be seen in a dynamic perspective. By more intensive cultivation of the land, increasing returns per hectare may be realized without loss of soil fertility. Nevertheless, Hayami and Ruttan include Boserup in the conservation model, because the inputs into agriculture are forthcoming from the agricultural sector itself. The provision of agricultural inputs by the industrial sector dates from after the 'second agricultural revolution' in the nineteenth century.

The urban industrial impact model

The urban industrial impact model in its modern form was formulated by T. W. Schultz (1953). Schultz argued that productivity, agricultural incomes and growth of production are highest close to urban centres. This is because product markets and markets for factors of production function better in the vicinity of areas with rapid urban and industrial development. This leads to a more efficient allocation of production factors in agriculture.

Hayami and Ruttan consider the empirical evidence for this relationship to be inconclusive and its relevance for poorer developing countries rather limited. A possible policy implication for developing countries would be to spread urbanization and industry as much as possible over an entire country. This would be preferable to the growth of megacities. Decentralization of urbanization and rural industrialization would intensify the linkages between agriculture and industry, which are positive for agricultural growth.

Irrespective of whether the distance to urban centres is really an important variable, the degree to which agricultural markets contribute to efficient allocation is of obvious significance to agricultural development (Ellis, 1988, p. 75). With respect to West Africa, Hill argues that in some regions rural markets actually function quite well. One should not confuse production for the market with urbanization (Hill, 1986). Lal and Myint (1996) speak of institutional underdevelopment, when lack of transport infrastructure, lack of information and inadequate channels of distribution isolate farmers from wider markets and stifle incentives to increase productivity.

The diffusion model

There are not only huge differences in agricultural technology and productivity between countries, but also within countries, regions, and even within villages. The diffusion model takes such differences as its point of departure. International and national diffusion of most advanced technologies can help narrow the gap between 'best practice' and the average farmer. *Inter alia*, the possibilities of transfer to developing countries of agricultural technologies developed in Western countries are featured.

The policy implications of this model include a strong emphasis on the construction of systems of agricultural extension and education. In many economically advanced countries (e.g. the Netherlands and the United States) there are highly developed networks of agricultural education and extension that allow for very rapid diffusion of new agricultural technologies. In many developing countries, substantial efforts have been made to build up systems of agricultural extension.

An important assumption of the diffusion model is that farmers do not adopt new technologies because they are ignorant or ill-informed. This assumption is by no means justified. Farmers in developing countries are often better informed about local economic, ecological, and social conditions than the extension workers sent out to educate them. According to Schultz (1964), farmers work quite efficiently and rationally, given the difficult conditions of their existence. They are poor but efficient.

New seeds and agricultural techniques that perform well in laboratories or model farms often turn out to be less successful in the field. They are often insufficiently adapted to local conditions. This is especially the case when technologies and seeds developed in the West are transferred to developing countries. Farmers are therefore justified in treating innovations with a healthy degree of suspicion.

With the introduction of new varieties, numerous 'secondary functions' of existing varieties – provision of hay, fodder, building materials, fuel, and so on – are often forgotten. Also, traditional agricultural practices tend to minimize risk, which is of great importance to the survival of small farmers. In recent years, it is argued that agricultural innovation should try to build on existing local practices.

High-payoff input model

This model finds its inspiration in the work of Theodor Schultz (1964). As mentioned, Schultz maintained that traditional farmers act rationally. Given the conditions in which they have to operate, they allocate their resources optimally. Within the constraints of a traditional economy there are not many opportunities to realize increases in output and productivity.

Schultz therefore argued that new inputs coming from outside the agricultural sector should be made available to farmers with government support and subsidies. In this approach the emphasis was on stimulating technological progress that was adapted to local circumstances, the development of high yielding varieties of maize, wheat and rice with high returns per harvest, and the search for the optimal conditions under which new varieties would flourish. These conditions included the application of chemical fertilizers, irrigation and water control.

Schultz and his numerous followers argued in favour of investment in the following:

1. Agricultural research centres producing new, well-adapted technical knowledge.
2. Industrial activities oriented towards agriculture. The industrial sector should develop and produce new agricultural inputs and supply them to farmers.
3. Agricultural education and extension which help farmers to apply the technologies and use the new inputs.

The high-payoff input model incorporates the preceding three models – conservation, urban industrial impact, and diffusion. The new inputs contribute to maintaining soil fertility when land use is intensified. Well-functioning factor and product markets are a prerequisite for the adequate utilization of new inputs and technologies. Where small peasants have insufficient access to new inputs due to market imperfections, cheap agricultural credit should be made available. Attention should also be paid to transport infrastructure and the development of market systems through which agricultural surpluses can be traded. Schooling and agricultural extension are explicitly included in the high-payoff input approach, as in the diffusion model. However, there is much more emphasis in the high-payoff input model on adapting new technologies to local conditions. The name of the model, finally, refers to the positive relationship between investments in agricultural research, schooling and extension, and the high returns of the new inputs. According to Schultz, the returns to agricultural investment in research, development and extension are much higher than returns to investment in industry.

The theory of induced technological development

According to Hayami and Ruttan, even Schultz's high-payoff input model has its limitations. Insufficient attention is paid to the direction of technological development and the process of institutional change. Technological development does not happen in a vacuum. Its course is influenced among others by the relative scarcity of factors of production. If market prices of production factors reflect their relative scarcity, farmers will prefer technologies that economize on the most scarce production factors. If agricultural research institutions are responsive to farmers' needs and preferences and there are effective interactions between farmers, research institutions and industrial producers of agricultural inputs, farmers' preferences for certain types of technological development will be translated into research programmes and incorporated in production plans of suppliers of agricultural inputs. The responsiveness of research and development institutions to local farmers' needs is an institutional characteristic. Under these conditions, a relative scarcity of labour will induce labour-saving technological development. This has been the path followed in the United States and also in England since the late nineteenth century. When labour is plentiful and land is scarce, technological development will be directed towards land saving. Land saving technology includes:

1. Biological technology, in particular selective breeding of plants and development of new varieties.
2. Chemical technology, including organic and inorganic fertilizers that add nutrients for plant growth to the soil, and pesticides and herbicides.
3. Development of land and water control.

Examples of this path of technological development include the Netherlands, Denmark, late-nineteenth-century Japan, and Taiwan between 1900 and 1940.

If the research system is closed and hierarchical, induced technological development will be less influenced by the relative scarcity of production factors. This may easily lead to technological developments that are insufficiently adapted to local conditions in developing countries. Thus the process of institutional development in the field of research, development and extension work is also an important determinant of the nature of technological development.

Hayami and Ruttan point to the fact that the process of induced technological change is not a gradual process – even under the best of conditions – but rather a succession of dynamic disequilibria. It is comparable to the process of 'unbalanced growth' analyzed by Hirschman and discussed in Chapter 7. Changes in relative scarcity and changes in technology can also induce changes in agricultural institutions, such as large landownership, labour relations, market characteristics, credit institutions and the organization of research and extension.

9.2.4 Increase in yields per harvest: the green revolution

The high-payoff input model is closely related to the third way of increasing agricultural production introduced at the beginning of section 9.2: increasing returns per harvested crop.[6] This model is often also called the 'green revolution'. The green revolution refers to breakthroughs in research into new varieties of maize, wheat and rice which, together with a set of complementary inputs, may result in great increases in the yields per harvest. When new varieties shorten the crop cycle from sowing to harvesting, the green revolution also allows for more crops per year and thus contributes to further intensification of agriculture and increase of output per unit of land.

The green revolution has the following characteristics:

- The development of new plant varieties with high yields that have been adjusted to local conditions: for example, Mexican wheat varieties that are highly sensitive to fertilizer use, not very sensitive to sunlight, more resistant to diseases, and with short stems. The dwarf varieties introduced in India in 1965 had yields of 4,450 kg per hectare on experimental plots, compared to yields of 1,200 kg per hectare for older varieties. Outside experimental stations yields of 3,200 kg per hectare were also quite impressive (Dixon, 1990).
- Use of industrially manufactured fertilizers, pesticides, and herbicides.
- Land-saving innovations.
- Increased volume of – relatively cheap – investments in agricultural research; a positive attitude towards science-based agriculture.
- The organization of an effective system of agricultural extension.
- Investments in irrigation and water control.
- The development of delivery systems for new seeds and inputs.
- The development of credit institutions and facilities which enable farmers to purchase the new inputs.
- Complementarities between the different inputs: research, new seeds, industrial inputs, irrigation, education and extension, delivery, and credit facilities.

The complementarities between all these so-called non-conventional inputs form one of the basic characteristics of the green revolution. When some elements are lacking, the potential increases in yields will not be realized.

The green revolution is associated with two well-known institutes for agricultural research: the International Rice Research Institute (IRRI) founded in 1960 in Los Banos in the Philippines and the International Maize and Wheat Improvement Centre (Centro Internacional de Mejoramiento de Maiz y Trigo) CIMMYT in Mexico. In the 1950s the CIMMYT developed high-productive varieties of maize and wheat.

The success of wheat research promoted research into rice varieties. In the 1960s new varieties of rice were developed at the IRRI. The work at these institutes was initially financed by the Rockefeller Foundation. Since 1971 it has been financed and supervised by the CGIAR (Consultative Group on International Agricultural Research). Today the CGIAR supervises the work of an international network of thirteen agricultural research institutes (Colman and Nixson, 1986, p. 217; Oasa, 1987).

The initial technological breakthroughs led to dramatically increased yields per crop. Also, the rapid maturing of dwarf varieties allowed for more harvests per year. The enthusiasm about these breakthroughs was translated into political rhetoric by the term 'green revolution'. This term suggests that technological breakthroughs might lessen the need for fundamental social reorganization and prevent the rise of revolutionary movements.

In rice production there were green revolutions long before the 1950s and 1960s: in medieval China, in Japan between 1881 and 1920, Taiwan between 1900 and 1940, and Korea in the 1920s. The early varieties developed by IRRI were based on genetic materials drawn from China, Taiwan, Japan and Indonesia. Semi-dwarf wheat originated in Japan in the 1800s (Parayil, 1992). In their famous article 'The role of agriculture in economic development', Johnston and Mellor (1961) analyzed the rapid increase in agricultural production and productivity in Japanese agriculture between 1881 and 1920. According to their estimates, production increased by 77 per cent while the area of land used for agriculture was expanded by only 21 per cent. The yields per hectare increased by 46 per cent, per capita food production by 20 per cent. The Japanese example shows how technological developments of mainly biological nature can lead to substantial increases in yields per hectare and per head of the population in a densely populated area (van der Meer and Yamada, 1990, p. 73ff.). Nevertheless, the sudden increases in productivity achieved in the research institutes in the 1950s and 1960s had the character of a technological breakthrough.

In India, new wheat seeds were introduced in 1965 from which the yields per hectare were far in excess of the yields of traditional varieties. New rice varieties were introduced in the Philippines in 1966 and spread rapidly to different Asian countries. By 1970 the new strains were being cultivated over an area of 10 million hectares. Within a few years Pakistan ceased to be dependent on food imports from the United States and India became self-sufficient in food.

The success of the green revolution in the 1960s and the euphoria that followed gave rise to a wave of criticism. Part of this criticism concerned technical matters. Outside the experimental fields and laboratory conditions, yields of newly developed varieties were often disappointing. The seeds performed poorly under less than optimum conditions (Griffin, 1976; Pearse, 1977; Glaeser, 1987). The new varieties were susceptible to diseases, pests and weather conditions. They were not sufficiently adjusted to local conditions. This issue was strongly emphasized by, among others, Chambers (1983) who stated that often valuable local knowledge and insights were lost due to international research programmes and their recommendations. Dixon gives an interesting example of the rejection by farmers of a new, fast growing variety of sorghum in Ethiopia. The new variety grew faster but had less stem and leaves than existing varieties. Stems and leaves were traditionally used as roofing material and fodder. Agricultural researchers had neglected the secondary functions of sorghum (Dixon, 1990, p. 97). Furthermore, critics pointed to the dangers of the loss in genetic diversity due to the introduction of several standardized varieties (genetic erosion). Diversity acts as an insurance policy against natural calamities, climatic influences and plant diseases. The new production techniques turned out to have various environmental hazards (Barrow, 1995). Topsoils were eroded due to intensive use. The use of nitrogenous fertilizers resulted in eutrophication of freshwater streams and lakes. Pesticides created health problems. Applications of fertilizer ran into diminishing returns (Glaeser, 1987; Oasa, 1987). Finally, it was claimed that the nutritional value of new varieties, particularly of rice, was lower than that of traditional varieties and food crops.

Technical problems and criticisms gave rise to the search for technical solutions: developing disease-resistant plants, better adjustment to local conditions, setting up gene banks, biological pest control, improved nitrogen absorption of new varieties, and so forth. In response to criticisms, new agricultural research institutes were developed, focusing on specific crops, climatic conditions or problems. According to Oasa (1987), there was a shift from the search for new breakthroughs, to a second generation of research of a more incremental nature. The new approach tries to achieve better integration of technological change with social factors and environmental constraints.

The most fundamental criticisms of the green revolution are of a political-economic nature (Griffin, 1976, 1981; Pearse, 1977; Pinstrup-Anderson, 1982; Pinstrup-Anderson and Hazell, 1985; Glaeser, 1987). These criticisms state that the introduction of the green revolution leads to increased rural inequality, increased landlessness and to impoverishment of the rural masses. The criticisms include the following elements:

1. Large farmers have better access to new inputs than small peasants. The green revolution therefore makes for more inequality. First, large farmers have financial reserves which they can use to purchase expensive new inputs. Second, they have relationships and contacts with government officials and agricultural extension institutions. They have easier access to cheap loans, information, and water supplies. This applies to India, for example, where coalitions between medium-sized and large farmers and government officials have emerged (Cassen, 1978), and to Bangladesh (Bol, 1983). Despite its emancipatory rhetoric, the dominant political party in post-war India, the Congress Party, was totally dependent in rural areas on the support of large landowners. This explains why so many attempts at land reform were unsuccessful from their inception (Frankel, 1978).

2. The position of small peasants is threatened by the increasing cost of inputs. To purchase new inputs they are forced to contract loans and go into debt. They become more and more dependent on the sale of their surplus production on the market.

When yields or prices are disappointing in a given year they may be forced to sell their land. Peasants have less access to land, capital, new seeds and complementary inputs such as water and fertilizer. In many countries they are also dependent on large landowners for credit. Thus the green revolution increases rural inequality and landlessness. Sometimes poor peasants are not dispossessed of land, but have to lease out their lands to the expanding classes of rich farmers and work on these lands as farm labourers.

3. When prices fall due to the increase in total production, small peasants who were unable to apply the new technologies, will be worse off. This is also conducive to inequality.

4. Due to their economic power large landowners pay too little for their production factors land and capital. For example, they have access to subsidized credit, so they will use methods that are too capital intensive. Large farmers tend to employ less farm labour and try to withdraw from traditional sharecropping arrangements. All these factors together make for increasing landlessness, concentration of landownership and rural unemployment (for example, in India, see Singh, 1982). Also, the total volume of production may be lower than is the case when production factors are allocated more efficiently.

5. Farmers in developing countries become more and more dependent on a few agricultural multinationals that have a monopoly on the provision of new seed varieties.

6. Production for export may have negative effects on women's allocation of time and energy. The best plots of land are reserved for cash crops, which are often cultivated by males. Food production is shifted to land of marginal quality, often located far from the household dwelling. In many African countries, food production is the preserve of women. Their position can be affected negatively by the shift to export crops. In addition to their household duties, they have to travel long distances to cultivate their fields.

7. The green revolution involves increasing production for the market and exports. According to the critics, it is conceivable that an increase in production per hectare goes hand in hand with decreased availability of food in a given region, especially when the landless labourers have insufficient means to buy food. Thus the green revolution may be lead to impoverishment and malnutrition.

This criticism contains some valuable elements. Introduction of technological changes, with no regard for power relationships, class structures and institutions, may result in reinforcement of dualism and increasing inequality. However, in some cases the initially even-handed critical analysis of the green revolution by authors like Griffin was replaced by a complete rejection in the 1970s and 1980s. A typical example is provided by an article by Boelens (1980). Here the green revolution is considered as an international conspiracy of the capitalist agribusiness, at the expense of human values and food requirements in developing countries.

In reply to the often one-sided criticisms of the green revolution, numerous counter-arguments have been put forward (see, for example, Hayami and Ruttan, 1985; Pinstrup-Anderson and Hazell, 1985; Ellis, 1988).

First, the argumentation of critics is often fragmentary, based on case studies rather than aggregates. There is a tendency, especially amongst anthropologists, to idealize traditional agricultural systems. Second, technological change is an absolute must when population is increasing rapidly. If technology does not change and population increases rapidly, marginal returns to agricultural efforts will decrease. This inevitably results in a decrease in food availability per head of the population.

Critics like Griffin remarked that there are no significant differences in production trends before and after the introduction of new varieties. Therefore, they concluded that the outcomes of the new technologies were rather disappointing. Hayami and Ruttan (1985), however, note that this argumentation contains serious logical flaws. One should not compare the situation before and after the introduction of new varieties, since population density is changing over time. What one should compare is the productivity trend with a growing population *without* technological change and the productivity trend with population growth *with* technological change. In absence of new technologies, per capita production and production per hectare would have been much lower than is presently the case.

It is true that larger farmers introduce new varieties sooner than small peasants. After some years, however, there is usually a diffusion of the new technologies to other categories of farmers. Small farmers and peasants also start to adopt the new varieties and apply the new technologies. There is nothing intrinsically capital intensive about the green revolution (Hayami and Ruttan, 1985). It can be applied just as well on small as on large farms. The above-mentioned example of Japan illustrates the labour-intensive potential of the new techniques. In post-war Indonesia and China, technological innovation also appears to contribute to expansion of employment in agriculture. In these countries, the relatively equal distribution of land is also a positive factor in this respect.

Finally, growth of agricultural production may result in lower prices for food. As production for own consumption becomes less important, an increasing part of the rural population of developing countries is dependent on the purchase of foodstuffs on the market. The poor thus benefit from lower food prices, both in urban and in rural areas.

In conclusion one may say that increases in productivity and technological change in agriculture are absolutely essential to feed a growing world population. Nowadays, this is no longer disputed, even by critics of the green revolution (Glaeser, 1987). In particular, in sub-Saharan Africa there is great need for technological advances in semi-arid agriculture that might contribute to agricultural growth, as happened previously in Asia and Latin America. More research in this field is urgently needed. Moreover, older research focused primarily on maize, wheat, and rice, while in many developing countries other food crops provide the basic foodstuffs (e.g. tuberous crops like cassavas, sweet potatoes, potatoes, yams, taro, and tree crops like sago palm, plantain, and breadfruit). Research into these crops is still very underdeveloped.

The critical debate on the green revolution still continues, but international research has also to some extent – at least on paper – responded to earlier criticisms (Oasa, 1987).[7] There is more emphasis on the ecological consequences of new technologies and new approaches, such as the farming systems approach, trying to integrate ecological, social and technological factors. Attempts are made to adapt existing traditional technologies and practices to present-day requirements. Since 1972 there is a specialized research institute for crops in the semi-arid tropics (ICRASAT) in Hyderabad, India. In 1976 the International Centre for Agricultural Research in Dry Areas was founded in Beirut. Since 1974 the International Board for Plant Genetic Resources (IBPGR) focuses on genetic diversity. For various crops and kinds of livestock there are specialized research institutes located in different parts of the world.[8] Also, in the international research effort, there are attempts to focus on technologies which are useful and feasible for smaller, resource-poor farmers.

In the introduction of technological innovations, an increase in rural inequality in some stages of the process of agricultural development is probably inevitable, as wealthy and less risk-averse farmers will tend to adopt new, highly productive technologies at an earlier stage than poor, risk-vulnerable small farmers and peasants. In light of the political economic criticisms discussed, however, more attention should be paid to the institutional and political aspects of technological change. Institutions should be designed to promote technological developments which are more in line with factor proportions. When labour is abundant, labour-intensive technological improvements should be sought. Small farmers should get easier access to credit facilities. Subsidized credit to wealthy farmers should be abolished. Land reforms could help improve the position of peasants and landless rural workers. Policy should ensure that not only the urban population, but also people in rural areas benefit from lower prices for food.

9.2.5 Summary

Table 9.7 summarizes the effects of expansion of the agricultural area and increases in yields per unit of land since 1961. The increase in yields per hectare incorporate the effects of increased cropping frequency and higher yields per crop.

During the past 30 years, 8 per cent of the increase in world production can be explained by the expansion of cultivated area.[9] In Africa and Latin America, however, these percentages are much higher. This means that increases in agricultural production in these regions may conflict with the aim of preserving tropical forests and woodlands. On the other hand, intensification of production and increasing yields per harvest may also threaten the environment, since intensification involves the use of increasing amounts of chemical fertilizers, pesticides and herbicides which pollute the soil and ground water (World Bank, 1992a, p. 134; Barrow, 1995, p. 194 ff.). According to the World Bank, the greatest challenge for agricultural policy

Table 9.7 Contributions of increases in cultivated area and in yields to growth of cereals production, 1961–1990

	Average production 1988–90 (million tons)	Yields per hectare 1988–90 (tons/ha)	Production growth since 1961–63 attributable to:		
			Total (%)	Expansion of area (%)	Increase in yields per hectare (%)
Developing countries	1,315	2.3	118	8	92
Sub-Saharan Africa	57	1.0	73	47	52
East Asia	499	3.7	189	6	94
South Asia	261	1.9	114	14	86
Latin America	105	2.1	111	30	71
Middle East and North Africa	41	1.4	68	23	77
Middle and Eastern Europe and former USSR	336	2.2	76	−13	113
High income countries	543	4.0	67	2	98
World	1,858	2.6	100	8	92

Source: World Bank, *World Development Report 1992*, Oxford and New York, Oxford University Press, 1992a, p. 135.

is to increase production and at the same time to protect the natural environment. When population increases to an estimated 9 billion people in 2030, cereal production – which accounts for 90 per cent of the world demand for food – should be increased by a factor 1.6. This is a very difficult, but not impossible task.

Summarizing, we observe that agricultural production increased in the long run due to expansion of cultivated area, increases in cropping frequency and improved yields per crop. In the past, the most important factors were expansion of cultivated area, increases in cropping frequency, and intensification of land use by applying more labour per unit of land. In many regions these avenues of production expansion have not yet been exhausted. But as the limits to labour intensification are being reached (e.g. in Asian countries like Indonesia and China), the emphasis will increasingly shift to the increase of yields per crop by means of technological innovation. As mentioned, technological innovation in turn may lead to further intensification of production: for example, in glasshouse production of vegetables, and in intensive cattle and poultry breeding. There is no reason why technological change in future years should not continue to allow food production to expand more rapidly than population. Still, there are numerous economic, institutional, and environmental barriers to production growth. There is a continued need for agricultural research into new agricultural technologies that are well adapted to local conditions.

9.3 *Food consumption*

In the introduction to this chapter it was shown that world food production exceeds the growth of world population. With the exception of sub-Saharan Africa, this also holds for food production in developing countries. However, this does not mean that the appalling problems of malnutrition and starvation in developing countries are in any way close to a solution.

In his famous book, *Poverty and Famines*, Amartya Sen (1981) argues that the occurrence of starvation and malnutrition does not depend only on food production and food availability, but also on people's actual *entitlements* to food. These entitlements may be based on one's own labour (a family producing for its own needs), on landownership (the owner of land is entitled to part of the harvest), on purchasing-power (money that has been earned is used to purchase food), and on legislation or government measures (e.g. food rationing, food distribution, social security). Analyzing two famous famines (the Bengal famine from 1942 to 1944, and the famine in Ethiopia from 1972 to 1974), Sen shows that neither famine was due primarily to insufficient production of food per head of population. In both famines, a slight shortfall in production led to widespread speculation, food hoarding and skyrocketing of prices. Food distribution systems failed in moving food surpluses to deficit areas. Consumers also lacked the financial means to buy food at its inflated prices. If governments had imported limited amounts of food and taken the responsibility for its distribution, prices could have been brought under control and famines could have been averted. Since independence in 1947, India has pursued such policies. Unlike what has happened in China, there have been no large-scale famines in India in the post-war period (Sen, 1982). A relatively open society and timely identification of food shortages are the prerequisites for success of a policy aimed at preventing famines. Sen's exposition illustrates the importance of prices. Poor people may profit greatly from price decreases due to production growth (see section 9.2.4).

Van der Meer (1983) makes a distinction between malnutrition and starvation. Malnutrition refers to a situation where, during longer periods of time, the diet is insufficient for people to lead a healthy and productive life. Starvation is a situation in which people die due to an acute shortage of food.

Malnutrition typically occurs in rural areas prior to the harvesting season. In sparsely populated areas, with no scarcity of land, undernourishment results from shortfalls in production in terms of quantity or quality. In densely populated areas, social inequality and unequal access to the means of production play a more important role. Even when the volume of food production is sufficient, the poor and landless may have too little purchasing-power to realize their entitlements to food. Thus, in some areas undernourishment may increase while production is growing.

Famines are mainly caused by crop failures, natural disasters, wars, civil wars, and social disruption. Again, it is not always the absolute shortage of food at an aggregate level that causes famine. Rather, famines are associated with situations in which people in given areas are unable to effectuate their entitlements to food.

In the twentieth century, great famines occurred primarily in China, the USSR and India (Arnold, 1988). In 1920–21, a famine in China led to 0.5 million casualties. In 1943 the Chinese province of Honan was struck by a famine resulting in between 2 and 3 million casualties. The latest great Chinese famine took place from 1958 to 1961. The estimates of number of casualties during this period vary from 16 to 30 million. Between 1942 and 1944 a famine killed 3 million people in Bengal, part of former British India. In 1921 a famine claimed between 1 and 3 million lives in the Soviet Union. Between 1932 and 1934, 5 million persons died due to famines that resulted from Stalin's forced agricultural collectivization. A famine hit Bangladesh in 1974; here the number of deaths was estimated to be between 300,000 and 1 million. The Ethiopian famine in 1984–85 led to over 1 million casualties.

In sparsely populated areas, famines are also caused by shortcomings in infrastructure. When there are localized shortages of food due to crop failures, poor infrastructure and malfunctioning distribution systems will hamper the transport of food from surplus areas or other countries. In densely populated areas, infrastructure is usually better. These areas can import food whenever there are shortages. In such conditions, famines are primarily caused by social disruption, government policy failures, civil wars, rebellions, and international wars. Countries where social disruption resulted in famine include Cambodia, Bangladesh, Biafra, Ethiopia, Somalia, and the Sudan. At the time of writing Burundi and Rwanda are threatened by famine.

The degree of openness of a society is also of the greatest importance. In China massive famines could occur between 1958 and 1961 without any knowledge of them reaching the outside world and the international community. In India, on the other hand, imminent famines rapidly led to mobilization of national and international relief actions (Sen, 1982). Due to improved medical facilities, better infrastructure, better communication facilities, and international relief organizations, the number of deaths due to famines since 1950 has declined in comparison with the first half of the twentieth century.

Tables 9.8 and 9.9 present rough trends in availability of food in developing countries. Average food availability is calculated as the sum of domestic food production (in calories) plus food imports and minus food exports, divided by total population. Table 9.8 shows that the average amount of calories available per person at world level increased from 96 per cent of average requirements in 1961–63 to 113 per cent of average requirement in 1988–90. Especially in Asia and the Near East the availability of food calories improved considerably. In Africa the caloric situation is less favourable. There was little change in the 1980s. In 1988–90, only 95 per cent of the average caloric requirements were being met.

It should be stressed that these data are averages. When one considers separate countries, it turns out that during the 1980s the per capita food availability decreased in no less than one-third of all developing countries. Half of the countries experiencing a decline are in Africa, and one-third in Latin America and the Caribbean (FAO, 1991b, p. 12). On the other hand, there were fifty-six developing countries – including China – with more than 2,600 calories per head of the population at the end of the 1980s, against thirty-nine countries in the early 1980s.

Table 9.8 Average availability of calories, 1961–1990

Country/region	Kilocalories per person per day				As a % of average requirements[a]			
	1961–63	1969–71	1979–81	1987–89	1961–63	1969–71	1979–81	1987–90
Africa[b]	2,117	2,138	2,180	2,204	91	92	94	95
Latin America	2,363	2,502	2,693	2,690	98	104	112	112
Near East	2,237	2,437	2,845	2,954	91	99	116	121
Far East[c]	1,825	2,029	2,245	2,442	80	89	98	107
Asian market economies	1,967	2,063	2,199		89	93	99	
Asian centrally planned economies	1,687	2,003	2,325		72	85	99	
Developing countries	1,940	2,117	2,324	2,473	84	91	100	107
Developed countries	3,031	3,195	3,287	3,404	118	125	128	133
World	2,287	2,433	2,579	2,697	96	102	108	113

Notes:

[a] The average caloric requirement differs from country to country. It depends on average height, age and sex distribution of the population, climatic conditions and average requirement of physical effort. The average caloric requirement is the number of calories required for normal, productive functioning in a society.

[b] Excluding Arab countries, which are included in the Near East.

[c] Since 1990 FAO statistics no longer distinguish between market economies and centrally planned economies.

Sources: Calories from FAO (1993a), *Production Yearbook 1992*; data on calories in market economies and centrally planned economies from FAO (various), *Production Yearbook 1988*. Average caloric requirements calculated from FAO (1975), *State of Food and Agriculture* 1975, p. 76. The caloric requirements for the Far East are calculated as the average of centrally planned and market economies. Table 9.8 is an adapted version of a table compiled by P. van der Eng.

Access to food is very unequally distributed, not only among countries, but also among regions within a country and even among the members of a single household (men versus women, adults versus children). As explained above, not all individuals are equally capable of effectuating their entitlements to food. Availability of calories does not equal consumption, not even at aggregate levels (Alexandratos, 1988, p. 57).[10]

Within households, young children in particular are likely to be exposed to malnutrition. Further, part of the available food is lost due to problems of transport or storage. Thus a sufficient average availability of food does not necessarily preclude widespread malnutrition and hunger.

Table 9.9 contains data on numbers and percentages of undernourished people in ninety-eight developing countries with market economies. China and other centrally planned developing countries are not included in the table. When caloric intake is less than 80 per cent of average caloric requirements, there are serious health hazards and dangers of arrested growth. When caloric intake is between 80 and 90 per cent of average requirements, there are no direct health risks, but the calories consumed are insufficient to lead an 'active working life' (World Bank, 1986a; van der Eng, 1992).

Table 9.9 indicates that the percentage of undernourished people shows a downward tendency between 1969 and 1985 in all regions except sub-Saharan Africa. Nevertheless, the absolute numbers of undernourished people increased. Using the 90 per cent criterion, the number of undernourished people increased by 15 million between 1969–71 and 1979–81, reaching 475 million. Between 1979–81 and 1983–85 another 37 million were added to this total. The estimated number for the year 2000 is 532 million people.

The majority of undernourished people can be found in the Far East; this is closely related to the vast population. Yet the share of this region in malnutrition shows an obvious downward tendency. In sub-Saharan Africa the number of undernourished people increases rapidly. In 1983–85 in this region, one in every three individuals was undernourished. In all developing countries together, a fifth of the total population was undernourished to a certain extent (FAO, 1990). World Bank estimates (1986a) are higher than those published by the FAO due to differences in definitions and the fact that more countries are included. The global trends are comparable. For 1980 the World Bank (1986a) estimated that 730 million people – that is, 34 per cent of the world population – did not get sufficient calories to lead an active working life.

Concluding remarks on agricultural policy

The above data illustrate the urgent need for further improvements in the world food situation. Since the 1970s the climate of opinion with respect to the potential contributions of agriculture to development has gradually become more positive. In several countries, increasing attention has been paid to the agricultural sector in development policy. Attempts have been made to counter the 'urban industrial bias'.

Table 9.9 Malnutrition in eighty-nine developing countries, 1969–2000[a]

	1969/1971	1979/1981	1983/1985	2000
Population with less than 80% of average caloric requirement				
In % of population				
Sub-Saharan Africa	23.5	21.9	26.0	20.3
Near East/N.Africa	15.7	6.7	5.6	4.6
Asia[b]	19.5	15.6	14.3	8.7
Latin America	12.7	9.8	9.5	8.0
Total	18.6	14.7	14.6	10.5
Numbers (millions of people)				
Sub-Saharan Africa	63	78	105	137
Near East/N.Africa	28	16	15	18
Asia[b]	190	191	191	155
Latin America	35	35	37	43
Total	316	320	348	353
Population with less than 90% of average caloric requirement				
In % of population				
Sub-Saharan Africa	32.6	30.6	35.2	28.7
Near East/N.Africa	22.9	10.8	9.1	7.6
Asia[b]	28.7	23.5	21.8	13.9
Latin America	18.5	14.6	14.2	11.6
Total	27.0	21.8	21.5	15.6
Numbers (millions of people)				
Sub-Saharan Africa	86	110	142	194
Near East/N.Africa	41	25	24	29
Asia[b]	281	288	291	246
Latin America	51	52	55	62
Total	460	475	512	532

Notes:
[a] Excluding centrally planned developing countries.
[b] Excluding Near Eastern Asian countries.

Source: Alexandratos (1988), 66. Alexandratos defines malnutrition thresholds in relation to the basal metabolism rate (BMR). The BMR is the energy requirement of a person who is fasting and completely inactive in a warm environment. Serious malnutrition is defined as less than 1.2 BMR, and malnutrition as less than 1.4 BMR. Recalculation into percentage of average requirement from van der Eng (1992).

The examples of India, China and Indonesia illustrate that it pays for developing economies to give more attention to agriculture. In these densely populated countries it proved possible to realize substantial increases in agricultural production per hectare and per head by combining new inputs, infrastructural investment, and institutional changes. Influential pessimistic predictions about agricultural involution and the negative prospects for agricultural growth (Geertz, 1963) have proved to be unfounded.

On the production side, price policies should provide positive incentives for farmers to increase their production and productivity. In addition, policy should focus on maintenance and improvement of agricultural infrastructure with respect to water control, land development, and storage and distribution. Finally, investments in agricultural research and extension remain of considerable importance.

In the international arena, economically advanced countries should provide less protection to their agricultural sector and reduce subsidies on agricultural exports to developing countries. Such exports are dumped on developing country markets at prices far below world market prices. They provide strong disincentives to agricultural producers in developing countries and have negative effects on agricultural development.

On the consumption side, entitlements to food should be extended. This can be done among others by improving access to land or by stimulating off-farm employment in the rural sector for those who can no longer find employment in agriculture. This subject will be taken up again in the following sections on rural development. In times of temporary food shortages, governments and the international community should intervene in the market to prevent prices from soaring, disequilibria from getting out of hand and famines breaking out. But permanent intervention in the form of subsidized food for the urban population should be phased out.

9.4 *Rural development versus agricultural development*

Rural development is a broader concept than agricultural development in two senses. First, rural development refers not only to economic changes, but also to transformations and changes in wider rural societies. A multidisciplinary approach is therefore called for. It is especially interesting to combine economic studies on agricultural development with anthropological and sociological studies of processes of socio-economic change in rural areas. Second, rural development indicates that economic activities in rural areas are not limited to agriculture. Though agriculture is a defining characteristic of rural areas, rural populations have always been involved in other economic activities such as trade, handicraft production and services. More recently public services and rural industries have also been established in rural areas. Non-agricultural activities are becoming more and more important. The interrelationships between these various activities are studied in the context of rural development. Without claiming to be a comprehensive study, the following sections will provide an introduction to some interesting aspects of changes in rural communities.

The study of rural development is interesting for quite a few reasons. Table 9.10 shows that the shares of agriculture in the total labour force are still quite high, though they have been declining over the years. The shares are highest in Asian countries, followed by African countries. Much lower shares are found in Latin America. The shares of the rural population in the total population are even higher than those of agriculture in the labour force. In 1995, 63 per cent of the total population of developing countries lived in rural areas.

Table 9.10 Shares of rural population, agricultural labour force, and agricultural production, 1965–1995

Country/region[a]	Share rural population (%)				Share agricultural labour force (%)			Share agricultural production (%)				Rural population (millions)			
	1950	1965	1980	1995	1965	1980	1993[b]	1960	1965	1980	1993	1950	1965	1980	1995
Bangladesh	95.8	93.8	88.7	80.5	83.7	74.8	65.5	61.0	53.0	52.0	30.0	40.0	54.7	78.3	103.2
China	89.0	81.8	80.4	69.8	81.6	68.9	61.0	28.0	38.0	30.0	19.0	493.7	596.5	800.8	863.7
India	82.7	81.2	76.9	73.2	72.9	71.1	63.2	50.0	44.0	38.0	31.0	295.9	402.1	530.0	681.6
Indonesia	87.6	84.2	77.8	67.5	70.5	57.2	50.4	45.0	51.0	25.0	19.0	69.7	90.1	117.4	135.9
Pakistan	82.5	76.5	71.9	65.3	59.8	50.7	47.4	46.0	40.0	30.0	25.0	32.6	43.7	61.4	88.1
Philippines	72.9	68.4	62.6	54.3	58.0	51.8	45.3	26.0	26.0	22.0	22.0	15.3	21.9	30.5	37.6
South Korea	78.6	67.6	43.1	22.4	55.1	36.4	16.7	40.0	38.0	17.0	7.0	16.0	19.3	16.4	10.1
Thailand	89.5	87.1	82.9	74.6	81.7	70.9	66.3	40.0	32.0	26.0	10.0	17.9	26.7	38.7	43.5
Turkey	78.7	65.9	56.2	31.2	74.5	62.5	48.8	41.0	34.0	23.0	15.0	16.4	20.5	25.0	19.4
Argentina	34.7	23.9	17.1	12.5	18.3	13.0		17.0	17.0	9.0	6.0	5.9	5.3	4.8	4.3
Brazil	64.0	49.6	33.8	21.3	48.5	31.0	24.2	16.0	19.0	10.0	10.0[d]	34.2	41.8	41.0	34.3
Chile	41.6	28.3	18.8	14.1	26.6	16.5	19.1	11.0	9.0	8.0	2.5	2.4	2.1	2.0	
Colombia	62.9	46.5	36.1	27.3	44.7	34.2	31.2[c]	34.0	27.0	22.0	17.0[d]	7.5	8.6	9.6	9.6
Mexico	57.3	45.1	33.7	24.7	49.6	36.5	22.6	16.0	14.0	9.0	8.0	15.7	19.3	22.36	13.1
Peru	64.5	48.1	35.4	27.8	49.7	40.0		26.0	18.0	12.0	11.0	4.9	5.5	6.1	6.6
Venezuela	46.8	30.2	16.7	7.1	29.6	16.0	11.4	6.0	6.0	5.0	5.0	2.3	2.7	2.5	1.5

Egypt	68.1	59.3	56.2	55.2	53.4	37.6	42.5	30.0	29.0	18.0	18.0	13.8	17.4	23.0	32.3
Ghana	85.5	73.9	68.8	63.7	61.0	55.8		41.0	44.0	60.0	48.0	4.2	5.8	7.4	11.1
Ivory Coast	86.8	76.9	65.2	56.4	80.6	65.2		43.0	47.0	31.0	37.0	2.4	3.5	5.3	8.1
Kenya	94.4	91.4	83.9	72.3	86.1	81.0		38.0	35.0	33.0	29.0	5.9	8.9	14.0	20.2
Nigeria	89.9	83.0	72.9	60.7	72.1	68.1	45.0[c]	63.0	55.0	27.0	34.0	29.6	40.4	57.2	77.1
Tanzania	96.2	94.7	85.2	75.6	91.5	85.6		57.0	46.0	45.0	56.0	7.6	11.2	15.8	23.3
Zambia	91.1	76.7	60.2	56.9		52.3		11.0	14.0	14.0	34.0	2.2	2.8	3.5	5.3
Africa[e]	87.3	81.2	74.1	66.3								182.4	242.2	333.3	465.2
Latin America	58.4	46.5	35.0	25.8								96.4	115.9	125.6	124.2
Asia	85.8	80.3	76.1	67.7								1,109.5	1,415.1	1,878.0	2,220.5
Developing countries total	83.0	76.6	71.2	62.8								1,398.4	1,786.7	2,356.2	2,835.5

Notes:

[a] Regional figures, including all developing countries for which data are available; [b] 1993 or the most recent year since 1988 for which data are available; [c] 1986; [d] 1990; [e] excluding South Africa; [f] excluding Japan.

Sources:

Share and absolute size of rural population from United Nations (1993).

Share of agricultural labour force in total labour force 1965 and 1980 from: World Bank, *Trends in Developing Economies*, various issues (until 1992). Peru 1980 from Maddison (1989); 1993 from World Bank (1995a), *World Development Report, 1995*, table A-2.

Share of agriculture in total population: 1960, 1965 and 1993 from World Bank, *World Development Report*, various issues (until 1995); 1980 from *World Tables 1992* and *World Tables 1995* (Venezuela, Ivory Coast, Kenya and Zambia). *World Development Report* data mainly at purchaser prices, *World Tables* data at factor cost.

The absolute numbers of inhabitants of rural areas in developing countries have increased from 1.8 billion in 1965 to 2.8 billion in 1995. Only in a few exceptional cases does the number of rural inhabitants show a decline (e.g. Argentina). In a UN (1993) report on urbanization, the growth of the rural population is expected to continue till 2015, after which it begins to decline slowly. Apart from the demographic importance of the rural sector, the study of rural development is also crucial because so much poverty is concentrated in rural areas.

Table 9.10 also shows that the share of agricultural production in national income is much lower than the share of agriculture in the total labour force. This has to do with two factors. First, labour productivity in the agricultural sector is lower than in other sectors. Second, many persons who are registered as employed in agriculture, are also active in other sectors of the economy. For example, 10 to 20 per cent of the male agricultural labour force also has some part-time employment in the rural industrial sector (UNDP, 1988).

Especially in Asian and African countries the rural population share is much higher than the agricultural labour force share. Again this is due to the fact that so many rural people depend primarily on some kind of off-farm employment for their livelihood.[11] For example, the United Nations organization UNDP has estimated that 25 per cent of primary employment in rural areas refers to non-agricultural activities (UNDP, 1988, quoted in Druijven, 1990).

9.4.1 Changes in rural societies

In the course of economic and social development, societies in which agriculture predominates change into societies in which industry and services become more important. While in the past most people used to live in rural conditions, more and more people have come to live in an urban environment. The share of agriculture in national output and employment tends to decline.

The shifts from the countryside to the city and from agricultural to other economic activities are not the only transformations. Rural societies themselves undergo change. Rural areas are increasingly less isolated from the outside world due to improved transport, trade, mobility, communications and the emergence of new media. As the money economy expands, the importance of commercial production for the market increases at the expense of non-market production for own-consumption needs. In many rural areas, mobility increases as a result of migration and migrant labour. Traditional redistributive arrangements and institutions within village communities come under pressure due to commercial production for the market. Social relationships within families, between villagers, and between social groups and classes undergo change. Traditional diffuse patterns of rights and obligations between powerful patrons and their rural clients become more businesslike with the expansion of the money economy.

Both increasing population density and commercialization of agriculture put great pressure on traditional farming systems and traditional rights to the use of land. When extensive agricultural practices are maintained unchanged, increasing population density may result in erosion and impoverishment of the soils. Processes of social differentiation take place, resulting in more unequal distribution of the access to land and rising landlessness. Non-agricultural activities such as rural industries, trade, and services gain in importance. The central authority of the national state penetrates ever deeper into rural communities through regulation and taxation.

Thus rural development refers to the whole complex of economic, social, and cultural changes taking place in rural societies in the course of these processes. Long (1977, p. 4) defines rural development as 'the processes by which rural populations of the Third World are drawn into the wider national and international economy and with the accompanying social transformations and local-level responses'.

9.4.2 Three perspectives on rural development

In the social sciences one can distinguish three important theoretical approaches to rural development (Long, 1977; Druijven, 1990), as follows:

1. The modernization approach which emphasizes cultural obstacles to development.
2. The incorporation approach which stresses the changes that take place in traditional rural communities under the influence of penetration of (capitalist) market relations.
3. The transactionalist approach, which concentrates on the ways in which individuals in various circumstances respond to the challenges and changes they are faced with.

Modernization theories

Modernization theory was the predominant approach in the 1950s and 1960s. Modernization theories interpret rural development as a transformation process from a traditional to a modern community, under the influence of economic and technical developments (Moore, 1963). Driving forces for change are: technological development, commercialization of agriculture, the rise of cash crops and agricultural wage labour, and industrialization and urbanization.

From this perspective, modernization implies a process of differentiation and specialization. Diffuse, multifunctional, personal social relationships are replaced with specialized, one-stranded, anonymous social relationships. Extended families make way for nuclear families. The family loses many of its functions with regard to education and socialization to specialized educational institutions. Consumption and production which were integrated in the household are gradually separated. Families' activities become more concentrated on emotional gratification. A social hierarchy based on ascription (family of origin, social background) changes into a hierarchy more based on achievement criteria. Specialized political and religious institutions are established. The need arises for new mechanisms of integration within the context of national societies, such as political parties, unions, bureaucracies, and so on. When integration does not keep up with differentiation, social strains and tensions are the result.

The prime objection to this view is the implicit unilinear path running from a traditional pole to modern pole, which is assumed to be the same for all societies. This unilinear perspective does not do justice to the diversity of circumstances and development paths in societies, lumped together under the heading 'traditional'. It also underemphasizes the amount of individual ingenuity, creativity and entrepreneurship to be found in a great variety of cultural contexts. Further, there are also numerous examples of modern economic developments that contribute to the preservation of traditional cultural and social arrangements, rather than to their disruption (see Kuper, 1984). Some modernization theorists such as Eisenstadt (1970) try to distinguish different traditional settings and different paths of modernization, but the bipolarity of traditional versus modern continues to be the framework of analysis.

At present it is hard to find unequivocal supporters of unabashed modernization theory. Nevertheless, the question whether there are 'cultural barriers' to development, which derives from modernization theory, remains of interest. In a series of publications in the 1960s, the anthropologist Foster (1965, 1975) defended the thesis that the concept of *limited goods* functions as a cultural barrier to economic and social change in traditional societies. The external reality is seen as something that human beings are unable to control. People find it hard to imagine that total welfare could increase as the result of individual efforts. The total amount of goods and welfare is seen as limited. This implies a zero-sum game in which the success of one person is a threat to the welfare of other individuals. There are not many feelings of solidarity within such traditional village communities. Cooperation is riddled with mutual mistrust because it may result in claims to authority by some of the participants. Economic success gives rise to jealousy. It sets off redistributive mechanisms such as the obligation to organize social festivities or to support relatives. Thus the idea that the total amount of goods is limited makes for conservatism and forms a barrier to entrepreneurship.

The main problem with this theory is a tendency towards overgeneralization. It is conceivable that, under certain conditions of uncertainty or risk, the notion of a limited store of goods crystallizes into a powerful cultural element that inhibits change. But, as Long points out, there are also many instances where traditional cultural elements are quite compatible with modern economic behaviour. Economists like Myint (1980) and Higgins (1959) have pointed out that entrepreneurship emerges all over the world whenever there are new opportunities for trade due to improvements in transport, communication, and infrastructure.

Incorporation theories

Incorporation theories are much more historical in nature than modernization theories. They study the effects of the penetration of a capitalist market economy in various non-capitalist agrarian societies in different historical periods (see Frank,

1969; Long, 1977; Dixon, 1990; Druijven, 1990). The term 'incorporation' refers to the ways in which non-capitalist or pre-capitalist societies become involved in international market relationships.

Dixon (1990, p. 39 ff.) presents an interesting overview of different processes of incorporation. Incorporation took place through the establishment of plantation economies by colonists using native or imported slave and contract labour to cultivate export crops. In countries such as South Africa, Kenya, Zimbabwe and Algeria, settlement colonies (see Chapter 2) were created, where white settlers appropriated the most fertile lands. The indigenous population was resettled on 'native' reserves, which were overcrowded and had infertile lands. The dispossessed native population served as a labour reserve for settler farming activities.

The example of the plantations was frequently followed by small-holder peasants who also started to cultivate export crops. Opinions differ as to whether or not this occurred voluntarily. According to incorporation theory, colonial tax levies in cash forced smallholders to cultivate cash crops. Also, colonial authorities often imposed obligations on peasants to supply labour to plantations or to deliver a quota of export crops in kind (e.g. sugar). More positive incentives were provided by the availability of new consumer goods and new agricultural inputs, which could only be acquired by means of money.

The incorporation theories, mainly of a neo-Marxist bent, emphasize the negative aspects of the penetration of the market economy in pre-capitalist societies. Survival strategies, which offered protection against crop failures and other risks in traditional societies, are disrupted. Aspects of traditional societies that are incompatible with the market economy are undermined. Behavioural patterns which can be made subservient to the market economy are preserved. For example, land scarcity in Latin American *minifundia* simply forces peasants to offer their labour cheaply to large landowners.

Modernization theories are primarily concerned with social relations within the village community. Incorporation theory focuses on the chains of dependence and exploitation, which extend far outside the village community. After colonies gained their independence, foreign-owned plantations were often nationalized – but dependence remained. Dependency theories argued that a few multinational agribusinesses had a monopoly on the processing, distribution and marketing of agricultural export crops and the supply of new seeds, fertilizers, machinery and other inputs.

Like modernization theories, incorporation theories suffer from a tendency to overgeneralization. The emphasis on the disruptive effects of the market economy goes hand in hand with a certain idealization of harmonious pre-capitalist relationships. Production for the market can also provide an escape from traditional constraints and power relationships. Also, insufficient justice is done to examples of successful agricultural development in different periods and countries. For example, during the late colonial period cocoa exports had very positive effects on the economic development of Ghana. More generally, primary exports from tropical countries provided a stimulus to economic development in the late nineteenth century (see Chapter 8). Rice production in Indonesia provides an example of very successful agricultural development, despite the gloomy predictions of the 1960s (see Geertz, 1963). In recent years, several Asian countries have become self-sufficient in fertilizers.

Transactionalist and decision-making theories

Long criticizes both modernization theories and incorporation theories for their tendency to depict rural populations as helpless victims, whether of traditional cultural obstacles or of external exploitation (Long, 1977; see also Druijven, 1990). He argues for an analysis of the differential responses to change shown by individuals and social categories within a population. As a third perspective on rural development, he distinguishes the *transactionalist approach*, which analyzes the active strategies of the poorest, the less poor, and the rich. In this approach special attention is paid to entrepreneurship and the manipulation of networks of clients and middlemen. This approach provides a more active picture of the rural population.

Anthropological studies of entrepreneurship in 'traditional' societies, such as Hill's study of Ghanaian cocoa farmers (Hill, 1986), also give a much more dynamic image of rural communities and a more realistic assessment of potential resources of entrepreneurship and creativity. Simultaneously, more insight is gained in the degree of inequality and diversity within rural communities. Some people follow more effective strategies than others; there are both winners and losers.

The emphasis in transactionalist approaches is on survival strategies, in which people are flexible with regard to the use of their labour and can search for alternative sources of employment outside the agricultural sector, in trade, services and crafts production. Ceremonial obligations, which were primarily interpreted as redistributive mechanisms in modernization theories, are reinterpreted here as investments in social relations and networks. These social investments are made in order to achieve certain goals in the future. The transactionalist approach in anthropology (see, for example, Barth 1966; Boissevain, 1974) provides a bridge to economic models of decision-making in rural households.

9.4.3 The peasant economy

In the discussion of rural development, peasants play an important role. As early as the 1920s the Russian agronomist Chayanov drew attention to interesting differences between the economic behaviour of large, commercial farmers producing for the market and small peasants producing mainly for their own consumption (Chayanov, 1966; see also Kitching, 1982). In his publications Chayanov defended Russian peasants against the communist reproach that they were capitalist farmers (*kulaks*). He did so by stressing the differences between capitalist farms and peasant agriculture. On such grounds, Chayanov rejected collectivization of agriculture.

A profit-maximizing commercial farmer will expand employment up until the point where the additional financial returns to the last agricultural worker equal the wage rate. The wage rate is in part determined by wages being paid outside the agricultural sector. Russian peasants at the start of this century, however, did not produce for the market, but for their own subsistence. They used their own and their family's labour power, rather than wage labour. There were hardly any opportunities for full-time paid employment outside agriculture, so no implicit wage could be determined.

According to Chayanov, under such circumstances financial returns and wages have little meaning for a peasant household. The peasant does not weigh financial returns against the financial cost of labour. Rather, he looks at the amounts of food needed to feed the family and the amounts of backbreaking physical labour required to produce this food. Since the labour of the peasant and his family does not 'cost' any money, he will continue to work until he can provide sufficiently for the subsistence of his household. Equilibrium is reached when the disutility of additional drudgery matches the utility of additional family consumption. At this point, the peasant will stop increasing his labour input. The labour input per hectare depends on family size and, in particular, on the number of dependants in the household (i.e. children and the elderly). The more mouths to be fed, the more work will be done. Labour input per hectare is also determined by the availability of land and the possibilities of part-time paid employment outside agriculture.

Other things being equal, the Chayanov model implies that a small self-supporting peasant will use more labour per unit of land and will realize a greater production per unit of land than a commercial farmer producing for the market. He will not stop working when the value of his output is less than his implicit wage. He will continue to work till he has produced enough to feed his family. Of course other things are hardly ever equal, in particular with respect to the amount of capital and the kind of technology employed. Nevertheless, it is a common finding that yields per hectare on small and medium-sized farms are generally higher than on large farms. This does not hold for very small farms, with too little land to farm efficiently.

In a study incorporating data on a large number of countries, Berry and Cline (1979) found that both financial returns per hectare and real production per hectare are inversely related to the land area available to a farmer. The authors concluded (p. 29) that redistribution of land from larger to smaller farmers would lead to an increase of total agricultural output and employment. Redistribution would reduce underutilization of labour on tiny plots of land. Also, there would be an increased demand for the labour services of the landless rural workers. Land reform will be discussed in more detail in section 9.5.

Characteristics of peasant economies

Inspired in part by Chayanov's work, a group of authors associated with the *Journal of Peasant Studies* has tried to identify general characteristics of the peasant economy, which call for a specific theoretical analysis (Shanin, 1971, 1973, 1974; see also Wolf, 1966).

Peasants are small farmers, producing primarily for own consumption with the use of family labour. The peasant family is both a unit of production and of consumption. There is a relatively low-level occupational specialization, although there is a division of labour between age groups and sexes. Peasants work with little capital. Ownership of land is not individualized. Households have rights of access to communal land on the basis of their membership in a village community. Access to communal land is allocated by the village authorities (Scott, 1976). A portion of agricultural surpluses is reserved for ceremonial obligations like feasts, religious rituals, payment of bride money, burials, and so forth. Credit is hard to obtain, markets are underdeveloped, and risks are high for households living close to subsistence levels. Security, therefore, is valued higher than innovativeness.

Peasants live in relatively closed village communities. Nevertheless, there are at least two kinds of links with the outside world. First, there is always some contact with the world outside the village through kinship ties and rural marketplaces. Second, there are always relationships with powerful outsiders who appropriate part of the agricultural surpluses, whether in kind, money, or labour These outsiders can be feudal or prebendal landlords, colonial administrators, large landowners or modern tax collectors and bureaucrats. Peasant societies are to found both in pre-industrial Europe and in present-day developing countries.

According to Wolf (1966), 'peasant economies' stand midway between isolated tribal communities of primitive agriculturalists, hunters and gatherers and fully integrated market economies. Many studies of changes in rural societies focus on the transformations of peasant economies. How do peasant economies respond when confronted with the rise of centralized state power and the penetration of market relationships (Moore, 1966; Wolf, 1966; Scott, 1976; Popkin, 1979; Ellis, 1988)?

Ellis (1988, p. 3) estimates – without any mention of sources – that over a billion people belong to peasant households, most of these in developing countries. On the basis of a survey of the literature, he distinguishes the following characteristics of the *peasant society*:

- Peasant society represents a transition from relatively dispersed, isolated and self-sufficient communities of farmers or pastoralists to fully integrated market economies.
- Although relatively isolated, peasant society is part of a larger economic and political system. Peasants are exposed in some degree to market influences. They stand in relations of subordination to powerful political outsiders (Wolf, 1966).
- Internal differentiation. Within peasant communities there are numerous differences in social and economic status. In particular, there are important differences between men and women.
- Peasants obtain their livelihood from the land, mainly by the cultivation of crops. This distinguishes them from landless labourers, pastoralists or nomads.
- A peasant household is both a unit of production and a unit of consumption. Households are, at least to some extent, self-sufficient. The degree of self-sufficiency varies strongly. Production for own consumption does not preclude part of harvest being traded on the market.
- The primary source of labour is family labour. This characteristic distinguishes peasant households from capitalist farms employing wage labour. But this does not rule out the use of some hired labour in peak periods.

- In some way or other, peasants have access to land to provide in their livelihood. This distinguishes them from landless agricultural workers and industrial labourers. Land is allocated on the basis of non-market criteria. Allocation depends on the social status of the household within the village community.
- Peasants are partially integrated into markets for products and factors of production. They stand with one leg in the non-market village economy and one leg in a market economy. The markets on which peasants are active are imperfectly functioning markets. This has to do with poor infrastructure (transport, communications), insufficient information, and power relationships that constrain peasants' freedom of choice. This implies that the supply of agricultural products responds only weakly to changes in price levels. In this context, Lal and Myint (1996) use the term *institutional underdevelopment*. They argue for expansion of agricultural exports since this tends to diminish institutional underdevelopment.
- Partial integration into markets implies that non-market criteria of reciprocality still play an important part in transactions between peasant households.

According to Ellis, partial integration into imperfectly functioning markets is the principal characteristic of peasant economies. It distinguishes peasants from commercially oriented family farmers who trade their entire product and purchase all their inputs on the market. On the other hand, access to the production factor land distinguishes peasants from landless agricultural labourers. In rural societies, peasants function alongside the commercial family farmers, who are more closely integrated into markets, and labourers working for wages on plantations or lands of large landowners. Also, as mentioned, agriculture is not the only source of livelihood in rural areas, though this is somewhat underemphasized in literature on peasants.

Diversity of local conditions

In generalizations on rural development, there is – in spite of all qualifications and denials – a tendency to think in terms of a traditional–modern polarity. On the one side, one distinguishes the traditional self-supporting pre-capitalist agricultural society, with communal rights to land and redistributive institutions within villages. On the other side, one distinguishes a modern money-and-market economy in which farmers produce commercially for the market.[12] This schematic conception is present both in modernization theories, which stress the institutional and cultural obstacles to change, and in radical and Marxist literature on peasant societies, which analyzes the penetration of money economy into traditional peasant societies and the associated processes of disruption.

In her book, *Development Economics on Trial*, the anthropologist Polly Hill (1986) launches a ferocious and delightful attack on universal developmental generalizations such as the transition from self-sufficiency to production for the market, the penetration of the money economy, increasing inequality, migration from rural to urban areas, the transition from communal land rights to private ownership of land, intensification of agriculture according to Boserup, and the unfounded thesis of Theodor Schultz that traditional peasants are efficient. Such generalizations do insufficient justice to the great diversity of agricultural circumstances in developing countries and the dynamic entrepreneurship which can often be found among members of so-called traditional societies. Often the generalizations are not only wrong, but they may even be harmful when they lead to inadequate policy recommendations that do not take the variations in local conditions into account.

Development economists and agricultural economists generalize because this is how they have been trained. They were nurtured on 'universal generalizations' and 'development schemes'. In as much as they do any empirical research at all, they base themselves on completely unreliable statistics (see section 9.1) and make little effort to become intimately familiar with the rural societies about which they are writing.

For example, Hill shows that in some regions farmers have been involved in market production for centuries. Both in West Africa and in south India money has played an important role in economic transactions far back in history. Rural marketplaces in the Sudan date back to the fourteenth century. The subsistence economy is a myth. So-called traditional rural societies in the past have always known numerous non-agricultural activities – in trade, services and handicraft production. Extensive and intensive agricultural activities can coexist side by side in one and the same region.[13] In West Africa, rural markets developed earlier than urban oriented markets. It is incorrect to state that the market economy penetrated rural areas from urban centres. In West Africa, migration from one rural area to another is at least as important as migration from rural to urban areas. In some rural societies there are communal rights to land use; in others, there has long been private ownership of land and land has long been freely saleable. These two types of land use can coexist.

In rural societies one finds a great variety of farmers: farmers who have rights to cultivate communal land owned by the village, clan, or tribe; agricultural labourers who receive wages to work on land that is owned by others; predominantly self-sufficient family farmers who rent or own their land; commercial family farms producing for the market; and large commercial farms and plantations using hired wage labour. The distinctions between these categories are rather vague and there is much overlap. Self-sufficient farmers or their relatives, for example, often also work as hired workers on land owned by others. Both rich and poor farmers participate in non-agricultural activities, like trade and crafts. Rich farmers do so because non-agricultural activities are so profitable, poor farmers because they cannot survive on agriculture alone. The richest farmers enjoy the greatest trading advantages. Further, there are great differences in the amounts of land available to different farmers, and a great variety of land tenure institutions: individual ownership, rights of use, sharecropping arrangements, lease relations, and so on.

The term *peasant economy* as a blanket term for all these different types of agricultural activities is therefore inappropriate and misleading. It denies significant intra-village inequalities in power, wealth, income and status. It disregards the differences between cattle-raising societies and crop-raising societies, between irrigated agriculture and rain-fed agriculture, and differences in natural circumstances and climatic conditions.

Next, the focus on peasant economies also neglects the differentiation between males and females within village communities. For example, in West Africa there are generally two separate economic spheres. Women are responsible for food production and often engage in trade. Men are responsible for the raising of cash crops and cattle breeding.

Hill prefers terms such as country people, farmers, cultivators to 'peasant'. The connotations of the term *peasant* are derogatory. It does not do justice to the inventiveness, creativity, and entrepreneurial spirit that Hill observed in her empirical research among country people. In this respect, Polly Hill comes very close to the positions of development economists such as Schultz, Lewis and Myint whom she criticizes so fiercely.

Hill's polemic is refreshing. It encourages readers to take into account the variety of local conditions in rural communities. Generalizations should relate to specific agrarian systems (e.g. dry grain farming in densely populated regions). However, Hill has a tendency to misrepresent the positions she is attacking and to exaggerate the differences of opinion. Like Hill, Schultz – one of Hill's black sheep – pointed to entrepreneurial qualities and creativity among farmers. Boserup (1970) was one of the early authors to analyze the role of women within rural communities. Marxist studies also emphasize rural inequalities.

Finally, there is a risk that Hill's love for anthropological detail may end up in no more than ethnographic description and a rejection of all attempts to generalize and to formulate hypotheses on rural development. In my opinion, Ellis's synthesis of the characteristics of peasant societies, described earlier, meets most of Hill's objections. The characteristics of peasant societies are no longer defined in absolute terms but leave scope for variation. For example, the transition from self-sufficiency to production for the market is seen as a continuum. The use of family labour does not exclude the hiring of wage labour, nor are family members themselves barred from working as paid labourers on other farms. The existence of off-farm employment is acknowledged, as are the differences between households. Finally, Ellis admits that the peasant household is only one of many types of rural households, albeit an important one. Provided they are applied carefully, the characteristics of the peasant economy may contribute to a better understanding of processes of rural change.

9.4.4 Rationality, risk and survival strategies in peasant societies

Increases in agricultural production and productivity are prerequisites for improvements in living conditions in rural areas. Production may be raised through expansion of the amounts of production factors (land, labour, agricultural equipment), more efficient use of existing means of production, or introduction of new techniques of production. The crucial question is to what degree peasant societies are willing and able to increase efficiency and introduce new technologies. Ever since Boeke (1955) pointed to the 'limited needs' in Indonesian society, there is a tradition that stresses the cultural obstacles to increases in efficiency, to entrepreneurship, and to innovation. We have come across this view in the discussion of the diffusion model and modernization theories.

In his pioneering work, *Transforming Traditional Agriculture*, Theodor Schultz (1964), later awarded the Nobel prize in economics, objected to this point of view. On the basis of fieldwork conducted by other researchers, he concluded that 'traditional farmers' use their production factors efficiently, given their circumstances. According to neoclassical economic theory, 'efficient' means that the marginal returns to the factors of production equal their marginal costs. The implication is that there are no cultural barriers to efficiency. Traditional farmers know exactly what they are doing and use their available factors of production in a rational fashion. They have a profound knowledge of the possibilities of traditional agriculture. Within the constraints of traditional economy, society and technology, there are few opportunities to increase efficiency and productivity. The level of productivity is very low, but they are doing the best they can. Peasants live close to subsistence. They are unable to make large investments in new agricultural technologies (seeds, fertilizers, pesticides, irrigation, and so on). In Schultz's words, farmers are 'poor but efficient'.

Schultz sees an important role for government in stimulating the development of new, highly productive technologies and making them available to farmers in traditional agriculture. The entrepreneurship among farmers is sufficient to ensure that new technologies will be adopted if they are likely to pay off. But economic incentives for the use of new technologies have to be created and negative incentives like inadequate access to credit or too low prices for agricultural products should be eliminated (Schultz, 1978).

Schultz's view has been severely criticized by anthropologists such as Adams (1986) and Polly Hill. Schultz bases himself on a limited number of ethnographical studies that are not very representative; what is more, he does not always interpret them correctly. Adams' most serious objection is that Schultz pays no attention to the cultural context in rural societies, to values and attitudes, and to social stratification. Peasants may act efficiently, but their efficiency depends on their culturally determined perceptions of reality and their informedness about technology, credit, and price movements of products and inputs. Character traits and motivations are also of great importance. In daily practice, there are great differences between farmers in the same village, with respect to economic performance and efficiency. According to Adams, Schultz also pays too little attention to the significance of production for own needs – analyzed by Chayanov – and the significance of risk in poor rural societies.

Cultural factors are stressed in James C. Scott's (1976) study, *The Moral Economy of the Peasant*. Scott belongs to the so-called *substantivist* tradition in anthropology (Polyani, 1957), which stresses reciprocity in exchange relationships and the differences between traditional multifunctional relationships and modern impersonal single-stranded relationships in a capitalist economy, in which rational calculation of costs and benefits prevails.

Unlike modernization theorists, Scott places little emphasis on obstacles to modernization. He stresses the survival functions of traditional institutions in Southeast Asia. Peasants exist at the margin of subsistence. Crop failures are an immediate threat to their bare survival. In their choice of production techniques, the essential criterion is safety and minimization of risk, rather than maximum output. This is why they cultivate different crops on scattered strips of land. They prefer to cultivate food crops rather than cash crops, the returns on which may fluctuate with market conditions.

The social institutions of rural communities were traditionally oriented to stability and the assurance of a minimum standard of living to the inhabitants. There were communal lands which were periodically redistributed amongst the cultivators. The village community also allocated taxes and levies imposed by royal rules, governments, or landlords. There were obligations for villagers to support each other with labour when this was needed (work sharing). Norms of reciprocity were very important. There were redistributive social obligations for the richer villagers. They were expected to be charitable, sponsor ceremonial celebrations and festivities, donate to shrines and help indigent kin.[14] Decision-making within village communities was aimed at reaching consensus.

Subsistence insurance was not confined to the village. Tenancy and sharecropping relations between peasants and powerful landlords also had survival aspects. Traditionally, the rent consisted of a fixed share of the harvest. This meant lower rents when harvests were bad and high rents when they were good. Furthermore, in times of need rich patrons had a certain obligation to provide food to their starving tenants or to forgo the collection of rent. In exchange, peasants had obligations to their patrons, such as showing respect, providing corvée labour and political support.

Scott writes that in Southeast Asia a *moral economy* and a *subsistence ethic* had developed, in which survival was a central element. This subsistence ethic provided guidelines for individual actions. Though there was considerable inequality within the village, and between villagers and external elites, there was also a moral claim to a guaranteed minimum income. According to Scott, this 'moral' survival economy was undermined by two tendencies: political centralization and penetration of the market economy. Political centralization involved the introduction of fixed taxes on land, not varying with harvest returns. The risk of output fluctuations was shifted onto the peasants. Commercialization introduced the uncertainties of fluctuating market prices. Local crafts and services, which provided alternative sources of income in bad times, were disrupted due to increased competition from without. Where possible, influential groups tried to reduce common use of communal land and introduce individualized ownership. Finally, traditional paternalistic relationships between patrons and peasants became more impersonal and contractual. Guarantees for survival were undermined. Risks were shifted to the peasants. According to Scott, it was not the increase in inequality in itself, but rather the weakening of traditional guarantees for survival which provided an explanation for the large-scale peasant uprisings in Southeast Asia during the first part of the present century. (For a more general formulation of this perspective, see Moore, 1966.) Peasants revolt when their traditional moral expectations of support by fellow-villagers and patrons in times of need are violated.

Scott's view has been fiercely criticized by Samuel Popkin (1979) in his study, *The Rational Peasant*. Popkin accuses authors like Scott, Wolf, and other substantivists of the idealization of traditional peasant societies and traditional power structures. For them, capitalist penetration was the main culprit, disrupting traditionally harmonious relationships and survival arrangements.

Popkin, on the contrary, argues that 'traditional' peasants in Vietnam – just as people elsewhere – are constantly engaged in the rational pursuit of their interests. They try to increase their welfare through short-term and long-term investments, including investments in social relations and social networks. Popkin's political economy approach is an example of the so-called *formalist* tradition in anthropology. This tradition insists that peasant societies can be analyzed with the same analytic tools as social relations in Western societies.

Within villages there are continuous conflicts and feelings of mutual distrust. As in every social setting, some villagers try to profit from communal arrangements as 'free riders', without making any contribution of their own. Traditional savings institutions are constantly threatened by the suspicion that some may benefit more than others. Also every village community has its outsiders who are denied access to communal land. In sum, the moral economy approach seriously underestimates the extent of inequality, competition, and conflict within village communities.

Popkin interprets the often paternalistic relationships between patrons and clients not as a result of cultural or moral factors, but rather as relations of dependence. In these relations, landlords have succeeded in monopolizing all external relations of peasants – with regard to credit, purchase of inputs, marketing of surpluses, and processing of agricultural products. The guarantees they offer peasants in times of need serve to maintain their dependence. The penetration of market relations offers peasants the chance to escape the monopoly power of local landlords. Often rich farmers and landlords try to block peasants' access to markets, fearing the peasants' increasing independence.

Popkin agrees that risk avoidance is a predominant feature of peasant society. However, he interprets it more as an individual survival strategy. Peasants are risk-averse. But this does not necessarily mean that they will never invest or make a gamble. If the potential loss is small, and there is a chance of a big outcome, peasants are quite willing to gamble. Penetration of the money economy and the centralized state, therefore, is not always perceived as a threat. Sometimes it offers new opportunities and escape from traditional relations of subordination.

Popkin's criticism is supported by empirical research by Haggis *et al.,* (1986) into peasant revolts in Asia. These authors conclude that peasant revolts did not start as a reaction to the disappearance of the moral economy. It was not necessarily the poorest peasants who revolted. Often richer farmers who felt their opportunities were being restricted, played an important role. Much political turmoil was not directed towards the restoration of traditional 'moral' relations. Class struggle and nationalist elements also played a role. Haggis *et al.* (1986) also come to the conclusion that Scott gives a too rosy view of the 'moral economy' of traditional relations of dependence and subordination.

By stressing the calculating aspects of peasants behaviour, Popkin narrows the gap between the thought of economists and anthropologists. Starting from pure neoclassical principles of utility maximization, the economist Lipton arrived at an analysis of risk aversion very similar to that of Popkin (Lipton, 1966). In many developing countries, the large variability of rainfall makes it impossible to predict the volume of production. Many peasants live close to subsistence levels. A crop failure may force them to borrow money for food and result in loss of land or even starvation. New inputs and technologies demand large investments, while returns vary from year to year. Though these investments might result in higher average returns, they may cause severe indebtedness in years of bad harvests. Therefore, the calculating behaviour of peasants is determined by a risk-averse *survival algorithm*. Traditional varieties with low but stable yields are preferred over newer varieties involving more uncertainty. Peasants also prefer to pay interest in kind rather than in money. Even if this costs them more, they are insured against sudden falls in the price of grains. Finally, Lipton points to the inequality relations, due to which peasants have less access to water, seeds, fertilizer, herbicides and pesticides which are all required to achieve higher yields. All in all, there is no contradiction between highly risk-averse behaviour and an extremely rational consideration of costs and benefits. The lesson that can be derived from Lipton's analysis is that policy measures which reduce peasants' risks, like cheap credit or buffer food stocks, will increase their willingness to innovate.

I feel that the more individualistic approach to peasant institutions and behaviour is rather convincing. If one considers changes in agriculture since the end of the nineteenth century, it seems obvious that peasants all over the world have responded dynamically, innovatively, and rationally whenever they were offered new opportunities. Still, it would be incorrect to neglect cultural constraints altogether, as many economists tend to do. Behaviour, which is a rational response to challenges in a given situation, tends to crystallize into cultural patterns, patterns of behaviour, and institutions. These, in turn, influence future responses and choices. Individual behaviour is also determined by internalized norms, which are culturally transmitted. One should also not forget that cultural norms and institutions within societies are often maintained by means of powerful social sanctions. The very perception of the alternatives between which one has to choose, is partly determined by culture and institutions (North, 1993). Also, the options and alternatives themselves are institutionally determined. If market institutions have not developed, peasants will not be able to respond to modern economic incentives. The cultural and the individualistic approaches are not as opposed as would seem to be the case at first sight.

9.5 *Land reform*

Access to land is one of the central themes in the study of rural development. In many developing countries, landownership and access to land is distributed very unequally. Inequality tends to increase in the course of time and the number of landless people in rural areas is on the rise (Griffin, 1981; Singh, 1982, for Southeast Asia; Ghai and Radwan, 1985, for African countries). A more equal distribution of land could contribute to a decrease in rural poverty since improved access to land would enable the poor to support themselves. Moreover, redistribution of land may also contribute to increased productivity.

In section 9.4.3 it has already been noted that smaller farmers generally cultivate their fields more efficiently than larger farmers and realize higher yields per hectare. A recent survey article concludes: 'Most of the work on the relationship between farm size and productivity strongly suggests that farms that rely mostly on family labour have higher productivity levels than large farms operated primarily with hired labour' (Binswanger *et al.*, 1995, p. 2664). Unlike industry, the agricultural sector has relatively few economies of scale. Therefore, large-scale agriculture is not more productive than small-scale agriculture. Besides, many large landowners do not employ their production factors very efficiently. They often live in urban areas and are not personally involved in agricultural production. They are characterized by highly consumptive lifestyles. Frequently, ownership of land is no more than a safe way of investing money. Peasants employ more labour per hectare than large landowners, have higher cropping frequencies, and higher yields per crop.

Most researchers are of the opinion that redistribution of land may contribute to a more equitable distribution of income, to a reduction of poverty, and to increases in productivity (Dorner, 1972; Alexandratos, 1988; Binswanger *et al.*, 1995). In countries where access to land has been distributed more equally – such as China, Japan, Korea and Taiwan – agricultural development has been more successful than in countries where there is a wide gap between large landowners with modern farm management and small peasants who cannot afford new inputs. In this context, Johnston and Kilby (1975) refer to a unimodal versus a bimodal agricultural development strategy. They warn, however, that there is no question of a simple choice between one kind of agricultural policy or another. Countries that have pursued a unimodal agricultural strategy benefited from initial conditions which were the outcome of unique historical circumstances. There is also no complete consensus that the effects of redistribution of land are positive under all circumstances. Myint (1980) argues, for instance, that larger, modern-oriented farmers are often the bearers of agricultural innovation. He believes one has to accept the associated inequalities. In this perspective, increasing landlessness is the consequence of productivity improvements in agriculture.

When referring to land reform, redistribution of land from large to smaller landowners is the first thing that comes to mind. However, land reform comes in many forms, depending on the kind of land tenure relationships in a country. In addition to land redistribution, land reforms can include: cadastral land reforms in which land rights are more clearly defined, improvements in the status of sharecroppers, bringing new land into cultivation, collectivization and decollectivization.

In several sub-Saharan African countries there is a tradition of common rights to land use.[15] Land is not for sale. Rights to cultivate land are in principle allocated to members of the community by chiefs of clans, village elders, and so on. Such land tenure relations date back to the time when population densities were low, land was abundant, and extensive agriculture was practised with long periods of fallow. When cultivation becomes more intensive and land more scarce, common rights to land form a disincentive for individual investment in improvement of soil fertility. The value of land goes up and conflicts break out over land rights (van Hekken and Thoden van Velzen, 1972). There is a pressure for institutional change. Gradually more individualized property rights to land begin to emerge (Boserup, 1965; North and Thomas, 1973; Feeny, 1982, 1987; North, 1990).

During the colonial period, the authorities had already introduced *cadastral land reform*, that is, registration of individual ownership titles and consolidation of scattered plots of land. In addition, where possible new land was brought into cultivation. Private ownership of land was to the advantage of colonists and plantation owners, who successfully laid claim to the most fertile lands. But attempts were also made to register ownership titles on behalf of native farmers. This type of land reform was continued after independence. It is interesting to note, though, that traditional practices of land allocation continued to function long after the formal legal relationships had changed.

In the post-war period, the significance of foreign-owned plantations declined. Many plantations were *expropriated*. Expropriated land was taken into collective use or was allocated to individual cultivators. Where possible, new lands were brought under cultivation, as in the pre-war period. Allocation of newly cultivated and expropriated lands among African farmers sometimes led to an increase in rural inequality, rather than its decline (Ghai and Radwan, 1985); one example is the 'million acre scheme' in Kenya, which primarily benefited large farmers.

Many Latin American countries are characterized by an extremely unequal distribution of landownership (see Dorner, 1972; Furtado, 1976; Maddison *et al.*, 1992), which has its origin in the pattern of Spanish and Portuguese colonization in the sixteenth century. On the one hand, there are vast estates owned by large landowners (*latifundia*); on the other, there are tiny plots of land owned by peasants (*minifundia*). The latter are too small to provide a decent living for peasant households, and peasants are therefore forced to offer their labour to the large landowners. The large landowners thus have their land cultivated or their cattle grazed by agricultural labourers. Sometimes the agricultural labourers are even allocated small plots of land to cultivate for their own use in exchange for their labour services.

On the large estates, cultivation of land is extensive and relatively capital intensive. The available reserves of labour are underutilized. Output per unit of land is not very high. At the same time, the smallest farms are so tiny that their productivity is also low. Under such circumstances, radical *redistribution* of landownership, creating more small and medium-sized farm holdings of viable size, could contribute to an improvement in the living standards of the poor and increased production per unit of land.

Mexico is the best-known example of a Latin American country where radical land reforms have taken place and large estates have been expropriated. The 1915

Land Reform Act gave rise to a type of communal landownership by the village community, the *ejido*. The *ejido* gave villagers rights to cultivate land, while pastures and woodlands remained in common use. In Mexico the inequality of access to land is now less marked than in other large Latin American countries. In addition to the *ejidos*, however, there is still also private landownership. Lands of the highest quality are usually owned by individuals. Other countries where land reforms have been implemented are Bolivia, Cuba, Chile (under Allende), El Salvador, and Nicaragua.

In many South and Southeast Asian countries, colonial practices and administrative centralization have long ago resulted in the diminishing importance of traditional communal rights to land. Except in communist countries, most land is in the hands of private owners. Despite inequality of landownership, actual access to land is less unequal than in Latin America. A lot of land is rented out in some form to peasants who cultivate the land on their own account. The peasants pay rent in money or in kind as a share of the crop. Under such circumstances, land reforms are especially concerned with improvements in the *legal status of tenant farmers* and in the reduction of the rent or the crop share owed to the landowner. When the position of tenant farmers is legally precarious or when a large portion of every increase in production automatically goes to the landowner, tenant farmers have little incentive to invest in increased productivity and technological innovation.[16]

In Asia, the most radical land reforms were implemented in China after the revolution of 1949. In the process of land reform an estimated 900,000 farmers – justly or unjustly classified as large farmers – lost their lives. Initially, expropriated land was reallocated to individual farmers, but in the 1950s, agricultural cooperatives were established. In 1958 the agricultural sector was completely collectivized, and large communes were established, sometimes including over a million people.

With respect to the *redistribution of land*, Dorner (1972) and Hayami and Ruttan (1985) warn against inflated expectations. It is true that, other things being equal, peasants can realize higher yields per hectare by cultivating the land more intensively than large farmers. But like the 'vent for surplus' effects, the effects of land redistribution are once and for all. If new inputs, and the means to purchase and use them, are not made available to the peasants, agricultural development will stagnate after land reform. As was already noted, larger farmers are more likely to employ new techniques than peasants. For land reform to succeed, the total institutional structure has to be adjusted, so that small peasants and farmers gain access to credit, schooling, extension, new inputs, and water without being faced with unacceptable risks.

During the past twenty years, great emphasis has been put on the expansion of credit facilities for small farmers and on increasing their access to new inputs, with good reason. Nevertheless, time and again the larger farmers succeed in getting a disproportionate part of the available credits and resources, due to their good political contacts, their social standing and power, their higher creditworthiness, and their better education (Bol, 1983). The risks involved in granting credit to small peasants are so high that financial institutions mainly focus on larger, creditworthy farmers. In the end, the net effect of many credit programmes is the granting of subsidized credit to the wealthier farmers, which makes for capital intensive agriculture rather than the opposite.

Although many developing countries in Africa, Asia and Latin America profess to pursue a policy of equalizing access to land, not much redistribution has occurred in practice. Almost everywhere, the close political ties between large landowners, representatives of the government, and dominant political movements prevent the realization of land reform. This holds for countries such as India (Cassen, 1978; Frankel, 1978), the Philippines, Brazil, Argentina, Kenya, and Zambia. Attempts at gradual reform through legislation are effectively sabotaged.

There are past instances of sweeping redistribution of land: China in 1949 (Hsu, 1982); Taiwan and Korea after World War II (Griffin, 1976); Mexico after the Mexican revolution; and Japan in the Meiji reforms after 1867 and again during the initial years of World War II. Such radical land reforms all took place in exceptional periods in history, when the whole social fabric was in turmoil. In revolutionary countries, the new regimes implemented land reforms with the use of widespread coercion and physical violence. In other cases, societies had been seriously disrupted as a result of wars, occupations, or external threats, all circumstances in which the resistance of powerful landed elites could be overcome. Yet one should realize the high cost of these changes in terms of human life and human suffering.

9.6 *Collectivization and cooperatives*

I stated above that there are few economies of scale in agriculture. This does not mean that there are none. Some crops such as sugar and bananas have economies of scale in processing and distribution. These products have to be processed or shipped within hours of harvesting to avoid deterioration. Therefore plantation production of such products continues to be of importance (Binswanger *et al.*, 1995). Certain activities and investments exceed the financial capacity of smaller individual farmers. These may include the construction of irrigation systems or the purchase of capital goods such as tractors and farm machinery. Finally, there may be economies of scale with respect to the marketing of output and the purchase of inputs. The individual small farmer's position is weak compared to that of large purchasers and sellers.

Such arguments provide the theoretical justification for the formation of agricultural cooperatives. When many small farmers cooperate, they will be able to purchase inputs more cheaply and to sell their products at better prices. They can profit from common investment in agricultural machinery, land improvement and water control.

In centrally planned economies like the Soviet Union and China the foundation of cooperatives was merely a step on the way to complete collectivization of agriculture. In the Soviet Union and Romania, the authorities believed in the creation of a collectivized industrial agricultural system in which economies of scale could be achieved through massive infusions of capital goods and large-scale production. Like other post-war industrialization strategies and development theories, Marxist theory was pervaded with negative evaluations of 'backward' agriculture and a glorification of the industrial sector. In China, one of the considerations for collectivization was the fact that extremely large-scale infrastructural works and irrigation systems were required, which could only be realized by a massive mobilization of labour. Consequently, communes were established which at their apex included more than one million people per commune (Hsu, 1982). With regard to the infrastructural aspects, some degree of success for this policy cannot be denied.

However attractive collectivization of agriculture may be in theory, the problems of worker motivation and efficient allocation turn out to be insuperable in practice. In the Chinese communes the links between efforts and rewards were completely severed. Other than fear and political mobilization, there was no incentive to work. Work points, which were the basis of rewards, were allocated according to political criteria. The forced introduction of communes during the Great Leap Forward in 1958–60 resulted in a famine in which, according to some estimates, as many as 30 million people died of hunger.

After 1960, Chinese agriculture was gradually decentralized. The introduction of a 'responsibility system' in 1978 led to a period of explosive growth of agricultural output. Under the responsibility system, Chinese farmers were allowed to sell the surpluses that remained after fulfilment of obligatory delivery quotas, at market prices. This provided them with strong incentives to increase their production. As yet, land remained in public ownership, but individual farmers acquired the right to cultivate well-defined plots of land for periods of ten to twenty years.

The absence of a clear relationship between effort and reward is the main problem in all large-scale collectivized agriculture, both in developing countries like Cuba and Tanzania, and in former socialist countries in Eastern Europe. It is one of the main diseconomies of scale. In former socialist countries in Eastern Europe, for example, the small plots of land that were privately cultivated had vastly higher productivity than collectivized agriculture. In agriculture the family farm, whether or not supplemented by hired labour, has proved to be the most efficient form of organization, both in comparison with large-scale collectivized agriculture and with large landownership. There is, however, still a valid case for voluntary cooperation and cooperatives in developing countries. In agrarian development projects, attempts are currently being made to build on existing traditional informal forms of cooperation, like credit cooperatives and grain banks.

9.7 *Non-agrarian activities and integrated rural development*

In this final section I will return to the topic of non-agricultural activities in rural communities (see for example, Druijven, 1983, 1990; Hogg, 1984; Teszler, 1984; Dixon, 1990). Druijven distinguishes between *off-farm employment* and *non-farm employment*. Off-farm employment refers to all activities of members of farming households outside their own household, including paid work within the agricultural sector. Non-farm employment refers to employment outside the agricultural sector, whether as side employment or as primary activity.

Non-agricultural activity in itself is not a recent phenomenon. In the past there has always been a wide range of non-agricultural activities in rural societies, like trade, transport, services, and traditional crafts. Still, several important changes can be discerned.

First, there are technical changes. Traditional methods of craft production change under the influence of new technical possibilities. For example, tailors can use pedal sewing machines or even electrically driven ones. The range of goods supplied in the informal sector undergoes change. For instance, waste products like old tyres are reworked into sandals (Teszler, 1984). Existing traditional crafts activities are replaced by rural industries.

Second, the importance of non-agricultural employment increases over time. According to an estimate by Eicher and Staatz (1984), between 30 and 50 per cent of the rural population in developing countries is now dependent on industrial and non-agricultural activities as a primary or secondary source of employment. New lines of activity are emerging, such as maintenance of motorcycles, bicycles and cars (Teszler, 1984), and putting-out arrangements, where some stages of industrial production are performed at home. New sources of employment include, among others, public works road construction, construction of communal facilities, irrigation and other infrastructural works. These often offer temporary employment outside agricultural peak periods. In services there are numerous activities in the informal sector. Furthermore, jobs are also being created in health care, education, administration, and agricultural extension. Finally, employment in rural industry is growing. In part, this has to do with traditional production in small brickyards, carpentries, or potteries. But there are also small-scale rural factories. These factories are often established in smaller cities, but provide employment for the rural population.

Third, as part of the ongoing division of labour, the numbers of people who depend on non-agricultural activities as their primary means of support is increasing.

Integrated rural development focuses on the whole scale of activities existing in rural areas. Proponents of an integrated rural development argue that government policies should transcend sectoral limits. A sectoral approach implies that the Department of Agriculture is responsible for the agricultural policy, the Department of Education for the education policy, the Department of Health for health care policy, and the Department of Industry for industrial policy. In the integrated approach, one tries to coordinate all activities within a certain region. Rural industries require better education for their employees and improved infrastructure and energy supply. Public services contribute to employment. At local levels, the positive interactions and linkages between agriculture and industry can be exploited to the full (Hogg, 1984). Rural industries are especially suited to local production of goods needed in rural areas: products meeting basic needs (e.g. processed food, shoes, clothing, building materials, basic medicines, bicycles, household utensils), or agricultural inputs (e.g. simple agricultural implements, pumps, chemical fertilizers). Precisely because the distance to the market is smaller, production is more easily adjusted to local needs. In addition, rural industries often use locally produced inputs, (e.g. food, textile fibres, wood, clay, raw materials).

China is one of the countries that paid considerable attention to the promotion of rural industries (Druijven, 1983). The underlying notion was that this might help limit migration to the cities and narrow the gap between rural and urban areas. Some of the rural industries were even located within communes. Others functioned as autonomous rural industries, producing steel, machinery, cement, and energy.

Despite substantial efforts, the share of rural industries in total industrial production is still quite modest. Also, labour productivity in such industries is considerably lower than in larger-scale industries. Especially during the Great Leap Forward between 1958 and 1960, numerous small-scale steel factories were established. The steel manufactured here was of such inferior quality that many of them were sooner or later forced to close down. Attempts to decentralize industry were also not always in line with comparative cost advantages and locational advantages of different regions.

In theory an integrated rural development policy seems to offer only advantages. However, as with all development strategies, one should not be misled by 'development rhetoric'. In practice, it turns out to be exceedingly difficult to transcend sectoral boundaries in policy. The pursuit of an integrated policy can easily result in immense bureaucratic coordination problems exceeding the available administrative capabilities.

QUESTIONS FOR REVIEW

1. To what extent has the Malthusian prediction that food production cannot keep up with population growth been validated in the course of the twentieth century?
2. To what extent does an increase in food production in a country imply that the consumption of food is also increasing and that undernourishment and malnutrition are on the decrease?
3. Discuss the three ways in which agricultural output can be increased. What were the most common routes to growth of output in the past? What is the most applicable route in the present?
4. Discuss Ester Boserup's theory of the impact of increasing population density on changes in agricultural technology. What lessons can be derived from Boserup's analysis?
5. Discuss the five models of agricultural development of Hayami and Ruttan.
6. What are the defining characteristics of the 'green revolution'? Provide a summary of the debate on the advantages and disadvantages of the green revolution.
7. What is the difference between rural development and agricultural development?

8. Discuss the differences between the three approaches to rural development: the modernization approach, the incorporation approach and the transactionalist approach.
9. What are the characteristics of a peasant economy? Summarize the debate on the advantages and disadvantages of the use of the concept of peasant economy.
10. Why do small farmers in developing countries generally prefer to minimize risks, rather than maximize output? What kind of strategies do they pursue in order to minimize risks?
11. What is integrated rural development?

Notes

1. Rice, for example, is grown both as a food crop and as a cash crop.
2. It would be preferable to compare food crop trends with non-food crop trends, rather than food crop trends and total crop trends, but FAO data were not available in that format.
3. This section has been inspired to a considerable extent by an article by C. van der Meer (1983), 'Voedselvoorziening en agrarische ontwikkeling' (Food supply and agricultural development), and an article by P. van der Eng (1992), 'Food supply and agricultural development' (1992).
4. Unfortunately there are large inconsistencies between the data from vol. 44 (*1990*) and vol. 48 (*1994*) of the FAO *Production Yearbook* (FAO, 1991a, 1995), especially for South America. For instance in vol. 44, cultivated area in South America in 1979 was 130.1 million hectares, against a figure of 97 million hectares for 1978 from vol. 48.
5. Closed forest is forest where tree crowns cover at least 20 per cent of the land area. In open forests the tree crowns cover 5 to 20 per cent of the land.
6. Diffusion of technology and more efficient allocation can also take place within more traditional agricultural systems. These 'models' are not necessarily associated with recent technological breakthroughs in agriculture.
7. According to Oasa (1987), who represents the critical strand in the literature, the response is real but insufficient. It does not tackle the fundamental political economic contradictions.
8. These institutes include the International Potato Centre in Peru, the International Livestock Centre for Africa in Ethiopia and the West African Rice Development Association in Monrovia, Liberia.
9. With respect to the total agricultural production the contribution of expansion of farm land between 1961 and 1988 is considerably larger than it is with respect to corn, 26 per cent (see Gillin and Krane, 1989).
10. Alexandratos (1988) writes that the estimated availability of calories for developing countries as a whole is higher than what would appear to be realistic on the basis of evolution of per capita incomes.
11. In addition, demographical factors such as the number of dependants per member of the labour force, may also play a role.
12. My attempts above to give a brief summary of trends of change in rural societies could also be easily misunderstood as a sketch of the transition from 'traditional' to 'modern'.
13. In her polemic sharpness, Hill does not always do justice to her opponents. For example, as early as 1965 Boserup explicitly pointed out that different intensities of land use can coexist in the same region, due to differences in soil quality and natural circumstances (Boserup, 1965: 57 ff.).

14. Scott does not idealize the traditional village community to the extent his critics suggest. He believes the redistributive obligations are enforced through expressions of envy, gossip, and social control. Dependence on community support entails loss of status.
15. Hill, however, points out that in parts of West Africa some land is freely traded.
16. In post-war literature, tenant relations were considered to be less efficient than cultivation of the land by its owner. However, in particular in areas where markets for products and production factors are quite underdeveloped, tenancy relations may effectively spread the risks over the tenant farmer and his/her landlord (see Hayami and Ruttan, 1985: 391 ff.).

10 State formation and political aspects of development

This chapter will focus on the processes of state formation in developing countries. Until recently, most economists ignored the relationships between state formation and economic development. Nevertheless, political and economic developments are closely interconnected. For example, it is of little use to discuss the economic development of Nicaragua in the 1980s without taking the war with the United States into consideration. Also, it is not much use analyzing the economic development of African countries, if one does not realize that many countries on the African continent are in a state of open or latent civil strife or international conflict. At the moment of writing (late 1995), this applies to countries such as Algeria, Angola, Burundi, Liberia, Mozambique, Nigeria, Rwanda, Somalia, and the Sudan.

The political aspects of development will be discussed from two perspectives with which the reader will by now be familiar. In the first place, the interactions between state formation and economic development will be analyzed. In this context an interesting paradox comes to the fore. The tasks and demands now facing the government apparatus in developing countries are heavier and more comprehensive than ever before in economic history. At the same time, the apparatus of government is less well equipped to fulfil these tasks.

In the second place, the characteristics of state formation and political development will be discussed as important independent aspects of development. In Chapter 1 it was argued that 'development' is much more than economic change alone. Themes like national independence, effectiveness of government policy, political democratization, and political participation are all included in a broader conception of development. In this chapter the following themes and topics will be discussed: concepts of state and nation (section 10.1); classical perspectives on the relationships between the state and the economy (section 10.2); state formation as a prerequisite for economic development: European patterns of development (section 10.3); specific characteristics and problems of state formation in developing countries (section 10.4);

the state as a motive force in economic development and industrialization (section 10.5); interactions between political and economic developments (section 10.6); and the state as a potential obstacle to economic development in sub-Saharan Africa (section 10.7).

10.1 *Concepts*

In *Social Change in the Twentieth Century*, Daniel Chirot (1977, pp. 11–15) provides useful definitions of concepts such as 'state' and 'nation'. Following Max Weber, Chirot defines the state as a social system with a set of *rules* enforced by a *permanent administrative body* (the apparatus of government).[1] This body is the highest source of authority in the wider social system. It claims the right to make collective decisions and to enforce them. A similar definition can be found in van den Hoogen (1992), according to whom the distinguishing characteristics of a state include a territory, a population, and a sovereign authority that can impose rules and decisions on its own citizens. In the international political system, *states* are the most important political actors.

A *nation* is a group of people who feel they have so much in common that they should have their own state. The joint element may be religion, culture, language, common descent, or shared historical experiences (see also Kellas, 1991). In this context, the important thing is the subjective feeling that people share common descent or history from which they derive their claim to statehood. Van den Berghe (1981) defines a nation as a politically conscious ethnic group.

The term *society* may have many different meanings. In the context of state formation and nation building, the term 'society' refers to the population that is controlled by a state or the population that forms a nation or both. A *country* refers to a well-defined geographical territory that is effectively controlled by a state. Effective control is the usual criterion for international diplomatic recognition of a country.

The term *nation-state* refers to the overlap of the population that is controlled by a state, and the population with shared feelings of belonging. This overlap is by no means self-evident. Nationalism – the idea that each nation should have its own independent state – is a relatively recent phenomenon, dating, in its modern form, from the nineteenth century. Prior to the nineteenth century most people used to identify more with village, region, or kin, than with larger territorial political units. In Europe, politics were mainly dominated by royal and noble elites. Kinship relationships within these elites played an important role in politics.

I do not mean to infer that there were no nationalist feelings or movements prior to the nineteenth century. Examples which immediately come to mind are French popular resistance to English domination in the fifteenth century, inspired by Joan of Arc, the Dutch revolt against Spanish rule in the sixteenth and seventeenth centuries, or French nationalism following the French Revolution in the eighteenth century. Still, important specific characteristics of modern nationalism were lacking, like the use of modern means of communication and organization to mobilize large numbers of people into mass movements and the underpinning of mass movements by nationalist ideologies.

There are nations without their own state, like the Jews before the establishment of the state of Israel, the Kurds, and the Palestinians. There are also movements which seek to unite larger groups with an appeal to their common identity, such as pan-Slavism or pan-Arabism. There are also *multinational states* in which several national groups with a distinctive 'we-feeling' coexist within a territory controlled by a single state apparatus. Well-known examples are the Habsburg monarchy till 1918, the Ottoman empire till 1918, the former Yugoslavia, the former Soviet Union, and present-day India.

Finally, there are also examples of *multi-ethnic states.* These states comprise various ethnic groups that are characterized by ethnic 'we-feelings', but do not claim their own separate states (see van den Berghe, 1981, p. 61). The Frisians in the Netherlands and the Welsh in Great Britain are examples of such groups. Often countries like the United States and Brazil are also called multi-ethnic states. Most European societies have become more multi-ethnic since World War II as a result of immigration.

All these concepts represent sliding scales, rather than absolutes. Within multi-ethnic states, nationalist sentiments may develop which may give rise to separatist movements. On the other hand, in processes of state formation separate groups may also develop common national identities. Although the term 'nation' sometimes has biological undertones of common descent or kinship, national awareness often develops as a result of shared historical experiences. In *The Embarrassment of Riches*, Simon Schama (1988) has impressively shown how Dutch national feelings were cultivated in the seventeenth century, resulting in the emergence of a Dutch national identity.

Chirot makes a distinction between core societies and peripheral societies, which is also of relevance for an understanding of state formation processes in developing countries.[2] In countries in the core of world society, state, nation, society and geographical boundaries tend to coincide. Examples of highly integrated nation-states are Denmark, France, Great Britain, Japan, the Netherlands and the United States. The main characteristic of such nation-states is a relatively high degree of political autonomy in national decision-making,[3] together with strong cultural integration and associated feelings of cultural self-confidence, at times bordering on complacency and feelings of superiority. Such 'strong states' are also characterized by effective government institutions (Thomas, 1987). From an economic point of view, core states are generally rich, highly industrialized and have a diversified economy.

On the periphery of world society, states and nations coincide to a far lesser extent. Many states are multi-ethnic or multinational. Country borders cut across ethnic boundaries. People are more likely to relate to tribe, village, or region than to a some far-off national state or national government. The unity of the national state is constantly threatened by nationalistic separatist movements, civil wars, and external interference. The capacity of the state apparatus to make and implement collective decisions is weakly developed. There is greater dependence on external influences than in core countries. Internally, there is a large degree of cultural heterogeneity. Externally, one is confronted with the cultural challenge of the West and penetration by Western cultural influences. Van den Hoogen points out that attempts to establish a strong, central authority in developing countries may actually become a source of conflict and violence (van den Hoogen, 1992). There is resistance not only to authoritarian government, but also to the very notion of nation-building itself. In economic terms, peripheral states are poorer, less industralized, and less diversified in their economic structure.

In recent years, we have become more aware of the fragility of nation-states, even in core states of the world economy. In almost all Western counties, the unity of the nation-state has become less self-evident. Movements for regional autonomy and separatist movements have gained in strength and importance. Examples include Scotland, Wales, the Basque Provinces, Catalonia, Corsica and Brittany, Flanders, the Walloon provinces, Northern Italy, Southern Tyrol, and Quebec. In the United States, Australia, and Western Europe cultural integration has weakened and identification with the dominant culture has declined among members of so-called ethnic minorities. This holds both for peoples who have been living in a country for ages like Indians and Spanish Americans, Australian Aborigines and Afro-Americans, and more recent immigrants. In particular in Western Europe, cultural heterogeneity increased rapidly during the post-war period due to migration flows from former colonies and other regions. Not only does the nation-state become less self-evident due to increased internal cultural and ethnic diversity, the latitude for independent national policy also diminishes due to supranational influences.

In several former communist states a destructive and, until recently, unthinkable process of national disintegration has unfolded since 1989. The Soviet Union, Czechoslovakia, and Yugoslavia broke up into smaller states. Within these new political entities ethnic groups struggled for ascendency or claimed their own autonomy. In Yugoslavia this resulted in a civil war in which various groups of Slavic descent (including Catholic Croats, Orthodox Serbs, and Islamic Serbs) fought each other ferociously and applied ethnic cleansing to create ethnically homogeneous regions. Similar processes took place in Georgia, Tadzhikistan, Azerbaijan and Chechenya. The demographer Keyfitz argues that the formation of smaller, ethnically homogeneous states is nothing but a continuation of the worldwide process of decolonization and breakdown of empires (Keyfitz, 1991). The borders of the present existing states are accidental. For some nations like the Kurds, the Tamils, and the Kashmiris, it was simply bad luck that the process of state formation was consolidated before they were granted states of their own.

This is a dangerous notion. It ignores the fact that most regions in the world are ethnically mixed. The smaller the political entities claiming national independence, the sharper and more murderous the conflicts between the various 'nations' within the borders of the 'state'. The ultimate consequence of Keyfitz's perspective is the acceptance of ethnic cleansing by victors in ethnic struggles.

These developments are taking place as this text is being written and it is not clear what their outcomes will be. They illustrate once again the fruitlessness of simple dichotomies opposing highly developed and less developed political units, and the tendency to think of development as a process of irreversible change from 'less developed' to 'more developed' (Chirot, 1977, p. 185 ff.).

10.2 *Marxist and Weberian perspectives on the state*

In the Marxist tradition, class relationships – the contradictions and conflicts between social groups and categories which have objective economic interests in common – are the central focus. Together with technological change (forces of production), class relationships form the substructure of society. The dynamics of class relationships and class conflicts ultimately determine what happens in the superstructure of society: culture, religion, law, and the state.[4] Reduced to its bare bones, this view implies that at a given moment in time the activities of the members of the state apparatus are completely determined by the interests of the ruling class. For instance, the state in capitalist society is said to be no more than the executive committee of the ruling class of capitalists and the bourgeoisie. In a feudal society the state represents the interests of the landed gentry and feudal landlords. After a socialist revolution, class contradictions would be abolished and the state would finally wither away (Marx, 1955).

This short summary does no justice to the discussions and polemics within the Marxist tradition concerning the interactions between the state and class relationships. Several neo-Marxist writings point in particular to the *relative autonomy* of the state apparatus. This implies that the state apparatus has a certain margin of freedom in relation to other social institutions. Political decisions and government actions have an independent measure of influence on the course of social and economic development (see, for example, Skocpol, 1979).

In addition, both Marxists and neo-Marxists stress the fact that government officials may be regarded a separate 'class' with its own interests. Government actions and policies are in part determined by this interest group (Dahrendorf, 1963; Skocpol, 1979; Bardhan, 1984). In his analysis of communist states, Djilas even uses the term 'the new class' for politicians and bureaucrats who function within the state apparatus. Their position in government is the basis for their social and material privileges (Djilas, 1957; Lane, 1971). Nevertheless, one may safely conclude that in the Marxist and neo-Marxist tradition the functioning of the state is ultimately primarily determined by the interests of dominant groups and classes in the economic sphere.

The Marxist perspective provides a useful counterbalance to the notion that the state is a neutral institution, standing above social parties, which produces rules and decisions more or less in a social vacuum, with the goal of improving social welfare.[5] The Marxist perspective is a source of inspiration for the empirical study of the social constraints within which governments must operate and the influence of classes, interest groups and pressure groups on government actions and policies (Alavi, 1979). The idea of the state as an arena for contending economic and social interest groups, including interest groups from within the state apparatus itself, has found wide acceptance. It is now also the prevailing perspective among non-Marxist political scientists. However, the simple Marxist class categories have been left behind. In their place, we see, both within and without the apparatus of government, a multitude of interest groups, lobbies and pressure groups, whose influence can be analyzed (Buchanan and Tullock, 1962; Olson, 1965; Tullock, 1965; Frey, 1978). One of the non-Marxist founders of this 'new political economy' was Joseph Schumpeter (1946) with his *Capitalism, Socialism and Democracy*.

Another important source of inspiration for present-day studies of the state is the work of Max Weber (1922). Unlike Marx, Weber emphasized that political power is not a mere reflection of economic power. The political sphere has an autonomy of its own, in relation to the economic sphere.[6] There is no question of the state withering away. On the contrary, Weber predicted that the state would become increasingly important within the context of a long-term process of bureaucratization and rationalization. The general tendency towards bureaucratization would be reinforced in countries where socialist revolutions would take place.

Although Weber was very concerned about the consequences of continued bureaucratization and rationalization, 'bureaucracy' itself does not have a negative connotation in his work. 'Bureaucracy' represents a newer and more efficient form of organization in which the activities of large numbers of people are coordinated in a network of specialized functions. In a bureaucracy, decisions are made on the basis of formal rules and precedents, rather than on the basis of the fancies and favours of royal sovereigns or personal obligations and ties between people. Job qualifications are defined as objectively as possible, and functions are ordered in a hierarchical structure. Recruitment for functions is based on objective criteria such as competence, education, and experience, irrespective of personal relationships and ties. In theory, personal connections, relationships of kin and social background play no role. There is a complete separation between the bureaucratic office and the personal sphere of the functionary. Finally, fulfilling a function in a bureaucracy is a full-time and fully paid, professional activity. According to Weber, the bureaucratic form of organization was more rational (i.e. non-arbitrary) than previous forms of organization. In its functioning it was more effective and more predictable. Both in its functioning in the political and in the economic domain, bureaucracy was superior to other forms of organization. It made for greater effectiveness and predictability. Bureaucratic organization was not only a characteristic of the modern state apparatus, but also of large modern capitalist enterprises. Thus, bureaucratization, was an aspect of successful economic and political development.

Again unlike Marx, Weber considered state formation as one of the important *prerequisites* of economic development. State formation in Europe involved centralization of power and rule-making, and pacification of the territory within the borders of the national state in the making. Political centralization implied the abolition of all sorts of local legislation, toll barriers, privileges, tariffs, and rules that hampered the emergence of national markets and the growth of trade. Local currencies were abolished and replaced by national currencies. The right to impose taxes became the monopoly of national authorities. Pacification implied that incessant conflicts and wars between local rulers gradually made way for a central power that acquired a monopoly on the use of violence. Only the army and the police had the legitimate right to apply violence, on behalf of the central authority.

It is clear that pacification within a larger territory is an essential prerequisite for an expansion of trade and markets, an increase in investment, and for economic growth in general. Where there are wars, conflicts, and sporadic violence, no one's property will be safe. Few people will be prepared to take the risks involved in long-term investments. Trade can only flourish when the transport of goods is not obstructed and when people can be sure that their property rights will be respected. Entrepreneurship will only make its appearance if people have some guarantee that future benefits of risky investments in the present accrue to those who have taken the risks.

Political centralization, uniformity of regulation at a national level, and the development of a well-functioning government bureaucracy increase predictability, which is a prerequisite for rational calculations of costs and benefits in a market economy. Legal protection of individual ownership rights by central rules, sanctioned by the central apparatus of violence, contributes to entrepreneurship and investment in capital goods and technical innovation. In the long term, these lead to an increase in collective welfare (North and Thomas, 1973).

10.3 *Processes of state formation in Europe*

In *Über den Prozess der Zivilisation*, Norbert Elias (1969) – building on insights of Max Weber and historians like Bloch, Lefèbre, and Pirenne – presents an analysis of centuries-long processes of centralization and state formation in Europe and, in particular, in what is now known as France.

The European states developed out of the highly decentralized feudal system that had emerged in Europe after the fall of the Roman Empire. The linchpin of this system consisted of local feudal landlords. They lived off agricultural surpluses produced in their territory and provided their serfs and dependants with some form of military protection against the depredations of other lords, robber barons, and overseas raiders. The peasants farmed primarily for their own consumption and were obliged to transfer part of their agricultural surpluses to their feudal landlord and his household. Although there was some trade, the small feudal domains were largely self-sufficient. The lords in turn were in vassalage to superior liege lords and sovereigns to whom they owed military support in times of war, in which event lords would then mobilize their serfs to serve as foot soldiers. The feudal value system had mystical elements which at a later stage could be called upon by monarchs to legitimize strong central authority (Wallerstein, 1974).

Feudal landlords strove continually to make their rights to land hereditary and to increase their autonomy from liege lords. At the same time they tried to expand their own spheres of influence and to make others subject to their authority. For many centuries, the feudal system fluctuated between centralization and decentralization. Sometimes local rulers would succeed in gaining military superiority and expanded the territory under their control in processes of centralization. However, these processes of centralization were rather precarious. Military expansion required funds and manpower, both of which had to be withdrawn from the local economy. This perpetually threatened to undermine the economic basis of political expansion (cf. Elvin, 1973, for China). The centralized rule over larger areas also involved considerable costs like the support of a centralized administrative apparatus, and the maintenance of systems of transport and communication. These costs could easily exceed the carrying capacity of the economic base.[7]

Feudal lords who supported a sovereign in his expansionist campaigns were frequently granted part of the conquered lands as a fief. The sovereign claimed the supreme authority over these lands. His vassals, however, always tried to gain hereditary rights to their land and to increase their independence from central authority. For such reasons, processes of centralization alternated with processes of decentralization and disintegration. A telling example of the difficulty of maintaining a central apparatus of government is the way in which early rulers like Charlemagne had to travel around the country with their courts. Agricultural surpluses were simply insufficient to support a large, permanent court in a central seat of government. The sovereign and his court were fed from the yields of the lands of the vassals who received the honour of a royal visit.

From the twelfth century onwards the scales tipped in favour of centralization. Certain royal dynasties gradually succeeded in establishing their authority over other feudal lords, subjecting more and more regions to their rule. For example, the Duchy of the Île de France eventually became the nucleus of the later kingdom of France, London would become the centre of a British kingdom and Madrid of a Spanish kingdom. The new national kingdoms that came into being were much smaller than the old empires of Rome or China, but they were more strongly centralized and were administered more effectively (Wallerstein, 1974; see also Chapter 2).

In the process of centralization, the balance of power between social classes underwent great change. In a feudal society one can distinguish: (1) the landed classes (the nobility and the clergy);[8] (2) the serfs who worked the land, transferred parts of their agricultural surpluses to the landlords, and provided them with various labour services; (3) the sovereign and his court; and (4) the rising classes of traders, financiers, artisans, and urban citizens.

Especially alliances between bourgeois groupings and the royal courts have been of decisive importance in processes of centralization. Financial support by merchant bankers and taxes on urban economic activities provided the sovereign with independent means and increased his power *vis-à-vis* the nobility. The possibility of funding standing mercenary armies made it less necessary to appeal to feudal loyalties for military manpower and support. This also worked in favour of centralizing tendencies.

Between the twelfth and the seventeenth centuries centralizing tendencies prevailed and feudalism was converted into centralized royal absolutist states, which were the forerunners of modern national states. These processes of centralization involved struggles for two important monopolies: the *monopoly of violence* and the *tax monopoly*. Central authorities increasingly claimed the right to impose taxes on their subjects, and the taxation rights of local feudal rulers and urban authorities were gradually curtailed. Sovereigns who succeeded in setting up an effective central bureaucracy had a head start in the battle for the tax monopoly.

The military pacification of larger areas involved the establishment of a monopoly of violence. Only the military and the police had the right to exercise violence on behalf of central authorities. Attempts were made to curb the use of violence by individuals, groups, and local rulers (see, for example, Tilly, 1975, p. 27 ff.).

For complex reasons – including demographic fluctuations and the gradual emergence of an economy based on trade, crafts, and manufacturing centring on towns – the influence of the feudal landed nobility started to wane from the late Middle Ages onwards. The fourteenth century, in particular, was a century of crisis in the feudal system. At the same time the influence of the commercial middle classes was growing. By the time the power and influence of these two social categories were more or less in balance, the central sovereign could act as an arbiter. His power and latitude increased dramatically.

Members of the feudal nobility were losing out in the economic sphere, but their social standing was still very high. They spent part of their time at the king's court, cultivating an exclusive and refined lifestyle (Elias, 1979). The commercial bourgeoisie became more powerful economically, but its members were not yet taken seriously socially. The central monarchy could play off these rival classes against each other.

In the sixteenth and seventeenth centuries centralization trends culminated in royal absolutism. The seemingly unlimited power of the crown reached its peak in France under the Sun King, Louis XIV. Here, the contending classes were most evenly balanced. All over Europe there were similar processes of centralization and concentration of power. However, in countries where either the bourgeoisie (as in England or in the Low Countries) or the landed nobility (as in German states) had more influence, the position of the central monarch was correspondingly less strong (see Moore, 1967; Elias, 1969, p. 1229 ff.)

Once a central authority with an effective monopoly of violence and a tax monopoly had been established, a *process of democratization* got under way in which the absolute power of the crown was gradually circumscribed. Bourgeois groupings, which had to raise most of the taxes, played a significant role in this process. The sovereign increasingly came to be answerable to institutions in which taxpayers were represented. Democratization was also furthered by the continuing social ascent of bourgeois groups and the continuing decline of the nobility. The sovereign was no longer able to play these two groups off against each other. At later stages, other social classes, such as the emerging working classes, also participated in the process of democratization.

The process of democratization also involved a gradual separation of the private and public functions of the crown. Initially, there was not much difference between public funds and the private fortune of the sovereign. Later, however, a distinction developed between the sovereign's personal finances and the finances of the state, for which the sovereign was accountable to representative bodies.[9] The central administrative apparatus also became more independent from the central sovereign. From a loose collection of people with personal ties and obligations to the sovereign, it was transformed into a professional bureaucracy. Democratization in the nineteenth century took the form of the rise of political mass movements. Ever larger groups participated in the political process and the struggle for universal suffrage began.

From the mid-eighteenth century onwards *nationalist movements* and *ideologies* arose, emphasizing the connection between a people (nation) and a state. This type of nationalism replaced earlier feelings of identification with region, village, or town. Nationalist sentiments also came to predominate among members of political elites, between whom there had previously been shared feelings of supranational loyalty based on kinship, social class and interpersonal relations.

In the twentieth century, modern nationalism – the idea that all peoples or nations are entitled to their own independent states – was to be an important force in the colonial struggles for independence from Western colonizers.

European processes of state formation have a number of specific characteristics that make them different from processes of state formation in other parts of the world. First, centralization did not emanate from one single centre, but from various focal points within Europe. Second, centralization never led to the establishment of an all-embracing European empire. Parallel processes of centralization resulted in a multitude of national states, competing with each other for technological advance, military supremacy, and economic and political expansion. Third, the European states were strong and effectively centralized, compared to larger but more loosely organized political entities such as, for instance, the Chinese Empire. Finally, rising bourgeois groups, who were the bearers of a money-and-market economy, had a relatively independent position. They were never completely subordinated to a central political authority, as was case in the great empires of the past. In the competition between states, political leaders actually depended in part on the support of their entrepreneurial classes. These classes supported the new strong states in their financial needs and in their competition with other states. The states in turn supported their entrepreneurial groups in their urge for external economic expansion. Initially, the European expansion in the world was economic rather than political in nature.

In *The Social Origins of Dictatorship and Democracy*, Barrington Moore (1967) analyzes differences in state formation processes in France, Germany, and England, which are closely associated with differences in the balance of power between social classes and groups. In France, the French Revolution led to the dramatic overthrow of the *ancien régime* by a popular movement led by bourgeois groupings whose social ascent and emancipation had been blocked. In England, this process was more gradual and less violent. The bourgeoisie and the nobility intermixed. The nobility participated in the modern market economy and the bourgeois classes underwent the cultural influences of the upper classes. In Germany, the process of state formation was altogether different. Partly as a result of the Thirty Years' War in the seventeenth century, the degree of political centralization had lagged behind and political unity was not achieved until very late. The landed nobility retained much of its influence, and the development of the middle classes was weak. When Germany achieved political integration in the second half of the nineteenth century under Prussian leadership, and strove for rapid economic development, a kind of coalition was formed between the landed nobility (the Junkers) and the rising working classes. Partly bypassing the middle classes, there was a policy of radical economic modernization and industrialization 'from the top down'.

In Great Britain and France, the development of capitalism, industrialization and the rise of the middle classes in France and England were associated with the rise of parliamentary democracy. According to Barrington Moore, the insecure position of the middle classes in Germany weakened democratic tendencies and contributed to the rise of fascism. Barrington Moore draws some very interesting parallels between German and Japanese economic and political development. In both cases, modernization was initiated from above by groups originating in old feudal elites. In both cases, there was a reactive kind of nationalism in response to external challenges and the examples of established and economically successful nation-states.

10.4 *State formation in developing countries*

In section 10.3, attention was paid to the notion, deriving from Max Weber, that state formation – characterized by pacification, centralization and the development of a monopoly of violence, a tax monopoly, and effective government institutions – is a prerequisite for economic development (see also Righart *et al.*, 1991, chapters 2 and 3).

In many developing countries since 1945 the state has not been completely consolidated and the national territory not fully pacified. In many Latin American, African, and Asian states the tax monopoly is underdeveloped, especially with respect to income taxes. The fiscal basis of the state is often weak (O'Connor, 1973). Wealthy citizens pay little or no income tax. Government revenues are highly dependent on taxes on land and agricultural production, tariffs on exports and imports, and, in some cases, financial aid from abroad. An important source of government revenue is monetary financing of expenditures. This form of financing is passed on to citizens in the form of inflation tax or *seigniorage* (see de Haan *et al.*, 1993). According to Myrdal (1968), many newly independent states were 'soft states', by which he means that governments did not have effective means to implement policy intentions and to impose binding obligations on their citizens. Myrdal refers in particular to non-communist states in South and Southeast Asia, though his analyses are also relevant for an understanding of state formation in Latin America and Africa.

In the following sections, attention will be paid to the specific characteristics and problems of state formation processes in developing countries. Here it can already be stated that political instability, malfunctioning of government, war and civil strife are at least as important as purely economic factors in explaining economic stagnation in developing countries. The interactions between processes of state formation and economic development will be discussed in more detail in section 10.6.

10.4.1 The importance of external penetration in processes of state formation

In Western Europe the nation-state was the outcome of centuries-long processes of decentralization and centralization from within, with modern political institutions gradually developing out of local traditions. With the exception of a limited number of countries such as China, Japan, Thailand, Persia, Ethiopia and Turkey, this is not the way states were formed in developing countries.[10] Usually the impetus for state formation in developing countries was *penetration from outside* by a foreign ethnic group (Goldthorpe, 1979, chapter 12; van Benthem van den Bergh, 1980; Sandbrook and Barker, 1985). The current borders of many developing countries have been decisively influenced by colonialism (Davidson, 1992)

These borders often contain a multiplicity of ethnic groups that hardly identify with the national state. Furthermore, ethnic tensions and divisions have been exacerbated by the classical divide-and-rule policies of colonial regimes. In some respects the ethnic and tribal divisions are even the product of modern influences (Davidson, 1992). Traditional ethnic ties were used by various groups in colonial and postcolonial times for purposes of modern political mass mobilization.

The legitimacy of the new state institutions is often limited. The internal pacification of the territory has not yet been completed, the tax monopoly is poorly developed, and the effectiveness of national state institutions is low. Moreover, especially in Africa, the colonial intermezzo has been brief. In this respect, also, modern state institutions have had relatively little time to take root (Sandbrook and Barker, 1985).

The following examples illustrate the significance of external penetration in state formation. Before the colonial period, India was a hotchpotch of principalities. In the fifteenth century there had been a large Muslim empire in the centre and north of India, the Mogul empire, which could have been the potential core of a future nation-state. However, after the arrival of the English, this empire disintegrated into a multitude of smaller kingdoms and principalities. Initially, British influence was concentrated in Bengal. In the nineteenth century British India was centralized as a colonial empire. This empire included the territory of present-day India, Pakistan, Bangladesh and Burma. After decolonization, Burma became an independent state. Religious differences between Muslims and Hindus resulted in a bloody division of the rest of British India into India and Pakistan. After a civil war in 1971 Pakistan broke up into two parts, Bangladesh and present-day Pakistan.

The current unified state of Indonesia came into existence in a similar way as a result of Dutch colonial centralizing impulses in the nineteenth century. A multitude of 'native' principalities, which had been politically independent until then, were united under colonial rule in a process that involved numerous wars and uprisings. The last of these wars was the Atjeh war at the end of the nineteenth century. During and after the struggle for independence, nationalist leaders took the colonial borders as their point of departure for postcolonial state formation. Even the annexation of Dutch New Guinea by Indonesia in 1963 was justified by Sukarno with reference to the fact that New Guinea had been part of the Dutch colonial empire. It should therefore also be part of the new state of Indonesia. The bloody occupation and annexation of East Timor was also justified by the idea that the borders of the Indonesian state should coincide with the areas formerly ruled by Europeans (including, in this case, the Portuguese).

In Indochina, the modern borders of states like Vietnam, Laos, and Cambodia were determined by the brief period of French rule from the mid-nineteenth century onwards. Here, too, national boundaries and ethnic dividing lines do not always coincide.

In Latin America, the present-day states came into existence after the disintegration of the Spanish and Portuguese colonial empires during the first decades of the nineteenth century. The former viceroyalty of New Granada broke up into Colombia, Ecuador, and Venezuela. The viceroyalty of Peru was divided into Peru, Chile and Bolivia. Attempts by Simon Bolivar, the leader of the struggle for independence, to form a Great Colombian republic uniting New Granada and Peru, failed. In 1903 Panama broke away from Colombia, partly on the instigation of and with the support of the United States.

Mexico evolved out of the viceroyalty of New Spain, which had included Central America, the Spanish West Indies, and, for some time, Venezuela. Here, too, attempts to maintain larger political units failed. The central American states broke away from Mexico between 1820 and 1830. In a war between 1845 and 1848 Mexico lost half its territory to the United States (Texas, New Mexico, California, Arizona, Nevada, and Utah). Argentina, Paraguay, and Uruguay developed out of the viceroyalty of Rio de la Plata. Brazil gained its independence from Portugal in 1822. Dom Pedro, the son of the last Portuguese king, became the first emperor of independent Brazil.

In each Latin American country the political scene was dominated by descendants of white colonists and immigrants. For a very long time, descendants of the original Indian population, imported slaves and contract labourers hardly participated in the political process, and to this very day they are underrepresented in politics. Since independence, the military have played an important role in politics in most countries. There has been widespread political instability. Foreign powers frequently intervened in order to safeguard their economic and political interests. There have also been numerous internal wars and conflicts that led to adjustments of national borders. Nevertheless, it is clear that modern processes of state formation in Latin America commenced at an earlier stage than in Africa and Asia. Despite the considerable ethnic diversity in Latin America, most territorial borders of the countries in this region are not in question. It remains a problem that the legitimacy of national institutions is limited.

The consequences of external penetration for the process of state formation have been most extreme in Africa and the Middle East. In Africa borders were determined both by military conquest and by diplomatic negotiations between the European powers, which started with the Berlin conference of 1884/1885 (see Jackson and Rosberg, 1986, p.6). In a brief period in the late nineteenth century the whole of Africa was colonized in the 'Scramble for Africa'. This process was completed by 1900. In 1914 there were only two independent countries in Africa: Abyssinia and

Liberia. In the Middle East the European powers entered the vacuum left after the fall of the Ottoman Empire, and established a multitude of colonies and protectorates. Both in Africa and in the Middle East the present borders are often straight lines on a map that ignore natural circumstances or ethnic composition. These lines were drawn on maps with rulers by representatives of the great colonial powers. In their land hunger, military rivalry and mutual competition, the great powers divided up the land among themselves. In particular, countries with few colonies elsewhere, like Germany and France, were eager to get a stake.

It is definitely not true there were no African states prior to the colonial period (Sandbrook and Barker, 1985; Davidson, 1992; Schoenmakers, 1992). There has been a rich diversity of political forms of organization, kingdoms, empires, and confederations. I mention but a few: the medieval realms in the savannas of Ghana and Mali, the ancient kingdoms of Nubia and Ethiopia, the seventeenth-century kingdom of Buganda in present-day Uganda, the Asante kingdom in Ghana, founded at the end of the seventeenth century, the nineteenth-century Lozi kingdom in present-day Zambia, the great kingdom of Benin from the twelfth to the nineteenth centuries, the Kaabu empire from the sixteenth to the nineteenth centuries in the region of Guinea Bissau, the Zulu empire in the nineteenth century, and many more.

The absence of the written word outside the Egyptian-Arabic sphere of influence, however, restricted the strength of most states, since writing is a prerequisite for a permanent, centralized systems of bookkeeping and administration. Except for warfare, conquest and the taking of slaves, the impact of pre-colonial states on everyday life in agricultural and nomadic societies was much more limited than that of modern state-formations. The territorial size of precolonial states was also usually rather small. Pre-colonial political formations might possibly have formed a basis for political centralization from within, but they were unable to resist the colonial penetration from Europe, from the second half of the nineteenth century onwards.

Apart from kingdoms, empires, and tribal confederations, many peoples in Africa lived in decentralized tribal configurations with no central political leadership – so-called *acephalous* political units (Mair, 1967). Their loyalty was to village, region or tribe rather than to remote and unfamiliar concepts such as empires or national states. Colonial bureaucracies in Africa were tiny and were far removed from local communities. The borders of the colonies cut across a rich variety of traditional political institutions, confederations, and tribal communities. In the process of decolonization in the decades following World War II, these extremely heterogeneous societies were transformed into independent national states, with inexperienced bureaucracies and imported political institutions. These states quickly degenerated into personal regimes (see section 10.7).

Linguistically, external influences on the process of state formation have also been of importance. In the process of gradual political centralization in Europe, the local dialect of the dominant centre usually developed into a national language over the centuries. However, there was no linguistic unity in many former colonies. For want of a national language, the language of the colonial rulers was used as a common means of communication. This situation was continued after independence. After all, a choice of the language of one of the principal ethnic or cultural groups could easily spark off feelings of resentment among other ethnic groups. Thus English became a national language in India, Pakistan, and former British colonies in Africa like Ghana, Nigeria, and Zimbabwe. French became the national language of the former West African colonies of France. Portuguese is now the national language of Brazil.

In Indonesia, the nationalist movement chose Bahasa Indonesia – a variant of Malay, used as a trade language – as the national tongue as early as 1928. Both Dutch and Javanese, the language of the dominant ethnic group in Indonesia, were rejected as the national language. By now, Dutch has almost disappeared in Indonesia, except among people of fifty years and older. As the internationally oriented language, it has been replaced by English. In this respect, Indonesia is a unique example of successful cultural decolonization. In a somewhat similar fashion, Israel succeeded in establishing modern Hebrew as the national language for Jewish immigrants coming from all over the world.

It is interesting to note that in their fight against Western colonialism, independence movements took colonial borders as given. The pursuit of 'national' independence was strongly influenced by Western ideas about nationalism and national states. It was based on the assumption that the population of a colony was a nation (van Benthem van den Bergh, 1980).

10.4.2 Internal political stability

In the former colonies, nationalist resistance against foreign rule created a sense of national solidarity. However, when the tangible opponent disappeared with the departure of the colonial rulers, contradictions between different ethnic groups and 'nations' within the borders of the newly independent states usually intensified. This was, and still is, an important and continuing source of political instability. Central authorities often regard expressions of ethnic, tribal, religious, cultural, and linguistic individuality as a threat to the political unity of the national state. These expressions, therefore, are suppressed, frequently by force. This may lead to an intensification of political conflicts and to the rise of new nationalist separatist movements. Thus the very process of state formation itself can become a source of political conflict and instability (van den Hoogen, 1992).

The instability of new states is augmented by the contradiction between the 'accumulation function' and the 'legitimation function' of the state (O'Connor, 1973). According to O'Connor, governments have to choose between conflicting objectives: the use of state power in support of capital accumulation by entrepreneurial classes on the one hand, and, on the other, maintenance of social harmony by means of government expenditures. In capitalist states, this contradiction results in a permanent fiscal crisis.

The greater the role of the government in the economy, the deeper the tension between these two functions. The legitimation function of the state implies that the government should not take any measures that will lastingly alienate politically important groups of the population. Maintaining social harmony may, however, require policies that hamper economic growth, such as food subsidies, creation of employment in the government sector and subsidies to urban industry. However, such measures also lead to a too extensive public sector, large fiscal deficits, and inflation. In the long term, these factors have negative effects on economic growth (e.g. in Brazil and Mexico; see Maddison *et al.*, 1992). The implementation of a policy of structural adjustment aimed at limiting the role of the government, restricting fiscal deficits, cutting subsidies and liberalizing the economy, jeopardizes the very political survival of regimes in many countries.

In her pioneering study, *States and Social Revolutions*, Theda Skocpol (1979) discerns a similar tension between the necessities of levying taxes for purposes of warfare, putting government finance on a sound basis and economic modernization on the one hand, and maintaining the support of crucial sections of the population on the other hand. She explains the sudden and seemingly inexplicable fall of regimes in the French and Russian revolutions and the 1911 revolution in China by the fact that governments were forced to implement unpopular economic reforms in order to cope with external challenges. These reforms conflicted with the interests of those groups that had been the most loyal allies of the ruling regime up till then. Thus, at a crucial juncture, a regime would suddenly lose the support of these groups, and would become more vulnerable to political opposition from other groups and classes.

10.4.3 External political interference

Not only is the political unification of many developing countries the result of external colonization from the West, but also after decolonization, processes of state formation continued to be characterized by external intervention and interference. Radical authors have even coined the term 'neocolonial relations'. External interference may be of an economic or a political nature. External economic interference may be the result of factors such as the operations of multinational enterprises, foreign investors, or conditions imposed by international economic institutions such as the IMF, the World Bank, or the large trade blocks of the rich countries (OECD, EU). In the following section, however, I will focus on political and military interference. Internal political instability invites political interference from without. External interference augments internal political instability. Initially, minor differences between ethnic groups within a country may easily acquire geopolitical dimensions.

The Cold War between East and West found its counterpart in conflicts between the 'clients' of the two blocs. These clients were often recruited on an ethnic basis in the pursuit of geopolitical objectives. Regional powers like South Africa, Vietnam, India, Libya, Iraq, Iran and Syria also tried to widen their spheres of influence. Their interventions in internal political conflicts in other countries exacerbated ethnic conflicts. Simultaneously, political leaders of ethnic groups solicited external military and political support in their struggles for control over the new national institutions. External interference made internal conflicts bloodier, less controllable and longer.

The list of developing countries in which external interference since World War II played a role in processes of state formation or national disintegration is long. The following examples illustrate the importance of external interference during this period (for Africa, see, for example, Gavshon, 1981; David, 1987):

- The war between Somalia and Ethiopia over the Ogaden from 1977 to 1978. Until 1977 the Americans offered military support to Ethiopia and the Soviet Union to Somalia. After the Somalian invasion of the Ogaden in 1977, the Soviet Union and Cuba supported Ethiopia by means of military supplies, advisers, and Cuban soldiers. The United States ended their support to Ethiopia and, in time, started to support Somalia. Eventually, the invasion of the Ogaden was withstood, and millions of ethnic Somalis fled across the Somalian border. In Somalia, politics degenerated into clan warfare, which persists to this very day.
- The struggle for the secession of Eritrea from Ethiopia which took place from 1962 to 1992. Until 1974 Haile Selassie received large-scale US support. Since 1977, Eritrean resistance against the communist regime of Haile Mariam Mengistu has been supported by the Islamic countries and indirectly by the United States.
- The Angolan civil war after the fall of the Portuguese regime in 1974. The MPLA government of Agostinho Neto and Dos Santos received large-scale military support from the Soviet Union and Cuba. The opposition of Holden Roberto's FNLA and Jonas Savimbi's Unita was supported by South Africa and the United States. For a while the FNLA was also supported by China. South African support even took the form of a military invasion. Large numbers of Cuban soldiers fought on the government side.
- The secession of Biafra from Nigeria. During the Nigerian Civil War (1967–1970) about the secession of Biafra, the United States offered some military support, albeit covertly, to the secessionist movement, whereas the British and the Soviet Union supported the regime in Lagos.
- The conflict over mineral-rich western Sahara between Morocco and the Polisario independence movement supported by Algeria.
- The Kurdish struggle for autonomy or independence in Turkey, Iran and Iraq. In their mutual conflicts the Turkish, Iranian and Iraqi regimes constantly supported separatist movements in the other countries with a view to weakening their opponents. Internally, even the peaceful pursuit of Kurdish autonomy was suppressed, for it was regarded as a threat to national unity. Presently, Kurdish autonomy is being supported by the international community in Iraq, to keep up the pressure on the Baghdad regime of Saddam Hussein.
- Zaire, where France, England and Belgium in 1960 first supported the secessionist movement of Moise Tshombe in Katanga, an area rich in minerals, while the United States and the Soviet Union supported the Democratic Republic under the first president Patrice Lumumba. Later the United States collaborated in the overthrow of the Lumumba regime when it oriented itself more towards the Soviet Union. The United States supported a takeover by Mobutu. In 1977/1978 there was another secessionist movement in Katanga, initiated by Angolan exiles.

This uprising was suppressed by Mobutu with the help of Moroccan troops and French logistic support. A second invasion from Katanga in 1978 was suppressed with the assistance of French and Belgian troops and American logistic support.

- Afghanistan, where the Soviet Union intervened militarily in favour of a communist government and where Islamic and Western countries supported various oppositional groups and factions.
- Cambodia, where the Americans, the Chinese and the Vietnamese tried to exert their influence in changing coalitions during different periods in time.
- Vietnam, where the French, the Americans and American-supported regimes fought nationalist independence movements and communist revolutionary movements, supported by China and the Soviet Union from 1945 to 1973.
- Korea, where the United States and several Western allies fought a full-scale war against the Chinese in 1950–1952; this war eventually resulted in the division of the former Japanese colony of Korea into present-day North and South Korea.
- Chad, where factions supported by the French and the Libyans fought for control.
- The war between Iran and Iraq where the Western countries initially supported the Iraqis in their war against the deeply anti-American Muslim-fundamentalist regime of the Ayatollah Khomeini. Later in the Gulf War in 1991, an international coalition under the leadership of the United States violently put an end to the sudden Iraqi annexation of the oil-rich sheikdom of Kuwait.
- Sri Lanka, where Tamils from the Indian federal state of Tamil Nadu supported the struggle for independence of the Tamil minority, originating in India. The Indian government, however, later sided with the central Sri Lankan authorities and was even briefly involved in an unsuccessful attempt at peace enforcement in Sri Lanka.
- Kashmir, where the claims of Pakistan and India and Muslims and Hindus clashed, in both the Pakistan-ruled and Indian-ruled parts of Kashmir.
- Nicaragua, Cuba, Chile, the Dominican Republic, Panama and Grenada, where the United States tried to prevent the establishment of communist regimes by means of either open or covert military and political intervention. In the case of Nicaragua a complete army of Contras was organized and funded by the United States for the violent overthrow of the Sandinist regime.
- Lebanon, where interference by Syria, Iran, the Palestinians and Israel caused the fragile balance achieved between various groups to be destroyed, resulting in a protracted and totally destructive civil war.
- Mozambique, where the South Africans and the Rhodesians gave military support to the opposition movement Renamo. Cuba and several Eastern European countries supported the government of Samora Machel.

This list – by no means complete – illustrates the importance of East–West competition and regional power balances in exacerbating conflicts within and between new states in Asia, Africa and the Middle East and older states in Latin America. For the superpowers, their mutual rivalry was more important than the question of whether the regimes or movements they supported were in any way worthy of their support.

Table 10.1 provides rough figures on internal and external conflicts in developing countries and the numbers of victims involved. Between 1945 and 1990, 21 million people were killed in internal and external conflicts – 12 million in internal conflicts, and 10 million in external warfare. In some countries (including Algeria, Angola, Guinea Bissau, Indonesia, Cameroon, Kenya, Mozambique, Morocco, Tunisia and Vietnam), the majority of casualties occurred in the fight for independence against colonial rulers.

Table 10.1 Wars and war casualties, 1945–1990

	Civil wars		International wars	
	Number of years[a]	Number of casualties	Number of years[b]	Number of casualties
Latin America		696,000		7,000
Argentina	5	19,000	1	1,000
Bolivia	1	2,000		
Brazil	1	1,000		
Chile	3	28,000		
Colombia	20	323,000		
Cuba	2	5,000		
Dom. Republic	1	3,000		
El Salvador	12	75,000		
Guatemala	26	141,000		
Honduras			1	5,000
Jamaica	1	1,000		
Nicaragua	10	80,000		
Panama			1	1,000
Paraguay	1	1,000		
Peru	8	17,000		
Middle East		372,000		672,000
Cyprus			1	5,000
Egypt			5	79,000
Iraq	12	117,000		
Iran	12	88,000	9	500,000
Israel			2	24,000
Jordan	1	10,000		
Kuwait			1	1,000
Lebanon	3	102,000	9	63,000
Syria	1	20,000		
Turkey	4	5,000		
Yemen	11	30,000		

Table 10.1 (*continued*)

	Civil wars		International wars	
	Number of years[a]	Number of casualties	Number of years[b]	Number of casualties
South Asia		865,000		2,338,000
Afghanistan			12	1,300,000
Bangladesh			1	1,000,000
India	11	816,000	6	38,000
Pakistan	5	9,000		
Sri Lanka	8	40,000		
Far East		4,636,000		6,057,000
Burma	9	22,000		
Cambodia	9	1,156,000	12	65,000
China	12	2,508,000	6	102,000
Indonesia[c]	7	536,000	10	155,000
Philippines	21	44,000	18	40,000
Korea	2	2,000	4	3,000,000
Laos	14	30,000		
Malaysia	11	13,000		
Taiwan	2	25,000	1	1,000
Vietnam[c]	6	300,000	23	2,694,000
Sub-Saharan Africa		5,513,000		705,000
Angola[c]	30	396,000		
Burundi	2	115,000		
Cameroon[c]			6	32,000
Chad	8	7,000		
Ethiopia			17	609,000
Ghana	1	1,000		
Guinea Bissau[c]	13	15,000		
Kenya[c]	12	15,000		
Liberia	2	15,000		
Madagascar			2	15,000
Mozambique[c]	10	1,050,000	11	30,000
Nigeria	7	2,006,000		
Rwanda	10	105,000		
Sudan	17	1,006,000		
Somalia	3	55,000		
Uganda	16	610,000	2	3,000

Table 10.1 (*continued*)

	Civil wars		International wars	
	Number of years[a]	Number of casualties	Number of years[b]	Number of casualties
Western Sahara			13	16,000
Zaire	6	100,000		
Zambia	1	1,000		
Zimbabwe	10	16,000		
North Africa		2,000		206,000
Algeria[c]	2	2,000	9	200,000
Morocco			4	3,000
Tunisia[c]			3	3,000
Total		12,081,000		9,985,000

Notes:

[a] Total number of years during which a civil war or an internal conflict took place in a country. Internal conflicts include government terror against civilians.

[b] Total number of years during which an international war took place. Wars have been allocated to the country on whose territory the war was mainly fought.

[c] Including the period of the struggle for independence.

Sources: Sivard (1991), 22–5. Subdivision into civil wars and international wars on the basis of Small and Singer (1982), 80 and 222.

One of the most striking features of Table 10.1 is the large number of victims of internal conflicts in relation to absolute population size in sub-Saharan Africa (over 5.5 million). Casualties were also high relative to population in the Middle East, mainly due to external wars. In absolute numbers, most people were killed in internal and external conflicts in east Asia. In Asia as a whole, external wars caused more casualties than internal conflicts.[11] Finally, though Latin America is generally known as a violent continent, the number of casualties here is relatively low. Researchers argue whether the number of violent conflicts in developing countries shows a declining trend in the course of time (Kende, 1972; Starr and Most, 1985). Starr and Most come to the conclusion that no long-term increase or decrease can be discerned. Rather, there is a cyclical trend, with a peak between 1965 and 1968. In the period covered by their research, the locus of conflicts has unmistakably shifted from Europe to developing countries, and the importance of internal conflicts has increased in comparison to classical wars between countries.

At the end of the 1980s it was widely expected that the thaw in East–West relations and the end of the Cold War would contribute to a pacification of internal conflicts within and wars between developing countries. So far this expectation has not yet materialized. In retrospect, it turned out that the East–West conflict not only exacerbated conflicts and tensions, but also had some stabilizing functions. With the disappearance – at least for the time being – of the East–West opposition and the sudden collapse of the Soviet empire, regional conflicts and internal ethnic and cultural tensions increased rather than decreased. This is manifest in the continued fighting in Angola in the early 1990s, in the failed attempt by Saddam Hussein of Iraq to annex Kuwait, in the ethnic conflicts preceding the first free elections in South Africa, in the continued civil war in Afghanistan, in the secessionist movements in India (in the Punjab) and Sri Lanka (the Tamils), in civil wars in Liberia, Somalia, and the Sudan, and in wholesale ethnic slaughter in Rwanda and Burundi.

In India the differences between Muslims and Hindus has deepened since 1991 due to the rise of Hindu-fundamentalist movements. In North Africa and the Middle East, tensions between fundamentalist Muslim movements – which can to some extent be interpreted as a cultural response to Western penetration – and nationalist regimes have increased, for example, in Algeria, Tunisia, Egypt and Jordan. In Algeria this has degenerated into a bloody civil war.

The resurgence of nationalist sentiments led to the disintegration of the Soviet Union, Yugoslavia and Czechoslovakia, and to intensified social tensions within almost all of the new smaller political entities. The smaller the new nation, the more hostile it seems to be to its minorities. The civil war in former Yugoslavia between 1991 and 1995 is said to have claimed between 200,000 to 300,000 victims. Worldwide, the number of refugees fleeing from areas of civil strife is also on the increase.

At the same time, there are also examples of countries where the improvement in East–West relations allowed for breakthroughs in longstanding ethnic and political conflicts. Examples include the recent – uncertain – movements towards pacification in Cambodia, Angola and Mozambique, the election of a multiracial government in Namibia, the abolition of the apartheid regime in South Africa and the breakthrough in the relations between Palestinians and Israelis in September 1993.

Thus there are two diametrically opposed trends. On the one hand, the weakening of East–West tensions leads to a strengthening of centrifugal forces and a strong resurgence of nationalism, cultural contradictions and separatist movements. The scope for outside intervention has increased rather than decreased, now that regional powers are less dependent on the international superpowers. On the other hand, the decline of East–West tensions contributes elsewhere to processes of pacification. This is the case in regions and countries where superpowers had backed different countries, parties or factions in their attempts to expand their spheres of influence.

It is hard to predict which of these two trends will predominate in the long run. In any event, the examples discussed above provide an indication of the overwhelming importance of external political and military interference in the post-war period and its impact on state formation processes in developing countries.

10.4.4 The role of the military in politics

The military play a prominent role in the political process of many developing countries, even when they are not formally in power (Goldthorpe, 1979; Clapham and Philip, 1985; Finer, 1988).[12] The importance of the military in the post-war period is illustrated by the 1982 figures in Table 10.2 on political regimes in developing countries in 1982 (derived from Kidron and Smith, 1983).

Table 10.2 distinguishes between one-party states, military regimes, personal rule by a sovereign or an absolute ruler, restricted parliamentarism and multiparty systems. The 1982 data derived from Kidron and Smith (1983) have been updated using similar data from CIA (1995), *World Fact Book.*

In 1982, thirty-one countries had a military regime; sixteen of these were African. Twenty-seven countries had a one-party system; fourteen of these were located in Africa. In seventeen countries there was a system of personal rule; eight of these were in the Middle East. Military influence is not restricted to countries with a military regime. In one-party states and in systems of personal rule, they usually also play an important role behind the scenes.

In a more recent survey Kidron and Smith (1991) distinguish between military regimes, regimes dominated by the military, and other regimes. A regime dominated by the military is a regime in which civilian institutions are formally restored, but in which real power still lies with the military. Although the subdivisions in the two sources are hard to compare, the number of purely military regimes appears to have decreased since 1982. In 1990 there were only eleven countries with a military regime, compared to thirty-one in 1982. However, another twenty-six countries had a regime that was dominated by the military.

In the 1995 data, the number of military regimes has declined to nine. The latest data do not indicate the number of military dominated regimes, but it should be not too dissimilar to that of 1990. The preliminary 1995 data do suggest a resurgence of democratic multiparty systems. Seventeen of the thirty African states have recently had their first multiparty elections.

How democratic all of these political systems really are can only be determined by a closer analysis than is possible here, but the figures probably suggest a too optimistic picture.[13] Multiparty elections in developing countries are often anything but fair and free, corruption and electoral manipulation are widespread, and the military continue to be an important force behind the scenes. Nevertheless, the data do point to an interesting development. They suggest an unmistakable decline in the legitimacy of various forms of authoritarian rule: one party systems, military dictatorships, and so forth. This trend is most marked in Latin America, but can also be seen in other regions.

Explanations for the important role of the military in the politics of developing countries in the post-war period are of two kinds, having to do with (1) characteristics of societies and political systems; (2) characteristics of the military system.

The complexity of economic and political institutions in advanced industrial societies functions as a constraint to possible military intervention in politics. The lower degree of institutional complexity in many developing countries and the weaker development of other national political institutions allows a greater involvement of

Table 10.2 Political regime in developing countries in 1982 and 1995

	One-party state		Military regime		Personal rule		Restricted parliamentary system		Multiparty democracy		Non-classifiable		Total	
	1982	1995	1982	1995	1982	1995	1982	1995	1982	1995	1982	1995	1982	1995
Africa	14	1	16	8	6	2	3	2	5	30	2	3	46	46
Asia	9	3	4	1	2	2	3	1	5	15		1	23	23
Latin America	1	1	9		1		7		8	24			25	25
Middle East	3	2	2		8	5	3	3	1	6			17	16
Total	27	7	31	9	17	9	15	6	19	75	2	4	111	110

Source: 1982: Kidron and Smith (1983); 1995: CIA (1995).

the military in politics (Finer, 1988). The unstable nature of political systems and their inability to accommodate sectional interests peacefully creates a political climate in which military intervention becomes thinkable. However, as societies and economies become more complex and differentiated in the course of their development, government by the military becomes more and more difficult. The recent trend towards restoration of civilian governments in Latin America seems to fit this line of reasoning. Military regimes in countries such as Brazil and Argentina proved unable to pursue effective economic policies in an increasingly complex economic environment, and they ended up relinquishing their power to civilian regimes.

The second category of explanatory factors refers to characteristics of military institutions themselves. First, the military have control over the means of violence. Potentially, this allows them to play a political role. Secondly, the military are a subsector of society, which is, in certain respects, more 'modern' than other subsectors (Shils, 1964; Bienen, 1971; Janowitz, 1981; Finer, 1988). For example, in Latin America in the 1920s, military officers had higher levels of education than comparable groups in civilian society (Philip, 1985). The military have access to modern technologies, and modern communications and means of transport. They have a modern hierarchical and centralized organization structure, a tradition of internal discipline and a strong corporate spirit.

The self-image of military officer classes is one of standing above the daily wear and tear of politics, political parties and interest groups. They see themselves as the ultimate safeguard of national interests. The military outlook involves an element of puritanism and a measure of contempt for the corruption, indecisiveness and decadence which the military associate with civilian rule (Janowitz, 1981). Thus the military come to see themselves as a factor contributing to the modernization of society and to economic development (Bienen, 1971). Examples of this attitude can be found, for example, amongst members of military elites in Argentina, Brazil, Chile, Indonesia, Pakistan, Thailand and South Korea.

The takeover of power by the military often takes the form of a coup d'état against the civilian government. To justify their intervention in politics, the military can appeal to deep-seated popular feelings of resentment concerning corruption in politics. Of course, this does not necessarily mean that military regimes are any less corrupt than their civilian predecessors. In Latin America the alleged or real threat of left-wing revolutionary movements often served as a justification for military takeovers. A third motive for intervention is the protection of the autonomy of the army against interference by civilian politicians (Philip, 1985). Sometimes, the military reacted to cuts in military expenditures, sometimes to attempts to politicize the military forces, and sometimes, to attempts to introduce political patronage by controlling the recruitment of officers. Finally, factions in civilian politics sometimes actively sought the support of the military in their rivalry with other factions and parties.

In South America the military have played an important role in politics since 1822. During the first years of political independence, *caudillos* competed for power, frequently leading informal armies. Later the officers' corps was professionalized through the establishment of military academies. Politicians hoped that professionalization would contribute to a more neutral army. Compulsory military service was introduced for the recruitment of common soldiers. Officers originated from a single class of landowners, and formed an internally homogeneous and highly united group of professionals. Professionalization helped differentiate military institutions from civilian institutions and society. According to Philip (1985), by 1920 the military were one of the best-organized forces in society. They were highly trained and felt isolated from and superior to civilians.

Between 1922 and 1932 there was a wave of military coups d'état in South America, partially as a result of the collapse of civilian governments during the great depression. Vargas came to power in Brazil, Peron in Argentina, Benavides in Peru, Terra in Uruguay. Even in Chile, with its tradition of civilian government, Ibanez became the military president from 1927 to 1932. Sometimes with interruptions, elsewhere continuously, military regimes ruled Latin America until the 1980s. The longest period of military rule was in Argentina where regimes controlled by the military stayed in power from 1930 until the inauguration of Alphonsin in 1983. Some military regimes – like that of Juan Peron – pursued populist policies with which they tried to win the support of the poor masses in the city and the trade unions.

Military coups, however, do not lead to more stable governments. Once the legitimacy of civilian government has been eroded, the military coup may give rise to a succession of military coups. Usually, military governments are as much affected by corruption as civilian governments. Again and again dissatisfied groups emerge, often from the lower military ranks, attempting to take over power by force.

Luttwak (1979) presents an overview of the total number of military coups in developing countries from 1945 to 1977. All in all, there have been 271 attempted coups, 147 of these were successful and 124 unsuccessful. In Africa there were 98 attempted coups, of which 44 were successful. In Latin America 95 coup attempts took place, of which 57 were successful.

Another estimate by Finer (1988) for the period between 1962 and 1980 comes to a total of 152 coups. In 1980 there were thirty-seven countries in which the government had come to power through a coup d'état, and 25 per cent of all independent states had a military government. Military regimes ruled over 55 per cent of the Latin American population and almost two-thirds of the population of the Arab states in North Africa and the Middle East. Similar figures obtain for sub-Saharan Africa (Finer, 1988).[14] Ghana tops the list with 5 successful coups, 6 attempted coups and 13 political conspiracies, between 1965 and 1985 (Fosu, 1992).

Table 10.3 presents recent data on successful coups since 1945; unsuccessful coup attempts are not included here. Due to differences in definitions, the number of successful coups for the period until 1977 is higher than in Luttwak (198 versus 147). In this table, too, political instability is highest in Africa and Latin America. The average number of coups per year is significantly lower in the second period than in the first (3.7 per year versus 6.0 per year).

Table 10.3 Successful coups in developing countries, 1945–1990

	1945–1977	1978–1990	1945–1990
Africa	64	26	90
Asia	28	7	35
Latin America	76	14	90
Middle East	30	1	31
Total	198	48	246

Sources: Data made available by de Haan and Siermann (1993). Original source Luttwak (1979), Taylor and Hudson (1972), Taylor and Jodice (1983), Banks (various issues), Steinberg (various issues).

10.4.5 One-party states

Another characteristic of political systems in developing countries is the frequent occurrence of one-party states in the post-war period. In 1982 there were twenty-seven one-party states throughout the world, fourteen of which were in Africa (see Table 10.2). In a one-party state the ruling party professes to be the personification of national aspirations and tries to channel all political activity within the party. Thus, the party integrates trade unions, youth movements, women's movements, and so on.

Communist countries like China, Vietnam, Laos and Cuba are good examples of one-party states. In such political systems the military are subordinate to the primacy of politics, even when individual military men fulfil important political functions. The party organization penetrates all sections of the military organization. The line between one-party systems and multiparty democracies is not always easy to draw. For instance, India has a well-functioning parliamentary system of government. Nevertheless, until very recently the Congress Party had been in power continuously since 1947.

The rapid rise of one-party states in Africa after independence is quite striking. Initially, Western-style parliamentary institutions were introduced in most countries after the proclamation of independence. However, before long, all power was taken over by a single party, usually under the leadership of a charismatic leader who had played an important role in the struggle for independence. Other parties were forbidden or subsumed under the dominant party. It is interesting to note that the transition from parliamentary systems to one-party states was not restricted to countries that became independent in the immediate post-war period, but also occurred in countries which gained their independence in the late 1970s, like Angola, Mozambique and Zimbabwe.

There are several possible explanations for the rise of one-party states in Africa (Coleman and Rosberg, 1964; Zolberg, 1966).

1. The legacy of centralized, bureaucratic and authoritarian colonial rule.
2. The tribal and ethnic heterogeneity of many of the new states. In the absence of traditions of national identification, political party organization often followed

ethnic dividing lines. Political opposition was regarded as a threat to the unity of the state.

3. Strong one-party states were considered indispensable for the realization of national integration between regional and tribal groupings and the creation of bonds between new national political elites and an electorate with little sense of national identification.
4. In the struggle for independence one movement usually emerged as the most powerful or influential. This movement would obtain an 'aura of legitimacy' for its contributions in the struggle for independence (Coleman and Rosberg, 1964, p. 658). As political movements were generally weakly developed, the first nationalist movements would acquire a decisive head start. At an early stage, they were recognized as discussion partners by colonial rulers in search of representatives of the population with whom they could negotiate (Zolberg, 1966).
5. With respect to ideology, there were strong socialist and communist influences on the new political movements. There was a generalized distrust of Western economic and political institutions. This is hardly surprising since both markets and Western political institutions were associated with colonial oppression. Communist ideology in particular provided a powerful underpinning to the notion of a one-party state.
6. In many countries, leaders genuinely felt that they needed to find alternatives to Western capitalist solutions and that they had to search for a new synthesis between traditional African political institutions and modern political institutions. Sometimes attempts were made to anchor the dominant political party in village meetings, urban district meetings, or other base level groupings (e.g. youth groups, women's groups) who sent delegates to higher branches of the party. Worsley interprets the 'African socialism' of leaders like Julius Nyerere in Tanzania, Léopold Senghor in the Ivory Coast, and Sékou Touré in Guinea as a variant of 'populist ideologies' of rural populations threatened by the penetration of industrial and financial capital (Worsley, 1967, p. 118 ff.).
7. Internal instability and external political interference reinforced the tendency towards the establishment of one-party states.

One-party states do not provide for a peaceful transfer of power by means of elections. As a result, the initial idealism of nationalist movements often degenerated into monopolization of power by one ethnic group or even absolute rule by a strong man (see section 10.7). The one-party state became increasingly dependent on military support, or it was overthrown in a military coup. The state itself was increasingly at stake in conflicts between ethnic groups, struggling for control of the state apparatus.

As indicated above, in the 1980s there has been a tendency towards restoration of civilian governments and a (re)introduction of multiparty systems. In most cases this trend was the result of the inability of one-party states and military regimes to cope adequately with the economic and political challenges facing them. In Latin America this trend is unmistakable, in Africa more uncertain. Several African countries have recently held multiparty elections, but the dominant parties of the post-war period find it hard to give up power. They have usually made use of their hold on the government bureaucracy and the means of mass communication in order to gain an advantage in the electoral process. It is too early to say whether the move towards multiparty elections is permanent.

10.4.6 Rapid growth of the public sector

In all developing countries the size of the apparatus of government has increased substantially. Most of the rapid growth of employment in services (see Table 3.7, p. 85) is accounted for by the growth of government employment. This has much to do with the building up of a social infrastructure of education, extension and medical care and with the increased role of the government in the economy during the post-war period.

The new educational systems produced an increased outflow of graduates with firm expectations of a guaranteed job in the public sector. The fear of political turmoil was one of the motives for governments to continue to employ many of these graduates. A government job was also considered as a reward for political loyalty and political services. As the legitimacy of one-party rule and military regimes declined, public employment became an important source of political patronage. This aspect of government would become a serious impediment to the effective functioning of the public sector.

10.4.7 'Soft states'

The debate on the 'soft state' was opened by Nobel prize winner Gunnar Myrdal (1968) in his study, *Asian Drama: An inquiry into the poverty of nations*, dealing with India in particular and Southeast Asian states in general. The term 'soft state' implies that the government does not have the effective instruments to translate policy intentions into actual policy, and to impose binding obligations on its citizens. This situation is caused partly by a lack of legitimacy of political institutions.

Powerful interest groups (e.g. large landowners, civil servants, trade unions, foreign enterprises, members of the high castes) manage to emasculate any policy that runs counter to their interests. For example, in India the legislation on land reform has never really been implemented, in part because at local levels the dominant Congress Party was controlled by landed interests. Further, the rich groups in Latin America and Asia pay little or no income taxes, as there is no effective system of taxation. For its revenues, the government depends on taxes that are easily collected, like taxes on land, agricultural production, or exports and imports. Because of the underdeveloped income tax system, government is continuously threatened by a *fiscal crisis* (O'Connor, 1973). For their financial requirements, governments depend on deficit finance and monetary financing of governmental expenditures. This makes for inflation and economic instability.

There are few feelings of loyalty to the government or the state among the masses of the population. Therefore, it is hard for governments to mobilize the efforts of large groups of people for infrastructural works or community development. Myrdal has a distinct preference for stronger states, like China, which seemed to be more capable of mobilizing their citizens for developmental purposes, but has little regard for the potentially disastrous consequences of flawed policies in strong states. For example, we should remember the casualties of the Great Leap Forward in China between 1958 and 1960 when tens of millions of people died due to forced industrialization and collectivization of the agricultural sector (see Bannister, 1984), and the horrors of the Cultural Revolution between 1966 and 1969 when the Chinese regime persecuted millions of its educated citizens and intellectuals (see Leys, 1978; Chang, 1991).

An interesting characteristic of 'soft states' is the abundance of regulatory instruments in the economic sphere. Myrdal aptly describes how one set of regulations calls forth further regulations. When a government starts restricting imports and controlling financial transactions with foreign countries – as a result of a shortage of foreign exchange – it is forced to develop a licensing system for the establishment of new enterprises or the expansion of existing ones. When government plans determine the prices of inputs and final products, they must also draw up rules to ration and allocate inputs and outputs to enterprises. Subsidizing of some economic enterprises implies that other enterprises do not receive any subsidy. This means that government officials will have to spend part of their time impeding the activities of new enterprises in favour of enterprises that are already being subsidized.

Since it is difficult to devise detailed rules for every conceivable situation, the rules leave considerable latitude for discretionary decisions by officials. This can easily result in arbitrariness and corruption. Large domestic and foreign firms in particular will try to influence key decisions to their own advantage. Since public officials are often underpaid, they are vulnerable to bribery.

Also, in many developing countries with mixed economies there was, until recently, a marked degree of animosity and distrust between the large collective sector and the private sector (e.g. in Peru, Argentina, Mexico and India). This led to even further attempts at regulation of the economy in the name of public interest. At the same time, private enterprises did their best to evade public regulations or to influence them to their advantage. In India the large enterprises were most successful in safeguarding their interests under this regulatory regime – whether by corruption or by other means. One of the explicit objectives of government policy in India was to prevent the rise of monopolies in the private sector. Nevertheless, the concentration ratios in the private sector (i.e. the shares of the largest enterprises in total output) tended to increase. Often the largest enterprises obtained monopolies through their access to licences.

Thus, at many levels of government corruption is the rule rather than the exception. In turn, this reduces the effectiveness of the government, and further undermines civilian faith in government, legal security and the rule of law. From high to low, people turn to patron–client relationships, in which people render each other services and favours, rather than appealing to formal legal rights or procedures. The predictability of government behaviour declines and bureaucracy is replaced by a 'personalist system' in which networks of personal relationships are the determining factor. The most extreme example of a totally corrupt machinery of government was the system of *cronyism* in the Philippines under the regime of Ferdinand Marcos, where huge amounts of public funds and development aid disappeared into private pockets.

10.5 *The role of government in economic development*

With regard to the economic role of the government in development, there is an interesting paradox of a *weak state with heavy tasks*. In the economically advanced countries of today, the role of the state in economic development in the nineteenth century was relatively restricted. The main tasks of government were the maintenance of law and order, the defence of private property and external defence (the so-called night watch state). In comparison, the role of the state in the economic process in today's developing countries is much greater. The demands on the functioning of the state apparatus are much higher. At the same time, the apparatus of government is less well equipped to fulfil these heavier demands.

It is indisputable that the role of government in the economic process has increased, both in poor and in rich countries (Gerschenkron, 1962; Myint, 1980; White, 1984; Maddison, 1986). In *Economic Backwardness in Historical Perspective*, Alexander Gerschenkron (1962) offers an interesting explanation for this phenomenon. As a result of technological development, the required scale of investment is becoming ever larger. The time span between the moment of committing financial resources and the moment an investment starts to yield a return grows longer. Thus it becomes more difficult and risky for individual private enterprises to mobilize the necessary funds for investment. During the Industrial Revolution in eighteenth-century England self-financing by firms was the main source of investment. In nineteenth-century Germany large banks and financial conglomerates (*das Finanzkapital*) together with the government were the institutions which mobilized the necessary funds for investment (see Tilly, 1986). In late nineteenth-century Russia the risks of huge investments in railways and industry had become so large that they were mainly borne by government in cooperation with foreign investors. In Japan the government also played a crucial role in initiating processes of capital accumulation in the industrial sector. Thus, in late development the task of the government is not only to create a favourable environment for private economic activities (legal security, predictability, pacification) but also to help mobilize savings and to act as an investor itself, where private investment is insufficient.

In developing countries, there are some additional considerations. First, it was believed that there was a shortage of entrepreneurship in the private sector. Entrepreneurial classes were weakly developed. There were no groups in the private sector who would generate sufficient investment. The state had to compensate for the shortage of entrepreneurship by acting as an investor itself. Second, there were enormous backlogs with respect to infrastructure, education and health care. Improvements in these fields required additional government efforts. Third, there was a policy goal of accelerated development in order to narrow the gap between rich and poor countries. This also called for a more active role on the part of government. In the Latin American context, this role is sometimes referred to as *developmentalism* (Urquidi, 1993). Notions concerning external effects and complementarities, discussed in Chapter 7, play a central role in this approach.

On the basis of their historical experiences, developing countries associated capitalism, market mechanisms, and international trade with colonialism and foreign oppression. There was a deep distrust of the free market and a search for alternative paths of development. In the post-war years the Soviet Union served as a model of a poor and backward country which had succeeded in industrializing rapidly by means of socialist planning.

10.5.1 The role of the state in economic development: five examples

This section provides illustrations of the role of the state in economic development in a discussion of the developmental experiences of Japan, China, Brazil, South Korea and India.

Japan

The government played an extremely important role in the economic development of Japan after the Meiji restoration in 1868 (Maddison, 1969; Pilat, 1994). The feudal system based on landownership by samurai, daimyo and the shogun was abolished (the shogun alone owned about one-fourth of all land). The large landowners were compensated with government obligations and were encouraged to invest their financial resources in industry. Land was redistributed to the actual cultivators, on whom land taxes were imposed. The financial system was reformed, and compulsory education was introduced in 1872.

The government played a decisive role in the process of industrialization, with investments in the military industry, shipbuilding and heavy industry. The government share in total investment was high. A pattern developed in which the government took the initiative for large-scale investments in industry. Once these industries started to function, they were sold off to the private sector. Large-scale investments were also made in the Japanese colonies (Korea, Taiwan, Manchuria). The government stimulated the growth of modern, very large industrial conglomerates (*zaibatsu*) that maintained strong ties with the government.

The Japanese government pursued an active policy of research and development. Foreign investments were impeded, but Japan managed to obtain technological know-how by inviting foreign scientists and technical specialists and by organizing study tours to Western countries.

Traditionally, the government paid a great deal of attention to schooling, education and technological development. Both agricultural growth and participation in international trade were promoted at an early stage. In agriculture, a lot of attention was paid to the linkages between agricultural and industrial development. During recent decades, however, overprotection of agriculture has led to increasing inefficiencies in this sector (van der Meer and Yamada, 1990).

In the Japanese model of industrialization, it is not quite clear whether government sets the course for private enterprise or whether private enterprise determines the direction of public policy. Rather, there was an intensive interaction between public and private sector. The government actively pursued an industrialization policy in which key industries with bright prospects were identified and supported. 'Sunset' industries were drastically cut back.

The Japanese industrial sector has a dual structure with small labour intensive, market-oriented firms acting as subcontractors for large, capital intensive firms pursuing long-term strategic objectives. Until recently these large companies offered their employees *lifetime employment*. In such a dual structure many of the risks of economic fluctuations are shifted to the small labour-intensive enterprises operating on the market.

The rapid economic and industrial development of Japan is an example of industrialization and modernization imposed from above (Moore, 1967). Members of the feudal class of samurai took control of the state apparatus during the Meiji reforms and took the initiative in transforming and modernizing the entire economy and society. In this process the commercial middle classes played a less important role than they did earlier in European history.

China

In communist China the role of the government in industrialization and economic development was even greater than in Japan. After the 1949 revolution all industrial enterprises were brought under public ownership. Large-scale land reforms were implemented. The land of large landowners was nationalized without compensation and redistributed among the peasants. After that, the agricultural sector was collectivized step by step, starting with voluntary cooperatives in the early 1950s and ending with the establishment of immense communes, sometimes involving over a million people in 1958–60 (Hsu, 1982). Initially, economic policy followed the example of the Soviet Union. The emphasis was on the development of heavy industries. In Marxist terminology this branch was referred to as 'Sector I': the production of machines to produce machines.

National five-year plans were introduced in which the physical production goals for all industries were laid down and industries were allocated predetermined amounts of inputs. These plans had been based on input–output models with fixed technical coefficients and a complete elimination of price mechanisms. Just like Japan, China succeeded in realizing a high level of savings. All investment was done via the public sector.

A difference compared with Soviet Russian development is that China paid more attention to agriculture. To be sure, agriculture was allocated a relatively modest part of total investment compared with heavy industry (Kitching, 1982). Still the rural population was successfully mobilized for large-scale infrastructural works like land reclamation, terracing, road construction and irrigation works (see Rawski, 1979; Hsu, 1982).

Although the land reforms initially provided the communist regime with a degree of legitimacy amongst the peasant population, the collectivization of agriculture eventually turned out to be a great failure. Links between effort and reward were completely severed. In 1978 a liberalization of the agricultural sector commenced, which led to an explosive growth in agricultural production. Simultaneously, inefficiency in the industrial sector was on the increase.

It seems possible – albeit often at great human and economic cost[15] – to build up a basic industrial sector by means of central planning and collective mobilization of savings. At later stages of industrial development, however, the planning system seems to be too inflexible to respond to differentiated and varying consumer needs.

Since the mid-1980s attempts are being made in China to gradually liberalize industry as well. This is not done by privatizing existing large public enterprises, but rather by permitting the rise of new market-oriented enterprises and by stimulating foreign investment. The past decade has seen very rapid growth of industrial production (Szirmai and Ren, 1995), but the performance of the public sector industries is still lagging behind. It is not clear whether the state-owned basic industries would be able to survive if exposed to open market competition. At present no moves are being made to privatize this sector of the economy, because of fear of the employment consequences of privatization.

Brazil

Brazil is a well-known example of a country that pursued a strong policy of import substituting industrialization (Furtado, 1976; Maddison *et al.*, 1992). Brazilian economic policy has sometimes been characterized as *state capitalism*.

From the mid-nineteenth century revenues from agricultural exports, in particular coffee, created a domestic market for industrial consumer goods. Political power, however, was controlled by agricultural oligarchies to whom industrialization was of little interest. A new phase of economic development began in 1930 when Getulio Vargas came to power after a military coup d'état. During this period, export prices of primary products fell and the flow of imports from Europe dried up. The government chose to pursue a strong policy of import substitution which protected Brazilian industries against foreign competition. This was realized by means of exchange rate policy, rationing and the allocation of foreign currencies, import tariffs on consumer goods, and subsidies on investment. Just like in Japan, private and public interests were entwined, with the government itself acting either as an investor or as a partner in joint ventures. A characteristic of Brazilian economic policy is its relative openness to foreign investment. Foreign investors often formed *joint ventures* with domestic private companies and public enterprises. Many of these joint ventures acquired monopolies on the protected domestic market.

A populist industrialization strategy was pursued in which the political elites maintained ties with organized labour. Industrial workers got preferential treatment over the rural population. Workers were organized into a kind of corporative state unions, which served among other things to control the production factor labour.

There was some degree of planning of economic activity and a high degree of state participation in investment. There were large government investments in the mining sector. Macroeconomic policy was highly expansionary. Growth was given precedence over macroeconomic stability and controlling inflation.

Between 1929 and 1980 Brazil (together with Mexico) ranked among the fastest growing economies in the world. Within a relatively brief period of time, Brazil succeeded in establishing a diversified industrial sector. Because of the great income inequality the poor benefited little from the economic growth. But even critics of the Brazilian economic miracle must admit that the poor suffered more from the economic stagnation of the 1980s, than from the unequally distributed growth in earlier decades.

After 1980 the shortcomings of Brazilian economic policy became manifest. Prolonged protection of domestic industry had resulted in great inefficiencies, inflexibilities and low levels of capacity utilization. The industrial sector was too inward-looking and had not succeeded in penetrating foreign markets. Macroeconomic instability increased, inflation reached astronomic levels and Brazil proved to be incapable of servicing its debt. The inflow of new capital stagnated. Currently, Brazil is faced with the dual challenge of stabilizing its economy and at the same time engaging in deregulation and privatization of part of the large public-owned sector of the economy. The economic problems facing the country are not incomparable to those of the former centrally planned economies in Eastern Europe.

South Korea

South Korea is another example of an economy where the state played a large role in the process of industrialization (Amsden, 1989; Pilat, 1994). According to Amsden and Pilat, government policy has been of crucial importance in the process of accelerated growth that has taken place in South Korea since 1953. In many respects, the role of the government in South Korea is similar to that in Brazil and Japan. The government actively participated in planning industrial activities through subsidies, credit facilities, protectionist tariffs, price controls and public investment. The government taxed the middle classes, without offering much in the way of social services for broad groups in the population. This provided the government with abundant financial means for investment. It encouraged the establishment of very large industrial conglomerates (*chaebol*).

Like Brazil, South Korea experienced a period of import substitution during which the domestic industry was protected against foreign competition. The difference with Brazil is that the South Korean government started to support and subsidize export-oriented activities as early as the 1960s. Government policy stopped discriminating in favour of firms that produced for the domestic market. Another difference is the far greater degree of discipline involved in subsidizing private companies. The government consistently refused to bail out large companies in financial difficulties. Weakly performing sectors of industry were forced to restructure. Subsidies and other kinds of government support were made dependent on performance criteria in terms of production growth, increase in productivity and penetration into export markets.

According to Amsden's – not undisputed – interpretation, the government succeeded in identifying potentially successful branches of activity and supported these by means of subsidies and price policies. The government pursued a policy of 'getting prices wrong' in order to stimulate investments which would be profitable in the long run. This meant that short-term prices deviated from free-market prices. In the long term the policy was market-oriented, because only efficiently producing enterprises would receive continued support. Monopolistic price-fixing by large conglomerates was not allowed. The outward orientation of industrial policy meant that South Korean products had to be competitive in international markets. Amsden points to a possible relationship between the authoritarian nature of the 'strong' South Korean state and the success of its economic policy. However, she sees no reason why a 'strong' state should not be compatible with political democracy (Amsden, 1989, p. 18). She does not elaborate further on this optimistic conclusion.

India

After the attainment of independence in 1947, India pursued economic development in accordance with a model referred to as *Indian socialism* (Maddison, 1974; Cassen, 1978; Bardhan, 1984). This model had some typical characteristics. On the one hand, it emphasized the development of traditional crafts, like spinning, weaving and small-scale industry in the tradition of Mahatma Gandhi. In this respect, policy tried to build on traditional Indian patterns of craft production. Home-spun clothing even became the symbol of the Indian struggle for independence. On the other hand, Jawaharlal Nehru strove to establish heavy industry along the lines of the Soviet planning model. Physical production objectives were laid down in a series of five-year plans. Socialism was to be realized by means of huge government investments in heavy industry. It was believed that the required volume of investment exceeded the capabilities of the private sector. Especially in the second five-year plan from 1956–61, heavy industries were given high priority. The private sector was allowed to continue its operations, but a rapidly expanding apparatus of government tried to control and regulate private economic activities.

One of the explicit objectives of regulation was to prevent monopolization and the domination of the Indian economy by large foreign investors and large domestic enterprises. Paradoxically, though, the largest companies profited most from government regulation. Through their contacts within the bureaucracy and through corruption, they often succeeded in establishing monopolies or acquiring licences.

The degree of concentration in the economy increased substantially. Smaller companies were not able to make their way through the red tape and the intricacies of government bureaucracies. There were long-standing complaints from the private sector that private entrepreneurs were bound hand and foot by government regulations. Nevertheless, the pressure for change was not very strong, as the largest companies benefited from the niches and monopolies which were the inadvertent consequence of government regulation.

The Indian industrialization model cannot be denied a certain measure of success. India succeeded in building up a diversified industrial infrastructure with a large share of capital goods and intermediate goods in total output. In addition, there were substantial investments in education, research and development. After the mid-1960s, more attention was also paid to agricultural development.

As in China, the establishment of basic industries like steel plants and power stations proved to be possible by means of central planning. In the later stages of industrial development, however, the planning model in India also turned out to be overly inflexible. From the 1970s, industrial development in India stagnated. Production was plagued by industrial unrest, logistic problems and insufficient utilization of capacity. Protectionism was conducive to inefficiency.

The emphasis on the capital goods industry required high levels of production in other sectors of the economy in order to generate sufficient demand for capital goods. But, domestic purchasing-power was insufficient to create a growing market for consumer goods industries – in part, due to low income levels in the agricultural sector. Indian industries were not sufficiently competitive for international markets. The protection of the traditional craft production also involved great waste, as these activities were not viable without protection. Furthermore, distrust of foreign investors reduced the inflow of foreign capital. In comparison with other Asian countries, growth of the Indian economy in the post-war period has been sluggish.

According to Bardhan (1984), the economic problems were caused especially by the fact that government policy was insufficiently insulated from the influence of powerful interest groups, as the legitimacy of government acquired in the struggle for independence was gradually eroded. Political contradictions between agricultural interests, the interests of professionals within the civil service and the interests of industrial capital, paralyzed government policy. They channelled government spending into wasteful direct and indirect subsidies that had to keep the different interest groups satisfied. The mobilization of investable financial resources – in itself fairly successful – led to government consumption, rather than more government investment. Bardhan sees declining public investment as an important explanation for the slow down in industrial growth in the 1960s and 1970s.

Another characteristic of Indian socialism was the strong emphasis on equality and land reform. The rhetoric of egalitarianism, however, had few consequences in practice. Through their hold on the Congress Party at local levels, powerful landed interests succeeded in frustrating the implementation of land reform measures. Despite a policy of preferential recruitment of untouchables and other underprivileged groups, the highly inegalitarian caste system remained extremely influential. In India there has been much talk about 'democratic planning' from the bottom up. In practice, however, there has been little participation of the population in the process of economic planning.

Since the mid-1980s, India has also participated in the worldwide trend towards deregulation, strengthening of market incentives and a reduction of the role of the government in the economy. The tensions between the public sector and the private sector are increasingly regarded as one of the impediments to economic development and an increased inflow of foreign investment. Many observers attribute the relatively slow economic growth in India – compared with other Asian economies such as Korea, Malaysia, Thailand, Indonesia and Taiwan – to the negative influences of a cumbersome and ineffective apparatus of a government with great discretionary powers and a considerable degree of corruption.[16]

These five examples illustrate that the role of the government in recent processes of industrialization has been larger than previously in history – irrespective of political system or ideology. They also illustrate that overprotection of domestic production and the elimination of economic incentives for efficient production and allocation result in economic stagnation. In the 1990s the orthodox feeling is that the role of the state should be reduced, that economies should be deregulated, and that economies should be more exposed to national and international competition. Still, opinions are greatly divided on the question of whether and to what extent government itself can function efficiently and in a market-conforming way. Authors like Amsden and Bardhan point to South Korea in order to illustrate the fact that governments can indeed act in a market-oriented manner and can promote efficient and dynamic economic behaviour.

10.6 *Interactions between economic and political developments*

In this section we will discuss briefly three aspects of the relationships between economic and political developments in developing countries: the effects of political instability on economic growth; the effects of both economic growth and stagnation on political instability; and the relationships between authoritarian characteristics of political systems and economic growth.

10.6.1 Political instability and economic stagnation

In section 10.2 I discussed the importance of internal pacification as a prerequisite for economic development. The absence of violence within a state is one of the principal aspects of political stability. Kuznets (1966, p. 451) stresses that a minimum degree of political stability is required for entrepreneurial individuals to be assured of a stable relation between their efforts and their rewards. Only then will they be prepared to invest in future production. Political instability, social unrest and abuse of civil rights hampers long-run capital accumulation. It results in capital flight and a brain drain, with the most skilled and best-educated members of the labour force emigrating in search of better economic opportunities (Fosu, 1992; de Haan and Sierman, 1996). Political instability, whether in the form of political turmoil or unpredictable changes in regimes and governments, causes economic stagnation.

It is not hard to find examples of political conflicts and political instability resulting in economic stagnation: for example, the famines in Ethiopia and Somalia, the total collapse of the economy of Uganda under Idi Amin, and the economic stagnation in countries like Cambodia, Angola and Somalia. In quantitative, comparative studies many researchers observe a negative relationship between indicators of political instability and economic growth. For example, McGowan and Johnson (1984) find a negative correlation between an index of political instability and growth of per capita income in thirty-nine countries in sub-Saharan Africa. Fosu (1992) distinguishes between countries with relatively high political stability and countries with relatively low political stability in sub-Saharan Africa. He comes to the conclusion that, other things being equal, annual economic growth is at least 1 per cent lower in the 'high political instability' countries. In a recent survey de Haan and Sierman (1996) also note a negative correlation between political instability (represented by the frequency of changes of government) and economic growth in sub-Saharan Africa. With respect to Asian countries there is an indirect negative relationship between instability and growth via an investment variable. With respect to Latin America, de Haan and Sierman find no significant relationships.

10.6.2 Economic development and political instability

Just as political stability is a prerequisite for economic development, economic development is one of the prerequisites for political stability. Only when there is economic growth, capital accumulation and an increase in productivity, can an effective government administration be financed and can the government play a mediating role in conflicts between social groups and classes. In economic stagnation, the government is threatened by a fiscal crisis and is forced to take sides in clashes of interest between social classes. This may manifest itself in increased repression of workers, unions, peasants and opposition movements (Anglade and Fortin, 1985). It may also manifest itself in attempts at economic reform, which sometimes alienate the very groups on which a regime relies for support (Skocpol, 1979).

Surprisingly, under certain circumstances economic growth may also give rise to political instability (Terhal, 1992). In accordance with Kuznets's well-known U-curve hypothesis, income inequality tends to increase during the early stages of industrialization and to decrease in later stages (Kuznets, 1955; see also section 7.4.1). As an explanation of the tendency towards increased inequality in early stages of industrialization, Ahluwalia (1976) points to the emergence of a new production factor, capital, with an extremely high productivity. Ownership of and access to this new production factor has a skewed distribution. Thus economic growth leads to increasing inequality between those groups who benefit from the increase in productivity associated with the new factors of production and the groups who do not. Thus growth and industrialization can give rise to political tensions and conflicts.

In the long term, Ahluwalia suggests, these political tensions will result in a certain redistribution of the access to the new production factors and to decreasing inequality.

Terhal emphasizes that such redistribution does not occur automatically. Rapidly increasing inequality may just as well result in escalating political conflict and lasting political instability. Terhal identifies the following two groups as crucial in processes of social conflict.[17]

1. *The mobile but unsatisfied group.* This group includes people whose position has improved economically, but who remain unsatisfied.
2. *The stagnating immobile group.* This includes a considerable group of poor people whose position remains more or less stagnant.

The groups that experience economic improvement in absolute and relative terms may still be dissatisfied, if their aspirations to achieve equal footing with older ruling elites are frustrated. The groups whose economic situation remains unchanged in absolute terms, may accept increasing inequality for quite a long time. They hope that sooner or later they will enjoy the same social and economic improvements that they can see other groups enjoying at present.[18] However, if such expectations remain unfulfilled for too long, a dramatic switch may take place in which acquiescence and hope are replaced by extreme frustration (Hirschman, 1973). When both these forms of frustration and dissatisfaction occur simultaneously, a politically explosive situation can arise, especially when economic dividing lines coincide with ethnic or geographic divisions.

According to Terhal, political elites can try to mitigate social tensions by co-opting the economically rising groups and increasing their access to political power and social status. At the same time, a regime can increase its legitimacy amongst the poor masses, who are not profiting much from economic growth, by a process of political democratization. Terhal quite rightly observes, by the way, that the political tensions associated with economic growth will be even deeper in conditions of economic stagnation.

In conclusion, it can be stated that political instability may result from economic growth as well as from economic stagnation. In the literature on social conflict there is no consensus on the question whether political instability is greatest under circumstances of rapid growth, declines in the rate of growth or straightforward economic stagnation (see Szirmai, 1988, chapter 9). Under present circumstances, continued economic stagnation would seem to be the most important threat to political stability in many developing countries.

10.6.3 Is there a relation between authoritarian regimes and economic development?

A review article by Sirowy and Inkeles (1990) summarizes the ongoing debate on the relation between democratic regimes and economic growth. One position states that there is a degree of tension between democratic institutions and the requirements of economic development in developing countries, especially in the case of late industrialization. A policy aimed at capital accumulation and rapid economic growth cannot be too democratic since accumulation and a sober macroeconomic policy require sacrifices a poor population can hardly be expected to make voluntarily. Long-term economic growth can only be achieved if the political system can be insulated from the short-term wishes of the people. Examples of countries with more or less autocratic regimes that achieved high economic growth rates include China, Indonesia, Taiwan, Thailand and South Korea. Bardhan (1984) blames slow economic growth in India on the political regime's incapacity to insulate itself sufficiently from the influences of interest groups. O'Donnell (1979) argues that bureaucratic authoritarian regimes are most capable of meeting the challenges of late industrialization. These challenges include, among other things, pursuing an import-substitution policy, building up intermediate and capital goods industries, achieving political predictability and stability, and pursuing sober macroeconomic policies. From this perspective, economic growth should precede political democratization.

Other authors defend the thesis that political democratization, civilian freedoms and economic growth have historically reinforced each other. Political pluralism is a prerequisite for economic pluralism and the flowering of entrepreneurship – in developing countries as well. Scully (1988) states that between 1960 and 1980 open societies with political civilian and economic freedoms grew three times as fast as societies in which these freedoms were restricted. There are many examples of authoritarian regimes that continued to pursue ineffective or harmful economic policies, in part due to the absence of democratic checks and controls. This assumption is embedded in present foreign policies of Western countries and international institutions when they include political democratization and improved observance of human rights as conditions for financial support and trade advantages.[19]

Quantitative empirical research has not yet resulted in any consensus about these questions. Studies contradict each other, depending on the definitions used, the time span covered, the sample of countries included and the research methods employed. The complexity of the debate is increased by the fact that protection of private property and a market economy (indicators of economic freedoms) may well coexist with the absence of any form of political democracy. Sirowy and Inkeles conclude that there is no support for the hypothesis that political democracy leads to more rapid economic growth. There are just as many studies claiming that there is no significant relation between democracy and growth, as there are studies claiming that there is a negative relationship between these two factors.

This debate, however interesting, does not do sufficient justice to the fact that democratization and the observance of human rights are of crucial importance as independent objectives of development, irrespective of their economic significance.

10.7 *The state as an obstacle to economic development*

In previous sections we saw that the role of the government in developing countries may be more important today than previously in history. Also, several issues have been raised with regard to the functioning of the apparatus of government and the political process in developing countries. In this section we take a closer look at the position of a number of authors (Sandbrook and Barker, 1985; Jackson and Rosberg, 1986; Sandbrook, 1986) who claim that in sub-Saharan Africa the state itself has become an obstacle to economic development.

According to Sandbrook and to Jackson and Rosberg, many African states are characterized by a system of *personal rule*. Personal rule is the answer of the political leaders to the question of how to rule predominantly rural populations, only marginally integrated into national markets and national societies, under conditions in which national political institutions have little legitimacy. Since independence, the various ethnic groups have few feelings of loyalty towards the central state apparatus. National borders have little to do with ethnic and cultural dividing lines. Often the effective control of the state over its territory only exists in name. Under such circumstances, it is hardly surprising that parliamentary institutions and multiparty systems never took root, and the state adapted itself to the particularist norms of a multi-ethnic society.

Colonial bureaucracies were very small and had limited tasks. The higher positions in the administration were all filled by European expatriates. Middle positions in the civil service, commerce, trade and industry were predominantly occupied by members of minorities: Lebanese, Syrians and Indians. After the achievement of independence, government bureaucracies were rapidly Africanized and simultaneously expanded, in spite of the initially inadequate supply of trained and experienced officials. Bureaucratic characteristics of the civil service were soon diluted and replaced by networks of personal relations, which Sandbrook, and Jackson and Rosberg refer to as *neopatrimonialism*[20] or *personal rule*. The administration was commercialized. Officials exploited their positions for financial returns. Political leaders used public funds for private purposes and for those of friends, family and clients. The political classes lived in relative luxury, financed among others by bribes from foreign companies in return for trading concessions. According to Rosberg and Jackson (1986, p. 23), Mobutu, lifetime head of state of Zaire, used 150 million dollars from the central bank for private ends between January 1977 and March 1979, while in the period 1979–83 under Shehu Shagari's democratically elected government of Nigeria, between 5 and 7 billion dollars were appropriated by government officials,

Personal rule has the following characteristics:

1. A strong man (the ruler, often the president). The person of the ruler is identified with the nation. All strategic positions within the political system, the government bureaucracy, the police force and the military are occupied by individuals who are personally loyal to the ruler. These individuals are usually recruited from the ethnic group of the political ruler.
2. Patron–client relationships running through the entire apparatus of government, from top to bottom. At all levels individuals maintain and strengthen their positions by granting personal favours to loyal clients in the form of jobs, use

of government funds and opportunities for corruption and enrichment. In return for political favours the private sector is expected to reciprocate.
3. Armed forces that are personally loyal to the political ruler.

Due to these characteristics, the young African states lack the capabilities to create the conditions for capital accumulation. The economic rationality of state actions is low. The government administration and the public enterprises (*parastatals*) are characterized by mismanagement, inefficiency and widespread corruption. An impersonal, predictable and bureaucratically rational functioning of the state apparatus becomes impossible.

Public means are squandered and entrepreneurial efficiency is discouraged. Easy profits can be made by political manipulation. Much human creativity and entrepreneurial talent is directed at manipulating the political system in order to obtain subsidies, licences and market monopolies. Rent-seeking behaviour comes in the place of economic efficiency and the search for economically productive investment opportunities. Foreign companies make their investments dependent on government-guaranteed monopolies.

Personal rule is usually an unstable form of political organization. Mostly, the ruler depends on a single ethnic group to maintain his power. This group profits from the control of the apparatus of government to the exclusion of other groups. Other groups are prone to resort to violent opposition. Coups d'état and military revolts are quite common. The strong men seek military and financial support from foreign powers. Their opponents do the same, soliciting support from competing foreign powers to the further detriment of political stability.

The state is in an almost permanent fiscal crisis. The need for revenues to maintain the system of patronage is high. Wealthy citizens succeed in evading income taxes. For their financial requirements, governments are forced to impose heavy taxes on peasants, exports and imports. The agricultural marketing boards (discussed in Chapter 9) are also used for such purposes. In some countries (e.g. Uganda under Idi Amin), the financial burdens imposed on the peasants were so heavy that they withdrew from the official market economy, started trading on parallel black markets or even moved back to subsistence production. This eroded the tax base even further.

According to Sandbrook, personal rule prevailed in most African countries in the early 1980s. The exceptions were militant socialist states such as Angola or Tanzania, where socialist ideology provided a degree of legitimacy. Sandbrook stresses the fact that political systems in Africa, as elsewhere, also show considerable variation. There are relatively strong states – Botswana, the Ivory Coast, Cameroon, Kenya, Malawi and Senegal – and extremely weak states – Chad, Ghana, Nigeria, Somalia and Zaire.[21] Moreover, he emphasizes quite rightly (especially in Sandbrook and Barker, 1985), that the roots of the economic crisis in sub-Saharan Africa are manifold and not limited to politics. Factors contributing to economic problems include the unfavourable international economic environment, the scarcity of natural resources, poor soil conditions, sustained droughts and rapid population growth. These factors interact with state formation processes. Economic stagnation leads to greater malfunctioning of government institutions. Characteristics of the state apparatus may result in further economic stagnation, resulting in a downward spiral.

Given the characteristics of state and politics in sub-Saharan Africa, Sandbrook argues in favour of a more limited role for the public sector in the economy. This would leave more scope for a healthy development of the private sector. The government should concentrate on a selected number of key issues only. Reducing the size of the public sector is not enough.[22] The effectiveness of the smaller government apparatus has to be increased if the state is to contribute to the conditions for successful capital accumulation. Further, the government and the political system should try to regain some legitimacy in the eyes of the people. The very recent trend towards more multiparty elections (see Table 10.2) should be seen in this light.

The key question remains, however, whether the political conditions are ripe for reform and whether there is a real political will to move from systems of neopatrimonial personal rule to systems of impersonal bureaucratic management and effectively functioning administration. The challenge of a policy of political structural adjustment is just as great as that of economic structural adjustment.

10.8 *Evaluation: the economic role of government in developing countries*

In conclusion to this chapter, a few remarks are in order concerning the future role of the state in the economy:

1. Reduction of the dominant role of the state in the economic process seems advisable. Regulation of the private sector, which gives rise to misallocation of scarce resources, should be diminished. Government protection of inefficient domestic industries should not be continued indefinitely. Structural adjustment is not only an economic recipe: it also involves reorganization of the political system.
2. The effectiveness of the apparatus of government should be increased. The government should take on less economic tasks and execute the remaining tasks more effectively. When corruption impedes the normal execution of government functions, privatization of these functions should be considered. An example of this is provided by the delegation of customs activities in Indonesia to a Swiss company. Key functions of government are increasing political stability, preservation of internal peace and order, and increasing the predictability of the economic processes. Stability and predictability are preconditions for increased investment and capital accumulation in the private sector.
3. Nevertheless, the role of the state in the economic process will be greater than was previously the case in earlier periods of economic history. Even the critics of political systems in developing countries, like Sandbrook, are agreed on this. The state retains important tasks with respect to investment in infrastructure, schooling, health care, environmental protection, promotion of agricultural

research and development, organization of agricultural education, promotion of industrial research and development – also for the benefit of small-scale industries – and improvement of the urban infrastructure. In addition, the state still has a role in mobilizing investment and functioning as a negotiating partner for powerful foreign investors.

4. Following the example of Southeast Asian states, developing country governments should not continue to protect inefficient enterprises indefinitely. Government policies should be more in conformity with market signals. They should stimulate those activities in the private sector which are successful on national or international markets (see World Bank, 1993).

QUESTIONS FOR REVIEW

1. Provide definitions of the concepts of state, nation, society and nation-state. Give examples of states which are not nation-states and nations which are not nation-states.
2. Discuss the differences between the Marxist and the Weberian perspectives on the role of the state in socio-economic development.
3. What are the most important differences between processes of state formation in developing countries and earlier processes of state formation in Western Europe?
4. Why have the military played such a prominent role in politics in many developing countries?
5. Why is the role of the state in economic development in present-day developing countries greater than the role of the state in the development of Western countries in the eighteenth and nineteenth centuries? To what extent is the increased importance of the state a stimulus for or an obstacle to economic development?
6. Analyze the mutual interrelationships between economic growth and political stability or instability.

Notes

1. There is some conceptual confusion about the distinction between 'state' and 'state apparatus'. The term state as used above (e.g. the Dutch state or the Chinese state) refers to the wider social system or society, the common rules of which are established in the political process. These rules are implemented and enforced by a permanent administrative body (the 'state apparatus'). However, elsewhere, for instance in Marxist literature the 'state' is also used to refer to the 'apparatus of government' (which includes the civil service, the army, the police, and such political institutions as the political executive, the head of state, the judiciary, parliament and other representative organs).

2. The terms 'core' and 'peripheral' derive from theories of dependence in which conditions in developing countries are primarily explained by external influences (see section 3.4). The use of these terms, however, does not necessarily imply acceptance of these theories.
3. Since national states are part of networks of international interdependence, autonomy in national decision-making is always a matter of degree. For example, the national autonomy of European countries is constrained by supranational institutions such as the European Union. The latitude for national economic policies in small countries such as the Netherlands or Belgium is determined by developments in the international economy.
4. State in this section refers to the 'state apparatus': government and political institutions (see n. 1).
5. This notion of the state as a neutral arbiter is part of the intellectual tradition of post-war social democracy in Western Europe.
6. In this respect, modern neo-Marxist authors were not only inspired by Marx, but also by his intellectual opponent Weber.
7. The tension between productive capacity and the costs of political expansion in feudal society is also found in much greater empires. It has been well analyzed by authors such as Paul Kennedy (1989), Marc Elvin (1973), and Immanuel Wallerstein (1974). Kennedy uses the term 'imperial overstretch'.
8. Elias does not pay much attention to the role of the clergy in processes of state formation, nor to the protracted conflicts between 'secular' and 'religious' powers. The clergy based part of its social influence on its religious functions. But, the clergy also lived off the revenues of its estates and as such can be seen as belonging to the landed classes.
9. A similar differentiation developed in the economic sphere between the private property of the entrepreneur and the assets of the firm.
10. Van den Berghe (1981) rightly points out that European states did not develop out of stateless societies. Almost all European states developed out of the fragmentation or decentralization of older political entities or empires, or the merging of existing, smaller political entities. That is why I have emphasized both processes of decentralization and centralization. There are also European examples of states whose borders have been determined by external forces, like former Yugoslavia and former Czechoslovakia.
11. From the preceding discussion, it should by now be clear that is difficult to make unambiguous distinctions between external warfare and internal conflicts.
12. This section has been inspired by Goldthorpe's (1979) excellent chapter on political characteristics of states in the poor countries and the literature quoted in Goldthorpe's chapter.
13. It is not clear whether the classification criteria of the 1995 data are identical to those of 1982. So, any conclusions from this table can only be very tentative.
14. These figures exclude regimes which only survive thanks to military backing as in Jordan and Morocco, or regimes where the military have temporarily withdrawn from politics as in Guatemala and the Dominican Republic.
15. Sometimes disastrous mistakes were made, like the attempt at forced industrialization during the Great Leap Forward.
16. Bardhan (1984) gives a similar critical analysis of the role of the government in relative stagnation. However, his conclusions are different. He does not argue in favour of liberalization. Rather he pleads for a more efficient government and an increase in public investment. Bardhan still defends the leading role of government in late industrial development. In his opinion, India should model its behaviour on South Korea and should try to insulate government policy from manipulation by interest groups.
17. In total Terhal identifies four groups: the disadvantaged and impoverished; the stagnating immobile; the mobile satisfied; and the mobile but unsatisfied.
18. Hirschman (1973) calls this the 'tunnel effect'. He draws an analogy with car drivers in a traffic jam before a tunnel: if they see cars moving in the other lane, they hope and

expect that cars in their own lane will also start moving sooner or later.

19. Foreign policies of the Western countries show little consistency in this respect. Sometimes, human rights are emphasized. At others, they are played down when the economic interests of the countries involved are threatened, e.g. in the recent relations between the United States and China in 1995.
20. The term 'patrimonialism' derives from Max Weber (1922) and refers to a form of traditional authority, in which one owes obedience to the person of the ruler, rather than to rules, principles or procedures. Tradition is the prime source of legitimacy and circumscribes the power of the ruler. The term 'patrimonial' refers to the fact that members of the administrative apparatus are recruited from amongst the ruler's family, kin, tribe, etc. Another characteristic is the absence of a distinction between the personal and the public sphere. Neo-patrimonialism or personal rule is a political system in which patrimonial rulers have no constitutional or traditional legitimacy.
21. Uganda, which was high on Sandbrook's list of weak states in the early 1980s, has since then made a remarkable political and economic recovery.
22. According to Sandbrook, the share of the government in the national income in sub-Saharan Africa is not exceptionally large in comparison with other developing countries and with affluent countries. What is rather more crucial in this respect is the regulating nature of government activities.

11 International economic and political relations since 1945

In Chapter 2, the concept of the *international economic order* was introduced. International economic orders are characterized by typical patterns of flows of goods and services, financial capital and people. Other characteristics include the intensity of relationships between economies and the institutional structure of these relationships. It turned out to be difficult to disentangle the political, institutional and economic aspects of international orders. In this chapter I return to a discussion of the international aspects of development. The emphasis will be on developments in international economic relations and their significance for developing countries after 1945. In addition to the economic aspects of the post-war international economic order, I will also deal with the political and institutional aspects such as the international balance of power, international organizations and international conventions and treaties.

This chapter is structured as follows. First, important economic and political characteristics of post-war international relations will be discussed (section 11.1). A brief chronological outline of the development of important international organizations and institutions will be given in section 11.2. In the second half of this chapter, three partly overlapping stages in the development of international relations since 1944 will be identified: the period of liberalization of world trade (1944–1973), the rise and eclipse of the policy goal of a New International Economic Order (1960–1982), and the period of debt crisis and structural adjustment (1982 to the present day). These stages will be discussed both chronologically and thematically. Section 11.3 presents a brief summary of the theoretical argument for free trade. Sections 11.4 to 11.6 summarize the arguments of the critics of free trade and the debates on a New International Economic Order. The debt crisis and its consequences is discussed in section 11.7, and data on international financial flows to and from developing countries are presented. In the concluding section (11.8) attention is given to structural adjustment policies and their consequences.

11.1 *Characteristics of international relations since 1945*

11.1.1 Economic aspects

Important characteristics of the international economic order since 1945 are as follows (Grassman and Lundberg, 1981; Krueger, 1990b; Maddison, 1985; Bhagwati, 1988): rapid growth of international trade; breaking the mould of the colonial pattern of trade; the modest share of developing countries in international trade; financial flows from rich countries to poor countries; liberalization of international trade; and growth of per capita national income in both rich and poor countries.

Rapid growth of international trade

Between 1950 and 1973, international trade increased very rapidly (Bhagwati, 1988; Maddison, 1989). This increase went hand in hand with a strong liberalization of international trade and a reduction of trade restrictions for industrial imports to advanced capitalist countries. In developing countries, which were building up their industrial sectors, industrial protectionism remained the rule.

With respect to agriculture, the advanced economies continued to follow highly protectionist policies in which expensive production by domestic producers was protected against foreign competition and agricultural exports were massively subsidized. Since the mid-1970s, there has been some revival of industrial protectionism in the advanced economies, particularly through non-tariff restrictions on imports. However, there is no question of a return to the protectionism of the pre-war period.

The period of rapid growth of international trade and per capita income between 1950 and 1973 came to an end with the first oil crisis in 1973. After 1973, the growth of world trade slowed down (see Table 11.1). A second dramatic hike in oil prices in 1979 further contributed to the retardation of the growth of the world economy and world trade.

Table 11.1 Growth rate of world exports

1720–1820	0.9
1820–1929	3.5
1929–1950	0.3
1950–1973	7.3
1973–1985	3.2
1985–1993	5.3
1973–1993	4.0

Sources: 1720–1973: Maddison (1982), 254; 1973–1985: IMF (1992); 1993: IMF (1995).

Breaking the mould of the colonial pattern of trade

The colonial pattern of international trade involved an international division of labour. Developing countries exclusively exported primary products and economically advanced countries exported manufactured products. In the post-war period this pattern started changing. The share of industrial products in the total exports of developing countries increased strongly. Certain Southeast Asian countries succeeded in penetrating the European and US markets for industrial products (OECD, 1979). This trend, however, is restricted to a number of rapidly industrializing developing countries. In poor countries in sub-Saharan Africa the share of primary exports still remains high.

A modest share of developing countries in international trade

The expansion of international trade till 1973 was mainly accounted for by the advanced industrial countries (Thoburn, 1977; Bhagwati, 1988). In 1966, the share of these countries in world exports was no less than 71 per cent. The share of the poorest countries in international trade was modest and declined even further between 1960 and 1977 (Lewis, 1978; Streeten, 1984). Between 1973 and 1986 the exports of Latin American and Asian developing countries increased faster than those of OECD countries (Maddison, 1989). Around 1980 the share of advanced industrial countries in world exports had decreased to 66.1 per cent (World Bank, 1987; Bhagwati, 1988).

Financial flows from rich to poor countries

In a reversal of earlier patterns between 1913 and 1950, there was a substantial net inflow of capital to developing countries between 1950 and 1982. This meant that these countries could afford to import more than they exported. Such financial inflows can contribute to the expansion of the productive potential, especially if these resources are used for productive investments in infrastructure and capital goods or for imports of intermediate goods. Using net capital inflows for consumptive purposes or defence expenditures, however, is less conducive to future growth. This pattern of net capital inflows was interrupted after 1982 – as will be shown later on in this chapter. In the years following the debt crisis of 1982 there was a net outflow of financial resources from poor to rich countries.

Liberalization of international trade

In comparison with older international economic orders, there was a high degree of freedom in the trade of goods and services, and in movements of capital. Both trade flows and capital flows increased. Mobility of labour, however, remained restricted.

Growth of per capita national income in rich and poor countries

Between 1950 and 1973, national income and per capita income increased rapidly both in rich and in poor countries. Per capita income in the richer countries increased faster than in poorer countries, so that international disparities also increased. Between 1973 and 1982 the growth of per capita incomes decelerated, particularly in the economically advanced countries which pursued restrictive economic policies. In Asia and Latin America, economic growth continued. In sub-Saharan Africa, it stagnated. If oil-rich Nigeria is left out of consideration, average per capita income declined in this period (Toye, 1993).

After 1982, growth trends in different parts of the world diverged. In the economically advanced countries there was a modest economic recovery, although the growth rates of per capita income remained lower than before 1973. Several large Asian economies experienced extremely rapid economic growth (World Bank, 1993a). Latin America experienced economic stagnation in the aftermath of the debt crisis. In countries such as Argentina and Venezuela per capita incomes decreased on average by 2.5 per cent per year between 1980 and 1989. In Brazil real per capita income was the same at the end of the period as at the beginning (Hofman, 1993). Sub-Saharan Africa experienced long-term stagnation (World Bank, 1989a). On average, per capita income here decreased by 1.6 per cent per year (Elbadawi *et al.*, 1992, p. 35). For Africa and Latin America the 1980s are often considered to be a 'lost decade'.

11.1.2 Political aspects

From a political point of view, decolonization was one of the main characteristics of the period after World War II (Grimal, 1978; Morris-Jones and Fisher, 1980; Emmer, 1992). Between 1945 and 1976 the Asian and African colonies of Great Britain, Belgium, the Netherlands, France, and Portugal achieved their independence. In the Middle East, decolonization mainly took place in the interwar period. Before 1919, regions like Syria, Lebanon, Iraq, Palestine, Kuwait and Jordan had been part of the Ottoman Empire. After World War I, they were ruled as mandates in name of the League of Nations by Great Britain and France (e.g. Lebanon, Syria). Between 1930 and 1947 these mandate territories were granted independence: Iraq in 1930, Syria and Lebanon in 1946, Jordan and Israel in 1947.

The decolonization of Asia took place between 1947 and 1957. India and Pakistan became independent in 1947, Burma in 1948 and Malaysia in 1957. In Vietnam Ho Chi Minh proclaimed independence in 1945 in the wake of the Japanese departure. France, however, was loath to relinquish its authority to a communist-oriented nationalist movement. It waged war against the Viet Minh until it was defeated at Dien Bien Phu in 1954. In the same year Vietnam was partitioned into North and South Vietnam and the question of unification was deferred to the future. The French colonies of Laos and Cambodia also became independent in 1954. In South Vietnam, after 1954, an anticommunist government was strongly supported by the United

States, who waged a full-scale but unsuccessful war to prevent a communist takeover of South Vietnam from within and from North Vietnam. The United States eventually withdrew from Vietnam after the Paris peace agreements of 1973. In 1976 North and South Vietnam were reunited under a communist regime.

On the African continent, decolonization commenced with the independence of Ghana in 1957. Between 1957 and 1980 all African colonies, with the exception of the South African mandate of Namibia, became independent, sometimes after bloody conflicts. The Portuguese colonies of Mozambique, Guinea-Bissau and Angola were the last to gain their independence, which was not recognized until 1976.

Rhodesia (formerly Southern Rhodesia) is a special case. Here white settlers unilaterally proclaimed their independence in 1965 in order to prevent power from passing to representatives of the black population. In 1980, internal resistance and external pressure resulted in a transfer of power to a government under the leadership of Robert Mugabe and the declaration of the independence of the republic of Zimbabwe.

Many processes of decolonization involved bitter struggles. These were often the result of the presence of large numbers of European settlers who fiercely resisted independence. Such was the case, for example, in Algeria, Mozambique, Angola, Rhodesia and Kenya. A second reason for wars of decolonization was when the former colonial powers could not transfer power to the preferred political successors, which was the case in Vietnam, Malacca and the Dutch East Indies (Emmer, 1992).

Some million people of European descent had settled in French Algeria. These settlers, initially together with the French government, opposed the independence movement FNL in a bloody war between 1954 and 1962. In the Portuguese colonies, also, over 800,000 Europeans had settled. They strove to maintain the political ties with their homeland. In general, the decolonization of the British colonies involved less bloodshed than those of other colonizers. Kenya is the exception, here. Between 1952 and 1955 there was violent resistance to British rule on the part of the Mau-Mau movement, in the course of which the British interned 50,000 Kikuyus in camps (Grimal, 1978). British policy was aimed not so much at preventing the independence of Kenya, but rather at safeguarding the privileges of the European settlers.

In Vietnam the French resisted the transfer of power to the communist-oriented nationalist movement Viet Minh. In Burma and Malacca the British government also resisted independence movements, fearing the establishment of communist regimes. In Malacca independence was not granted until 1957 after the threat of communism had diminished. Sukarno proclaimed the independence of the Dutch East Indies on 17 August 1945, on the eve of the Japanese capitulation. The Dutch wars against Indonesian independence were partly inspired by the wish to restore pre-war colonial relations, but also in part by differences of opinion with regard to the political constitution of the future independent state (a federalist solution versus the strong unified state claimed by the leaders of the independence movement). Indonesian military resistance and growing international pressure, especially by the United States, finally resulted in the Netherlands recognizing the independence of Indonesia in 1949.

According to Emmer (1992), decolonization is generally the result of three factors: increasing resistance to foreign rule within colonies; decreasing willingness to rule colonies in the home countries; and international pressure. In the period immediately following World War II not only the Soviet Union but also the United States actively supported the process of decolonization. Later, however, fear of communist regimes in the newly independent states came to play a significant role in US foreign policy. Thus the delayed decolonization of the Portuguese colonies in Africa was not only explained by the dictatorship of Salazar in Portugal, but also by US fears of an expansion of the communist sphere of influence in Africa.

Initially, in the years after World War II, it was assumed that colonial rule was one of the main sources of economic and social underdevelopment. It was widely hoped and expected that decolonization would lead to rapid economic development (Franck and Munangsangu, 1982; Meier, 1984). When this did not materialize quickly, some observers blamed this on neocolonial relations of economic dependence. Disappointing economic outcomes also led to a call for a new and more just international economic order. Since the 1980s the climate of opinion has once again changed. The quality of domestic economic policy in developing countries presently receives more emphasis. This shift of opinion has been influenced by the marked differences in economic performance in developing countries in different parts of the world, which will be discussed in further detail in section 11.8.

Another important characteristic of international relationships in the post-war period is the great increase in the number of international intergovernmental organizations and international treaties. In 1939 there were 80 international organizations, and in 1990 there were 293 (Baehr, 1992). National states founded international organizations to pursue common objectives and to improve international coordination. With the exception of the European Union, these organizations are not supranational. The participating states retain their sovereignty. The coordinating potential of international organizations is limited due to the absence of binding regulatory powers. Their effective functioning is dependent on the voluntary cooperation of sovereign states, and in particular, the economically, politically, and militarily powerful ones.

From an analytical point of view, an important characteristic of the international order is the combination of increasing interdependence of people, societies and states on the one hand and, on the other, a poorly developed capability for international political coordination (Streeten, 1984). International trade has increased strongly. The economies of poor countries have become highly dependent on those of the rich countries. The disappearance of rain forests, the global warming due to the emission of CO_2 gases, damage to the ozone layer by CFCs, radiation risks associated with nuclear power stations and nuclear wastes, all indicate that the ecological consequences of economic activities have now become global. Due to improved transport, international mobility is increasing strongly. As a result of improved communications, the dissemination of new ideas and technologies proceeds more rapidly and cultures are ever more subject to influences from other cultures.

Given this increased interdependence, the capability of international institutions to fulfil a coordinating and regulating role has lagged behind. The creation of a network of international organizations, institutions and treaties may be regarded as a first – uncompleted – step in the direction of international coordination.

One can make a comparison with the formation of national states, as analyzed in the previous chapter. In processes of state formation, political power is centralized by means of internal consolidation or external penetration. Centralization results in a monopoly of the means of violence and, in due time, in some measure of democratization of the control over the state apparatus. There is a process of uniformization in which a national legal system replaces a diversity of local customs and regulations. Laws and regulations are enforced by the state through its monopoly of violence. The state finances its expenditures through its monopoly on taxation.

In world society there is no comparable process of international centralization and pacification. Perhaps the *Pax Britannica* in the nineteenth century came closest to some kind of international centralization. At that time, British economic, military, technical, and cultural hegemony in the world resulted in a long period of relative international and national pacification. This cannot be said for the much shorter period of American dominance since World War II. First, until 1991 the Soviet Union was a rival centre of power. Secondly, decolonization led to a proliferation of independent states in a non-pacified world. Between 1945 and 1976 there have been no less than 104 wars. Between 1945 and 1990 there have been 22 million casualties in wars and internal conflicts (see Chapter 10). Most of the international wars had an East–West dimension.

A factor of political importance in post-war international relations was the founding of the movement of non-aligned countries at the Bandung conference of 1955. This movement received a new impetus when China joined it after its rift with the Soviet Union in 1960. Since 1966, this movement has more or less organized itself in international organizations as the 'Group of 77'. The formation of this bloc was stimulated by the initial success of the cartel of oil producing countries (OPEC) in 1973. Since the 1970s, however, the bloc of developing countries has broken up into a diversity of groups with differing interests (see van Dam, 1984). These include oil-exporting countries, oil-importing countries, newly industrialized countries or regional blocs like the ASEAN, the organization of American States (OAS), and the countries associated with the European Union through the Lomé agreements. The political importance of developing countries as a united bloc has declined substantially.

The period since 1945 is characterized by the rise and decline of the Soviet power bloc and the Soviet sphere of influence, by tensions between rich countries on the northern hemisphere and poor countries on the southern hemisphere, and by tensions between poor countries themselves. Only the direct conflicts between East and West have more or less been pacified as a result of the threat of mutual nuclear destruction. Wars mainly occurred in developing countries. After the disintegration of the Soviet Union, the United States is the only remaining superpower. Nevertheless, at least in the short run, this has not resulted in a more pacified international order.

Despite the lack of an international monopoly of violence, the post-war period has seen several initiatives towards the creation of an international political order and the formation of an international legal order. But these initiatives have been hard to sustain, precisely because there is no centralized monopoly of violence and there are no independent sources of finance for international institutions. The international legal order depends almost entirely on voluntary agreements between sovereign states. They may negotiate international treaties and agree to implement them with help of the organs of the national state. For example, a European agreement to reduce overfishing is implemented by national governments with respect to their own fishermen. Apart from concluding international treaties and conventions, states may also found international organizations and institutions. In some cases they may voluntarily transfer some of their prerogatives to these institutions, as, for instance, in the case of the European Union. Finally, states may voluntarily agree to submit their disputes to international arbitration. Such procedures can crystallize into international common law (Franck and Munansangu, 1982).

The development of an international legal order depends on the voluntary cooperation of national states. If powerful states are not willing to cooperate, international organizations will be paralyzed. If one of the parties involved in a conflict is unwilling to bring this conflict before the International Court of Justice in the Hague, the court is powerless. A well-known example is the US refusal to allow a complaint concerning the laying of mines in Nicaraguan waters to be judged by the International Court. A further problem is the fact that international institutions do not have the independent power to implement their decisions. For example, for many years South Africa ignored UN resolutions concerning the independence of Namibia without suffering any consequences. International organizations are also powerless against large-scale violations of human rights. Only if coalitions of powerful states are prepared to sanction violations of international norms and other powerful states do not oppose them actively, can some decisions of international bodies actually be enforced.

11.2 *International organizations since 1945*[1]

Table 11.2 presents a chronological overview of a series of important international treaties, resolutions and events, which is illustrative of developments in international economic relations since 1944.

Many new international organizations were founded in the post-war period. In this context, it is meaningful to distinguish between a cluster of specialized financial institutions dominated by the rich countries, and the United Nations and its numerous specialized daughter organizations in which decisions are reached by majority vote and developing countries have much more influence on policy (Schrijver, 1985).

The UN family includes the FAO (Food and Agriculture Organization), the UNIDO (United Nations Industrial Development Organization), the UNCTAD (United Nations Conference on Trade and Development), UNESCO (for education, science and culture), UNICEF (the children's emergency fund), the WHO (the World Health Organization), UNITAR (training), the ILO (International Labour Organiz-

Table 11.2 Important international organizations, treaties and conferences, 1944–1995

1944	Bretton Woods Conference: • IMF (International Monetary Fund); • IBRD (International Bank for Reconstruction and Development) (World Bank).
1945	Founding of the United Nations at the San Francisco Conference: • General Assembly; • Security Council; • ECOSOC (Economic and Social Council).
1947	General Agreement on Tariffs and Trade (GATT) signed in Geneva.
1947–1948	Drawing up of the Havana Charter for the International Trade Organization (ITO).
1948	Founding of the Organization of American States (OAS).
1949	Founding of the North Atlantic Treaty Organization (NATO).
1949	Second round of GATT negotiations on tariff reductions (Annecy).
1951	Third round of GATT negotiations on tariff reductions (Torquay).
1955	Founding of the movement of non-aligned countries at Bandung.
1955	GATT gets a permanent status.
1955	Founding of the Warsaw Pact.
1956	Fourth round of GATT negotiations on tariff reductions (Geneva).
1956	Founding of the International Finance Corporation (IFC), a subsidiary of the World Bank for the stimulation of private foreign investment in developing countries.
1957	Signing of the treaty of Rome: founding of the European Economic Community (EEC) by six states: Belgium, the Federal Republic of Germany, France, Italy, Luxembourg and the Netherlands.
1960	Founding of the International Development Association (IDA), a subsidiary organization of the World Bank: this organization issues soft loans to developing countries.
1960–1961	GATT: Dillon Round.
1961	Founding of the Organization for Economic Cooperation and Development (OECD), with Western European countries, the USA, Canada and Japan as its members.
1961	The UN proclaims the First Development Decade.
1963	Founding of the Organization of African Unity (OAU).
1964	UNCTAD 1 (United Nations Conference on Trade and Development). First Unctad Conference in Geneva. Establishment of the group of 77 non-aligned countries within the UN. Raúl Prebisch, secretary-general of the ECLAC, calls for a new international economic order.
1964–1976	GATT: Kennedy Round. With respect to GATT negotiation rounds up to and including the Kennedy Round, it is generally assumed that tariff reductions for products from developing were lower than for other products. During the Kennedy Round the largest tariff reductions were negotiated for advanced technologies and capital intensive products.
1965	Founding of the UNDP (United Nations Development Programme) which centred on technical assistance to developing countries and the financing of development projects.
1965	Addition of a new chapter 'Trade and Development' to the GATT agreements. The requirement of reciprocity was abandoned for developing countries.
1968	Second UNCTAD conference in New Delhi.
1971	Collapse of the Bretton Woods fixed exchange rate system.

Table 11.2 (*continued*)

1971	Lima declaration of ministers of the G77 on targets for industrial production. Objective: by the year 2000, 25 per cent of world industrial production should be produced in developing countries.
1971–1976	GATT: gradual introduction of the Generalized System of Preferences (GSP) to facilitate the exports of industrial products from developing countries to the industralized countries.
1972	Third UNCTAD conference in Santiago de Chile.
1973	Oil crisis.
1973	In a speech in Nairobi the president of the World Bank, Robert McNamara, calls attention to the basic needs of millions of people living in absolute poverty.
1973–1979	GATT negotiations: Tokyo Round. Tariffs reduced by 30 per cent.
1974	Sixth special meeting of the General Assembly of the UN. Acceptance of a resolution on a New International Economic Order. A 'Charter of the Economic Rights and Duties of States' is formulated.
1974	Multi-fibre Arrangement. 'Voluntary' import restrictions for textile exports from developing countries.
1975	Lomé Convention signed in February 1975 by the EEC and 63 ACP countries (former European colonies in Africa, the Caribbean and the Pacific). The agreement includes a series of non-reciprocal trade concessions by the EEC and the setting up of two funds for the stabilization of export revenues of developing countries.
1975	UN resolution on 'Development and International Economic Cooperation'.
1976	UNCTAD IV in Nairobi.
1976	World employment conference by the ILO in Geneva calls for an emphasis on basic needs in development policy.
1979	UNCTAD V in Manila.
1979	Second oil crisis.
1979	World Bank introduces Structural Adjustment Loans (SALs).
1980	Treaty on an Integrated Programme for Commodities. Today, in 1995, the treaty has not yet been ratified by the required 90 states and therefore is still not being implemented.
1980	Publication of the Brandt report: *North-South: A programme for survival.* Emphasis on mutual interests of rich countries and developing countries.
1980	Prime minister Michael Manley of Jamaica refuses to meet IMF conditions for further financial support. First political conflict about 'conditionality'.
1981	World Bank introduces Sectoral Adjustment Loans (SECALs).
1982	Signing of a comprehensive treaty on maritime law, in Jamaica in December 1982. Among others, this treaty deals with the common exploitation of natural resources of the seabed outside territorial waters. This agreement has not been signed by the US, the United Kingdom and the Federal Republic of Germany. It has not been implemented.
1982	Mexico postpones payments of its debt service. Start of the debt crisis. Since 1982 the IMF and the World Bank increasingly emphasize 'structural adjustment policies' as a condition for obtaining new loans.
1983	Third ACP-EEC treaty signed in Lomé.
1985	Baker Plan introduced in Seoul: *A Programme for Sustained Growth*. The Plan argues for renewed capital flows to developing countries. Recognition of the fact that a solution of the debt crisis depends on resumption of economic growth.
1986–1993	GATT: Uruguay Round on liberalization of international trade. Completed

Table 11.2 (*continued*)

	15 December 1993. Agricultural products and services are included in the agreements for the first time. Agreement on the creation of the International Trade Organization.
1986	IMF: Structural Fund Facility (SAF) to finance structural adjustment programmes.
1987	IMF: Extended Structural Fund Facility (ESAF) to finance sectoral structural adjustment programmes.
1989	Fourth ACP-EEC agreement signed in Lomé.
1989	Brady Plan launched in March 1989. First step towards voluntary debt reduction as a contribution to the resumption of economic growth.
1991	Disintegration of the Soviet Union.
1992	United National Conference on Environment and Development (UNCED) in Rio de Janeiro. At this conference resolutions are passed on pressing global environmental issues such as reduction of CO_2 emissions, CFCs and deforestation.
1993	Mexico, the US and Canada agree on a North American free trade treaty (NAFTA).
1993	Treaty of Maastricht. The European Economic Community is transformed into the European Union. Agreement on the introduction of a common European currency by 1989.
1993	15 December. Conclusion of the GATT Uruguay Round. Agreement on the setting up of the World Trade Organization.
1994	World Population Plan of Action adopted by the United Nations Conference on Population and Development in Cairo, September 1994.
1995	Start of the World Trade Organization in Geneva.

Sources: Schrijver (1985); also Meier (1984); Bhagwati (1988); Hermes (1992); Teunissen (1990); Fey (1985); Johnson (1967).

ation), and many more.[2] Formally all specialized UN organizations fall within the compass of the responsibility of the Economic and Social Council of the UN. These organizations have to submit annual reports to the council. In practice, however, they are largely independent (Nerfin, 1985).

The financial institutions dominated by the rich countries include the institutions of General Agreement on Tariffs and Trade (GATT), the International Monetary Fund (IMF), the World Bank and its subsidiaries, the Asian Development Bank, the Inter-American Development Bank, the International Development Association (IDA) and the International Finance Corporation (IFC), the OECD and the periodic meetings of the leaders of the seven richest industrialized countries (the G7). In theory, as specialized UN organizations, the International Monetary Fund and the World Bank are accountable to the Economic and Social Council of the UN. But, the number of votes in these organizations depends on financial resources provided by the participating countries. This means that policy decisions of these organizations are determined by the rich countries. The founding of these organizations actually preceded the founding of the United Nations.

A recurrent motive in the succession of international conferences, resolutions and treaties is the interaction between policy orientations aimed at a liberal international order based on free trade and claims for a new, more just international order based on international regulation. The institutions dominated by the affluent countries championed free trade. United Nations organizations and meetings dominated by developing countries called for a new international economic order. In turn, the World Bank, the IMF and the GATT responded to these claims with new policies (cf. Schrijver, 1985). In the late 1980s, developing countries started to realize that participation in the international economy and the opening up of the domestic economy to international competition had some advantages. At the same time, strangely enough, protectionist tendencies seemed to be on the increase in the economically advanced countries (Krueger, 1990b).

The foundations for the institutional structure of the post-war liberal international economic order were laid at a conference in Bretton Woods in 1944 (Burk, 1990). Forty-four countries were represented at this conference, among which were twenty-one developing countries, although these only played a very minor role in the debates. At the conference, agreements were reached on a system of stable exchange rates, with the dollar as the base currency and with currencies convertible to gold at fixed rates. The International Monetary Fund was set up to safeguard international financial stability. The IMF provided financial support to countries faced with sudden deficits in their balance of payments. The initial task of the new International Bank for Reconstruction and Development (World Bank) was to provide funding for economic reconstruction of war damages. The Bank started operations in 1946 and gradually shifted its focus of attention to developing countries after 1950. The Bank concentrated mainly on investment in infrastructure. By 1981 the total of outstanding loans was over 5 billion dollars (Meier, 1984). Voting power in institutions like the IMF and the World Bank depends on the amount of financial resources contributed by the member countries.

With the IMF and the World Bank, the General Agreement on Tariffs and Trade (GATT) became the third pillar of the liberal international economic order. In the GATT treaty signed in Geneva in October 1947, 123 separate trade agreements between twenty-three advanced economies were combined into a single agreement (Fey, 1985). Important principles underlying this agreement include the following:

- Governments should refrain from interference in international trade. They may only impose tariffs on imports.
- Quantitative restrictions and trade barriers are only permitted under specified conditions.
- Reciprocity: tariff reductions have to be reciprocal.
- Non-discrimination: trade advantages granted to one country have to be granted to all other countries. This is also referred to as the 'most favoured nation clause'.

The GATT agreement was meant as a temporary agreement in anticipation of the founding of an International Trade Organization (ITO) with broader responsibilities. From November 1947 to March 1948 a charter for this organization was negotiated in Havana. In these discussions, representatives of developing countries played a more prominent role than in the GATT negotiations. The concept for the ITO charter, therefore, also included a chapter on 'Economic development and recovery', which paid attention to foreign direct investment and to protection of infant industries. In another chapter, the subject of agreements to stabilize commodity prices was broached. The Havana conference ended in a conflict between developing countries and economically advanced countries. The ITO was never established. Therefore, in 1955 the GATT institutions, originally intended as temporary, received a permanent status.

Not counting the Uruguay Round concluded in December 1993, GATT negotiations took place in seven rounds. Between 1947 and 1979 these seven rounds led to a reduction in the average import tariffs by no less than 92 per cent (Bhagwati, 1988). Until the Uruguay Round agricultural products were excluded from the negotiations. Tariff reductions referred mainly to industrial products. The GATT agreements also included procedures to solve trade disputes between participating countries. The reduction of trade barriers mainly affected trade between the rich countries. Developing countries continued to protect their industrial sectors.

The reductions of tariffs continued beyond 1973, but they were increasingly offset by the growth of non-tariff barriers to imports to rich countries. Non-tariff barriers include 'voluntary agreements on the restriction of exports', appeals to 'anti-dumping clauses' of the GATT, and imposition of restrictive quality and environmental requirements. However, according to Bhagwati (1988), there has been no relapse into the protectionism of the interwar period. The liberalization of the 1950s and 1960s has not been undone. But the further reductions of import tariffs after 1973 have been balanced by increases in other forms of protectionism.

In part due to tariff reductions, trade between economically advanced countries increased twice as fast as their real output. Growth of trade was also helped by the decreasing costs of transport and communication. Important exceptions to the liberalization of international trade were agriculture and textiles. Until recently, the US and European policy with respect to agricultural products was highly protectionist. Attempts were made to protect the textile industry in the rich countries against imports from low-wage countries by means of the so-called Multifibre Arrangement of 1974, and its predecessors. In practice, developing countries were quite successful in evading these import restrictions in the 1980s. Exports of textiles and clothing from developing countries to the OECD countries increased annually by 13 and 20 per cent respectively (Krueger, 1990b).

The United Nations was founded in 1945 at a conference in San Francisco. Initially, its main objective was to safeguard international peace and security. It had only fifty-one member states. Only four developing countries in Africa and Asia were represented. Between 1945 and 1965, sixty-five former colonies became independent and joined the UN as sovereign member states. More and more, the focus of UN attention shifted to problems of development. By 1992, of the 180 UN member states, 152 were developing countries (UN, 1993a, 1993b). The principal organs of the UN are as follows:

- The General Assembly, where each state has one vote.
- The Security Council, with the victors of World War II (the United States, France, Great Britain, the Soviet Union and China) as permanent members, each with the power of veto.
- The Economic and Social Council (ECOSOC), which, in principle, coordinates the work of the numerous specialized UN organizations.

From the fact that they provide most of the financial funding for the work of the UN organizations, the rich countries derive a certain degree of influence. Still, on basis of the 'one country, one vote' principle, developing countries have a great deal of influence within UN organizations, with respect to both policy-making and staff recruitment. Through specialized organizations like the United Nations Conference on Trade and Development (UNCTAD) and through the General Assembly of the UN, developing countries can make themselves heard and can express their criticisms of the liberal international economic order.

At the first UNCTAD conference in Geneva in 1964, a bloc of seventy-seven non-aligned developing countries was formed. With Raúl Prebisch as one of their main spokesmen, they called for a new international economic order. In this new order, the position of developing countries in the system of international trade would be strengthened and their access to markets in developed countries would be improved. The call for a New International Economic Order (NIEO) became stronger and stronger at subsequent UNCTAD conferences. The pursuit of the NIEO received a substantial boost when a cartel of petroleum-exporting countries (OPEC) managed to raise oil prices dramatically in 1973. In 1974, the General Assembly of the UN accepted a resolution on the formation of a new international economic order. One of the important demands included in this resolution, was more voting power for developing countries in the financial institutions dominated by the rich countries. The pursuit of a NIEO reached its zenith in an agreement on an Integrated Programme for Commodities in 1980 and an agreement on the common exploitation of the natural resources of the seabed in 1982.

The demand for more votes in financial institutions was never met by the rich countries. But in other ways the financial institutions responded to the pressure for change. As early as 1955 it was accepted that developing countries could temporarily protect their domestic industries while trade barriers in the rich countries were being reduced. The justification for this exception was the 'infant industry' argument. In 1965 an additional chapter was added to the GATT agreements in which the reciprocity requirement was dropped for developing countries. Developing countries do not have to reciprocate tariff reductions in rich countries. Between 1971 and 1976 a system of Generalized Preferences was developed, in which industrial exports from developing countries were given a measure of preferential access to markets in rich countries. However, the effects of these measures on export growth in the poorest countries were disappointing.

The World Bank increasingly turned into a real development bank. It not only financed infrastructural projects, but also increasingly supported agricultural, industrial and educational projects. In 1956, the International Finance Corporation (IFC) was established as a separate subsidiary to promote private investment in developing countries. 1960 saw the founding of the International Development Association (IDA), which issued soft loans to developing countries on favourable conditions. Since 1973 the emphasis has shifted, at least in theory, to poverty alleviation (see Chenery *et al.*, 1974; van Dam, 1989). This change was heralded in a speech by the President of the World Bank, Robert McNamara, in October 1973. McNamara argued for policies to increase the productivity and the employment chances of the very poor. From the late 1960s until the late 1970s the share of infrastructural projects in World Bank lending decreased from 60 per cent to 33 per cent. By 1980, 50 per cent of all World Bank loans were used to finance rural development, education, population projects, urbanization, water supply and nutrition (Meier, 1984).

The tasks of the IMF were initially restricted to monetary stabilization. Developing countries received no special attention. Later, the IMF also started focusing on the economic problems of developing countries. Separate facilities were created to assist developing countries with balance of payments problems and to compensate for shortfalls in export revenues. In recent years, the bulk of IMF loans goes to developing countries.

Among the responses to the call for a new international economic order, one should mention a series of agreements between the EEC and former colonies in Africa, the Caribbean and the Pacific (the ACP countries). In the so-called Lomé agreements, an attempt was made to provide a framework for policy dialogue between developing countries and rich European countries. Special funds were established to help stabilize export revenues from agricultural and mining exports of developing countries (STABEX and SYSMIN). Exports from ACP countries were granted preferential access to European markets and the resources for financing development projects were expanded. As will be shown later, these measures have had little impact. The shares of the ACP countries in the European markets have declined, particularly in comparison with the shares gained by other developing countries excluded from the Lomé agreements (Fitzpatrick, 1983). The movement toward a NIEO reached its peak around 1980 with a draft treaty on an Integrated Programme for Commodities. This programme was meant to stabilize prices of primary exports at a high level through the creation of buffer stocks.

Neither this programme nor the above-mentioned treaty on the exploitation of the seabed has ever been implemented. The reasons for this are manifold. In the first place, it is an illusion that developing countries have joint interests. The interests of oil-exporting countries, oil-importing countries, newly industrialized countries and agricultural exporters, and richer and poorer countries, all show considerable divergence. This prevented these countries from presenting a united front to rich countries in international negotiations. Secondly, there was resistance on the part of the rich countries, and in particular, by the United States and Great Britain (Johnson, 1967). The United States, for example, refused to sign the maritime treaty on the joint exploitation of the resources of the seabed. This treaty would have provided the UN with independent sources of income, and would have rendered the organization less dependent on its rich sponsors. In the third place, there was increasing criticism of the contents of the NIEO proposals themselves (see section 11.6). Finally, the NIEO disappeared from the international agenda as result of the debt crisis that broke out in 1982.

After 1982 all attention went to the debt crisis, which threatened world financial stability. The inflow of private financial capital to developing countries came to an end. Official financial institutions like the IMF and the World Bank increasingly started attaching conditions to the provision of new credit. These conditions implied that developing countries had to pursue 'structural adjustment policies', which were aimed at improving their balance of payments, reducing the role of government, deregulating the economy and stimulating an export-orientation. The 1980s were completely dominated by the debate on structural adjustment policy (see Lensink, 1995), a policy that found backing in the remarkable economic success of several Asian countries where sober macroeconomic policies had been followed and export-orientation had been encouraged. Structural adjustment policies are consistent with the resurgence of liberal perspectives on both national and international economic policy.

Krueger (1990b, 1993) rightly points to the paradoxical situation that developing countries are turning to the market under pressure from international financial institutions, while there is a simultaneous revival of protectionist tendencies in the rich countries that stood at the cradle of the post-war liberal economic order. Until 1979, subsequent GATT negotiation rounds had managed to reduce average import tariffs on manufactured goods to 5 per cent (Fey, 1985). At the same time, protectionist tendencies resurfaced along with the stagnation of economic growth in the rich countries after 1973. Apart from excluding agriculture and services, the GATT agreements included numerous clauses of exception to which the protectionist interests could appeal. One of the clauses referred to the right to take countermeasures in cases of 'dumping' by another country. 'Dumping' is a very elastic concept. Between 1980 and 1985 the EEC countries, the United States and six other advanced economies appealed to anti-dumping provisions 1,155 times in order to restrict imports from other countries. There were another 425 appeals to anti-subsidy provisions (Bhagwati, 1988). Another exception to free trade is provided by situations in which there is the danger of 'serious injury to domestic producers'. In such cases, temporary relaxation of GATT rules is possible. With this clause as a fall-back, rich countries can blackmail developing countries into signing 'voluntary' agreements on export quotas. Another threat to the liberal international order is the rise of trade blocs with internal free trade and intensified protectionism at the outside borders (Krueger, 1993).

Although the fear of revived protectionism is not without grounds, Bhagwati interprets recent protectionist measures differently. He sees them as a peace offering by liberally oriented governments to domestic pressure groups, rather than as a fundamental break with a free-trade regime. Developing countries are quite successful in evading protectionist measures. In spite of the deceleration of the growth of world trade after 1973, world trade between 1973 and 1983 increased faster than world production. The increase in non-tariff restrictions did, however, compensate for the further reduction of import tariffs that have been realized in GATT negotiations after 1973.

At the formal level, liberalization of trade has recently received a further impetus from the successful completion of the protracted negotiations of the GATT Uruguay round in December 1993. For the first time, agriculture has been also been included in the package of tariff reductions. Trade in services has also been liberalized. Finally, agreement has been reached on the establishment of a World Trade Organization (WTO), originally scheduled for 1948. The WTO started operations on 1 January 1995

11.3 *The principle of international free trade*

The international economic order since 1945 is based on the principle of free trade. The arguments in favour of international free trade derive from classical economists like Adam Smith and David Ricardo. The basic arguments have remained unchanged in spite of numerous elaborations and refinements. This section will provide a very brief summary of the argument.

Let us assume that there are two countries, A and B, and two goods, for example, food and clothing. For simplicity's sake, we also assume that the production of these two goods only requires labour. This means that the costs of the goods can be expressed in labour hours.[3] When country A can produce food more cheaply than country B and country B can produce clothing more cheaply than country A, it is evident that both countries will benefit from the international trade in food and clothing. The classical economists, however, have shown that the two countries will also benefit from international trade, even when country A produces both products more cheaply than country B. According to the *law of comparative advantage*, the two countries should specialize in producing those products in which they are most efficient in relative terms.

The following example, taken from Samuelson and Nordhaus (1989, p. 903 with permission of the McGraw Hill companies), illustrates this principle (see Table 11.3). By employing one day of labour, country A can produce either one unit of food or half a unit of clothing. If the price of the product is expressed in labour units, one hunit of food in country A can be traded for half a unit of clothing in the absence of international trade. In country B, one labour day will produce one-third of a unit of food and one-fourth of a unit of clothing. This means that in the absence of international trade, one unit of food can be traded for three-quarters of a unit of clothing.

In our example, country A is more efficient (cheaper) in absolute terms than country B in the production of both goods. However, in relative terms, one gets less

Table 11.3 Advantages of international trade

	Labour days required for the production of: One unit of food	One unit of clothing
Country A	1	2
Country B	3	4
Terms of trade of food and clothing, without international trade		
Country A		1 : 1/2
Country B		1 : 3/4
Terms of trade of food and clothing, with international trade		
Country A		1 : 3/4
Country B		1 : 1/2

clothing per unit of food in country A (half a unit of clothing for one unit of food), than in country B (three-quarters of a unit of clothing for one unit of food). This means that country A is relatively more efficient at producing food and country B is relatively more efficient at producing clothing. Thus international trade will benefit both countries. If country A specializes in the production of food and exports part of it to country B, one day's work will produce one unit of food, which can then be traded for three-quarters of a unit of clothing. This is more than the half a unit of clothing which one can get in the absence of international trade. If country B specializes in producing clothing and exports part of it to country A, it will be able to trade one unit of clothing for two units of food. Again, this is more than the one and one-third units of food it would get in the absence of international trade. For both countries, therefore, international trade is profitable. In addition, specialization in production often gives rise to economies of scale, which make production even cheaper.

In the twentieth-century version of the theory of comparative advantage, the emphasis is on the proportions of the factors of production, capital and labour (see Kol and Mennes, 1990). Countries with surplus labour and a scarcity of capital will produce labour-intensive products relatively cheaply, and will have a comparative advantage in such products. Countries with an abundance of capital and a shortage of labour will have a comparative advantage in capital-intensive products. This theory is also known as the Heckscher–Ohlin–Samuelson theory.

The essence of the theory of comparative cost advantage is that international trade is beneficial to all parties involved: it increases total welfare. The most powerful argument against comparative advantage is that it reinforces existing patterns of production and specialization. If a developing country has a comparative advantage in a limited number of primary products, it will remain dependent on them. The possibility of importing industrial products relatively cheaply from abroad makes it difficult to build up a domestic industrial sector.

11.4 *Criticisms of the liberal international order*

Despite the rapid growth of the world trade and per capita incomes in the 1950–73 period, there was increasing dissatisfaction with the liberal international economic order on the part of developing countries (see Johnson, 1967; Lewis, 1978; Seers, 1979; Brandt *et al.*, 1980; Streeten, 1984; Schrijver, 1985). The essence of their criticisms was the argument, deriving from Friedrich List, that powerful countries with a highly developed economy benefit more from international free trade than poor countries. Developing countries had profited insufficiently from the growth of the world economy, and, within developing countries, growth had largely bypassed the poorest classes of the population. The international order should be restructured in such a way that the masses of the population in poor developing countries could profit from international trade. Exports should provide developing countries with the financial resources needed for development. This would make them less dependent on development aid ('trade, not aid').

Criticisms of the liberal economic order include the following elements (Bhagwati, 1977; Corden, 1979; Myint, 1980; Streeten, 1984).

- In the post-war period, neither decolonization nor development aid resulted in sufficient economic growth in developing countries. Although most countries had achieved their formal political independence, economically they felt as just dependent on the dominant rich countries as before. There was widespread disappointment about development aid. On the one hand, the amount of aid fell far short of the original target of 0.7 per cent of the gross national product of the donor countries. On the other hand, countries became increasingly irritated with the paternalism and meddling in internal affairs that seems inextricably connected with development aid.
- Economic growth in developing countries did not result in much decrease in poverty due to the extremely unequal distribution of incomes (ul Haq, 1976).
- The share of the poorest developing countries in world exports decreased. Excluding oil-exporting countries, the share of the low-income countries in world trade decreased from 3.6 per cent in 1960 to 1.5 per cent in 1977 (Streeten, 1984, p. 474).
- Most prices of primary exports of developing countries showed downward trends, both in absolute terms and relative to prices of imported manufactured goods
- Prices of primary exports of developing countries fluctuated strongly in the short run, so that export revenues were very unstable.
- International income inequality increased, since per capita incomes in the rich countries increased faster than those in the poor countries.
- Large multinational enterprises contributed to a drain of resources. They tend to repatriate their profits abroad, contribute little to the domestic economy, and maintain the economic dependence of the developing countries.

As an alternative to the liberal international economic order, the New International Economic Order (NIEO) was launched at the first meeting of the UNCTAD in 1964. The NIEO encompassed a comprehensive set of measures formulated by Raúl Prebisch, the Secretary-General of the Economic Commission for Latin America (ECLA) and representatives of the group of seventy-seven non-aligned countries. The NIEO was further elaborated at successive UNCTAD conferences. The call for a new international order was strengthened by the short-lived but spectacular success of the OPEC oil cartel, which managed to increase oil prices drastically in 1973 and 1979.

The policy proposals for the New International Economic Order include the following:

1. Commodity agreements for primary exports of developing countries:
   (a) First, it is proposed to create buffer stocks of important commodities. When world prices fall below certain critical levels, the commodities are bought up at guaranteed minimum prices. If prices go up again, the buffer stocks are sold on the market.
   (b) In the second place, it is proposed to provide compensatory finance in case of wildly fluctuating export revenues. If export revenues of a country drop below critical limits, the programme will compensate for the shortfalls. When revenues are high, payments are made to the compensatory fund.
   (c) In the third place, it is proposed to provide financial resources for the setting up of primary resource processing industries in developing countries.
   (d) Finally, export prices of developing countries are to be indexed to the prices of their imports, to avoid deterioration of the terms of trade.

   The overall objective of commodity agreements is to stabilize primary export prices and export revenues in the short term and to improve the terms of trade for developing countries in the long term.
2. Reducing protectionism on the part of the advanced industrial economies.
3. Preferential (and non-reciprocal) access to the markets of industrialized countries for manufactured exports from developing countries. The developing countries retain the right to protect their domestic industries. The goal of these measures is to increase the share of developing countries in world manufacturing production and manufactured exports.
4. Recognition of the right of developing countries to establish producer cartels in order to raise the prices of their primary export products. The model for such cartels is the Organization of Petroleum-Exporting Countries (OPEC).
5. Recognition of the right of developing countries to exploit their own natural resources. This includes the right to nationalize foreign enterprises.
6. Increase in the share of developing countries in world transport.
7. Formulation of a code of conduct for multinational enterprises, including requirements such as: reinvestment of part of their profits, training of local employees, transfer of technology, respect for local rules and laws, cooperation with local entrepreneurs and subcontractors and domestic sourcing.
8. Expansion of internal financial resources available for development programmes from international organizations such as the World Bank and the IMF.

9. Debt reduction for the poorest developing countries.
10. More votes for developing countries in international financial institutions.
11. Independent sources of funding for international organizations like the United Nations. Proposals for the joint exploitation of the natural resources of the seabed.
12. Increasing trade flows between developing countries (so-called South-South trade).

These proposals were eventually included in a resolution on the New International Economic Order, which was accepted by the UN General Assembly in 1974. The commodity agreements have been worked out in the 1980 draft treaty for an Integrated Programme for Commodities and in a 1982 draft treaty on the exploitation of natural resources of the seabed. Neither of these treaties has ever been implemented.

11.5 *Lomé agreements*

In 1975, the first of a series of agreements between the EEC and the former European colonies in Africa, the Caribbean and the Pacific (the ACP countries) was concluded in Lomé. These agreements tried to realize some of the ideas of the new international economic order. The Lomé agreements developed out of a dialogue between rich countries and developing countries. Among others, they comprise a European development fund for developmental projects; a fund for the stabilization of revenues from primary agricultural exports from developing countries (STABEX); and a fund for the stabilization of revenues from mining exports (SYSMIN). In addition, agreements were reached on preferential access to European markets for manufactured exports from the ACP countries. Despite high hopes and initial enthusiasm the results of these Lomé agreements have been highly disappointing. The stabilization funds were soon exhausted as more and more claims were made, while no money was ever paid back as originally intended. Also, the funds were paid out to governments rather than to producers, so that there were no incentives to increase production or to improve productivity. Moreover, the funds functioned automatically. There were no conditions with regard to macroeconomic policies. Despite preferential access to European markets, market shares of the ACP countries declined. At the same time, Asian developing countries excluded from the Lomé agreements succeeded in improving their market shares. Some critics point to European protectionism as a possible cause of the disappointing outcomes, but over time, the theoretical framework underlying the new international economic order itself came to be criticized.

11.6 *Criticisms of the new international order*

Somewhere in the late 1970s, a turning point occurred in the debates on economic development. There was increasing criticism of the market-distorting impacts of government planning in developing countries and of attempts to regulate international trade in the context of the NIEO.

First, some critics deny that there is a systematic deterioration in the terms of trade for exports from developing countries (Johnson, 1967; Myint, 1980; Spraos, 1980). Though the debate on the terms of trade continues (Sapsford, 1985, 1988; Sarkar, 1986), I concluded in Chapter 8 that no systematic law-like patterns can be discerned. The terms of trade vary from period to period, country to country and product to product. Countries with a flexible production structure and a diversified export package are less affected by prices movements than countries with inflexible production structures and dependence on a single export product (monocultures). According to Myint, export pessimists have made too much of the low income elasticity of the demand for primary products.[4] Western demand for some exotic agricultural products (e.g. mangoes, kiwi fruit, lichis) actually increases as incomes go up. Moreover, price elasticity (the relation between changes in quantities demanded of a product and changes in its price) may be more important for a developing country than aggregate income elasticity. The prices of primary exports turn out to be no more unstable than those of manufactured goods or capital goods. Finally, one should not forget that many developing countries no longer exclusively export primary products.

Experience has shown that attempts to stabilize commodity prices above their market levels, through commodity agreements or price cartels, are hardly ever successful in the long run. If prices are higher than free market equilibrium prices, extra supply is elicited till the commodity fund is exhausted or prices collapse. This happened with oil. Attempts to stabilize the prices of commodities such as tin, cocoa or coffee also failed.

The Lomé agreements illustrate that preferential access to markets does not guarantee successful export performance. Efficient low-cost industrial production in Asian countries has been able to compete in European markets. Manufactured exports have been quite successful in penetrating Western markets for industrial consumer goods without any preferential access. Emphasizing the right of developing countries to continue to protect their domestic industries indefinitely may prolong the existence of non-viable industries.

Attempts to increase the voting power of developing countries in international financial institutions have met with fierce resistance from the countries who provide the funds. These attempts are in conflict with the ever stricter conditions that the IMF and the World Bank attach to the provision of financial support. Finally, the demise of the new international economic order was also furthered by the increasing heterogeneity of developing countries. Attempts to legislate a comprehensive framework for the international order clashes with the diversity of interests and circumstances in developing countries (van Dam, 1984). The bloc of non-aligned countries no longer speaks with one voice.

Foreign direct investment

One of the topics about which the climate of opinion has changed dramatically is foreign direct investment. In the 1970s, multinationals and foreign investors were regarded with great suspicion. There was fear of foreign domination of the economy and of a drain on domestic resources by profit repatriation and transfer pricing. The right to nationalize foreign enterprises was included in the resolutions on the new international order. There was also a call for a code of conduct for multinationals.

At present, developing countries are vying with each other to attract foreign direct investment, including formerly closed economies such as China and India. Foreign direct investment can bring financial resources into a country without increasing the volume of debt. Direct foreign investment, however, comprises more than financial flows alone. It includes a total package of finance, management experience, transfer of technology and skills, marketing expertise and access to world markets (Dunning, 1988; Helleiner, 1989; Gillis *et al.*, 1992).

The right to nationalize multinational enterprises emphasized in the NIEO is inconsistent with the goal of attracting more direct foreign investment. The threat of nationalization indeed has adverse effects on the behaviour of multinationals. They will charge an 'uncertainty premium' and go for maximum short-term profits that will be repatriated as soon as possible. Enterprises will only display a less 'predatory' behaviour, if their long-term prospects are more certain.

Since the 1970s, some progress has been achieved in drawing up codes of conduct for multinational enterprises. Such codes specify the obligations of multinationals, such as training local staff, reinvesting part of their profits, respecting domestic legislation, subcontracting, using local intermediate goods and entering into joint ventures with domestic investors. On the other hand, the codes also offer more certainty to foreign investors. This is not to say that foreign direct investment is above criticism; multinationals sometimes raise all their capital on domestic markets, while repatriating part of their profits. A sizeable minority of foreign investment projects costs more, in terms of the opportunity cost of the resources used, than the earnings generated (Helleiner, 1989). The distribution of benefits between the multinational and the host country still depends in part on bargaining. Once a multinational has committed its resources and the host country has gained more experience, the latter's bargaining position can improve (Vernon, 1977). Clear delineation of the rights and obligations of multinational companies and governments continues to be an objective of negotiations within the UN Centre for transnational corporations (Helleiner, 1989).

In the post-war period, the importance of foreign direct investment fluctuated. Its share in net capital flows was quite high in the 1950s and 1960s, reached a low point in the early 1980s and recovered after that. The debt crisis created new interest in direct foreign investment. In 1988, FDI was 19 per cent of net capital flows (Gillis *et al.*, 1992). New forms of foreign direct investment have also developed, such as joint ventures, licensing agreements, franchising, management contracts and subcontracting.

The eclectic theory of multinational investment (Dunning, 1988) gives three explanations for foreign direct investment. First, there are unique firm-specific characteristics, which explain the foreign firms' advantages over domestic firms.

These include intangible factors such as technologies and management skills, economies of scale, servicing networks and access to markets. A second set of factors refers to locational advantages as determined by labour costs, transport costs, availability of natural resources, tariff protection and other government policies in the host country. The third set of factors, which Dunning calls internalization advantages, is very interesting. A foreign firm has to choose between selling its firm-specific advantages to local firms or setting up lines of production itself. In a nutshell, Dunning argues that the uncertainties of markets lead foreign firms to prefer the internal hierarchy of the multinational organization to market transactions between independent firms. The very attempt to internalize market uncertainties and imperfections again indicates that there is considerable leeway for bargaining. Developing countries often attempt to 'unpackage' the total direct investment package in order to select those aspects that are most to their advantage.

11.7 *The debt crisis*[5]

In 1982 Mexico suspended the payment of its debt service due to insufficient foreign exchange. Other developing countries and countries in Eastern Europe were also unable to keep up payments on debt. Private banks responded by a sudden reduction in the supply of new credit. The debt crisis was a fact. There were two aspects to this crisis: a threat to the stability of the global financial system; and a threat to the economic development of poor countries. After 1982, all attention was focused on coping with the consequences of the debt crisis. The immediacy of that crisis effectively ended the faltering debate on the new international economic order. In this section, some important aspects of the debt crisis will be discussed briefly.

11.7.1 The debt cycle

In our puritan way of thinking, debts have negative connotations. In some stages of economic development, however, it is quite normal to incur debts. The accumulation of a stock of capital goods and the building up of industry and infrastructure in developing countries is facilitated by a substantial inflow of capital from abroad. This inflow may take the form of direct foreign investment, development aid or loans from governments, international financial institutions or private banks. Unlike foreign direct investment, loans result in increasing foreign indebtedness. As long as the borrowed funds are invested economically, debt causes few problems. Economic investment implies that borrowed resources contribute more to the growth of national income than they cost in terms of interest payments. Interest payments can be financed from the increase in national income. According to Lewis (1978), the absolute volume of debt is of no significance. As long as loans are invested economically, the more debt the better.

With respect to foreign capital flows, Lewis distinguishes four stages of the debt cycle (see also World Bank, 1985; Hermes, 1992, p. 29). During the first stage new borrowing exceeds debt service payments, so that interest payments, principal repayments and additional investment can all be financed from new loans.[6] The country imports more goods and services than it exports. During the second stage new borrowing exceeds repayments of outstanding loans, but it is less than total debt service. The volume of foreign debt is still increasing. During the third stage there is a surplus on the current account of the balance of payments and the volume of foreign debt starts to decrease. In the final stage of the debt cycle a country becomes a net creditor.

Debts only become a problem when loans are used unproductively (e.g. for consumptive purposes, for the financing of wasteful government bureaucracies, or for investments with dubious returns). Debts become even more of a problem when they only serve to finance debt service payments on previous debts. Then the volume of debt increases, while no new financial resources become available for investment in future production.

During most of the post-war period, developing countries were at the first stage of the debt cycle. Tables 3.5, 11.5 and 12.4 in this book point to a steady flow of capital to developing countries and sustained deficits on their trade balance of goods and services. Until 1977, the relationship between foreign finance and development was a positive one. Around 1977, this situation changed for many Latin American and African countries. Economic growth faltered and a perverse situation arose. Developing countries had to go ever deeper into debt to finance debt service payments on outstanding debt, while their export revenues were shrinking and their economies were stagnating.

11.7.2 Causes of the debt crisis

The debt crisis was the result of a complex of internal and external causes (Maddison, 1985; Wood, 1985; Buiter and Srinivasan, 1987; Griffin, 1988; Hermes, 1992; Lensink, 1993, chapter 2). After 1973 the growth of world economy and world trade slowed down. Increased oil prices fuelled inflation. The Western countries responded to inflation by pursuing restrictive fiscal and monetary policies at the expense of growth and employment. Developing countries were faced with declining export revenues, deteriorating terms of trade for their export products, and, except for oil exporting countries, rising energy bills.

Nevertheless many developing countries, in particular in Latin America, responded differently from the Western countries. In anticipation of a recovery of world economic growth, they tried to stimulate their economies through expansive fiscal and monetary policies. Deficits on the current account of the balance of payments were increasingly financed by loans from the private banking sector. Compared to the 1950s and 1960s, the share of foreign direct investment – which does not increase foreign indebtedness – in the capital flows to developing countries declined strongly. Initially this was compensated for by loans from official financial institutions and governments (Lensink, 1993), but the volume of finance supplied from these sources fell far short of financial requirements. Also, by borrowing from private banks, developing countries could evade the increasingly strict conditions imposed by the World Bank and the IMF (Wood, 1985).

Private banks were eager to provide loans to developing countries. They had accumulated huge amounts of petrodollars which were being 'recycled' into the banking system by the oil-exporting countries. Private banks even pursued aggressive marketing strategies to expand their loans to developing countries. Due to high inflation, real interest rates were low, sometimes even negative. The loans usually consisted of short-term credits with variable interest rates.

Until 1979, expansionary macroeconomic policies in Latin America appeared to be quite successful. Latin American countries managed to keep up the momentum of economic growth, though at the price of high inflation. But the anticipated recovery of the world economy failed to materialize, especially in 1979 when oil prices again quadrupled, and a new and even more serious depression followed (Maddison, 1985). Under the influence of the restrictive monetary policies of the Reagan administration, real interest rates suddenly soared. Since many loans were short term and interest rates variable, the debt service suddenly went up. More and more loans had to be contracted, just to meet debt service obligations.

As debt problems cumulated, the Latin American economic policies of the 1970s turned out to be less successful than initially assumed. There had been large-scale economic mismanagement. Many of the funds borrowed had been squandered on inefficient subsidies or non-profitable government projects.[7] In addition, government resources were used to maintain systems of political patronage. Due to huge government deficits and loose monetary policies, inflation increased sharply. High inflation disrupted domestic markets, discouraged the inflow of new foreign direct investment and stimulated capital flight. Unlike Southeast Asia, where outward-oriented policies had long been pursued, the protection of inefficient domestic industries in Latin America had been continued for too long. Domestic economic structures had become rigid and attempts to penetrate export markets met with insufficient success. Thus insufficient revenues from exports made the financing of debt service with new loans inevitable.

In the debates on the debt crisis, Latin American countries play a central role. It was their inability to meet their debt service payments that triggered the debt crisis. In Africa, private lending was of little importance. For foreign finance, African countries depended primarily on loans from foreign governments and international institutions. In absolute terms, the volume of debt was much smaller than in Latin American countries. Nevertheless, economic problems on the African continent had been mounting since 1975. A combination of poor economic policies – with respect to agriculture as well as industry and international trade – unfavourable natural circumstances, and an unfriendly international economic climate resulted in a long period of economic stagnation.

11.7.3 Quantitative data on the debt crisis

Tables 11.4 to 11.6 are meant to give the reader an idea of the magnitude of the debt crisis and the problems involved. Table 11.4 presents data on trends in debt burdens in twenty-two countries between 1982 and 1993. The sixteen countries in the upper part of the table are classified as 'severely indebted' in the World Bank (1995) publication *World Debt Tables 1994/1995*. Severely indebted countries (SICs) are defined as countries where the present value of total debt service is over 80 per cent of GNP and/or over 220 per cent of the value of exports.[8] *Debt service* comprises repayments of long-term debt, interest on long-term debt, annual repayments of and charges for IMF credit, and interest on short-term debt.

Of the sixteen severely indebted countries included in Table 11.4, eleven countries were classified as 'heavily indebted' (HICs) in 1982, although the definitions for 1982 were not the same as those for 1993.[9] In 1982, five countries – Algeria, Nigeria, Zaire, Bulgaria and Poland – were not yet classified as heavily indebted. In these countries the debt situation has deteriorated dramatically in eleven years.[10] Algeria is a special case. In 1991 it was classified as severely indebted. Its debt had increased from 17.6 billion dollars in 1982 to 28.2 billion in 1991. After 1991, the volume of debt declined quite substantially. In 1993, Algeria was no longer classified as severely indebted. Nevertheless, the debt service export ratio remained very high at 77 per cent.

In the bottom half of the table, one finds six countries that were considered heavily indebted in 1982 and are no longer included in either the severely indebted or the moderately indebted category in 1993. The debt situation in these countries has improved. They illustrate that one should not only look at the volume of foreign debt, but should see debt in relation to other variables like national income or exports. For example, South Korea has a foreign debt of over 47 billion dollars, but it is no longer regarded as a severely indebted country. In a dynamic economy such as the South Korean one, *debt service* (interest payments and repayment of debts) does not cause great problems. Debts are only a problem when debt service obligations become an impediment to resumption of economic growth and development. In a situation of *debt overhang* there is little incentive to work at improving the economic situation, as all the fruits of growth accrue to foreign financial institutions.

The case of Mexico is especially interesting. Mexico triggered the debt crisis in 1982. In 1993, it had accumulated a huge foreign debt of 118 billion dollars. Nevertheless, in 1993 it was no longer listed as a severely indebted country, according to the *World Debt Tables* criteria.

In the last four columns of Table 11.4 foreign debt is expressed as a percentage of GNP, and annual debt service as a proportion of export earnings, for 1982 and 1993. The data illustrate that a considerable part of export earnings in developing countries may be absorbed by debt servicing.

In terms of the debt service to exports ratio, Algeria tops the list in 1993 with 77 per cent, followed by Peru (64 per cent) and Argentina (48 per cent).[11] There are several countries with high debt–GNP ratios and relatively low debt service–export

Table 11.4 Countries with heavy debt burdens, 1982–1993 ($m)

	Total foreign debt[a]		Total debt service[b]		Debt as % of GNP		Debt service as % of exports	
	1982	1993	1982	1993	1982	1993	1982	1993
Countries with heavy debt burdens in 1993[c]								
Argentina	43,634	74,473	4,875	7,947	84	30	50	48
Brazil	92,990	132,749	19,092	10,743	35	24	81	24
Ecuador	7,705	14,110	2,144	921	67	102	78	26
Nicaragua	2,913	10,445	201	116	112	762	44	29
Peru	10,712	20,328	2,037	2,774	45	52	49	64
Algeria[d]	17,636	25,757	4,563	9,146	40	57	31	77
Ivory Coast	7,862	19,146	1,309	964	111	244	46	30
Morocco	12,535	21,430	1,640	2,614	85	82	43	31
Nigeria[ef]	12,954	32,531	2,092	1,831	17	101	16	29
Sudan[fg]	7,216	16,560	296	20	97	273	29	5
Syria[h]	6,148	19,975	502	283	38	117	17	5
Tanzania[g]	2,915	7,522	158	155	51	285	29	25
Zaire[ei]	5,078	11,280	542	28	38	142	32	–
Zambia	3,688	6,788	411	349	102	232	31	33
Bulgaria[ej]	4,041	12,250	1,721	295	23	125	15	6
Poland[ej]	33,336	45,306	2,045	1,692	49	53	15	11
Subtotal	271,363	470,650	43,628	39,878				
Total 48 SIC's	404,470	665,995	64,342	40,338		51		22
Total developing countries	738,688	1,811,777	70,459	199,006	36	40	16	17

Table 11.4 *(continued)*

	Total foreign debt[a]		Total debt service[b]		Debt as % of GNP		Debt service as % of exports	
	1982	1993	1982	1993	1982	1993	1982	1993
Countries with heavy debt burdens in 1982, but not in 1993[k]								
Egypt	29,525	40,626	1,898	2,407	124	105	21	15
Former Yugoslavia	19,900	11,314	4,077	16	32	–	21	–
Mexico	86,019	118,028	15,684	20,900	53	36	57	33
Portugal[f]	13,598	36,942	2,443	5,553	61	50	29	18
Romania	10,003	4,456	2,910	355	21	18	23	6
South Korea	37,330	47,203	6,348	9,173	52	14	22	9

Notes:

[a] Including short-term debt.
[b] Repayment of debts and interest payments on debts.
[c] Categorized as 'severely indebted countries' (SICs) in 1993 according to the *World Debt Tables 1994/95* criteria.
[d] Algeria classified as SIC in 1991, but no longer so in 1993. Not heavily indebted in 1982 (see note [c]).
[e] Countries that were classified as SICs in 1993 but were not classified among the 'highly indebted countries' (HICs) in 1982. The criteria for 1982 and 1993 are not the same. The HICs in 1982 included countries that were classified as 'severely indebted' in 1993, but also countries that were classified as 'moderately indebted' (MICs) in 1993.
[f] Debt service–export ratio from 1992 instead of 1993.
[g] debt–GNP ratio from 1992 instead of 1993.
[h] debt–GNP ratio from 1991 instead of 1993.
[i] debt-GNP ratio from 1990 instead of 1993.
[j] Data for 1985 instead of 1982.
[k] Countries that were classified as 'highly indebted' in 1982 and that were neither 'severely indebted' nor 'moderately indebted' in 1993.

Sources: 1982: World Bank (1993b), *World Debt Tables 1992–1993*; 1993: World Bank (1995), *World Debt Tables 1994–1995*. Zambia debt–GNP and debt service–export ratios from *World Debt Tables 1993–1994*.

ratios. These include Nicaragua, Sudan, Syria, Bulgaria and Tanzania. These low ratios either reflect some form of debt default or agreements with international financiers, deferring debt service payments to some future date. Another factor of importance is the restructuring of debt, with an increasing share of official loans with low interest rates.

Of the 16 countries with severe debts in 1993 in Table 11.4, five are Latin American and nine are African. Among the severely indebted countries are both oil-exporting countries like Nigeria and Algeria and oil-importing countries. Until 1991, oil-exporting Mexico was also in this category. In the oil-importing countries the increase in oil prices in 1973 and 1979 was one of the factors contributing to the debt crisis. The oil-exporting countries had incurred huge debts before 1982. They subsequently suffered from the collapse of oil prices during the 1980s.

In terms of absolute volume, debts are highest in the three largest Latin American countries: Brazil, Mexico and Argentina. Compared to most developing countries, average per capita incomes are relatively high in these countries. Debt–GNP ratios are by far the highest in African countries like Tanzania, the Sudan, the Ivory Coast and Zambia, and in small Latin American countries like Nicaragua and Panama. The debt service–export revenue ratio in 1993 is highest in Algeria, Peru and Argentina.

In sixteen of the twenty-two countries included in Table 11.4, the debt service as a percentage of export earnings has decreased since 1982. This suggests a certain measure of success of the economic stabilization programmes aimed at restoring the equilibrium on the balance of payments in the short term (for a further discussion of this topic, see section 11.8). But debt default or deferment of debt service also contributed to the declining ratios, as mentioned above. Debts as a percentage of GNP have increased severely in eight of the nine African countries. In Latin America, they decreased in four of the six countries included in Table 11.4.

In the mid-1980s a paradoxical situation arose in which there was a net capital outflow from developing countries to rich countries. This switch is illustrated in Tables 11.5 and 11.6. Table 11.5 presents an overview of net financial flows to developing countries between 1970 and 1994. Table 11.6 presents data for twenty-three selected developing countries between 1980 and 1993. These tables only refer to debt flows. Foreign direct investment and portfolio investment flows are excluded.

For an understanding of these tables some terms need to be defined. Debts are subdivided into *long-term debts* with a maturity of more than one year and *short-term debts* with a maturity of less than one year. Consistent long-run time series are only available for long-term debts. The figures in the two tables therefore refer predominantly to long-term debts. Table 11.5 also includes some data on total debts, including short-term debts and IMF credits for the period since 1980. Total debts are much higher than long-term debts, but the general trends are comparable. Table 11.5 distinguishes between net capital flows on debt and net transfers on debt. *Net capital flows on debt* refer solely to the balance of new loans disbursed and principal repayments of old loans. Interest payments are left out of consideration. *Net transfers on debt* equal net capital flows minus interest payments on existing loans. It is conceivable that net capital flows are positive, while net transfers, taking interest

Table 11.5 Debts and financial flows in developing countries, 1970–1994 ($bn)[a]

	1970	1975	1980	1982	1985	1986	1987	1988	1989	1990	1991	1992	1993	1994[b]
Long-term debts														
Total long-term debts	62	162	427	561	809	916	1,128	1,127	1,151	1,226	1,286	1,329	1,424	1,538
New loans	13	44	105	116	96	100	120	125	122	136	137	160	179	190
Of which, private[c]	8	29	77	83	62	61	71	76	74	80	79	111	125	130
Total debt service	8	24	75	96	114	123	142	153	146	151	150	155	168	175
Repayments	6	15	43	48	58	69	84	88	86	92	90	98	110	110
Of which, private[c]	5		35		45	52	61	63	61	65	61	67	79	75
Interest payments	2	9	32	48	56	54	58	65	60	59	60	57	58	65
Net capital flows[d]	7	29	62	68	38	31	36	37	36	44	48	62	69	79
Net transfers[e]	4	21	30	20	−18	−23	−21	−28	−24	−15	−13	5	12	15
Long- and short-term debts														
Total debt stock			572	753	991	1,089	1,369	1,375	1,427	1,539	1,627	1,696	1,812	1,945
Net capital flows	16[g]		112[g]		45	29	44	43	55	63	74	96	105	108
Net transfers on debt					−27	−38	−29	−39	−24	−15	−7	21	29	25

Notes:
[a] This table includes data for 116 developing countries reporting to the World Bank. The data for 1975 and 1982 refer to 111 developing countries.
[b] Tentative estimate.
[c] Including publicly guaranteed loans from private creditors.
[d] Balance of new loans disbursed and principal repayments (also referred to as net flows on debt).
[e] Net capital flows minus interest payments on debt (discrepancies due to rounding errors).
[f] Including IMF credit.
[g] Data on short-term debt from WDT (1995).

Sources: 1970, 1980, 1985 and 1986: World Bank (1993b), *World Debt Tables 1992/1993*. 1975 from *WDT* (1989); 1982 from *WDT* (1990); 1987–1994 from *WDT* (1995).

payments into account, are negative. This implies that the flow of money out of a developing country exceeds the flow of money into a country.[12]

The total of long-term debts of the 116 developing countries reporting to the World Bank increased from 62 billion dollars in 1970 to 561 billion dollars in 1982. By 1994 the total long-term debt had increased further to 1,538 billion dollars. Including short-term debts, the 1994 total amounted to 1,945 billion dollars.[13] Of course, the nominal volume of debt also depends on the exchange rate. If the value of the dollar drops, as in 1985–87, 1990 or 1995, the dollar value of debt contracted in other foreign currencies will go up.

Table 11.5 shows that the strong growth of private credit from 1970 onwards came to an end in 1982. After 1982, private financial institutions were no longer willing to provide additional credit. Most of the loans provided in the 1980s served to finance the repayment of earlier loans. The balance of not publicly guaranteed private loans – a category not included separately in Table 11.5 – even became negative.

It is interesting to note the differences between net capital flows and net transfers. Net capital flows remained positive during the entire period 1970–94. The volume of new loans exceeded the sum of repayment of earlier loans and the outflow of capital to other countries. The net long-term capital inflow decreased from 68 billion dollars in 1982 to 31 billion dollars in 1986. After that it picked up again, increasing in nominal terms to 108 billion dollars by 1994. Hermes (1992) has calculated that, expressed in constant 1988 dollars, the real value of capital inflows between 1981 and 1989 halved.

The picture is different for net transfers, which include interest payments. Net transfers became negative after 1984. Instead of a net flow of resources from rich to poor countries, characteristic of the post-war economic order, there was an outflow of resources from poor to rich countries. This net outflow reached its peak in 1988. Since then there has been a recovery. Between 1992 and 1994 the aggregate net transfers on debt became positive again.[14]

In Table 11.6 the differences in regional trends are quite striking. The outflow of resources hit Latin American and African countries far harder than Asian countries. In Asia, net transfers were hardly ever negative and improved substantially in the 1990s. Latin America suffered very heavily, especially between 1984 and 1988. Mexico, for example, was faced by an enormous capital flight. The situation in Latin America is very volatile. When economic prospects improve, flight capital can return to a country, but it is also quick to leave again. Negative net transfers in Chile and South Korea have a different meaning than in other countries. In the late 1980s favourable economic developments formed the basis for repayment of part of foreign debts. For South Korea, the declining ratio of debt to national income is clearly visible in Table 11.4.

Data on net total resource flows, including private direct investment and portfolio investment are represented in Table 12.4 of the next chapter. This table confirms the general trends discussed here, but provides more country detail.

Table 11.6 Net transfers with respect to long-term debt for selected developing countries ($m)*

	1980	1982	1984	1986	1988	1989	1990	1991	1992	1993
Bangladesh	547	518	439	806	575	705	662	460	354	191
China	1,609	−6	461	4,207	5,135	3,509	3,740	2,723	8,394	10,183
India	893	1,182	1,654	1,126	1,720	897	−605	1,082	−1,186	−201
Indonesia	431	914	620	−840	18	2	1,275	−536	1,480	−2,951
Pakistan	460	816	275	150	300	574	352	232	624	804
Philippines	733	678	28	−635	−1,545	−1,099	−677	−1,022	−1,218	−506
South Korea	790	−16	966	−4,363	−5,142	−3,987	−1,628	2,678	1,780	−133
Thailand	1,349	608	657	−1,237	−1,047	582	435	1,233	−299	−1,684
Turkey	1,373	−263	152	235	1,004	−1,580	−1,625	−2,330	−229	2,408
Argentina	1,518	3,325	−3,283	−3,064	−2,237	−1,886	−3,811	−3,941	−1,071	4,585
Brazil	−1,640	−1,400	−2,243	−6,295	−9,515	−8,206	−3,203	−4,391	943	2,963
Chile	1,171	−515	−776	−594	−59	−615	158	−1,766	−549	−263
Colombia	498	551	737	657	−594	−1,277	−1,509	−1,553	−2,074	−1,320
Mexico	2,241	199	−8,626	−7,123	−9,024	−8,117	334	−3,874	−6,319	−2,478
Peru	−382	731	585	84	46	−11	−32	−425	−132	−223
Venezuela	314	−1,331	−2,414	−3,764	−3,373	−1,934	−2,517	−1,186	−143	−1,139
Egypt	2,114	3,167	1,623	600	302	−792	−821	−150	−819	−755
Ghana	112	27	12	244	182	167	228	278	199	147
Ivory Coast	737	953	368	−313	140	188	469	46	−68	−139
Kenya	263	60	−53	115	148	302	138	−124	43	−44
Nigeria	979	2,010	−1,450	−421	−1,133	−571	−2,406	2,503	−3,031	−1,266
Tanzania	319	259	176	167	186	131	230	159	76	89
Zambia	275	160	142	212	61	34	−6	−145	37	63
Total 9 Asian countries	8,185	4,431	5,252	−551	1,018	−397	1,929	4,520	9,648	8,111
Total 7 Latin American countries	3,720	1,560	−16,020	−20,099	−24,756	−22,046	−10,580	−17,136	−9,345	2,125
Total 7 African countries	4,799	6,636	818	604	−114	−541	−2,168	−2,439	−3,563	−1,905
Total 23 countries	16,704	12,627	−9,950	−20,046	−23,852	−22,984	−10,819	−15,055	−3,260	8,331

Note: * Net transfers on long-term capital flows minus interest payments on long-term debts (or new loans minus principal repayments and interest payments).

Sources: 1980–1991: World Bank (1993b), *World Debt Tables 1992/1993*; 1984 from *WDT 1991–92*; 1992–93 from *WDT, 1994–95*.

Reactions to the debt crisis

One of the immediate consequences of the debt crisis was a sudden drop in the flow of private capital to developing countries. When new loans were forthcoming, they served mainly to finance existing debt service. Finance for new investments or imports of indispensable intermediate inputs was scarce. Thus the debt crisis contributed to the stagnation of economic growth in many African and Latin American developing countries. The debt crisis also threatened the stability of the international banking system and consequently the entire international financial system. Many private banks, especially in the United States, had pursued reckless credit policies. Their existence was jeopardized when countries in Latin America and Eastern Europe suspended debt service payments in the wake of Mexico.

During the first years after 1982, therefore, international efforts were aimed mainly at preventing the imminent collapse of the financial system. Later, attention shifted to the consequences of the debt crisis for developing countries. The International Monetary Fund played a prominent role in the prevention of an international financial crisis. It imposed rigorous changes in domestic economic policy as conditions for balance of payments support, new loans and agreements on debt rescheduling. Since private capital flows had dried up, developing countries could no longer get around the 'conditionality' of official financial institutions. The World Bank had formerly operated independently of the IMF and had focused on long-term investment projects. Now it also made its loans conditional on acceptance of IMF policy recommendations. These recommendations are generally referred to as *structural adjustment policies.* Their short-term aim is to improve the balance of payments and reduce government deficits (*stabilization*). The long-term objective is to achieve a more dynamic and flexible economic structure (*structural adjustment*).

In the short term, the goal was to cut back on developing country imports in order to reduce deficits in the balance of payments. This would decrease the need for external finance. Between 1982 and 1985 these policies were fairly successful (Hermes, 1992). Deficits in the balance of payments were indeed reduced, not so much by growth of exports but by a decline in imports. Private banks, which had overexposed themselves in developing countries during the 1970s, increased their reserves for non-repayable debts. By 1985 it was clear that a collapse of the international financial system had been averted. After 1985, debt service as a percentage of export revenues also started to go down (see Table 11.4).

The consequences of stabilization policies were less positive for developing countries. The restrictions on imports of semi-finished goods and capital goods led to stagnating production. In some Latin American countries and most countries in sub-Saharan Africa, per capita incomes fell sharply. Economic stagnation triggered a debate on how to mitigate or avoid the negative consequences of the debt crisis for developing countries. In this debate, two conflicting points of view can be distinguished (Wood, 1985; Buiter and Srinivasan, 1987; Griffin, 1988).

Griffin argued that the debt crisis and economic stagnation were very much the result of external factors such as slower growth of the world economy, deteriorating terms of trade, protectionism by advanced countries, and irresponsible policies of private banks. Since enormous debt service hinders all attempts to restore economic growth, debt relief or debt forgiveness is essential.

Buiter and Srinivasan (1987) severely criticized this point of view. According to them, the main causes of economic stagnation and rising debt were bad economic management and profligate economic policies in the large Latin American countries. These countries had high budget deficits and pursued inefficient protectionist policies, which resulted in inflexible economic structures. Major debtors such as Brazil, Argentina and Mexico are much richer than the poor Asian countries which pursued more prudent and effective macroeconomic policies. Their financial problems are caused in part by capital flight. Debt relief would mean rewarding economic mismanagement and punishing countries that pursued more effective policies and paid their debts. In Latin American countries, structural adjustment policies have to restore the confidence of international finance. Then financial flows will resume and capital flight will be reversed.

Buiter and Srinivasan agree that financial aid flows to very poor African countries should be increased. But they regard debt restructuring in Latin America as a disguised subsidy to the American banking system.

Both parties in the debate acknowledge that resumption of economic growth in developing countries requires renewed net transfers of resources. However, one point of view stresses outright cancellation or reduction of debts; the other point of view emphasizes the implementation of programmes of structural adjustment as a condition for new loans or the restructuring of earlier ones.

Two plans have been of considerable importance in the official responses to the debt crisis, as follows:

1. The Baker Plan in 1985 (*A Programme for Sustained Growth*).
2. The Brady Plan in 1989 for voluntary debt reduction.

The Baker Plan

This plan was put forward by the American Secretary of the Treasury Baker. It assumes that revival of economic growth is only possible if the net inflow of financial resources to developing countries is resumed. The plan argues for cooperation between the IMF, the World Bank and private banking institutions. Private institutions are encouraged to grant new loans. Precondition for the expansion of credit is the pursuit of adjustment policies. The aim is resumption of net capital inflows. At this point, debt reduction is not yet on the table. The adjustment policies in the Baker Plan are not limited to short-term stabilization, as was the case between 1982 and 1985. The plan also strives to improve the working of markets in the long term, by reducing protection and opening up the economy to foreign investment and foreign competition.

The Baker Plan has only been moderately successful. Private banks have been reluctant to cooperate voluntarily and the recommendations for structural adjustment have been only partly realized. Most of the funds went to just three countries: Brazil, Mexico and Argentina. Moreover, the renewed net inflow capital was still modest.

In the meantime, it was realized that debt reduction should also be considered. In the poor African countries the debt burden was so heavy, that the problems could not be solved without outside help. A beginning was made with debt relief and cancellation of part of debts. As almost all loans had been supplied by governments' official financial institutions, policy here was not dependent on the cooperation of the private banking system. Similar policies were proposed with respect to severely indebted Eastern European countries such as Poland and Bulgaria. Further, private banks realized they were better off with repayment of a portion of outstanding debts than with default on total debt. They started participating in plans and measures for voluntary debt reduction.

The Brady Plan

The Brady Plan of 1989 focuses on voluntary debt reduction in a country-by-country approach. The IMF and the World Bank reserved finances for this purpose. Private banks were persuaded to write down the value of risky outstanding loans. The main argument for debt reduction is a decrease in the so-called *debt overhang*. If a country has an excessive foreign debt, all benefits of domestic policy reforms accrue to foreign creditors. This undermines the political will to implement painful adjustment measures. Debt reduction may increase the willingness and capability to meet part of future debt service obligations. Another advantage is that more financial means are available for investment in future growth. The creditors themselves will benefit more from partial repayment of debt than from no repayment at all.

Several techniques for the reduction of debt have been developed in recent years. They include buying back outstanding debts at reduced prices, selling debt on the second-hand market for debts, debt–equity swaps in which loans are exchanged for equity shares, reducing debt in exchange for environmental protection measures (debt for nature swaps), replacing short-term debt by long-term debt with lower interest rates, and many others. The willingness to implement structural adjustment packages negotiated with the IMF remains a precondition for all types of debt-reduction deals.

Between 1985 and 1990 debt reduction has totalled 25 billion dollars. In relation to the total volume of debt, this is merely a drop in the ocean. At the same time there have also been countries where economic growth has resumed, so that debt service becomes less of a problem in spite of the high volume of debt. It can be expected that the trend towards cancelling of debts of the poorest countries will be continued in the near future, though always on the condition of structural adjustment.

Since the second half of the 1980s, capital flows to many developing countries have resumed. This could already be seen in Tables 11.5 and 11.6, which present net resource flows on debt. The exception in these tables is Africa, where these flows remain negative. A more complete picture is presented in the next chapter in Table 12.4. This table includes private direct investment, portfolio investment and aid flows. By the early 1990s, even in Africa the net total resource flows have turned positive again (see also Lensink, 1995).

11.8 *The debate on structural adjustment policies*

11.8.1 Objectives

There are five main objectives of structural adjustment policy (Selowsky, 1987), as follows:

1. Improvement of the external balance between imports and exports. This goal is pursued by reductions in expenditures, depreciation of overvalued exchange rates, and shifts in expenditure to domestically produced goods and services.
2. Rationalization of the public sector and cuts in government expenditures, in particular in expenditures on loss-making public enterprises.
3. Structural adjustments in the production structure aimed at a more efficient allocation of production factors, greater flexibility and sustained growth.
4. Stable incentives for private enterprise, liberalization of the economy and reinforcement of market mechanisms.
5. Opening up of the economy to international competition.

11.8.2 Structuralism versus neoliberalism: structural adjustment as a reaction to post-war trends in development policy.

Structural adjustment policy is in sharp contrast to the central ideas underlying development strategies between the 1950s and the 1970s. In these strategies, discussed in Chapters 7 to 9, government was assigned a critical role in initiating development. The government was a large-scale investor itself and tried to coordinate private sector investment by means of planning. It had to protect the industrial sector against cut-throat international competition in order to give domestic industries time to mature.

The pleas for government interventionism were based on a *structuralist interpretation* of the economic conditions in poor countries (Urquidi, 1993; see also Chapter 3). Structuralism assumes that the conditions for a beneficial functioning of the market mechanism are absent in developing countries, because there are so many restrictions, bottlenecks and imperfections. For instance, there is insufficient infrastructure, insufficient education for productive participation in the economy, and a lack of entrepreneurship. Underdeveloped financial markets cannot supply potential entrepreneurs with sufficient finance. The risks of traditional agriculture restrict the opportunities for innovation. Under such circumstances, a free-market economy will not motivate people to engage in new productive activities. Rather, it will cause their situation to deteriorate. Structuralist policies aim at the supply side of the economy. But from the structuralist perspective, reinforcement of the supply side in developing countries requires government intervention to compensate for market imperfections (Mosley, 1991; Toye, 1993). Structuralist notions thus justify extensive government intervention in the economy.

Modern structural adjustment policy is a frontal attack on post-war structuralist policies. Advocates of structural adjustment believe that many African and Latin American governments pursued policies which gave rise to increasing economic imbalances and distorted markets. In some developing countries the interventionist state itself had become an obstacle to economic dynamism. Although the debate on the role of the government is far from concluded, previous chapters have shown that such criticism is not completely unfounded.

In the explanations of economic stagnation in the 1980s, less importance is ascribed to external causes such as decreasing export prices or the stagnation of the world economy. The emphasis is mainly on internal factors and domestic policies. It is emphasized that several Asian developing economies performed very well during the 1980s in spite of unfavourable external circumstances. It is argued that countries which converted from *inward looking* to *outward looking* development strategies at an early stage did better economically than countries that continued to pursue inward-looking policies (see Chapter 7).

It is extremely interesting that the advocates of structural adjustment policy also use structuralist arguments, in spite of their preference for free markets; hence the term 'structural' adjustment. Their arguments suggest that the supply side of the economy does not function properly, due to bottlenecks, constraints and market imperfections. Economic institutions do not stimulate productive behaviour. Therefore, countries must explicitly pursue a structural policy aimed at increasing their productive capacities and the efficiency of the production structure. But in this case, government policies, excessive regulation and intervention in the market are identified as the prime causes of economic inflexibility. The traditional structuralist argument is thus stood on its head (Toye, 1993).

11.8.3 Structural adjustment, IMF and the World Bank

The discussion of structural adjustment predates the debt crisis (Lensink, 1995). As early as 1979 the World Bank introduced the financial instrument of structural adjustment loans (SALs). The World Bank was highly dissatisfied with its project-related financial flows. Too many funds were spent on large-scale capital intensive projects of dubious effectiveness (Toye, 1993). Far from all projects were completed. After official completion, sometimes insufficient means were available to continue the projects. Developing countries were not so much in need of new project aid, but rather of additional means for the completion and upkeep of existing infrastructural projects. As prices did not reflect real scarcity relations due to distorted markets, it was almost impossible to formulate good projects and to weigh their costs and benefits.

The structural adjustment loans were designed to make new, non-project-related funds available, and at the same time, to formulate conditions with respect to reinforcement of market mechanisms, strengthening economic incentives, improving macroeconomic policies and liberalizing the economy.

After the debt crisis, the pressures to implement structural adjustment policies increased. The roles of the World Bank and the IMF converged. Initially, the World

Bank had focused on medium- and long-term project aid and the IMF on short-run financial support for countries with balance of payments difficulties. Now the World Bank moved from project to programme lending and the IMF created instruments for medium-term structural adjustment (Lensink, 1995). The World Bank and the IMF coordinated their actions and both set structural adjustment as a condition for the provision of new loans. A country had first to turn to the IMF for a stand-by arrangement through which means are made available to finance deficits in the balance-of-payments. Only after IMF conditions had been met could a country apply for adjustment loans from the World Bank aimed at long-term restructuring of the economy. Between 1979 and 1991, ninety-nine developing countries received structural adjustment loans from the World Bank.

11.8.4 Stabilization and structural adjustment

Although the term 'structural adjustment' is frequently used to refer to both *economic stabilization policy* and *structural adjustment policy* in a more restricted sense, it is useful to distinguish clearly between these two kinds of policy (Mosley, 1991; Hermes, 1992; Lensink, 1993).

The aims of stabilization policies are to restore the external balance on the balance of payments and to reduce inflation. Imports should be restricted and exports should be promoted. Financial means that were employed to finance imports thus become available for debt servicing. Stabilization is realized by means of measures that influence the demand side of the economy. Demand is restricted by measures such as tax increases, reduction of government deficits and government expenditures, abolition of government subsidies, higher prices for government services, wage policies, tight monetary policies, increases in interest rates and, especially, depreciation of overvalued exchange rates. Depreciation makes imports more expensive and exports cheaper.

Structural adjustment measures are measures directed towards long-run improvements in the supply side of the economy, so that production can increase and economic subjects can respond better to economic incentives. Structural adjustment packages often include stabilization measures, but their scope is wider. The long-run aim is to reduce the role of the state and liberalize the whole economy, so that prices actually reflect scarcity and promote more efficient economic behaviour. Discrimination against agriculture in favour of the industrial sector should be ended. Restrictions on trade and capital flows should be phased out. Protection of domestic industry by means of tariffs and quotas should be reduced. Domestic firms should be exposed more to foreign competition and should try to penetrate export markets. Exports should follow the lines of comparative advantage.

Of course, stabilization programmes and structural adjustment programmes are complementary. The imbalances in the economy that result in financial crisis in the short term are partly due to the inadequacy of domestic supply with respect to domestic demand. This will result in inflation and deficits on the current account of the balance of payments. In the long term, removal of structural impediments and increased flexibility of the production structure are the best way to prevent financial crisis from recurring (Husain, 1993).

11.8.5 Structural adjustment policy measures

In negotiations with the IMF and the World Bank, a set of economic reform measures is drawn up for each specific country. The provision of new loans is made dependent on the acceptance of the package of reforms. The concrete package differs from country to country, depending on the circumstances. The most frequently used measures are set out below (Selowsky, 1987; Mosley, 1991; Mosley *et al.*, 1991; Doroodian, 1993; Greenaway and Morrisey, 1993; Toye, 1993; Lensink, 1995).

Liberalization of domestic markets

Less price controls; less wage legislation; abolition of the practice of indexing wages to inflation; abolition of minimum wage regulations.

Trade policy

1. Depreciation of overvalued exchange rates. A cheaper currency makes imports more expensive and exports cheaper. Import-substituting domestic production becomes more profitable.
2. Liberalization of trade policy by abolishing import quotas; import tariff systems are made more transparent and tariffs themselves are reduced. At first sight, abolition of import restrictions seems to conflict with the aim of reduction of balance-of-payments deficits. But when exchange rates are determined by market forces, growth of imports will lead to depreciation of the exchange rate. This in turn makes for recovery of the external balance. Liberalization of imports also undermines monopoly positions of traders who profited from import-licensing under the protectionist regime. Domestic producers are exposed to international competition.
3. Striking a balance between incentives for import substituting production and incentives for export production.

The public sector, fiscal policy, government expenditure, public enterprises

1. Reforms of the budgetary and fiscal system, aimed at a better control of government expenditure and a more effective collection of taxes.
2. Reducing government expenditures and government deficits.
3. Restructuring the priorities in government investment. More priority to investment in the agricultural sector.
4. Increasing the government's capacity to formulate and execute government investment programmes; increasing the general efficiency of government.

5. Increasing the output and efficiency of loss-making public enterprises (*parastatals*).
6. Privatization of public enterprises and public activities.
7. Liberalization of price policy.
8. Reducing subsidies for energy and food. Increasing taxes on consumer goods.

Capital market

1. Liberalization of domestic and foreign capital markets.
2. Deregulation of interest rates. Higher interest rates elicit higher domestic savings. Higher interest costs lead to a more efficient use of capital in the production process.
3. Creating new financial institutions; privatization or restructuring of government controlled banks.

Agricultural policy

1. Increasing agricultural prices in order to stimulate agricultural production.
2. Abolishing or limiting the role of state marketing boards that used to have a monopoly on the trade in food and export products. Liberalization of agricultural trade.
3. Reducing subsidies for agricultural inputs.

Industrial policy

Intensifying incentives for efficient production in the industrial sector, among others by refusing to bail out unprofitable firms and investment projects.

Energy policy

Increasing the domestic prices of energy to relieve the government budget; promoting the domestic supply of energy.

11.8.6 The effectiveness of structural adjustment programmes

Since 1979, ninety-nine countries had received World Bank loans as part of structural adjustment programmes (SAPs). For years the success of the structural adjustment policy has been fiercely debated. Two central question in this debate are: (1) To what degree does structural adjustment contribute to economic recovery? (2) Are the social consequences of adjustment policies acceptable? Unfortunately, it is hard to provide unambiguous empirical answers to these questions. First, by no means all adjustment measures agreed upon are actually implemented. Second, there are countries which do not receive adjustment loans but nevertheless implement their own adjustment policies (e.g. India). Third, circumstances and the initial conditions differ from country to country. Fourth, policy is only one of the factors impinging on economic and social development.

In the literature, the following factors are identified as important to the success of adjustment policies (Edwards, 1990; Mosley, 1991; Mosley *et al.*, 1991; Greenaway and Morrissey, 1993; Lensink, 1995):

1. *Implementation.* Is a government really prepared to implement painful measures? Isn't drawing up a SAP just a feint to obtain new loans? On average, only 60 per cent of all reform measures agreed upon are actually implemented (Mosley, 1991). In the nine countries studied by Mosley *et al.* (1991), the implementation percentages vary from 25 to 90 per cent. Stabilization measures are generally easier to implement than structural reform measures, which often meet with resistance from powerful interest groups whose 'rents' are threatened.

2. *Credibility of government policy.* Is the government able to convince private entrepreneurs that it will continue to carry out adjustment policies in spite of their unpopularity? If credibility is lacking, positive responses from the private sector are very unlikely. Frequent changes in policy have negative effects on economic development.

3. *The sequencing of adjustment measures* (Greenaway and Morrissey, 1993). If policies are implemented in the wrong order, they may harm the economy. This is illustrated by the following five examples. Abolishing controls over capital flows before reforming domestic financial markets can result in capital flight. Without prior reduction of budget deficits, liberalization of financial markets will lead to inflation. A sudden increase in interest rates may also increase government expenditures. Without macroeconomic stabilization, liberalization of trade leads to a deterioration of the economic situation. Liberalization of trade without depreciation of the currency leads to increasing deficits on the balance of payments. Sooner or later these will force the government to intervene again.

In the literature, the following sequence is suggested as most fruitful (Edwards, 1990; Greenaway and Morrissey, 1993; Toye, 1993; Lensink, 1995, pp. 228 ff.):

1. Reform policies start with macroeconomic stabilization, depreciation of exchange rates, tackling inflation and reducing government deficits. Almost all authors stress the importance of reducing budget deficits and depreciating the currency as the first step in the process of reform.
2. Liberalization of the domestic real economy: liberalization of prices and liberalization of labour markets.
3. Reform of domestic financial markets. If financial markets are liberalized before step 2, financial resources may be wasted on unproductive activities.
4. Liberalization of foreign trade. According to some authors, efficient allocation of production factors only takes place if the financial system is already well

developed. But other authors argue that financial liberalization should come after trade liberalization in order to avoid resources being squandered on import substitution. Thus the sequence of steps 3 and 4 is still disputed.

5. The last stage involves liberalization of international capital flows. If one does this before domestic financial markets have been liberalized, there will be capital flight because domestic interest rates are still too low.

Effects of structural adjustment policy

With respect to the effects of the structural adjustment policy, opinions in the literature vary from favourable (World Bank, 1989b; Husain, 1993) to extremely critical (Cornia *et al.*, 1987, 1992; Elbadawi, 1992; Elbadawi *et al.*, 1992). I agree with Mosley that any country which is faced with external shocks and increasing deficits on its balance of payments will sooner or later be forced to implement some kind of economic adjustment policy. However, this does not inevitably mean that they have to turn to international financial institutions such as the IMF or the World Bank.

In a large-scale evaluation study, Mosley *et al.* (1991) conclude that countries which have implemented far-reaching structural adjustment policies are generally more successful in terms of economic growth and balance of payments. The effects on export performance are not all that clear (Greenaway and Morrissey, 1993).

Of the ninety-nine structural adjustment programmes, forty-four were drawn up for extremely poor countries in sub-Saharan Africa. The results in this region are definitely disappointing. It is true that African countries which have implemented more drastic adjustment programmes do not perform as poorly as other countries, but trends of economic stagnation have by no means been reversed. An earlier optimistic World Bank report on the success of structural adjustment policies in Africa (World Bank, 1989b) has been severely criticized (Mosley and Weeks, 1992). In a review of the most recent studies on structural adjustment in Africa, Lensink (1995) concludes that there are modest positive effects on GDP growth, mixed results with respect to export growth, and disappointing effects on savings and investments. But the methodological problems of ascertaining the impacts of structural adjustment remain great. In addition to economic policy, numerous other factors also play an important role in this region, like constant political turmoil, ethnic conflicts, droughts and an unfavourable international economic climate.

It is worrying that many studies conclude that there are adverse effects of structural adjustment programmes on investment levels. The reason for this, of course, is that reductions in government expenditures also affect government investment. Contrary to what was anticipated, this was not compensated for in the short term by increases in private investment. In the long term, a decline in investment rates is incompatible with the goals of increasing productive capacity. At the same time, the decline in investment is also interpreted by some as the result of stricter criteria being applied to unprofitable projects.

Social consequences of adjustment policy

In 1987, Cornia *et al.* (1987) published their study, *Adjustment with a Human Face.* In this study they criticized the social consequences of adjustment programmes. Cutbacks in government expenditure were realized at the expense of education, health care and food and energy subsidies for the very poor. Thus structural adjustment policy did not only lead to further impoverishment, but also to insufficient investment in human capital, which endangers the opportunities of future economic growth. The authors pleaded for a more gradual implementation of structural adjustment policy and for compensatory finance to deal with the social consequences of expenditure cuts. Their call has been heeded by UN organizations like UNICEF and the Economic Commission for Africa. In the design of new adjustment programmes the World Bank today also pays more attention to the consequences for poverty, at least on paper.

A counter-argument is that subsidies, educational facilities and health care services in developing countries are usually not accessible to the poorest. Because of the urban-industrial bias, urban inhabitants and relatively privileged persons, such as students, civil servants or industrial employees, are the main beneficiaries of public services and subsidies. An adjustment policy that cuts back on subsidies may raise the price of agricultural products and improve the terms of trade for the rural areas. This would actually improve the situation of some of the poor who depend on agriculture for their living.

The question is not whether structural adjustment policies have negative social consequences. In the short term, it is almost certain that they do. More important is the question as to whether adjustment policy leads to an improvement in economic dynamics in the long term (Gunning, 1988). The worst case is a situation in which adjustment policy takes its toll on the poor without much hope of resumption of economic growth. This seems to characterize the situation in the present-day Russian Federation in its transition from a centrally planned economy to a market economy (Menshikov, 1993).

Is Africa different? Pros and cons of structural adjustment

Mosley (1991) presents a very clarifying distinction between adjustment programmes in middle-income countries and adjustment programmes in the poorest African countries with a stagnating economy. In middle-income countries, structural reforms may help transform a too inward-looking economy into a more export-oriented economy. In this respect, Turkey and the Philippines have been very successful. In countries like Chile, Mexico, Indonesia and, at an earlier stage, South Korea, adjustment policies met with positive outcomes.

In the poorest developing countries the inward-oriented strategy is not the main problem. Rather the problem lies in the fact that the agricultural infrastructure, the transport system and the capital stock have been neglected. In sub-Saharan Africa the cutbacks in government expenditure have been realized at the expense of essential investments in agricultural infrastructure, schooling and agricultural education. If prices of food and export crops are no longer controlled and state marketing boards are abolished, farmers will not necessarily respond by increasing their production. Farmers' ability to respond to market incentives is restricted by factors such as a sparse and scattered population, bad roads, poor transport and communication, insufficient agricultural schooling and education, insufficient agricultural research, and poor possibilities for marketing (Helleiner, 1992b). Helleiner even argues for maintaining the state marketing boards for agricultural exports. Otherwise farmers will not be able to market their products on the international market. Helleiner is convinced that investment in infrastructure is at least as important as higher prices. Both Mosley and Weeks (1992) and Helleiner (1992b) conclude that African countries which liberalized agricultural prices without simultaneously increasing government investment in infrastructure performed worse economically than other African countries.

Combined with increased investment in the rural infrastructure and agricultural services, price liberalization may lead to remarkably positive results. An example of this was provided by Nigeria between 1986 and 1991 (Husain, 1993). During this period the value of food imports decreased from 2.5 million dollars to 300–400 million dollars per year due to increased agricultural self-sufficiency.

According to Mosley, structural adjustment in the poor countries in sub-Saharan Africa does not require reduced government intervention. He and other authors of this school actually argue for an increased role of government and more investment in education, schooling and infrastructure. Provided governments can be made more efficient, government intervention is what is needed to combat market imperfections associated with poor infrastructure, an inadequate and dated capital stock, and insufficient education to guarantee participation in economic life. The traditional structuralist arguments are still very much alive here.

The argument for more infrastructural investment is quite convincing. What is less convincing is the faith in an increased role of government in the economic process. It is not enough to say that governments should become more efficient than in the past. In the light of the criticism of the functioning of the state apparatus in sub-Saharan Africa in Chapter 10, it is open to serious doubt as to whether African governments can fulfil the dynamic role suggested by Mosley and Helleiner. A more restricted role for governments remains a central issue on the agenda of the very poor countries in Africa.

QUESTIONS FOR REVIEW

1. Discuss the characteristics and institutions of the liberal international order, devised at the Bretton Woods conference in 1944. What were the tasks assigned to the IMF and what were the tasks assigned to the World Bank?

2. What were the main criticisms of the liberal international economic order on the part of the advocates of a new international economic order in the 1960s and 1970s?
3. What were the most important policy proposals for a new international economic order? Why have we heard so little about the new international economic order since the early 1980s?
4. What are the primary objectives of structural adjustment policies? Compare structural adjustment policy proposals with the characterstics of orthodox post-war development strategies.
5. What are the differences between structural adjustment policies and economic stabilization policies? Are there also similarities between the two?
6. Summarize the debate on the (positive or negative) consequences of structural adjustment policies in different parts of the developing world.

Notes

1. This section has been inspired to an important extent by a review article by N. Schrijver (1985), 'De Verenigde Naties, de internationale economische organisaties en ontwikkelingssamenwerking' (The United Nations, international economic organizations and development cooperation).
2. Among others: the International Civil Aviation Organization, the Universal Postal Union, the International Telecommunication Union, the International Maritime Organization, the World Meteorological Organization, the World Organization for Intellectual Property.
3. This assumption is not essential. It is only used to explain the principle of free trade as briefly as possible.
4. The idea that the demand for primary products does not increase in proportion to the increase in average per capita incomes.
5. In writing this section, I have made extensive use of a recent publication *De internationale schuldencrisis* (The international debt crisis) by Hermes (1992).
6. Debt service is the sum of repayments of principal and interest payments in a given period.
7. Unlike what is generally assumed, a considerable part of the loans was used to keep up investment and consumption, according to Hermes (1992). However, this tells us little about the efficiency of investments.
8. The present value of debt service is the sum of all debt service due during the lifetime of a loan, discounted to current dollar values using the interest rates of the loans. In 1993 the category of SICs included 48 countries. The top panel of Table 11.4 includes fourteen severely indebted countries with the largest absolute volume of debt, plus Tanzania and Zambia as examples of two very heavily indebted small African countries. The data in Table 11.4 themselves are annual data, rather than discounted present values.
9. The list of 'heavily indebted countries' of 1982 includes both 'severely indebted countries' (SICs) and 'moderately indebted countries' (MICs) of 1993. Unlike in 1993, four criteria of indebtedness were used. The 1982 criteria refer to the value of debt service in a given year, rather than to the discounted value of debt service.
10. Algeria is a special case. It was classified as severely indebted in 1991, but no longer so in 1993. This oil-rich country has been retained in the table because of the relatively large volume of its debt.

11. The annual figures are sometimes very erratic, though. For instance, Nicaragua had a debt service to exports ratio of 112 per cent in 1991, against 29 per cent in 1993. Syria had a debt service to exports ratio of 27 per cent in 1991, against 5 per cent in 1993.
12. Strangely enough, interest receipts are not included in net transfers. Net transfers on debt also exclude financial flows associated with direct foreign investment.
13. One hundred and sixteen developing countries participate in the World Bank Debt Reporting System. Developing countries that were part of the former Soviet Union are also included.
14. Using OECD data, Hermes (1992) concludes that aggregate net transfers turned positive as early as 1986. The difference in dating depends in part on definitions. The OECD data include both interest payments and dividend payments. They refer not only to payments, but also to receipts. The patterns, however, are similar. Moreover, the unfavourable position of Latin American countries in the 1980s is rightly emphasized.

12 Foreign aid and development

In this final chapter I turn to the role of foreign aid in development. The central issue is whether and to what extent aid can make a positive contribution to development.[1] The decision to discuss foreign aid at the end of this book is a deliberate one. After all, development is determined by a complex of factors, including historical experiences, natural circumstances, demographic factors, power structures and processes of state formation, institutions and attitudes, international economic relations and economic policy. Foreign aid is just one of many factors. At best, its contribution can only be marginal. The original theories of economic aid formulated in the 1950s and the 1960s by authors such as Chenery and Strout, Rostow and Rosenstein-Rodan, recognize this explicitly. They state that under certain conditions foreign aid may contribute to an *acceleration* of growth and development, but it cannot transform processes of stagnation into dynamic processes of development. In the debates between the supporters and opponents of foreign aid this tends to be forgotten.

Until quite recently, the desirability of development aid was not questioned in the political debate. In the 1980s all donors together granted a total of approximately 60 billion dollars per year in official development assistance. In 1987, the United States was the largest donor in absolute terms, followed by Japan, France, Germany, Italy, the Netherlands, Denmark and the United Kingdom, in that order. Net aid flows as a percentage of gross national income were highest in Norway (1.1 per cent), the Netherlands (1 per cent), Sweden (0.9 per cent) and Denmark (0.9 per cent). In the United States aid was only 0.2 per cent of GNP (Krueger *et al.*, 1989, table 3.1).

Despite the substantial resources involved, the budgets for foreign aid were exempted from expenditure cuts in most countries until the late 1980s. Although there has been a lively debate on the effectiveness of aid flows, the basic idea of development aid was supported by political parties across the political spectrum and by the general public. It was not until the early 1990s that this consensus on development aid started to unravel.

This chapter is structured as follows. Section 12.1 examines the motives for granting foreign aid. After a discussion of different sources and types of aid in section 12.2, section 12.3 concentrates on the objectives and expected outcomes of aid. Underlying development aid are theories of development and its bottlenecks. Implicitly or explicitly these theories provide justifications for different kinds of aid. These theories are also discussed in section 12.3. Development aid is provided in different areas of policy concern: health care, education, legal development, administrative capacity, economic development, and so on. In keeping with the focus of the whole book, the emphasis in this chapter is on the contribution of various kinds of aid to the economic dynamics of developing countries. Section 12.4 presents a brief outline of the history of development aid. Quantitative data on aid flows are presented in section 12.5. In the final section (12.6) the debate between supporters and opponents of development aid is summarized. Attention is paid to radical criticisms which interpret foreign aid as an instrument to prolong the dependence of poor countries and to keep them subordinated to the interests of the rich countries. Subsequently, attention is paid to the criticisms of proponents of the free market who see development aid as one of the obstacles to development. Finally, this section presents the mainstream perspective on development and its response to criticisms from the radical left and the neoliberal right. The mainstream claim is that in spite of many shortcomings, aid on balance makes a positive contribution to development. The central question in the debate is whether development aid, in spite of its stated aims of reducing poverty and misery and increasing the autonomy of people in developing countries, does in fact contribute to continued dependence.

12.1 *Why foreign aid?*

The debate on development aid has been complicated by a failure to distinguish clearly between the principles and moral motives underlying aid and the assessments of its effects and results (Riddell, 1987, chapters 2, 3, and 4). A statement to the effect that given the urgency of the poverty issue and the enormous income gap between rich and poor countries, governments have a moral obligation to provide aid, implicitly assumes that the effects of aid are positive. For if foreign aid was thought to have negative effects on development, the moral case for aid would automatically become invalid.

If the contributions of aid to development are disappointing, the question has to be asked whether this is due to the inherent shortcomings of aid or whether it depends on the specific ways in which aid is provided. For instance, a topical issue is whether aid from governments to governments is the most suitable way of providing aid. In sum, our judgements concerning the desirability of aid depend on our perspectives on the empirical reality of which aid is a constituent part. Here I will first discuss the different motives underlying foreign aid. In section 12.6, I will discuss the empirical consequences of aid.

The following kinds of motives for development aid can be distinguished: moral motives; references to mutual interests; commercial motives; and political and strategic motives (Riddell, 1987; Hoebink, 1988, 1990a, 1990b).

Moral motives

Moral motives for development aid include the following:

- *Humanitarian motives* Given widespread poverty, malnutrition and unacceptable living conditions in many developing countries, there is a moral obligation to provide aid. These motives take some criterion of absolute human needs as their point of departure.
- *Egalitarian motives* From an egalitarian point of view, the extreme inequalities between rich and poor countries, and rich and poor people, and the widening gaps between rich and poor in the world economy, are morally unacceptable. The rich have a moral duty to help the poor. Development aid is seen as an equalizing transfer payment.
- *International solidarity* It is not self-evident that criteria of need and egalitarian justice should be applied on a global scale. It can be argued that the main task of a state is to provide for the welfare of its own citizens, according to the criteria of justice within the society. The moral argument for development aid includes the proposition that moral obligations transcend the borders of national societies. In its most extreme version this argument states that we are all members of a new global society.
- *Reparation of past wrongs* In the past, rich Western countries have exploited poor countries and have harmed their chances of development through colonialism and external intervention. As the Western world is responsible for the underdevelopment of poor countries, Western countries have a moral obligation to repay past debts. From this perspective, development aid is a kind of compensation payment.

Mutual interests

Poor countries and rich countries are mutually interdependent in global society. Economic and social development in poor countries is not only in the interest of the citizens of these countries. It is also in the interest of rich countries and their citizens (see Brandt *et al.*, 1980, 1983). The mutual interest motive is expressed in different modalities, as follows:

- The world economy is increasingly an interdependent whole. Economic development and increasing per capita incomes in poor countries create new markets for imports from rich countries. Economic stagnation in poor countries has negative effects on economic growth in the rich countries.

- Global environmental problems caused by pollution, depletion of resources, population growth and economic growth threaten the welfare and development prospects of both rich and poor countries. Protection of the global environment and sustainable development are common interests (e.g. the report, *Our Common Future*, Bruntland *et al.*, 1987).
- The enormous gaps in income levels in the world economy may lead to destructive conflicts between the rich countries in the North and the poor countries in the South. Avoiding such conflicts by promoting economic development in poor countries is also in the interest of the rich countries.
- A special version of the mutual interest motive is the prevention of massive immigration from developing countries to the economically advanced countries. This line of reasoning states that if economic conditions in developing countries improve as a result of development aid, migration flows to the rich countries, which are experienced as threatening, will come to an end.

Commercial motives

Development aid is seen as an instrument of export promotion. Development aid is used to support firms exporting to developing countries, and to help develop new export markets. It is hard to draw the boundary between commercial motives and mutual interests. Sometimes the only motive is blatant self-interest, with firms in rich countries lobbying for support and foreign aid functioning as a form of export credit in disguise. Sometimes there is a genuine conviction that the promotion of economic development in a developing country is compatible with an expansion of exports to this country.

Political and strategic motives

Foreign aid is frequently an instrument of foreign policy, aimed at cementing the political ties between donors and client countries. Former European colonial powers tried to maintain or reinforce their political, economic and cultural ties with their former colonies through development aid. For the United States, preventing countries from falling within the communist sphere of influence was clearly an important motive for foreign aid. In the 1960s and 1970s most US foreign aid went to South Korea and South Vietnam. In the 1970s, the lion's share of aid was provided to Egypt and Israel. Foreign aid was one of the main instruments of US foreign policy in the Middle East. Eighty per cent of aid from the former Soviet Union was allocated to Cuba, Mongolia and Vietnam. Most French development aid went to its former colonies in Africa. In the early period of Dutch development aid, a large proportion was reserved for (former) colonies.

For a public justification of their aid policies, governments tend to appeal primarily to moral motives. But in practice, all the motives mentioned above play a role in maintaining broad political and social support of foreign aid policy. In a lucid analysis of the ethical and moral arguments for foreign aid, Riddell (1987, pp. 12–16) identifies the following seven propositions which together constitute the argument that there is a moral obligation for governments to provide foreign aid to developing countries:[2]

1. On the basis of comparisons between domestic standards of living in rich countries and those in developing countries, potential donors accept that there are problems in developing countries which provide a moral basis for action.
2. Direct intervention can help solve such problems.
3. External financial and/or technical assistance contributes to a development strategy aimed at solving these problems.
4. Aid flows from government to government contribute to the solution of problems.
5. There is a moral obligation to give aid to defined categories of countries, and – through the governments of these countries – to defined groups within these countries.
6. The moral obligation to provide aid to identified countries is so strong that the use of funds for foreign aid is justified in the light of other legitimate claims on a government's financial resources.
7. The resources furnished by means of foreign aid actually help promote development or have the potential of doing so in the future, based on the learning experiences of past mistakes.

Each of these propositions can be challenged by critics and is open to discussion. The criticism of the moral motives for aid has been formulated by contract theorists, such as Nozick, Bauer and Hayek, applying procedural theories of justice. From this perspective, all inequalities in outcomes and rewards obtained by individual effort and according to just procedures are justified. Redistribution of outcomes on the basis of needs or egalitarian criteria is rejected as unjust. Only when inequality is the result of unjust acquisition in the past may there be a basis for compensation in the present. However, here the debate shifts to the empirical domain. The critics of egalitarian and needs-based criteria are convinced that differences in economic development are explained by differences in skills, talents, efforts, institutions and policies, and not by past exploitation.

A second line of criticism is that governments are only responsible for their own citizens and have no obligations to citizens of other countries. A third category of arguments, formulated in particular by Peter Bauer, refers to the fact the aid is provided on a government-to-government basis. Even if one subscribes to the moral argument in favour of aid, which Bauer certainly does not, there may still be good reasons for being opposed to intergovernmental aid flows. In practice, according to Bauer, aid means that poor people in rich countries are taxed in order to subsidize rich people and members of political elites in poor countries. Once again, the discussion about principles of justice is mixed with discussion about empirical realities.

Without doing sufficient justice to the interesting debate on the moral foundations of development aid – well summarized by Riddell – I will take the moral arguments for development aid as my point of departure. In the rest of the chapter the focus will be on the empirical discussion concerning the effects of aid on development. This means that little attention will be paid to other motives underlying foreign aid. These will only enter the discussion when they have effects on the primary objective of development aid: that is, contributing to an improvement in the living conditions and economic dynamics in developing countries.

12.2 *Development aid: sources and categories*

The Development Assistance Committee (DAC) of the Organization for Economic Cooperation and the Development (OECD) presents an annual survey of aid flows to developing countries in the *Geographical Distribution of Financial Flows to Developing Countries* (GDFF). In this publication, official development assistance (ODA) is defined as: financial flows to developing countries provided by official agencies, with the objective of promoting the economic development and welfare of developing countries and with a grant element of at least 25 per cent.

The following *sources* of development aid can be distinguished:

- Aid provided by advanced industrialized countries united in the OECD. This aid is coordinated by the *Development Assistance Committee.*
- Aid provided by Arab oil-producing countries. These aid flows increased in the 1970s when oil prices were raised. In the 1980s these flows declined again. Presently only three countries are specifically listed in the GDFF (OECD, 1995) as bilateral donors: Saudi Arabia, Kuwait and the United Arab Emirates. But there are also multilateral flows from the Arab countries.
- Aid from the formerly centrally planned countries united in the CMEA (Council for Mutual Economic Assistance). The amounts were quite modest. Eighty per cent of aid offered by the former Soviet Union was allocated to just three countries: Cuba, Vietnam, and Mongolia.[3] These aid flows have dried up since the mid-1980s and are presently no longer distinguished as a separate category.
- Aid provided by voluntary development organizations (non-governmental organizations; NGOs). These flows can be quite substantial. In the Netherlands, voluntary organizations provide aid to the extent of 250 to 300 million Dutch guilders annually (Kruyt and Koonings, 1988).[4]

DAC statistics on development assistance refer primarily to aid provided by OECD member countries of the DAC and Arab countries. Aid offered with other than developmental objectives (e.g. military assistance) is excluded. Aid flows include both outright grants (in money or kind) and soft loans with a grant element of at least 25 per cent. Loans without this grant element, like export credits, are not defined as part of official development assistance. The concessionality of a loan – the softness or grant element – is the difference between the costs of a loan (depending on the maturity of the loan, the grace period before first repayment and the annual interest) and the costs a borrower would have to pay at market rates. For practical purposes, the reference interest rate for commercial loans is set at 10 per cent. The grant element in development assistance is different for each country, yet it is rather high (in 1991 an average 87 per cent; see OECD, 1995). Aid is not always financial. it sometimes consists of goods (food, machines, fertilizers) or services (technical experts, teachers). In such cases, the value of the goods and services is included in the statistics.

The OECD records both bilateral aid which is provided directly on a country-to-country basis, and multilateral aid through international organizations. Important sources of multilateral aid are: the International Development Association (IDA), a subsidiary organization of the World Bank, which issues soft loans for development objectives; regional development banks; the World Health Organization (WHO); the International Fund for Agricultural Development (IFAD); and the European Development Fund. Multilaterally funded technical aid is offered by the United Nations Development Programme (UNDP) and the Food and Agriculture Organization (FAO). There are also specific Arab-financed multilateral agencies such as the Opec Fund for International Development (OFID).

In general, governments find it easier to put their stamp on aid policy in bilateral aid relations than via aid provided through multilateral agencies. Bilateral aid also offers more opportunities for support to domestic producers and exporters in the donor country. The distinction between bilateral and multilateral aid is not absolute, however. Much bilateral aid is coordinated on a recipient country basis via international donor consortia. The European Development Fund is also a mixture of bilateral and multilateral aid.

The following *categories* of aid can be distinguished (Cassen, 1986): project aid; programme aid; food aid; and technical cooperation.

Project aid

Under the heading of project aid, support is provided for a consistent set of activities, with a specified duration and a well-defined objective. Project aid makes available specific capital assets or pieces of technical assistance. An important aspect of project aid refers to infrastructural works, such as roads, harbours, dams, irrigation projects, energy projects, or telecommunications projects. In addition, projects include both large-scale and small-scale industrial projects, agricultural projects, integrated rural development projects, education projects, population projects, health projects, projects for women, and so forth.

Programme aid

In the case of programme aid, financial support is provided to governments in the form of financial grants or concessional loans in support of economic policy programmes. Programme aid may be provided for the benefit of the entire economy or for specific sectors. In the latter case, the developing country government receives financial resources to execute certain policies in one specific sector – education, agriculture, small-scale industry, and so on. Programme aid leaves more to the discretion of the recipient than project aid. It is easier to disburse quickly, which makes it a more flexible instrument. Programme aid can be offered in the form of balance-of-payments support. It is usually linked to policy dialogue.

Food aid

Food aid is concerned with the provision of food in kind from the agricultural surpluses of the rich countries. This food is provided either free of charge or at low price. Apart from emergency aid in case of natural disasters and famines, food aid is also offered when the food production in a country fails to meet the demand for food. Food may also be provided to people in exchange for work on roads, infrastructure, or municipal facilities (*Food for Work*).

Technical cooperation

Technical cooperation involves providing technical services of 'experts' and 'teachers'. The boundary between technical cooperation and project aid is not quite clear since elements of technical cooperation are included in almost all projects. However, projects mainly refer to physical capital goods which are supplied or for which money is provided. Technical aid refers to 'experts' who contribute to engineering design and construction of capital projects, the transfer of knowledge, education and educational institution building, institutional development or technology transfer. Scholarships, short training programmes and education services of international educational institutions in donor countries are also considered part of technical cooperation.

In theory, programme aid could also be used to pay for services of technical experts or for investments in education. Most often, however, technical aid is provided in the form of payment of the salaries of experts posted in developing countries.

The distinction between project aid and programme aid is a matter of the form in which aid is provided. Food aid and technical cooperation are mentioned separately because of their specific substantive characteristics and because of the fact that most donor countries have separate programmes for these kinds of aid.

12.3 *Theories and objectives*

Discussions of foreign aid are implicitly or explicitly based on theories of economic development, in which aid flows can fulfil certain functions (Bruton, 1969; Bauer, 1981; Cassen, 1986; Riddell, 1987; Krueger *et al.*, 1989; Bos, 1990; Lesink, 1993). Together with normative considerations, these theories determine the specific goals and objectives one hopes to realize by means of development aid.

The foundations of theories on the role of foreign aid in development were laid in the 1950s and 1960s. As sketched in the chapter on industrialization strategies (Chapter 7), the prevailing assumption was that developing countries were caught in vicious cycles of poverty. Due to low per capita incomes, savings were low. Due to low savings rates, investment was low, so that there were little prospects for future growth of national income and development of the industrial sector.

Capital was seen as the scarce factor in development. What was required was a large-scale investment programme in industry and infrastructure, that would help economies break out of their vicious circles (Millikan and Rostow, 1957; Rosenstein-Rodan, 1961; Rostow, 1971).

In this situation, an influx of foreign capital could contribute to increased investment, without the necessity of a simultaneous decline in domestic consumption. Aid would come in two forms: capital goods and industrial inputs; and technical aid to promote the transfer of knowledge and skills. Starting from growth targets established in national plans, the required levels of savings and investments were calculated by means of fixed capital–output ratios (see Chapter 7). Given the domestic savings ratios, the need for foreign capital could be determined. Development aid would have to provide part of the required foreign capital. It was assumed that private capital markets would be unable to meet the foreign finance requirements of developing countries. Distrust of the market dominated development strategies. This formed a justification for government intervention and financial aid flows from governments to governments.

The two-gap model of Chenery and Strout

The most complete formulation of the line of thinking described above is Chenery and Strout's (1966) *two-gap model* (see also Chenery and Adelman, 1966; Chenery and MacEwan, 1966; Bruton, 1969; Chenery, 1979). Transformation of the economic structure requires a large inflow of external financial resources in a short period of time. Foreign aid can contribute to the acceleration of economic growth and structural transformation by relieving crucial bottlenecks in the process of development. This would increase the efficiency of the use of domestic economic resources.

Chenery and Strout distinguish two *gaps*: the savings gap, and the foreign exchange gap. As mentioned above, economic growth requires large investments in industry and infrastructure. Domestic savings are insufficient to meet investment requirements. This is Chenery and Strout's first gap. The inflow of foreign financial resources, of which foreign aid is part, can compensate for the shortage of domestic savings. In this respect, the crucial assumption is that the inflow of aid does not result in a decline of domestic savings (see Bruton, 1969). If they do decline, the inflow of development aid will result in an increase in domestic consumption, but the investment and growth goals will not be realized. In 1979 Chenery adjusted his theories to allow for the possibility that part of the inflow of resources is consumed, so that the increase in total investment is less than the additional inflow of resources from abroad (Chenery, 1979).

Chenery and Strout's second gap refers to the shortage of foreign exchange. In a situation where a new industrial sector and infrastructure is being built up, most of the machines, capital goods, raw materials, and intermediates have to be imported from abroad. This requires foreign exchange. Even when sufficient levels of domestic savings have been realized, exports may yield insufficient foreign exchange to finance these imports. In this line of reasoning, development aid is necessary to finance the import of the required goods (and services and technical assistance) from economically advanced countries. The larger of the two gaps determines the aggregate need for foreign finance.

In the *two-gap model* there is a strong emphasis on the amounts of capital needed and the scale of investment required.[5] The question of the efficiency and effectiveness of investment is hardly raised. It should be stressed that the role of development aid in the total strategy is a fairly limited one. Foreign aid is part of total capital flows to developing countries. Under certain favourable conditions, it may contribute to an acceleration of growth and development by relieving specific bottlenecks. The idea was that both the large-scale investment push and development aid should be of relatively short duration (some ten to fifteen years). Once sustained economic growth had been achieved, the private capital market would be able to meet the financial requirements of developing countries. Although the assumptions of the Chenery and Strout model have been strongly criticized, some kind of 'gap analysis' still underlies modern debates on the financial requirements of developing countries (Lensink, 1993a).

Poverty reduction

One of the important objectives of development aid is the improvement of the living conditions of the poor in developing countries. Initially, it was thought that eventually economic growth would sooner or later automatically lead to a reduction in poverty. It was accepted that income inequality would increase in the early stages of development. Economic growth and industrialization require increased savings rates and increased savings rates imply shifts in income shares from poor classes who consume all their income to rich classes who are willing to save and invest (e.g. Lewis, 1954). But as economic growth got under way and per capita incomes started increasing, the advantages of growth would *trickle down* to large sections of the population, as had happened in nineteenth-century Western Europe. Also, the income distribution tended to become more equal at later stages of development (Kuznets, 1955; see also Szirmai, 1988, chapters 2 and 6).

In the 1960s and 1970s, the *trickle-down* assumption was fiercely criticized. It was believed that even in countries that experienced rapid growth the poorer sections of the population profited little, due to increasing income inequality. Power structures and vested interests stood in the way of the benefits of growth trickling down automatically. The assumption that only the rich save, while the poor consume, also came in for criticism. Poor people are eager to invest in increasing their productivity, rich classes are sometimes characterized by wasteful consumptive lifestyles.

A strategy of growth and redistribution was proposed in which production factors were to be reallocated to poor sections of the population (Chenery *et al.*, 1974; ILO, 1976). Key phrases were 'redistribution with growth' and 'basic needs strategy'. More credit for small peasants and better access to land would increase agricultural output and productivity. More credit and technological support for small businesses would have favourable employment consequences. Better systems of health care for the poor – an investment in human capital – would result in increased labour productivity of the working population. Redistribution and growth were thus considered as complementary rather than conflicting objectives.

The empirical foundations for this debate were rather weak, though. It was a highly ideological debate, in which preoccupations existing within the rich countries were projected onto the developing countries (van Dam, 1978). When growth in Latin America stagnated in the 1980s, it turned out that the poorest were the principal victims of economic stagnation. Their situation was worse than it had been in the previous period of economic growth and dynamism, despite the unequal distribution of the benefits of growth.

Since the early 1970s, policy statements on development aid concentrated increasingly on direct poverty reduction and on reaching target groups of the poor. In practice, only a limited part of funds targeted to the poor actually reached their destination. In Dutch aid policy, poverty reduction was the prime goal between 1973 and 1977. Nevertheless, Hoebink (1988) estimates that only some 6 to 7 per cent of aid to Sri Lanka (a focus of Dutch aid) actually reached the designated poverty groups. In other countries these percentages were even lower.

In my opinion, this does not mean that all arguments for increasing the resources of the poor are invalid. On the contrary, in the chapters on health, education and agricultural development, it was argued that investments in human capital can increase productivity and contribute to growth. What is being questioned is the independent scope for aid policy in this respect and the tendency to play down the benefits of growth. Also, it is unlikely that any direct attack on poverty will be effective in the absence of adequate macro- and microeconomic policies.

Technical assistance and investments in human capital

In the 1950s and 1960s there was a debate between the proponents of capital transfers and the proponents of technical assistance (Krueger *et al.*, 1989). The supporters of capital transfers emphasized the required size of the investment effort. They focused on increasing the investment rate and increasing the availability of physical capital goods and intermediate inputs. Supporters of technical assistance pointed to the importance of the transfer of knowledge and technical know-how. They argued that, through knowledge of new methods of production and more adequate and efficient use of existing means of production, output would increase. Theoretically speaking they emphasized the role of technical efficiency and technological development in growth of output.

In practice, it is obvious that capital transfers and technical assistance are closely connected. It is useless to provide capital goods without training and schooling on how to use them effectively. It is also useless to increase levels of knowledge and proficiency when there are no physical means of production to which such knowledge can be applied. Development projects, therefore, often included combinations of capital transfers and technical assistance.

In the course of time, technical assistance was reinterpreted in the broader sense as an investment in human capital. It was not limited to the transfer of existing Western technologies, by sending Western experts abroad. Rather it involved an increase in levels of education in the broadest possible sense, so that the capabilities to absorb new technologies and insights would be increased (see Chapter 6). Investment in human capital would also make it easier to adapt technologies to local circumstances in developing countries.

The formulation of the theory of human capital has been influenced by *theories of agricultural development* inspired by the work of the Nobel Prize winner Theodor Schultz (1964; see also Chapter 9). Schultz emphasized the importance of so-called non-conventional inputs into the agricultural sector. What he considered most important was not an increased supply of capital goods, but rather investment in agricultural education, extension and agricultural research. Following Schultz, it was realized that an expansion in agricultural research capacity in and for the benefit of developing countries could lead to breakthroughs in agricultural productivity (Hayami and Ruttan, 1985). In this context, it is important that agricultural technologies should be well adapted to local circumstances. According to Schultz, investment in human capital is a broad concept. It involves informing farmers about new techniques, training agricultural extension workers, and setting up educational and research institutions which are closely linked to extension networks. Thus investment in human capital shades into investment in *institution building*. Schultz and his followers have shown that such investments in human capital and institution building can have very high returns.

Technical assistance is also provided in the form of doctors, nurses and family-planning workers. In particular, if this kind of technical assistance also involves the sustained training of health personnel and other experts, it can also be considered as an investment in human capital. As explained in Chapters 4 and 5, investments in the health of adults and children can contribute to economic dynamism and increased productivity.

Improving macroeconomic policy: policy dialogue and programme aid

Since the early 1980s, policymakers have realized that it does not make much sense to consider only the effects of a series of isolated development projects. Any positive impacts of development projects are nullified if bad macroeconomic policies are being pursued, or if institutions at the microlevel are hostile to entrepreneurship, investment or growth of production and productivity. For example, it is not much use to provide capital to a country where inflation is running so high and expectations are so uncertain that entrepreneurs and financiers try to move all their resources out of the country. It is pointless to finance costly investments in irrigation if the prices of agricultural products are kept so low that there are no incentives for farmers to increase their production. If prices do not reflect scarcity relations, it also becomes impossible to make decent cost-benefit evaluations of projects.

As has been indicated in Chapter 11, many developing countries, in particular in Latin America and Africa, have pursued ineffective macroeconomic policies. Excessive protection of domestic industries and overvalued exchange rates led to non-viable industries and an inability to compete on international markets. Preferential treatment of manufacturing and artificially low prices for agricultural products hampered the development of the agricultural sector. Too much government intervention, a poorly functioning administrative apparatus, huge deficits on government budgets, and loose monetary policies were conducive to macroeconomic instability. As stressed by authors like Krueger (1978), Balassa (1978), and Bhagwati (1985a), countries that started exporting early, pursued sober macroeconomic policies, and depreciated their exchange rates, performed much better economically than other countries.

Foreign aid since the early 1980s, therefore, is increasingly linked with a 'policy dialogue' aimed at improvement of macroeconomic policy and institutional reform (OECD, 1985). In this context there has been a shift from project aid to programme aid (Cassen, 1986). The dialogue element in programme aid is considered of great importance, as the success of policy reforms requires the active commitment and involvement of policymakers in developing countries. Financial support is provided to governments for the implementation of structural adjustment programmes aimed at macroeconomic stabilization and deregulation of the economy. A restoration of market mechanisms and a reduced role for government is part of almost all reform programmes. Of course, this does not mean that the debate on the role of government in economic development is concluded.

Development aid may have three different functions within the context of policy dialogue. First, the traditional objectives of development projects are more likely to be realized, if developing countries pursue better policies. Second, foreign aid and other financial flows may be used to put pressure on policymakers in developing countries to engage in policy reform. This is referred to by the term *conditionality*. Third, programme aid may help mitigate the adverse effects of structural adjustment policies (Riddell, 1987). For instance, balance-of-payments support may allow firms to import the inputs they need, so that production will not needlessly stagnate. As shown in the previous chapter, the need for aid is probably greatest in the poorest countries, where the adaptive capacity of the economy is the least developed.

Part of aid flows may be used for consumptive purposes or to maintain educational and health services that would otherwise be subject to expenditure cuts. At the same time, critics of policy dialogue argue that the availability of financial support diminishes the pressure to restore the health of government finances in developing countries. If the apparatus of government itself is an obstacle to development (see Chapter 10), providing more programme aid will not be of much help.

12.4 *The emergence of foreign aid*

In the period immediately after World War II, the first priority was the reconstruction of war damage in Europe. The United States provided massive support to Western European countries by means of the Marshall Plan. The success of the Marshall Plan created a positive climate with regard to the role of international financial flows in economic development (Krueger *et al.*, 1989, chapter 1). The differences between the reparation of war damages in economically advanced areas and the transformation of economic structures in poor countries were hardly taken into account.

The official involvement of the United States in development aid dates back to January 1949 when President Harry S Truman gave his inaugural address. In the fourth point of his address Truman announced a new programme for making the benefits of scientific and industrial progress in the affluent countries available to developing countries. The emphasis was on technical assistance. This so-called Point Four programme was later enacted in legislation, although the budgeted resources remained much lower than those set aside for the Marshall Plan. In 1950 Congress allocated $34.5 million to technical assistance. It was not until about 1960 that resource transfers to developing countries reached levels approximating those of the Marshall Plan.

The United States was not alone in starting foreign aid in 1950. In the same year the World Bank issued its first development loan to Colombia, and the Expanded Program of Technical Assistance (UNEPTA) of the UN started up. Later this programme would be replaced by the United Nations Development Programme (UNDP).

In January 1950, Great Britain and the Commonwealth members Australia, Canada and New Zealand committed themselves to providing foreign aid by signing the Colombo Plan. Aid was intended especially for the countries that used to be part of former British India. India, in particular, became a testing ground for foreign aid and theories of development.

Other (ex)colonial powers in Europe, like France, Belgium and the Netherlands, also started to provide foreign aid. After some time their example was followed by the countries defeated in World War II – Germany, Japan and Italy. In these countries, foreign aid commenced once their economies had recovered from the damage caused by the war.

By 1960, multilateral institutions like the World Bank, the International Finance Corporation and the International Development Association (IDA) had become the main sources of external financial flows to developing countries. Around 1960, the United States was responsible for more than half of all bilateral and multilateral development aid. Most of the rest was supplied by four former colonial European powers: France, England, Belgium and the Netherlands.

Prince (1976) stresses the continuity between the post-war development aid of European countries and the pre-war colonial policies, particularly in the field of technical assistance. In France and Great Britain, development aid was closely tied in with decolonization and the objectives of decolonization policy. An important goal of pre-war French colonial policies had been the assimilation of colonized peoples into French culture. In the postcolonial period French foreign aid flows concentrated on Francophone Africa. Elements of assimilation policy resurfaced in aid policies. There was a strong emphasis on the spread of French language and culture, on education by French experts and on maintaining the economic ties with France. Until 1993 the currencies in French West Africa were directly linked to the French franc.

The long-term objective of British colonial policies in the twentieth century was the association of former colonies in a Commonwealth of English-speaking countries. The system of administration was based on *indirect rule*. In comparison with France, Great Britain intervened less in the internal political and social affairs of its colonies. Foreign aid was seen as a continuation of gradual preparations for independence in the context of the Commonwealth during the pre-war period. Therefore, aid flows were strongly centred on Commonwealth countries.

In the case of the Netherlands, there was a sudden rift with Indonesia in 1949 after the so-called police actions of 1947–49. The Netherlands attempted to restore its damaged international prestige by participating on a large scale in multilateral technical assistance which was beginning at that time. The Netherlands had a reservoir of experience in the form of colonial training programmes, unemployed colonial civil servants and technical experts. It was quite successful in finding employment for its experts in multilateral aid programmes (van Soest, 1975; Teszler, 1978). As a small country, the Netherlands made use of development aid as a distinguishing characteristic of its foreign policy. The small Scandinavian countries did likewise.

Reasons for the United States to expand their bilateral aid in the 1950s and 1960s included, among others, the fear of Chinese communist expansion in Asia and the influence of the Cuban revolution in Latin America. Because of the Cold War, large amounts of aid were provided to countries on the periphery of the communist bloc, such as Greece, Turkey, South Korea, Taiwan, South Vietnam and Laos. In 1960 President Kennedy launched the *Alliance for Progress*, a programme for economic development and cooperation in Latin America. The same year saw the foundation of the Peace Corps, an initiative that would soon be copied by other countries.

Development aid from the OECD countries was institutionalized in the Development Assistance Committee (DAC) in 1960. The DAC coordinated and recorded aid-related efforts by the OECD countries. More and more OECD countries started to provide foreign aid, while the US share in total aid flows gradually declined. In 1960 the US share in total OECD foreign aid was 57.5 per cent; in 1987 it had dropped to 21.5 per cent. As a percentage of gross national income US aid in 1987 was only 0.2 per cent, the lowest percentage of all OECD countries except Austria and Portugal (Krueger *et al.*, 1989, p. 35).

12.5 *Quantitative data on aid flows*

As a background for the debate on aid, this section provides quantitative data on the magnitude and geographical distribution of aid flows, on aid as a proportion of total resource flows, and on aid as a percentage of national income in developing countries.

12.5.1 Long-term trends in the magnitude and geographical distribution of aid flows

Table 12.1 presents data on the total volume of official development assistance from OECD, OPEC countries and CMEA countries. Aid flows from voluntary organizations have not been included in the table. At constant 1991 dollars the value of the total aid flows between 1960 and 1980 doubled. As mentioned before, the share of the largest donor, the United States, decreased substantially during this period. The number of countries providing aid increased, as did the volume of aid per country. The 1970s were characterized primarily by a strong growth of aid flows from oil-exporting countries. The aid from the Soviet Union and former socialist countries in Eastern Europe has always been rather modest and is now nonexistent. In the 1980s the growth of aid flows came to an end. Aid flows stabilized at around 60 billion dollars per year.

Most aid goes to low-income countries. Aid flows to the least developed countries increased strongly between 1975 and 1992. The regional data show a strong increase in aid to African countries, while aid flows to Asia show a downward tendency, with the exception of aid to China.

Since 1991 there have been increasing aid flows to several of the newly independent states of the former Soviet Union and to former communist countries in Eastern European. OECD statistics started including these flows in 1994 (in the *GDFF 1987–1993*). With the exception of negligible sums for the Asian republics of the former Soviet Union, these flows are not included in the totals of Tables 12.1 to 12.3, but they are of increasing importance. Between 1990 and 1993, net disbursements of official aid to Eastern European countries in transition grew from 1.3 billion to 4.9 billion current dollars.[6]

Table 12.2 presents further information on the distribution of aid over different regions. This table is not directly comparable to Table 12.1 as it refers to aid from OECD countries only. Compared to their shares in developing country population, two regions are overrepresented in the aid flows: sub-Saharan Africa, and North Africa and the Middle East. Around 1991 the share of these regions in aid was three times as high as their share in population. For the Middle East this is explained by the strategic importance of the region. Foreign political considerations determine the magnitude of aid flows to Israel, Jordan and Egypt. The overrepresentation of sub-Saharan Africa has to do with the deep economic problems of this region and the extent of poverty here. In proportion to its population share, Asia is highly underrepresented in aid flows.

12.5.2 Development aid in proportion to total resource flows

Table 12.3 contains information on the share of development aid in total net financial flows to developing countries. This share fluctuates considerably. In the 1970s the

Table 12.1 Net receipts of development assistance by income category and region, 1960–1992 (at constant 1991 prices and exchange rates) ($bn)[a]

	1960–61	1970	1975–76	1980	1982	1984	1986	1988	1990	1991	1992[b]
All developing countries	30.1	40.6	53.0	61.9	58.9	59.0	60.1	56.6	61.8	60.6	57.3
Income category[cd]											
Low-income countries			31.9	32.9	34.7	29.2	31.6	32.1	35.9	34.5	33.6
Least developed countries			9.5	12.3	14.1	14.3	15.9	16.0	15.9	14.8	14.8
Lower-middle income countries						14.3	12.6	10.4	11.7	10.5	9.2
Higher-middle income countries						4.6	5.1	3.5	4.0	4.7	4.3
Region											
Total Africa[e]						19.5	20.0	19.9	26.1	24.7	23.3
Sub-Saharan Africa			10.6	14.8	16.5	14.3	16.0	16.5	18.1	17.2	16.7
Total Asia[e]			18.0	16.6	17.7	17.8	20.2	17.7	15.6	14.5	13.8
Low-income countries						11.3	12.2	13.0	12.2	12.5	12.3
North Africa and the Middle East			13.9	14.3	12.3	10.6	9.3	5.9	12.0	12.0	10.9
Latin America			5.9	6.2	7.6	6.9	5.2	4.9	5.5	6.0	5.8

Notes:

[a] Net capital flows: new grants and loans minus repayments of outstanding loans.

[b] Provisional estimate.

[c] Countries have been classified on the basis of their 1991 GNP. The least developed category comprises the low-income countries, excluding China, India, Nigeria, Indonesia and a few small countries.

[d] The sum of all subcategories is far less than the total. Not all aid has been registered per category. Not all countries have been included in the categories.

[e] North Africa is also included in the total for Africa, the Middle East in the total for Asia.

Sources: 1984–1992 from OECD (1993a); *Financing and External Debt of Developing Countries 1992*, Paris, 1993. 1975–1982 from OECD, *Financing and External Debt 1985*, Paris, 1986. 1970 from OECD (1993b). *Development Cooperation 1992*, Paris, 1993.

Table 12.2 Distribution of net official development assistance from OECD countries, by region[a]

Region	Share (%)				Share in total population 1993 (%)	Net aid 1993 ($bn)
	1975–76	1980–81	1985–86	1992–93		
Sub-Saharan Africa	26	30.8	33.8	36.4	12.0	18.0
Asia	34	35.6	30.9	29.8	69.2	14.3
Oceania	6	4.6	3.7	3.0	0.1	1.6
North Africa and the Middle East	18	15.4	18.3	14.6	5.6	6.4
Latin America	14	10.2	12.1	10.9	10.8	5.5
Southern Europe[b]	1	3.4	1.2	5.3	2.3	3.0
Total	99	100.0	100.0	100.0	100.0	48.8

Notes:

[a] Net ODA from OECD DAC members (OECD countries excluding Mexico, Greece, Iceland and Turkey). Bilateral and multilateral official development aid excluding non-allocated items.

[b] Including Turkey.

Source: 1975–1976 from OECD (1986) *Financing and External Debt 1985* (table III.5), Paris, 1986, 1980–93: OECD, *Development Cooperation 1992* (table 20), Paris, 1992 and OECD, *Development Cooperation 1994* (table 39), Paris, 1994.

Table 12.3 Net development aid as a percentage of total net inflow of financial resources, 1960–1992, by income category and region*

	1960–61	1970	1975–76	1980	1982	1984	1986	1988	1990	1991	1992[b]
All developing countries	56.1	44.7	30.5	29.2	28.9	40.1	55.6	49.3	43.2	44.2	34.2
Income category[c]											
Low-income countries			71.3	70.2	64.7	56.5	67.7	57.1	56.9	65.1	61.9
Least developed countries			80.4	75.0	90.0	77.8	93.7	90.1	86.4	97.4	102.5
Lower-middle income countries						48.5	59.4	57.9	36.3	34.8	28.6
Higher-middle income countries						9.4	22.6	12.6	13.5	11.2	7.1
Region											
Total Africa[e]						67.6	63.9	66.2	84.5	98.0	100.8
Sub-Saharan Africa			47.7	59.2	57.9	87.1	53.7	66.8	85.7	92.5	98.3
Total Asia[e]			47.6	41.7	37.0	38.3	58.9	45.1	25.8	26.6	22.1
Low income countries						40.8	56.4	44.9	31.0	42.5	37.6
North Africa and the Middle East			49.1	56.9	63.4	61.9	77.6	66.6	97.5	131.9	67.8
Latin America			10.6	6.8	8.9	13.9	22.6	20.7	23.3	19.8	12.0

Note:
* Net total resource flows include ODA, other official flows, private capital flows (including guaranteed export credits, private direct investment, private portfolio investment, private bank loans).
b, c, e see Table 12.1.

Sources: See Table 12.1.

relative importance of development aid decreased when private banks increased their loans to developing countries on a very large scale. Between 1982 and 1986 the share of development aid increased to 56 per cent of the net resource flow. This was especially caused by curtailment of private lending and foreign direct investment after the debt crisis. Subsequently, the trend reversed and the share of aid in net total resource flows declined again. In 1992 it stood at 34 per cent.

Regardless of the trends, Table 12.3 shows that development aid accounts for a substantial part of the total inflow of financial resources into developing countries. Especially in the category of the LDCs and in Africa, development aid accounts for an extremely large share of the total net resource inflow. In 1992 the share was even above 100 per cent. This means that the net aid flow was higher than the net total resource flow. The balance of the other financial flows (other official financial flows and private flows) was negative in that year.

Tables 12.4 and 12.5 present similar data, but now for twenty-three selected developing countries. Table 12.4 contains the absolute figures on net aid flows and net total resource flows. In Table 12.5, net aid flows have been expressed as a percentage of the total resource flows. The concept of net total resource flows in these two tables is broader than the financial flow concepts employed in Tables 11.5 and 11.6 of Chapter 11. The tables in Chapter 11 refer to net flows and net transfers on debt. The tables here also include foreign direct investment and foreign portfolio investment.

Unfortunately, the data on the total resource flows in Tables 12.4 and 12.5 – taken from the OECD publication, *Geographical Distribution of Financial Flows to Developing Countries* – are not consistent with those from the OECD publications used in Table 12.3. Due to differences in the definitions applied, the total resource flows in Tables 12.4 and 12.5 are much smaller, and accordingly, the shares of development aid are far higher. Still these tables are interesting since they provide country detail lacking in the other sources and illustrate how much the importance of development aid in the total of resource flows can vary from country to country and from year to year.

Several countries in Table 12.4 have a net outflow of resources in certain years. In such years the outflow of financial resources is caused either by debt service obligations or by capital transfers to other countries. Examples of countries with a substantial net outflow of financial resources are Mexico and Nigeria in 1985, Brazil and Chile in 1987, Argentina and Colombia in 1989, and Brazil and Colombia in 1991. Capital transfers to foreign countries are a response to uncertain economic prospects. (Non-registered capital flight is not even taken into account.) Net capital outflows from Taiwan in 1985, 1987, 1991 and 1993 and South Korea in 1987 and 1989 can be interpreted differently. They are caused by repayments of outstanding debt and foreign direct investment abroad as part of successful economic development. Taiwan and South Korea have become major sources of foreign direct investment in other developing countries such as India and China.

In Table 12.5, net aid flows have been expressed as a percentage of net total resource flows. What immediately meets the eye are the extremely large shares of

Table 12.4 Net official development assistance and net total resource flows in selected developing countries, 1976–1993 (current $m)*

	1976		1980		1985		1987		1989		1991		1993	
	ODA	Total	ODA	Total	ODA	Total	ODA	Total	ODA	Total	ODA	Total	ODA	Total
Bangladesh	532	537	1,283	1,280	1,131	1,099	1,790	1,764	1,807	1,818	1,889	2,029	1,386	1,483
China			66	324	940	2,297	1,382	4,283	2,077	5,617	1,999	5,133	3,273	7,699
India	1,824	1,836	2,147	2,408	1,592	2,507	1,703	3,363	1,778	5,056	2,745	4,378	1,503	2,130
Indonesia	669	2,676	950	1,758	603	1,683	1,246	3,160	1,839	4,787	1,874	5,766	2,026	3,967
Pakistan	1,277	1,363	1,130	1,372	770	897	820	915	1,446	2,661	1,371	2,207	1,065	1,691
Philippines	187	1,085	300	971	460	583	732	913	825	1,205	1,054	1,666	1,491	3,344
South Korea	218	1,429	139	818	−9	1,592	11	−2,438	52	−807	55	2,825	−35	2,928
Taiwan	−21	118	−4	439	−10	−518	−9	−305	2	732	3	−1,410	7	−1,184
Thailand	169	207	418	1,114	486	857	470	885	722	2,278	722	3,690	614	2,345
Turkey	138	633	952	1,827	181	1,132	379	2,415	144	1,336	1,623	2,846	463	5,065
Argentina	31	520	19	2,773	39	2,119	100	960	212	−1,504	300	265	283	5,446
Brazil	111	3,743	85	4,369	123	1,326	289	−786	207	3,802	183	−3,647	239	3,714
Chile	8	−60	−10	409	40	125	21	−203	62	−19	126	373	184	608
Colombia	77	252	90	833	62	326	78	123	68	−327	123	−310	109	−187
Mexico	63	1,299	56	4,463	145	−1,700	156	1,895	99	3,793	278	7,153	402	15,343
Peru	74	350	203	625	316	−1	294	152	310	32	614	349	561	1,228
Venezuela	−0	−340	15	1,303	10	−941	19	2,146	60	492	31	2,171	50	1,003
Egypt	1,829	2,077	1,387	2,329	1,760	2,897	1,726	2,535	1,545	2,106	5,025	4,232	2,304	2,793
Ghana	64	67	193	227	196	193	413	500	718	912	882	997	621	74
Ivory Coast	108	415	210	918	118	261	241	337	396	25	633	555	766	664
Kenya	162	411	397	557	430	526	560	688	1,064	1,464	921	1,082	923	870
Nigeria	53	155	36	1,201	32	−251	69	1,707	345	2,265	263	1,027	280	761
Tanzania	268	337	679	864	484	556	900	953	918	855	1,083	1,076	948	925
Zambia	62	129	318	376	329	529	426	357	374	569	883	751	875	849
Subtotal	7,901	19,241	11,058	33,557	10,227	18,094	13,817	26,318	17,069	39,148	24,677	45,204	20,337	63,557

Note: * Net total resource flows: ODA, other official flows and private capital flows (including guaranteed export credits, private direct investment, private portfolio investment, private bank loans).

Sources: OECD (1995), *Geographical Distribution of Financial Flows to Developing Countries (GDFF) 1989/1993*; 1976: *GDFF 1984*; 1980: *GDFF 1987*. *GDFF* is the only source presenting detailed and comprehensive data by country.

Table 12.5 Net official development assistance as a percentage of net total resource flows in selected developing countries, 1976–1993

	1976	1980	1985	1987	1989	1991	1993
Bangladesh	99.0	100.2	102.9	101.5	99.4	93.1	93.5
China		20.4	40.9	32.3	37.0	38.9	42.5
India	99.3	89.2	63.5	50.6	35.2	62.7	70.6
Indonesia	25.0	54.0	35.8	39.4	38.4	32.5	51.1
Pakistan	93.7	82.4	85.8	89.6	54.3	62.1	63.0
Philippines	17.2	30.9	78.9	80.2	68.5	63.3	44.6
South Korea	15.3	17.0	−0.5[a]	[b]	[b]	1.9	−1.2[a]
Taiwan	−17.6[a]	−0.8[a]	[ab]	[ab]	0.3	[b]	[b]
Thailand	81.7	37.6	56.7	53.1	31.7	19.6	26.2
Turkey	21.7	52.1	16.0	15.7	10.8	57.0	9.1
Argentina	5.9	0.7	1.9	10.4	[b]	113.2	5.2
Brazil	3.0	2.0	9.3	[b]	5.4	[b]	6.4
Chile	[b]	−2.4[a]	32.3	[b]	[b]	33.7	30.2
Colombia	30.4	10.8	18.9	63.5	[b]	[b]	[b]
Mexico	4.9	1.3	[b]	8.2	2.6	3.9	2.6
Peru	21.1	32.5	[b]	193.9	980.4	175.8	45.7
Venezuela	0.1	1.2	−1.1	0.9	12.2	1.4	5.0
Egypt	88.1	59.5	60.8	68.1	73.4	118.7	82.5
Ghana	95.0	84.7	101.3	82.5	78.7	88.5	838.6
Ivory Coast	26.1	22.9	45.1	71.4	1,594.8	114.4	115.2
Kenya	39.3	71.2	81.8	81.4	72.7	85.1	106.1
Nigeria	34.5	3.0	[b]	4.1	15.2	25.6	36.7
Tanzania	79.3	78.6	87.0	94.4	107.4	100.7	102.5
Zambia	48.0	84.6	62.1	119.5	65.7	117.6	103.0

Notes:
[a] Net ODA is negative. When net total financial receipts are positive, the sign is negative.
[b] There is a net outflow of total financial resources. When net ODA is positive the sign is negative. In this case, percentages have not been reproduced.

Sources: See Table 12.4.

aid in the total resource flows for African countries like Egypt, Ghana, the Ivory Coast, Tanzania and Zambia and in Asia for Bangladesh. These countries depend almost exclusively on foreign aid for an inflow of foreign financial resources.

In Asia we note a strong decrease in the share of aid to Thailand and decreases in India and Pakistan until 1989, after which the shares go up again. These fluctuations illustrate the short run volatility of capital flows. In such countries like Taiwan and South Korea, which were successful in their economic development, the share of development aid is very small and in some years even negative when earlier aid loans are being repaid.

The negative signs in Table 12.5 require some explanation. The sign may be negative when the net aid flow is negative and the net total resource flow positive (note a). The percentages are usually very low. The sign may also be negative when the net total resource flow is negative and the aid flow is positive. These negative percentages have not been reproduced in the table since they are meaningless. The original absolute figures, however, can be found in Table 12.4.

12.5.3 Net development assistance as a percentage of gross domestic product

In Table 12.6 the inflow of aid has been related to gross domestic product. In fifteen of the twenty-three countries the share of foreign aid in GDP in 1993 was below 2.5 per cent. In the large Latin American countries the role of foreign aid has always been marginal. In Asian countries, the shares of aid in GDP have tended to decline since 1976, reflecting the increasing importance of private capital flows and foreign direct investment. Only in Bangladesh does the share of aid remain high.

Table 12.6 Net development assistance as a percentage of gross domestic product in selected developing countries, 1976–1993

	1976	1980	1985	1987	1989	1991	1993
Bangladesh	7.2	9.9	7.2	10.2	8.8	8.1	5.8
China	0.0	0.0	0.3	0.5	0.6	0.5	0.8
India	1.9	1.2	0.7	0.7	0.6	1.1	0.6
Indonesia	1.7	1.2	0.7	1.6	1.9	1.6	1.4
Pakistan	9.6	4.8	2.5	2.5	3.6	3.0	2.1
Philippines	1.1	0.9	1.5	2.2	1.9	2.3	2.8
South Korea	0.8	0.2	−0.0	0.0	0.0	0.0	−0.0
Thailand	1.0	1.3	1.2	0.9	1.0	0.7	0.5
Turkey	0.3	1.7	0.3	0.4	0.1	1.1	0.3
Argentina	0.1	0.0	0.0	0.1	0.3	0.2	0.1
Brazil	0.1	0.0	0.1	0.1	0.0	0.0	0.0
Chile	0.1	−0.0	0.2	0.1	0.2	0.4	0.4
Colombia	0.5	0.3	0.2	0.2	0.2	0.3	0.2
Mexico	0.1	0.0	0.1	0.1	0.0	0.1	0.1
Peru	0.5	1.0	2.0	1.1	1.2	2.0	1.4
Venezuela	−0.0	0.0	0.0	0.0	0.1	0.1	0.1
Egypt	13.7	6.1	5.1	4.9	4.6	15.3	5.9
Ghana	2.3	4.3	4.3	8.1	13.7	12.6	10.2
Ivory Coast	2.3	2.1	1.7	2.3	4.2	6.7	8.2
Kenya	4.7	5.5	7.0	7.0	12.8	11.5	16.7
Nigeria	0.1	0.0	0.0	0.3	1.1	0.8	0.9
Tanzania	9.2	13.2	7.0	25.5	32.3	37.9	39.9
Zambia	2.3	8.2	14.6	20.5	9.4	26.2	23.7

Note:
[a] GDP at market prices.

Source: See Table 12.4. Gross domestic product from World Bank (1995), *World Tables 1995*.

The significance of foreign aid in the African countries included in the table is quite considerable. In 1993 the share of foreign aid in four of the seven African countries was over 10 per cent of GDP. In Tanzania the share even reached the almost unbelievable figure of 40 per cent of GDP in 1993. When aid–GDP ratios are so high, it is clear that most of government expenditures and investments will be financed by foreign aid flows.

12.5.4 Reduction of the real value of aid by tying

A substantial part of bilateral foreign aid is 'tied' aid. The recipient of tied aid is obliged to spend it on the purchase of goods and services in the donor country. This means that development aid functions as an export credit. Tying reduces the total value of aid, because the recipient is not free to use the financial resources provided to buy the cheapest and best goods and services available on international or domestic markets. Often the prices of imports from the donor country will be 20 to 30 per cent above world market prices. Moreover, it is very likely that the recipients of aid are forced to buy goods that are not really suited to their needs and local circumstances. Furthermore, a country may end up with many different and incompatible brands of the same product from different countries. Estimates of the percentage by which tying reduces the value of aid vary. Sometimes developing countries use foreign aid to finance goods they would have imported anyway. The resources saved can then be used freely for other purposes, so the negative effects of tying are diminished (Jepma, 1992).

Jay and Michalopoulos (1989, p. 74) conclude that on average 45 per cent of all official development assistance from OECD countries (both bilateral and multilateral) could be classified as tied in 1985–86. Jepma (1992, p. 7) estimates that in 1988, 50 to 55 per cent of all bilateral aid from European Community countries was tied aid. In addition, donors may influence expenditure patterns of developing countries by providing aid for specific sectors in which their own industry or expertise is well represented. Thus it is very likely that Dutch aid for dredging projects finds its way back to the Netherlands even if it is formally untied. Sending out 'experts' from donor countries also automatically means that a large portion of project costs consists of the salaries of citizens of the donor country itself. Hancock (1991) estimates that there are presently some 80,000 highly paid expatriate experts working in Africa, more than in the colonial period. Worldwide, a total of 150,000 expatriates is employed per year.

The proportion of foreign aid that thus flows back to the donor country (the 'flow-back percentage') may therefore exceed the tying percentage. Hoebink, for example, estimates that the flow-back percentage for West German and British aid is 60 to 75 per cent. With respect to Dutch aid this used to be about 90 per cent in the early 1970s. Since the 1980s the Dutch flow-back percentage has been reduced to 55 per cent due to an increased willingness to finance local costs and local personnel in developing countries (Hoebink, 1988, pp. 235 and 330).

12.5.5 The volume of aid: conclusion

Although foreign aid flows represent a very modest percentage of the national income of the donor countries, the quantitative survey presented above indicates that aid flows are not without importance in international economic relations. Foreign aid forms a substantial part of the total capital flows between rich countries and developing countries (see also Lensink, 1993a).

In most large Latin American and Asian countries the role of foreign aid as a percentage of GDP is limited. Yet especially in the poorest African countries the inflow of aid represents a considerable percentage of GDP. Aid is not a marginal phenomenon here. It represents one of the central facts of economic life. The debate on the quality and the effects of aid is not just academic. It touches on the economic prospects of the poorest African countries.

12.6 *Perspectives on development aid*

The basic idea underlying development aid is that it contributes to building up the productive potential and the institutional structure of a country in order to promote the self-reliance of that country. This immediately brings us to the central dilemma involving all aid relations: the tension between dependence and self-reliance. The debate on the pros and cons of development aid boils down to the following issue: Does aid ultimately contribute to emancipation and economic dynamism, or does it ultimately result in a permanent dependence of the aid recipient, which forms an obstacle to autonomous social and economic dynamics?

Basically, three positions can be distinguished in the debate on aid:[7]

1. The orthodox view that development aid on balance contributes to economic and social development and to the solution of socio-economic problems in developing countries.
2. The radical left view that development aid promotes the penetration of capitalist market relationships in developing countries and consequently leads to the sustained dependence and underdevelopment of these countries.
3. The right-wing neoliberal view that development aid hinders economic growth and development since it maintains inefficient government intervention and obstructs the unfolding of dynamic market relationships.

The orthodox or mainstream attitude is prevalent among governments in donor countries, governments in aid-receiving countries, officials in national and international development organizations and development bureaucracies, aid workers, young idealistic intellectuals and students, and – until very recently – among the general public in the rich countries. Until recently there was a widespread consensus on the desirability of development aid. This consensus was partly maintained by intensive publicity campaigns funded from budgets for development aid. The support for aid was not based on its proven effectiveness. Rather, it was based on the moral need to do something about the problems of abject poverty, hunger, malnutrition, disease and inequality in world society.

In the orthodox approach there are two central ideas. First, aid provides additional resources which would otherwise not have been available for development. Second, it contributes to the mobilization of latent resources in developing countries. Within the mainstream, however, there is a great variety of opinions and points of view. Some people favour project aid, others programme aid. Some are supporters of poverty alleviation, others of investment in infrastructure. Some would like to provide aid without conditions, others prefer to increase conditionality.

Even within the mainstream there has been growing criticism of ineffectiveness, inefficiency, and waste in development aid (e.g Jepma, 1988).[8] Some critics argue that under a smoke screen of idealistic motives, rich countries do nothing but pursue their national interests. Other authors criticize the lack of coordination and coherence in aid policies. Often the criticism is that aid is poorly adapted to local economic, social, and cultural circumstances. The organizational structure of development organizations and the relations between developmental bureaucracies are subjected to critical analysis (Quarles van Ufford *et al.*, 1988).

Representatives of developing countries complain about the paternalist or even neocolonialist nature of foreign aid. They argue that aid should be made available to governments, organizations and individuals with no strings or demeaning conditions attached. Developing countries should determine their own priorities.

At the same time, the notion is gaining ground that aid is only of use within the framework of an effective economic and social government policy. If the policy framework is not right, a string of separate projects can never be very successful. This line of reasoning leads to more and more conditions being attached to aid. This is referred to as 'conditionality' or 'policy dialogue'. It was already noted above that there has been a shift from project aid to programme aid, and that programme aid is increasingly provided on certain conditions. These conditions refer primarily, though not exclusively, to economic policy. The observation of human rights by governments may also be a condition for aid, but Western policy in this respect is very erratic.

A common characteristic of these mainstream approaches is that the principle of the desirability of aid itself is not questioned. The critics concentrate on the reform, reorganization or change of specific aspects of aid policy.

More fundamental are the criticisms by representatives of left-wing radical and right-wing liberal perspectives on development aid. From both perspectives, foreign aid is explicitly considered as an obstacle to development. The critics are not concerned with reforming aid but rather with abolishing it. Besides important differences, there are also interesting similarities between the radical and the liberal criticisms of foreign aid. Both point to the perpetuation of dependence as a central characteristic of aid relations. Thus the debate on aid shows some interesting parallels with the left- and right-wing criticisms of the Western European welfare states in the 1980s.

The criticism from the left reached its peak in the 1970s in the context of a general radicalization of the intellectual climate. The neoliberal criticism became louder during the 1980s. At present, criticism by right-wing liberals is the most fundamental challenge to the development establishment. The following sections present an overview of this debate. Section 12.6.1 discusses the arguments of the left-wing radical critics; section 12.6.2 pays attention to the criticism by right-wing liberals. Section 12.6.3 focuses on project aid and its critics. Section 12.6.4 deals with responses from the mainstream to its critics from the left and the right. In this section attention is also paid to the results of empirical research into the effects of foreign aid.[9]

12.6.1 Radical criticisms of development aid

The criticisms of development aid from the radical left (Griffin, 1970, 1987; Griffin and Enos, 1970; Hayter, 1971, 1981; Mende, 1973; Zeylstra, 1975; Lappé *et al.*, 1980; Griffin and Gurley, 1985; Hayter and Watson, 1985) was formulated mainly in the 1970s. This criticism should be seen against a backdrop of the emergence of theories of underdevelopment and dependence discussed in Chapters 2 and 3. In these theories, poverty and social disintegration in developing countries are seen as the consequences of Western economic and political expansion. Unlike the trend in Western countries, in developing countries the spread of capitalist market relations only leads to further impoverishment. Tiny wealthy elites in business and government benefit from capitalist penetration. They ally themselves with foreign interests and help maintain the chains of exploitation in developing countries. From this perspective, foreign aid is one of the many ways in which developing countries are made subject to the Western capitalist sphere of influence. Foreign aid helps maintain repressive regimes that exploit their own people. Foreign aid serves primarily to promote the further penetration of capitalist market relations in developing countries, from which only the rich countries can benefit. It also maintains the dependence of the poor on the rich and of poor countries on rich countries.

The radical leftist criticism also contains a range of more specific objections to development aid and its workings in practice. Lappé *et al.* (1980) state that aid never reaches the kind of people for whom it is officially intended. Official aid is provided by governments to governments. Aid flows running via the powerful will never reach the powerless. Credit meant for poor peasants is provided to rich farmers. Most benefits of irrigation works go to large landowners. Funds for development end up in the bank accounts of politicians. Ultimately, aid results in a reinforcement of the positions of the more powerful at all levels of society. Only a drastic revolutionary change in the power structure could create a situation in which aid also has positive effects for the poor.

The thesis of Lappé *et al.*, that development aid provided through governments and ruling elites hardly ever reaches the poor, finds support in numerous less ideologically pronounced empirical studies. Bol (1983) has shown for Bangladesh and Hoebink (1988) for Tanzania and Sri Lanka how little aid actually reaches the poor, even when this is one of the main objectives of aid policy. In part this can be explained by the interests of Western donors, who use foreign aid as an instrument of export policy. It also has to do with the nature of power and inequality structures in developing countries. To implement a development project successfully one needs the cooperation of powerful and influential key figures at national, regional and local levels. But their interests are usually not served by improvements in the conditions of the poorest groups. This, by the way, also applies to other aspects of domestic policy in developing countries (Myrdal, 1971; Frankel, 1978).

Hayter (1971) argued, in *Aid as Imperialism*, that development aid in Latin America was one of the means of imposing capitalist market relations on developing countries. She was one of the first to note that aid was provided on condition that Western policy prescriptions were followed. Countries that tried to pursue alternative policies which focused on the needs of the poor, like Cuba and Chile, were cut off from aid, boycotted economically and attacked militarily.

For Mende (1973), the key to economic development lies in the domestic mobilization of resources for investment. Only then can a truly autonomous and dynamic process of economic development start. Alienated ruling elites in developing countries, however, lack the capacity to start the process of internal mobilization of people and financial resources. In order to maintain their positions, they depend on foreign aid and support from abroad. Mende comes to the conclusion that development aid hardly ever has any positive effects. It merely helps maintain the *status quo*. Foreign aid thus weakens the capacity for domestic mobilization of savings and self-reliant development.

Lappé *et al.* mention food aid as an example of aid that discourages domestic production. The provision of large quantities of cheap food to developing countries relieves affluent countries of their agricultural surpluses. However, domestic production of food in developing countries becomes unprofitable. Thus developing countries become permanently dependent on food imports. This criticism of food aid is echoed by numerous later studies (e.g. Jackson, 1982; Boserup, 1983).

Griffin (1970; see also Griffin and Enos, 1970) launched an explicit attack on orthodox theories of aid in which expansion of the resources available for investment is a central element (see section 12.3). On the basis of a cross-section analysis, he concludes that there is a negative correlation between the inflow of development aid and the volume of domestic savings. His data also point to an absence of positive correlations between the magnitude of aid flows on the one hand and investment rates and economic growth on the other.

In a more recent publication, Griffin (1987) concludes that in twelve African countries foreign aid crowds out domestic savings. Development aid is spent by governments, partly for consumptive purposes, partly on defence expenditures, and partly on wages. When aid is earmarked for investment, domestic means which become free are used for consumption. Even in those cases where investment increases slightly as a result of aid flows, this has no positive consequences for economic growth. This is because donors have a distinct preference for large-scale capital-intensive prestige projects that are ill-adapted to local circumstances. These projects have high capital–output ratios and contribute little to growth of output. Thus development aid encourages an inefficient use of resources in the economy. Recipients of large aid flows, such as Bangladesh, Ethiopia, Zaire, Haiti and the Sudan, grow more slowly than countries that receive less aid.

Like many other critics, Griffin observes that aid does not reach the poor in spite of all developmental rhetoric. Aid helps to maintain corrupt and repressive regimes. In their economic policies these regimes tend to neglect agriculture, the sector in which most of the poor people have to eke out a living. Developing countries would benefit more from less aid and more independence, better access for their exports to the protected markets of rich countries, and stronger governments that would have better chances of mobilizing domestic savings.

12.6.2 Neoliberal criticism of development aid

Just like radical leftist criticism of development aid, right-wing neoliberal criticism is part of a more comprehensive perspective on society, the economy and economic development. From this perspective, the main engine of growth and development consists of the efforts of creative and enterprising individuals in free markets. Intervention in the market discourages individual entrepreneurship and an efficient allocation of resources. Development aid is one of the guises of interventionism. Therefore it is one of the obstacles to economic growth.

The right-wing liberal perspective on economic development goes back to the work of the economists Friedrich Hayek and Milton Friedman. In the 1980s it was specifically elaborated with regard to development aid. The main authors of this school are Lal (1978, 1983), Krauss (1983a, 1983b), and Bauer and Yamey. Today, in contrast to the 1970s, neoliberal criticism is the main challenge to foreign aid. This is partly due to the disintegration of the communist bloc and the loss of credibility of centralized planning as a development strategy.

The most influential representative of this movement is Peter Bauer, who criticized the assumptions of foreign aid in a long series of publications (Bauer, 1976, 1981, 1984, 1988; Bauer and Yamey, 1981, 1986). Bauer's point of view is characterized by the following quotation: 'Aid promotes the delusion that a society can progress from indigence to prosperity without the intermediate stage of economic effort and achievement' (1981, p. 107). According to Bauer, all countries that experienced economic growth did so without foreign aid. They realized economic growth because they had the right skills, attitudes, motivations and institutions at their disposal. Foreign aid cannot help create such capabilities, but it can form an obstacle to their development. According to Bauer, the market is the bearer of economic growth. Development aid reinforces the positions of interventionist governments who have hostile attitudes towards the market.

Bauer presents a sharp, humorous, though not systematically empirically grounded, criticism of almost all aspects of development aid. His criticisms, which are representative of the entire range of neoliberal attacks on aid, can be summarized in the following five points:

1. *Savings are not a bottleneck for economic development*. Bauer argues that there is no shortage of savings in developing countries. Rather, there is an insufficient capacity to absorb investment. If there are sufficient opportunities for economically productive investment, domestic and foreign entrepreneurs and suppliers of capital will mobilize the resources needed. For example, if an investment in infrastructure contributes to increased productivity in the long run, the government can easily borrow money on the capital market and finance interest and repayments from future increases in tax receipts. Even under the most favourable circumstances, the positive impact of development aid is therefore restricted. It saves some of the costs of loans for investments, which would have been undertaken anyway in the absence of aid.

However, the fact that aid is 'free' increases the chances of waste and inefficient use of financial resources. Aid stimulates investment in unprofitable projects that do not contribute to the growth of the economic potential of a country, while increasing the indebtedness of a country (if aid is not provided as a grant).

Together with the left-wing critics, Bauer is of the opinion that considerable portions of aid are used for consumptive purposes, the upkeep of patron–client relationships, payments of civil servant salaries, or investments in unrealistic prestige projects.

2. *Development aid does not contribute to poverty alleviation.* Official development assistance is provided to governments rather than to individuals. For governments in developing countries the interests of the poor seldom have high priority. For example, the European aid flows provided in compensation for shortfalls in agricultural export revenues never ended up in the hands of the farmers themselves. It was the governments that profited. According to Bauer, foreign aid means taxing the poor in rich countries for the benefit of the rich in poor countries. If foreign aid has to be provided at all, Bauer prefers to channel it through non-governmental organizations. They are less dependent on the cooperation of governmental institutions in developing countries. There is a greater chance that some of the money reaches the people it is intended for. However, non-governmental organizations (NGOs) sometimes show the same failings as governmental aid organizations – waste, bureaucracy, dependence on powerful intermediaries, and so forth (see, for example, Kruyt, 1988).

3. *Foreign aid strengthens the position of regimes guilty of large scale violations of human rights.* Development is provided to regimes in total disregard of their record on human rights and tolerance of political opposition. Thus the regimes of Papa Doc in Haiti and Mobutu in Zaire have been large-scale recipients of aid. Not infrequently, the recipient governments are also hostile to the most entrepreneurial and economically successful ethnic groups in their country, which are discriminated against and are sometimes even deported en masse.[10] Examples that come to mind are the position of the Chinese in Indonesia, Malaysia and Thailand, and the position of Indian minorities in East Africa.

4. *Foreign aid reinforces the position of governments pursuing anti-market policies*

harmful to economic development. Governments receiving aid pursue policies discriminating against the agrarian sector. They protect inefficient and unviable industries by means of import substitution policies. They intervene in markets through extensive regulation, licensing or support of poorly run parastatals. They are hostile to private entrepreneurs and foreign investors. They pursue inadequate macro-economic policies characterized by huge government deficits, high inflation and overvalued exchange rates. And finally, they use aid as an instrument to safeguard their personal privileges and to secure their hold on power.

5. *Development aid stimulates the politicization of the whole society in developing countries.* According to Bauer, this is the most fundamental objection to aid. Aid causes resources to be channelled to the government. Creative individuals are tempted to use all their talents to acquire subsidies and manipulate public resources, licences and regulations to their own benefit. This causes conflicts between ethnic groups that have access to the machinery of government and ethnic groups that do not. Economic entrepreneurship aimed at seeking new opportunities for productive activity in the private sector is discouraged. 'Rent- seeking', the search for monopoly profits through governmental licences and regulations, becomes the norm for entrepreneurial behaviour.

It is interesting to see how many elements the criticisms from the left and from the right have in common. According to both schools of thought, aid never reaches the poor; aid crowds out domestic savings; aid helps maintain repressive regimes; and aid preserves the dependence of poor countries on rich countries. The crucial difference between the two perspectives, however, lies in their evaluation of the market. Left-wing critics regard aid as the handmaiden of exploitative capitalist market relationships in developing countries. Right-wing critics believe profoundly in the workings of the market economy. Foreign aid is seen as an obstacle to the unfolding of the market mechanism.

The main shortcoming of both perspectives is that if one does not subscribe fully to *a priori* notions about the market – that capitalist market relations frustrate development, and government intervention in markets is an obstacle to development – the argumentation is not convincing. On the basis of impressionistic and selectively chosen examples, advocates of both perspectives come to very far-reaching general conclusions that do not stand up to closer empirical analysis.

12.6.3 Criticism of development projects

A useful contribution to the debate is the fierce attack on the practice of development aid by the journalist Graham Hancock (1991), in *Lords of Poverty*. This book contains a horrifying catalogue of the things that can go wrong in development projects. To name but a few:

- Repeated shipments of food aid consisting of food stocks unfit for human or animal consumption.

- A shipment of polystyrene igloos to tropical regions in Africa.
- Shipments of electric blankets to tropical Africa under the terms of emergency aid.
- Supply of medicines for which the expiry dates had been exceeded by more than fifteen years.
- Large dams in river basins that caused the flooding of the dwellings of hundreds of thousands of people, displaced millions of people, severely damaged the environment, and silted up within short periods of time.
- Unsuccessful transmigration projects that caused deforestation and erosion and offered migrants little chance of making an acceptable living.
- Large shipments of trucks to Africa, of which 95 per cent were out of operation within a few months.
- Large-scale energy projects which are ill-adapted to the local circumstances.
- Capital-intensive fishing projects in regions where cheap labour was easily available.
- Roads constructed without the necessary bridges across rivers.
- Experts whose expertise was based solely on the colour of their skin.
- A nuclear plant built on a geological fault line in an earthquake-prone area in the Philippines (George, 1988).
- Defence procurement in the donor country as a condition for aid.

Hancock shows convincingly that these are not incidental mistakes. They occur with great regularity all over the world. His book also provides a wealth of concrete examples to illustrate that much financial aid is spent on salaries of expatriate experts living a life of relative luxury in developing countries, or on imports of luxury consumer goods from Western countries, or is appropriated by members of the elites in developing countries. Hancock, too, stresses how little aid actual reaches the poor. Finally, he presents numerous examples of corrupt and totally inefficient regimes that have been supported liberally by means of development aid, including Mobutu in Zaire, Bokassa in the Central African Republic, Ferdinand Marcos in the Philippines and Papa Doc in Haiti. Often these regimes were also guilty of large-scale violations of human rights.

Like other authors discussed above, Hancock comes to the conclusion that development aid mainly serves the interests of donor governments, Western businesses and members of development bureaucracies and governmental organizations in both rich countries and developing countries.

12.6.4 The mainstream response to criticism

In response to the growing stream of criticism, the international aid establishment has started paying more attention to the quality and effectiveness of aid flows. The World Bank and national development organizations have commissioned thousands of evaluation studies and have set up research projects to examine the effectiveness of aid. Three recent authoritative studies in the mainstream tradition deal extensively with all the criticisms of foreign aid and try to formulate recommendations for its improved effectiveness. The studies are *Does Aid Work?* by R. A. Cassen (1986), *Foreign Aid Reconsidered* by R. C. Riddell (1987), and *Aid and Development* by A. O. Krueger *et al.* (1989). These studies subscribe to much of the criticism of development aid. Yet, on balance, their final conclusions are more positive.

Riddell in particular rightly emphasizes that expectations concerning aid have been too high. Development aid in itself cannot create economic growth, nor can it reverse patterns of economic stagnation. As one of the many factors impinging on development, foreign aid may – under favourable circumstances – contribute to some acceleration of economic development. At the microlevel, evaluation studies suggest that the majority of development projects contribute positively to development. At the macroeconomic level, the results of empirical studies are very contradictory. There is no conclusive evidence for the hypothesis of a positive correlation between aid and economic growth. However, there is also no evidence for the opposite conclusion that aid is detrimental to economic development. In countries implementing effective economic policies, the net contribution of foreign aid seems positive. According to the three studies, critical analysis of foreign aid can help us to learn not only from past mistakes and past failures, but also from past successes. The notion that development aid cannot be reformed or improved is rejected outright.

The debate on development projects

In his review of a large number of evaluation studies, Cassen (1986, 1988) concludes that about two-thirds of all development projects evaluated have been more or less successful in the light of the originally stated objectives.[11] Cost-benefit analyses often show returns of 10 per cent and higher. For instance, 80 per cent of all evaluated projects funded by the International Development Agency proved to have returns of over 10 per cent. Of the examined samples of loans provided by the Asian Development Bank and the Inter American Development Bank 60 per cent met their objectives and another 30 per cent met them partially.

In general, formal evaluations and cost-benefit analyses give a more positive picture of projects, than qualitative assessments by eye witnesses and participants (cf. Roth, 1993). It is hard to reach definitive conclusions. It almost seems as if the publications are coming from two completely different planets. It is even more confusing when critics such as Hancock freely quote from evaluations by international organizations when it suits their argument, but reach completely different conclusions to the organizations themselves.

The moral outrage of critical observers like Hancock or Susan George does not always contribute to the clarity of the argument. As Schumpeter wrote, the process of economic development is a process of creative destruction, with both 'winners' and 'losers'. When pros and cons are not dispassionately weighed, an extremely negative picture easily emerges. For example, Hancock criticizes structural adjustment programmes in general because they result in declining real incomes in the short term. This misses the point. Even the most successful adjustment programmes will cause problems in the short term.

On the other hand, cost-benefit analysis also has some serious limitations, especially in conditions in which the price mechanism does not function properly. The use of arbitrary 'shadow prices' offers ample opportunities to calculate oneself into economic success (see, for example, Bol, 1983, for a criticism of cost-benefit analysis of development projects). Riddell points out that the objectives of projects are often poorly defined, or even mutually contradictory. In such circumstances, it is hard to say whether a project is a success or a failure. He also estimates that not more than 10 per cent of all development projects has been evaluated. How representative the evaluated projects are, is not known.

Often the long-run effects of projects are hard to determine. Some projects have unintended positive results and learning effects that were not foreseen in the project design. For instance, a project, may not reach the very poor as intended, but can contribute to economic dynamics, technology transfer or learning in other ways. One should also not forget how often investment projects are unsuccessful in Western countries. The chaotic process of 'learning by doing' is essential to economic development. This includes inevitable failures and disappointments. When potentially high returns are associated with high risks of failure, there is a strong case for using development finance.

Cassen rejects the so-called *fungibility thesis*. This thesis states that aid does not really finance the high-priority investments it ostensibly pays for. These would have been carried out anyway. Rather, development aid finances more marginal investments or consumption, using the funds released from the high-priority projects.

Cassen puts forward four arguments against the fungibility thesis. First, the number of investment projects in a developing country is not static. As investment increases, new investment opportunities continue to arise. Some worthwhile investment projects would not even exist in the absence of aid. For instance, complicated irrigation or hydroelectric projects could not be realized without technical cooperation with foreign donors. In the second place, even if there is some replacement of investment, the notion that the recipient country has sufficient resources to finance all high priority projects is evidently not correct. Many authors besides Cassen stress that national and international capital markets are far from perfect. The fact that there are very profitable investment projects does not mean that private finance will be automatically forthcoming. In the third place, there are complementarities between investments (see Chapter 7). Investment projects financed by foreign aid may make other investments in the private sector more profitable. Finally, it is no great problem if some part of financial aid is used for expansion of consumption in a very poor country, as long as a substantial part of the aid flow is available for additional investment.

Cassen also pays attention to the reasons why projects fail. These include lack of coordination, conflicting objectives, imperfections in project design, expenditure deadlines, insufficient attention to maintenance and insufficient feedback and learning from past mistakes.

A common problem is the lack of coordination between donors and a lack of coordination capabilities in the recipient country. In some of the poorest developing countries, aid workers from different donor countries stumble over each other. The projects from different countries are not integrated and heavy burdens are imposed on the scarce administrative capabilities of the receiving countries. A second reason for project failure is conflicting objectives. All authors agree that the pursuit of commercial objectives or foreign policy objectives has a negative effect on the chances of success of development projects. Many projects fail due to technical imperfections in the project design and the neglect of local circumstances (cf. Cochrane, 1979). Far too often, projects make insufficient use of local expertise and knowledge.

Another cause of project failures is the pressure on donor organizations to spend their allocated budgets before the budgetary period runs out. This pressure to spend makes for built-in waste and inefficiency. It is a characteristic of all aid targets, which specify that certain sums have to be disbursed by certain dates. In the early years of Dutch development policy, the available funds grew more rapidly than the numbers of civil servants responsible for foreign aid. In combination with expenditure targets, this was later identified as an important source of inefficiencies.

A frequently heard complaint is that development aid focuses too much on new projects and too little on the continuation and upkeep of existing projects. Thus there is a systematic tendency to reserve insufficient funds for maintenance, spare parts, energy costs and the costs of local personnel. Donors expect the local costs of projects to be funded from the budgets of the aid recipients. But these budgets are inadequate for such purposes, especially when governments are forced to cut back on expenditure under the terms of structural adjustment programmes. Thus newly built roads soon become impassable due to a lack of maintenance, and newly constructed energy facilities operate at a fraction of their capacity. At the recipients' end, the shortage of administrative capacity is identified as a problem, especially in combination with a preference for large-scale prestige projects.

Finally, Cassen points to lack of sufficient feedback and learning effects from past experience. Not enough lessons are learned from past mistakes (see also OECD, 1985; Burki and Ayres, 1986). There is too little feedback from evaluation studies to new project design. There is almost no exchange of information between different national and international organizations concerned with development aid. Krueger and her co-authors (1989) are slightly more positive about the learning effects in project aid. Many of the criticisms – especially with respect to the excessively large-scale nature of industrial and infrastructural projects – refer primarily to projects from the early years of development aid. In more recent projects, the criticisms have been taken more to heart.

The mainstream literature also identifies the areas in which development aid has been relatively successful. One of them is agricultural development. In many developing countries in Asia and Latin America, the growth of agricultural production exceeded the growth of the population (see Chapter 9). This was realized in part due to investments in agricultural research, education, extension, irrigation and land improvement, all financed by development aid. Agricultural research financed from international aid flows made a significant contribution to the advances of the green revolution and to the growth of agricultural production and productivity.

Positive results have also been achieved in the field of infrastructure – in spite of many disappointments. Infrastructural investment in roads, harbours, telecommunications systems, dams and energy supply is an essential component in all development strategies. Such investments can seldom be financed via private capital markets.

Another area where aid has made a worthwhile contribution is education. Around 10 per cent of all World Bank loans go to education and educational projects. The rapid expansion of the educational systems in developing countries since World War II (as described in Chapter 6) was facilitated by foreign aid flows. Despite many disappointments, it is clear that education in developing countries benefited from technical and educational assistance. In a country such as India, success has been achieved in building up an independent research infrastructure of high quality.

A fourth area of relative success is that of family planning and health-care policy. Though population growth in many countries is still much too high (see Chapter 4), this does not mean that the resources invested in family planning have been wasted. The dramatic decreases in death rates discussed in Chapter 5 are in part the result of a multitude of projects that contributed to the transfer of medical technologies and the spread of new knowledge about disease and health care.

Riddell examines the criticisms of food aid (Riddell, 1987, pp. 228–36). Although there have been many failures, there have also been examples of success. According to Riddell, these are not restricted to emergency aid, but also include other food aid programmes and projects. He recognizes the danger of food aid acting as a disincentive to domestic food production. He concludes that the way in which food aid is provided may be more important than the question of whether such aid should or should not be provided.

On the other hand, the mainstream defenders of project aid also admit that there are many areas in which the results of project aid have been very disappointing. There has been a marked lack of success in integrated rural development programmes (Ruttan, 1989a), due to the difficulties of coordinating activities of various government organizations and departments. Special problems were encountered in the extension of small-scale pilot projects into general practice on a regional or national scale. There were also negative experiences with credit programmes aimed at small farmers. These projects often failed to appreciate the role of traditional credit institutions, and resources hardly ever reached the intended target groups. A final area of project failure is found in cattle-breeding projects.

Regionally, the success rate of projects has been the highest in South and Southeast Asia. Project aid in sub-Saharan Africa has been significantly less successful than in other areas of the world.

Macroeconomic effects of development aid

At the macrolevel it is fruitful to consider foreign aid as part of the aggregate inflow of financial resources to developing countries, characterizing the post-war international economic order (see Tables 3.5 on p. 83, 12.3 and 12.4). This inflow is one of the differences between the post-war period and the period between 1913 and 1950 when there were capital outflows from many colonies to the rich countries (Maddison, 1989).[12] Potentially, a net resource inflow offers developing countries the opportunity of importing new means of production and adopting new technologies. In the post-war period the net inflow of financial resources, of which aid flows were a part, contributed to an economic climate that was favourable to growth and dynamism.

With regard to the specific contribution of development aid, the macroeconomic debate focuses on the relationships between the amounts of aid a country receives and its savings, investments and economic growth. The empirical studies in this field are contradictory (see Riddell, 1987, pp. 102–27). Griffin (1970) and Griffin and Enos (1970) observe a negative relationship between aid and domestic savings, and aid and economic growth. Papanek (1972, 1973), finds a positive relation, as does Heller (1975). Rana and Dowling (1988, 1990) note modest but positive effects of development aid. In 1980, Mosley found no statistically significant relationships for all developing countries together. For the thirty poorest countries in his sample, however, there was a positive relation between aid and growth. In a later study Mosley (1987) found no significant relations at all. A negative relationship between aid and savings rates is reported by Gupta and Islam (1983). In a recent study of African countries, Lensink (1993a, 1993b) concludes that there is a positive relation between aid and economic growth. The positive, direct effects on aid flows and growth are, however, partially offset by a significant negative effect on savings.[13]

Riddell concludes that neither the claims of the critics of aid, nor those of the unabashed supporters of aid, can be substantiated empirically. He endorses Papanek's conclusion that no causal conclusions can be derived from the statistical analyses. First, development aid is modest in proportion to national income in most developing countries. Other economic and non-economic factors are far more important. It is very difficult to isolate the independent effects of aid. Second, one of the reasons for providing aid is that some countries are in great economic difficulties. Table 12.1 shows that aid to Asian countries is decreasing, while aid flows to the poorest African countries with serious economic problems are on the increase. Of course, one cannot conclude from this that there is an inverse relationship between aid and economic stagnation. Rather, the magnitude of aid flows is influenced by the intractability of the economic problems.

Like Cassen, Riddell concludes that the theoretical debate also does not provide unambiguous answers. As explained above, Cassen and Riddell argue that the fungibility thesis is not convincing. This thesis states that highly profitable investments would also have been realized without foreign aid, so the contribution of aid is limited. Cassen and Riddell argue that there are more potentially profitable investment projects in developing countries than can be financed from the available financial resources. Therefore, the extra resources provided as foreign aid can really make a difference to the investment effort.

There are no theoretically convincing reasons why there should necessarily be a negative relationship between aid and domestic savings. Under some conditions, the availability of aid could result in a decline in domestic savings. Whether this occurs in reality depends very much on the nature of domestic economic policy. In the conclusion to his book, Riddell argues for a balanced approach to development aid, in which the effects of aid are analyzed country by country and from period to period. Aid cannot set economic growth in motion. At best, it can help accelerate growth and assist directly or indirectly in some alleviation of poverty. Strangely enough, this careful and balanced conclusion is followed by a less restrained plea for an increase in official aid flows.

The supporters of aid also point to a number of countries where massive infusions of aid contributed to rapid economic development. In this context, the experiences of Taiwan, South Korea, India, Indonesia, Colombia, Brazil and Thailand are often mentioned. In these countries, foreign aid is said to have contributed to infrastructure, the road system, energy supply, agricultural productivity and the restoration of the balance between agriculture and industry. Other examples of positive impacts are provided by countries such as Lesoto, Botswana, Malawi and Bangladesh, which initially could not have survived as independent states without outside help.

None of these examples is undisputed, however. Some observers believe that in South Korea, large-scale development aid in the 1950s and 1960s contributed to the build up of infrastructure and the educational system, which were prerequisites for later economic growth. Other observers argue that the economic development of South Korea did not really begin until after 1960, when the United States curtailed financial aid and South Korea was forced to pursue more effective economic policies.

An important conclusion of all three studies discussed in this section is that the success of foreign aid depends to an important extent on the *development policies* pursued in the countries receiving aid. At the macrolevel, policies should aim at macroeconomic stability, bringing government finances under control, deregulation of the economy and a change from an inward-orientation to more export-oriented development (see Chapter 11). At the microlevel, the goal should be the development of institutions and policies that provide positive incentives to the economic efforts of individuals. It is against this background that Cassen and Krueger argue for programme aid and policy dialogue rather than project aid. This signifies a change in the role of aid. Programme aid is provided to support countries in the implementation of the necessary policy reforms. It may also help mitigate the negative social consequences of structural adjustment policies. If there are no changes in policy, development projects – regardless of their individual merits – will not contribute much to a change in the underlying economic dynamics. If foreign aid contributes to a reorientation of policy, its impact should be judged as positive, irrespective of the returns to development projects. If, on the other hand, foreign aid only provides policymakers with the means to postpone painful measures of reform, its net effects are negative.

12.6.5 Epilogue: an attempt at evaluation

A part of the extensive literature on the pros and cons of development aid has been udiscussed above. The tentative conclusions I have derived from this debate can be summarized in the following points:[14]

1. There are strong moral considerations that support the provision of development aid. These considerations gain in strength if aid on balance makes positive contributions to development and the solution of concrete problems in developing countries.
2. The fact that large amounts of aid are wasted is in itself not an argument against aid. Considering the urgency of developmental problems, a considerable degree of waste is acceptable, as long as aid realizes some part of its developmental objectives (see also point 5 below). Of course, one should always try to increase the effectiveness of aid.
3. The fact that development aid also serves the interests of the donor countries is not an important argument against aid provided that aid on balance contributes to the realization of developmental objectives. However, when the interests of the donor countries conflict with the realization of these objectives, aid programmes should be discontinued.
4. The fact that aid does not immediately reach the poor is no reason to discontinue aid as long it contributes on balance to the economic dynamism of the recipient countries. An important proposition in this whole book is that in the long run a dynamic economy is the main prerequisite for reducing poverty.
5. Development aid should be discontinued if it can be shown to be an obstacle to development. This may be the case when foreign aid is directly responsible for the continuation of regimes pursuing disastrous economic and social policies resulting in economic stagnation and widespread human suffering. Furthermore, especially in countries which pursue very inadequate economic policies and where government expenditures are overwhelmingly financed by aid flows, there is a clear relationship between foreign aid and policy failure. In such cases, reductions in the volume of aid or even discontinuation of the aid relationship should be considered.
6. If the provision of goods as part of aid is a disincentive to the production of these goods in the developing countries themselves, these kinds of aid should be discontinued. In this context I refer mainly to food aid in other than emergency situations.
7. Countries where net foreign aid flows exceed 10 per cent of gross domestic product are in danger of becoming too dependent on aid. When human talents are exclusively oriented towards aid flows and their use, aid itself turns into a long-run obstacle to autonomous economic development. Reduction of aid flows to below critical levels should be seriously considered, though any concrete figure still seems arbitrary.
8. Western countries bear part of the responsibility for situations in which many people in developing countries have become dependent on aid flows. Countries engaging in policy reform should therefore be able to rely on continued support for longer periods of time, even if the long-run goal is a reduction of aid flows.

Aid flows should be not be discontinued from one day to another (with the possible exception of extreme situations mentioned under point 5). Rather, aid should be used to encourage reform (conditionality). In these cases, however, policy reform should be aimed at reducing the dependence on foreign aid flows in the longer run.

9. Even when government-to-government aid flows are discontinued, continuation of direct aid to poverty groups by non-governmental organizations can be defended. Non-governmental agencies are usually more effective at channelling the aid to the groups for which it is intended, but this certainly does not mean that such agencies should be excluded from critical scrutiny.
10. There is a strong humanitarian case for continuation of emergency aid in the case of disasters, floods or famines. Again, a condition is that a reasonable part of aid meets its objectives and reaches the target groups for which it is intended (see point 2). Also the availability of aid should not undermine incentives for production (see point 5).
11. On balance one may conclude that aid flows during the post-war period have made positive contributions to development in several countries. It is more worth while to devote one's energy to improving the effectiveness of aid than to argue for its discontinuation.
12. Nevertheless, the criticisms discussed in this chapter have shown that aid relations between donor countries and developing countries leave much to be desired. It is quite justified that quantitative targets for foreign aid, such as reserving a fixed percentage of national income for aid, come in for serious criticism. Moreover, a significant proportion of development aid flows back to the rich donor countries, while much aid is of questionable effectiveness and much has been supplied to countries pursuing counterproductive macroeconomic policies. Given these circumstances, improving the effectiveness of foreign aid has a higher priority than maintaining or increasing the volume of aid flows.
13. Development aid can never be a decisive factor in economic growth and development. Economic development can only be achieved through the efforts and policies of individuals and their governments. In the context of effective national and international policies, however, foreign aid may also make a positive contribution to development.

QUESTION FOR REVIEW

1. Discuss the different motives for providing foreign aid to developing countries.
2. Discuss the theoretical foundations for providing foreign aid to developing countries.
3. Discuss the importance of foreign aid as a proportion of total financial flows to developing countries and as a percentage of gross domestic product in different developing countries and regions.

4. Summarize the main characterstics of the radical left-wing and neo-liberal right-wing criticisms of foreign aid.
5. Discuss the fungibility thesis.
6. What are the main points of the orthodox defence of foreign aid?
7. To what extent does the effectiveness of aid depend on development policies and development strategies?

Notes

1. In this chapter, the terms 'development aid', 'development assistance' and 'foreign aid' are used interchangeably.
2. Reproduced in abbreviated form.
3. Within the former Soviet Union there were several republics and regions which are comparable to developing countries. The expenditures of the former Soviet Union included flows which are comparable to development aid, but which have not been registered as such.
4. The distinction between official aid flows and voluntary aid flows is not always clear cut. Some aid organizations are entirely funded by voluntary donations of citizens. Other non-governmental aid organizations are heavily subsidized by governments. In the Netherlands, four of the largest NGOs receive about three-quarters of their revenues from the government.
5. As explained in Chapter 7, Chenery and Strout also argue in favour of technical aid as a complement to aid for capital accumulation. The shortage of human capital could actually be seen as the third gap of the Chenery–Strout model.
6. The latest edition of OECD (1995), *Geographical Distribution of Financial Flows to Developing Countries, 1989–1993*, has a separate chapter on thirteen Eastern European countries 'in transition': the three Baltic Republics, the Czech Republic, the Slovak Republic, Poland, Russia, Belarus, Hungary, Moldova, Romania and Bulgaria. The aid flow is designated Official Aid (OA), but it meets the same criteria as Official Development Assistance (ODA). The Asian republics of the former Soviet Union are included as developing countries in Asia.
7. See Riddell's excellent summary of the debate in *Foreign Aid Reconsidered* (1987).
8. For the Netherlands, see Berlage and Renard, 1993; Bol, 1983; Breman, 1986; Van Dam, 1989a, 1989b; Emmerij, 1984; Haan, 1989; Hoebink, 1988; Jepma, 1984, 1988; Kruyt and Vellinga, 1983; Lensink, 1993b; Quarles van Ufford *et al.*, 1988; Roth, 1993; Tims, 1985, 1989; Vingerhoets, 1986; Zoomers, 1992. The debate in the Netherlands is interesting, because this is one of the countries where public support for foreign aid was strongest. But similar literatures exist for other countries.
9. The classification of authors in schools is fraught with difficulties. Many empirically oriented studies contain conclusions which are in keeping either with the radical left-wing or the liberal right-wing criticisms. But an author is usually not classified as such unless he explicitly concludes that aid is an obstacle to development.
10. A well-known example is the deportation of 50,000 people of Indian descent from Uganda by dictator Idi Amin.
11. In the fifteen years preceding 1987 the DAC recorded over 9,000 project evaluations (Riddell, 1987: 185).
12. In the middle of the 1980s many developing countries experienced an outflow of resources, but presently the pattern of a net inflow seems to have resumed.

13. The language of statistical analysis is sometimes misleading. A positive relationship between aid flows and growth suggests that there is growth. In fact, many sub-Saharan African countries in recent years experienced declining per capita incomes.
14. The empirical results and theoretical analyses are so contradictory that it is illusory to expect to arrive at unambiguous conclusions. The final choices are inevitably value laden. Nevertheless, in order to avoid being too noncommittal, I have chosen to specify the reasoned conclusions I have derived from these important debates.

Bibliography

Chapter 1

Ahluwalia, M. S., N. G. Carter and H. Chenery (1979), 'Growth and poverty in developing countries', in H. Chenery (ed.), *Structural Change and Development Policy*, New York and Oxford: Oxford University Press, 462–514.

Alexandratos, N. (1988), *World Agriculture toward 2000*, Belhaven, NC and London: Food and Agriculture Organization.

Allen, R. D. G. (1980), *An Introduction to National Accounts Statistics*, London: Macmillan.

Bauer, P. T. (1976), *Dissent on Development*, London: Weidenfield & Nicholson.

Beckerman, W. (1974), *In Defense of Economic Growth*, London: Jonathan Cape.

Beckerman, W. (1993), 'Is economic growth still desirable?', in A. Szirmai, B. van Ark and D. Pilat (eds), *Explaining Economic Growth: Essays in honour of Angus Maddison*, Amsterdam: North Holland, 77–100.

Berry, A., F. Bourguignon and C. Morrisson (1983), 'The level of world inequality: how much can one say?', in *The Review of Income and Wealth*, 3 September, 217–42.

Brandt, W. *et al.* (1980), *North-South: A progamme for survival*, London: Pan Books.

Brandt, W. *et al.* (1983), *Common Crisis: North–South cooperation for world recovery*, London: Pan Books.

Brundtland, G. H. *et al.* (1987), *Our Common Future*, The World Commission on Environment and Development, Oxford: Oxford University Press.

Bunyard, P. (1985), 'World climate and tropical forest destruction', *The Ecologist*, **15**, 125–36.

Chenery, H., M. S. Ahluwalia, C. L. G. Bell, J. H. Duloy and R. Jolly (1974), *Redistribution with Growth*, New York: Oxford University Press.

Chirot, D. (1977), *Social Change in the Twentieth Century*, New York: Harcourt, Brace & Jovanovich.

Dam, F. van (1978), 'Mode in het ontwikkelingsvraagstuk' (Fashions in development), in *Economisch Statistische Berichten*, 17 May, 496–500.

Dam, F. van (1989), 'Het ontwikkelingsvraagstuk op hoofdpunten bezien' (Main issues in development), in *Economisch Statistische Berichten*, 31 May, 529–33.

Diamond, S. (1974), *In Search of the Primitive: A critique of civilization*, New York: Transaction Books.

Elias, N. (1970), 'Problemen van distantie en betrokkenheid' (Problems of detachment and involvement), in N. Elias, *Sociologie en geschiedenis en andere essays*, Amsterdam: Van Gennep.

Ettinger, J. van, T. H. Jansen and C. J. Jepma (1989), 'Climate, Environment and Development', paper for the international steering committee for the preparation of The Ministerial Conference on Atmospheric Pollution, November.

Haq, M. ul (1976), *The Poverty Curtain: Choices for the Third World*, New York: Columbia University Press.

Higgins, B. and J. D. Higgins (1979), *Economic Development of a Small Planet*, New York: Norton.

ILO (1976), *Employment Growth and Basic Needs: A one world problem*, Geneva: ILO.

Jones, E. L. (1988), *Growth Recurring: Economic change in world history*, Oxford: Clarendon Press.

Kravis, I. B., A. Heston and R. Summers (1982), *World Product and Income*, Baltimore: Johns Hopkins University Press.

Kuznets, S. (1966), *Modern Economic Growth*, New Haven: Yale University Press.

Lewis, A. (1950), *The Theory of Economic Growth*, London: Allen & Unwin.

Meadows, D. H., D. L. Meadows, J. Randers and W. W. Behrens (1972), *The Limits to Growth*, New York: Universe Books.

Myint, H. (1980), *The Economics of the Developing Countries*, 5th edn, London: Hutchinson.

Myrdal, G. (1968), *Asian Drama: An inquiry into the poverty of nations*, Harmondsworth: Penguin.

Myrdal, G. (1971), *The Challenge of World Poverty*, New York: Vintage Books.

North, D. C. and R. P. Thomas (1973), *The Rise of the Western World*, Cambridge: Cambridge University Press.

OECD (1979), *The Impact of the New Industrializing Countries*, Paris: OECD.

Reynolds, L. G. (1986), *Economic Growth in the Third World*, New Haven: Yale University Press.

Seers, D. (1979), 'The meaning of development', in D. Lehman, (ed.), *Development Theory: Four critical studies*, London: Cass, 9–30.

Streeten, P. (1972), *The Frontiers of Development Studies*, London: Macmillan.

Summers, R. and A. Heston (1991), 'The Penn world table, mark 5: an expanded set of international comparisons, 1955–1988', *Quarterly Journal of Economics*, May.

Szirmai, A. (1993), 'Introduction', in A. Szirmai, B. van Ark and D. Pilat (eds), *Explaining Economic Growth: Essays in Honour of Angus Maddison*, Amsterdam: North Holland, 1–34.

UNDP (1991), *Human Development Report 1991*, New York and Oxford: Oxford University Press.

UNSO (1968), *A System of National Accounts*, Studies in Methods, series F, no. 2, rev. 3, New York: United Nations Statistical Office.

World Bank (1986), *World Development Report 1986*, Oxford and New York: Oxford University Press.

World Bank (1989a), *World Development Report 1989*, Oxford and New York: Oxford University Press.

World Bank (1989b), *Sub-Saharan Africa: From crisis to sustainable growth*, Washington, DC: World Bank.

World Bank (1990), *World Development Report 1990: Poverty*, Oxford and New York: Oxford University Press.

World Bank (1992), *World Development Report 1992: Development and the Environment*, Oxford and New York: Oxford University Press.

World Bank (1993), *World Development Report 1993*, Oxford and New York: Oxford University Press.

World Bank (1995), *World Development Report 1995: Workers in an integrating world*, Oxford and New York: Oxford University Press.

Worsley, P. (1964), *The Third World*, Weidenfeld & Nicholson.

Chapter 2

Bairoch, P. (1980), 'Le bilan économique du colonialisme: mythes et réalités', in L. Blussé, H. L. Wesseling, G. D. Winius (eds), *History and Underdevelopment: Essays on underdevelopment and European expansion in Asia and Africa*, Leiden: Centre for the History of European Expansion, 29–41.

Baker, C. (1981), 'Economic organization and slump in South and Southeast Asia', in *Comparative Studies in Society and History*, **23**, 325–49.

Baran, P. (1957), *The Political Economy of Growth*, New York: Monthly Review Press.

Boserup, E. (1965), *The Conditions of Agricultural Growth*, New York: Aldine.

Boserup, E. (1981), *Population and Technology*, Chicago: University of Chicago Press.

Braudel, F. (1978), 'Expansion of Europe and the *longue durée*', in H. L. Wesseling (ed.), *Expansion and Reaction*, Leiden: Leiden University Press.

Breman, J. (1985), *Arbeidsmigratie en transformatie in koloniaal Azië* (Labour migration and transformation in colonial Asia), Comparative Asian Studies Programme, Working Paper No. 7, Rotterdam: CASP.

Cipolla, C. M. (1981), *Before the Industrial Revolution: European society and economy, 1000–1700*, 2nd edn, London: Methuen.

Curtin, P. D. (1969), *The Atlantic Slave Trade: A census*, Madison: University of Wisconsin Press.

Darby, H. C., and H. Fullart (1970), *The New Cambridge Modern History Atlas*, Cambridge: Cambridge University Press.

Davis, K. (1951), *The Population of India and Pakistan*, Princeton: University of Princeton.

Elias, N. (1969), *Über den Prozess der Zivilisation*, vol. ii, 2nd edn, Bern: Franke Verlag.

Elvin, M. (1973), *The Pattern of Chinese Past*, Stanford Calif.: Stanford University Press.

Emmer, P. C. (1986), 'The meek Hindu: the recruitment of Indian indentured labourers for service overseas, 1870–1916', in P. C. Emmer (ed.), *Colonialism and Migration: Indentured labour before and after slavery*, Dordrecht: Nijhoff, 3–18.

Engerman, S. L. (1986), 'Servants to slaves to servants: contract labour and European expansion', in P. C. Emmer (ed.), *Colonialism and Migration*, Dordrecht: Nijhoff, 263–94.

Fage, J. D. (1969), *A History of West Africa: An introductory survey*, 4th edn, Cambridge: Cambridge University Press.

Fage, J. D. (1977), 'Slavery and the slave trade in the context of West African history', in Z. A. Konczacki and J. M. Konczacki (eds), *An Economic History of Tropical Africa*, vol. i, *The Pre-Colonial Period*, London: Cass, 166–78.

Fieldhouse, D. K. (1982), *The Colonial Empires: A comparative survey from the eighteenth century*, 2nd edn, London: Macmillan.

Furtado, C. (1976), *Economic Development of Latin America*, 2nd edn, Cambridge: Cambridge University Press.

Gerschenkron, A. (1962), *Economic Backwardness in Historical Perspective*, Cambridge, Mass.: Harvard University Press.

Hopkins, A. G. (1973), *An Economic History of West Africa*, London: Longman.

Jones, E. L. (1988), *Growth Recurring: Economic change in world history*, Oxford: Clarendon Press.

Kennedy, P. (1989), *The Rise and Fall of Great Powers*, New York: Vintage Books.

Landes, D. (1969), *The Unbound Prometheus: Technological changes and industrial development in Western Europe from 1750 to the present*, Cambridge: Cambridge University Press.

Lewis, A. (1954), 'Economic development with unlimited supplies of labour', *The Manchester School of Economic and Social Studies*, **22**, 139–91.

Lewis, W. A. (ed.) (1970), *Tropical Development 1880–1913*, London: Allen & Unwin.

Lewis, W. A. (1978a), *Growth and Fluctuations 1870–1913*, London: Allen & Unwin.

Lewis, W. A. (1978b), *The Evolution of the International Economic Order*, Princeton: Princeton University Press.

Lin, J. Y. (1995), 'The Needham Puzzle: Why the industrial revolution did not originate in China', *Economic Development and Cultural Change*, **43**, (2), January.
Lovejoy, P. E. (1982), 'The volume of the Atlantic slave trade: a synthesis', *Journal of African History*, **33**, 473–501.
McEvedy, C. and R. Jones (1978), *Atlas of World Population History*, Harmondsworth: Penguin.
McNeil, W. H. (1989), 'European expansion and warfare since 1500', in J. A. de Moor and H. L. Wesseling (eds), *Imperialism and War*, London: Brill.
Maddison, A. (1982a) *Phases of Capitalist Development*, Oxford University Press: Oxford.
Maddison, A. (1982b), 'International economic orders past and present: the West and the rest since 1500', *Syllabus Leergang Ontwikkelingsproblematiek*, Mimeographed, University of Groningen, Groningen, 23–38.
Maddison, A. (1983), 'A comparison of levels of GDP per capita in developed and developing countries, 1700–1980', *Journal of Economic History*, **43**, (1), March, 27–41.
Maddison, A. (1985), *Two Crises: Latin America and Asia, 1929–1938 and 1973–1983*, Paris: OECD.
Maddison, A. (1989), *The World Economy in the 20th Century*, Paris: OECD.
Maddison, A. (1995), *Monitoring the World Economy*, Paris: OECD Development Centre.
Myers, R. H. and M. R. Peattie (1984), *The Japanese Colonial Empire, 1895–1945*, Princeton: Princeton University Press.
Myint, H. (1980), *The Economics of the Developing Countries*, 5th edn, London: Hutchinson.
North, D. C. and R. P. Thomas (1973), *The Rise of the Western World*, Cambridge: Cambridge University Press.
Palmer, R. R. and J. Colton (1978), *A History of the Modern World*, 5th edn, New York: Knopf.
Perkins, D. W. (1969), *Agricultural Development in China, 1368–1968*, Edinburgh: Edinburgh University Press.
Reynolds, L. G. (1986), *Economic Growth in the Third World: An introduction*, New Haven: Yale University Press.
Slicher van Bath, B. H. (1989), *Indianen en Spanjaarden: Een ontmoeting tussen twee werelden, Latijns-Amerika, 1500–1800* (Indians and Spaniards: A meeting between two worlds, Latin America, 1500–1800), Amsterdam: Bakker.
Streeten, P. (1984), 'Approaches to a new international order', in C. K. Wilber (ed.), *The Political Economy of Development and Underdevelopment*, 3rd edn, New York: Random House, New York, 473–97.
Wallerstein, E. (1974), *The Modern World System*, New York: Academic Press.
Weber, M. (1920), 'Confuzianismus und Taoismus', *Gesammelte Aufsatze zur Religionssoziologie*, **1**, Mohr, Tübingen, 1920.
Williams, E. (1964), *Capitalism and Slavery*, 2nd edn, London: Deutsch.
Wolf, E. R. (1982), *Europe and the People without History*, Berkeley: University of California Press.

Chapter 3

Abramovitz, M. (1956; repr. 1989), 'Resource and output trends in the United States since 1870', *American Economic Review*, **46** (2), May, 5–23; repr. in *id.*, *Thinking about Growth and Other Essays on Economic Growth and Welfare*, Cambridge: Cambridge University Press.
Baran, G. A. (1957), *The Political Economy of Growth*, New York: Monthly Review Press.
Baumol, W. J., S. A. B. Blackman and E. N. Wolff (1989), *Productivity and American Leadership*, Cambridge, Mass.: MIT Press.
Boeke, J. H. (1953), *Economics and Economic Policy of Dual Societies as Exemplified by Indonesia*, New York: Institute of Pacific Relations.

Chirot, D. (1977), *Social Change in the Twentieth Century*, New York: Harcourt, Brace & Jovanovich.
Colman, D. and F. Nixson (1985), *Economics of Change in Less Developed Countries*, 2nd edn, Oxford: Phillip Allen, Barnes and Noble Books.
Denison, E. F. (1967), *Why Growth Rates Differ*, Washington, DC: Brookings Institution.
DGBAS (1993), *Statistical Yearbook of the Republic of China*, Taipeh: Directorate General of Budget, Accounting and Statistics.
DGBAS (1994), Executive Yuan, *National Income of Taiwan Area of Republic of China*, Taipeh: Directorate General of Budget, Accounting and Statistics.
Dos Santos, T. (1970), 'The structure of dependence', *American Econonic Review*, **60** (2), May, 231–6.
Durkheim, E. (1973; first pub. 1897), *Le Suicide*, Press Universitaires de France.
Fagerberg, J. (1994), 'Technology and international differences in growth rates', *Journal of Economic Literature*, **32**, September, 1147–75.
Fieldhouse, D. K. (1973), *Economics and Empire, 1830–1914*, Ithaca: Cornell University Press.
Frank, A. G. (1969), *Capitalism and Underdevelopment in Latin America*, rev. edn, New York: Monthly Review Press.
Frank, A. G. (1971), *The Sociology of Underdevelopment and the Underdevelopment of Sociology*, London: Pluto Press.
Gerschenkron, A. (1962), *Economic Backwardness in Historical Perspective*, Cambridge, Mass.: Harvard University Press.
Hoselitz, B. F. (1960), *Sociological Aspects of Economic Growth*, New York: The Free Press.
Hunt, D. (1989), *Economic Theories of Development: An analysis of competing paradigms*, New York: Harvester.
Inkeles, A. (1969), 'Making men modern: on the causes and consequences of individual change in developing countries', *American Journal of Sociology*, **75** (2), September, 208–25.
Inkeles, A. and D. Smith (1974), *Becoming Modern*, Cambridge, Mass.: Harvard University Press.
Kastelein, T. J. (1983), *Economische Theorieën over Economische Ontwikkeling en Koloniën uit de 18e, 19e en begin 20e eeuw* (Economic Theories on Economic Development and Colonies from the 18th, 19th and Early 20th Century), mimeographed, Department of Economics of the University of Groningen, Groningen.
Kendrick, J. W. (1961), *Productivity Trends in the United States*, National Bureau for Economic Research, Princeton: Princeton University Press.
Kuznets, S. (1965), *Economic Growth and Structure*, London: Heinemann.
Lewis, W. A. (1950), *Theory of Economic Growth*, London: Allen & Unwin.
Lewis, W. A. (1954), 'Economic development with unlimited supplies of labour', *The Manchester School of Economic and Social Studies*, **22**, 1954, 139–91.
Lewis, W. A. (1978), *Evolution of the International Economic Order*, Princeton: Princeton University Press.
Lucas, R. E. (1988), 'On the mechanics of economic development', *Journal of Monetary Economic*, **22**, 3–42.
Maddison, A. (1970), *Economic Progress and Policy in Developing Countries*, New York: Norton.
Maddison, A. (1986), 'Notes on developing country performance', mimeographed, University of Groningen, Groningen.
Maddison, A. (1987), 'Growth and slowdown in advanced capitalist economies', *Journal of Economic Literature*, **25**, June, 649–98.
Maddison, A. (1989), *The World Economy in the Twentieth Century*, Paris: OECD.
Maddison, A. (1995), *Monitoring the World Economy*, Paris: OECD Development Centre.
Moore, W. E. (1963), *Social Change*, Englewood Cliffs, NJ: Prentice Hall.
Mitchell, B. R. (1982), *International Historical Statistics: The America's and Australasia*, London: Macmillan.

Myint, H. (1980), *The Economics of the Developing Countries*, 5th edn, London: Hutchinson.
Myrdal, G. (1968), *Asian Drama: An inquiry into the poverty of nations*, Harmondsworth: Penguin.
North, D. C. (1990), *Institutions, Institutional Change and Economic Performance*, Cambridge: Cambridge University Press.
North, D. C. (1993), 'The ultimate causes of growth', in A. Szirmai, B. van Ark and D. Pilat (eds), *Explaining Economic Growth: Essays in honour of Angus Maddison*, Amsterdam: North Holland, 65–75.
North, D. C. and R. P. Thomas (1973), *The Rise of the Western World: A new economic history*, Cambridge: Cambridge University Press.
OECD, *National Accounts*, various volumes, Paris: OECD.
Prebisch, R. (1962), 'The economic development of Latin America and its principal problems', *Economic Bulletin of Latin America*, 7 (1), February.
Romer, P. (1986), 'Increasing returns and long-run growth', *Journal of Political Economy*, **94** (5), 1002–37.
Romer, P. (1990), 'Endogenous technological change', *Journal of Political Economy*, **95** (5), October, S71–102.
Rostow, W. W. (1960), *The Stages of Economic Growth*, Cambridge: Cambridge Unversity Press.
Rostow, W. W. (ed.) (1965), *The Economics of Take-Off into Sustained Growth*, London: Macmillan.
Schumpeter, J. A. (1976; first pub. 1943), *Capitalism, Socialism and Democracy*, London: Allen & Unwin.
Smith, A. (1961; first pub. 1776), *An Inquiry into the Nature and Causes of the Wealth of Nations*, ed. E. Cannan, London: Methuen.
Solow, R. M. (1956), 'A contribution to the theory of economic growth', *Quarterly Journal of Economics*, **70** (1), February, 65–94.
Solow, R. M. (1957), 'Technical change and the aggregate production function', *Review of Economics and Statistics*, **39** (3), August, 312–20.
Solow, R. M. (1991), 'New directions in growth theory', in B. Gahlen, H. Hesse, H. J. Ramser and G. Bombach (eds), *Wachstumstheorie und Wachstumspolitik: Ein neuer Anlauf*, Tübingen: Mohr/Siebeck, 3–17.
Urquidi, V. (1993), 'The developmentalist view', in A. Szirmai *et al.*, *Explaining Economic Growth*, 447–66.
Weber, M. (1969; first pub. 1905), *Die Protestantische Ethik*, ed. J. Winckelmann, Munich: Siebenstern.
World Bank (various), *World Development Report*, Oxford and New York: Oxford University Press.
World Bank (various), *World Tables*, Baltimore and London: Johns Hopkins University Press.

Chapter 4

Becker, G. S. (1960), 'An economic analysis of fertility', in National Bureau for Economic Research (ed.), *Demographic and Economic Change in Developed Countries*, Princeton: Princeton University Press.
Beckerman, W. (1993), 'Is economic growth still desirable?', in A. Szirmai, B. van Ark and D. Pilat (eds), *Explaining Economic Growth: Essays in honour of Angus Maddison*, Amsterdam: North Holland, 77–100.
Birdsall, N. (1988), 'Economic approaches to population growth', in H. Chenery and T. N. Srinivasan (eds), *Handbook of Development Economics*, vol. i, Amsterdam: Elsevier, 477–542.

Bongaarts, J. (1982), 'The fertility-inhibiting effects of the intermediate fertility variables', *Studies in Family Planning*, **13** (6/7), June/July, 179–89.
Bongaarts, J. and R. G. Potter (1983), *Fertility, Biology and Behavior: An analysis of the proximate determinants*, New York: Academic Press.
Boserup, E. (1965), *The Conditions of Agricultural Growth*, London: Allen & Unwin.
Boserup, E. (1981), *Population and Technology*, Chicago: University of Chicago Press.
Boserup, E. (1983), 'The impact of scarcity and plenty on development', *Journal of Interdisciplinary History*, **14** (2), 383–407.
Brown, L. R. and H. E. Young (1990), 'Feeding the world in the nineties', in L. R. Brown *et al.* (eds), *State of the World 1990*, New York and London: World Watch Institute.
Brundtland, G. H. *et al.* (1987), *Our Common Future*, World Commission on Environment and Development, Oxford: Oxford University Press.
Caldwell, J. C. and P. Caldwell (1985), 'Cultural forces tending to sustain high fertility in tropical Africa', in *PHN Technical note* 85-16, Population, Health and Nutrition Department, Washington, DC: World Bank.
Caldwell, J. C. and P. Caldwell (1987), 'The cultural context of high fertility in sub-Sahara Africa', *Population and Development Review*, **13** (3), September, 409–36.
Cipolla, C. M. (1978), *An Economic History of World Population*, 7th edn, Harmondsworth: Penguin.
Coale, A. J. and E. M. Hoover (1958), *Population Growth and Economic Development in Low-Income Countries*, Princeton: Princeton University Press.
Durand, J. D. (1977), 'Historical estimates of world population: an evaluation', *Population and Development Review*, **3** (3), 253–95.
Easterlin, R. A. (1978), 'The economics and sociology of fertility: a synthesis', in C. Tilley (ed.), *Historical Studies of Changing Fertility*, Princeton: Princeton University Press.
Ehrlich, P. R. and A. H. Ehrlich (1990), *The Population Explosion*, New York: Simon Schuster.
Goodstadt, L. (1982), 'China's one child family', *Population and Development Review*, **8**, 37–50.
Hansen, B. and G. A. Marzouk (1965), *Development and Economic Policy in the U.A.R. (Egypt)*, Amsterdam: North Holland.
Keating, M. (1993), *Agenda for Change: A plain language version of Agenda 21 and the other Rio agreements*, Geneva: Centre for Our Common Future.
Kelley, A. C. (1988), 'Economic consequences of population change in the Third World', *Journal of Economic Literature*, **26**, December, 1685–728.
Kirsten, E., E. W. Buchholtz and W. Köllman (1956), *Raum und Bevölkerung in der Weltgeschichte*, Würtzburg: Ploetz.
Kuznets, S. (1980), 'Recent population trends in less developed countries and implications for internal income inequality', in R. A. Easterlin (ed.), *Population and Economic Change in Developing Countries*, Chicago: University of Chicago Press, 471–515.
Leibenstein, H. (1954), *A Theory of Economic Demographic Development*, Princeton: Princeton University Press.
Maddison, A. (1989), *The World Economy in the Twentieth Century*, Paris: OECD.
Maddison, A. (1995), *Monitoring the World Economy*, Paris: OECD Development Centre.
Meadows, D. H., D. L. Meadows, J. Randers and W. W. Behrens (1972), *Limits to Growth*, New York: Universe Books.
Meer, C. L. J. van der (1983), 'Voedselvoorziening en Agrarische Ontwikkeling' (Food supply and agricultural development), in C. L. J. van der Meer (ed.), *Landbouw en Ontwikkeling*, The Hague: VUGA, 177–206.
Myint, H. (1980), *The Economics of the Developing Countries*, 5th edn, London: Hutchinson.
Nelson, R. (1956), 'A theory of the low level equilibrium trap in underdeveloped economies', *American Economic Review*, **46**, 894–908.
Oldeman, L. R., V. W. P. van Engelen and J. H. M. Pulles (1991), 'The extent of human-induced

soil degradation', in L. R. Oldeman, R. T. A. Hakkeling and W. G. Sombroek (eds), *World Map of the Status of Human-Induced Soil Degradation: An explanatory note*, 2nd rev. edn, Wageningen: International Soil Reference and Information Centre.

Simon, J. (1982), *The Ultimate Resource*, Princeton: Princeton University Press.

Szereszewski, R. (1965), *Structural Changes in the Economy of Ghana*, 1891–1911, London: Weidenfeld & Nicolson.

Todaro, M. P. (1981), *Economic Development in the Third World*, 2nd edn, New York: Longman.

United Nations (1988), *World Population Prospects*, 1986, New York: UN.

United Nations (1989), *World Population Prospects*, 1988, New York: UN.

United Nations (1993a), *World Population Prospects: The 1992 revision*, New York: UN.

United Nations (1993b), *World Urbanization Prospects: The 1992 revision*, New York: UN.

United Nations (1994), *Population, Environment and Development*, New York: UN.

United Nations Population Division (1994), *World Population Plan of Action*, Department for Economic and Social Information and Policy Analysis, New York: United Nations.

Willis, R. (1973), 'A new approach to the economic theory of fertility', *Journal of Political Economy*, March/April, S14–S64.

World Bank (1984), *World Development Report 1984*, part 2, 'Population change and development', Oxford and New York: Oxford University Press.

World Bank (1992), *World Development Report 1992: Development and the environment*, Oxford and New York: Oxford University Press.

World Bank (1994), *World Population Projections 1994–95*, Baltimore and London: Johns Hopkins University.

World Bank (1995), *World Tables 1995*, Baltimore and London: Johns Hopkins University Press.

Chapter 5

Baldwin, R. E. and B. A. Weisbrod (1974), 'Disease and labor productivity', *Economic Development and Cultural Change*, **22** (3), 414–35.

Bardhan, P. (1993), 'Economics of development and the development of economics', *Journal of Economic Perspectives*, 7 (2), Spring, 129–42.

Barlow, R. (1979), 'Health and economic development: a theoretical and empirical review', *Human Capital and Development*, **1**, 45–75.

Caldwell, J. C. (1984), 'Introductory remarks on interactions between health, mortality and development', *Mortality and Health Policy: Proceedings of the expert group on mortality and health policy*, 1984 International Conference on Population, New York: United Nations, 106–11.

Caldwell, J. C. (1986), 'Routes to low mortality in poor countries', *Population and Development Review*, **12** (2), 171–221.

Chambers, R. (1982), 'Health, agriculture and rural poverty: why seasons matter', *Journal of Development Studies*, **18** (2).

Cornia, G. A. (1984), 'A summary and interpretation of the evidence', *World Development*, **12** (3), 381–91.

Deolalikar, A. B. (1988), 'Do health and nutrition influence labor productivity in agriculture? Econometric estimates for south India', *Review of Economics and Statistics*, **70** (2), May.

Frederikson, H. (1969), 'Feedbacks in economic and demographic transition', *Science*, **166**.

Frenk, J., T. Frejka, J. L. Bobadilla, C. Stern, J. Sepulveda and M. José (1989), 'The epidemiologic transition in Latin America', *International Population Conference*, vol. 1, New Delhi 1989, Liège: IUSSP, 419–32.

Hardiman, M. and J. Midgley (1982), *The Social Dimension of Development: Social policy and planning in the Third World*, Chichester: Wiley.

Johansson, S. R. and K. Mosk (1987), 'Exposure, resistance and life expectancy: disease and death during the economic development of Japan, 1900–1960', *Population Studies*, **41** (2), July, 207–36.

Kadt, E. de and M. Lipton (1988), *Agriculture–Health Linkages*, offset publication no. 104, Geneva: World Health Organisation.

Keyzer, M. A. (1993), 'Welfare assessment of the efficiency wage argument', Development Economics Seminar paper no. 93-3/13, November, Institute of Social Studies, The Hague.

Leibenstein, H. (1957), *Economic Backwardness and Economic Growth: Studies in the theory of economic development*, New York: Wiley.

Leisinger, K. M. (1989), *Poverty, Sickness and Medicines: An unholy alliance? Development policy health and the role of the pharmaceutical industry in the Third World*, Geneva: Federation International de l'Industrie du Medicament.

McKeown, T. (1976), *The Modern Rise of Population*, London: Arnold.

McKeown, T. (1978), 'Fertility, mortality and causes of death: an examination of issues related to the modern rise of population', *Population Studies*, **32** (3), 535–42.

McKeown, T. (1979), *The Role of Medicine*, Oxford: Blackwell.

McKeown, T. (1988), *The Origins of Human Disease*, Oxford: Blackwell.

Maurice, J. and A. M. Pearce (eds) (1987), *Tropical Disease Research: A global partnership*, Geneva: WHO.

Mosley, W. H. (1983), 'Primary care: Rhetoric and reality', *Populi*, **10** (3), 41–54.

Mosley, W. H. (1984), 'Child survival: research and policy', *Population and Development Review*, **10**, suppl., 3–23.

Mosley, W. H. (1985a), 'Biological and socio-economic determinants of child survival: a proximate determinants framework integrating fertility and mortality variables', *Congrès International de la Population*, Florence 1985, Liège: Ordina Editions, 189–208.

Mosley, W. H. (1985b), 'Will primary health care reduce infant and child mortality? A critique of some current strategies, with special reference to Africa and Asia', in J. Vallin and A. D. Lopez (eds), *Health Policy, Social Policy and Mortality Prospects*, Liège: Ordina Editions, 103–38.

Mushkin, S. (1962), 'Health as an investment', *Journal of Political Economy*, **70** (5), October, 129–57.

Netherlands Development Cooperation (1988), *Primary Health Care: Evaluation of Dutch-supported activities in the field of extramural health care since 1975*, The Hague: Ministry of Foreign Affairs, Directoraat General Internationale Samenwerking.

Norren, B. van and H. A. W. van Vianen (1986), *The Malnutrition–Infections Syndrome and its Demographic Outcome in Developing Countries*, publication no. 4, The Hague: Programming Committee for Demographic Research.

Omran, A. R. (1971), 'The epidemiologic transition: a theory of the epidemiology of population change', *Millbank Memorial Fund Quarterly*, **49**, 509–38.

Popkin, B. M. (1978), 'Nutrition and labor productivity', *Social Science and Medicine*, **12C** (3/4), 117–25.

Preston, S. H. (1975), 'The changing relation between mortality and level of economic development', *Population Studies*, **29** (2), 231–48.

Preston, S. H. (1976), *Mortality Patterns in National Populations*, New York: Academic Press.

Sreter, S. (1988), 'The importance of social intervention in Britain's mortality decline *c.*1850–1914: a re-interpretation of the role of public health', *Social History of Medicine*, **1** (1), April, 1–38.

United Nations (1953), *Demographic Yearbook*, New York: UN.

United Nations (1960), *Demographic Yearbook*, New York: UN.

United Nations (1963), *Demographic Yearbook*, New York: UN.

United Nations (1979), *Demographic Yearbook*, hist. suppl., New York: UN.

United Nations (1984), *Mortality and Health Policy: Proceedings of the expert group on*

mortality and health policy, International Conference on Population 1984, Department of International Economic and Social Affairs, New York: UN.
United Nations (1985), *World Population Trends, Population and Development, Interrelations and Population Policies, 1983: Monitoring report*, vol. i, New York: UN.
United Nations (1986), *World Population Prospects: Estimates and projections as assessed in 1984*, New York: UN.
United Nations (1988a), *World Population. Trends and Policies, 1987: Monitoring report*, New York: UN.
United Nations (1988b), *Mortality of Children under Age 5: World estimates and projections, 1950–2025*, Population studies no. 105, New York: UN.
United Nations (1993a), *World Population Prospects: The 1992 revision*, New York: UN.
United Nations (1993b), *World Urbanization Prospects: The 1992 revision*, New York: UN.
United Nations (1994), *Aids and the Demography of Africa*, Department for Economic and Social Information and Policy Analysis, New York: UN.
United Nations/ESCAP (1985), *Mortality and Health Issues*, New York: UN.
Vallin, J. (1989), 'Conclusion: théorie(s) de la baisse de la mortalité et situation Africaine', in G. Pison, E. van de Walle and M. Sala-Diakanda, *Mortalité et société en Afrique au sud du Sahara*: travaux et documents, cahier no. 124, Paris: Presses Universitaires de France.
Walsh, J. A. (1990), 'Estimating the burden of illness in the Tropics', in: K. S. Warren and A. F. Mahmoud (eds), *Tropical and Geographical Medicine*, New York: McGraw-Hill, 185–96.
WHO (1978), *Primary Health Care: Report of the International Conference on Primary Health Care*, Health for All Series, no. 1, Geneva: World Health Organization.
WHO (1981), *Global Strategy for Health for All by the Year 2000*, Health for All Series, no. 3, Geneva: World Health Organization, 74–6.
WHO (1987), *Evaluation of the Strategy for Health for All by the Year 2000: Seventh report on the world health situation*, vol. i, *Global Review*, Geneva: World Health Organization.
WHO (1993), *Implementation of the Global Strategy for Health for All by the Year 2000. Second Evaluation: Eighth report on the world health situation*, vol. i, *Global Review*, Geneva: World Health Organization.
World Bank (1983), *World Tables 1983*, Baltimore and London: Johns Hopkins University Press.
World Bank (1984), 'Population change and development', in *id.*, *World Development Report 1984*, Oxford: Oxford University Press.
World Bank (1990), *World Development Report 1990*, Oxford and New York: Oxford University Press.
World Bank (1992), *World Development Report 1992*, Oxford and New York: Oxford University Press.
World Bank (1994a), *World Development Report 1994*, Oxford and New York: Oxford University Press.
World Bank (1994b), *World Population Projections 1994–95*, Baltimore: Johns Hopkins University Press.

Chapter 6

Abernethy, D. (1969), *The Political Dilemma of Popular Education: An African case*, Stanford: Stanford University Press.
Abramovitz, M. (1956), 'Resource and output trends in the United States since 1870', *American Economic Review*, May.
Altbach, P. G. and G. P. Kelly (1978), *Education and Colonialism*, New York/London: Longman.

Altbach, P. G. (1982), 'Servitude of the mind? Education, dependency and neocolonialism', in P. G. Altbach, R. F. Arnove and G. P. Kelly (eds), *Comparative Education*, New York: Macmillan, 469–84.
Anderson, C. A. and M. J. Bowman (1976), 'Education and economic modernization in historical perspective', in L. Stone (ed.), *Schooling and Societies: Studies in the history of education*, Baltimore: Johns Hopkins University Press.
Barro, R. J. (1989), 'Economic growth in a cross section of countries', *The Quarterly Journal of Economics*, **106**, 407, 433.
Becker, G. S. (1964), *Human Capital: A theoretical and empirical analysis, with special reference to education*, New York and London: Columbia University Press.
Berg, I. (1970), *Education and Jobs: The great training robbery*, New York: Praeger.
Blaug, M. (1972), *The Economics of Education*, Harmondsworth: Penguin.
Blaug, M. (1976), 'The empirical status of human capital theory: a slightly jaundiced survey', *Journal of Economic Literature*, September, 827–56.
Blaug, M. (1979), 'Economics of education in developing countries: current trends and new priorities', *Third World Quarterly*, January, 73–83.
Blaug, M. (1985), 'Where are we now in the economics of education?', *Economics of Education Review*, **4** (1), 17–28.
Blaug, M. (1990), *The Economic Value of Higher Education*, NIAS, Uhlenbeck Lecture VIII, Wassenaar: Netherlands Institute for Advanced Studies in the Humanities and Social Sciences.
Blaug, M., R. Layard and M. Woodhall (1969), *Causes of Graduate Unemployment in India*, London: Penguin/Allen Lane.
Bowles, S. and H. Gintis (1976), *Schooling in Capitalist America*, New York: Basic Books.
Bowman, M. J. and C. A. Anderson (1963), 'Concerning the role of education in development', in C. Geertz (ed.), *Old Societies and New States: The quest for modernity in Africa and Asia*, Glencoe, Ill.: The Free Press.
Bowman, M. J. and C. A. Anderson (1973), 'Human capital and economic modernisation in historical perspective', in F. C. Lane (ed.), *Proceedings of the Fourth International Conference of Economic History, 1968*, Paris: Mouton.
Carnoy, M. (1974), *Education as Cultural Imperialism*, New York: David McKay.
Coombs, P. (1985), *The World Crisis in Education: The view from the 1980s*, Oxford and New York: Oxford University Press.
Coombs, P. and M. Ahmed (1974), *Attacking Rural Poverty: How nonformal education can help*, Baltimore: Johns Hopkins University.
Curle, A. (1964), *World Campaign for Universal Literacy: Comment and Proposal*, Occasional Papers in Education and Development, Graduate School of Education, Harvard University.
Denison, E. F. (1962), *The Sources of Economic Growth and the Alternatives Before Us*, New York: Committee for Economic Development.
Denison, E. F. (1967), *Why Growth Rates Differ*, Washington, DC: Brookings Institution.
Dore, R. (1976), *The Diploma Disease: Education, qualification and development*, London: Allen & Unwin.
Easterlin, R. A. (1981), 'Why isn't the whole world developed?', *Journal of Economic History*, **41**.
Evenson, R. E. and L. E. Westphal (1995), 'Technological Change and technology strategy', in J. Behrman and T. N. Srinivasan (eds), *Handbook of Development Economics*, vol. IIIA, Amsterdam: North Holland, 2209–99.
Fägerlind, I. and L. J. Saha (1989), *Education and National Development: A comparative perspective*, 2nd edn, Oxford: Pergamon.
Foster, P. (1965a), *Education and Social Change in Ghana*, London: Routledge & Kegan Paul.
Foster, P. (1965b), 'The vocational school fallacy in development planning', in C. A. Anderson and M. J. Bowman (eds), *Education and Economic Development*, Chicago: Aldine, 142–6.

Foster, P. (1980), 'Education and social inequality in sub-Saharan Africa', *Journal of Modern African Studies*, **18**, 201–36.

Freire, P. (1970), *Pedagogy of the Oppressed*, New York: Seabury Press.

Gillis, M., D. H. Perkins, M. Roemer and D. R. Snodgrass (1992), *Economics of Development*, 3rd edn, New York and London: Norton, Ch. 9.

Hallak, J. (1990), *Investing in the Future: Setting education priorities in the developing world*, UNESCO/International Institute for Education Planning, Paris and Oxford: UNDP.

Hanley, S. B. (1990), 'The relationship of education and economic growth: the case of Japan', in G. Tortella (ed.), *Education and Economic Development Since the Industrial Revolution*, Valencia: Generalitat Valenciana.

Hardiman, M. and J. Midgley (1982), *The Social Dimensions of Development: Social policy and planning in the Third World*, Chichester: Wiley, 182–210.

Heinink, A. L. and J. M. B. Koetsier (1984), 'Onderwijs in de derde wereld: hefboom voor ontwikkeling?', (Education in the Third World: the driving force of development?) *INFO, Informatiebladen van het Instituut voor Onderwijskunde*, **15** (2), March, 73–86.

Hobsbawm, E. (1969), *Industry and Empire*, London: Penguin.

Illich, I. (1974), *Deschooling Society*, New York: Harper & Row.

Jones, P. W. (1988), *International Policies for Third World Education: UNESCO, literacy and development*, London and New York: UNESCO.

Komenan, A. G. (1987), *Improving the Efficiency of Education in Developing Countries*, Washington, DC: World Bank, annex 'World education indicators'.

Krieger, M. (1988), 'African policy linking education and development: standard criticisms and a new departure', *International Review of Education*, **34** (3), 293–311.

Lind, A. and A. Johnston (1986), *Adult Literacy in the Third World: A review of objectives and strategies*, Education Division Documents no. 32, Stockholm: SIDA.

Lucas, R. E. (1988), 'On the mechanics of economic development', *Journal of Monetary Economics*, **22**, 3–42.

Maddison, A. (1987), 'Growth and slowdown in advanced capitalist economies', *Journal of Economic Literature*, **25**, June, 649–98.

Mankiw, T., D. Romer and D. Weil (1992), 'A contribution to the empirics of economic growth', *Quarterly Journal of Economics*, **107**, 407–38.

Mitch, D. (1990), 'Education and economic growth', in G. Tortella (ed.), *Education and Economic Development*, *op. cit.*

Naik, J. P. (1975), *Equality, Quality and Quantity: The elusive triangle in Indian education*, Bombay: Allied Publishers.

Nicholas, S. (1990), 'Literacy and the Industrial Revolution', in G. Tortella (ed.), *Education and Economic Development*, *op. cit.*

Nuñez, C. (1990), 'Literacy and economic growth in Spain, 1860–1977', in G. Tortella (ed.), *Education and Economic Development*, *op. cit.*

Ooijens, J. and P. van Kampen (1989), *Analfabetisme en alfabetisering in Latijns Amerika en het Caribisch gebied* (Illiteracy and Literacy Education in Latin America and the Caribbean), Verhandelingen no. 46, December, The Hague: CESO.

Pilat, D. (1994), *The Economics of Rapid Growth: The experience of Japan and Korea*, Aldershot: Elgar.

Psacharopoulos, G. (1985), 'Returns to education: a further international update and implications', *Journal of Human Resources*, **20** (4), 583–604.

Psacharopoulos, G. (1989), 'Why education reforms fail: a comparative analysis', *International Review of Education*, **35**, 179–95.

Psacharopoulos, G. (1993), *Returns to Investment in Education: A global update*, Policy Research Working Papers in Education and Development, WPS, 1067, Washington: World Bank.

Psacharopoulos, G., and A. H. Arriagada (1986), 'The educational composition of the labour

force', *International Labour Review*, **125** (5), 561–74.
Romer, P. (1986), 'Increasing returns and long-run growth', *Journal of Political Economy*, **94** (5), 1002–37.
Sandberg, L. G. (1982), 'Ignorance, poverty and economic backwardness in the early stages of European industrialization: variations on Alexander Gerschenkron's grand theme', *Journal of European Economic History*, **11**, 675–98.
Sandberg, L. G. (1990), 'Education and economic growth: voices from Valencia', in G. Tortella (ed.), *Education and Economic Development*, *op. cit.*
Schultz, T. W. (1961), 'Investment in human capital', *American Economic Review*, **51**, January, 17ff.
Schultz, T. W. (1971), *Investment in Human Capital: The role of education and research*, New York: The Free Press.
Schultz, T. W. (1988), 'Education, investment and returns', in H. Chenery and T. N. Srinivasan (eds), *Handbook of Development Economics*, vol. i, Amsterdam: North Holland, 543–630.
Solow, R. M. (1957), 'Technical change and the aggregate production function', *Review of Economics and Statistics*, **39** (3), 312–20.
Thompson, E. P. (1963), *The Making of the English Working Class*, Vintage: New York.
Tortella, G. (ed.) (1990), *Education and Economic Development Since the Industrial Revolution*, Valencia: Generalitat Valenciana.
UNESCO (1983), *Trends and Projections of Enrolment, 1960–2000 (as assessed in 1982*, Division of Statistics on Education, Office of Statistics, March, Paris: UNESCO.
UNESCO (various), *Statistical Yearbook*, Paris: UNESCO.
Williamson, B. (1979), *Education, Social Structure and Development: A comparative analysis*, London: Macmillan.
Wolff, E. and M. Gittleman (1993), 'The role of education in productivity convergence: does higher education matter?', in A. Szirmai, B. van Ark and D. Pilat (eds), *Explaining Economic Growth: Essays in honour of Angus Maddison*, Amsterdam: North Holland.

Chapter 7

Ahluwalia, M. S. (1976), 'Inequality, poverty and development', *Journal of Development Economics*, **3**, September, 307–42.
Amsden, A. (1989), *Asia's Next Giant: South Korea and late industrialization*, New York and Oxford: Oxford University Press.
Bacha, E. L. (1979), 'The Kuznets Curve and beyond; growth and changes in inequalities', in E. Malinvaud (ed.), *Economic Growth and Resources*, vol. i, London: Macmillan.
Baran, P. (1957), *The Political Economy of Growth*, New York: Monthly Review Press.
Bardhan, P. (1984), *The Political Economy of Development in India*, New Delhi: Oxford University Press.
Bos, H. C. (1984), 'The role of industry and industrial policies in the third development decade', in P. K. Gosh (ed.), *Industrialization and Development*, Westport, Conn.: Greenwood Press.
Boserup, E. (1965), *The Conditions of Agricultural Growth*, New York: Aldine.
Breman, J. (1980), *The Informal Sector in Research: Theory and practice*, Rotterdam: CASP.
Bruton, H. J. (1969), 'The two-gap approach to aid and development: comment', *American Economic Review*, **59**, June, 439–46.
Chenery, H. and I. Adelman (1966), 'Foreign aid and economic development: the case of Greece', *Review of Economics and Statistics*, February.
Chenery, H. and A. MacEwan (1966), 'Optimal patterns of growth and aid: the case of Pakistan', *Pakistan Development Review*, Summer.
Chenery, H. and A. Strout (1966), 'Foreign assistance and economic development', *American Economic Review*, **56**, 679–733.

Chenery, H. and T. N. Srinivasan (1988), *Handbook of Development Economies*, vol. i, Amsterdam: North Holland.

Chenery, H., S. Robinson and M. Syrquin (1986), *Industrialization and Growth: A comparative study*, New York: Oxford University Press.

Clark, C. (1940), *The Conditions of Economic Progress*, London: Macmillan.

Cline, W. R. (1982), 'Can the East Asian model of development be generalized?', *World Development*, **10** (2).

Dijk, M. P. van (1980), 'De informele sector van Ouagadougou en Dakar: de ontwikkelingsmogelijkheden van kleine bedrijven in twee Westafrikaanse hoofdsteden' (The informal sector of Ouagadougou and Dakar: the development opportunities of small enterprises in two West African capitals), dissertation, Free University of Amsterdam.

Fei, J. C. H. and G. Ranis (1964), *Development of the Labor Surplus Economy: Theory and Policy*, Homewood, Ill.: Irwin.

Furtado, C. (1976), *Economic Development of Latin America*, 2nd edn, Cambridge: Cambridge University Press.

Gersowitz, M. (ed.) (1983; first pub. 1967), *Selected Writings of Sir W. A. Lewis*, New York: New York University Press.

Gillis, M., D. H. Perkins, M. Roemer and D. R. Snodgrass (1992), *Economics of Development*, 3rd edn, New York: Norton.

Gosh, P. L. (1984), *Industrialization and Development*, Westport, Conn.: Greenwood Press.

Hart, K. (1973), 'Informal income opportunities and urban employment in Ghana', in R. Jolly, E. de Kadt and F. Wilson (eds), *Third World Employment: Problems and strategy*, Harmondsworth: Penguin.

Higgins, B. (1968; first pub. 1959), *Economic Development*, New York: Norton.

Higgins, B. and J. D. Higgins (1979), *Economic Development of a Small Planet*, New York: Norton.

Hirschman, A. O. (1988, first pub. 1958), *The Strategy of Economic Development*, Boulder, Colo. and London: Westview Press.

Hofman, A. (1993), 'Economic Development in Latin America in the 20th century: a comparative perspective', in A. Szirmai, B. van Ark and D. Pilat (eds), *Explaining Economic Growth: Essays in honour of Angus Maddison*, Amsterdam: North Holland.

Hughes, H. (1984), 'Industrialization and development: a stocktaking', in P. K. Gosh (ed.), *Industrialization and Development*, *op. cit.*, 5–29.

ILO (1972), *Employments, Income and Equality: A strategy for increasing productive employment in Kenya*, Geneva: International Labour Organization.

Kirkpatrick, C. (1987), 'Trade policy and industrialization in LDCs', in N. Gemmell (ed.), *Surveys in Development Economics*, Oxford: Blackwell.

Kitching, G. (1982), *Development and Underdevelopment in Historical Perspective*, London: Methuen.

Krueger, A. O. (1978), *Foreign Trade Regimes and Economic Development*, Cambridge, Mass.: Ballinger.

Krueger, A. O. (1984), 'The newly industrializing countries: experience and lessons', in M. Dutta (ed.), *Studies in United States–Asia Economic Relations*, Durham, NC: Acorn Press, 253–74.

Krueger, A. O., C. Michalopoulos and V. W. Ruttan (1989), *Aid and Development*, Baltimore and London: Johns Hopkins University Press.

Kuznets, S. (1955), 'Economic growth and income inequality', in *American Economic Review*, **45** (1), 1–28.

Kuznets, S. (1966), *Modern Economic Growth*, New Haven: Yale University Press.

Kuznets, S. (1971), *Economic Growth of Nations: Total output and production structure*, Cambridge, Mass.: Harvard University Press.

Leibenstein, H. (1954), *A Theory of Economic Demographic Development*, Princeton: Princeton University Press.

Lewis, W. A. (1954), 'Economic development with unlimited supplies of labour', *Manchester School of Economic and Social Studies*, **22**, 139–91.
Lewis, W. A. (1955), *Theory of Economic Growth*, London: Allen & Unwin.
Lewis, W. A. (1978), *The Evolution of the International Economic Order*, Princeton: Princeton University Press.
Lewis, W. A. (1983a; first pub. 1967), 'Reflections on unlimited labor', in M. Gersowitz (ed.), *Writings of Sir W. A. Lewis*, *op. cit.*, 421–43.
Lewis, W. A. (1983b, first pub. 1967), 'Unemployment in developing countries', in M. Gersowitz (ed.), *Writings of Sir W. A. Lewis*, *op. cit.*, 411–21.
Little, I. M. D., T. Scitovsky and M. Scott (1970), *Industry and Trade in Some Developing Countries*, New York: Oxford University Press.
Maddison, A. (1982), *Phases of Capitalist Development*, Oxford: Oxford University Press.
Maddison, A. (1987), 'Growth and slowdown in advanced capitalist economies: techniques of quantitative assessment', *Journal of Economic Literature*, **25**, 647–98.
Maddison, A. (1989), *The World Economy in the Twentieth Century*, Paris: OECD.
Maddison, A. (1991), *Dynamics of Capitalist Development*, Oxford: Oxford University Press.
Myint, H. (1980), *The Economics of the Developing Countries*, 5th edn, London: Hutchinson.
Nelson, R. (1956), 'A theory of the low level equilibrium trap in underdeveloped economies', *American Economic Review*, **46**, 894–908.
Nurkse, R. (1953), *Problems of Capital Formation in Underdeveloped Countries*, New York: Oxford University Press.
Pack, H. (1988), 'Industrialization and trade', in H. Chenery and T. N. Srinivasan, *Handbook of Development Economics*, vol. i, Amsterdam: North Holland, 334–80.
Pilat, D. (1994), *The Economics of Rapid Growth: The experience of Japan and Korea*, Aldershot: Elgar.
Rawski, T. G. (1979), *Economic Growth and Employment in China*, New York and Oxford: World Bank/Oxford University Press.
Riddle, D. I. (1986), *Service-Led Growth: The role of the service sector in world development*, New York: Praeger.
Rosenstein-Rodan, P. (1943), 'Problems of industrialization of east and south-east Europe', *Economic Journal*, June–September, 201–11.
Rosenstein-Rodan, P. (1961), 'Notes on the Theory of the "Big Push"', in H. S. Ellis (ed.), *Economic Development for Latin America*, London: Macmillan, 55–66.
Rostow, W. W. (1971; first pub. 1960), *The Stages of Economic Growth*, 2nd edn, Cambridge: Cambridge University Press.
Rubinson, R. (1976), 'The world economy and the distribution of income within states: a cross national study', *American Sociological Review*, **41**, August, 611–23.
Syrquin, M. (1988), 'Patterns of structural change', in H. Chenery and T. N. Srinivasan, *Handbook of Development Economics*, *op. cit.*, 205–73.
Szirmai, A. and R. Ren (1995), Chinese Manufacturing Performance in Comparative Perspective, 1980–1992, Research Memorandum 581 (GD-20), Groningen: Groningen Growth and Development Centre.
Thirlwall, A. P. (1994), *Growth and Development with Special Reference to Developing Economies*, 5th edn, London: Macmillan.
Todaro, M. (1969), 'A model of labor migration and urban unemployment in less developed countries', *American Economic Review*, **59** (1), March, 138–48.
UNIDO (1990), *Handbook of Industrial Statistics 1990*, Vienna: United Nations Industrial Development Organization.
UNIDO (1995), *International Yearbook of Industrial Statistics*, Vienna: United Nations Industrial Development Organization.
Verbruggen, H. (1985), Gains from Export-Oriented Industrialization with Special Reference to South East Asia', dissertation, Free University, Amsterdam.

World Bank (1985), *World Development Report 1985*, Oxford and New York: Oxford University Press.
World Bank (1990), *World Development Report 1990*, Oxford and New York: Oxford University Press.
World Bank (1993), *World Tables 1993*, Baltimore: Johns Hopkins University Press.
World Bank (1995), *World Development Report 1995*, Oxford and New York: Oxford University Press.

Chapter 8

Amin, S. (1974), *Accumulation on a World Scale*, New York: Monthly Review Press.
Bairoch, P. (1975), *The Economic Development of the Third World since 1900*, Berkeley: University of California Press.
Baldwin, R. E. (1956), 'Patterns of development in newly settled regions', *Manchester School of Economic and Social Studies*, May.
Bardhan, P. (1984), *The Political Economy of Development in India*, New Delhi: Oxford University Press.
Bautista, R. M. (1989), 'Domestic terms of trade and agricultural growth in developing countries', in N. Islam (ed.), *The Balance between Industry and Agriculture in Economic Development, Factors Influencing Change: Proceedings of the Eighth World Congress of the International Economic Association*, vol. v, Delhi: Macmillan.
Bhagwati, J. (1958), 'Immiserizing growth: a geometrical note', in *Review of Economic Studies*, 25, 201–5.
Boserup, E. (1981), *Population and Technology*, Chicago: University of Chicago Press.
Boserup, E. (1985), 'The primary sector in African development', in M. Lundahl (ed.), *The Primary Sector in Economic Development*, London: Croom Helm.
Cassen, R. H. (1978), *India, Population, Economy, Society*, London: Macmillan.
Caves, R. E. (1965), '"Vent for surplus" models of trade and growth', in R. E. Baldwin *et al.* (eds), *Trade, Growth and the Balance of Payments*, Chicago: Rand McNally.
Eicher, C. K. and L. W. de Witt (eds) (1964), *Agriculture in Development*, New York: McGraw-Hill.
Emmanuel, A. (1972), *Unequal Exchange: A study of the imperialism of trade*, New York: Monthly Review Press.
Fei, J. C. H. and G. Ranis (1964), *Development of the Labor Surplus Economy: Theory and policy*, Homewood, Ill.: Irwin.
Gillis, M., D. H. Perkins, M. Roemer and D. R. Snodgrass (1992), *Economics of Development*, 3rd edn, New York: Norton.
Grilli, E. R. and Maw, Chen Yang (1988), 'Primary commodity prices, manufactured goods prices, and the terms of trade of developing countries: what the long run shows', *The World Bank Economic Review*, 2 (1), 1–47.
Griffin, K. (1987), *World Hunger and the World Economy*, London: Macmillan.
Hayami, Y. and V. Ruttan (1985), *Agricultural Development: An international perspective*, Baltimore and London: Johns Hopkins University Press.
Helleiner, G. K. (1992), 'Structural adjustment and long-term development in sub-Saharan Africa', in F. Stewart, S. Lall and J. Wamful (eds), *Alternative Development Strategies in Sub-Saharan Africa*, Hong Kong: Macmillan.
Hirschman, A. O. (1977), 'A generalized linkage approach to economic development, with special reference to staples', in Manning Nash (ed.), *Essays on Economic Development and Cultural Change in Honor of Bert F. Hoselitz*, Economic Development and Cultural Change, Supplement to vol. 25.
Hirschman, A. O. (1988; first pub. 1958), *The Strategy of Economic Development*, New Haven: Yale University Press.

Horesh, E. and S. Joekes (1985), 'The impact of primary exports on the Ghanaian economy', in M. Lundahl (ed.), *The Primary Sector*, *op. cit.*
IMF (various), *International Financial Statistics Yearbook*, Washington, DC: International Monetary Fund.
Islam, N. (1989a), 'Introduction to Part I: relative price changes in agriculture and industry', in *id.*, *The Balance between Industry and Agriculture*, *op. cit.*
Islam, N. (ed.) (1989b), *The Balance between Industry and Agriculture: Economic Development, Factors Influencing Change*, Proceedings of the Eighth World Congress of the International Economic Association, vol. v, Delhi: Macmillan.
Johnston, B. F. (1970), 'Agriculture and structural transformation in developing countries: a survey of research', *Journal of Economic Literature*, **3**, 369–404.
Johnston, B. F. and J. W. Mellor (1961), 'The role of agriculture in economic development', *American Economic Review*, **51**, September, 566–93.
Jorgenson, D. W. (1961), 'The development of a dual economy', *Economic Journal*, June, 309–34.
Jorgenson, D. W. (1967), 'Surplus agricultural labour and the development of a dual economy', *Oxford Economic Papers*, **19**, November, 288–312.
Jorgenson, D. W. (1969), 'The role of agriculture in economic development: classical versus neoclassical models of growth', in C. Wharton (ed.), *Subsistence Agriculture and Economic Development*, Chicago: Aldine.
Kuznets, S. (1965), *Economic Growth and Structure*, London: Heinemann.
Lensink, R. (1995), *Structural Adjustment in Sub-Saharan Africa*, Longman: London.
Lewis, W. A. (1954), 'Economic development with unlimited supplies of labour', *The Manchester School of Economic and Social Studies*, **22**, 139–91.
Lewis, W. A. (1969), *Aspects of Tropical Trade, 1883–1965*, Stockholm: Almquist & Wicksell.
Lewis, W. A. (1970), *Tropical Development, 1880–1913*, London: Allen & Unwin.
Lewis, W. A. (1978a), *Growth and Fluctuations*, 1870–1913, London: Allen & Unwin.
Lewis, W. A. (1978b), *The Evolution of the International Economic Order*, Princeton: Princeton University Press.
Lipton, M. (1977), *Why Poor People Stay Poor: Urban bias in world development*, London: Temple Smith.
Lord, M. J. (1989), 'Primary commodities as an engine for export growth in Latin America', in N. Islam (ed.), *The Balance between Industry and Agriculture*, *op. cit.*
Lundahl, M. (ed.) (1985), *The Primary Sector in Economic Development*, London: Croom Helm.
McBean, A. I. (1989), 'Agricultural exports of developing countries: market conditions and national policies', in N. Islam (ed.), *The Balance between Industry and Agriculture*, *op. cit.*
Maddison, A. (1989), *The World Economy in the Twentieth Century*, Paris: OECD.
Manarungsan, S. (1989), Economic development of Thailand, 1850–1950: Response to the challenge of the world economy, dissertation, University of Groningen.
Meier, G. M. (1968), *The International Economics of Development*, New York: Harper.
Meier, G. M. (1989), 'The old and new export pessimism: a critical survey', in N. Islam (ed.), *The Balance between Industry and Agriculture*, *op. cit.*
Mellor, J. W. (1976), *The New Economics of Growth*, Ithaca, NY: Cornell University Press.
Mellor, J. W. and B. F. Johnston (1984), 'The world food equation: interrelations among development, employment and food consumption', *Journal of Economic Literature*, **22**, 531–74.
Mosher, A. T. (1966), *Getting Agriculture Moving: Essentials for development and modernization*, New York: Praeger.
Myint, H. (1959), 'The "classical theory"' of international trade and the underdeveloped countries', *Economic Journal*, **68**, 317–37.
Myint, H. (1975), 'Agriculture and economic development in the open economy', in L. G. Reynolds (ed.), *Agriculture in Development Theory*, New Haven: Yale University Press.

Myint, H. (1980), *The Economics of the Developing Countries*, 5th edn, London: Hutchinson.
Myrdal, G. (1957), *Economic Theory and Underdeveloped Regions*, London: Duckworth.
Nicholls, W. H. (1964), 'The place of agriculture in economic development', in C. K. Eicher and L. W. de Witt (eds), *Agriculture in Development*, *op. cit.*
Nurkse, R. (1962), *Patterns of Trade and Development*, the 1959 Wicksell Lectures, Oxford: Blackwell.
Ohkawa, K. and H. Rosovsky (1964), 'The role of agriculture in modern Japanese economic development', in C. Eicher and L. W. de Witt (eds), *Agriculture in Development*, *op cit.*, 45–68.
Prebisch, R. (1950), *The Economic Development of Latin America and its Principal Problems*, Department of Economic Affairs, New York: United Nations.
Ranis, G. (1989), 'Macro policies, the terms of trade and the spatial dimension of balanced growth', in N. Islam (ed.), *The Balance between Industry and Agriculture*, *op. cit.*
Rawski, T. G. (1979), *Economic Growth and Employment in China*, New York and Oxford: World Bank/Oxford University Press.
Reynolds, L. G. (ed.) (1975a), *Agriculture in Development Theory*, New Haven: Yale University Press.
Reynolds, L. G. (1975b), 'Agriculture in development theory: an overview', in *id.*, *Agriculture in Development Theory*, *op. cit.*
Rostow, W. W. (1960), *The Stages of Economic Growth*, Cambridge: Cambridge University Press.
Sapsford, D. (1985), 'The statistical debate on the net barter terms of trade between primary commodities and manufactures: a comment and some statistical evidence', *The Economical Journal*, **95**, September, 781–8.
Sapsford, D. (1988), 'The debate over trends in the terms of trade', in D. Greenaway (ed.), *Economic Development and International Trade*, London: Macmillan, 117–30.
Singer, H. W. (1950), 'The distribution of gains between investing and borrowing countries', *American Economic Review*, **41**, 473–86.
Spraos, J. (1980), 'The statistical debate on the net barter terms of trade between primary commodities and manufactures', *The Economic Journal*, **90**, March, 107–28.
Sarkar, P. (1986), 'The Singer–Prebisch hypothesis: a statistical evaluation', *Cambridge Journal of Economics*, **10**, 355–71.
Thirlwall, A. P. (1994), *Growth and Development with Special Reference to Developing Economies*, 5th edn, London: Macmillan.
Thoburn, J. T. (1977), *Primary Commodity Exports and Economic Development: Theory, evidence and a study of Malaysia*, London: Wiley.
Timmer, C. P. (1969), 'The turnip, the new husbandry and the English agricultural revolution', *The Quarterly Journal of Economics*, **83**, 375–95.
Timmer, C. P. (1988), 'The agricultural transformation', in H. Chenery and T. N. Srinivasan (eds), *Handbook of Development Economics*, vol. i, Amsterdam: North Holland, 276–331.
World Bank (1989), *Sub-Saharan Africa: From crisis to sustainable growth*, Washington, DC: World Bank.
World Bank (1995), *World Tables 1995*, Baltimore: Johns Hopkins University Press.

Chapter 9

Adams, J. (1986), 'Peasant rationality: individuals, groups, cultures', *World Development*, **14** (2), 273–82.
Alexandratos, N. (1988), *World Agriculture towards 2000*, Belhaven, NC and London: Food and Agriculture Organization.

Anthony, K. M. A. (1979), *Agricultural Change in Tropical Africa*, Ithaca, NY: Cornell University Press.
Arnold, D. (1988), *Famine: Social crisis and historical change*, Oxford: Blackwell.
Barth, F. (1966), *Models of Social Organisation*, London: Royal Anthropological Institute.
Barrow, C. J. (1995), *Developing the Environment, Problems and Management*, London: Longman.
Berry, R. and W. R. Cline (1979), *Agrarian Structure and Productivity in Developing Countries*, Baltimore: Johns Hopkins University Press.
Binswanger, H. P., K. Deininger and G. Feder (1995), 'Power distortions, revolt and reform in agricultural land relations', in J. Behrman and T. N. Srinivasan (eds), *Handbook of Development Economics*, vol. 3B, Amsterdam: Elsevier, 2659–772.
Boeke, J. L. (1955), *Economie van Indonesië*, Haarlem: Tjeenk Willink.
Boelens, J. (1980), 'De groene revolutie: een kapitale aangelegenheid' (The green revolution: a capital affair), *Intermediair*, **16** (6), 8 February, 41–51.
Boissevain, J. (1974), *Friends of Friends: Networks, manipulators and coalitions*, Oxford: Blackwell.
Bol, D. (1983), *Economen en armoede: Moedwil en misverstand in de ontwikkelingshulp* (Economists and Poverty: Bad faith and misunderstandings in development aid), Amsterdam: Van Gennep.
Booth, A. (1988), *Agricultural Development in Indonesia*, Sydney: Allen & Unwin.
Booth, A. and R. M. Sundrum (1985), *Labour Absorption in Agriculture: Theoretical analysis and empirical investigations*, Oxford: Oxford University Press.
Boserup, E. (1965), *The Conditions of Agricultural Growth*, New York: Aldine.
Boserup, E. (1970), *Women's Role in Economic Development*, New York: St Martin's.
Boserup, E. (1981), *Population and Technology*, Chicago: University of Chicago Press.
Boserup, E. (1983), 'The impact of scarcity and plenty on development', *Journal of Interdisciplinary History*, **14** (2), Autumn, 383–407.
Boserup, E. (1990), *Economic and Demographic Relationships in Development: Essays selected and introduced by T. Paul Schultz*, Baltimore and London: Johns Hopkins University Press.
Bunyard, P. (1985), 'World climate and tropical forest destruction', *The Ecologist*, **15**, 125–36.
Cassen, R. A. (1978), *India, Population, Economy, Society*, London: Macmillan.
Chambers, R. (1983), *Rural Development: Putting the last first*, Harlow: Longman Scientific and Technical.
Chayanov, A. V. (1966), 'On the theory of non-capitalist economic systems', in D. Thorner, B. Kerblay and R. F. Smith (eds), *The Theory of Peasant Economy*, Homewood, Ill.: Irwin, 1–28.
Colman, D. and F. Nixson (1986), *Economics of Change in Less Developed Countries*, 2nd edn, Oxford: Philip Allan.
Dixon, C. (1990), *Rural Development in the Third World*, London and New York: Routledge.
Dorner, P. (1972), *Land Reform and Economic Development*, Harmondsworth: Penguin.
Druijven, P. C. J. (1983), *Rurale industrialisatie in de Volksrepubliek China* (Rural industrialisation in the People's Republic of China), Geografisch en Planologisch Instituut, Bijdragen tot de Sociale Geografie en Planologie, no. 6, Amsterdam: Free University.
Druijven, P. C. J. (1990), Mandenvlechters en mezcalstokers in Mexico' (Basket weavers and mescal distillers in Mexico), dissertation, Amsterdam: Free University.
Eicher, C. K. and J. M. Staatz (eds) (1984), *Agricultural Development in the Third World*, Baltimore and London: Johns Hopkins University Press.
Eisenstadt, S. N. (1970), 'Social change and development', in S. N. Eisenstadt (ed.), *Readings in Social Evolution and Development*, Oxford: Pergamon.
Ellis, F. (1988), *Peasant Economics: Farm households and agrarian development*, Cambridge: Cambridge University Press.
Eng, P. van der (1992), 'Food supply and agricultural development', in W. P. M. F. Ivens (ed.), *World Food Production Textbook*, Heerlen: Open University.

Eng, P. van der (1993), 'Agricultural growth in Indonesia since 1880', dissertation, Groningen: University of Groningen.
FAO (1975), *State of Food and Agriculture, 1975*, Rome: Food and Agriculture Organization.
FAO (1981), *Agriculture Towards 2000*, Rome: Food and Agriculture Organization.
FAO (1988), *An Interim Report on the State of Forest Resources in the Developing Countries*, Rome: Food and Agriculture Organization.
FAO (1989), *State of Food and Agriculture, 1989*, Rome: Food and Agriculture Organization.
FAO (1990), *State of Food and Agriculture, 1990*, Rome: Food and Agriculture Organization.
FAO (1991a), *Production Yearbook*, vol. 44, *1990*, Rome: Food and Agriculture Organization.
FAO (1991b), *State of Food and Agriculture, 1991*, Rome: Food and Agriculture Organization.
FAO (1993a), *Production Yearbook*, vol. 46, *1992*, Rome: Food and Agriculture Organization.
FAO (1993b), *State of Food and Agriculture, 1993*, Rome: Food and Agriculture Organization.
FAO (1995), *Production Yearbook*, vol. 48, *1994*, Rome: Food and Agriculture Organization.
FAO (various), *Production Yearbook*, Rome: Food and Agriculture Organization.
Feeny, D. (1982), *The Political Economy of Productivity: Thai agricultural development 1880–1975*, Vancouver and London: University of British Columbia Press.
Feeny, D. (1987), 'The development of property rights in land: a comparative study', in R. H. Bates (eds.), *Toward a Political Economy of Development: A rationalist perspective*, Berkeley: University of California Press.
Foster, G. (1965), 'Peasant society and the image of limited good', *American Anthropologist*, **67**, April, 293–315.
Foster, G. (1975), *Traditional Cultures and the Impact of Technological Change*, New York: Harper & Row.
Frank, A. G. (1969), *Capitalism and Underdevelopment in Latin America*, rev. edn, New York: Monthly Review Press.
Frankel, F. R. (1978), *India's Political Economy, 1947–1977*, Princeton: Princeton University Press.
Furtado, C. (1976), *Economic Development of Latin America*, Cambridge: Cambridge University Press.
Geertz, C. (1963), *Agricultural Involution: The processes of ecological change in Indonesia*, Berkeley: University of California Press.
Ghai, D. and S. Radwan (eds) (1985), *Agrarian Policies and Rural Poverty in Africa*, Geneva: ILO.
Gillin, E. D. and J. Krane (1989), 'Where does the increase in crop production come from?', *FAO Quarterly Bulletin of Statistics*, **2** (4), pp. iii–iv.
Glaeser, B. (1987), 'Agriculture between the green revolution and ecodevelopment: which way to go?', in B. Glaeser (ed.), *The Green Revolution Revisited: Critique and alternatives*, London: Allen & Unwin, 1–9.
Goudsblom, J. (1992), *Vuur en beschaving* (Fire and civilization), Amsterdam: Meulenhof.
Griffin, K. (1976), *The Political Economy of Agrarian Change*, London: Macmillan.
Griffin, K. (1981), *Land Concentration and Rural Poverty*, 2nd edn, London: Macmillan.
Haggis, J., S. Jarret, D. Taylor and P. Mayer (1986), 'By the skin of their teeth: a critical examination of James Scott's *The Moral Economy of the Peasant*', *World Development*, **14** (12), 1435–55.
Harrison, P. (1992), *The Third Revolution: Population, environment and a sustainable world*, Harmondsworth: Penguin.
Hayami, Y. and V. W. Ruttan (1971), *Agricultural Development: An international perspective*, Baltimore: Johns Hopkins University Press.
Hayami, Y. and R. W. Ruttan (1985), *Agricultural Development: An international perspective*, rev. edn, Baltimore: Johns Hopkins University Press.
Hekken, P. M. van and H. U. E. Thoden van Velzen (1972), *Land Scarcity and Rural Inequality in Tanzania*, The Hague: Mouton.

Helleiner, G. K. (1992), 'Structural adjustment and long-term development in sub-Saharan Africa', in F. Stewart, S. Lall and J. Wamful (eds), *Alternative Development Strategies in Sub-Saharan Africa*, Hong Kong: Macmillan.

Higgins, B. (1959), *Economic Development Problems, Principles and Policies*, New York: Norton.

Hill, P. (1986), *Development Economics on Trial: The anthropological case for a prosecution*, Cambridge: Cambridge University Press.

Hogg, M. V. (1984), 'Industrialization and rural development: an analysis of basic issues', in P. K. Gosh (ed.), *Industrialization and Development*, Westport, Conn.: Greenwood Press, 153–83.

Hsu, R. C. (1982), *Food for One Billion: China's agriculture since 1949*, Boulder, Colo.: Westview Press.

Hunter, G. (1974), *Modernizing Peasant Societies*, London: Oxford University Press.

Husain, I. (1993), 'Structural Adjustment and the Long-Term Development of Sub-Saharan Africa', paper presented at the International Seminar of Structural Adjustment and Long-Term Development in Sub-Saharan Africa: Research and Policy Issues, DGIS, The Hague, 1–3 June.

Jepma, C. J. (1993), *Deforestation in the Humid Tropics: A socio-economic approach*, Groningen: Stichting International Development Economics.

Johnston, B. F. (1970), 'Agricultural and structural transformation in developing countries: a survey of research', *Journal of Economic Literature*, 8, June, 369–404.

Johnston, B. F. and P. Kilby (1975), *Agriculture and Structural Transformation: Economic strategies in late-developing countries*, New York: Oxford University Press.

Johnston, B. F. and J. W. Mellor (1961), 'The role of agriculture in economic development', *American Economic Review*, pp. 566–93.

Kitching, G. (1982), *Development and Underdevelopment in Historical Perspective*, London: Methuen.

Kuper, A. J. (1984), 'African culture and African development', in C. A. O. van Nieuwenhuijze (ed.), *Development Regardless of Culture*, Leiden: Brill.

Lal, D. and H. Myint (1996), *The Political Economy of Poverty, Equity and Growth*, Oxford: Oxford University Press.

Leite, L. L. and P. A. Furley (1985), 'Land development in the Brazilian Amazon', in J. Hemming (ed.), *Change in the Amazon Basin II*, Manchester: Manchester University Press.

Lipton, M. (1966), 'The theory of the optimizing peasant', *Journal of Development Studies*, 4, 327–51.

Long, N. (1977), *An Introduction to the Sociology of Rural Development*, London: Tavistock.

Maddison, A. (1989), *The World Economy in the Twentieth Century*, Paris: OECD.

Maddison, A. *et al.* (1992), *The Political Economy of Poverty, Equity and Growth: Brazil and Mexico*, Oxford: Oxford University Press.

Manarungsan, S. (1989), 'Economic development of Thailand 1850–1950: Response to the challenge of the world economy', dissertation, University of Groningen.

Meer, C. L. J. van der (1981), 'Rural development in northern Thailand', dissertation, University of Groningen.

Meer, C. L. J. van der (1983), 'Voedselvoorziening en agrarische ontwikkeling', (Food supply and agricultural development), in C. L. J. van der Meer (ed.), *Landbouw en ontwikkeling* (Agriculture and development), The Hague: Vuga, 177–205.

Meer, C. L. J. van der and S. Yamada (1990), *Japanese Agriculture: An economic comparative analysis*, London: Gower.

Mellow, J. W. (1966), *The Economics of Agricultural Development*, Ithaca, NY: Cornell University Press.

Moore, B. (1966), *Social Origins of Democracy and Dictatorship*, Harmondsworth: Penguin.

Moore, W. E. (1963), *Social Change*, Englewood Cliffs, NJ: Prentice Hall.

Myers, N. (1989), *Deforestation Rates in Tropical Forests and their Climatic Implications*, London: Friends of the Earth.

Myers, N. (1991), 'Tropical forests: present status and future outlook', *Climatic Change*, **19**, September, 3–32.

Myint, H. (1980), *The Economics of the Developing Countries*, 5th edn, London: Hutchinson.

North, D. C. (1990), *Institutions, Institutional Change and Economic Performance*, Cambridge: Cambridge University Press.

North, D. C. (1993), 'The ultimate sources of economic growth', in A. Szirmai, B. van Ark and D. Pilat (eds), *Explaining Economic Growth: Essays in honour of Angus Maddison*, Amsterdam: North Holland.

North, D. C. and R. P. Thomas (1973), *The Rise of the Western World: A new economic history*, Cambridge: Cambridge University Press.

Oasa, E. K. (1987), 'The political economy of international agricultural research: a review of CGIAR's response to criticisms of the "green revolution"', in B. Glaeser (ed.), *The Green Revolution Revisited: Critique and alternatives*, Allen & Unwin: London, 13–55.

Parayil, G. (1992), 'The green revolution in India: a case study of technological change, *Technology and Culture*, 33, 737–56.

Pearse, A. (1977), 'Technology and peasant production: reflections on a global study, *Development and Change*, **8**.

Perkins, D. H. (1969), *Agricultural Development in China 1368–1968*, Chicago: Aldine.

Perkins, D. H. (1984), *Rural Development in China*, Baltimore: World Bank/Johns Hopkins University Press.

Pinstrup-Anderson, P. (1982), *Agricultural Research and Technology in Economic Development*, London and New York: Longman.

Pinstrup-Anderson, P. and P. B. R. Hazell (1985), 'The impact of the green revolution and prospects for the future', *Food Review International*, **1** (1), 1–25.

Polyani, K. (1957), *The Great Transformation*, Boston: Beacon Press.

Popkin, S. L. (1979), *The Rational Peasant: The political economy of rural society in Vietnam*, Berkeley: University of California Press.

Rawski, T. G. (1979), *Economic Growth and Employment in China*, New York and Oxford: World Bank/Oxford University Press.

Revelle, R. (1975), 'Will the Earth's land and water resources be sufficient for future populations?', *The Population Debate: Dimensions and Perspectives. Papers of the World Population Conference*, Bucharest 1974, vol. ii, New York: United Nations, 3–14.

Schultz, T. W. (1953), *The Economic Organisation of Agriculture*, New York: McGraw-Hill.

Schultz, T. W. (1964), *Transforming Traditional Agriculture*, New Haven and London: Yale University Press.

Schultz, T. W. (1968), *Economic Growth and Agriculture*, New York: McGraw-Hill.

Schultz, T. W. (1978), 'On economics and politics of agriculture', in T. W. Schultz (ed.), *Distortions and Agricultural Incentives*, Bloomington, Ind.: Indiana University Press, 1–23.

Scott, J. C. (1976), *The Moral Economy of the Peasant, Rebellion and Subsistence in South East Asia*, New Haven: Yale University Press.

Sen, A. (1981), *Poverty and Famines*, Oxford: Clarendon Press.

Sen, A. (1982), 'How is India doing?', *New York Review of Books*, 16 December, 41–5.

Shanin, T. (ed.) (1971), *Peasants and Peasant Societies*, Harmondsworth: Penguin.

Shanin, T. (1973), 'The nature and the logic of the peasant economy, part I: a generalization', *Journal of Peasant Studies*, **1** (1), October, 63–80.

Shanin, T. (1974), 'The nature and the logic of the peasant economy, part II: diversity and change; part III: policy and intervention', *Journal of Peasant Studies*, **1** (2), January, 186–206.

Singh, I. (1982), *The Landless Poor in South Asia: Proceedings of the 18th Conference of the International Association of Agricultural Economists*, Jakarta 1982.

Slicher van Bath, B. (1960), *De Agrarische Geschiedenis van West-Europa, 500–1850* (The Agrarian History of Western Europe, 500–1850), Utrecht: Aula.

Teszler, R. (1984), 'Blotevoetenindustrie en plattelandsontwikkeling' (Barefoot industry and rural development), *Internationale Spectator*, **38** (12), December, 702–12.
The World Commission on Environment and Development (1987), *Our Common Future*, Oxford and New York: Oxford University Press.
Thorner, D., B. Kerblay and R. E. F. Smith (1966), *A. V. Chayanov: The theory of peasant economy*, Manchester: Manchester University Press.
Timmer, C. P. (1988), 'The agricultural transformation', in H. Chenery and T. N. Srinivasan (eds), *Handbook of Development Economics*, vol. i, Amsterdam: North Holland.
UN (1989), *Prospects of World Urbanization*, New York: United Nations.
UN (1993), *World Urbanization Prospects: The 1992 revision*, New York: United Nations.
UNDP (1988), *Development of Rural Small Industrial Enterprise: Lessons from experience*, joint study by UNDP, Government of the Netherlands, ILO, UNIDO, Vienna.
UNEP (1993), *Ecoforum*, 17 (1/2), 17 May, 12.
Vries, J. de (1975), 'Peasant demand patterns and economic development, Friesland, 1550–1750', in E. Janes and W. Parkers (eds), *European Peasants and their Market*, Princeton: Princeton University Press.
Wolf, E. R. (1966), *Peasants*, Englewood Cliffs, NJ: Prentice Hall.
World Bank (1986a), *Poverty and Hunger: Issues and options for food security in developing countries*, Washington, DC: World Bank.
World Bank (1986b), *World Development Report 1986, Part II*, Oxford: Oxford University Press.
World Bank (1989), *Sub-Saharan Africa: From crisis to sustainable growth, a long-term perspective study*, Washington, DC: World Bank.
World Bank (1990a), *World Development Report 1990*, Oxford: Oxford University Press.
World Bank (1990b), *Trends in Developing Economies*, Washington, DC.
World Bank (1992a), *World Development Report 1992*, Oxford: Oxford University Press.
World Bank (1992b), *Trends in Developing Economies*, Washington, DC.
World Bank (1992c), *World Tables 1992*, Baltimore and London: Johns Hopkins University Press.
World Bank (1995a), *World Development Report 1995*, Oxford: Oxford University Press.
World Bank (1995b), *World Tables 1995*, Baltimore and London: Johns Hopkins University Press.
World Resources Institute (1990), *World Resources 1990–1991*, Oxford: Oxford University Press.

Chapter 10

Ahluwalia, M. S. (1976), 'Inequality, poverty and development', in *Journal of Development Economics*, 3 (4).
Alavi, H. (1979), 'The state in post-colonial societies: Pakistan and Bangladesh', in H. Goulborne (ed.), *Politics and the State in the Third World*, London: Macmillan, 38–70.
Amsden, A. (1989), *Asia's Next Giant: South Korea and late industrialization*, New York and Oxford: Oxford University Press.
Anglade, C. and C. Fortin (1985), 'The state and capital accummulation in Latin America: a conceptual and historical introduction', in C. Anglade and C. Fortin (eds), *The State and Capital Accummulation in Latin America*, vol. i, Brazil, Chile, Mexico: University of Pittsburgh Press.
Banks, A. (ed.) (various), *Political Handbook of the World*, New York: McGraw-Hill.
Bannister, J. (1984), 'Analysis of recent data on the population of China', *Population and Development Review*, **10**, 241–71.
Bardhan, P. (1984), *The Political Economy of Development in India*, Oxford: Blackwell.

Benthem van den Bergh, G. van (1980), *On the Dynamics of Development of Contemporary States: An approach to comparative politics*, ISS Occasional Paper, November, The Hague: Institute of Social Studies.

Berghe, P. L. van den (1981), *The Ethnic Phenomenon*, New York and Oxford: Elsevier.

Bienen, H. (1971), *The Military and Modernization*, Chicago: Aldine/Atherton.

Buchanan, J. and G. Tullock (1962), *The Calculus of Consent: Logical foundations of constitutional democracy*, Michigan University Press: Ann Arbor.

Cassen, R. C. (1978), *India: Population, Economy, Society*, London: Macmillan.

Chang, J. (1991), *Wild Swans: Three Daughters of China*, New York: Doubleday.

Chirot, D. (1977), *Social Change in the Twentieth Century*, New York: Harcourt, Brace & Jovanovich.

CIA (1995), *World Factbook 1995*, World Wide Web server, address:
http://www.odci.gov/cia/publications/95fact.

Clapham, C. and G. Philip (eds) (1985), *The Political Dilemmas of Military Regimes*, London: Croom Helm.

Cohen, Y. (1985), 'The impact of bureaucratic-authoritarian rule on economic growth', *Comparative Political Studies*, **18**, 123–36.

Coleman, J. S. and C. B. Rosberg Jr. (eds) (1964), *Political Parties and National Integration in Tropical Africa*, Berkeley: University of California Press.

Dahrendorf, R. (1963), *Class and Class Conflict in Industrial Society*, London: Routledge & Kegan Paul.

David, S. R. (1987), 'The use of proxy forces by major powers in the Third World', in S. G. Neuman and R. E. Harkavy (eds), *The Lessons of Recent Wars in the Third World*, Lexington, Mass.: Heath.

Davidson, B. (1992), *The Black Man's Burden: Africa and the curse of the nation-state*, North Wootton.

Djilas, M. (1957), *The New Class: An analysis of the Communist system*, New York: Praeger.

Doel, J. van den (1978), *Democratie en welvaartstheorie* (Democracy and Welfare Theory), 2nd edn, Alphen a/d Rijn: Samsom.

Elias, N. (1969), *Über den Prozess der Zivilisation*, 2nd edn, Bern: Franke Verlag.

Elias, N. (1979), *Die höfische Gesellschaft*, 4th edn, Darmstadt and Neuwied: Luchterland.

Elvin, M. (1973), *The Pattern of Chinese Past*, London: Stanford University Press.

Finer, S. E. (1988), *The Man on Horseback*, 2nd enlarged edn, Boulder, Colo.: Westview Press.

Fosu, A. K. (1992), 'Political instability and economic growth: evidence from sub-Saharan Africa', *Economic Development and Cultural Change*, **40**, July, 829–41.

Frey, B. D. (1978), *Modern Political Economy*, Oxford: Martin Robertson.

Furtado, C. (1976), *The Economic Development of Latin America*, Cambridge: Cambridge University Press.

Gavshon, A. (1981), *Crisis in Africa: Battleground of East and West*, Boulder, Colo.: Westview Press.

Gerschenkron, A. (1962), *Economic Backwardness in Historical Perspective*, Cambridge, Mass.: Harvard University Press.

Goldthorpe, J. (1979), *De derde wereld* (The Third World), The Hague: Vuga, 257–79.

Goulborne, H. (1979), *Politics and State in the Third World*, London: Macmillan.

Haan, J. de and C. L. J. Sierman (1993), 'Political instability, freedom and economic growth: some further evidence', *Economic Development and Cultural Change*, **44** (2), January.

Haan, J. de, D. Zelhorst and O. Roukens (1993), 'Seignorage in developing countries', *Applied Financial Economics*, **3**, 307–14.

Harkavy, R. E. and S. G. Neuman (1985), *The Lessons of Recent Wars in the Third World*, vol. i, Lexington Books, Lexington, Mass.: pp. 33–52.

Hirschman, A. (1973), 'The changing tolerance for income inequality in the course of economic development', *World Development*, **1** (12), December, 29–36.

Hoogen, T. J. van den (1992), 'Security and Third World states: a conceptual analysis', *Development and Security*, no. 38, Centre for Development Studies, December, University of Groningen.
Hsu, R. C. (1982), *Food for One Billion: China's agriculture since 1949*, Boulder, Colo.: Westview Press.
Jackson, R. and C. Rosberg (1982), *Personal Rule in Black Africa*, Berkeley: University of California Press.
Jackson, R. and C. Rosberg (1986), 'Sovereignity and underdevelopment: juridical statehood in the African crisis', *The Journal of Modern African Studies*, **24** (1), 1–31.
Janowitz, M. (ed.) (1981), *Civil–Military Regimes: Regional perspectives*, London: Sage.
Kellas, J. G. (1991), *The Politics of Nationalism and Ethnicity*, London: Macmillan.
Kende, I. (1972), *Local Wars in Asia, Africa and Latin America, 1945–1969*, Studies of Developing Countries no. 60, Budapest: Center for Afro-Asian Research.
Kennedy, P. (1989), *The Rise and Fall of the Great Powers*, New York: Vintage Books.
Keyfitz, N. (1991), *The Demography of the Fission of Empires*, Population Research Centre, November, Groningen.
Kidron, M. and D. Smith (1983), *The War Atlas: Armed conflict – armed peace*, London: Heinemann.
Kidron, M. and D. Smith (1991), *The New State of War and Peace*, New York: Simon & Schuster.
Kitching, G. (1982), *Development and Underdevelopment in Historical Perspective*, London: Macmillan.
Kuznets, S. (1955), 'Economic growth and income inequality', *American Economic Review*, **45** (1), 1–28.
Kuznets, S. (1966), *Modern Economic Growth: Rate, structure and spread*, New Haven: Yale University Press.
Lane, D. (1971), *The End of Inequality? Stratification under state socialism*, Harmondsworth: Penguin.
Leys, S. (1978), *Ombres Chinois*, Paris: Laffont.
Luttwak, E. (1979), *Coup d'Etat: A practical handbook*, London: Wildwood House.
McGowan, P. J. and T. H. Johnson (1984), 'African military coups d'etat and underdevelopment: a quantitative historical analysis', *Journal of Modern African Studies*, **22** (4).
Maddison, A. (1969), *Economic Growth in Japan and the USSR*, New York: Norton.
Maddison, A. (1974), *Class Structure and Economic Growth in India and Pakistan*, London: Allen & Unwin.
Maddison, A. (1986), 'Marx and Bismarck: capitalism and government, 1883–1953', in H. J. Wagener and J. W. Drukker (eds), *The Economic Law of Motion of Modern Society*, Cambridge: Cambridge University Press.
Maddison, A. *et al.* (1992), *Brazil and Mexico: The political economy of poverty, equity and growth*, a World Bank Comparative Study, Oxford: Oxford University Press.
Mair, L. (1967), *Primitive Government*, Harmondsworth: Penguin.
Marx, K. (1955; first pub. 1848), *The Communist Manifesto*, New York: Appleton Century Cross.
Meer, C. L. J. van der and S. Yamada (1990), *Japanese Agriculture: An economic comparative analysis*, Aldershot: Gower.
Moore, B. Jr. (1967), *Social Origins of Dictatorship and Democracy: Lord and peasant in the making of the modern world*, Harmondsworth: Penguin.
Myint, H. (1980), *The Economics of the Developing Countries*, 5th edn, London: Hutchinson.
Myrdal, G. (1968), *Asian Drama: An inquiry into the poverty of nations*, Harmondsworth: Penguin.
North, D. C. and R. P. Thomas (1973), *The Rise of the Western World: A new economic history*, Cambridge: Cambridge University Press.

O'Connor, J. (1973), *The Fiscal Crisis of the State*, New York: St Martin's Press.
O'Donnell, G. (1979), *Modernization and Bureaucratic-Authoritarianism in South American Politics*, Berkeley: University of California Press.
Olson, M. (1965), *The Logic of Collective Action*, Cambridge, Mass.: Harvard University Press.
Petras, J. (1977), 'State capitalism and the Third World', *Development and Change*, **8**, 1–17.
Philip, G. (1985), 'Military rule in South America: the dilemmas of authoritarianism', in C. Clapham and G. Philip (eds), *The Political Dilemmas of Military Regimes*, London: Croom Helm.
Pilat, D. (1994), *The Economics of Rapid Growth: The experience of Japan and Korea*, Aldershot: Elgar.
Rawski, T. G. (1979), *Economic Growth and Employment in China*, World Bank, New York and Oxford: Oxford University Press.
Righart, H. *et al.* (1991), *De trage revolutie: Over de wording van industriële samenlevingen* (The Slow Revolution: On the origin of industrial societies), Boom: Open Universiteit.
Sandbrook, R. (1986), 'The state as an obstacle to development', *World Development*, **14** (3), 309–22.
Sandbrook, R. and J. Barker (1985), *The Politics of Africa's Economic Stagnation*, Cambridge: Cambridge University Press.
Schama, S. (1988), *The Embarassment of Riches*, New York: Fontana Press.
Schoenmakers, H. (1992), Staatsvorming, rurale ontwikkeling en boeren in Guinée Bissau (State formation, rural development and peasants in Guinea Bissau), dissertation, Catholic University, Nijmegen.
Schumpeter, J. (1946), *Capitalism, Socialism and Democracy*, London: Allen & Unwin.
Scully, G. W. (1988), 'The institutional framework and economic development', *Journal of Political Economy*, **96**, October, 652–62.
Shils, E. (1964), 'The military in the political development of new states', in J. Johnson (ed.), *The Military and Society in Latin America*, Palo Alto, Calif.: Stanford University Press.
Sirowy, L. and A. Inkeles (1990), 'The effects of democracy on economic growth and inequality: a review', *Studies in Comparative International Development*, **25** (1), Spring, 126–57.
Sivard, R. (1991), *World Military and Social Expenditures*, Washington, DC: World Priorities.
Skocpol, T. (1979), *States and Social Revolutions*, Cambridge, Mass.: Cambridge University Press.
Small, M. and J. D. Singer (1982), *Resort to Arms, International and Civil Wars, 1816–1980*, Beverly Hills: Sage.
Starr, H. and B. A. Most (1985), 'Patterns of conflict: quantitative analysis and the comparative lessons of Third World wars', in Harkavy and Neuman, *Lessons of Recent Wars in the Third World*, *op. cit.*, 33–52.
Steinberg, S. H. (various), *The Statesman Yearbook*, London: Macmillan.
Szirmai, A. (1988), *Inequality Observed: A study of attitudes towards income inequality*, Aldershot: Avebury.
Szirmai, A. and R. Ren (1995), *China's Manufacturing Performance in Comparative Perspective*, Groningen Growth and Development Centre, Research Memorandum 581 (GD 20), Groningen.
Szirmai, A., B. van Ark and D. Pilat (eds) (1993), *Explaining Economic Growth: Essays in honour of Angus Maddison*, Amsterdam: North Holland.
Taylor, C. L. and M. C. Hudson (1972), *World Handbook of Political and Social Indicators*, New York: Yale University Press.
Taylor, C. L. and D. A. Jodice (1983), *World Handbook of Political and Social Indicators*, New Haven: Yale University Press.
Terhal, P. (1992), 'Economic growth and political insecurity: towards a multidisciplinary approach', *Development and Security*, no. 36, August 1992, Centre for Development Studies, Groningen.

Thomas, C. (1987), *In Search of Security: The Third World in international relations*, Boulder, Colo.: Lynne Rienner.
Tilly, C. (ed.) (1975), *The Formation of National States in Western Europe*, Princeton: Princeton University Press.
Tilly, R. (1986), 'Financing industrial enterprise in Great Britain and Germany in the nineteenth century: testing grounds for Marxist and Schumpeterian theories?', in Wagener and Drukker, *Economic Law of Motion of Modern Society*, *op. cit*.
Tullock, G. (1965), *The Politics of Bureaucracy*, Public Affairs Press, Washington, DC.
Urquidi, V. (1993), 'The Developmentalist Perspective', in: Szirmai, van Ark and Pilat.
Wagener, H. J. and J. W. Drukker (eds) (1986), *The Economic Law of Motion of Modern Society: A Marx, Keynes, Schumpeter Centennial*, Cambridge: Cambridge University Press.
Wallerstein, I. (1974), *The Modern World System*, Academic Press: New York.
Weber, M. (1992), *Wirtschaft und Gesellschaft*, Tübingen: Mohr.
White, G. (1984), 'Development states and socialist industrialisation in the Third World', *Journal of Development Studies*, **20**, 97–120.
World Bank (1993), *The East Asian Miracle: Economic growth and public policy*, Oxford: Oxford University Press.
Worsley, P. (1967), *The Third World*, 2nd edn, London: Weidenfeld & Nicholson.
Zolberg, A. R. (1966), *Creating Political Order: The party states of West Africa*, Chicago: Rand McNally.

Chapter 11

Baehr, P. R. (1992), 'De rol van internationale organisaties sinds 1945' (The role of international organisations since 1945), in D. F. J. Bosscher, H. Renner, R. B. Soetendorp and R. Wagenaar (eds), *De wereld na 1945* (The World since 1945), Utrecht: Het Spectrum, Aula.
Bhagwati, J. N. (1977), *The New International Order: The North–South debate*, Cambridge, Mass.: MIT.
Bhagwati, J. N. (1988), *Protectionism*, Cambridge, Mass.: MIT Press.
Brandt, W. *et al* (1980), *North–South: A programme for survival*, London: Pan Books.
Buiter, W. H. and T. N. Srinivasan (1987), 'Rewarding the profligate and punishing the prudent and poor: some recent proposals for debt relief', *World Development*, **15** (3), 411–17.
Burk, K. (1990), 'The international environment', in A. Graham and A. Seldon, *Government and Economies in the Postwar World*, London: Routledge.
Chenery, H. *et al.* (1974), *Redistribution with Growth*, London: Oxford University Press.
Cline, W. R. (1988), 'International debt: progress and strategy', *Finance and Development*, **25**, June, 9–11.
Corden, W. (1979), *The NIEO Proposals: A cool look*, London: Trade Policy Research Centre.
Cornia, G. A., R. Jolly and F. Steward (eds) (1987), *Adjustment with a Human Face*, Oxford: Clarendon Press.
Cornia, G. A., R. van der Hoeven and T. Mkandawire (eds) (1992), *Africa's Recovery in the 1990s: From stagnation and adjustment to human development*, New York: St Martin's Press/UNICEF.
Dam, F. van (1978), 'Mode in het Ontwikkelingsvraagstuk' (Fashions in development), *Economisch Statistische Berichten*, 17 May, 496–500.
Dam, F. van (1984), 'Honderd jaar ontwikkelingsvraagstuk' (The issue of development: one hundred years), *Economisch Statistische Berichten*, 162–8.
Dam, F. van (1989), 'Het ontwikkelingsvraagstuk op hoofdpunten bezien' (Main issues in development), *Economisch Statistische Berichten*, 31 May, 529–33.

Dam, F. van (1992), 'Noord–Zuid: balans van veertig jaar' (North–South: an Evaluation after forty years), *Internationale Spectator*, June, 318–23.

Dolman, A. J. (1983), 'De internationale economische orde: achtergrond en geschiedenis' (The international economic order: background and history), *Wending*, March, 146–54.

Doriye, J. and M. Wuyts (1992), *Aid, Adjustment and Sustainable Recovery: The case of Tanzania*, Working Paper no. 6, Department of Economics, March, London: School of Oriental and African Studies.

Doroodian, K. (1993), 'Macroeconomic performance and adjustment under policies commonly supported by the International Monetary Fund', *Economic Development and Cultural Change*, **41** (4), July, 349–864.

Dunning, J. (1988), 'Trade, location of economic activity and the multinational enterprise: a search for an eclectic approach', in J. Dunning, *Explaining International Production*, Unwin Hyman: London, 13–40.

Edwards, S. (1990), 'The sequencing of economic reform: analytical issues and lessons from Latin America', *The World Economy*, **13**, 1–14.

Elbadawi, I. A. (1992), *Have World Bank-Supported Adjustment Programs Improved Economic Performance in Sub-Saharan Africa*', Policy Research Working Papers, WPS 1001, October, Washington: World Bank.

Elbadawi, I. A., D. Ghura and G. Uwugaren (1992), *Why Structural Adjustment has not Succeeded in Sub-Saharan Africa*?', Policy Research Working Papers, WPS 1000, October, Washington: World Bank.

Emmer, P.C. (1992), 'De contractie van het Westen: de dekolonisatie na 1945' (Contraction of the West: decolonisation after 1945), in D. F. J. Bosscher, H. Renner, R. B. Soetendrop and R. Wagenaar (eds), *De Wereld na 1945*, Utrecht: Het Spectrum, Aula.

Fey, J. N. (1985), 'GATT – Een vlucht naar voren?' (GATT – an escape forwards?), *Internationale Spectator*, **39** (11), November, 670–8.

Fitzpatrick, J. (1983), *Trade and the Lomé Convention*, Lomé briefing no. 9, EEC: Lomé.

Franck, T. M. and M. M. Munansangu (1982), *The New International Economic Order: International law in the making*, New York: United Nations Institute for Training and Research.

Gillis, M., D. H. Perkins, M. Roemer and D. R. Snodgrass (1992), *Economics of Development*, 3rd edn, New York: Norton.

Grassman, S. and E. Lundberg (eds) (1981), *The World Economic Order: Past and present*, London: Macmillan.

Greenaway, D. and O. Morrissey (1993), 'Structural adjustment and liberalisation in developing countries: what lessons have we learned?', *Kyklos*, **46**, 241–61.

Griffin, K. (1988), 'Toward a cooperative settlement of the debt problem', *Finance and Development*, June, 12–14.

Grimal, H. (1978), *Decolonization: The British, French, Dutch and Belgian Empires, 1919–1963*, London: Routledge & Kegan Paul.

Gunning, J. W. (1988), 'Structurele aanpassing en armoedebestrijding: de rol van de Wereldbank' (Structural adjustment and poverty prevention; the role of the World Bank), *Internationale Spectator*, December, 751–5.

Haq, M. ul. (1976), *The Poverty Curtain: Choices for the Third World*, New York: Columbia University Press.

Helleiner, G. K. (1989), 'Transnational corporations and direct foreign investment', in H. Chenery and T. N. Srinivasan, *Handbook of Development Economics*, vol. ii, Amsterdam: North Holland, 1387–439

Helleiner, G. K. (1992a), 'The IMF, the World Bank and Africa's adjustment and external debt problems: an unofficial view', *World Development*, **20**, June, 779–92.

Helleiner, G. K. (1992b), 'Structural adjustment and long-term development in sub-Saharan Africa', in F. Stewart, S. Lall and J. Wamful (eds), *Alternative Development Strategies in Sub-Saharan Africa*, Hong Kong: Macmillan.

Hermes, C. L. M. (1992), *De internationale schuldencrisis* (The international debt crisis), Groningen: Wolters-Noordhoff.
Hill, T. (1985), *Lomé II is Dead, Long Live Lomé III*, Lomé briefing no. 22, EEC: Lomé.
Hofman, A. (1993), 'Economic development in Latin America in the 20th century', in A. Szirmai, B. van Ark and D. Pilat (eds), *Explaining Economic Growth*, Amsterdam: North Holland, 241–66.
Husain, I. (1993), Structural Adjustment and the Long-Term Development of Sub-Saharan Africa', paper presented at the International Seminar of Structural Adjustment and Long-Term Development in Sub-Saharan Africa: Research and Policy Issues, DGIS, The Hague, 1–3 June.
IMF (1992), *International Financial Statistics Yearbook*, Washington, DC: IMF.
IMF (1995), *International Financial Statistics*, February, Washington, DC: IMF.
Johnson, H. G. (1967), *Economic Policies towards Less Developed Countries*, Washington, DC: Brookings Institute.
Kol, J. and L. B. M. Mennes (1990), 'Internationale handel-theorie en beleid' (International trade theory and policy), *Economische Statistische Berichten*, 21 November, 1088–93.
Krueger, A. O. (1990a), *Perspectives on Trade and Development*, New York and London: Harvester Wheatsheaf.
Krueger, A. O. (1990b), *Theory and Practice of Commercial Policy 1945–90*, Working Paper no. 3569, December, Cambridge, Mass.: National Bureau of Economic Research.
Krueger, A. O. (1992), *Economic Policy Reform in Developing Countries*, Cambridge, Mass. and Oxford: Blackwell.
Krueger, A. O. (1993), *Free Trade Agreements as Protectionist Devices: Rules of origin*, Cambridge, Mass.: National Bureau of Economic Research.
Krueger, A. O. and R. Duncan (1993), *The Political Economy of Controls: Complexity*, NBER, Cambridge, Mass.: National Bureau of Economic Research.
Lensink, R. (1993), *External Finance and Development*, Groningen: Wolters-Noordhoff.
Lensink, R. (1995), *Structural Adjustment in Sub-Saharan Africa*, London: Longman.
Lewis, A. (1978), *The Evolution of the International Economic Order*, Princeton: Princeton University Press.
Maddison, A. (1982), 'International economic orders past and present: the West and the rest since 1500', *Syllabus Leergang Ontwikkelingsproblematiek*, mimeographed, University of Groningen, Groningen, 23–38.
Maddison, A. (1985), *Two Crises: Latin America and Asia 1929–38 and 1973–83*, Paris: OECD.
Maddison, A. (1989), *The World Economy in the Twentieth Century*, Paris: OECD.
Meier, G. (1984), *Emerging from Poverty: The economics that really matters*, New York and Oxford: Oxford University Press.
Menshikov, S. (1993), 'The "socialist experiment"' and transition towards the market', in Szirmai, van Ark and Pilat, *Explaining Economic Growth*, *op. cit.*, 467–84.
Morris-Jones, W. H. and G. Fischer (1980), *Decolonisation and After: The British and French experience*, London: Frank Cass.
Mosley, P. (1991), 'Structural adjustment: a general overview 1980–89', in V. N. Balasubramanyam and S. Lall (eds), *Current Issues in Development Economics*, London: Macmillan.
Mosley, P. and J. Weeks (1992), *Has Recovery Begun? Africa's adjustment in the 1980s revisited*, Working Paper no. 29, Department of Economics, November, London: School of Oriental and African Studies.
Mosley, P., J. Harrigan and J. Toye (1991), *Aid and Power: the World Bank and policy based lending*; vol. i, *Analysis and Policy Proposals*; vol ii, *Case Studies*, London: Routledge.
Myint, H. (1980), *The Economics of the Developing Countries*, 5th edn, London: Hutchinson.
Nerfin, M. (1985), 'The future of the United Nations system: some questions on the occasion of an anniversary', *Development Dialogue*, 1, 1–23.
OECD (1979), *The Impact of the Newly Industrializing Countries*, Paris: OECD.

Samuelson, P. and W. D. Nordhaus (1989), *Economics*, 13th edn, New York: McGraw-Hill.
Sapsford, D. (1985), 'The statistical debate on the net barter terms of trade between primary commodities and manufactures: a comment and some statistical evidence', *The Economic Journal*, **95**, September, 781–8.
Sapsford, D. (1988), 'The debate over trends in the terms of trade', in D. Greenaway (ed.), *Economic Development and International Trade*, London: Macmillan, 117–30.
Sarkar, P. (1986), 'The Singer–Prebisch hypothesis: a statistical evaluation', *Cambridge Journal of Economics*, **10**, 355–71.
Schrijver, N. (1985), 'De Verenigde Naties, de internationale economische organisaties en ontwikkelingssamenwerking' (The United Nations, international economic organizations and development cooperation), *Syllabus Leergang Ontwikkelingsproblematiek*, mimeographed, University of Groningen, Groningen.
Seers, D. (1979), 'The meaning of development', in D. Lehman (ed.), *Development Theory: Four Critical Studies*, London: Frank Cass, 9–30,
Selowsky, M. (1987), 'Adjustment in the 1980s: an overview of the issues', *Finance and Development*, **24**, June, 11–13.
Spraos, J. (1980), 'The statistical debate on the net barter terms of trade between primary commodities and manufactures', *The Economic Journal*, **90**, March, 107–28.
Streeten, P. (1984), 'Approaches to a new international economic order', in C. K. Wilber (ed.), *The Political Economy of Development and Underdevelopment*, 3rd edn, New York: Random House.
Szirmai, A., B. van Ark and D. Pilat (eds) (1993), *Explaining Economic Growth: Essays in honour of Angus Maddison*, Amsterdam: North Holland.
Teunissen, P. J. (1990), 'Een ambigue wereld. Compendium: Sociologie van de internationale betrekkingen' (An ambiguous world. Compendium: Sociology of the international relations), mimeographed, Groningen.
Thoburn, J. T. (1977), *Primary Commodity Exports and Economic Development: Theory*, evidence and a study of Malaysia, New York: Wiley.
Toye, J. (1993), 'Structural adjustment: context, assumptions, origin and diversity', paper presented at the International Seminar of Structural Adjustment and Long-Term Development in Sub-Saharan Africa: Research and Policy Issues, DGIS, The Hague, 1–3 June.
United Nations Economic Commission for Africa (1989), *Statistics and Policies: ECA preliminary observations on the World Bank 'Africa's adjustment and growth in the 1980s'*, April, Addis Ababa: ECA.
United Nations (1993a), *Stateman's Yearbook*, New York: United Nations.
United Nations (1993b), *Monthly Bulletin of Statistics*, March, New York: United Nations.
Urquidi, V. (1993), 'The Developmentalist View', in: Szirmai, van Ark and Pilat, *Explaining Economic Growth*, *op. cit.*, 447–65.
Verloren van Themaat, J. P. (1985), 'Lomé III: Oplossing van de jaren '70 voor de problemen van de jaren '80' (Lomé III: solution of the 1970s for the problems of the 1980s), *Internationale Spectator*, **39** (3), 121–6.
Vernon, R. (1977), *Storm over Multinationals: The real issues*, Cambridge, Mass.: Harvard University Press.
Wood, R. (1985), 'The aid regime and international debt: crisis and structural adjustment', *Development and Change*, **16**, 179–212.
World Bank (1985), *World Development Report 1985*, Oxford: Oxford University Press.
World Bank (1987), *World Development Report 1987*, Oxford: Oxford University Press.
World Bank (1989a), *Sub-Saharan Africa: From crisis to sustainable growth*, Washington, DC: World Bank.
World Bank and UNDP (1989b), *Africa's Adjustment and Growth in the 1980s*, Washington, DC and New York: World Bank/UNDP.
World Bank (1993a), *The East Asian Miracle*, Washington, DC: World Bank.
World Bank (1993b), *World Debt Tables 1992–1993*, Washington, DC: World Bank.

World Bank (1995; previous issues), *World Debt Tables 1994–1995*, Washington, DC: World Bank.

Chapter 12

Balassa, B. (1978), 'Exports and economic growth: further evidence', *Journal of Development Economics*, 5, June, 181–9.
Bauer, P. T. (1976), *Dissent on Development*, London: Weidenfeld & Nicholson.
Bauer, P. T. (1981), *Equality, the Third World and Economic Delusion*, London: Weidenfeld & Nicholson.
Bauer, P. T. (1984), *Reality and Rhetoric*, London: Weidenfeld & Nicholson.
Bauer, P. T. (1988), 'Comment on R. A. Cassen, aid evaluation: its scope and limits', in C. J. Jepma (ed.), *North–South Cooperation in Retrospect and Prospect*, London: Routledge & Kegan Paul, 182–6.
Bauer, P. T. and B. Yamey (1981), 'The political economy of foreign aid', *Lloyds Bank Review*, October, 1–15.
Bauer, P. T. and B. Yamey (1986), *Development Forum*, **14** (3), April, United Nations, Geneva.
Beek, L.J. M. van (1985), 'Ontwikkelingshulp tussen overheid en particulier initiatief: het mede financieringsprogramma 1965–1985' (Development aid between government and private initiative: the cofinancing programme 1965–1985), *Internationale Spectator*, **39**, December, 749–57.
Berlage, L. and R. Renard (1993), *Evaluatie van Ontwikkelingshulp in België en Nederland* (Evaluation of Development Aid in Belgium and the Netherlands), Research Paper in Economic Development no. 24, Leuven: Centrum voor Economische Studieën.
Bhagwati, J. N. (1985a), 'Foreign trade regimes', in *id.*, *Dependence and Interdependence: Essays in development economics*, vol. ii, ed. G. Grossman, Oxford: Blackwell, 123–38.
Bhagwati, J. N (1985b), 'The tying of aid', in *id.*, *Dependence and Interdependence: Essays in development economics*, vol. ii, ed. G. Grossman, Oxford: Blackwell, 204–51.
Bhagwati, J. N. (1985c), 'Alternative estimates of the real cost of aid', in *id.*, *Dependence and Interdependence: Essays in development economics*, vol. ii, ed. G. Grossman, Oxford: Blackwell: 252–68.
Bhagwati, J. N. (1985d), 'Substitution between foreign capital and domestic saving', in *id.*, *Dependence and Interdependence: Essays in development economics*, vol. ii, ed. G. Grossman, Oxford: Blackwell, 269–76.
Bol, D. (1983), *Economen en armoede: Moedwil en misverstand in de ontwikkelingshulp* (Economists and Poverty: Bad faith and misunderstandings in development aid), Amsterdam: Van Gennep.
Bos, H. C. (1990), 'Ontwikkelingseconomie' (Development eonomics), *Economisch Statistische Berichten*, 5 December, 1160–7.
Boserup, E. (1983), 'The impact of scarcity and plenty on development', *Journal of Interdisciplinary History*, **14** (2), 383–407.
Brandt, W. *et al.* (1980), *North–South: A programme for survival*, London: Pan Books.
Brandt, W. *et al.* (1983), *Common Crisis: North–South cooperation for world recovery*, London: Pan Books.
Breman, J. (1986), 'Over hobbies en lobbies: de uitbesteding van de Nederlandse ontwikkelingshulp' (On hobbies and lobbies: farming out Dutch development aid), *Internationale Spectator*, **40** (6), June, 353–63.
Brundtland, G. H. *et al.* (1987), *Our Common Future*, The World Commission on Environment and Development, Oxford: Oxford University Press.
Bruton, H. J. (1969), 'The two-gap approach to aid and development: comment', *The American Economic Review*, **59**, June, 439–46.

Burki, S. J. and Ayres, R. (1986), 'A fresh look at development aid', *Finance and Development*, **23** (1), March, 6–10.
Cassen, R. A. (1986), *Does Aid Work?*, Oxford: Clarendon Press.
Cassen, R. A. (1988), 'Aid evaluation: its scope and limits', in C. J. Jepma (ed.), *North–South Cooperation in Retrospect and Prospect*, London: Routledge & Kegan Paul, 167–81.
Chenery, H. (1979), *Structural Change and Development Policy*, New York: Oxford University Press.
Chenery, H. and I. Adelman (1966), 'Foreign aid and economic development: the case of Greece', *Review of Economics and Statistics*, February.
Chenery, H. and A. MacEwan (1966), 'Optimal patterns of growth and aid: the case of Pakistan', *Pakistan Development Review*, Summer.
Chenery, H. and A. M. Strout (1966), 'Foreign assistance and economic development', *American Economic Review*, **56**, September, 679–733.
Chenery, H., M. S. Ahluwalia, C. L. G. Bell, J. H. Duloy and R. Jolly (1974), *Redistribution with Growth*, New York and Oxford: Oxford University Press.
Clay, E. J. and H. Singer (eds) (1983), *Food Aid: Food for thought*, IDS Bulletin, vol. 14, no. 12, April.
Clay, E. J. and H. Singer (1985), *Food Aid and Development Issues and Evidence*, Rome Occasional Papers no. 3, September, Rome: World Food Programme.
Cochrane, G. (1979), *The Cultural Appraisal of Development Projects*, New York and London: Praeger.
Dam, F. van (1978), 'Mode in het ontwikkelingsvraagstuk' (Trends in the issue of development), *Economisch Statistische Berichten*, 17 May, 496–500.
Dam, F. van (1989a), 'Het ontwikkelingsvraagstuk op hoofdpunten bezien' (Main issues in development), *Economisch Statistische Berichten*, 31 May, 529–33.
Dam, F. van (1989b), 'Zin en onzin over projecthulp' (Sense and nonsense in project aid), *Internationale Spectator*, **43** (6), June, 372–3.
Dam, F. van (1992), 'Noord–zuid: balans van veertig jaar' (North–south: an evaluation after forty years), *Internationale Spectator*, **46** (6), June, 318–23.
Emmerij, L. J. (1984), 'Ontwikkelingssamenwerking op een kruispunt? Noodzaak tot omvorming van het Nederlandse beleid en apparaat' (Development cooperation at crossroads? The need to change Dutch policy and apparatus), *Internationale Spectator*, **38**, March, 121ff.
Frankel, F. R. (1978), *India's Political Economy, 1947–77*, Princeton: Princeton University Press.
George, S. (1988), *A Fate Worse than Debt*, London and New York: Penguin.
Griffin, K. (1970), 'Foreign capital, domestic savings and economic development', *Bulletin of the Oxford Institute of Economics and Statistics*, **32** (2), May, 1970, and 'reply' in **33** (2), May.
Griffin, K. (1987), 'Doubts about aid', in *id.*, *World Hunger and the World Economy*, London: Macmillan, pp. 235–54.
Griffin, K. and J. L. Enos (1970), 'Foreign assistance: objectives and consequences', *Economic Development and Cultural Change*, **18**, April.
Griffin, K. and J. Gurley (1985), 'Radical analyses of imperialism, the Third World and the transition to socialism', *Journal of Economic Literature*, **23** (3), September.
Griffin, K. and A. R. Khan (1985), 'Poverty in the Third World: ugly facts and fancy models', *World Development*, **6** (3), March.
Gupta, K. L. and M. A. Islam (1983), *Foreign Capital, Savings and Growth*, Dordrecht: Reidel.
Haan, L. J. (1989), 'Over de kwaliteit van de ontwikkelingssamenwerking' (On the quality of development cooperation), *Internationale Spectator*, **43** (6), June, 374–5.
Hancock, G. (1991), *Lords of Poverty*, London: Mandarin Paperbacks.
Hayami, Y. and V. W. Ruttan (1985), *Agricultural Development: An international perspective*, rev. edn, Baltimore: Johns Hopkins University Press.

Hayter, T. (1971), *Aid as Imperialism*, London: Penguin.
Hayter, T. (1981), *The Creation of World Poverty: An alternative view to the Brandt Report*, London: Pluto.
Hayter, T. and C. Watson (1985), *Aid: Rhetoric and reality*, London: Pluto.
Heller, P. S. (1975), 'A model of public fiscal behavior in developing countries: aid, investment and taxation', *American Economic Review*, **65**, June, 429–45.
Hoebink, P. (1988), *Geven en Nemen: De Nederlandse ontwikkelingshulp aan Tanzania en Sri Lanka* (Giving or Taking: Dutch development aid to Tanzania and Sri Lanka), Nijmegen: Stichting Derde Wereld Publikaties.
Hoebink, P. (1990a), 'Tussen militair, dominee en koopman: hulpbeleid van westerse landen' (Between soldier, clergyman and merchant: aid policies in Western countries), *Internationale Spectator*, **44**, March, 126–39.
Hoebink, P. (1990b), 'De Nederlandse ontwikkelingshulp' (Dutch Development aid), in R. Doom (ed.), *Derde wereld handboek: Deel I, noord–zuid en zuid–zuid in politiek perspectief*, Amsterdam: Amsterdam, Mets, 197–218.
Hommes, E. (1993), 'Ontwikkelingssamenwerking en buitenlands beleid' (Development cooperation and foreign policy), *Internationale Spectator*, **47** (1), 45–50.
ILO (1976), *Employment, Growth and Basic Needs: A one-world problem*, Geneva: International Labour Organization.
IMF (1993), *Statistical Yearbook*, Washington, DC: IMF.
Jackson, T. (1982), *Against the Grain: The dilemma of project food aid*, Oxford: Oxfam.
Jay, K. and C. Michalopoulos (1989), 'Donor policies, donor interests, and aid effectiveness', in A. O. Krueger *et al., Aid and Development*, Baltimore: Johns Hopkins University Press, 68–88.
Jepma, C. J. (1984), 'Ontwikkelingssamenwerking op het nieuwe spoor' (Development cooperation on a new track), *Internationale Spectator*, **38**, September, 504ff.
Jepma, C. J. (1985), 'Commentaar: ontwikkelingsbeleid en vooronderstellingen' (Comment: development policy and assumptions), *Internationale Spectator*, **39** (6), June, 347ff.
Jepma, C. J. (ed.) (1988), *North–South Cooperation in Retrospect and Prospect*, London: Routledge & Kegan Paul.
Jepma, C. J. (1992), EC-Wide Untying', *Development and Security*, no. 37, Centre for Development Studies, October, University of Groningen.
Krauss, M. (1983a), *Development without Aid*, New York: McGraw-Hill.
Krauss, M. (1983b), Transferring incomes versus transferring prosperity, report, January, Manhattan Institute for Policy Research.
Krueger, A. O. (1978), *Foreign Trade Regimes and Economic Development: Liberalization attempts and consequences*, Cambridge, Mass.: NBER/Ballinger.
Krueger, A. O. (1986), 'Aid in the development process', *World Bank Research Review*, **11** (1), 57–78.
Krueger, A. O., C. Michalopoulos and V. Ruttan (1989), *Aid and Development*, Baltimore and London: Johns Hopkins University Press.
Kruyt, D. (1988), 'De Sociologie van ontwikkelingsbureaucratieen' (The sociology of development bureaucracies), in D. Kruyt and K. Koonings (eds), *Ontwikkelingsvraagstukken: Theorie, beleid en methoden*, Muiderberg: Coutinho, 57–73.
Kruyt, D. and K. Koonings (eds) (1988), *Ontwikkelingsvraagstukken: Theorie, beleid en methoden* (Development Issues. Theory, policy, and methods), Muiderberg: Coutinho.
Kruyt, D. and M. Vellinga (1983), *Ontwikkelingshulp getest: Resultaten onder de loep* (Development Aid Examined: A closer look at the results), Muiderberg: Coutinho.
Kuznets, S. (1955), 'Economic growth and income inequality', *American Economic Review*, **45** (1), 1–28.
Lal, D. (1976), 'Distribution and development: a review article', *World Development*, **4** (9), 725–38.

Lal, D. (1978), *Poverty, Power and Prejudice: The North–South confrontation*, London: Fabian Society.

Lal, D. (1983), *The Poverty of Development Economics*, London: Institute of Economic Affairs.

Lappé, F. M., J. Collins, and D. McKinley (1980), *Aid as Obstacle: Twenty questions about our foreign aid and the hungry*, San Francisco: Institute for Food and Development Policy.

Lensink, R. (1993a), *External Finance and Development*, Groningen: Wolters Noordhoff.

Lensink, R. (1993b), 'Recipient government behavior and the effectiveness of development aid', *De Economist*, **141** (4), 543–62.

Lensink, R. and M. M. Antuma (1992), 'De effectiviteit van ontwikkelingshulp' (The effectiveness of development aid), photocopy, Groningen.

Lewis, W. A. (1954), 'Economic development with unlimited supplies of labour', *Manchester School of Economic and Social Studies*, **22**, 139–91.

Maddison, A. (1989), *The World Economy in the 20th Century*, Paris: OECD.

Mende, T. (1973), *From Aid to Recolonisation: Lessons of a failure*, London: Harrap.

Millikan, M. F. and W. E. Rostow (1957), *A Proposal: A key to effective foreign policy*, New York: Harper & Row.

Mosley, P. (1980), 'Aid savings and growth revisited', *Oxford Bulletin of Economics and Statistics*, **42** (2), May, 79–95.

Mosley, P. (1987), *Overseas Aid: Its defence and reform*, Brighton: Wheatsheaf Books.

Mosley, P., J. Harrigan and J. Toye (1991), *Aid and Power: the World Bank and policy-based lending*, vol. i, *Analysis and Policy Proposals*; vol. ii, *Case Studies*, London: Routledge.

Myrdal, G. (1971), *The Challenge of World Poverty*, New York: Vintage Books.

OECD (1985), *Twenty-Five Years of Development Cooperation: A review*, Paris: OECD.

OECD (1986), *Financing and External Debt of Developing Countries 1985*, Paris: OECD.

OECD (1993a), *Financing and External Debt of Developing Countries 1992*, Paris: OECD.

OECD (1993b), *Development Cooperation 1992*, Paris: OECD.

OECD (1994), *Development Cooperation 1994*, Paris: OECD.

OECD (1995; and previous issues), *Geographical Distribution of Financial Flows to Developing Countries 1989–1993*, Paris: OECD.

Papanek, G. F. (1972), 'The effect of aid and other resource transfers on savings and growth in less developed countries', *The Economic Journal*, **82** (327), September, 934–50.

Papanek, G. F. (1973), 'Aid, foreign private investment, saving and growth in less developed countries', *The Journal of Political Economy*, **81**, 120–30.

Papanek, G. F. (1983), 'Aid, equity and growth in South Asia', in J. Parkinson (ed.), *Poverty and Aid*, Oxford: Blackwell.

Prince, G. H. A. (1976), 'Ontwikkelingssamenwerking; als voortzetting van koloniaal beleid' (Development cooperation as a continuation of colonial policies), *Internationale Spectator*, **30** (3), March, 173–80.

Quarles van Ufford, P., D. Kruijt and T. Downing (eds) (1988), *The Hidden Crisis in Development: Development bureaucracies*, Amsterdam: Free University Press.

Rana, P. B. and J. M. Dowling (1988), 'The impact of foreign capital on growth: evidence from Asian developing countries', *The Developing Economies*, **26** (1), 3–11.

Rana, P. B. and J. M. Dowling (1990), 'Foreign capital and Asian economic growth', *Asian Development Review*, **8**, 77–102.

Riddell, R. C. (1987), *Foreign Aid Reconsidered*, Baltimore and London: Johns Hopkins/Curry.

Rosenstein-Rodan, P. (1961), 'International aid for underdeveloped countries', *Review of Economics and Statistics*, **43**, May, 107–38.

Rostow, W. W. (1971; first pub. 1960), *The Stages of Economic Growth*, 2nd edn, Cambridge, Mass.: Cambridge University Press.

Roth, D. (1993), 'Ontwikkelingshulp ter discussie: kwaliteitsdecreet of kwaliteitsdebat?' (Development aid in discussion: quality decree or quality debate?, *Internationale Spectator*, **47** (5), May, 274–80.

Ruttan, V. W. (1989a), 'Improving the quality of life in rural areas', in Krueger *et al.*, *Aid and Development*, *op. cit.*

Ruttan, V. W. (1989b), 'Why foreign economic assistance?', *Economic Development and Cultural Change*, 37, January.

Schrijver, N. and P. Terhal (1989), 'Het vierde ontwikkelingsdecennium: naar een andere opzet' (The fourth development decade: towards a different set-up), *Internationale Spectator*, **43** (12), December, 730–6.

Schultz, T. W. (1964), *Transforming Traditional Agriculture*, New Haven and London: Yale University Press.

Soest, J. van (1975), *Het begin van de ontwikkelingshulp in de Verenigde Naties en in Nederland 1945–1952* (Early Development Aid in the United Nations and the Netherlands, 1945–1952), Nijmegen: University of Nijmegen.

Stern, N. (1974), 'Professor Bauer on development', *Journal of Development Economics*, **1**.

Szirmai, A. (1988), *Inequality Observed: A study of attitudes towards income inequality*, Aldershot: Avebury Press.

Teszler, R. K. (1978), 'Nederlandse samenwerking met ontwikkelingslanden' (Dutch cooperation with developing countries), in E. H. v.d. Beugel *et al.*, *Nederlandse buitenlandse politiek: Heden en verleden* (Dutch Foreign Policies: Past and present), Baarn: In den Toren.

Tims, W. (1985), 'Commentaar: organisatie en doeltreffendheid van de Nederlandse ontwikkelingssamenwerking' (Comment: organisation and effectiveness of Dutch Development Cooperation), *Internationale Spectator*, **39** (12), December, 759ff.

Tims, W. (1989), 'Development cooperation: a Dutch preoccupation', *Internationale Spectator*, **43** (11), November, 714–17.

Vingerhoets, J. (1986), 'Het "nieuwe" hulpbeleid van minister Schoo' (The "new" aid policies of Minister Schoo), *Internationale Spectator*, **40** (3), March, 149–57.

White, H. (1992), 'The macroeconomic impact of development aid: a critical survey', *The Journal of Development Studies*, **28** (2), 163–240.

World Bank (1993), *World Tables 1993*, Baltimore: Johns Hopkins University Press.

World Bank (1995), *World Tables 1995*, Baltimore: Johns Hopkins University Press.

Zeylstra, W. G. (1975), *Aid or Development: The relevance of development aid to problems of developing countries*, Leiden: A. W. Sijthoff.

Zoomers, E. B. (1992), 'Effectiviteit van Nederlands ontwikkelingsbeleid: suggesties tot verbetering van de projectcyclus' (Effectiveness of Dutch development policy: suggestions for improvements in the project cycle), *Internationale Spectator*, **46**, March, 114–19.

Index